Cambridge
International AS and A Level

# Accounting

Ian Harrison

Acknowledgements:
The Publishers would like to thank the following for permission to reproduce copyright material:

Photo credits:
**p.84** © SIA KAMBOU/AFP/Getty Images; **p.158** © maxoido - Fotolia; **p.191** © Peter Horree / Alamy; **p.263** © Kaveh Kazemi/Getty Images; **p.269** © NAN - Fotolia.com; **p.291** © Per-Anders Pettersson/ Getty Images; **p.336** © poco_bw - Fotolia; **p.357** © Paylessimages - Fotolia.com; **p.387** © Asia Images Group Pte Ltd / Alamy; **p.485** © terex - Fotolia

Questions from the Cambridge International AS and A Level Accounting papers are reproduced by kind permission of Cambridge International Examinations.



Orders: please contact Bookpoint Ltd, 130 Milton Park, Abingdon, Oxon OX14 4SB.
Telephone: (44) 01235 827827. Fax: (44) 01235 400401. Lines are open 9.00–5.00, Monday to Saturday, with a 24-hour message answering service. Visit our website at www.hoddereducation.com


First published in 2015 by
Hodder Education
An Hachette UK Company
Carmelite House
50 Victoria Embankment
London
EC4Y 0DZ

Impression number 5 4 3 2 1
Year 2017 2016 2015



Cover photo © Justin Guariglia/Corbis
Illustrations by Integra Software Services Pvt. Ltd., Pondicherry, India
Typeset by Integra Software Services Pvt. Ltd., Pondicherry, India
Printed in Dubai

A catalogue record for this title is available from the British Library
**ISBN: 978 1444 181 432**

# Contents

# Student's CD contents

Additional questions
Interactive tests
Revision checklists
Examination structure
Glossary of command words
Planning your revision
Answers to Additional questions
Appendix 1: Ratios
Appendix 2: Layouts of financial statements

# Introduction

## The textbook

This book has been written with the needs of students in mind, and I have tried to maximise, as far as is possible, the achievement of positive learning. Also, the book has been developed based on my many years of experience as both an examiner and a teacher of the subject to Advanced Level students both in the UK and overseas.

The book has been endorsed by Cambridge International Examinations, listed as an endorsed textbook for students who study the Cambridge International Examinations syllabus 9706. The text covers the whole of the syllabus, organised and split in accordance with the examination papers in the syllabus, and follows as far as is possible the order in which topics appear in the published syllabus. The sections covered by each chapter are listed. Each area of the syllabus is given as a reference point.

## Syllabus coverage

The first 31 chapters cover the AS syllabus in its entirety. At the end of the AS Level syllabus chapters there are examination-style questions. Some of the questions are from past exam papers. Where appropriate the original questions have been modified to reflect recent changes in accounting terminology and practice. *Readers are advised that all topics in the AS section of the syllabus may also be examined at Advanced Level.*

Chapters 32 to 46 deal with topics that may be examined at Advanced Level. The examination-style questions at the end of the A Level chapters are written to reflect recent changes in accounting exam papers.

## Features of the book

Each chapter starts with the relevant syllabus statement. Throughout the chapters there are Examples and Worked examples, with answers, to illustrate the introduced concepts. They are followed by a few 'Now try ...' questions leading students to additional questions in the CD as well as some self-test questions, which allow students to further explore the concept and test themselves. Meanwhile, important terms are explained and sometimes tips are given to help students to better understand the related concepts. Each chapter ends with a summary, which covers all the key points.

**How the syllabus points are covered in the 46 chapters**

| AS Level content – Paper 1 and Paper 2 | | Additional A Level content – Paper 3 | |
|---|---|---|---|
| **Syllabus points** | **Chapters** | **Syllabus points** | **Chapters** |
| 1.1 | Chapters 1 – 7 and 14 | 1.1.1 | Chapter 32 |
| 1.2 | Chapters 6 and 19 | 1.1.2 | Chapter 33 |
| 1.3 | Chapters 10 – 12 | 1.1.3 | Chapters 34 and 35 |
| 1.4.1 | Chapters 9 and 18 – 20 | 1.1.4 | Chapter 36 |
| 1.4.2 | Chapters 15 – 17 and 22 | 1.1.5 | Chapter 37 |
| 1.4.3 | Chapters 23 and 24 | 1.2 | Chapter 38 |
| 1.4.4 | Chapter 25 and 26 | 1.3 | Chapters 39 and 40 |
| 1.5 | Chapter 27 | 1.4 | Chapter 41 |
| 2.1 | Chapters 20 and 28 | 1.5 | Chapter 42 |
| 2.2.1 | Chapter 28 | 2.1 | Chapter 43 |
| 2.2.2 | Chapter 29 | 2.2 | Chapter 44 |
| 2.2.3 | Chapters 29 and 30 | 2.3 | Chapter 45 |
| 2.3 | Chapter 31 | 2.4 | Chapter 46 |

## Key concepts

The 9706 syllabus is built around five fundamental concepts that should be applied to all accounting transactions. They are:

**A true and fair view**
The concept of true and fair view ensures that financial statements accurately and truthfully reflect the transactions of the business.

**Duality (double entry)**
The method of systematically recording transactions to show the giving and receiving of value.

**Consistency**
The treatment of similar transactions and items in the same way each year so that the results of business activity can be compared with previous results.

**Business entity**
The separation of the ownership of a business from the actual business itself. Only business assets and transactions are recorded in the business books of account.

**Money measurement**
The business financial records only deal with transactions that can be measured in monetary terms.

These key concepts will dictate the way that you study accounting. They underpin the work that you will study during your course. You should find that they provide themes that run through all the accounting topics that you study. The above icons appear in the text, indicating where each Key concept is covered,

When you are studying a topic, relate one or more of these key concepts to that topic.

# The Student's CD-ROM

There is a student's CD-ROM accompanying the book to help students further their study in accounting. It includes:

- Additional questions – they are referred to in the book as 'Now try …' questions which illustrate more about the concept where introduced and test if you have grasped the knowledge.
- Interactive tests – these are different types of questions such as true or false and multiple choice, designed to improve the understanding of accounting.
- Revision checklist to check if you have understood every syllabus point covered in the chapter.
- Answers to additional questions.
- Materials to help you prepare for the examinations in Accounting.

In accounting, there are certain layouts that you must learn so it is important that you practise questions based on each topic area on a regular basis. Use each piece of work in the book and the CD to build up a bank of knowledge and skills that you may be able to apply to subsequent pieces of work. As a subject, accounting is rather like a detective solving a crime; the pieces of information collected some weeks ago might help to solve today's problem. Most importantly, you must learn the concepts for each topic. This is usually easier that you might first think; the difficult part is applying the appropriate knowledge to the questions.

I hope you enjoy exploring in accounting and may you have good performance in your AS/A Level examinations.

Ian Harrison

# 1 The double-entry system

**Content**

**1.1 The accounting cycle**

- Explain and apply the principles of the double-entry system to record business transactions

**By the end of this chapter you should be able to:**

- use double-entry book-keeping to record financial transactions
- enter financial transactions into a ledger using debit and credit entries
- understand and explain the purpose of using a ledger
- understand and explain why a ledger is generally divided into three parts.

## 1.1 Debit and credit entries in the double-entry system

There are two main ways in which the managers of businesses record their financial transactions. They use either:

- a double-entry system of recording transactions
- a single-entry system of recording transactions.

This chapter looks at the double-entry system, which provides the accountant with the information needed in order to produce the data required to prepare an **income statement** that will show whether or not the business has been profitable. You will encounter the single-entry system in Chapters 22 and 23.

An **income statement** is a statement that calculates the profit that a business has made for a period of time (usually a financial year).

As the name implies, double-entry book-keeping recognises that there are two sides or aspects to every business transaction. See, for example, the two sides of each of the following transactions:

I fill my car with $20 of fuel.

- I receive the fuel.
- The filling station attendant puts the fuel into my vehicle.

I buy a pair of soccer boots costing $13.

- I receive the boots.
- The sports shop 'gives' me the boots.

**Tip**

Like all areas of study, accounting has its own jargon. Whenever a new word or term is introduced, an explanation or definition will be given. Make sure you read and understand what these terms mean and how they are used in accounting.

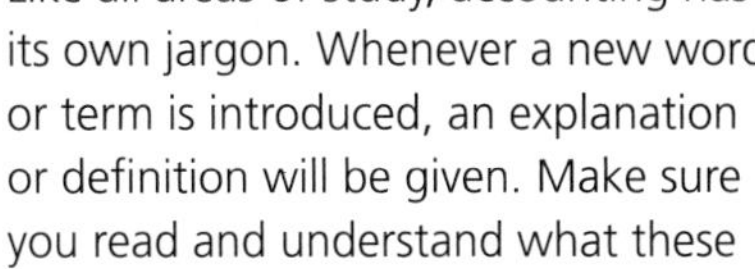

There are two more aspects to each of these transactions:

When I give the filling station attendant my $20

- she receives the cash
- I 'give' the cash.

When I give the shop assistant my $13

- he receives the cash
- I 'give' the cash.

This way of recording both sides of any transaction is known as the **dual aspect** principle of accounting.

A **ledger account** contains the detailed record of financial transactions undertaken by a business. Since all accounts appear in a ledger (or book), the term is often shortened to the single word **account**.

A **ledger** is the book where all accounts are kept.

All financial transactions involving the business are recorded in a format called a **ledger account** or simply an **account**.

You would find each account on a separate page in the **ledger**. In fact, if a great many transactions of a similar nature are undertaken, an account may spread over several pages.

For the sake of convenience this one book (the ledger) is divided into several smaller books. You can imagine that large businesses like the Toyota Motor Corporation or McDonalds could not possibly keep all their financial records in one book.

Initially, to make our task a little simpler, we shall keep all our records together. When the other books are introduced, you will see that it does make sense to split the ledger into several different parts.

Do not worry if all this seems a little strange. You will soon be familiar with it but it does require *practice*. The key to success in accounting is practice.

An account looks like a 'T' shape, like this:

| | |
|---|---|
| | |

Each account has two sides.

- The *left* side is known as the **debit** side.
- The *right* side is known as the **credit** side.

**An account**

| Debit | Credit |
|---|---|
| The debit side of an account is always the receiving side or the side that shows gains in value. | The credit side of an account is always the giving or losing side – the side that shows value given. |
| Debit is often abbreviated to Dr. | Credit is often abbreviated to Cr. |

**Dr** **An account** **Cr**

| Receives | Gives |
|---|---|
| or | or |
| Gains | Loses |

An account in the ledger would be headed thus:

**Dr** ******* **account** **Cr**

| | |
|---|---|
| | |

**Note**

There should always be a heading; if the account shown is not a personal account, the heading should include the word 'account'.

The golden rule of the game of 'double entry' is that every time you enter something on the debit side (left side) of an account you must enter an equivalent amount on the credit side (right side) of another account.

This is all fairly straightforward, but *it does require practice.*

**Worked example**

Bola owns a business selling meat. During one week the following financial transactions take place:

1 Bola purchases meat $210 from Scragg, a meat wholesaler. She will pay for the meat in a couple of weeks' time.
2 Bola's cash sales for the week amount to $742.
3 Bola supplies meat to the Grand Hotel $217. They will pay for the meat at the end of the month.
4 Bola pays the rent for her shop $75.
5 She pays her telephone bill $43.

**Required**

Enter the transactions in Bola's ledger.

**Purchases** are any items that are purchased with the intention of selling them to customers.

**Sales** are any items that are sold in the normal course of business to customers.

## Answer

1 Bola receives meat … and Scragg 'loses' the meat …

| Dr | Purchases account | Cr |
|---|---|---|
| $ | | |
| 210 | | |

| Dr | Scragg | Cr |
|---|---|---|
| | | $ |
| | | 210 |

2 Bola 'loses' (sells) some meat … and she gains cash …

| Dr | Sales account | Cr |
|---|---|---|
| | | $ |
| | | 742 |

| Dr | Cash account | Cr |
|---|---|---|
| $ | | |
| 742 | | |

3 Bola 'loses' meat … and the Grand Hotel gains the meat …

| Dr | Sales account | Cr |
|---|---|---|
| | | $ |
| | | 217 |

| Dr | Grand Hotel | Cr |
|---|---|---|
| $ | | |
| 217 | | |

4 Bola gains the use of her premises … and she 'loses' (pays) cash …

| Dr | Rent account | Cr |
|---|---|---|
| $ | | |
| 75 | | |

| Dr | Cash account | Cr |
|---|---|---|
| | | $ |
| | | 75 |

- This is can be a confusing entry because we are used to talking about 'paying rent'.
- Bola pays money to a landlord for the use of his building.
- Bola receives/gains the use of the premises.
- In cases like this, think of the cash entry first and then put in the second entry.

5 Bola gains the use of her telephone … and she loses cash ….

| Dr | Telephone account | Cr |
|---|---|---|
| $ | | |
| 43 | | |

| Dr | Cash account | Cr |
|---|---|---|
| | | $ |
| | | 43 |

- Another confusing entry. Bola receives/gains the use of the telephone.
- Bola gives the telephone company cash for the service they provide to her.

If you are uncertain about the telephone account ask whether Bola has gained cash or 'lost' cash. You know that Bola has paid cash to the telephone company so the cash has to be a credit entry (right side); the other entry has to be a debit entry (left side) according to the rules of double entry.

➤ Now try Question 1.

## 1.2 Treatment of similar transactions

If there are a number of similar transactions that need to be recorded, we enter them all in one account.

**Worked example**

Greta Teer owns and runs a store selling newspapers, magazines and candies. The following transactions took place over the past few days:

1 Cash sales of newspapers amounted to $68.

2 Cash sales of chocolate and candies amounted to $151.

3 Greta purchased candies, potato chips and soft drinks $135, paying cash to her wholesaler.

4 She paid $160 cash for local taxes.

5 Greta sold four boxes of potato chips to a local club for cash $30.

**Required**

Enter the transactions in Greta's ledger.

### Answer

| Dr | Sales account Cr |
|---|---|
| | $ |
| | 68 |
| | 151 |
| | 30 |

| Dr Cash account | Cr |
|---|---|
| $ | $ |
| 68 | 135 |
| 151 | 160 |
| 30 | |

| Dr Purchases account | Cr |
|---|---|
| $ | |
| 135 | |

| Dr Local taxes account | Cr |
|---|---|
| $ | |
| 160 | |

**Note**

All the transactions involving cash have been entered in one cash account. All the sales transactions have also been entered in one account.

➤ Now try Question 2.

It should be obvious that as well as keeping money in the business, the owners of businesses will bank money and will pay many bills by means of cheques. So, as well as having a cash account in the ledger, the business would also keep a bank account to record transactions using the business bank account.

**Worked example**

Sven Drax owns and runs a hotel. He supplies the following information:

1 Sven purchases a deep freeze unit $415, paying by cheque.

2 He purchases for cash $127 fruit and vegetables for the hotel restaurant.

3 Sven purchases petrol $45 for the hotel mini-bus using cash.

**Drawings** is the term used to describe the withdrawal of resources (cash or goods) from the business by the owner for private use outside the business.

4 He pays for a family holiday $1500 paying with a business cheque.
5 He pays $2178 cash takings into the bank account.

**Required**

Enter the transactions in the hotel ledger.

## Answer

**Freezer account**

| Dr $ | Cr |
|---|---|
| 415 | |

**Bank account**

| Dr $ | Cr $ |
|---|---|
| 2178 | 415 |
| | 1500 |

**Purchases account**

| Dr $ | Cr |
|---|---|
| 127 | |

**Cash account**

| Dr | Cr $ |
|---|---|
| | 127 |
| | 45 |

**Motor expenses account**

| Dr $ | Cr |
|---|---|
| 45 | |

**Drawings account**

| Dr $ | Cr |
|---|---|
| 1500 | |

**Sales (or takings) account**

| Dr | Cr $ |
|---|---|
| | 2178 |

**Note**

The freezer unit is not purchases – it is capital expenditure. There was not already an account, so *when in doubt open an account*. The cheque paid out to the holiday company is drawings – it is not a business expense.

**Self-test questions**

1 Every ____________ ____________ needs a corresponding debit entry.
2 Define the term 'account'.
3 In which account would goods purchased for resale be entered?
4 Denzil pays the rent on his factory with $300 cash. The entries to record this transaction are debit rent account $300; credit cash account $300. True/False?
5 Bradley pays the telephone bill $120 cash. The entries to record this transaction are debit cash account $120; credit telephone account $120. True/False?
6 Which side of an account is the 'receiving' side?
7 Which side of an account is the 'giving' side?

## 1.3 The division of the ledger

All accounts are entered in one book called the ledger. Because the number of accounts could run into many hundreds, it is more convenient to split the ledger into a number of different books.

**Credit customers** are people (or businesses) that we sell goods to; they will pay for their goods at some time in the future. The goods are sold on **credit**.

Until credit customers have paid for the goods that have been purchased, they are **trade debtors**. Trade debtors are collectively known as **trade receivables**.

**Credit suppliers** are people (or businesses) that we purchase goods from; we will settle the debt that we owe at some future date. The goods are purchased on **credit**.

A person or business supplying goods on credit is known as a **trade creditor** until the debt is settled. A number of trade creditors are collectively known as **trade payables**.

**Personal accounts** are accounts that record transactions with credit customers and credit suppliers.

**Nominal accounts**, **real accounts** and **liability accounts** will all be found in the general ledger.

**Nominal accounts** record expenses, profits, losses and gains.

**Real accounts** record the acquisition and disposal of **non-current assets** like land, buildings, equipment and vehicles.

**Liability accounts** record the acquisition and repayment of loans and overdrafts.

Can you think of how you might split the ledger to make it more manageable? We make it more manageable by grouping together similar accounts. We put:

- **credit customers'** accounts together in one ledger
- **credit suppliers'** accounts together in one ledger
- all other accounts in another ledger.

All transactions involving credit customers will be found in the **sales ledger** (also known as the **debtors' ledger**).

All transactions with credit suppliers will be found in the **purchases ledger** (also known as the **creditors' ledger**).

All other transactions will be found in the **general ledger**. (For those of you familiar with computerised accounts, the general ledger is often called the **nominal ledger** in accounting packages.)

Initially you will make mistakes when asked which accounts would appear in which ledger; do not worry about this – we have all made similar mistakes in the past.

The difficult ones are as follows:

- The sales account, which is *not* found in the sales ledger, is reserved for the **personal accounts** of our credit customers. The sales account would be found in the general ledger.
- The purchases account will *not* be found in the purchases ledger. It is reserved for the personal accounts of credit suppliers only. The purchases account would be found in the general ledger.

We only record credit transactions in the sales ledger and the purchases ledger.

- If a sale is made for cash it is *not* entered in the sales ledger.
- If something is purchased for cash it is *not* entered in the purchases ledger.

These transactions appear in the general ledger.

**Worked example**

1 Nadhim purchases goods for resale $73; he pays cash.

2 He sells goods $19 for cash.

**Required**

List the two entries in Nadhim's ledger for each transaction.

## Answer

| | Debits | Credits |
|---|---|---|
| 1 | Purchases account | Cash account |
| 2 | Cash account | Sales account |

When you go to a takeaway food store and you order your meal, the proprietor does not open an account for you; he simply takes your money and gives you your meal.

He debits – cash account (the sale of your meal would be included in his total cash sales for the day).

He credits – sales account (using the total sales figure for the day).

Remember that each account would be in a different ledger according to the classification we have discussed.

Each account would be shown on a separate page in the ledger. There is not enough space in this book to afford such a luxury. We will write the accounts on the same page.

➤ Now try Question 3.

**Worked example**

Siobhan Murphy provides the following information for the past few days:

1 Siobhan purchases a non-current asset $1450 from Adil on credit.

2 She sells goods $77 to Fiona, who pays by cheque.

3 She purchases goods for resale $510 from Zainab on credit.

4 She purchases goods for resale $65 from Joan for cash.

**Required**

Enter the transactions in Siobhan's ledger. (Indicate in which ledger each account would be found.)

## Answer

**Non-current assets account (GL)**

| Dr | Cr |
|---|---|
| $ | |
| 1450 | |

**Adil (PL)**

| Dr | Cr |
|---|---|
| | $ |
| | 1450 |

**Sales account (GL)**

| Dr | Cr |
|---|---|
| | $ |
| | 77 |

**Bank account**

| Dr | Cr |
|---|---|
| $ | |
| 77 | |

**Purchases account (GL)**

| Dr | Cr |
|---|---|
| $ | |
| 510 | |
| 65 | |

**Zainab (PL)**

| Dr | Cr |
|---|---|
| | $ |
| | 510 |

**Cash account (GL)**

| Dr | Cr |
|---|---|
| | $ |
| | 65 |

**Note**

- Customers' accounts and suppliers' accounts appear in the sales ledger (SL) and in the purchases ledger (PL) respectively – but only if the transactions are on credit.
- Accounts that are not personal accounts are found in the general ledger (GL).
- All debit entries have a corresponding credit entry.
- All credit entries have a corresponding debit entry.

Readers who have bank accounts will have observed that when they receive a bank statement from the bank, money paid out of the account is entered in the left column (debit) of the bank statement, while moneys received into the account are entered in the right column (credit). This causes problems initially.

After what has been said above, this might seem to be the wrong way round. So who is right? Well, both the bank statement and this book are correct. You need to remember that the bank statement is written from the point of view of the bank, not from your point of view.

More details on this are given in Chapter 12.

➤ Now try Question 4.

## Self-test questions

8 Every ____________ needs a corresponding credit entry.
9 Name the book in which all business transactions are entered.
10 List the three divisions of the ledger.
11 Explain the meaning of the term 'personal account'.
12 Name two 'real' accounts found in the ledger.
13 Name two 'nominal' accounts found in the ledger.
14 Name two 'liability' accounts found in the ledger.

## Chapter summary

- All business financial transactions are recorded in accounts.
- Accounts are recorded in a ledger.
- Non-personal accounts should contain the word 'account' in the heading, for example 'Motor expenses account'.
- Personal accounts only have the person's name or the name of a business in the heading, for example 'Patel and Co.'
- All transactions have a dual aspect.
- Every debit entry in an account in the ledger must have a corresponding credit entry.
- Every credit entry in an account in the ledger must have a corresponding debit entry.
- The ledger is divided into three parts because it is easier and more convenient to use in this form.
- The purchases ledger contains the accounts of suppliers with credit accounts.
- The sales ledger contains the accounts of customers with credit accounts
- The general ledger contains nominal, real and liability accounts.

# 2 The books of prime entry

**Content**

**1.1 The accounting cycle**

- Describe the functions of the books of prime entry

**By the end of this chapter you should be able to:**

- identify the five books of prime entry that deal with credit transactions
- use a cash book as a book of prime entry
- identify the source documents used to make entries in the books
- make entries in the six books to record financial transactions
- post entries from the books of prime entry to the ledgers
- understand the effect that trade discount has on entries in the books of prime entry.

The **books of prime entry** are also known as **subsidiary books** and **books of original entry**. There are six books of prime entry and they are:

**1** the purchases journal
**2** the sales journal
**3** the purchases returns journal
**4** the sales returns journal
**5** the general journal
**6** the cash book.

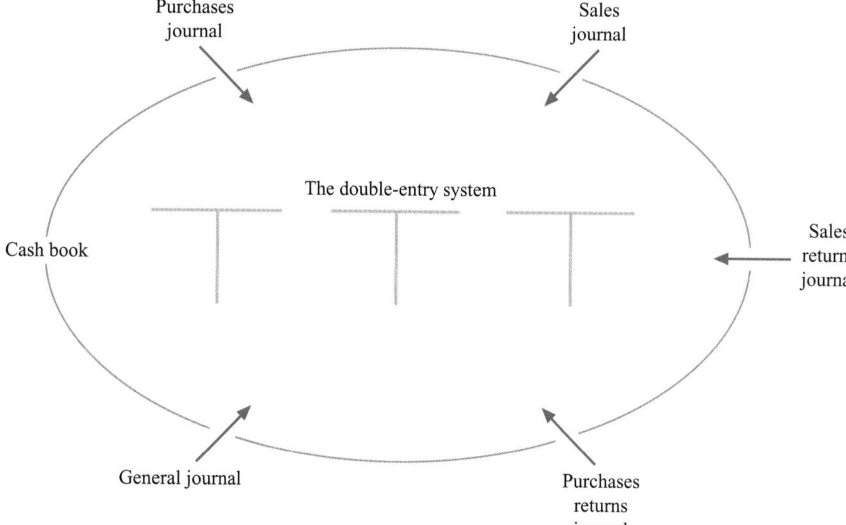


**Figure 2.1** The six books of prime entry

All transactions are first entered in a book of prime entry.

Each book of prime entry is made up of a list of similar types of transaction. The items are listed in the book until it is worthwhile to post the list to the ledger. Some of this may sound confusing; but when you have seen how the books work, things will become clear.

All transactions *must* be entered in one of the books of prime entry before they can be entered in the ledger.

So the cash book is used to get into the ground and it will also play its part in the game of double entry.

- The books of prime entry are used as a convenient way of entering transactions into the double-entry system.
- It is less efficient to make entries into the ledgers as they arise. It is too time consuming and that means it is generally more costly.
- It is better to collect the entries and categorise them into bundles of similar types and then to post from these books in bulk.

## 2.1 Recording credit purchases and sales

### 2.1.1 The purchases journal

The **purchases journal** is also known as the purchases day book.

When a purchases invoice is received from a supplier of goods it shows the goods that have been purchased and the price charged. The details are listed in the purchases journal.

The primary sources of information used to make entries in the books of prime entry are called **source documents**.

The purchases journal is a list of credit purchases made. The **source documents** are the purchase invoices received.

When it is convenient (this could be daily, weekly or monthly depending on the volume of purchases made by the business), the list of purchases is totalled and the total is posted to the *debit* side of the purchases account in the general ledger because the goods have been received.

Each individual supplier's ledger account in the purchases ledger is credited with the value of goods purchased (showing that the supplier has 'given' the goods).

**Tip**

As long as you remember the left side is debit and the right side is credit, you can leave Dr/Cr out when writing the ledger accounts.

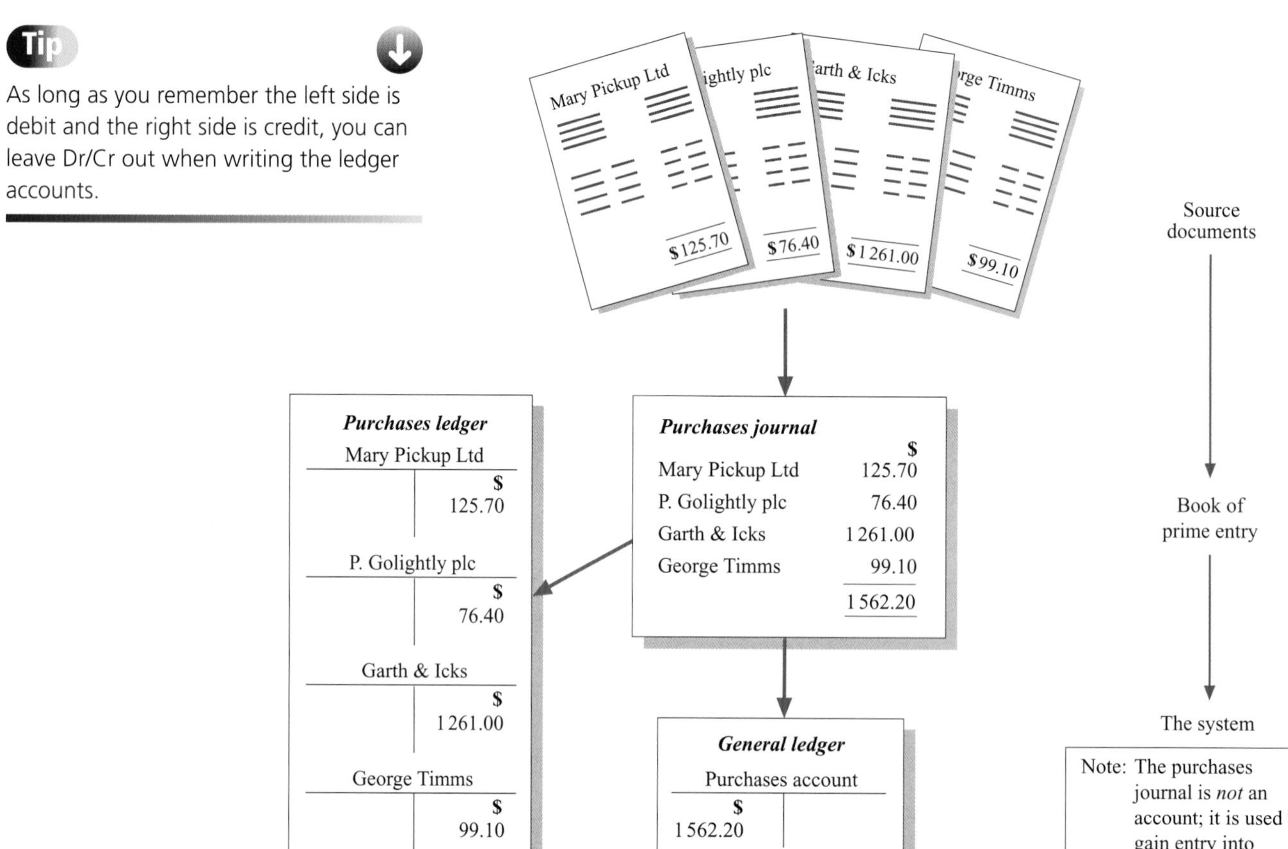


**Figure 2.2** The purchases journal

## 2.1.2 The sales journal

The **sales journal** is also known as the sales day book.

When goods are sold the supplier sends a sales invoice to the customer. The sales invoice itemises the goods that have been sold and the price of those goods.

A copy of this invoice is retained by the seller.

The copy sales invoice is the source document from which the sales journal is written.

The copy sales invoices sent to customers are used to prepare a list of the credit sales made.

When it is convenient (this could be daily, weekly or monthly depending on the volume of sales made by the business), the list is totalled and the total is posted to the *credit* side of the sales account in the general ledger because the goods have been 'given' to the customer.

Each individual customer's ledger account in the sales ledger is debited with the value of goods sold to them (indicating that the customer has 'gained' the goods).

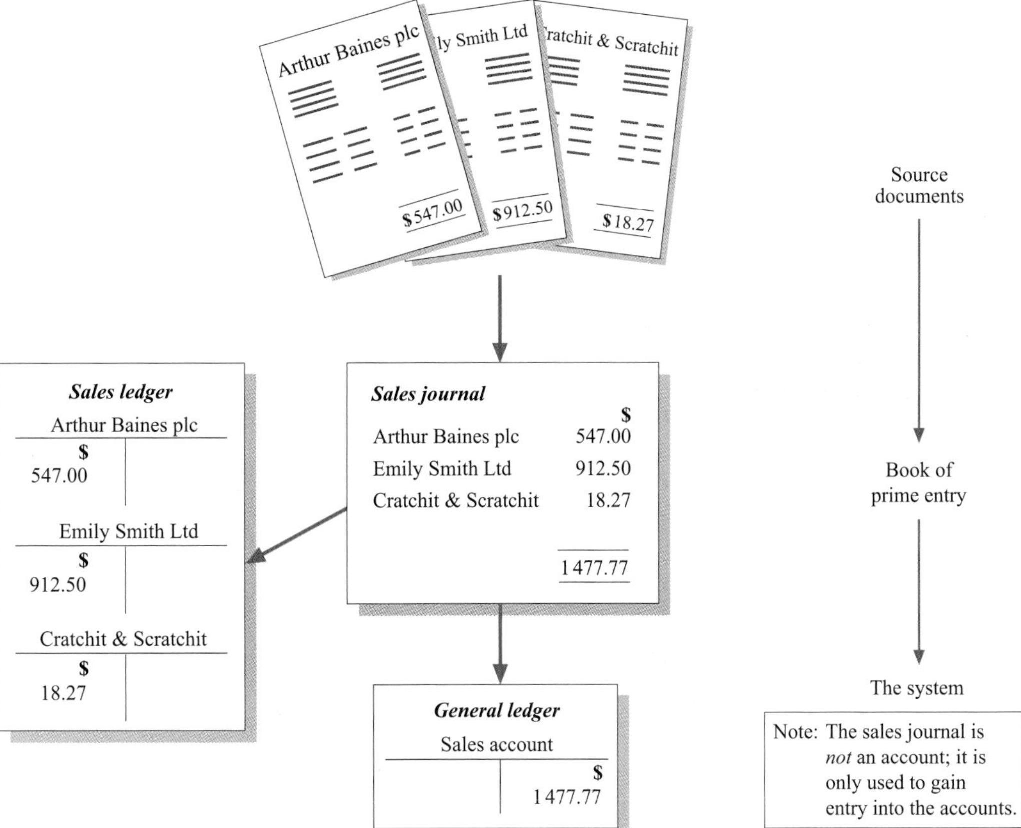


**Figure 2.3** The sales journal

# 2.2 Recording the return of goods

## 2.2.1 The purchases returns journal

The **purchases returns journal** is also known as the returns outwards journal or purchases returns book.

Sometimes, goods that have been purchased turn out to be faulty, the wrong colour, the wrong size or not useful in some other way. These goods will be returned to the supplier. The supplier in due course will send a credit note.

These credit notes are the source documents from which the purchases returns journal is written up.

The purchases returns journal is a list of all the credit notes received from suppliers. When it is convenient, the list is added and the total is posted to the credit of the **purchases returns account** (the returns have been sent back to the supplier).

**Note**

- The goods that have been returned are not posted to the credit side of the purchases account.
- Each individual entry in the purchases returns journal is then posted to the debit of the respective supplier's account in the purchases ledger (the suppliers receive the goods).

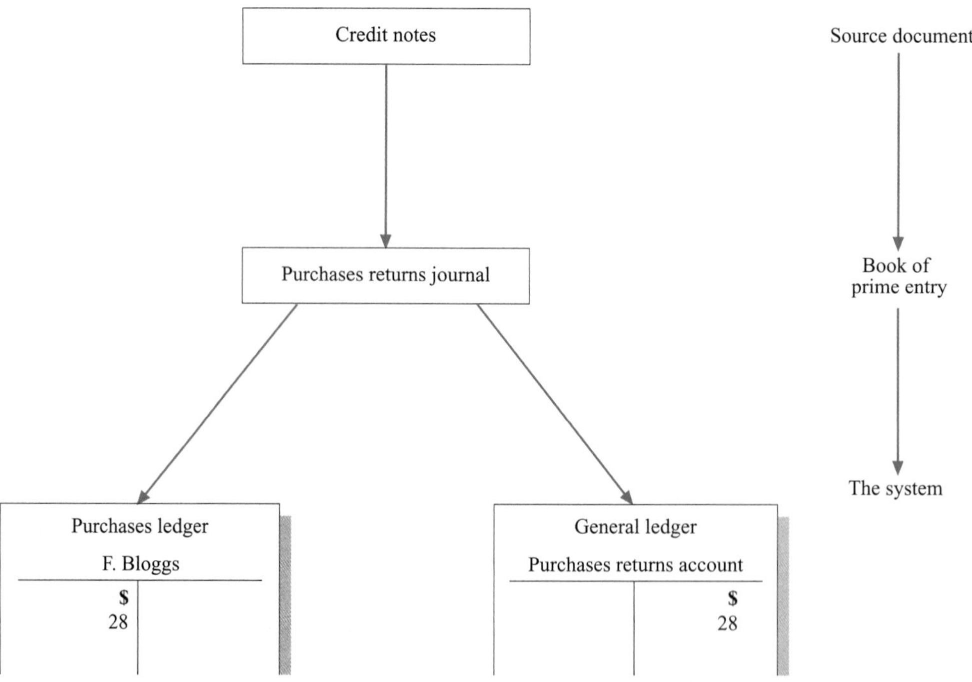


**Figure 2.4** The purchases returns journal

### 2.2.2 The sales returns journal

The **sales returns journal** is also known as the returns inwards journal.

Sales that are not acceptable are returned by the customer and a credit note is sent to the customer.

A copy of the credit note will be retained and this is the source document from which the sales returns journal is written up.

When convenient, the list is added and the total is posted to the debit of the **sales returns account** (the goods have been received).

**Note**

- The goods that have been returned are not debited to the sales account.
- Each individual entry in the sales returns journal is posted to the credit of the customer who returned the goods (they have 'given' the goods back to the supplier).

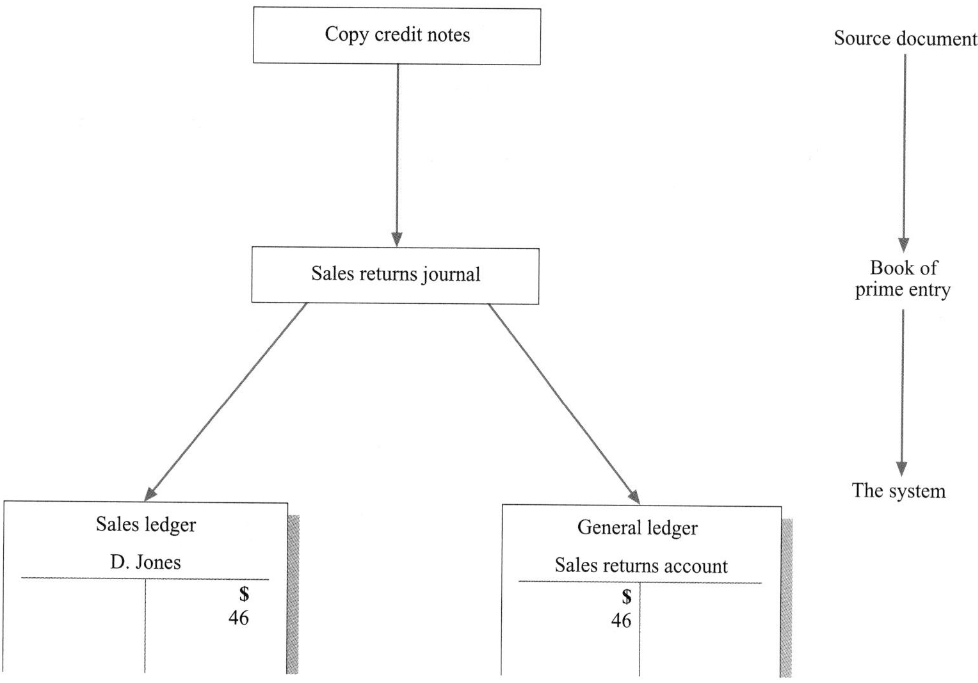


**Figure 2.5** The sales returns journal

## 2.3 The general journal and its uses

**Tip**

The general journal is usually referred to as 'the journal'.

The **general journal** is often a source of confusion for students. But do not worry – its uses are very limited and it is not as difficult as we often assume when we first contact it. It is, however, a topic that you need to be familiar with.

The general journal is used when we cannot comfortably find another book of prime entry to use.

Its layout is different from the other books of prime entry described above.

The 'folio' columns are often omitted in examination questions.

**Example**

**General journal**

| Date | Particulars | Folio | Debit | Credit |
|---|---|---|---|---|
| The date of the entries | The account to be debited | Ledger and page | Amount to be debited | |
| | The account to be credited | | | Amount to be credited |
| A description of why the transaction was necessary (the narrative) | | | | |

After the two entries have been entered in the general journal, an explanation of why the transaction was necessary is required. This is referred to as the **narrative**.
The general journal has six uses. It is used to record:

1. the purchase of non-current assets on credit
2. the sale of non-current assets on credit
3. the entries necessary to open ledger accounts when a business first comes into existence
4. the entries required to record the closing of ledger accounts when a business finally ceases to trade
5. the correction of errors
6. inter-ledger transfers.

The source documents used to write up the general journal would include:

- purchase invoices for capital expenditure
- sales invoices for sales of capital items.

Other source documents will be encountered as we progress with our studies.

**Worked example of use 1**

On 23 April 2014, Tamara purchased on credit an xtr/397 machine from Dextel and Co. for $12600.

**Required**

Prepare the entry in Tamara's general journal to record the transaction.

## Answer

**General journal**

| Date | Particulars | Folio | Debit | Credit |
|---|---|---|---|---|
| | | | $ | $ |
| 23 April 2014 | Machinery account | GL23* | 12600 | |
| | Dextel Ltd | PL26 | | 12600 |
| Purchase of Machine xtr/397 on credit from Dextel Ltd | | | | |

* Page numbers in the ledgers are for illustrative purposes.

Remember the use of the narrative explaining why entries in the ledgers are necessary.

## Worked example of use 2

On 6 September 2014, Hussain sold vehicle P341 FTX to Greg's garage for $230. Greg will settle the debt on 31 October 2014.

**Required**

Prepare the entry in Hussain's general journal to record the transaction.

### Answer

General journal

| Date | Particulars | Folio | Debit | Credit |
|---|---|---|---|---|
| | | | $ | $ |
| 6 September 2014 | Greg's garage | SL42 | 230 | |
| | Vehicles disposal account | GL11 | | 230 |
| Sale of vehicle P341 FTX to Greg's garage | | | | |

## Worked example of use 3

Marlene started in business on 1 January 2014 by paying $14000 into her business bank account.

**Required**

Prepare the entry in Marlene's general journal to record the transaction.

### Answer

General journal

| Date | Particulars | Folio | Debit | Credit |
|---|---|---|---|---|
| | | | $ | $ |
| 1 January 2014 | Bank account | GL1 | 14000 | |
| | Capital account | GL2 | | 14000 |
| Capital introduced by Marlene | | | | |

**Tip**

If you find it difficult to prepare journal entries, try drawing up 'T' accounts as you did in Chapter 1. Then from the accounts draw up the journal. In reality, the journal should be done first as it is the book of prime entry.

The other three uses are dealt with later:

- use 4 in Chapter 38 (closing the ledge accounts when a business ceases to trade)
- use 5 in Chapter 11 (correcting errors in the double-entry system)
- use 6 in Chapter 13 (making transfers from the sales ledger to the purchases ledger).

**Worked example**

On 2 August 2014, Jared purchases, on credit, a new machine for his business costing $5400 from Factre Ltd.

**Required**

Prepare the entries in Jared's general journal to record the transaction.

### Workings

If you are unsure how to tackle this question, draw up the 'T' accounts.

Jared gains a machine. Factre Ltd 'loses' the machine.

**Machinery account**

| $ | |
|---|---|
| 5400 | |

**Factre Ltd**

| | $ |
|---|---|
| | 5400 |

Which account has been debited? Which account has been credited?

If you can do this, then you can draw up the general journal.

### Answer

**General journal**

| Date | Particulars | Folio | Debit | Credit |
|---|---|---|---|---|
| | | | $ | $ |
| 2 August 2014 | Machinery account | GL19 | 5400 | |
| | Factre Ltd | PL41 | | 5400 |
| Purchase of new machine from Factre Ltd | | | | |

## 2.4 The cash book used as a book of prime entry

The final book of prime entry is the **cash book**. The cash book is dealt with in more detail in Chapters 4 and 5. It is sufficient to say at this stage that any cash (or bank) transactions will be entered in the cash book (and in another account in order to complete the double entry).

The cash book is not only part of our double-entry system, it is also a book of prime entry.

The source documents used to write up the cash book would include:

- cheque book counterfoils
- receipts received from suppliers who have dealt in cash
- copy receipts given to customers
- cash register till rolls.

Other source documents used to write up the cash book will be encountered in later chapters.

# 2.5 Trade discount

**Trade discount** is a reduction in the price charged to a customer who is also in business.

**Example**

Extrav plc sells a wooden kitchen cupboard to the general public for $300. Clyde is a kitchen designer and fitter. He purchases a kitchen cupboard from Extrav plc, to fit into one of his customer's kitchens for $240.

Clyde gets trade discount of $60. This trade discount expressed as a percentage would be 20 per cent.

Trade discount is not recorded in Extrav plc's ledger, nor is it recorded in Clyde's ledger.

In Clyde's purchases journal the entry would show:

| | $ |
|---|---|
| Extrav plc | 240 |

In Extrav plc's sales journal the entry would show:

| | $ |
|---|---|
| Clyde | 240 |

**Worked example**

The following are the prices of some kitchen cupboards as charged to the general public by Extrav plc and the rates of trade discount allowed to other different retail businesses.

| Name of customer | Model of cupboard | Retail price charged to the general public | Rate of trade discount |
|---|---|---|---|
| | | $ | % |
| Hay Bee Ltd | vh/13 | 1 490 | 25 |
| Sea Dee | bk/32 | 4 600 | 50 |
| M. Henn plc | jf/71 | 6 780 | 70 |
| Pea Queue Ltd | bo/22 | 630 | 10 |

**Required**

Prepare the entries in the sales journal of Extrav plc.

## Answer

**Sales journal**

| | $ |
|---|---|
| Hay Bee Ltd | 1 117.50 |
| Sea Dee | 2 300.00 |
| M. Henn plc | 2 034.00 |
| Pea Queue Ltd | 567.00 |
| | 6 018.50 |

Similarly, in the purchases journal of the customers of Extrav plc the amounts would be shown net of trade discount.

So in the purchases journal of Hay Bee Ltd we would find an entry:

| | $ |
|---|---|
| Extrav plc | 1 117.50 |

**Postings** to the respective ledgers would follow the lines shown earlier in this chapter.

**Posting** is the term used by accountants for entering transactions into the ledger accounts of a business.

## Self-test questions

1 Why is there a need to use books of prime entry?
2 Give an alternative name for the books of prime entry.
3 Give another name for the sales journal.
4 What is meant by the term 'posting'?
5 Which book of prime entry is also part of the double-entry system?
6 Name the source document used to prepare the purchases journal.
7 Name the source document used to prepare the sales returns journal.
8 Which two accounts are prepared from the entries in the sales journal?
9 Which two accounts are prepared from the entries in the purchases returns journal?
10 Explain how postings are made from the returns journal to the general ledger.
11 Name one use of the general journal.
12 How is trade discount entered in the books of prime entry?

➤ **Now try Question 1.**

## Chapter summary

- All business transactions must be first entered in a book of prime entry before they can be entered in the double-entry system.
- Five books of prime entry deal with credit transactions:
  - purchases journal
  - sales journal
  - purchases returns journal
  - sales returns journal
  - general journal.
- The five books of prime entry are 'lists' from which ledger accounts are compiled.
- The sixth book of prime entry is the cash book.
- The cash book deals with all cash and bank account transactions. It is also part of the double-entry system
- Trade discount is a reduction in price charged by a supplier to a customer who is in business.

# 3 The ledger accounts in detail

**Content**

**1.1 The accounting cycle**

- Prepare ledger accounts

**By the end of this chapter you should be able to:**
- make detailed entries in a ledger account.

## 3.1 Making detailed entries in ledger accounts

Up to now we have used 'T' accounts to record the two sides of a transaction. This is useful and it will give us the information that we require. However, it would be more useful if the 'T' accounts gave us more details of each transaction.
- It would be useful to know when the transaction took place.
- It would also be useful to be able to follow the whole transaction through to its completion, especially when a problem occurs in the system.

These problems are rectified by simple means.

Each entry should be preceded by:
- the *date* of the transaction
- a *description* stating where the corresponding entry can be located
- the *appropriate ledger and folio (page) number* of the 'other' entry.

An entry in a ledger account may look like this:

| Dr | | **An account** | | | | | Cr |
|---|---|---|---|---|---|---|---|
| | | | $ | | | | |
| 7 April | Sales | GL17 | 217 | | | | |

The transaction took place on 7 April. The 'opposite' entry (the credit entry) is in the sales account and can be found on page 17 of the general ledger.

| Dr | | | | **Another account** | | | Cr |
|---|---|---|---|---|---|---|---|
| | | | | | | | $ |
| | | | | 12 Sept | Purchases | GL28 | 416 |

Here the transaction took place on 12 September. The debit entry is in the purchases account, which is on page 28 of the general ledger.

If you are asked to prepare a ledger account, then your answer must have *all* the details. However, when you are working things out, you may use 'T' accounts because this is faster and just as accurate.
Many accountants and teachers use 'T' accounts to solve tricky problems and for general workings.

Try jotting down your workings using 'T' accounts. When you gain confidence in their use you will find that you can use them as a revision tool and for solving problems.

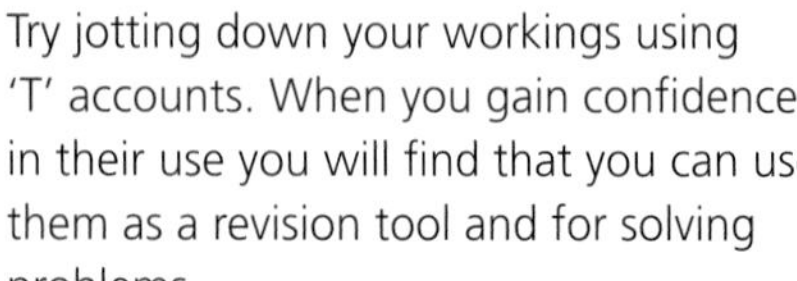

## 3.2 Using the books of prime entry

The information shown in ledger accounts is derived from one of the books of prime entry.

**Worked example**

The following transactions took place during the first week in October:

1 1 October: purchased goods for resale on credit from Arkimed plc $120
2 1 October: sold goods on credit to Morris & Co. $600
3 2 October: purchased vehicle on credit from Pooley Motors plc $17 400
4 4 October: sold goods on credit to Nelson plc $315
5 4 October: purchased goods for resale on credit from Bjorn & Co. $450
6 4 October: purchased goods for resale on credit from Darth & Son $170
7 7 October: sold goods on credit to Olivia Ltd $1340
8 7 October: returned damaged goods $38 to Arkimed plc
9 7 October: purchased goods for resale on credit from Charlene $320.

**Required**

a Identify the source document that has been used in each case to write up the book of prime entry.
b Write up the appropriate books of prime entry.
c Show the entries in each ledger account.

### Answer

a Purchase invoices: Transactions 1, 3, 5, 6, 9
Copy sales invoices: Transactions 2, 4, 7
Credit note: Transaction 8

b

**Purchases journal**

| | | | $ |
|---|---|---|---|
| 1 Oct | Arkimed plc | PL1 | 120 |
| 4 Oct | Bjorn & Co. | PL2 | 450 |
| 4 Oct | Darth & Son | PL3 | 170 |
| 7 Oct | Charlene | PL4 | 320 |
| | | | 1 060 |

**Sales journal**

| | | | $ |
|---|---|---|---|
| 1 Oct | Morris & Co. | SL1 | 600 |
| 4 Oct | Nelson plc | SL2 | 315 |
| 7 Oct | Olivia Ltd | SL3 | 1 340 |
| | | | 2 255 |

**Purchases returns journal**

| | | | $ |
|---|---|---|---|
| 7 Oct | Arkimed | PL1 | 38 |

**General journal**

| | | | Dr | Cr |
|---|---|---|---|---|
| | | | $ | $ |
| 2 Oct | Vehicles | GL4 | 17 400 | |
| | Pooley Mtrs plc | GL5 | | 17 400 |
| Purchase of vehicle from Pooley Motors plc | | | | |

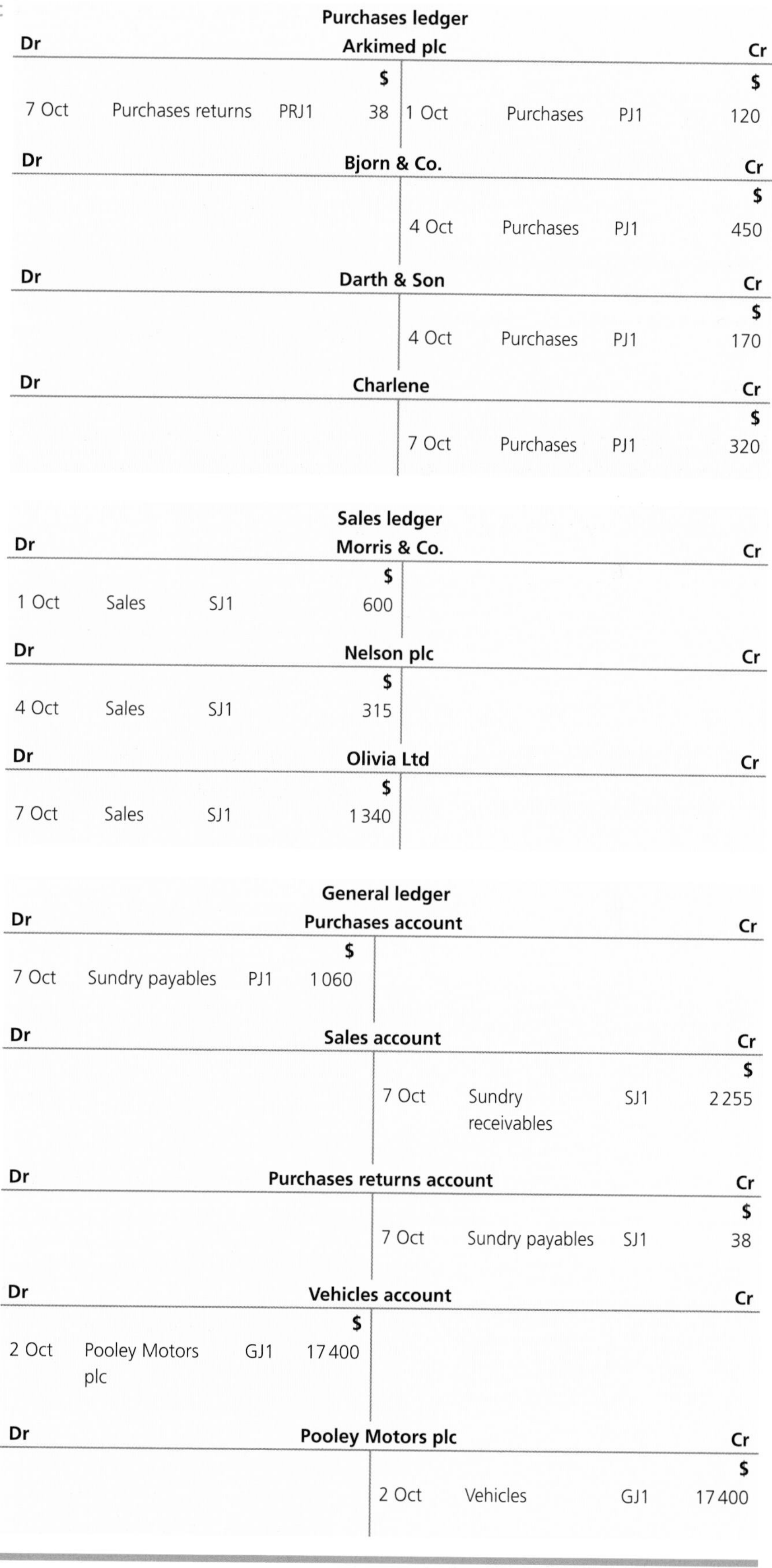

c

**Purchases ledger**

**Arkimed plc**

| Dr | | | $ | | | | $ Cr |
|---|---|---|---|---|---|---|---|
| 7 Oct | Purchases returns | PRJ1 | 38 | 1 Oct | Purchases | PJ1 | 120 |

**Bjorn & Co.**

| Dr | | | | | | | $ Cr |
|---|---|---|---|---|---|---|---|
| | | | | 4 Oct | Purchases | PJ1 | 450 |

**Darth & Son**

| Dr | | | | | | | $ Cr |
|---|---|---|---|---|---|---|---|
| | | | | 4 Oct | Purchases | PJ1 | 170 |

**Charlene**

| Dr | | | | | | | $ Cr |
|---|---|---|---|---|---|---|---|
| | | | | 7 Oct | Purchases | PJ1 | 320 |

**Sales ledger**

**Morris & Co.**

| Dr | | | $ | | | | Cr |
|---|---|---|---|---|---|---|---|
| 1 Oct | Sales | SJ1 | 600 | | | | |

**Nelson plc**

| Dr | | | $ | | | | Cr |
|---|---|---|---|---|---|---|---|
| 4 Oct | Sales | SJ1 | 315 | | | | |

**Olivia Ltd**

| Dr | | | $ | | | | Cr |
|---|---|---|---|---|---|---|---|
| 7 Oct | Sales | SJ1 | 1 340 | | | | |

**General ledger**

**Purchases account**

| Dr | | | $ | | | | Cr |
|---|---|---|---|---|---|---|---|
| 7 Oct | Sundry payables | PJ1 | 1 060 | | | | |

**Sales account**

| Dr | | | | | | | $ Cr |
|---|---|---|---|---|---|---|---|
| | | | | 7 Oct | Sundry receivables | SJ1 | 2 255 |

**Purchases returns account**

| Dr | | | | | | | $ Cr |
|---|---|---|---|---|---|---|---|
| | | | | 7 Oct | Sundry payables | SJ1 | 38 |

**Vehicles account**

| Dr | | | $ | | | | Cr |
|---|---|---|---|---|---|---|---|
| 2 Oct | Pooley Motors plc | GJ1 | 17 400 | | | | |

**Pooley Motors plc**

| Dr | | | | | | | $ Cr |
|---|---|---|---|---|---|---|---|
| | | | | 2 Oct | Vehicles | GJ1 | 17 400 |

The cash book is a book of prime entry. It contains the business cash account and the business bank account. We consider the cash book in much more detail in Chapter 4.

The following example uses the cash book as a book of prime entry:

**Worked example**

The following transactions took place during December:

1 December: paid rent using cash $250
2 December: paid local taxes by cheque $110
6 December: paid wages using cash $1782
13 December: paid wages using cash $1780
17 December: paid insurance premium by cheque $240
20 December: paid wages using cash $1780
27 December: paid wages using cash $1781
31 December: paid rent by cheque $250.

**Required**

a Enter the transactions in an appropriate book of prime entry.

b Show the necessary ledger accounts.

## Answer

a

**Cash book**

**Cash account**

| Dr | | | | | | | Cr |
|---|---|---|---|---|---|---|---|
| | | | | | | | $ |
| | | | | 1 Dec | Rent | GL1 | 250 |
| | | | | 6 Dec | Wages | GL4 | 1 782 |
| | | | | 13 Dec | Wages | GL4 | 1 780 |
| | | | | 20 Dec | Wages | GL4 | 1 780 |
| | | | | 27 Dec | Wages | GL4 | 1 781 |

**Bank account**

| Dr | | | | | | | Cr |
|---|---|---|---|---|---|---|---|
| | | | | | | | $ |
| | | | | 2 Dec | Local taxes | GL2 | 110 |
| | | | | 17 Dec | Insurance | GL3 | 240 |
| | | | | 31 Dec | Rent | GL1 | 250 |

b

**General ledger**

**Rent account**

| Dr | | | | | | | Cr |
|---|---|---|---|---|---|---|---|
| | | | $ | | | | |
| 1 Dec | Cash | CB1 | 250 | | | | |
| 31 Dec | Bank | CB1 | 250 | | | | |

**Local taxes account**

| Dr | | | | | | | Cr |
|---|---|---|---|---|---|---|---|
| | | | $ | | | | |
| 2 Dec | Bank | CB1 | 110 | | | | |

**Insurance account**

| Dr | | | | | | | Cr |
|---|---|---|---|---|---|---|---|
| | | | $ | | | | |
| 17 Dec | Bank | CB1 | 240 | | | | |

**Wages account**

| Dr | | | | | | | Cr |
|---|---|---|---|---|---|---|---|
| | | | $ | | | | |
| 6 Dec | Cash | CB1 | 1 782 | | | | |
| 13 Dec | Cash | CB1 | 1 780 | | | | |
| 20 Dec | Cash | CB1 | 1 780 | | | | |
| 27 Dec | Cash | CB1 | 1 781 | | | | |

Entering transactions in the books of prime entry and then the ledgers is not a difficult task; it just takes patience and the ability to enter transactions twice – once on the debit side of an account and once on the credit side of another account. Remember, *practice makes perfect.*

## Self-test questions

1 Identity the four pieces of information you would expect to find on the debit side of a ledger account.
2 Identify the four pieces of information you would expect to find on the credit side of a ledger account.
3 When would you use 'T' accounts?
4 Which source document would you use to write up the purchases returns journal?
5 Which type of account would you expect to find in the sales ledger?
6 Name a personal ledger.

➤ **Now try Question 1.**

## Chapter summary

- Ledger accounts must show date, details of a 'corresponding' entry, folio details and the amount of the transaction.
- 'T' accounts must only be used for revision purposes or as part of workings.
- All transactions must be entered in a book of prime entry before being posted to a ledger.

# 4 The cash book

**Content**

**1.1 The accounting cycle**

- Describe the functions of the books of prime entry

**By the end of this chapter you should be able to:**

- record cash and cheque payments
- record receipts of cash and cheques
- identify the source documents used to write up a cash book
- balance the cash and bank columns of a cash book
- make contra entries in a cash book.

## 4.1 The cash book

We have looked in some detail at the five books of prime entry used to access the double-entry system. The sixth and final book is the cash book. The cash book records *all* transactions concerning **money**.

**Money** can be in the form of cash, cheques, credit and debit card transactions.

You will have noticed in the section on double entry that the cash and bank accounts were used very frequently and as a result became very full with entries. Generally, in business these accounts are used more frequently than any other accounts. This means that it is sensible to remove these two accounts from the general ledger and keep them apart from the other accounts.

The cash and bank accounts are kept separately in one book – the cash book.

Because it is such an important and sensitive area of the business, all cash and cheque transactions are usually the responsibility of one senior or well-qualified person – the cashier.

## 4.2 Recording cash and cheque payments in a cash book

The accounts in the cash book work on double-entry principles like all other accounts.

- The debit (or receiving) side is found on the left.
- The credit (or giving) side is on the right.

The only differences in the layout of the cash book are that the debit entries are distanced from the credit entries by extra columns and information; and that the debit entries, generally, take up the whole of the left page while the credit entries take up the whole of the right page.

The layout is the same on both sides of the cash book:

**Example**

The debit side of the cash book looks like this:

**Cash book**

| Date | Particulars | Folio | Cash | Bank |
|---|---|---|---|---|

The credit side of the cash book looks like this:

**Cash book**

| Date | Particulars | Folio | Cash | Bank |
|---|---|---|---|---|

The whole cash book looks like this:

| Dr | | | | Cash book | | | | | Cr |
|---|---|---|---|---|---|---|---|---|---|
| **Date** | **Particulars** | **Folio** | **Cash** | **Bank** | **Date** | **Particulars** | **Folio** | **Cash** | **Bank** |
| (1) | (2) | (3) | (4) | (5) | (6) | (7) | (8) | (9) | (10) |

- Columns (1) and (6) give the date on which the transaction occurred.
- Columns (2) and (7) identify the account where the corresponding entry can be found.
- Columns (3) and (8) show the page of the ledger where the corresponding entry can be found.
- All cash received is entered in Column (4).
- All monies paid into the business bank account are recorded in Column (5).
- All cash payments made are recorded in Column (9).
- All payments made by cheque are recorded in Column (10).

**Worked example**

The following transactions took place in the first week of September:

1 September: paid R. Serth $34 cash

2 September: paid T. Horse $167 cash

3 September: paid V. Dole $78 cash.

**Required**

Enter the transactions in a cash book.

## Answer

| Dr | | | | Cash book | | | | | Cr |
|---|---|---|---|---|---|---|---|---|---|
| **Date** | **Particulars** | **Folio** | **Cash** | **Bank** | **Date** | **Particulars** | **Folio** | **Cash** | **Bank** |
| | | | | | | | | $ | |
| | | | | | 1 Sept | R. Serth | PL9 | 34 | |
| | | | | | 2 Sept | T. Horse | PL6 | 167 | |
| | | | | | 3 Sept | V. Dole | PL2 | 78 | |

**Worked example**

The following transactions took place in February:

3 February: paid rent $400 by cheque

7 February: paid Gary $67 by cheque

9 February: paid wages $832 by cheque.

**Required**

Enter the transactions in a cash book.

## Answer

| Dr | | | | | Cash book | | | | Cr |
|---|---|---|---|---|---|---|---|---|---|
| **Date** | **Particulars** | **Folio** | **Cash** | **Bank** | **Date** | **Particulars** | **Folio** | **Cash** | **Bank** |
| | | | | | | | | | $ |
| | | | | | 3 Feb | Rent | GL8 | | 400 |
| | | | | | 7 Feb | Gary | PL9 | | 67 |
| | | | | | 9 Feb | Wages | GL15 | | 832 |

## 4.3 Recording the receipt of cash and cheques in a cash book

**Worked example**

The following transactions took place during May:

4 May: cash received from Nigel $213

5 May: cash received from Harry $92

9 May: cash received from Hilary $729.

**Required**

Enter the transactions in a cash book.

## Answer

| Dr | | | | | Cash book | | | | Cr |
|---|---|---|---|---|---|---|---|---|---|
| **Date** | **Particulars** | **Folio** | **Cash** | **Bank** | **Date** | **Particulars** | **Folio** | **Cash** | **Bank** |
| | | | $ | | | | | | |
| 4 May | Nigel | SL12 | 213 | | | | | | |
| 5 May | Harry | SL7 | 92 | | | | | | |
| 9 May | Hilary | SL8 | 729 | | | | | | |

**Worked example**

The following transactions took place during January:

2 January: cheque received from Steve $249

3 January: cash sales banked $851

11 January: cheque received from Mustaf $29.

**Required**

Enter the transactions in a cash book.

## Answer

| Dr | | | | Cash book | | | | | Cr |
|---|---|---|---|---|---|---|---|---|---|
| Date | Particulars | Folio | Cash | Bank | Date | Particulars | Folio | Cash | Bank |
| | | | | $ | | | | | |
| 2 Jan | Steve | SL5 | | 249 | | | | | |
| 3 Jan | Cash sales | GL23 | | 851 | | | | | |
| 11 Jan | Mustaf | SL7 | | 29 | | | | | |

Once you have mastered the method of recording debit entries and credit entries it should be fairly straightforward to combine the two.

### Worked example

The following transactions took place during April:

2 April: cash received from Xavier, a customer, $458
4 April: motor repairs $530 paid using cash
6 April: cash received from Milly, a customer, $77
7 April: rent $210 paid using cash
9 April: insurance premium $156 paid using cash
12 April: cash sales $743.

**Required**

Enter the transactions in a cash book.

## Answer

| Dr | | | | Cash book | | | | | Cr |
|---|---|---|---|---|---|---|---|---|---|
| Date | Particulars | Folio | Cash | Bank | Date | Particulars | Folio | Cash | Bank |
| | | | $ | | | | | $ | |
| 2 Apr | Xavier | SL4 | 458 | | 4 Apr | Motor expenses | GL23 | 530 | |
| 6 Apr | Milly | SL13 | 77 | | 7 Apr | Rent | GL8 | 210 | |
| 12 Apr | Cash sales | GL2 | 743 | | 9 Apr | Insurance | GL11 | 156 | |

### Worked example

The following transactions took place in October:

3 October: paid Price, a supplier, $350 by cheque
6 October: a cheque for $450 received, an overpayment of rent
9 October: takings paid into bank $2187
11 October: Bliff, a customer, paid by cheque $639
12 October: a cheque received from Box $93 paid into the bank
17 October: local taxes $219 paid by cheque.

**Required**

Enter the transactions in a cash book.

### Answer

| Dr | | | | Cash book | | | | | Cr |
|---|---|---|---|---|---|---|---|---|---|
| Date | Particulars | Folio | Cash | Bank | Date | Particulars | Folio | Cash | Bank |
| | | | | $ | | | | | $ |
| 6 Oct | Rent | GL6 | | 450 | 3 Oct | Price | SL4 | | 350 |
| 9 Oct | Sales | GL17 | | 2 187 | 17 Oct | Local taxes | GL7 | | 219 |
| 11 Oct | Bliff | SL23 | | 639 | | | | | |
| 12 Oct | Box | PL14 | | 93 | | | | | |

It is now simply a matter of putting cash payments and cash receipts in the same book as cheque payments and monies paid into the bank.

**Worked example**

The following transactions have taken place:

1 November: cheque from Norman, a customer, $288 paid into bank
2 November: motor expenses paid by cheque $311
5 November: matthew draws a cheque for private use $150
10 November: cash sales $2 390
15 November: motor fuel purchased with cash $42
21 November: cheque paid into bank for Insurance refund $273
29 November: paid wages in cash $1 309
30 November: cash sales $5 630, paid directly into bank.

**Required**

Enter the transactions in a cash book.

### Answer

| Dr | | | | Cash book | | | | | Cr |
|---|---|---|---|---|---|---|---|---|---|
| Date | Particulars | Folio | Cash | Bank | Date | Particulars | Folio | Cash | Bank |
| | | | $ | $ | | | | $ | $ |
| 1 Nov | Norman | SL4 | | 288 | 2 Nov | Motor expenses | GL12 | | 311 |
| 10 Nov | Sales | GL9 | 2 390 | | 5 Nov | Drawings | GL23 | | 150 |
| 21 Nov | Insurance | GL11 | | 273 | 15 Nov | Motor expenses | GL12 | 42 | |
| 30 Nov | Sales | GL9 | | 5 630 | 29 Nov | Wages | GL7 | 1 309 | |

➤ Now try Question 1.

## 4.4 Source documents used to write up a cash book

The source documents used to write up a cash book are:

| Debit side | Credit side |
|---|---|
| Copy receipts | Receipts |
| Till rolls | Cheque book counterfoils |
| Bank paying-in book counterfoils | |

A further source of information to be used to write up the cash book is a copy of the details (recorded by the bank) of transactions made using the business bank account – but more of this source later.

**Self-test questions**

1 Draw out the headings used in a cash book.
2 On which side of a cash book would you enter a cheque received?
3 On which side of a cash book would a cheque payment be entered?
4 In which column would a cash sale be entered?
5 In which column would a cheque for the payment of rent be entered?

## 4.5 'Balancing' a cash book

At the end of an appropriate length of time, a cash book should be balanced. (The time when balancing takes place will generally depend on the size of the business and the number of transactions that are included in the cash book.)

Both of the balances in a cash book should be verified.

- How could you verify the cash balance brought down?
- How could you verify the bank balance that you brought down?

The balance brought down in the cash column should agree with the **cash in hand** at that date.

The bank balance in the cash book can be verified by reference to the bank statement.

The balances are brought down to start the 'new' time period.

Remember the cash balance will always be brought down as a debit. The bank balance brought down could be either a debit or a credit balance.

**Cash in hand** is the term used to describe the amount of cash held by a business at any one time. The cash in hand in a shop would be found in the tills. In a larger business it might be found in a safe.

A **balancing figure** is an amount that needs to be included in the debit side or credit side of an account to make the debit side equal to the credit side. The amount used to balance a cash book column is then used to 'start' the next time period.

**Worked example**

The cash book of Grey is shown:

| Dr | | | | Cash book | | | | | Cr |
|---|---|---|---|---|---|---|---|---|---|
| **Date** | **Particulars** | **Folio** | **Cash** | **Bank** | **Date** | **Particulars** | **Folio** | **Cash** | **Bank** |
| | | | **$** | **$** | | | | **$** | **$** |
| 1 Nov | Reid | SL6 | | 1 439 | 4 Nov | Wages | GL4 | | 428 |
| 6 Nov | Sales | GL9 | 1 270 | | 7 Nov | Hunt | PL6 | 73 | |
| 8 Nov | Gong | SL23 | | 451 | 11 Nov | Rent | GL6 | | 600 |
| 14 Nov | Potts | SL14 | | 349 | 16 Nov | Trig | PL16 | 38 | |

**Required**

Balance the cash and bank columns of the cash book on 16 November and carry any balances down.

### Answer

| Dr | | | | Cash book | | | | | Cr |
|---|---|---|---|---|---|---|---|---|---|
| **Date** | **Particulars** | **Folio** | **Cash** | **Bank** | **Date** | **Particulars** | **Folio** | **Cash** | **Bank** |
| | | | **$** | **$** | | | | **$** | **$** |
| 1 Nov | Reid | SL6 | | 1 439 | 4 Nov | Wages | GL4 | | 428 |
| 6 Nov | Sales | GL9 | 1 270 | | 7 Nov | Hunt | PL6 | 73 | |
| 8 Nov | Gong | SL23 | | 451 | 11 Nov | Rent | GL6 | | 600 |
| 14 Nov | Potts | SL14 | | 349 | 16 Nov | Trig | PL16 | 38 | |
| | | | | | 16 Nov | Balances c/d | | 1 159 | 1 211 |
| | | | 1 270 | 2 239 | | | | 1 270 | 2 239 |
| 17 Nov | Balances b/d | | 1 159 | 1 211 | | | | | |

**Tip**

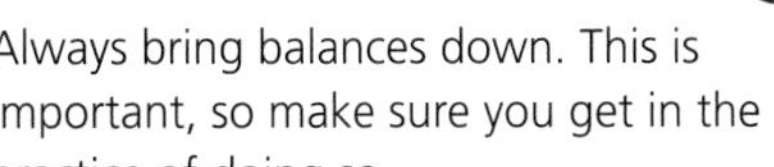

Always bring balances down. This is important, so make sure you get in the practice of doing so.

**Tip**

In ledger accounts, use 'Balance c/d' (carried down) for the balances above the total. Use 'Balance b/d' (brought down) for the balance below the total.

**Note**

Make sure that all four totals are on the same line. Balance the cash columns first; then balance the bank columns. Do not try to do them both at the same time.

➤ Now try Question 2.

## 4.6 Contra entries in a cash book

A transaction that appears on both the debit and credit sides of the double-entry system is called a **contra entry**. Contra entries have no effect on the well-being of the business.

Clearly, it is unsafe to keep large amounts of cash and cheques on the business premises for prolonged periods of time. The cashier will arrange for the monies received to be taken to a bank and deposited when the amount in the till or safe warrants it.

**Example**

The following is an extract from the cash book of Grant:

| Dr | | Cash book | | | | | | | Cr |
|---|---|---|---|---|---|---|---|---|---|
| **Date** | **Particulars** | **Folio** | **Cash** | **Bank** | **Date** | **Particulars** | **Folio** | **Cash** | **Bank** |
| | | | **$** | | | | | **$** | |
| 4 Jul | Cash sales | GL32 | 4397 | | 5 Jul | Purchases | GL7 | 48 | |
| 4 Jul | Bradley | SL51 | 74 | | | | | | |

Grant has more than $4000 cash on his premises – this represents a security risk. He pays $4000 into the business bank account on 5 July.

Talk yourself through this transaction.

Grant takes $4000 from the till ... the cash column 'loses' $4000.

| Date | Particulars | Folio | Cash | Bank |
|---|---|---|---|---|
| | | | **$** | |
| 5 Jul | Bank | C | 4000 | |

**Note**

- the date of the transaction
- the particulars telling where the 'corresponding' entry is to be found (in the bank column)
- 'C' is for 'contra' showing that Grant's business is neither better nor worse off because of the transaction
- $4000 in the cash column shows that cash has been 'lost'.

Grant takes the money to the bank and the bank receives the money.

| Date | Particulars | Folio | Cash | Bank |
|---|---|---|---|---|
| | | | | **$** |
| 5 Jul | Cash | C | | 4000 |

**Note**

- the date of the transaction
- the particulars telling where the 'corresponding' entry is to be found (in the cash column)
- 'C' is for 'contra' showing that Grant's business is neither better nor worse off because of the transaction
- $4000 in the bank column shows that money has been received into the bank account.

The effect on the business is the same as the effect on your finances that would occur if you removed a five-dollar bill from one pocket and put it into another pocket.

Another common contra entry in the cash book is the withdrawal of cash from the bank for use in the business. This transaction often occurs when cash wages need to be paid and the business has insufficient cash in the safe to make up the necessary wage packets. In fact, for security reasons, many larger businesses now pay wages and salaries directly into staff bank accounts so that large amounts of cash do not need to be transported from the bank and then kept on the business's premises.

**Example**

The following is an extract from the cash book of Diego:

| Dr | | | | Cash book | | | | | Cr |
|---|---|---|---|---|---|---|---|---|---|
| **Date** | **Particulars** | **Folio** | **Cash** | **Bank** | **Date** | **Particulars** | **Folio** | **Cash** | **Bank** |
| | | | | **$** | | | | | **$** |
| 12 Aug | Robson | SL32 | | 4574 | 11 Aug | Machinery | GL6 | | 2350 |
| 16 Aug | Nkomo | SL79 | | 5490 | | | | | |

Wages amounting to $4529 have to be paid in cash on 18 August. Diego withdraws this sum from the bank on 17 August.

If we talk ourselves through the process, the entries become clear:

Diego goes to the bank and withdraws $4529.

| Date | Particulars | Folio | Cash | Bank |
|---|---|---|---|---|
| | | | | **$** |
| 17 Aug | Cash | C | | 4529 |

He returns to his business premises and puts the cash in the safe:

| Date | Particulars | Folio | Cash | Bank |
|---|---|---|---|---|
| | | | **$** | |
| 17 Aug | Bank | C | 4529 | |

➤ Now try Question 3.

Many larger businesses now keep a cheque payments book and a cash receipts and lodgement book. This is certainly the case where the bulk of transactions are conducted through the bank account.

**Self-test questions**

6 What does the word 'contra' mean?

7 The cash book is not only a book of prime entry, it is also part of the ____________ system.

8 Fill in the gaps with 'debited' or 'credited'.

a Money taken from the safe and deposited in the bank would be ____________ in the cash column of the cash book and be ____________ in the bank column.

b Money withdrawn from the bank for use in the business would be ____________ in the cash column of the cash book and be ____________ in the bank column.

9 Which book of prime entry would you use to record a sale of goods on credit?

10 Name two source documents used to write up a cash book.

11 Is it possible to have a credit balance in the cash column of a cash book?

12 Is it possible to have a credit balance in the bank column of a cash book?

13 Under what circumstances do we write 'C' for contra against transactions in the cash book?

## Chapter summary

- The cash book is both a book of prime entry and it is part of the double-entry system.
- All transactions that involve cash and cheques are entered in the cash book.
- All cash transactions are entered in the cash columns.
- All transactions involving cheques are entered in the bank columns.
- All entries in a cash book need 'corresponding' entries in other ledger accounts to complete the double entry.
- Contra items have no effect on the worth of the business.
- Any balance shown in the cash column must be a debit balance.
- Balances shown in the bank column could be either a debit or a credit balance.

# 5 Discounts

**Content**

**1.1 The accounting cycle**

- Describe the functions of the books of prime entry

**By the end of this chapter you should be able to:**

- distinguish between trade discount and cash discount
- calculate both kinds of discount
- record cash discount allowed and cash discount received in ledger accounts
- use discount columns in a cash book as memorandum entries.

## 5.1 Types of discount

There are two types of discount available to businesses: **trade discount** and **cash discount**.

As we saw earlier, trade discount is a reduction in the price of goods charged by a manufacturer or distributor to another business. Trade discount is not recorded in the double-entry books of account.

Cash discount is a reduction in the price charged for goods when a credit customer settles their debt within a time given by the supplier. Cash discounts are available to encourage trade receivables to settle debts promptly.

**Example**

A customer owes $100.

A retailer may indicate that if the debt is settled before the month end, a cash discount of five per cent will be allowed.

The debtor pays before the month end, so only $95 needs to be paid – $100 less $5 cash discount.

Both the receipt of the money and the cash discount are recorded by the retailer and the customer.

## 5.2 Recording cash discounts allowed

The ledger accounts necessary to record cash discount allowed to credit customers are shown below:

**Worked example**

On 1 August Yung has three debtors. Her settlement terms allow a cash discount of five per cent to customers who settle their debts before the end, of August. (For illustrative purposes only, Yung does not keep a cash book.)

| Debtor | Amount owed | Date of payment by cheque |
|---|---|---|
| Georgi | $2 800 | 23 August |
| Ahmed | $80 | 17 September |
| Fatima | $360 | 29 August |

**Required**

Prepare the ledger accounts to record the settling of the debts due.

## Answer

**Sales ledger**

**Georgi**

| Dr | | | | | | | Cr |
|---|---|---|---|---|---|---|---|
| | | $ | | | | $ | |
| 1 Aug | Balance b/d | 2 800.00 | 23 Aug | Bank | GL1 | 2 660.00 | |
| | | | 23 Aug | Discount allowed | GL2 | 140.00 | |

**Ahmed**

| Dr | | | | | | | Cr |
|---|---|---|---|---|---|---|---|
| | | $ | | | | $ | |
| 1 Aug | Balance b/d | 80.00 | 17 Sept | Bank | GL1 | 80.00 | |

**Fatima**

| Dr | | | | | | | Cr |
|---|---|---|---|---|---|---|---|
| | | $ | | | | $ | |
| 1 Aug | Balance b/d | 360.00 | 29 Aug | Bank | GL1 | 342.00 | |
| | | | 29 Aug | Discount allowed | GL2 | 18.00 | |

**General ledger**

**Bank account**

| Dr | | | | | Cr |
|---|---|---|---|---|---|
| | | | $ | | |
| 23 Aug | Georgi | SL1 | 2 660.00 | | |
| 29 Aug | Fatima | SL3 | 342.00 | | |
| 17 Sept | Ahmed | SL2 | 80.00 | | |

**Discount allowed account**

| Dr | | | | | Cr |
|---|---|---|---|---|---|
| | | | $ | | |
| 23 Aug | Georgi | SL1 | 140.00 | | |
| 29 Aug | Fatima | SL3 | 18.00 | | |

You can see that discount allowed is credited to the customer's account, thus reducing the amount to be paid in settlement. It is debited to the discount allowed account in the general ledger. Ahmed did not qualify for a discount – he did not pay before the end of August.

## 5.3 Recording cash discount received

**Worked example**

Yung has three creditors on 1 August (for illustrative purposes only, Yung does not keep a cash book).

| Supplier | Amount owed | Cash discount available if payment made before 31 August |
|---|---|---|
| | $ | % |
| Hameed & Co. | 400 | 2 |
| BTQ plc | 7 400 | 5 |
| Carot Ltd | 200 | 3 |

Yung settled the amounts she owed by cheque on 26 August.

**Required**

The ledger accounts in Yung's books of account recording the payments made by her.

## Answer

**Purchases ledger**

**Hameed & Co.**

| Dr | | | | | | Cr |
|---|---|---|---|---|---|---|
| | | | **$** | | | **$** |
| 26 Aug | Bank | GL3 | 392.00 | 1 Aug | Balance b/d | 400.00 |
| 26 Aug | Discount received | GL4 | 8.00 | | | |

**BTQ plc**

| Dr | | | | | | Cr |
|---|---|---|---|---|---|---|
| | | | **$** | | | **$** |
| 26 Aug | Bank | GL3 | 7030.00 | 1 Aug | Balance b/d | 7400.00 |
| 26 Aug | Discount received | GL4 | 370.00 | | | |

**Carot Ltd**

| Dr | | | | | | Cr |
|---|---|---|---|---|---|---|
| | | | **$** | | | **$** |
| 26 Aug | Bank | GL3 | 194.00 | 1 Aug | Balance b/d | 200.00 |
| 26 Aug | Discount received | GL4 | 6.00 | | | |

**General ledger**

**Bank account**

| Dr | | | Cr |
|---|---|---|---|
| | | | **$** |
| 26 Aug | Hameed & Co. | PL1 | 392.00 |
| 26 Aug | BTQ plc | PL2 | 7030.00 |
| 26 Aug | Carot Ltd | PL3 | 194.00 |

**Discount received account**

| Dr | | | Cr |
|---|---|---|---|
| | | | **$** |
| 26 Aug | Hameed & Co. | PL1 | 8.00 |
| 26 Aug | BTQ plc | PL2 | 370.00 |
| 26 Aug | Carot Ltd | PL3 | 6.00 |

You can see that discount received is debited to the supplier's account, thus reducing the amount that Yung has to pay in settlement. The discounts are credited to the discount received account in the general ledger.

To summarise:

- Discount allowed is debited to the discount allowed account in the general ledger and is credited to the customer's account in the sales ledger.
- Discount received is credited to the discount received account in the general ledger and is debited to the supplier's account in the purchases ledger.

## 5.4 Entering cash discounts in the general ledger

To write up the discount accounts in the general ledger in the way outlined above means that all the accounts in the sales ledger must be scrutinised and all the accounts in the purchases ledger must also be examined and lists must be made of all the discounts allowed and discounts received in order to post them to the general ledger. This could be a huge task. We simplify our work by adding an extra column to those already found in the cash book.

We have already used a 'two-column' cash book (cash columns and bank columns). The principles used still hold good. We introduce a third column on the debit and credit sides for discounts, so that we now have a 'three-column' cash book.

The three-column cash book headings look like this:

| Date | Particulars | Folio | Discount | Cash | Bank | Date | Particulars | Folio | Discount | Cash | Bank |
|---|---|---|---|---|---|---|---|---|---|---|---|
| | | | | | | | | | | | |

**Memorandum columns** record information that is not part of the double-entry system.

The discount columns are **memorandum columns** only; they record the discounts but are not yet part of the double-entry system. This is a much more efficient way of collecting the information necessary to write up the discount accounts in the general ledger rather than examining every account in the sales ledger and every account in the purchases ledger.

*Note that we will now dispense with the folio columns in most examples and questions. You will not usually need to include them in your answers to questions.*

The entries to record the previous transactions in Yung's cash book would look like this:

**Example**

Dr — Cash book — Cr

| Date | Particulars | Discount | Cash | Bank | Date | Particulars | Discount | Cash | Bank |
|---|---|---|---|---|---|---|---|---|---|
| | | $ | | $ | | | $ | | $ |
| 23 Aug | Geogi | 140.00 | | 2660.00 | 26 Aug | Hameed & Co. | 8.00 | | 392.00 |
| 29 Aug | Fatima | 18.00 | | 342.00 | 26 Aug | BTQ plc | 370.00 | | 7030.00 |
| 17 Sept | Ahmed | | | 80.00 | 26 Aug | Carot Ltd | 6.00 | | 194.00 |
| 17 Sept | Balance c/d | | | 4534.00 | | | | | |
| | | 158.00 | | 7616.00 | | | 384.00 | | 7616.00 |
| | | | | | 18 Sept | Balance b/d | | | 4534.00 |

The cash and bank columns in the cash book are balanced as they were in the cash book of Grey in Chapter 4.

**Note**

- It is important to note that the discount columns are totalled. They are *not* compared and balanced since there is no connection between the entries in the two columns. One column refers to customers' accounts; the other column refers to suppliers' accounts.
- The discount columns are *memorandum* columns only – they are not part of the double-entry system.

The totals of the discount columns are then posted to the respective discount allowed and discount received accounts in the general ledger.

The purchases ledger accounts and the sales ledger accounts are the same as previously shown. However, the discount accounts would look like this.

**Example**

General ledger

Dr — Discount allowed account — Cr

| | | $ | | | |
|---|---|---|---|---|---|
| 17 Sept | Sundry debtors | 158 | | | |

Dr — Discount received account — Cr

| | | | | | $ |
|---|---|---|---|---|---|
| | | | 17 Sept | Sundry creditors | 384.00 |

**Note**

- The totals are used; the individual discounts are not shown.
- Notice also that two separate accounts are used.

## Self-test questions

1 Explain the term 'cash discount'.
2 Explain the term 'trade discount'.
3 Discount ____________ is debited to the discount ____________ account in the general ledger.
4 Discount ____________ is credited to the discount ____________ account in the general ledger.
5 On which side of the cash book would you find the discount allowed column?
6 On which side of the cash book would you find the discount received column?
7 Which columns of the cash book are balanced regularly?
8 Which columns of the cash book are not balanced?
9 What is meant by the term 'memorandum column'?

➤ **Now try Question 1.**

## Chapter summary

- Trade discount is not recorded in the books of account.
- Cash discount is a reward for prompt payment.
- Cash discount allowed is credited in the debtor's account and debited to the discount allowed account in the general ledger.
- Cash discount received is debited to the creditor's account and credited to the discount received account in the general ledger.
- To save time, both types of cash discount are listed in the cash book. The totals of the two columns are posted separately to the two discount accounts in the general ledger.
- The discount columns in the cash book are memorandum columns only – they are not part of the double-entry system.

# 6 Preparing simple financial statements

## Content

**1.1 The accounting cycle**

- Prepare ledger accounts and trial balance

**1.2 Accounting for non-current assets**

- Understand the treatment of capital and revenue incomes and expenditures

**1.4 Preparation of [simple] financial statements**

- Understand the need for and purpose of financial statements

**By the end of this chapter you should be able to:**

- prepare a simple income statement to reveal the profit or loss earned by a business
- prepare a simple statement of financial position.

The managers and owners of all businesses wish that their business will survive and flourish. In order that this might happen, the business must generate positive cash flows as these should ensure its short-term survival. All cash and bank transactions are recorded in a cash book. Balancing the cash and bank columns enable cash and bank surpluses and deficits to be recognised quickly. Short-term decisions regarding these surpluses and deficits can be then be made to benefit the business.

Profits should ensure survival of the business in the long term.

We have seen how all transactions are recorded in detail in the ledgers of a business, but the recording of cash and credit transactions in the ledger does not immediately reveal whether or not a business is profitable.

## 6.1 Balancing a ledger account

We have seen that every time we make a debit entry into our double-entry system we must also make a credit entry. If we follow this rule, then the total of all debit entries in the system must equal the sum of all credit entries.

A **trial balance** is a summary of all the entries in the double-entry system. It checks that each transaction has been entered once on the debit side of an account and once on the credit side of another account.

A **balancing figure** is an amount that needs to be included in the debit side or credit side of an account to make the debit side equal to the credit side.

The cash and bank columns of the cash book are balanced in the same way that ledger accounts are balanced.

**Example**

Dr **An account** Cr

| Dr | $ | Cr | $ |
|---|---|---|---|
| | 23 | | 45 |
| | 41 | | |
| | 16 | | |

The debit side of the account adds to $80.

The credit side adds to $45.

To make the account balance we need to insert $35 into the credit side.

The account now looks like this:

Dr **An account** Cr

| Dr | $ | Cr | $ |
|---|---|---|---|
| | 23 | | 45 |
| | 41 | | 35 |
| | 16 | | |
| | 80 | | 80 |

The account balances.

This process makes it look as though the debit entries were exactly the same amounts as the credit entries – not true!

The debit side totalled $35 more than the credit side. We need to reflect this when we start the account again. We carry the balance down.

We start anew with an opening balance of $35 on the debit side:

Dr **An account** Cr

| Dr | $ | Cr | $ |
|---|---|---|---|
| | 23 | | 45 |
| | 41 | | 35 |
| | 16 | | |
| | 80 | | 80 |
| | 35 | | |

The rules of our double-entry game say that every time we include a debit entry in the system we must also include a credit entry. We have done just that. We inserted a credit entry to make the account balance.

Our debit entry starts us off again:

**Worked example**

The following accounts are given:

Dr **Zog** Cr

| Dr | $ | Cr | $ |
|---|---|---|---|
| | 23 | | 53 |
| | 13 | | 41 |
| | | | 8 |

Dr **Melvyn** Cr

| Dr | $ | Cr | $ |
|---|---|---|---|
| | 12 | | 34 |
| | 25 | | 37 |
| | 73 | | |

Dr **Tan** Cr

| Dr | $ | Cr | $ |
|---|---|---|---|
| | 71 | | 90 |
| | 27 | | 38 |
| | 91 | | |

**Required**

Balance the accounts and carry down any balances.

### Answer

| Dr | Zog | Cr |
|---|---|---|
| | $ | $ |
| | 23 | 53 |
| | 13 | 41 |
| | *66* | 8 |
| | 102 | 102 |
| | | 66 |

| Dr | Melvyn | Cr |
|---|---|---|
| | $ | $ |
| | 12 | 34 |
| | 25 | 37 |
| | 73 | *39* |
| | 110 | 110 |
| | 39 | |

| Dr | Tan | Cr |
|---|---|---|
| | $ | $ |
| | 71 | 90 |
| | 27 | 38 |
| | 91 | *61* |
| | 189 | 189 |
| | 61 | |

When a balance is described as a debit balance or a credit balance, we are describing the balance required to start the account in the next time period; the balance that has been brought down.

In the example above:

- Zog's account has a credit balance of $66
- Melvyn's account has a debit balance of $39
- Tan's account has a debit balance of $61.

## 6.2 The trial balance

We prepare a list of all the balances that we extracted from the ledgers by balancing all the ledger accounts and carrying down any outstanding balances on each account. We list all the debit balances under a column headed debit and we list each credit balance in a column headed credit.

The debit column is totalled; the credit is totalled. The two columns should have the same total. This list is called a trial balance.

If we extract a trial balance, and the two sides total to the same figure, we can say with some certainty that every debit has a corresponding credit.

If the trial balance totals do not agree, then we can say with some certainty that there are some errors in the double-entry system.

Here are a couple of simple double-entry examples using 'T' accounts, followed by a very simple trial balance.

**Worked example**

The following transactions are for Geraint's business:

1 Geraint purchased goods for resale $153 from Buvcu on credit.

2 He sold goods $29 to Sangita on credit.

3 Geraint sold goods for cash $296.

4 He paid motor expenses $68 paying cash.

**Required**

Enter the transactions in Geraint's ledger. Carry down any balances and check the accuracy of the entries by extracting a trial balance.

### Answer

| Dr | Purchases account | Cr |
|---|---|---|
| | $ | |
| | 153 | |

| Dr | Buvcu | Cr |
|---|---|---|
| | | $ |
| | | 153 |

| Dr | Sales account | Cr |
|---|---|---|
| | | $ |
| | | 29 |
| | | 296 |

| Dr | Sangita | Cr |
|---|---|---|
| | $ | |
| | 29 | |

| Dr | Cash account | | Cr |
|---|---|---|---|
| | $ | | $ |
| | 296 | | 68 |

| Dr | Motor expenses account | | Cr |
|---|---|---|---|
| | $ | | |
| | 68 | | |

**Trial balance**

| | Debit | Credit | |
|---|---|---|---|
| | $ | $ | |
| Purchases | 153 | | *The account shows a debit balance; the trial balance shows a debit balance.* |
| Buvcu | | 153 | *The account shows a credit balance; the trial balance shows a credit balance.* |
| Sales | | 325 | *Sales have credit entries totalling $325; the trial balance shows this balance.* |
| Sangita | 29 | | *The account shows a debit balance; the trial balance shows a debit balance.* |
| Cash | 228 | | *The debit side is greater; the trial balance shows the debit balancing figure.* |
| Motor expenses | 68 | | *The account shows a debit balance; the trial balance shows a debit balance.* |
| | 478 | 478 | |

The trial balance has shown that we have entered our transactions accurately.

## Worked example

The following accounts have been extracted from a ledger:

| Dr | Cash account | | Cr |
|---|---|---|---|
| | $ | | $ |
| | 42 | | 100 |
| | 534 | | 458 |
| | | | 12 |

| Dr | Bank account | | Cr |
|---|---|---|---|
| | $ | | $ |
| | 365 | | 534 |
| | 912 | | 141 |
| | | | 69 |

| Dr | Rent account | | Cr |
|---|---|---|---|
| | $ | | |
| | 100 | | |

| Dr | Wages account | | Cr |
|---|---|---|---|
| | $ | | |
| | 458 | | |

| Dr | Sales account | | Cr |
|---|---|---|---|
| | | | $ |
| | | | 42 |
| | | | 365 |
| | | | 912 |

| Dr | Purchases account | | Cr |
|---|---|---|---|
| | $ | | |
| | 141 | | |
| | 69 | | |
| | 12 | | |

**Required**

Balance the ledger accounts. Carry down any balances and extract a trial balance to check the accuracy of the entries in the ledger.

## Answer

| Dr | Cash account | | Cr |
|---|---|---|---|
| | $ | | $ |
| | 42 | | 100 |
| | 534 | | 458 |
| | | | 12 |
| | | | 6 |
| | 576 | | 576 |
| | 6 | | |

| Dr | Bank account | | Cr |
|---|---|---|---|
| | $ | | $ |
| | 365 | | 534 |
| | 912 | | 141 |
| | | | 69 |
| | | | *533* |
| | 1277 | | 1277 |
| | 533 | | |

| Dr | Rent account | Cr |
|---|---|---|
| | $ | |
| | 100 | |

| Dr | Wages account | Cr |
|---|---|---|
| | $ | |
| | 458 | |

| Dr | Sales account | Cr |
|---|---|---|
| | $ | $ |
| | | 42 |
| | | 365 |
| | *1319* | 912 |
| | 1319 | 1319 |
| | | 1319 |

| Dr | Purchases account | Cr |
|---|---|---|
| | $ | $ |
| | 141 | |
| | 69 | |
| | 12 | *222* |
| | 222 | 222 |
| | 222 | |

**Trial balance**

| | Dr | Cr |
|---|---|---|
| | $ | $ |
| Cash | 6 | |
| Bank | 533 | |
| Rent | 100 | |
| Wages | 458 | |
| Sales | | 1319 |
| Purchases | 222 | |
| | 1319 | 1319 |

## 6.3 Calculating profit

We saw in Chapter 1 that accounts in a general ledger can be divided into nominal accounts, real accounts and liability accounts.

Information in the form of balances extracted from nominal accounts in a ledger can be used to calculate business profits. If the total of all revenues earned is compared to the total of all expenses incurred, the difference will reveal whether or not the business has made a profit or loss in the time period covered by the information.

**Worked example**

Balances taken from the nominal accounts in the ledger of Ong show the following information for a financial year:

- rent and local taxes paid $870; wages paid $56 000; payments for other expenses $8900
- purchase of goods for resale $121 500; sales for the year $193 000.

**Required**

Calculate whether or not Ong's business has been profitable over the year.

### Answer

Profit for the year $5730 (= Sales $193 000 – Expenses $187 270).

(Expenses = Purchases $121 500 + $870 + $56 000 + $8 900)

**Worked example**

The following information has been extracted from the nominal accounts in the ledger of Jethro after one year of trading:

- sales of goods: $116 000
- expenses incurred during the year – purchases of goods for resale: $59 600
- payments made – rent and local taxes: $2760; power: $8930; wages: $42 770; motor expenses: $2950; other expenses: $6840.

**Required**

Calculate whether or not Jethro's business has been profitable during the year.

## Answer

Jethro's business has not been profitable. It has made a loss of $7850 (= Sales $116 000 – Payments $123 850).

Sales $116 000 less Payments made during the year $123 850.

The calculation that we have just done can be shown more formally in an income statement.

**Tip**

An income statement shows how the business has performed over a period of time whereas the statement of financial position shows the financial position of the business on a particular date.
This point is identified in the headings – make sure that you use them as they are important.

**Tip**

In income statement, we use 'revenue' instead of 'sales'.

**Example**

Ubertus provides the following information which is a list of the nominal ledger balances he extracted from his ledger on 31 July 2014 after one year's trading.

- Sales: $279 988
- Purchases of goods for resale: $201 760
- Payments made – wages: $41 215; motor expenses: $8960; local taxes: $1800; advertising: $2430; insurances: $1540; other expenses: $9610.

Ubertus income statement for the year ended 31 July 2014 will include the information above:

**Ubertus**
**Income statement for the year ended 31 July 2014**

| | Dr | Cr |
|---|---|---|
| | $ | $ |
| Revenue | | 279 988 |
| *Less* expenses | | |
| Purchases | 201 760 | |
| Wages | 41 215 | |
| Motor expenses | 8 960 | |
| Local taxes | 1 800 | |
| Advertising | 2 430 | |
| Insurances | 1 540 | |
| Other expenses | 9 610 | |
| Total expenses | | 267 315 |
| Profit for the year | | 12 673 |

This is a very simple income statement.

The difference between the sales revenue generated and the cost of the goods sold is called **gross profit**.

We shall develop the layout in future chapters where we will consider adjustments to make the statement more accurate and reveal more information.

➤ Now try Question 1.

## 6.4 Statements to show financial position

There are other types of account in a general ledger.

Some accounts in the ledger record the purchase of assets; some record liabilities incurred by the business. Accounts in the purchases ledger show credit transactions with suppliers, while accounts in the sales ledger show credit transactions with customers. Balances from these accounts will be used to prepare a **statement of financial position**.

A statement of financial position lists the assets owned by a business and liabilities owed by a business. The total value of assets held must equal the total value of liabilities.

External liabilities are amounts owed to people or businesses that are not the owners. The difference between the amounts owed to external creditors and the assets held by a business is known as **capital** or **net assets**. It represents the amount of the owner's investment in their business.

**Worked example**

Heidi provides the following balances extracted from her general ledger:

Premises \$65 000; mortgage on premises \$35 000; vehicle \$12 000; amount owing to bank for vehicle purchase \$4000; bank balance \$1200.

**Required**

a Classify the information given into assets and liabilities.

b Calculate the value of Heidi's capital.

### Answer

a Assets: Premises, vehicle and bank balance (\$65 000 + \$12 000 + \$1200 = \$78 200)

Liabilities: Mortgage on premises and amount owing to bank for vehicle purchase (\$35 000 + \$4000 = \$39 000)

b Capital = Value of assets less value of liabilities

= \$78 200 – \$39 000

= \$39 200

Once again we can show the information in a more formal layout.

**Worked example**

Kamil provides the following information that he has extracted from his ledgers at 31 July 2014:

| | Dr | Cr |
|---|---|---|
| | $ | $ |
| Bank overdraft | | 2 200 |
| Long-term bank loan | | 8 000 |
| Machinery | 10 000 | |
| Mortgage on premises | | 25 000 |
| Premises | 40 000 | |
| Vehicle | 8 500 | |
| Trade payables | | 800 |
| Trade receivables | 1 500 | |

**Inventories** are goods that have been purchased for resale but have, as yet, not been sold.

**Additional information**

The inventory held at 31 July 2014 was valued at $2000.

**Required**

Prepare a statement of financial position at 31 July 2014.

## Answer

**Kamil**

**Statement of financial position at 31 July 2014**

| | $ | | $ |
|---|---|---|---|
| **ASSETS** | | **CAPITAL AND LIABILITIES** | |
| Inventory | 2000 | **Liabilities** | |
| Machinery | 10000 | Bank overdraft | 2200 |
| Premises | 40000 | Long-term bank loan | 8000 |
| Vehicles | 8500 | Mortgage on premises | 25000 |
| Trade receivables | 1500 | Trade payables | 800 |
| | | | 36000 |
| | | **Capital** (net assets – difference between the value of assets and external liabilities) | 26000 |
| **Total assets** | 62000 | **Total capital and liabilities** | 62000 |

The information detailed in business books of accounts can be used to show the profitability of the business and also to show its financial positions. A more formal and structured layout of a statement of financial position will be considered in greater detail in Chapter 14 (Section 14.3).

➤ Now try Question 2.

**Worked example**

Nonaki provides the following list of balances extracted from his ledgers at 30 November 2014, after his first year of trading:

| | Dr | Cr |
|---|---|---|
| | $ | $ |
| Bank overdraft | | 1700 |
| Sales | | 167880 |
| Purchases | 87500 | |
| Wages | 53710 | |
| Heating and lighting | 1900 | |
| Rent and local taxes | 4890 | |
| Vehicles | 9000 | |
| Motor expenses | 2540 | |
| Equipment | 6700 | |
| General expenses | 1780 | |
| Trade receivables | 3900 | |
| Trade payables | | 2340 |

**Additional information:**

Inventories held were valued at $4370 at 30 November 2014.

**Required**

Prepare:

a an income statement for the year ended 30 November 2014

b a statement of financial position at 30 November 2014.

**Workings**

The purchases shown in the income statement is a measure of the goods bought and used as sales. The figure of $87 500 is the value of the goods purchased for resale. However, the additional information tells us that not all of the goods were in fact sold. Goods to the value of $4370 remain unsold at the end of the financial year, so the purchases 'used' to generate profits was $83 130 ($87 500 *less* $4370).

## Answer

a

**Nonaki**

**Income statement for the year ended 30 November 2014**

| | Dr | Cr |
|---|---|---|
| | $ | $ |
| Revenue | | 167 880 |
| *Less* purchases | | 83 130 |
| Gross profit | | 84 750 |
| *Less* expenses | | |
| Wages | 53 710 | |
| Heating and lighting | 1 900 | |
| Rent and local taxes | 4 890 | |
| Motor expenses | 2 540 | |
| General expenses | 1 780 | 64 820 |
| Profit for the year | | 19 930 |

It is usual to put in subtotals for each separate area, e.g. non-current assets, current assets, non-current liabilities and current liabilities.

b

**Nonaki**

**Statement of financial position at 30 November 2014**

| | $ | | $ |
|---|---|---|---|
| **ASSETS** | | **CAPITAL AND LIABILITIES** | |
| Vehicles | 9 000 | **Liabilities** | |
| Equipment | 6 700 | Bank overdraft | 1 700 |
| Trade receivables | 3 900 | Trade payables | 2 340 |
| Inventories | 4 370 | | 4 040 |
| **Total assets** | 23 970 | **Capital** | 19 930 |
| | | **Total capital and liabilities** | 23 970 |

### Self-test questions

1 The 'left side' of an account adds to $349. The right side adds to $421. What balance would be shown on the account?
2 Would the account described above show a debit or a credit balance?
3 Explain the term 'trial balance'.
4 Explain why a trial balance should 'balance' if there are no errors in the books of account.
5 Identify two statements that can be prepared using information shown on a trial balance.
6 Which of the two statements is used to calculate profits?
7 Explain the term 'capital'.
8 Give another name for the term 'capital'.

➤ Now try Question 3.

## Chapter summary

- A trial balance is a summary of all the balances remaining in the books of account (usually extracted at the financial year end).
- The balances are arranged in a debit column and a credit column.
- The totals of the two columns should be the same.
- If they are equal, it generally indicates that every debit entry has a corresponding credit entry (see Chapter 10).
- The information contained in a trial balance can be used to prepare two statements: one calculating the profitability of the business and the other showing the assets and liabilities of the business.

# 7 Accounting principles, concepts and conventions

## Content

**1.1 The accounting cycle**

- Apply the accounting concepts underpinning the preparation of accounts: business entity, historic cost, money measurement, going concern, consistency, prudence, realisation, duality, materiality, matching and substance over form

**By the end of this chapter you should:**

- understand the generally accepted principles, concepts and conventions of: business entity; historic cost; money measurement; going concern; consistency; prudence; realisation; duality; materiality; matching (accruals); substance over form.

Over the years accounting has evolved rules that all accountants use when preparing the financial statements of a business. These rules are referred to as **accounting concepts** or **accounting principles**. Some of these principles are enshrined in law and in International Accounting Standards (IAS) laid down by major accounting bodies (see Chapter 36).

The application of these rules by all accountants means that the users of the financial statements can rely on the information they contain, safe in the knowledge that a set of financial statements prepared in Kingston, Kuala Lumpur, Karachi or Kalol for any type of business have been prepared using the same ground rules.

The concepts are an important topic: they underpin all of the work done by accountants. Make sure that you are familiar with them.

## 7.1 The business entity concept

The concept of the **business entity** states that only the expenses and revenues relating to the business are recorded in the business books of account. Transactions involving the private affairs of the owner are not part of the business and should not be included in the business books.

The owner's private electricity bills or private food bills should not be included as business expenditure.

If the business cheque book is used to pay the proprietor's private mortgage payments the amount should be included in the drawings account.

## 7.2 Historic cost

Traditionally financial statements have been prepared using **historic cost**. This means that all income, expenditure, assets and liabilities are recorded at the price paid for them at the date of the transaction. Unfortunately, as time goes by, the value of assets is understated and profits are overstated, especially in times of inflation.

Some of the advantages of using historic cost are that it is:

- objective
- easily understood
- easily applied to the double-entry system
- easy for external auditors to verify all transactions
- recognised by tax authorities.

Some of the disadvantages of using historic cost include:

- overstated profits due to failure to adjust for increased costs of replacing inventory or replacement of non-current assets
- understatement of non-current asset values, hence understatement of capital employed (this can be overcome by revaluing the assets).

Property, plant and equipment should be valued at cost in a statement of financial position. Cost includes the actual purchase price plus all other costs involved in bringing the asset to the location where it is to be used together with costs of making sure that the asset can perform its intended use. The asset is shown at historical cost less accumulated depreciation. Non-current assets may be shown on a statement of financial position at a revalued amount if the fair value can be measured reliably. The company must revalue all assets in a particular class. If a company has seven different factories, it cannot revalue just one of those factories. Future depreciation is calculated and provided on the revalued amount.

## 7.3 Money measurement

Only transactions that can be measured in monetary terms should be included in the business books of account. It is extremely difficult to put a value on:

- managerial efficiency and expertise
- the skill and efficiency of the workforce
- good customer relations
- good after-sales service.

## 7.4 The going concern concept

Unless we have knowledge to the contrary, we assume that the business will continue to trade in its present form for the foreseeable future. This means that we value all business assets at cost, not at what they would fetch if sold (but see IAS 16 in Chapter 36). If the business is going to continue, the assets will not be sold so sale value is irrelevant.

International Accounting Standard 1 (IAS 1) names the **going concern concept** as a fundamental accounting concept (see Chapter 36.)

## 7.5 The concept of consistency

The **concept of consistency** requires that once a method of treating information has been established the method should continue to be used in subsequent years' financial statements.

The application of this concept can be seen in Chapter 19 when methods of providing for depreciation of non-current assets are considered.

If information is treated differently each year then inter-year results cannot be compared. Trends cannot be determined.

## 7.6 Prudence

**Prudence** requires that revenues and profits are only included in the accounts when they are realised or their realisation is reasonably certain. This prevents profits from being overstated. If year end gross profit is overstated, then the profit for the year will also be overstated. If profits are overstated, a trader may withdraw more resources (money and goods) from the business than is wise.

This could lead to a position where assets could not be replaced when necessary or that trade payables could not be paid when due. However, the concept of prudence allows provision to be made for all known expenses or losses when they become known. For example, if damages were awarded against the business in a court case, the business could make a provision on the estimated amount that it might have to pay out in compensation.

## 7.7 The realisation concept

**Title** is the legal term for ownership. For example, title deeds to premises shows that the holder of the deeds is the owner of the premises.

The **realisation concept** states that profits are normally recognised when the **title** to the goods passes to the customer, not necessarily when money changes hands. This concept is an extension of the **matching** or **accruals concept** (see section 7.10).

**Example**

Fiona is an engineer. She is fairly certain that, in July, Jack will sign a contract to purchase machinery valued at $18000. The $18000 should not be included in Fiona's financial statements until the title to the machinery has passed to Jack.

When goods are sent to a customer on sale or return, a sale does not take place until the potential customer indicates that they wish to purchase the goods. Goods sent on a sale or return basis remain as inventory in the 'sender's' books of account.

## 7.8 Duality

Every financial transaction has a twofold effect on the position of the business as recorded in the books of account. The assets of a business are always equal to the liabilities. This effect is recognisable in the accounting equation (see Section 14.4) and in the double-entry book-keeping system. For example, when an asset is purchased either another asset is reduced or a liability is incurred.

## 7.9 The concept of materiality

If the inclusion or exclusion of information in a financial statement would mislead the users of that statement, then the information is **material**.

The **concept of materiality** recognises that some types of expenditure are less important in a business context than others. So, absolute precision in the recording of these transactions is not absolutely essential.

To spend much time in deciding how to treat a transaction of little consequence in the financial statements is detrimental to the well-being of the business – it would be a waste of time and resources.

Remember that capital expenditure is spending on non-current assets or their improvement. Revenue expenditure is spending on the normal running costs of a business. Non-current assets are used in a business for more than one financial time period. If we apply the matching concept we should spread the cost of a non-current asset over the years it is used to generate the profits.

**Example**

A business purchases a ruler. The ruler costs $0.45. It estimated that the ruler should last for three years. Technically, the ruler is a non-current asset and should therefore be classified as capital expenditure. To do this would be rather silly for such a trivial amount. The $0.45 would be treated as revenue expenditure and would be debited to either general expenses or office expenses.

This treatment is not going to have a significant impact on profits or the valuation of net assets on a statement of financial position – the absolute accuracy of its treatment is not material.

# 7.10 The matching concept

The **matching concept** is sometimes known as the **accruals concept**.

As accountants, we are concerned with the value of resources used by the business and the benefits derived from the use of those resources by the business in any one financial year. The value of the resources used in any time period may be different from the price paid to acquire the resources.

## Worked example

Juanita has a financial year end on 31 December 2014. The following amounts have been paid during the year ended 31 December 2014:

| | $ |
|---|---|
| Wages | 48 000 |
| Rent | 5 500 |
| Local taxes | 1 800 |
| Insurance | 2 100 |
| Motor expenses | 14 300 |

- Wages due to workers for work completed in the week 24–31 December 2014, but unpaid, amount to $970.
- Rent $500, for December 2014, was paid on 19 January 2015.
- Local taxes have been paid for the period ending 31 March 2015. $450 relates to 1 January – 31 March 2015.
- Insurance includes a premium $300 for the period 1 January – 28 February 2015.
- Motor expenses do not include $236 paid on 27 January 2015 for a vehicle service completed on 15 December 2014.

**Required**

Calculate the amounts to be included in an income statement for the year ended 31 December 2014 in respect of wages, rent, local taxes, insurance and motor expenses.

### Answer

- Wages: $48 970
  Juanita has used $48 970 skills and expertise of her workers during the year even though she has only paid them $48 000.
- Rent: $6000
  Juanita has had the use of premises worth $6000 to her; even though she had only paid $5500.
- Local taxes: $1350
  Juanita has used local government facilities valued at $1350 for the year. She has also paid $450 for the use of facilities in the following year – we are not, at the moment, interested in the figures relating to next year.
- Insurance: $1800
  The payment of $2100 includes $300 for insurance cover next year. This means that only $1800 refers to this year.
- Motor expenses: $14 536
  The service was completed in the year ended 31 December 2014 even though it was not paid for until the following year.

## 7.11 Substance over form

This principle ensures that financial statements observe the commercial substance of transactions rather than just their legal form. In most transactions commercial substance is the same as the legal form, but occasionally the accounting treatment is not a true reflection of the legal position.

For example, when a non-current asset is purchased using hire purchase, the asset legally remains the property of the seller until the final instalment has been paid. However, from a business accounting point of view, the asset can be regarded as belonging to the purchaser.

### Self-test questions

1 A business has just purchased a specialised piece of computerised manufacturing machinery for $240 000. It will be used for three years. It would certainly have no resale value because of its specialised nature. How should the machinery be valued? Cost: $240 000; resale value: $0; average value: $80 000.
2 Lopez says 'If we delay paying $45 000 for the purchase of a non-current asset until a couple of weeks after our financial year end our recorded profits will increase by that amount.' Is Lopez correct in his treatment of the purchase?
3 Why is there a need to be consistent in the treatment of accounting information?
4 What is meant by the term 'substance over form'?

➤ **Now try Questions 1–3.**

### Chapter summary

- Accounting concepts and principles are the basic rules of accounting. They should be applied to the recording of all transactions and the preparation of all accounting statements.

# 8 Closing down the double-entry system

## Content

### 1.1 The accounting cycle

- Explain and apply the principles of the double-entry system to record business transactions

### 1.4 Preparation of financial statements

1.4.2 Sole traders

- Prepare an income statement and statement of financial position for a sole trader from full or incomplete accounting records

**By the end of this chapter you should be able to:**

- close appropriate accounts in the general ledger
- transfer amounts from the nominal accounts in the general ledger to an income statement
- transfer a balance from an income statement to the proprietor's capital account
- show details of changes to capital as a calculation and in account format
- prepare an inventory account in the general ledger
- value inventory by using cost or net realisable value
- identify and calculate the effect that a change in inventory valuation will have on reported profits.

We have seen how the double-entry system works. The system relies on the basic principle:

'Every debit must have a corresponding credit.'

**Worked example**

The following transactions took place during the year ended 31 August 2014 for Ghola. All transactions were paid by cheque:

- 26 September 2013: purchase of vehicle $17500
- 30 September 2013: payment of rent $700
- 11 October 2013: purchase of vehicle $16900
- 17 October 2013: payment for advertising $120
- 1 November 2013: payment of wages $13200
- 23 November 2013: payment for advertising $2600
- 31 December 2013: payment of rent $700
- 1 February 2014: payment of wages $13700
- 31 March 2014: payment of rent $700
- 31 March 2014: payment of local taxes $1300
- 1 May 2014: payment of wages $12900
- 17 June 2014: payment for advertising $340
- 30 June 2014: payment of rent $700
- 1 August 2014: payment of wages $14600.

**Required**

Prepare accounts for wages, rent, local taxes, advertising and vehicles for the year ended 31 August 2014.

## Answer

| Dr | | Vehicles account | Cr |
|---|---|---|---|
| | | $ | |
| 26 Sept 2013 | Bank | 17 500 | |
| 11 Oct 2013 | Bank | 16 900 | |

| Dr | | Rent account | Cr |
|---|---|---|---|
| | | $ | |
| 30 Sept 2013 | Bank | 700 | |
| 31 Dec 2013 | Bank | 700 | |
| 31 Mar 2014 | Bank | 700 | |
| 30 June 2014 | Bank | 700 | |

| Dr | | Advertising account | Cr |
|---|---|---|---|
| | | $ | |
| 17 Oct 2013 | Bank | 120 | |
| 23 Nov 2013 | Bank | 2600 | |
| 17 June 2014 | Bank | 340 | |

| Dr | | Wages account | Cr |
|---|---|---|---|
| | | $ | |
| 1 Nov 2013 | Bank | 13 200 | |
| 1 Feb 2014 | Bank | 13 700 | |
| 1 May 2014 | Bank | 12 900 | |
| 1 Aug 2014 | Bank | 14 600 | |

| Dr | | Local taxes account | Cr |
|---|---|---|---|
| | | $ | |
| 31 Mar 2013 | Bank | 1300 | |

The credit entries corresponding to all the debit entries shown would appear in the bank account.

## 8.1 Closing accounts in the general ledger

**Nominal accounts** are general ledger accounts that record incomes and expenses such as purchases, sales, wages, rent payable, rent receivable, motor expenses, etc.

**Real accounts** are general ledger accounts in which the purchase and sale of non-current assets and cash and bank transactions are recorded. Real accounts would include land, premises, plant, machinery, office equipment, vehicles, cash and bank balances.

A **private ledger** is part of the general ledger and is kept separate. It contains accounts of a sensitive nature that the owner of a business does not wish others to see.

At the end of each financial year, we need to close down any accounts that we have finished with for the year in question. Not all accounts will be closed down. Some accounts contain information that is relevant to the business's activity in the future. In fact we only close down the **nominal accounts** in the general ledger since the information they contain will be used to calculate that year's profit. The **real accounts** will remain to carry their information through into the following year.

### How are the nominal accounts closed?

The nominal accounts are closed by transferring the balances on each account to the **income statement**, which should be found in the general ledger.

Ideally, the income statement ought to be in the general ledger. In reality it is rarely kept in the general ledger. The information contained is of a sensitive nature so it will generally be kept separately from the rest of the general ledger in a **private ledger**.

A private ledger is kept apart from the general ledger for obvious reasons. Other accounts that the owner of a business might wish to keep in a private ledger may include the capital account or an account that shows loan transactions, etc.

**Example**

The accounts shown in the books of account of Ghola, above, would be closed as follows:

The nominal accounts are transferred to the income statement. The transfers will close the accounts for the year in question and will leave them clear to start a new financial year.

The accounts and the income statement are as follows:

**Vehicles account**

| Dr | | | Cr | | |
|---|---|---|---|---|---|
| | | $ | | | |
| 26 Sept 2013 | Bank | 17500 | | | |
| 11 Oct 2013 | Bank | 16900 | | | |

**Rent account**

| Dr | | | Cr | | |
|---|---|---|---|---|---|
| | | $ | | | $ |
| 30 Sept 2013 | Bank | 700 | | | |
| 31 Dec 2013 | Bank | 700 | | | |
| 31 Mar 2014 | Bank | 700 | 31 Aug 2014 | Income statement | 2800 |
| 30 June 2014 | Bank | 700 | | | |
| | | 2800 | | | 2800 |

**Advertising account**

| Dr | | | Cr | | |
|---|---|---|---|---|---|
| | | $ | | | $ |
| 17 Oct 2013 | Bank | 120 | 31 Aug 2014 | Income statement | 3060 |
| 23 Nov 2013 | Bank | 2600 | | | |
| 17 Jun 2014 | Bank | 340 | | | |
| | | 3060 | | | 3060 |

**Wages account**

| Dr | | | Cr | | |
|---|---|---|---|---|---|
| | | $ | | | $ |
| 1 Nov 2013 | Bank | 13200 | 31 Aug 2014 | Income statement | 54400 |
| 1 Feb 2014 | Bank | 13700 | | | |
| 1 May 2014 | Bank | 12900 | | | |
| 1 Aug 2014 | Bank | 14600 | | | |
| | | 54400 | | | 54400 |

**Local taxes account**

| Dr | | | Cr | | |
|---|---|---|---|---|---|
| | | $ | | | $ |
| 31 Mar 2014 | Bank | 1300 | 31 Aug 2014 | Income statement | 1300 |
| | | 1300 | | | 1300 |

**Bank account**

| Dr | | | Cr | | |
|---|---|---|---|---|---|
| | | | | | $ |
| | | | 26 Sept 2013 | Vehicle | 17500 |
| | | | 30 Sept 2013 | Rent | 700 |
| | | | 11 Oct 2013 | Vehicle | 16900 |
| | | | 17 Oct 2013 | Advertising | 120 |
| | | | 1 Nov 2013 | Wages | 13200 |
| | | | 23 Nov 2013 | Advertising | 2600 |
| | | | 31 Dec 2013 | Rent | 700 |
| | | | 1 Feb 2014 | Wages | 13700 |
| | | | 31 Mar 2014 | Local taxes | 1300 |
| | | | 31 Mar 2014 | Rent | 700 |
| | | | 1 May 2014 | Wages | 12900 |
| | | | 17 Jun 2014 | Advertising | 340 |
| | | | 30 Jun 2014 | Rent | 700 |
| | | | 1 Aug 2014 | Wages | 14600 |

**Extract from income statement for the year ended 31 August 2014**

| | $ |
|---|---|
| Expenses | |
| Rent | 2800 |
| Advertising | 3060 |
| Wages | 54400 |
| Local taxes | 1300 |

Notice that credit entries are made using double-entry principles; each credit in a nominal account is matched by an entry in the income statement.

The vehicles account and bank account stay open since we will use these accounts next year.

The purchases, sales, purchases returns and sales returns accounts will be closed using the same technique but the balances on those accounts are transferred to the trading account of the income statement.

Not only does the closing of the nominal accounts provide us with information to enable us to calculate the profits made by the business, it also enables us to have a fresh start in the general ledger nominal accounts next year. Imagine if we did not tidy out these accounts on an annual basis, some accounts would have hundreds of thousands of entries after 20 years!

The rule is that all accounts providing us with information that is relevant to one financial year are closed down at the end of that year – the other accounts remain in the books of account as balances to start up the system again next year. All these remaining balances show the financial position of the business – in the **statement of financial position** on the final day of the financial year.

## 8.2 'Closing' the income statement

The income statement is also closed down at the end of each financial year. We can then prepare the next income statement in a year's time.

**Worked example**

The following list of balances has been extracted from the books of Patel, a trader, after his first year of trading:

**Purchases** are any items that are purchased with the intention of selling them to customers.

**Balances at 31 December 2014**

| | $ | $ |
|---|---|---|
| Purchases | 41 600 | |
| Sales | | 103 110 |
| Land and buildings | 60 000 | |
| Fixtures and fittings | 7 000 | |
| Vehicles | 21 000 | |
| Rent, local taxes and insurance | 5 430 | |
| Lighting and heating expenses | 7 980 | |
| Motor expenses | 9 260 | |
| Repairs and renewals | 1 780 | |
| Wages | 14 320 | |
| Trade receivables | 1 740 | |
| Trade payables | | 1 490 |
| Drawings | 2 170 | |
| Capital | | 70 000 |
| Cash | 480 | |
| Bank balance | 1 840 | |
| | 174 600 | 174 600 |

**Inventory** is goods held for resale that have not been disposed of during the financial year.

Inventory at 31 December 2014 was valued at $1010.

**Required**

a Identify the accounts that will be closed down at the end of the financial year by posting the amounts to an income statement.

b Prepare an income statement for the year ended 31 December 2014.

c Prepare a statement of financial position at 31 December 2014.

### Answer

a The following accounts will be closed (they are all nominal accounts): purchases, sales, rent, local taxes and insurance, lighting and heating, motor expenses, repairs and renewals and wages.

b

**Patel**
**Income statement for the year ended 31 December 2014**

| | $ | $ |
|---|---|---|
| Revenue | | 103 110 |
| *Less* Cost of sales | | |
| Purchases | 41 600 | |
| *Less* Inventory | 1 010 | 40 590 |
| Gross profit | | 62 520 |
| *Less* Expenses | | |
| Rent, local taxes and insurance | 5 430 | |
| Lighting and heating | 7 980 | |
| Motor expenses | 9 260 | |
| Repairs and renewals | 1 780 | |
| Wages | 14 320 | 38 770 |
| Profit for the year | | 23 750 |

- The income statement is 'closed' with the profit for the year calculation of $23 750.
- The profit for the year is entered on the credit side of the capital account in the general ledger, thus increasing the amount of capital invested in the business by the owner.

c

**Patel**
**Statement of financial position at 31 December 2014**

| | $ | $ |
|---|---|---|
| **ASSETS** | | |
| **Non-current assets** | | |
| Land and buildings | | 60 000 |
| Fixtures and fittings | | 7 000 |
| Vehicles | | 21 000 |
| | | 88 000 |
| **Current assets** | | |
| Inventory | 1 010 | |
| Trade receivables | 1 740 | |
| Bank balance | 1 840 | |
| Cash | 480 | 5 070 |
| **Total assets** | | 93 070 |
| **CAPITAL AND LIABILITIES** | | |
| **Capital** | | |
| Capital introduced | | 70 000 |
| *Add* Profit | | 23 750 |
| | | 93 750 |
| *Less* Drawings | | 2 170 |
| | | 91 580 |
| **Current liabilities** | | |
| Trade payables | | 1 490 |
| **Total capital and liabilities** | | 93 070 |

**Draft**: an attempt to prepare a statement or document which may need to be amended before it can be said to be a perfect copy.

Worked example

The following draft list of balances has been extracted from the books of account of Mischner on 30 June 2014 after her first year of trading. There are three missing figures. The accounts that will provide the missing figures are shown below the list.

**Draft list of balances at 30 June 2014**

| | $ | $ |
|---|---|---|
| Purchases | 128 360 | |
| Sales | | 317 830 |
| Premises | ? | |
| Fixtures and fittings | 17 000 | |
| Vehicles | 34 000 | |
| Wages | 119 000 | |
| Rent and local taxes | 14 670 | |
| Motor expenses | 21 630 | |
| Repairs | ? | |
| Lighting and heating expenses | 9710 | |
| General expenses | ? | |
| Trade receivables | 2 460 | |
| Trade payables | | 5400 |
| Drawings | 26 300 | |
| Capital | | 150 000 |
| Bank balance | 3 510 | |
| Cash in hand | 640 | |

Inventory at 30 June 2014 was valued at $6480.

**Dr Repairs account Cr**

| | | $ | |
|---|---|---|---|
| 3 Apr 2014 | Bank | 348 | |
| 19 May 2014 | Cash | 56 | |
| 12 June 2014 | Bank | 1 319 | |
| 27 June 2014 | Bank | 737 | |

**Dr General expenses account Cr**

| | | $ | |
|---|---|---|---|
| 7 Sept 2013 | Cash | 1 467 | |
| 24 Nov 2013 | Bank | 1 672 | |
| 3 Jan 2014 | Bank | 4 381 | |
| 17 Feb 2014 | Cash | 419 | |
| 9 May 2014 | Bank | 2 318 | |
| 7 June 2014 | Bank | 3 233 | |

**Dr Premises account Cr**

| | | $ | |
|---|---|---|---|
| 1 July 2014 | Balance b/d | 80 000 | |

**Required**

a Complete the list of balances and ensure that it balances.

b Close the relevant accounts shown.

c Prepare an income statement for the year ended 30 June 2014.

d Prepare a statement of financial position at 30 June 2014.

## Answer

a The balance totals are $473 230.

b The repairs account is closed by a credit entry of $2460; the general expenses account is closed by a credit entry of $13 490. The premises account should not be closed down – the premises will be used by the business in subsequent years.

c

| **Mischner**<br>**Income statement for the year ended 30 June 2014** | | |
|---|---|---|
| | **$** | **$** |
| Revenue | | 317830 |
| *Less* Cost of sales | | |
| Purchases | 128360 | |
| *Less* Inventory | 6480 | 121880 |
| Gross profit | | 195950 |
| *Less* Expenses | | |
| Wages | 119000 | |
| Rent and local taxes | 14670 | |
| Motor expenses | 21630 | |
| Repairs | 2460 | |
| Lighting and heating expenses | 9710 | |
| General expenses | 13490 | 180960 |
| Profit for the year | | 14990 |

d

| **Mischner**<br>**Statement of financial position at 30 June 2014** | | |
|---|---|---|
| | **$** | **$** |
| **ASSETS** | | |
| **Non-current assets** | | |
| Premises | | 80000 |
| Fixtures and fittings | | 17000 |
| Vehicles | | 34000 |
| | | 131000 |
| **Current assets** | | |
| Inventory | 6480 | |
| Trade receivables | 2460 | |
| Bank balance | 3510 | |
| Cash | 640 | 13090 |
| **Total assets** | | 144090 |
| **CAPITAL AND LIABILITIES** | | |
| **Capital** | | |
| Opening balance | | 150000 |
| *Add* Profit | | 14990 |
| | | 164990 |
| *Less* Drawings | | 26300 |
| | | 138690 |
| **Current liabilities** | | |
| Trade payables | | 5400 |
| **Total capital and liabilities** | | 144090 |

**Tip** 

If a question asks you to show a capital account, it should be in account form – not as a calculation as it would appear in a statement of financial position.

➤ Now try Question 1.

**Example**

Mischner's capital account in the general ledger would look like this:

**Dr — Capital account — Cr**

| | | $ | | | $ |
|---|---|---|---|---|---|
| 30 June 2014 | Drawings | 26 300 | 1 July 2013 | Bank | 150 000 |
| 30 June 2014 | Balance c/d | 138 690 | 30 June 2014 | Profit for year | 14 990* |
| | | 164 990 | | | 164 990 |
| | | | 1 July 2014 | Balance b/d | 138 690 |

* The profit for the year of $14 990 is entered in Mischner's capital account.

It is useful and usual to show all the details contained in the capital account in the statement of financial position, as we have done above and in previous examples.

## 8.3 The inventory account in the general ledger

Up to now the businesses that we have looked at have, in the main, been in the first year of trading. As part of our income statements and our statements of financial position, we have had to consider **inventories**.

**Inventories** are the goods that remain unsold at the end of a financial year.

Inventories are valued physically at the end of each financial year. Even if a trader keeps manual or computerised inventory records, the figures produced are not used in the end-of-year financial statements.

Despite what you might think, inventory records kept manually or on a computerised system will be inaccurate! Why? Because goods get stolen, they get damaged, some goods deteriorate, and these occurrences are not shown in our manual or computer records.

The most accurate way to value inventories is to count them manually and then value them – but more of that later.

After the trial balance is extracted from the ledgers, a value is placed on closing inventories – hence 'closing inventory' appears as an afterthought.

Closing inventory is deducted from the goods available for sale to obtain the cost of goods that the business has sold, in other words the cost of sales figure for the year. Closing inventory is a current asset and must be shown in the statement of financial position at the end of the financial year.

We have seen that the income statement is prepared using revenue incomes and expenditures by closing the nominal accounts in the general ledger. An inventory account appears in the general ledger and is prepared as follows:

At the financial year end inventories are valued and recorded as a debit in the account since they are assets.

**Example**

**Dr — Inventory account — Cr**

| | | $ | | | $ |
|---|---|---|---|---|---|
| End of Year 0 (now) | Deducted from cost of sales in income statement | 1 234 | | | |

At the end of the following year:

| Dr | | Inventory account | | | Cr |
|---|---|---|---|---|---|
| | | $ | | | $ |
| End of Year 0 (now) | Deducted from cost of sales in income statement | 1234 | Start of Year 1 | Added to cost of sales in income statement | 1234 |
| End of Year 1 | Deducted from cost of sales in income statement | 2345 | | | |

| Dr | | Inventory account | | | Cr |
|---|---|---|---|---|---|
| | | $ | | | $ |
| End of Year 0 (now) | Deducted from cost of sales in income statement | 1234 | Start of Year 1 | Added to cost of sales in income statement | 1234 |
| End of Year 1 | Deducted from cost of sales in income statement | 2345 | Start of Year 2 | Added to cost of sales in income statement | 2345 |
| End of Year 2 | Deducted from cost of sales in income statement | 3456 | | | |

The closing inventory is deducted from the current year's cost of sales (since it has not as yet been sold) and the balance in the inventory account is shown in the statement of financial position as a current asset.

## 8.4 Valuation of inventories

The overriding principle used in the **valuation of inventory** is that it is always valued at the lower of **cost price** or **net realisable value**.

At the end of the financial year a trader will physically count the items that remain as inventory (goods remaining unsold) in the business. A list is made of all the items. Each category of goods held has then to be valued.

- If closing inventory is *overvalued*, gross profit is *overvalued*.
- If gross profit is *overvalued*, then the profit for the year is *overvalued*.
- If closing inventory is *undervalued*, then gross profit is *undervalued*.
- If gross profit is *undervalued*, then the profit for the year is *undervalued*.

We can check this with a simple example.

**Example**

The following is the trading account of the income statement of Figaro:

- Closing inventory should be valued at $15.
- Sales amount to $50.

| Inventory overvalued | | Accurate inventory value | | Inventory undervalued | |
|---|---|---|---|---|---|
| | $ | | $ | | $ |
| Opening inventory | 10 | Opening inventory | 10 | Opening inventory | 10 |
| Purchases | 25 | Purchases | 25 | Purchases | 25 |
| | 35 | | 35 | | 35 |
| *Less* Closing inventory | 20 | *Less* Closing inventory | 15 | *Less* Closing inventory | 8 |
| Cost of sales | 15 | Cost of sales | 20 | Cost of sales | 27 |
| Gross profit | 35 | Gross profit | 30 | Gross profit | 23 |
| Sales | 50 | Sales | 50 | Sales | 50 |

Highest inventory valuation gives highest gross profit.

Lowest inventory valuation gives lowest gross profit.

**Tip**

Make sure that you understand the concept of net realisable value. Many students throw away their chances of success by being unable to calculate correctly the net realisable value of items of inventory.

The use of net realisable value causes problems for many students.

**Worked example**

The following information is available regarding inventory held by John at 31 August 2014.

| Components | Units held at year end | Cost price $ | Selling price $ |
|---|---|---|---|
| PX/117 | 21 | 16 | 20 |
| QR/2138 | 13 | 41 | 50 |
| T/1798C | 8 | 18 | 15 |
| S/5319 | 32 | 10 | 20 |

**Required**

Calculate the total value of the inventory of components held at 31 August 2014.

## Answer

Total value of inventory of components = $1309.

### Workings

| | $ |
|---|---|
| PX/117 at cost | 336 |
| QR/2183 at cost | 533 |
| T/1798C at realisable value (selling price) | 120 |
| S/5319 at cost | 320 |

**Note**

- Realisable value is selling price.
- Net realisable value is the realisable value net of (less) any expenses incurred in getting the goods ready for sale.

➤ Now try Question 2.

**Self-test questions**

1 Name the type of accounts that are closed down at the end of the financial year.
2 Why do some traders keep a private ledger?
3 What entries are required to close the following accounts?

| Account | Debit | Credit |
|---|---|---|
| Rent payable | | |
| Discount received | | |
| Purchases | | |

4 Insurance; purchases returns; carriage inwards; Orton, a debtor; wages. Identify the account that would *not* be closed at the end of a financial year.
5 Axel, a creditor; bank; advertising; capital; vehicles. Identify the account that would be closed at the end of a financial year.
6 Explain what is meant by the word draft in 'draft income statement'.
7 What is the overriding principle used in the valuation of inventory?
8 The application of this principle is an example of the ____________ concept.
9 If closing inventory is overvalued, gross profit will be ____________.
10 Explain how closing inventory is dealt with in financial statements.

➤ Now try Question 3.

## Chapter summary

- At the end of each financial year the nominal accounts in the general ledger are closed by transferring the balances to an income statement.
- Real accounts are not closed and are shown on the statement of financial position.
- The profit for the year is transferred to the capital account.
- Inventories are valued at the lower of cost or net realisable value.
- Net realisable value is the selling price of the items held less any costs that might be incurred in making the items ready for sale.

# 9 Accruals and prepayments

**Content**

**1.4 Preparation of financial statements**

1.4.1 Adjustments to financial statements
- Calculate the adjustments needed for accruals and prepayments

**By the end of this chapter you should be able to:**
- apply the accruals concept to relevant accounting information
- account for expenses owed at the end of a financial year
- account for expenditures paid in advance of the financial year
- record amounts owed and prepaid in the appropriate ledger accounts
- record revenues that are outstanding and revenues that are paid in advance in the books of account.

## 9.1 Accruals and prepayments

The **accruals concept** recognises the difference between the actual payment of cash and the legal obligation to pay cash. It also recognises the distinction between the receipt of cash and the legal right to receive cash.

A **trial balance** is a list of the totals of all ledger accounts as they appear in all the ledgers.

So far we have assumed that money spent and money received exactly matched the time period under review. For example, we have assumed that:
- rent paid in February was for the use of premises in February
- wages paid in July was payment for work done in July
- the figures shown in the **trial balance** prepared at 31 December 2014 showed all the incomes and all the expenses for the year ended 31 December 2014, nothing more and nothing less.

When calculating profit, accountants are interested in accounting for the resources that the business has used during the financial year to generate the revenue receipts for that same year.

When preparing financial statements, a trader must include all items of expenditure, paid and payable.

This sounds a little strange at first but it will soon become clear.

When we prepare a set of financial statements we need to include all the items that apply to the accounting period under consideration.

Some expenses listed in a trial balance are always paid in advance, for example:
- insurance has to be paid in advance
- local taxes are generally paid in advance.

Other expenses listed in a trial balance might not be paid up to date:
- part of rent payable may not yet have been paid
- wages earned for work already done may not be due to be paid until the next month.

An accountant will look at rent differently from the way a landlord or a tenant sees it.

# 9.2 Dealing with accrued expenses

**Example**

Lori runs a small store. She has signed a tenancy agreement with her landlord, stating that she can use the store premises for the next five years on payment of a rental of $6000 per annum payable quarterly in advance on 1 January, 1 April, 1 July and 1 October.

At 31 December 2014, Lori's financial year end, Lori has only paid her landlord $4500; she still owes the rent that was due to be paid on 1 October.

The amount shown on Lori's income statement as an expense for rent is $6000 since Lori has had the use of a resource (the store) worth $6000 to help her generate her profits.

---

An extract from Lori's trial balance at 31 December 2014 would show:

| | Dr | Cr |
|---|---|---|
| | $ | $ |
| Rent payable | 4500 | |

**Trade payables** are amounts owed to the suppliers of goods for resale.

**Other payables** are amounts owed to the suppliers of goods and services, other than those goods purchased for resale.

**Trade receivables** are amounts owed by credit customers who have not yet settled their account.

**Other receivables** are amounts owed by people (or businesses) who are not credit customers.

When we prepare the income statement for the year ended 31 December 2014, the entries shown above would show:

| Extract from income statement for the year ended 31 December 2014 | |
|---|---|
| | $ |
| Expenses | |
| Rent payable | 6000 |

But this cannot be totally correct. Lori has increased her debit entries by $1500 with no corresponding increase in her credit entries. She needs to include an extra credit in her financial statements – rent payable owed at the year end.

In the statement of financial position prepared at the year end, **trade payables** represent amounts owed to suppliers who have supplied goods but who have not yet been paid. Since the rent payable is owed at the date when the statement of financial position is prepared, this too must be a payable.

Lori has used her premises and not yet fully paid for their use. Rent payable must be shown as **other payables**: a current liability, along with the trade payables.

**Note**

- The statement of financial position has not been credited.
- The statement of financial position is not part of the double-entry system; it is merely a statement showing balances outstanding at the end of a financial year.
- The outstanding rent is included in current liabilities with other credit balances (for example, the trade payables).

A statement of financial position at 31 December 2014 would show:

| Statement of financial position at 31 December 2014 | |
|---|---|
| | $ |
| **Current liabilities** | |
| Other payables (rent) | 1500 |

## 9.3 Dealing with prepaid expenses

Sometimes a business will pay for services before it actually receives the services. Insurance, for example, has to be paid for before cover is provided. Some local taxes are also to be paid before the period for which they are due.

Since we are accounting for resources used in the period covered by the financial statements, any amounts paid in advance must be disregarded.

**Worked example**

An extract from Lori's trial balance at 31 December 2014 shows:

| | $ |
|---|---|
| Insurances | 2 300 |
| Local taxes | 1 200 |

- Insurance paid for January 2015 amounts to $100.
- Local taxes paid for the three months ending 31 March 2015 amount to $300.

**Required**

Prepare an extract from the income statement for the year ended 31 December 2014 showing the entries for insurance and local taxes.

### Answer

**Lori**

**Extract from income statement for the year ended 31 December 2014**

| | $ |
|---|---|
| Insurance | 2 200 |
| Local taxes | 900 |

Lori does not include the $100 paid for *next year's insurance cover* or the $300 for *next year's local taxes*. She only includes the payments made to acquire the resources that have been used to run her business this year.

But it cannot be right to reduce the two expenses without corresponding entries. We can reduce debits by increasing credits.

In effect Lori has credited insurance with $100; she has credited local taxes with $300. She needs to include two extra debits – two extra receivables.

Lori's statement of financial position at 31 December 2014 will show:

| | $ |
|---|---|
| **Current assets** | |
| Other receivables | 400 |

➤ Now try Question 1.

**Self-test questions**

1 The accruals concept is sometimes known as the ____________ concept.
2 Define an accrual.
3 Give two examples of accrued expenses at a financial year end.
4 How should an accrued expense be classified in a statement of financial position?
5 Define a prepayment.
6 Give an example of a prepayment at a financial year end.
7 How should a prepayment be classified in a statement of financial position?

## 9.4 Recording accrued expenses and prepaid expenses in the general ledger

We have seen that payments made to acquire goods and services for a business are not always perfectly matched to the receipt of the actual goods and services. Sometimes goods and services are received during a financial year but are not paid for until after the financial year end.

Accrued expenses and prepaid expenses must be recorded in the business books of account.

### Worked example

During the year ended 31 December 2014, Jahangir has paid wages of $443 408 to his staff. The summarised entries in the wages account are shown:

| Dr | Wages account | | Cr |
|---|---|---|---|
| | $ | | $ |
| Bank | 127 938 | | |
| Bank | 89 267 | | |
| Bank | 131 442 | | |
| Bank | 94 761 | | |

At the financial year end, Jahangir owes his workers $2793 for work completed during December 2014.

**Required**

a Complete the wages account for the year ended 31 December 2014.

b Show appropriate entries in the financial statements.

#### Workings

At the year end Jahangir owes his workers $2793. This accrued expense is owed at the financial year end – therefore it is a credit (a payable). It has to be shown as a credit in the books of account at the start of the next financial year.

| Dr | Wages account | | Cr |
|---|---|---|---|
| | $ | | $ |
| | | | |
| | | Balance b/d | 2 793 |

The rules of double entry mean we cannot make a credit entry without a corresponding debit entry. Enter a debit entry 'above the line' to complete the double entry.

| Dr | Wages account | | Cr |
|---|---|---|---|
| | $ | | $ |
| Balance c/d | 2 793 | | |
| | | | |
| | | Balance b/d | 2 793 |

Total the account and transfer the adjusted amount to the income statement.

The balance left on the account at the financial year end is shown on the statement of financial position as a current liability – the amount that still has to be paid to Jahangir's staff.

## Answer

a

| Dr | Wages account | | Cr |
|---|---|---|---|
| | $ | | $ |
| Bank | 127938 | | |
| Bank | 89267 | | |
| Bank | 131442 | | |
| Bank | 94761 | | |
| Balance c/d | 2793 | Income statement | 446201 |
| | 446201 | | 446201 |
| | | Balance b/d | 2793 |

b

**Extract from income statement for the year ended 31 December 2014**

| | $ |
|---|---|
| Expenses | |
| Wages | 446201 |

**Extract from statement of financial position at 31 December 2014**

| | $ |
|---|---|
| **Current liabilities** | |
| Other payables | 2793 |

### Worked example

Josie has paid $1798 for insurance at 31 December 2014. The summarised entries are shown. $340 has been paid in advance for insurance in 2015.

| Dr | Insurance account | Cr |
|---|---|---|
| | $ | |
| Bank | 610 | |
| Bank | 720 | |
| Bank | 468 | |

**Required**

a Prepare the insurance account for the year ended 31 December 2014.

b Show appropriate entries in the financial statements.

### Workings

At the financial year end the insurance company owes Josie $340; therefore it is a receivable. It has to be shown as a debit in the books of account at the start of the next financial year.

| Dr | Insurance account | | Cr |
|---|---|---|---|
| | $ | | |
| | | | |
| | | | |
| Balance b/d | 340 | | |

Remember every debit entry needs a corresponding credit entry.

| Dr | Insurance account | | Cr |
|---|---|---|---|
| | $ | | $ |
| | | Balance c/d | 340 |
| | | | |
| Balance b/d | 340 | | |

Now complete the account.

## Answer

a

| Dr | Insurance account | | Cr |
|---|---|---|---|
| | $ | | $ |
| Bank | 610 | Income statement | 1458 |
| Bank | 720 | | |
| Bank | 468 | Balance c/d | 340 |
| | 1798 | | 1798 |
| Balance b/d | 340 | | |

b

| Extract from income statement for the year ended 31 December 2014 | |
|---|---|
| | $ |
| Expenses | |
| Insurance | 1458 |

| Extract from statement of financial position at 31 December 2014 | |
|---|---|
| | $ |
| **Current assets** | |
| Other receivables | 340 |

# 9.5 Dealing with outstanding revenues and revenues paid in advance

## 9.5.1 Recording outstanding revenues

When revenue has been earned during a financial year but has not yet been received, the revenue due must be included in the financial statements.

**Example**

Lori sublets the rooms above her shop to Dan for a rental of $50 per week. At 31 December Dan owes two weeks' rent.

Lori's income statement would show a full year's rental income of $2600 even though she has only actually received $2500 from Dan.

When preparing an income statement, a trader must include all items of revenue received or receivable for the time period under review.

➤ Now try Question 2.

### 9.5.2 Recording revenues that are paid in advance

Sometimes commission receivable and rent receivable may be paid in advance. The amounts relating to *next year* will not be included in *this year's* financial statements.

**Worked example**

Hua works on commission for Henri. Hua has earned $5320 commission for the year ended 31 January 2015. At 31 January 2015, Hua has received commission payments of $6000.

**Required**

a State the amount to be entered in Hua's income statement for the year ended 31 January 2015.

b Calculate the amount to be shown in the statement of financial position at 31 January 2015. Name the section of the statement of financial position in which it will appear.

#### Answer

a The amount to be shown in the income statement is $5320. This should be shown as an addition to the gross profit.

b $680 is shown under current liabilities in the statement of financial position. (Hua owes Henri $680 at the end of the financial year.)

---

**Worked example**

Gerda sublets part of her premises to Colin for $6240 per annum. At Gerda's financial year end, 31 July 2014, Colin had paid $6600 rent.

**Required**

a State the amount to be entered in Gerda's income statement for the year ended 31 July 2014.

b Calculate the amount to be shown in the statement of financial position at 31 July 2014. Name the section of the statement of financial position in which it will appear.

#### Answer

a The amount shown in the income statement is $6240. This should be added to gross profit.

b $360 is shown as a current liability in the statement of financial position.

---

Amounts *owed* for expenses by a business at the financial year end are usually totalled and entered in the statement of financial position as a current liability. The total is shown as 'other payables'.

Amounts *paid in advance* for expenses by the business at the financial year end are usually totalled and entered in the statement of financial position as a current asset. The total is shown as 'other receivables'.

Amounts *owed* to a business for commission receivable and rent receivable are usually added to receivables.

**Self-test questions**

8 The amount of an expense on the trial balance is always entered in an income statement. True/False?

9 A receivable is a current asset. True/False?

10 A payable is a current asset. True/False?

11 Money paid for the next financial year's rent is a current asset. True/False?

12 Money received from a tenant for next year's rent is a current asset. True/False?

## Chapter summary

- We account for resources used during a financial year, not money paid to acquire those resources.
- The accruals concept recognises the difference between the actual payment of cash and the legal obligation to pay cash. Accruals are current liabilities. Prepayments are current assets.
- The concept also recognises the distinction between the actual receipt of cash and the legal right to receive cash. Cash received before it is due is a current liability. Cash owed but not yet paid is a current asset.

# 10 Control systems – the trial balance

**→ Content**

**1.1 The accounting cycle**

- Prepare ledger accounts and trial balance

**1.3 Reconciliation and verification**

- Reconcile and verify ledger accounts using documentation from internal and external sources

**By the end of this chapter you should be able to:**

- prepare a trial balance
- explain the uses and limitations of preparing a trial balance as a control system
- identify errors not revealed by extracting a trial balance.

## 10.1 The trial balance

We saw in Chapter 6 that we can list all the balances taken from the ledgers of a business to construct a trial balance. From the trial balance we could prepare a simple income statement and a simple statement of financial position. Although this is a useful way of obtaining information for use in preparing the two statements, it is not the primary function of extracting a trial balance from the ledgers.

**Worked example**

Sneh owns and runs a shop selling clothes. The following transactions have taken place:

- Sneh's cash sales amount to $612
- she purchases trousers from Caitlin $129 on credit
- Sneh sells a shirt and shoes to Upsala $76 on credit
- she pays rent for her shop $250 cash
- she purchases shoes $345, for resale, on credit from Rohit
- Sneh pays wages $166 using cash.

**Required**

Enter the transactions in Sneh's ledger. Carry down any balances. Extract a trial balance to check the accuracy of the entries.

## Answer

| Dr | Cash account (GL) | Cr |
|---|---|---|
| | $ | $ |
| | 612 | 250 |
| | | 166 |

| Dr | Sales acount (GL) | Cr |
|---|---|---|
| | | $ |
| | | 612 |
| | | 76 |

| Dr | Purchases account (GL) | Cr |
|---|---|---|
| | $ | |
| | 129 | |
| | 345 | |

| Dr | Caitlin (PL) | Cr |
|---|---|---|
| | | $ |
| | | 129 |

| Dr | Upsala (SL) | Cr |
|---|---|---|
| | $ | |
| | 76 | |

| Dr | Rent account (GL) | Cr |
|---|---|---|
| | $ | |
| | 250 | |

| Dr | Rohit (PL) | Cr |
|---|---|---|
| | | $ |
| | | 345 |

| Dr | Wages account | Cr |
|---|---|---|
| | $ | |
| | 166 | |

**Trial balance**

| | Dr | Cr |
|---|---|---|
| | $ | $ |
| Cash | 196 | |
| Sales | | 688 |
| Purchases | 474 | |
| Caitlin | | 129 |
| Upsala | 76 | |
| Rent | 250 | |
| Rohit | | 345 |
| Wages | 166 | |
| | 1 162 | 1 162 |

A trial balance is made up of the balances extracted from the ledger. It summarises the balances in all the ledgers.

If you consider the few trial balances that have been prepared a pattern has started to emerge.

➤ **Now try Question 1.**

## 10.1.1 Debit balances

- Assets are always debit balances. Examples in the worked example above are cash balances (an asset); debtors like Upsala (an asset) – he owes money to Sneh.
- Expenses are always debit balances. Examples above are the balance on the rent account; the balance on the wages account; the balance on the purchases account.

## 10.1.2 Credit balances

- Incomes and benefits are always credit balances. An example above is the balance on the sales account.
- Liabilities are always credit balances. The examples above are Caitlin and Rohit; they are creditors – Sneh owes them money.

You can learn where balances are entered on a trial balance by using a mnemonic. For example: **D**o **A**ll **E**lephants **C**hase **L**arge **I**talian **B**uffaloes. Perhaps you can devise your own mnemonics to help you remember key facts.

A trial balance will show balances thus:

| Debit balances | Credit balances |
|---|---|
| Assets | Liabilities |
| Expenses | Incomes |
| | Benefits |

**Worked example**

The following is a list of account headings found in Tayyiba's ledger.

Place a tick in the appropriate columns to show the category into which each item falls. Indicate whether a balance on the account would appear in the debit or credit column of her trial balance.

| Account name | Asset | Expense | Liability | Income or benefit | Debit | Credit |
|---|---|---|---|---|---|---|
| Wages | | | | | | |
| Premises | | | | | | |
| Biko, a credit supplier | | | | | | |
| Advertising | | | | | | |
| Sales | | | | | | |
| Bank overdraft | | | | | | |

## Answer

- Wages: Expense/Debit
- Premises: Asset/Debit
- Biko: Liability/Credit
- Advertising: Expense/Debit
- Sales: Income or benefit/Credit
- Bank overdraft: Liability/Credit

**Worked example**

The following balances have been extracted from the ledgers of Laksumana on 30 April 2015:

buildings $120 000; fixtures and fittings $45 000; van $14 500; motor expenses $4160; rent $7000; local taxes $2400; insurance $2100; cash in hand $120; balance at bank $3670; trade receivables $850; trade payables $1200; sales $260 000; purchases $140 000; capital $78 600.

**Required**

Prepare a trial balance at 30 April 2015 for Laksumana.

## Answer

**Laksumana**

**Trial balance at 30 April 2015**

| | Dr | Cr |
|---|---|---|
| | $ | $ |
| Buildings | 120 000 | |
| Fixtures and Fittings | 45 000 | |
| Van | 14 500 | |
| Rent | 7 000 | |
| Local taxes | 2 400 | |
| Insurance | 2 100 | |

| | | |
|---|---|---|
| Motor expenses | 4160 | |
| Cash in hand | 120 | |
| Balance at bank | 3670 | |
| Trade receivables | 850 | |
| Trade payables | | 1200 |
| Sales | | 260000 |
| Purchases | 140000 | |
| Capital | | 78600 |
| | 339800 | 339800 |

**Note**

- The debit and credit column totals are the same. So we can say with some certainty that whoever did the double-entry book-keeping probably made a debit entry for every credit entry. ('Probably' means that there could be some missing debit and/or credits of the same total value – these are known as **compensating errors**, which will be discussed later.)
- The debit column of the trial balance contains only assets and expenses; the credit column of the trial balance contains only liabilities and incomes or benefits.

**Self-test questions**

1 The debit side of a ledger account totals $242; the credit side totals $200. What is the balance on the account?
2 Generally, which side of a trial balance will have the most entries?
3 Liabilities are found on the ____________ side of a trial balance.
4 Incomes are found on the ____________ side of a trial balance.
5 In which ledger would you expect to find the account of Gisele, a supplier of goods on credit?
6 In which ledger would you expect to find the sales returns account?

## 10.2 Uses of the trial balance

The trial balance has only one function and that is to check the arithmetic accuracy of the double-entry system.

However, as you have seen in earlier chapters, the trial balance can be used as a list from which to prepare the financial statements. It is generally used to prepare an income statement and a statement of financial position.

## 10.3 Limitations of using a trial balance as a control system

The trial balance has certain limitations. Even if the trial balance totals do agree, that is no guarantee that there are no mistakes in the system. There are six types of error in the double-entry system that will not result in an incorrect trial balance. These are listed in Section 10.6.

If the totals of a trial balance disagree, you must run through a few checks in order to see that you have not made a simple error:

**1** Check that you have added the debit column correctly and also that you have added the credit column correctly.
**2** Check that there are lots more entries in the debit column than there are in the credit column. The debit column should only contain assets and expenses. The credit column should only contain liabilities and incomes or benefits.

3 If you cannot find the error, look at the totals. If the total of the debit column is smaller than the total of the credit column, check that you have not missed a debit balance. If the credit column total is the smaller of the two, check that you have not missed a credit balance.
4 If the error has not been found by going through the three previous points, divide the difference in the totals by two. Then look to see if an asset has been incorrectly placed in the credit column or if a liability has been placed in the debit column; items in the incorrect column will double the mistake.
5 If you divide the difference in trial balance totals by nine and your answer is a whole number, then the error could be what is known as a **transposition error**, for example $123 entered as $132 would give a difference in the trial balance totals of nine; $96 written as $69 would cause a difference in trial balance totals of 27, which is divisible by nine.

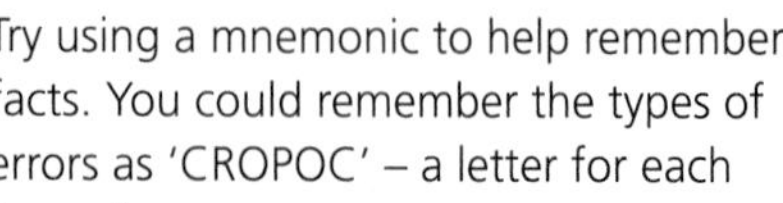

Try using a mnemonic to help remember facts. You could remember the types of errors as 'CROPOC' – a letter for each type of error:
**C**ommission
**R**eversal
**O**mission
**P**rinciple
**O**riginal entry
**C**ompensating

## 10.4 Errors that are not revealed by extracting a trial balance

There are six types of errors that are not revealed by extracting a trial balance:
1 errors of commission
2 reversal of entries
3 errors of omission
4 errors of principle
5 errors of original entry
6 compensating errors.

It is essential that you learn the names of these errors.

### 10.4.1 Errors of commission

Errors of commission arise when the correct amount is entered on the correct side of the wrong account.

If $600 rent was paid by cheque and the motor expenses account was debited with $600, the error would not be revealed by the trial balance.

### 10.4.2 Reversal of entries

This occurs when the correct figures are used but both entries are entered on the wrong side of the accounts used.

For example, if $70 of goods were purchased from P. Smith and P. Smith's account in the purchases ledger was debited with $70, and the purchases account in the general ledger was credited with $70, a trial balance would still balance.

### 10.4.3 Errors of omission

These errors occur when a transaction is completely missed from the ledgers. If a purchase invoice was destroyed there would be no entry in the purchases journal and therefore the purchases account in the general ledger would not contain the debit entry recording the transaction; neither would the supplier's account contain the credit entry. The debit entry is zero; the credit entry is zero. The debit and credit entries agree.

### 10.4.4 Errors of principle

These errors are when a transaction is posted to the incorrect class of account. For example, if a new vehicle was purchased and was inadvertently entered into the motor expenses account in the general ledger, this would not be revealed by the trial balance. Some readers may be confused by the difference between an error of commission and an error of principle.

- An **error of commission** will *not* affect profits and/or the validity of the statement of financial position.
- An **error of principle** *will* affect both the profit of the business and will either understate or overstate an entry on the statement of financial position.

You may wish to use this rule when trying to decide whether an incorrect posting is an error of commission or an error of principle.

For example, a vehicle costing $23 500 is posted incorrectly to the motor expenses account. Profit will be understated by $23 500. (Profit will be reduced by the 'extra' expense in the income statement.) The non-current assets shown on the statement of financial position will be understated by $23 500 also.

## 10.4.5 Errors of original entry

If a credit sale for $176 was entered in the sales journal as $167, then a debit entry of $167 would be recorded in the customer's account in the sales ledger and a credit entry of $167 would be entered in the sales account in the general ledger.

The debit entry is $167; the credit entry is $167. The debit and credit entries agree.

## 10.4.6 Compensating errors

Compensating errors cancel each other out. If the debit side of an account is totalled incorrectly and is $100 too much and another totally separate account with credit entries is incorrectly totalled by $100 too much, then no error will be revealed by extracting a trial balance.

**Worked example**

1 Vehicle repair paid by cheque $649

| Debit entry | Credit entry |
|---|---|
| Bank account $649 | Motor expenses account $649 |

2 Machine sold for $4 000

| Debit entry | Credit entry |
|---|---|
| Bank account $4 000 | Sales account $4 000 |

3 Goods purchased $29 from Trip & Co. on credit

| Debit entry | Credit entry |
|---|---|
| Purchases account $29 | Prit & Co. $29 |

4 Goods sold $76 on credit to Ricket

| Debit entry | Credit entry |
|---|---|
| Ricket's account $67 | Sales account $67 |

**Required**

Identify the types of errors listed above.

### Answer

1 Reversal of entries
2 Error of principle
3 Error of commission
4 Error of original entry (also compensating error)

➤ Now try Question 2.

## Self-test questions

7 A trial balance balances. This is proof that there are no mistakes in any ledger. True/False?
8 What is the purpose of extracting a trial balance from the ledgers?
9 Can a trial balance be used for any other purpose than checking for the accuracy of the double-entry system?
10 A trial balance is extracted from the general ledger. True/False?
11 On which side of a trial balance would you find rent receivable?

## Chapter summary

- A trial balance is extracted from the three ledgers.
- It is a summarised version of all the accounts extracted from the three ledgers.
- The debit column of a trial balance lists assets and expenses.
- The credit column of a trial balance lists liabilities, incomes and benefits.
- A trial balance checks the arithmetical accuracy of the double-entry book-keeping system.
- If the trial balance balances it is not a guarantee that the double-entry system is free of errors.
- There are six types of error that will not be disclosed by extracting a trial balance.
- The trial balance can also be used as a useful list from which to prepare the financial statements of a business.

# 11 Suspense accounts

**Content**

**1.3 Reconciliation and verification**

- Prepare ledger accounts and journal entries to correct errors using a suspense account and record the effects of these in the financial statements.

**By the end of this chapter you should be able to:**

- prepare and use a suspense account as part of the mechanism for correcting errors.

## 11.1 Using a suspense account

Although the prime function of a trial balance is to test the accuracy of our double-entry system, we often use a trial balance as a list from which we prepare financial statements. This saves us much time.

However, if the trial balance fails to balance, then any financial statements prepared from the trial balance will not balance either.

When the trial balance fails to balance, the difference between the total of the debit side and the total of the credit side is placed in a temporary account called a **suspense account**.

If the debit column of the trial balance has a smaller total than the credit column, we insert an item 'suspense account' in the debit column in order that the two columns will have the same total.

If the total of the credit column of the trial balance is smaller than the total of the debit column, then the amount for suspense account would be inserted in the credit column.

**Example**

Lara has extracted a trial balance. The totals of the debit and credit columns do not agree.

| | Debit column total | Credit column total |
|---|---|---|
| | $ | $ |
| | 123 456 | 132 546 |
| *Lara inserts a suspense account to make the trial balance balance* | 9 090 | |
| | 132 546 | 132 546 |

**Example**

Lawrence has extracted a trial balance from his ledgers. The totals of the debit and credit columns do not agree.

| | Debit column total | Credit column total |
|---|---|---|
| | $ | $ |
| | 890321 | 889617 |
| *Lawrence inserts a suspense account to make the trial balance balance* | | 704 |
| | 890321 | 890321 |

A word of warning: if you prepare a set of financial statements and those statements do not balance, run through the checks mentioned in Chapter 10. If you do not find the error, do not make the statement of financial position balance by inserting a suspense item. This wastes time and you are merely drawing attention to the fact that you have made an error.

We can then prepare a set of draft financial statements safe in the knowledge that they will balance (provided we do not make any errors in the preparation).

In the draft financial statements, a suspense account shown as a debit balance in the trial balance will be shown as a current asset in the statement of financial position.

If the suspense account has been included as a credit balance in the trial balance, it should be shown as a current liability on the statement of financial position.

Lara's suspense account balance would be shown as a current asset $9090 on her draft statement of financial position.

Lawrence's suspense account balance would be shown as a current liability $704 on his draft statement of financial position.

When the errors that have prevented the trial balance from balancing are found and corrected, the draft financial statements are amended and should be correct according to the information given.

When errors affecting the balancing of the trial balance are found, they will be entered in the suspense account (and in another account since we are using a double-entry system).

## 11.2 The correction of errors

Earlier we used the **general journal** as the book of prime entry to record:

- the purchase of non-current assets on credit
- the sale of non-current assets on credit
- the entries when a business first comes into existence.

A fourth use of the general journal, as a book of prime entry, is to record the correction of errors.

**Casting** is a term used by accountants for adding. **Undercast** means that a total is lower than it ought to be. **Overcast** means that a total is greater than it ought to be.

Remember that:

- not all errors affect the balancing of the trial balance
- when the errors are entered in the suspense account, the suspense account balance should be eliminated.

**Worked example**

On 31 March 2014 Vijay's trial balance failed to agree. The debit column total was $20500; the credit column totalled $21000. The difference was entered in a suspense account.

Since extracting the trial balance the following errors have been found:

1 The purchases account was undercast by $1000.

2 Goods sold on credit to J. Latino for $500 were debited to J. Latino's account. These goods had not been included in the sales journal.

**Required**

Prepare:

a general journal entries to correct the errors

b a suspense account showing the corrections that have been made.

**Workings**

When general journal entries are required, we ask ourselves questions as follows.

In the first example:

- Which account should be debited? Answer – purchases account
- Which account should be credited? Answer – suspense account

In the second example:

- Which account should be debited? Answer – suspense account
- Which account should be credited? Answer – sales account

## Answer

a

**General journal**

| | Dr | Cr |
|---|---|---|
| | $ | $ |
| 1 Purchases account | 1 000 | |
| Suspense account | | 1 000 |
| Correction of error: Purchases account undercast by $1000 | | |
| 2 Suspense account | 500 | |
| Sales account | | 500 |
| Correction of error: Sale of goods to Latino not included in sales journal | | |

b

**Suspense account**

| Dr | | | Cr |
|---|---|---|---|
| | $ | | $ |
| Trial balance difference | 500 | Purchases | 1 000 |
| Sales account | 500 | | |
| | 1 000 | | 1 000 |

**Worked example**

The totals on Maura's trial balance at 30 November 2013 failed to agree. The debit column totalled $230 161; the credit column totalled $189 521. The difference was entered in a suspense account. On further examination of the books of account, the following errors were found:

1 Motoring expenses $1700 had been entered in the vehicles account.

2 The total of the sales journal for July $16 320 had been posted to the debit side of the purchases account.

3 The total of rent received $4000 for the year had been entered as a debit entry in the rent payable account.

4 Maura had withdrawn goods for her own use $4700 during the year. These goods had been entered on the debit side of the purchases account.

**Required**

Prepare:

a journal entries to correct the errors

b a suspense account.

## Answer

a

**General journal**

| | Dr | Cr |
|---|---|---|
| | $ | $ |
| Motor expenses account | 1 700 | |
| Vehicles account | | 1 700 |
| Error of principle: Motor expenses included as capital expenditure | | |
| Suspense account | 32 640 | |
| Sales account | | 16 320 |
| Purchases account | | 16 320 |
| Posting error: Sales posted incorrectly to purchases account | | |
| Suspense account | 8 000 | |
| Rent receivable account | | 4 000 |
| Rent payable account | | 4 000 |
| Posting error: Rent receivable entered incorrectly in the rent payable account | | |
| Drawings account | 4 700 | |
| Purchases account | | 4 700 |
| Posting error: Drawings entered as purchases | | |

b

**Suspense account**

| Dr | $ | | Cr $ |
|---|---|---|---|
| Sales account | 16 320 | Trial balance difference | 40 640 |
| Purchases account | 16 320 | | |
| Rent receivable account | 4 000 | | |
| Rent payable account | 4 000 | | |
| | 40 640 | | 40 640 |

## Self-test questions

1 What is an error of original entry?
2 What does the term 'overcast' mean?
3 A trial balance balances. Therefore there are no mistakes in the ledgers. True/False?
4 What is the difference between an error of principle and an error of commission?
5 The debit column of a trial balance totals $230 150 and the credit column totals $230 000. What amount will be entered in a suspense account?
6 What does the mnemonic CROPOC stand for?
7 What does the term 'casting' mean?

➤ Now try Question 1.

## Chapter summary

- A suspense account is used to make the debit column total agree with the credit column total if the trial balance does not balance.
- When errors are rectified, the suspense account should 'disappear'.

# 12 Control systems – bank reconciliations

**Content**

**1.3 Reconciliation and verification**

- Prepare a bank reconciliation statement from relevant information.

**By the end of this chapter you should be able to:**

- explain the procedure used to check the accuracy of the entries made in the cash columns of a cash book
- check the accuracy of entries in the bank columns of a cash book
- identify and enter any bank transactions that may be missing from the bank columns of a cash book
- identify and correct any bank transactions incorrectly entered in the bank columns of a cash book
- prepare a bank reconciliation statement
- explain the reasons for preparing a bank reconciliation statement.

We have seen that the whole double-entry system can be checked by extracting a trial balance.

Remember that even if the trial balance does agree, it does not necessarily mean that there are no errors in the double-entry system. *All you can be sure of is that the double-entry system is arithmetically correct.*

Can you remember the six types of errors that are not revealed by extracting a trial balance? Remember CROPOC? If not, refer back to Chapter 10 (Section 10.6).

Altogether we use four checks to verify the accuracy of the system. The trial balance is generally prepared at the financial year end, although a trial balance could be extracted every day to see if the system is arithmetically correct. The other three checks are done at frequent intervals throughout the year.

Let us first look at the two checks that are used to verify the entries in the cash book.

## 12.1 Checking the accuracy of a cash balance shown in a cash book

We check the cash balance shown in the cash columns of the cash book frequently. Some businesses, like a small local store, would perhaps only check the cash balances on a weekly basis whereas some very large organisations may check the cash balances much more frequently.

How often would you check the cash balances in your tills if you were the owner of a store? It might depend on how much cash goes through each till. It might depend on how many staff had access to the tills and how trustworthy those members of staff are.

When checking the cash, we count all the money that is in the till and check the amount held against the total shown on the till roll. The two should be the same. It is done fairly frequently, because if there is a discrepancy it is much easier to remember what might have caused any difference. For example, money may have been taken from the till to pay a cleaner and no note has been made of the payment. It is much easier to remember this immediately after the event than, say, some four months later.

The cash in the till should not only agree with the till roll total but also should agree with the total of the cash columns in the cash book kept by the business.

This is the most frequent check undertaken by businesses. It is fairly straightforward and very easy to do.

## 12.2 Checking the accuracy of transactions recorded in the bank columns of a cash book

This topic often gives some students a few problems. How are the bank columns in a cash book written up? The bulk of banking transactions are undertaken by the bank on instructions given by the managers of the business. The instructions to undertake transactions involving the use of the banking system are given to the bank by:

- cheque – cheques are simply instructions given to the bank to take money from an account and give the money to someone else
- paying-in slip – these slips record the amount of cash and cheques paid into the business bank account.

When any bank transaction is undertaken, two records are kept of the transaction. One is recorded by the business in a cash book. The other record is kept by the bank. The two records kept are taken from different parts of a source document.

Records of every transaction are kept by the bank and the bank's customer.

### 12.2.1 Recording monies paid into a bank account

When money is paid into a bank the person paying in the money will fill in a slip showing the numbers and amounts of each type of coin and bank note deposited plus a list of all the cheques that are being paid in. The person fills in a counterfoil, which duplicates this information. The money and cheques are handed to the bank cashier, who checks the amounts for accuracy and then stamps the paying-in slip and the duplicate (the counterfoil or the stub). From this counterfoil, the debit entries are made in the cash book – so this is one of the source documents to write up the cash book.

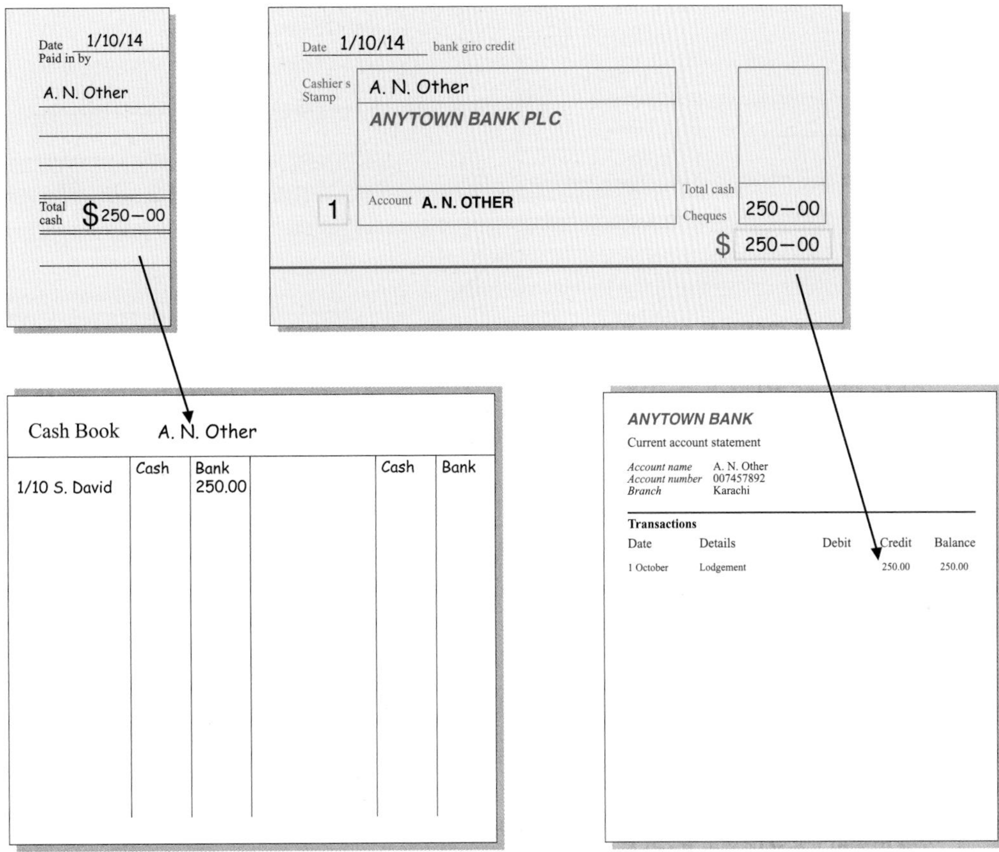


**Figure 12.1** Records of a transaction when money is paid into the bank

The bank uses the actual paying-in slip to show how much money and cheques have been deposited in the business bank account. These entries will appear as credit entries on a copy of the bank's records.

## 12.2.2 Recording monies withdrawn from a bank account

The **payee** is the person to whom a cheque is made payable.

The **drawer** is the person (or business) using a cheque for payment.

When payment is made by cheque, the cheque is filled out with the **payee**'s name, the date, the amount (both in words and in figures) and then the **drawer** signs the cheque and sends it to the creditor, the person who has been owed the money.

The cheque counterfoil is used as the source document to write up the credit bank column in the cash book.

The bank uses the cheque that has been sent to the payee (the creditor) to enter withdrawals from the business account. These withdrawals will be shown on the debit side of a copy of the bank's records.

A statement will be sent to the business on a frequent basis, usually at the end of every month but in the case of very large businesses the bank statement may be sent to the business on a weekly basis. A copy of the bank's records may be obtained electronically if the account is managed online.

**Note**

The fifth column on the bank statement (or copy of the bank's records) shows a running balance figure.

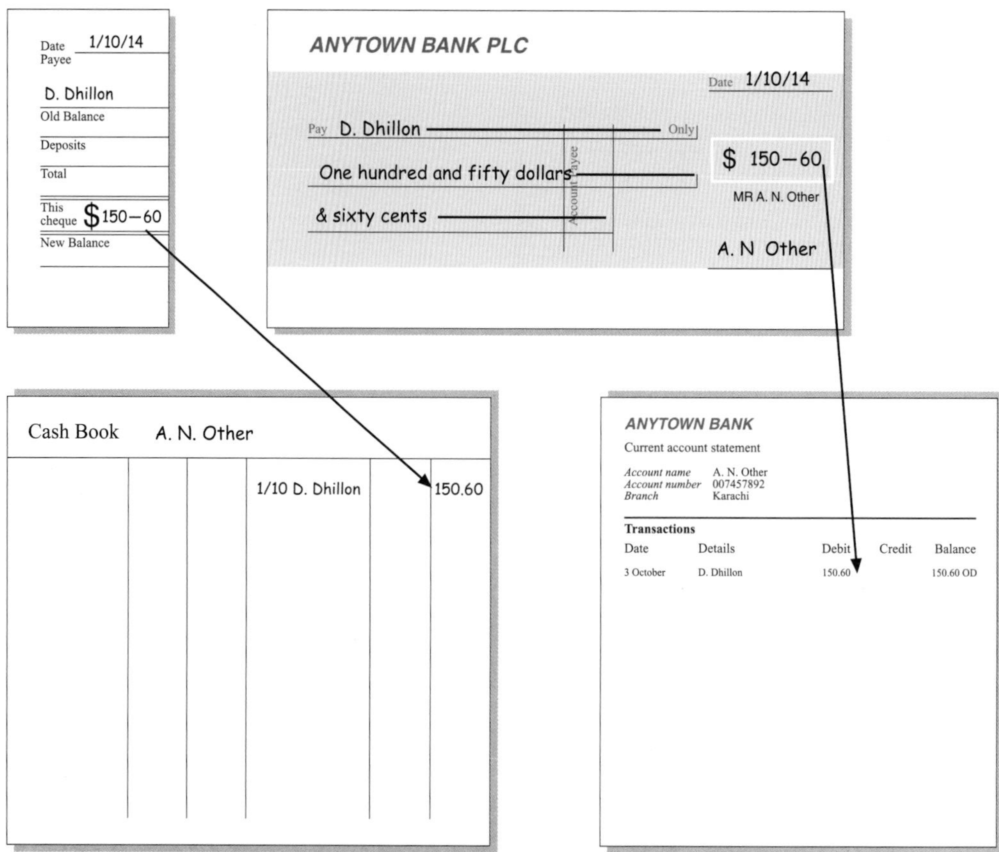


**Figure 12.2** Records of a transaction when a payment is made by cheque

## 12.3 Reasons why a cash book and bank statement might not show identical entries

The records kept by the bank and the cash book should be identical since the cash book is prepared from the counterfoils, which are duplicates of the original documents from which the bank draws up its bank statement. The bank statement is a copy of the account in the bank's ledger.

We have seen how entries using the banking system are recorded in the cash book.

- Cheques received are shown in the bank column on the debit side of the cash book.
- Cheques paid to suppliers of goods and services are shown in the bank column on the credit side of the cash book.

The amounts withdrawn from the bank account by cheque should appear as identical amounts in the bank column on the credit side of the cash book and in the debit column of the bank statement.

Amounts paid in should appear as identical amounts in the bank column on the debit side of the cash book and in the credit column of the bank statement. Can you think of any reasons why the cash book entries should not be identical to those shown in the bank's ledger?

The counterfoil might not agree with the cheque. The cheque might say $110 but the cheque counterfoil could say $101. So the cash book will show $101 and the bank statement will show $110. Which amount is correct? The bank will have taken

**Standing orders** are payments made automatically by a bank on behalf of customers. They are set amounts and may be paid weekly, monthly or annually.

**Direct debits** are payments made by the bank on behalf of customers. The authority to withdraw money from the account is given to the payee. The amounts withdrawn from the account are generally variable.

**Bank charges** are made by banks to cover the costs of maintaining the drawer's account.

**Interest on overdrafts**: the interest charged by banks when an account is overdrawn.

**Credit transfers** are amounts paid into an account directly through the banking system instead of by issuing a cheque.

**Dishonoured cheques** are cheques that have not gone through the drawer's bank account. Often this may be because the drawer has insufficient funds in their account to honour (pay) the cheque.

Learn these definitions. They are very important.

$110 out of the account since this is what the instruction (the cheque) says, so this is the correct amount and the counterfoil and cash book should be changed.

- The counterfoil might not have been filled in at all. The amount shown in the bank statement should be entered in the cash book.
- The bank may have made payments from the account on a **standing order** and the payment from the account has for the moment been overlooked by the drawer and not yet included in the business cash book. The amount should be entered as a payment in the bank column on the credit side of the cash book.
- The bank may have made payment from the account by **direct debit** and the payment from the account has been overlooked by the drawer. The amount should be entered as a payment in the bank column on the credit side of the cash book.
- The bank may have taken money from the account as **bank charges** and this amount has not yet been included in the business cash book. The amount should be included as a payment in the bank column on the credit side of the cash book.
- The bank may have made an interest charge for times when the bank statement shows a debit balance (i.e. the account has been overdrawn). The amount of interest charged should be entered as a payment in the bank column on the credit side of the cash book.
- The bank may have received deposits on behalf of the business directly through the banking system. Any **credit transfers** should be entered as receipts by debiting the bank column in the cash book.
- When a cheque is received, the cheque will be banked. It is entered in the bank column on the debit side of the cash book. If, subsequently, the cheque is dishonoured this fact will be shown on the bank statement. (This is referred to colloquially as a cheque that has 'bounced'.) The trader cannot adjust the bank account in the cash book until the trader is informed by the bank. If it is not also shown in the cash book, the **dishonoured cheque** should be entered as a payment in the bank column on the credit side of the cash book.
- The trader can make the following errors:
  - addition errors in either bank column of the cash book
  - entering the incorrect amount from the cheque and paying-in counterfoils
  - entering the correct amount on the incorrect side of the cash book.
- The bank could make the following errors:
  - entering a withdrawal that should have been debited to the account of someone else
  - entering a deposit that should have been credited to the account of someone else.

**Note**

It is highly unlikely that addition errors will take place in bank statements since they are, generally, computer generated.

A **bank reconciliation statement** is prepared to make sure that the entries in the bank columns of a trader's cash book are the same as those recorded by the bank in its ledger.

If we correct the differences all should be well.

Why is there a need to prepare a **bank reconciliation statement**?

We need to check that:

1. all transactions using banking facilities have been recorded
2. all transactions have been recorded accurately by both the business and the bank
3. all transactions have gone through the drawer's account kept at the bank.

**Clearing** a cheque refers to the passage of a cheque through the banking system. It involves the transfer of money from one account to another. This can take a few days if the accounts are held at different banks.

When a trader pays a supplier by cheque, this should be entered in the bank column on the credit side of the cash book (using the counterfoil as the source document) on the same date that the cheque was written. However, the bank may not show the cheque on the bank statement until several days later – this could be as much as a week later (days in the postal system plus days in the **clearing** system).

When the trader pays money into the business bank account, it will be immediately recorded in the trader's bank column in the cash book. However, the bank will not credit any cheques that are deposited to the trader's bank account until the cheques are cleared.

**Note**

The drawer's account shown on the bank statement is prepared from the actual cheques and paying-in slips received by them. If an error is made on the counterfoil, two different amounts will be recorded by the bank and by the trader.

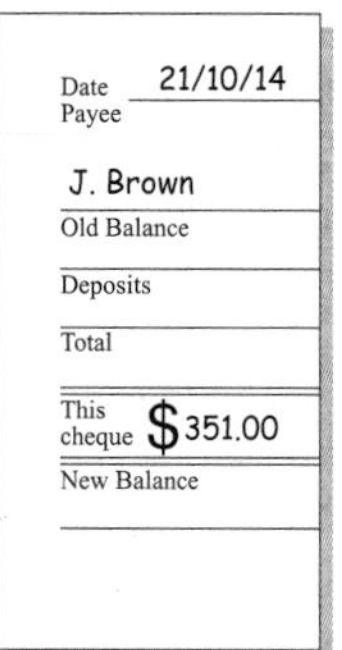


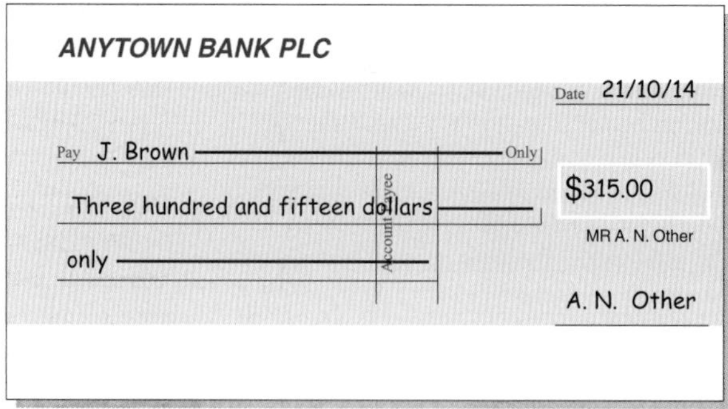


**Figure 12.3** Cheque (*right*) and counterfoil

Which is correct?

The bank will react to the instructions (the cheque), which are to remove $315 from the account and pay it to Brown.

After all the necessary adjustments have been made, the cash book should contain exactly the same information as the bank statement. Or should it? Well, it could, but in real life the likelihood of this happening is fairly remote because of the reasons outlined earlier.

**Lodgements** are payments made into the bank account.

**Unpresented cheques** have not yet been cleared and debited to the account at the bank.

Some deposits made by the trader on the day the bank statement is produced by the bank may not yet be recorded on the statement. These items are called '**lodgements** not yet credited by the bank'. Some cheques paid out by the trader and entered in the cash book will still be in the postal system, in the payee's office or in the bank clearing system. These cheques have yet to be presented at the trader's bank – they are called '**unpresented cheques**'.

So we have to reconcile (bring together) the two different amounts shown in the cash book and on the bank statement. This is done in a bank reconciliation statement. The statement is set out thus:

**Example**

Bank reconciliation statement at … *(the date when the reconciliation is prepared)*

Balance at bank as per cash book

*Add* Unpresented cheques

*Less* Lodgements not yet credited by the bank

Balance at bank as per the bank statement … *(date)*

**Tip**

Make sure that you learn the correct layout for a bank reconciliation statement.

## 12.4 Procedure used to prepare a bank reconciliation statement

**1** Balance the cash book. Remember only the cash and bank columns are balanced; the discount columns are totalled.
**2** Compare the bank columns of the cash book with the bank statement. Tick all the entries shown in the cash book and their corresponding entries in the bank statement.
**3** Bring the cash book up to date by:
  **a** entering payments made by the bank but not yet entered in the cash book in the bank column on the credit side of the cash book (standing orders, direct debits, bank charges, fees, interest and dishonoured cheques)
  **b** entering amounts received by the bank but not entered in the cash book in the bank column on the debit side of the cash book.
**4** Correct any errors discovered in the bank columns of the cash book.
**5** If the bank statement contains errors, inform the bank, make a note of the error and ask the bank for an adjusted bank statement balance.
**6** Prepare the bank reconciliation statement:

Bank reconciliation at … (*the date when the reconciliation is prepared*)

Balance at bank as per cash book

*Add* Unpresented cheques

*Less* Lodgements not yet credited by the bank

Balance at bank as per the bank statement … (*date*)

**Note**

The adjusted balance shown in the bank columns of the cash book is the balance to be shown in both the trial balance and the statement of financial position.

Remember to post all the items entered in the cash book adjustments to the appropriate accounts in the ledgers.

**Worked example**

The bank columns of P. Chene's cash book show the following details for April:

| Dr | | Bank | | | Cheque | Bank Cr |
|---|---|---|---|---|---|---|
| | | $ | | | | $ |
| 1 April | Balance b/d | 486.87 | 3 April | H. Pater | 341 | 34.22 |
| 7 April | H. Rajah | 345.51 | 4 April | T. Hannibal | 342 | 72.91 |
| 10 April | F. Thon | 56.32 | 17 April | C. Dob | 343 | 310.00 |
| 23 April | M. Singh | 178.54 | 22 April | D. Cols | 344 | 130.08 |
| 30 April | J. Cust | 12.55 | 24 April | N. Bedi | 345 | 54.01 |
| | | | 30 April | R. Edy | 346 | 145.37 |
| | | | 30 April | Balance c/d | | 333.20 |
| | | 1 079.79 | | | | 1 079.79 |
| 1 May | Balance b/d | 333.20 | | | | |

She received her bank statement on 3 May:

| Date | Details | Debit | Credit | Balance |
|---|---|---|---|---|
| | | $ | $ | $ |
| 1 April | Balance | | | 486.87 |
| 7 April | Lodgement | | 345.51 | 832.38 |
| 9 April | 342 | 72.91 | | 759.47 |
| 10 April | 341 | 34.22 | | 725.25 |
| | Lodgement | | 56.32 | 781.57 |
| 15 April | Direct debit (Insurance) | 45.66 | | 735.91 |
| 17 April | Credit transfer (M. Chorte) | | 61.00 | 796.91 |
| 23 April | Lodgement | | 178.54 | 975.45 |
| 29 April | 344 | 130.08 | | 845.37 |
| | 345 | 54.01 | | 791.36 |
| 30 April | Bank charges | 6.43 | | 784.93 |

**Required**

a Make any necessary adjustments to P. Chene's cash book.

b Prepare a bank reconciliation statement at 30 April.

## Workings

'Tick' all the items that appear both in P. Chene's cash book and on her bank statement.

- The item that remains unticked in the bank column on the debit side of the cash book is: Cust / $12.55
- The items that remain unticked in the bank column on the credit side of the cash book are: Dob / $310.00; Edy / $145.37
- The item that remains unticked in the credit column of the bank statement is: Chorte / $61.00
- The items that remain unticked in the debit column of the bank statement are: Standing order for insurance / $45.66; Bank charges / $6.43.

It is important that Chene's cash book is updated. The cash book is a vital part of her double-entry records so it should be correct and contain all the transactions relating to the business.

The three transactions remaining unticked on the bank statement have taken place. They remain unticked because *she has not yet recorded them in her cash book.*

The first task is *to record* the transactions in her cash book.

In real life the cash book would simply be extended for a few lines to enable the entries to be made.

Also, we should not forget to complete the double entry for these transactions (although it is purely for illustrative purposes, as the question did not ask for this):

| Dr | | | Chorte (SL) | | Cr |
|---|---|---|---|---|---|
| | | | | | $ |
| | | | 17 April | Bank | 61.00 |

| Dr | Insurance account (GL) | | Cr |
|---|---|---|---|
| | | $ | |
| 15 April | Bank | 45.66 | |

| Dr | Bank charges account (GL) | | Cr |
|---|---|---|---|
| | | $ | |
| 30 April | Bank | 6.43 | |

## Answer

a

**Cash book**

| Dr | | | | | Cr |
|---|---|---|---|---|---|
| | | **$** | | | **$** |
| 1 May | Balance b/d | 333.20 | 15 April | Insurance | 45.66 |
| 17 April | M. Chorte | 61.00 | 30 April | Bank charges | 6.43 |
| | | | 30 April | Balance c/d | 342.11 |
| | | 394.20 | | | 394.20 |
| 1 May | Balance b/d | 342.11 | | | |

**Note**

The balance of $342.11 is the balance to be entered on Chene's trial balance; it is also the balance to be shown as a current asset on her statement of financial position.

b

**Bank reconciliation statement at 30 April**

| | **$** | **$** |
|---|---|---|
| Balance at bank as per the cash book | | 342.11 |
| *Add* Unpresented cheques: | | |
| Dob | 310.00 | |
| Edy | 145.37 | 455.37 |
| | | 797.48 |
| *Less* Lodgements not yet credited: | | |
| Cust | | 12.55 |
| Balance at bank as per bank statement | | 784.93 |

**Tip** 

Never do more than what is asked for in a question. You are unlikely to be rewarded and you will penalise yourself by taking more time than is necessary.

We have reconciled the bank balance shown in the cash book with that shown in the bank statement. We can say with certainty that the transactions recorded in the bank columns of the cash book have been accurately recorded.

### Worked example

The bank columns of D. Dhillon's cash book are shown:

**Cash book**

| Dr | | | | | | Cr |
|---|---|---|---|---|---|---|
| | | **$** | | | | **$** |
| 1 Oct | Balance b/d | 127.63 | 2 Oct | M. Vaughan | 673 | 272.61 |
| 7 Oct | D. Paster | 367.42 | 4 Oct | C. Chan | 674 | 81.13 |
| 15 Oct | T. Henkel | 84.56 | 11 Oct | M. Vere | 675 | 364.42 |
| 15 Oct | B. Tain | 97.42 | 27 Oct | D. Perth | 676 | 182.09 |
| 31 Oct | M. Sond | 216.84 | 29 Oct | N. Lister | 677 | 12.13 |
| 31 Oct | Balance c/d | 18.51 | | | | |
| | | 912.38 | | | | 912.38 |
| | | | 1 Nov | Balance b/d | | 18.51 |

He received his bank statement on 4 November.

***ANYTOWN BANK PLC***

Current account statement

*Account name* D. DHILLON
*Account number* 007457892
*Branch* Karachi

**Transactions**

| Date | Details | Debit | Credit | Balance |
|---|---|---|---|---|
| 1 October | Balance | | | 127.63 |
| 3 October | Lodgement | | 367.42 | 495.05 |
| 7 October | 674 | 81.31 | | 413.74 |
| | Lodgement | | 84.56 | 498.30 |
| 10 October | Lodgement | | 97.42 | 595.72 |
| 15 October | 675 | 364.42 | | 231.30 |
| 16 October | 673 | 272.61 | | 41.31 OD |
| 31 October | Credit transfer G. Jackson | | 41.99 | 0.68 |
| | Stdg order Loan repmt | 150.00 | | 149.32 OD |
| | Dishonoured cheque | 12.48 | | 161.80 OD |
| | Bank charges | 27.56 | | 189.36 OD |

**Figure 12.4** Dhillon's bank statement

**Required**

a Make any adjustments to Dhillon's cash book.

b Prepare a bank reconciliation statement at 31 October.

## Answer

a

| Dr | | Cash book | | | Cr |
|---|---|---|---|---|---|
| | | $ | | | $ |
| 31 Oct | Credit transfer G. Jacks | 41.99 | 31 Oct | Balance b/d | 18.51 |
| | | | 4 Oct | Correction – C. Chan | 0.18 |
| | | | 31 Oct | s/o Loan repayment | 150.00 |
| | | | 31 Oct | Dishonoured cheque | 12.48 |
| 31 Oct | Balance c/d | 166.74 | 31 Oct | Bank charges | 27.56 |
| | | 208.73 | | | 208.73 |
| | | | 31 Oct | Balance b/d | 166.74 |

**Note**

- The amount paid to Chan has been increased – the bank has paid him $81.31, so the cash book has to record the payment.
- The dishonoured cheque has been credited in the cash book.
- The opening balance is a credit balance on the bank statement, indicating that Dhillon has money in the bank; at the end of October a debit balance is shown on the bank statement indicating that Dhillon is overdrawn.

b

**D. Dhillon**
**Bank reconciliation statement at 31 October**

| | | $ | $ | | |
|---|---|---|---|---|---|
| Balance at bank as per cash book | | | 166.74 | OD | |
| *Add* Unpresented cheques: | | | | | |
| | D. Perth | 182.09 | | | |
| | N. Lister | 12.13 | 194.22 | | *This positive amount added to a negative amount gives this positive result.* |
| | | | 27.48 | | |
| *Less* Lodgements not yet credited: | | | | | |
| | M. Sond | | 216.84 | | *This amount deducted gives a negative result.* |
| Balance at bank as per bank statement | | | 189.36 | OD | |

Once more we can now say that all the transactions recorded in the bank columns of the cash book have been recorded accurately.

## Self-test questions

1 Why would a trader prepare a bank reconciliation statement?
2 How often is a bank reconciliation statement prepared?
3 Explain the term 'drawer'.
4 What is a standing order?
5 What is the difference between a standing order and a direct debit?
6 What is meant by the term 'overdrawn'?
7 A bank statement shows a closing credit balance. Does this indicate that the business is running an overdraft?
8 Why are credit transfers often missing from the bank columns of the cash book?
9 Fill in the gaps.

**Bank reconciliation statement ________ 31 March 2015**

| | $ |
|---|---|
| Balance at bank as per cash book | 210 |
| ________ unpresented cheques | 156 |
| | _____ |
| ________ lodgements not yet credited | 99 |
| Balance at bank as per bank statement | _____ |

10 Explain why debit entries in a cash book are shown as credit entries on a bank statement.

➤ Now try Question 1.

## Chapter summary

- The cash balance shown in a cash book should be checked frequently.
- Bank reconciliation statements are prepared to check the accuracy of transactions recorded in the bank columns of the cash book.
- It is a two-stage operation – the cash book is updated first, then the actual reconciliation statement is prepared by adjusting the balance shown in the cash book for unpresented cheques and lodgements not yet credited in the bank statement.

# 13 Control systems – ledger control accounts

## Content

### 1.3 Reconciliation and verification

- Prepare sales and purchases ledger control accounts
- Reconcile control accounts and ledgers
- Outline the uses and limitations of control accounts

**By the end of this chapter you should be able to:**
- prepare sales ledger and purchases ledger control accounts
- enter and explain credit balances in a sales ledger control account
- enter and explain debit balances in a purchases ledger control account
- enter and explain the use of contra entries in control accounts
- make necessary entries to record bad debts
- explain the advantages and limitations of using control accounts as a control mechanism
- reconcile the balances shown in control accounts with a schedule of balances extracted from the personal ledgers.

We have seen that the arithmetical accuracy of the whole double-entry book-keeping system is checked by extracting a trial balance. Although in theory there is only one book used to record all double-entry transactions, we have seen that the ledger is actually divided into three parts. The bulk of all entries in the double-entry system are in the personal ledgers: the sales ledger and the purchases ledger.

Because there are so many entries in these two ledgers, there is great potential for errors to be made. **Control accounts** are used to check the accuracy of the entries made in each of the sales ledgers and in each of the purchases ledgers.

Each month a control account is prepared for each ledger. In this way, errors can be identified as being in one particular ledger in the month that they have occurred.

A control account summarises all the individual entries that have been made in the sales ledgers and the purchases ledgers in any particular month. Any entry in any sales ledger or purchases ledger will be duplicated in the control account.

The construction of a control account is the same whether or not it is maintained as part of the double-entry system or as a memorandum account.

## 13.1 Preparation of a sales ledger control account

If a business has a large number of credit customers it may divide the sales ledger according to geographical areas, customers of particular sales persons, alphabetically, etc. The sales journal would reflect any divisions of the sales ledger.

Some businesses use control accounts as part of their double-entry system. They maintain personal credit customers' accounts in detail as **memorandum accounts**.

These memorandum accounts are used:
- to send out monthly statements
- for credit control purposes, i.e. identifying bad debts and potential doubtful debtors.

**Memorandum accounts** record financial information in account form but they are not part of the double-entry system.

Other businesses use control accounts as memorandum accounts, using them only for control purposes.

The sales ledger control account is a replica, in total, of all the entries made in the individual sales ledger accounts. Any entries that appear in an individual debtor's account will appear in the control account for that ledger.

Here is a simple illustration:

**Worked example**

**Sales ledger**

| Dr | Clogg | | Cr |
|---|---|---|---|
| | $ | | $ |
| 1 May Sales | 50 | 9 May Cash | 48 |
| | | 9 May Disc alld | 2 |
| | 50 | | 50 |

| Dr | Saddler | | Cr |
|---|---|---|---|
| | $ | | $ |
| 7 May Sales | 60 | 7 May Sales returns | 29 |
| | | 14 May Bank | 20 |
| | | 31 May Bal c/d | 11 |
| | 60 | | 60 |
| 1 June Bal b/d | 11 | | |

**Required**

Prepare the sales ledger control account for the month of May.

## Answer

| Dr | Sales ledger control account | | | | Cr |
|---|---|---|---|---|---|
| | | $ | | | $ |
| 1 May | Sales | 50 | 9 May | Cash | 48 |
| 7 May | Sales | 60 | 9 May | Discount allowed | 2 |
| | | | 12 May | Sales returns | 29 |
| | | | 14 May | Bank | 20 |
| | | | 31 May | Balance c/d | 11 |
| | | 110 | | | 110 |
| 1 June | Balance b/d | 11 | | | |

**Tip**

The most common error made when working on control accounts is to reverse the entries.

If you can remember that the control account is an *exact replica of all the sales ledger entries*, you should not get the items required in preparing a control account on the wrong side. (This, of course, assumes that you understand on which side each of the entries appears in an individual account!)

In reality we cannot look at every individual account in a sales ledger and copy them into a sales ledger control account. Nor can we add each of the different categories of entries together – it would be too time consuming. We can, however, get the necessary figures in total by using the books of prime entry.

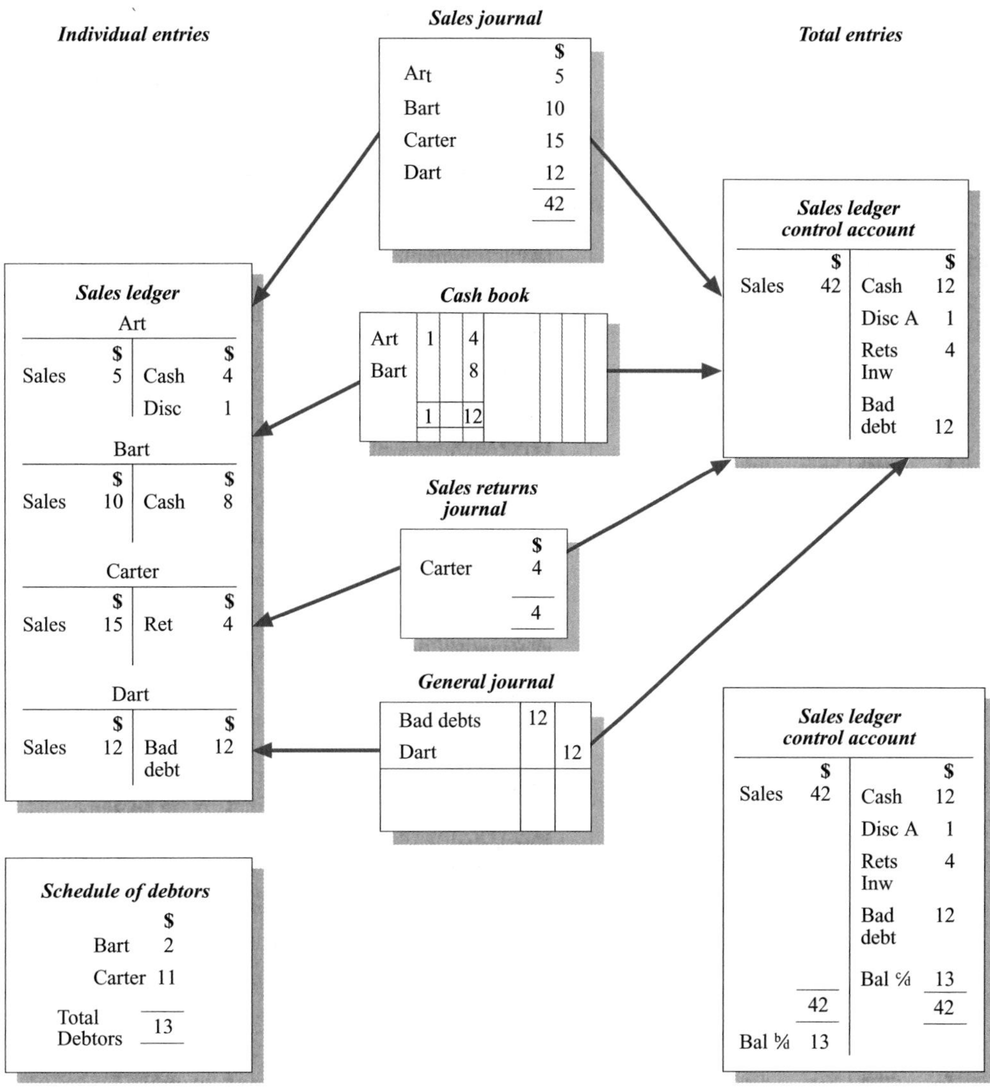


**Figure 13.1** The sales ledger control account

Worked example

## Example 1

Petra started business in May 2014. She provides the following totals from her books of prime entry on 31 May 2014:

credit sales $7300; cash sales $2100; sales returns $420; monies received from debtors $5400.

A schedule of trade receivables extracted from Petra's sales ledger on 31 May 2014 shows they owed $1480.

**Schedule of trade receivables** is a list of debtors' balances extracted from each sales ledger.

**Required**

Prepare a sales ledger control account for May 2014.

## Answer

| Dr | | Sales ledger control account | | | Cr |
|---|---|---|---|---|---|
| | | $ | | | $ |
| 31 May | Sales | 7300 | 31 May | Sales returns | 420 |
| | | | 31 May | Cash | 5400 |
| | | | 31 May | Balance c/d | 1480* |
| | | 7300 | | | 7300 |
| 1 June | Balance b/d | 1480 | | | |

* Figure included to make control account balance.

The total amount owed by trade receivables at the end of May according to the control account should be $1480. This figure should agree with the total of balances listed on the schedule of receivables – it does, so we can say that the sales ledger is arithmetically correct for the month of May 2014.

**Note**

- The $2100 (cash sales) should not be included – these do not appear in the sales ledger as the sales ledger is reserved only for credit customers.
- The $1480 debit balance should also be brought down on the sales ledger control account.

### Example 2

At the end of her second month of trading Petra provides you with the following information, which she has extracted from her books of prime entry on 30 June 2014:

credit sales $9400; cash sales $2750; monies received from credit customers $6200; discount allowed $610; sales returns $240.

**Required**

Prepare a sales ledger control account for June 2014. (Bring forward the trade receivables' balance from the May sales ledger control account.)

## Answer

| Dr | | Sales ledger control account | | | Cr |
|---|---|---|---|---|---|
| | | $ | | | $ |
| 1 June | Balance b/d | 1480 | 30 June | Cash | 6200 |
| 30 June | Sales | 9400 | 30 June | Discount allowed | 610 |
| | | | 30 June | Sales returns | 240 |
| | | | 30 June | Balance c/d | 3830 |
| | | 10880 | | | 10880 |
| 1 July | Balance b/d | 3830 | | | |

➤ Now try Question 1.

### Self-test questions

1 Explain the term 'trade receivables'.
2 A trade debtor is the same as a trade receivable. True/False?
3 Urooj owes you $100 for goods she purchased last month. Is she a trade debtor or a trade receivable?
4 Is trade discount entered on the debit or credit side of the sales ledger control account?
5 Sales returns is entered on the credit side of a sales ledger control account. True/False?

## 13.2 Preparation of a purchases ledger control account

The purchases ledger control account is a replica of all the entries made in the individual purchases ledger accounts.

Here is a simple illustration:

**Example**

| Dr | Saleem | | Cr |
|---|---|---|---|
| | $ | | $ |
| 13 July Cash | 347 | I July Purchases | 350 |
| Discount received | 3 | | |
| | 350 | | 350 |

| Dr | Toshak | | Cr |
|---|---|---|---|
| | $ | | $ |
| 19 July Cash | 20 | 7 July Purchases | 125 |
| 24 July Purchases returns | 18 | | |
| 31 July Bal c/d | 87 | | |
| | 125 | | 125 |
| | | 1 Aug Bal b/d | 87 |

| Dr | | Purchases ledger control account | | | Cr |
|---|---|---|---|---|---|
| | | $ | | | $ |
| 13 July | Cash | 347 | 1 July | Purchases | 350 |
| 13 July | Discount received | 3 | 7 July | Purchases | 125 |
| 19 July | Cash | 20 | | | |
| 24 July | Purchases returns | 18 | | | |
| 31 July | Balance c/d | 87 | | | |
| | | 475 | | | 475 |
| | | | 1 Aug | Balance b/d | 87 |

Once again this simple but effective illustration relies on the fact that you must understand what an individual account in a purchases ledger looks like.

We cannot look at every individual account in a purchases ledger and total them. We use totals that can be found in the books of prime entry.

**Worked example**

### Example 1

Yip started in business in February 2015. He provides the following totals from his books of prime entry on 28 February 2015:

credit purchases $9430; cash purchases $1790; purchases returns $105; monies paid by Yip to credit suppliers $8100.

A schedule of trade payables extracted from the purchases ledger on 28 February 2015 totals $1225.

**Schedule of trade payables (creditors)** is a list of creditors' balances extracted from each of the purchases ledgers.

**Required**

Prepare a purchases ledger control account for February 2015.

### Answer

| Dr | | Purchases ledger control account | | | Cr |
|---|---|---|---|---|---|
| | | $ | | | $ |
| 28 February | Purchases returns | 105 | 28 February | Purchases | 9430 |
| 28 February | Cash | 8100 | | | |
| 28 February | Balance c/d | 1225 | | | |
| | | 9430 | | | 9430 |
| | | | 1 March | Balance b/d | 1225 |

The trade payables at the end of February according to the control account should amount to $1225. This agrees with Yip's schedule, so we can say that his purchases ledger is arithmetically correct for the month of February.

Cash purchases were not included because they do not appear in the purchases ledger – the ledger is only used to record Yip's transactions with his credit suppliers.

### Example 2

Yip provides you with the following information, which has been extracted from his books of prime entry for March 2015, his second month of trading:

credit purchases $8600; cash purchases $2930; monies paid by Yip to credit suppliers $6800; discount received from trade payables $460; purchases returns $120.

**Required**

Prepare a purchases ledger control account for March 2015. (Bring forward the trade payables' balance from the February purchases ledger control account.)

### Answer

| Dr | | Purchases ledger control account | | | Cr |
|---|---|---|---|---|---|
| | | $ | | | $ |
| 31 March | Cash | 6800 | 1 March | Balance b/d | 1225 |
| 31 March | Discount received | 460 | 31 March | Purchases | 8600 |
| 31 March | Purchases returns | 120 | | | |
| 31 March | Balance c/d | 2445 | | | |
| | | 9825 | | | 9825 |
| | | | 1 April | Balance b/d | 2445 |

➤ Now try Question 2.

**Self-test questions**

6 Explain the term 'trade payables'.
7 Trade creditors are the same as trade receivables. True/False?
8 You owe Barbi $70 for goods you purchased last month. Is Barbi a trade payable or a trade creditor?
9 Is trade discount entered on the debit or the credit side of a purchases ledger control account?
10 Purchases returns is entered on the debit side of a purchases ledger control account. True/False?

## 13.3 Credit balances in a sales ledger

Usually, any closing balance in the account of an individual credit customer will be a debit. However, it is possible that an individual debtor account may end with a credit balance. How can this possibly happen?

**Worked example**

### Example 1

Phara sells $720 goods to Claude on 3 October 2014.

On 23 October 2014 Claude sends Phara a cheque for $720.

On 29 October 2014 Claude returns $30 of goods which have proved to be faulty.

**Required**

Prepare Claude's account as it would appear in Phara's sales ledger at 31 October 2014.

## Answer

The question asks for the account so it must be produced in detail, not as a 'T' account.

| Dr | | Claude | | | Cr |
|---|---|---|---|---|---|
| | | $ | | | $ |
| 3 October | Sales | 720 | 23 October | Bank | 720 |
| | | | 29 October | Sales returns | 30 |

You can see that at 31 October there is a credit balance in Claude's account, although this account is contained in Phara's sales ledger (her debtors' ledger).

In Phara's list of outstanding balances in the sales ledger at 31 October 2014 she will have to show this balance on Claude's account as a creditor. It will also feature in the sales ledger control account for October as a payable (creditor).

**Note**

Do not deduct this amount from Phara's total of trade receivables (debtors) at the end of the month. It must be included in a trial balance at 31 October 2014 and a statement of financial position prepared at 31 October 2014 with trade payables.

### Example 2

Toddy is a regular customer of Phara. He has paid $50 on the 24th of each month to Phara by standing order since 24 May 2014. On 6 September Phara sells $230 of goods to Toddy.

**Required**

Prepare the account of Toddy as it would appear in Phara's sales ledger at 30 September 2014.

## Answer

| Dr | | Toddy | | | Cr |
|---|---|---|---|---|---|
| | | $ | | | $ |
| 6 September | Sales | 230 | 24 May | Bank | 50 |
| | | | 24 June | Bank | 50 |
| | | | 24 July | Bank | 50 |
| | | | 24 August | Bank | 50 |
| 30 September | Balance c/d | 20 | 24 September | Bank | 50 |
| | | 250 | | | 250 |
| | | | 1 October | Balance b/d | 20 |

In Phara's list of outstanding balances in her sales ledger at 30 September 2014 the balance standing on Toddy's account will be shown as a credit $20 – he is a creditor at that date – and this should be shown accordingly on a trial balance extracted on 30 September 2014 or any statement of financial position prepared at 30 September 2014.

A credit balance could also appear in a debtor's account if the customer had made an overpayment or was allowed additional cash or trade discount after the account had been settled.

# 13.4 Debit balances in a purchases ledger

We have seen how credit balances can occur in sales ledger accounts; similar circumstances could result in debit balances appearing on the list of balances extracted from a purchases ledger.

Debit balances would appear in the purchases ledger if a trader:

- settled his or her account with a supplier and then returned faulty goods
- pays a fixed amount each month, which in total exceeds the amount of purchases made

- was allowed additional discount after settling the account
- had overpaid an outstanding balance.

Any credit balances in the sales ledger at a month end will be shown as credit balances in the sales ledger control account for that month.

Any debit balances in the purchases ledger at a month end will be shown as debit balances in the purchases ledger control account for that month.

## Worked example

Harvey provides the following information from his books of prime entry at 31 July 2014:

| | $ |
|---|---|
| Credit sales for July | 6930 |
| Monies received from credit customers during month | 5100 |
| Discounts allowed | 450 |
| Sales returns | 180 |

He provides the following additional information:

| | $ |
|---|---|
| Debit balances appearing in the sales ledger at 1 July 2014 | 2100 |
| Credit balances appearing in the sales ledger at 1 July 2014 | 30 |
| Creditor appearing in schedule of trade receivables' total at 31 July 2014 | 90 |

**Required**

Prepare the sales ledger control account for July 2014.

### Answer

**Sales ledger control account**

| Dr | | | | | Cr |
|---|---|---|---|---|---|
| | | $ | | | $ |
| 1 July | Balance b/d | 2100 | 1 July | Balance b/d | 30 |
| 31 July | Sales | 6930 | 31 July | Cash | 5100 |
| | | | 31 July | Discount allowed | 450 |
| | | | 31 July | Sales returns | 180 |
| 31 July | Balance c/d *(given)* | 90 | 31 July | Balance c/d *(missing figure)* | 3360 |
| | | 9120 | | | 9120 |
| 1 August | Balance b/d | 3360 | 1 August | Balance b/d | 90 |

## Self-test questions

11 Explain two reasons why debit balances might appear in a purchases ledger control account.

12 Is it possible for there to be both debit and credit balances on a sales ledger control account at the end of a month?

13 State a reason why there could be a credit balance on a sales ledger control account at the end of a month.

## 13.5 Contra entries in control accounts

**Contra** entries are sometimes called **set-offs**. A business may well be both a customer of and a supplier to another business.

**Example**

Niki had supplied Hoole with goods valued at $4300 on credit. Niki had also purchased $700 of goods for his business on credit from Hoole.

This would appear in Niki's books of account thus:

**Sales ledger**

**Hoole**

| Dr | $ | Cr | $ |
|---|---|---|---|
| Sales account | 4 300 | | |

**Purchases ledger**

**Hoole**

| Dr | $ | Cr | $ |
|---|---|---|---|
| | | Purchases account | 700 |

It would not seem sensible for Niki to send $700 to Hoole while demanding that Hoole pay $4300.

The usual procedure in cases like this is to transfer the smaller amount from one ledger to the other. The entries are:

**Sales ledger**

**Hoole**

| Dr | $ | Cr | $ |
|---|---|---|---|
| | | Transfer from purchases ledger | 700 |

**Purchases ledger**

**Hoole**

| Dr | $ | Cr | $ |
|---|---|---|---|
| Transfer to sales ledger | 700 | | |

This will close one account (in the purchases ledger) and reduce the balance owed by Hoole (in the sales ledger). The account now looks like this:

**Sales ledger**

**Hoole**

| Dr | $ | Cr | $ |
|---|---|---|---|
| Sales account | 4 300 | Transfer to purchases ledger | 700 |

**Purchases ledger**

**Hoole**

| Dr | $ | Cr | $ |
|---|---|---|---|
| Transfer from sales ledger | 700 | Purchases account | 700 |

All transactions should be recorded in a book of prime entry. Entries involving transfers should be entered in the journal:

**General journal**

| | | Dr | Cr |
|---|---|---|---|
| | | $ | $ |
| Hoole | PL26* | 700 | |
| Hoole | SL15* | | 700 |
| Transfer of credit balance in Hoole's account in purchases ledger to Hoole's account in sales ledger | | | |

* Folio details are for illustrative purposes.

The general journal is used for inter-ledger transfers. This is another use of the general journal as a book of prime entry, identified as use 6 in Section 2.3 of Chapter 2 on books of prime entry.

- All entries in the personal ledgers must also be shown in the control accounts.
- There will be an entry on the credit side of Niki's sales ledger control account.
- There will also be an entry on the debit side of Niki's purchases ledger control account reflecting the entries in the two personal ledgers.

Worked example

### Example 1

Erin has a debit balance of $100 in Ricardo's sales ledger and a credit balance of $30 in Ricardo's purchases ledger.

**Required**

Show the contra entries (set-offs) as they would appear in both Ricardo's sales ledger control account and his purchases ledger control account.

## Answer

**Ricardo: Sales ledger control account**

| Dr | | | Cr |
|---|---|---|---|
| | | | $ |
| | | Transfer from purchases ledger control account | 30 |

**Ricardo: Purchases ledger control account**

| Dr | | | Cr |
|---|---|---|---|
| | $ | | |
| Transfer to sales ledger control account | 30 | | |

### Example 2

Erick has a debit balance of $710 in Djarak's sales ledger and a credit balance of $1400 in Djarak's purchases ledger.

**Required**

Show how the contra (set-offs) would appear in both Djarak's sales ledger control account and his purchases ledger control account.

Tip

It does not matter whether the debit balance or the credit balance is greater when showing the contra in the control accounts:

- The sales ledger control account is always credited.
- The purchases ledger control account is always debited.

In the personal ledgers it is the smaller balance that is transferred.

## Answer

**Djarak: Sales ledger control account**

| Dr | | | Cr |
|---|---|---|---|
| | | | $ |
| | | Transfer to purchases ledger control account | 710 |

**Djarak: Purchases ledger control account**

| Dr | | | Cr |
|---|---|---|---|
| | $ | | |
| Transfer from sales ledger control account | 710 | | |

**Worked example**

Damien provides the following information taken from his books at 30 November 2014:

sales ledger balances 1 November $6340; purchases ledger balances 1 November $3960; credit sales for November $140 100; credit purchases for November $64 300; monies received from trade receivables for November $139 570; monies paid to trade payables in November $63 030; discounts allowed $350; discounts received $180; sales returns $900; purchases returns $600; transfers from sales ledger to purchases ledger $440.

**Required**

Prepare:

a a sales ledger control account showing clearly the closing balance of outstanding receivables at 30 November 2014

b a purchases ledger control account showing clearly the closing balance of outstanding trade payables at 30 November 2014.

## Answer

a

**Sales ledger control account**

| Dr | | | | | Cr |
|---|---|---|---|---|---|
| | | $ | | | $ |
| 1 November | Balance b/d | 6 340 | 30 November | Cash | 139 570 |
| 30 November | Sales | 140 100 | 30 November | Discount allowed | 350 |
| | | | 30 November | Sales returns | 900 |
| | | | 30 November | Transfer to purchases ledger control account | 440 |
| | | | 30 November | Balance c/d | 5 180 |
| | | 146 440 | | | 146 440 |
| 1 December | Balance b/d | 5 180 | | | |

b

**Purchases ledger control account**

| Dr | | | | | Cr |
|---|---|---|---|---|---|
| | | $ | | | $ |
| 30 November | Cash | 63 030 | 1 November | Balance b/d | 3 960 |
| 30 November | Discount received | 180 | 30 November | Purchases | 64 300 |
| 30 November | Purchases returns | 600 | | | |
| 30 November | Transfer from sales ledger control account | 440 | | | |
| 30 November | Balance c/d | 4 010 | | | |
| | | 68 260 | | | 68 260 |
| | | | 1 December | Balance b/d | 4 010 |

# 13.6 Bad debts and provision for doubtful debts

Practise preparing individual accounts from the sales ledger and the purchases ledger – control accounts are similar but use larger amounts of money.

A debt that cannot be paid should be written off (see Chapter 18). This entails crediting the individual debtor's account with the amount written off; thus 'balancing' the account.

Any entry in an individual debtor account must be duplicated in the sales ledger control account since the control account is a summary of all the entries that appear in the ledger.

**Worked example**

Reeta owes Belinda $540. Reeta cannot pay the amount that she owes. Belinda writes off the debt.

**Required**

Prepare:

a Reeta's account in the sales ledger

b the entry in the sales ledger control account.

If a question asks you to prepare both purchases ledger and sales ledger control accounts, do not attempt to prepare them at the same time. Extract relevant information to prepare a purchases ledger control account; when you have completed this task, extract information and prepare a sales ledger control account.

## Answer

**Reeta**

| | $ | | $ |
|---|---|---|---|
| Balance b/d | 540 | Bad debts account | 540 |

**Sales ledger control account**

| | | | $ |
|---|---|---|---|
| | | Bad debts | 540 |

**Provision for doubtful debts** (see Chapter 18) is not included in a sales ledger control account. Unlike a debt that is written off, the provision is not entered in specific individual debtors' accounts. Only transactions that appear in ledger accounts appear in control accounts. Therefore, if the provision does not appear in a personal ledger account, it will not appear in the control account.

## 13.7 Reconciling control accounts with ledgers

If a comparison of a trade receivables balance shown in a control account fails to agree with a total of trade receivables balances extracted from the sales ledger there must be an error or errors in either:

- the control account
- and/or the sales ledger concerned.

Similarly, if the trade payables balance in a control account does not agree with a schedule of trade payables balances extracted from the purchases ledger there must be an error or errors in either:

- the control account
- and/or the purchases ledger concerned.

Remember that some errors will affect both totals and some will affect neither total.

Steps must be taken to identify the transactions that have caused the difference in the two totals. Once identified a correction of the error(s) should reconcile the two totals. The two totals should be equal in an examination question!

Items that will affect the total of trade receivables balances extracted from the personal ledger include incorrect postings from the books of prime entry to the ledger.

Items that will affect the control accounts include errors in the books of prime entry that affect the totals shown in the book.

**Worked example**

Babita maintains a sales ledger control account. At the end of September 2014 she discovered that the schedule of trade receivables extracted from her sales ledger amounted to $6640 while her control account showed outstanding balances of $9138 on that date. An investigation revealed the following errors:

- The sales journal had been under cast by $1000.
- The debit balance on a customer's account $430 had been omitted from the schedule of trade receivables.

- Discount received $18 from Nimola had been entered correctly in the cash book but had been debited to Minola, a credit customer.
- Discount allowed $340 had not been entered in the control account.
- Sales returns $2800 had not been entered in the control account.
- A cheque received from Smythe for $650 had been entered in his account as $560

**Required**

Reconcile a corrected sales ledger control account balance with a corrected schedule of trade receivable balances.

## Answer

**Adjusted sales ledger control account for September**

| | $ | | $ |
|---|---|---|---|
| Balance b/d | 9 138 | Discount received | 18 |
| Sales | 1 000 | Discount allowed | 340 |
| | | Sales returns | 2 800 |
| | | Balance c/d | 6 980 |
| | 10 138 | | 10 138 |
| Balance b/d | 6 980 | | |

**Adjusted schedule of trade receivables balances at end of September**

| | $ |
|---|---|
| Incorrect balances | 6 640 |
| Balance omitted | 430 |
| Correction of transposition | (90) |
| Balance as per control account | 6 980 |

**Worked example**

On 30 June 2014 the purchases ledger control account for the month showed a credit balance of $2480. This amount did not agree with a schedule of trade payables extracted from the purchases ledger on that date. During July 2014 the following errors were revealed:

- An invoice received from a supplier $1230 had been correctly entered in the purchases journal but had been posted to the supplier's account as $2130.
- Goods valued at $190 returned to a supplier had been omitted from the books of account.
- A payment of $1890 to a supplier had been entered twice in the cash book and the supplier's account.
- A contra item $340 had only been entered in the purchases ledger.

**Required**

a Prepare the corrected purchases ledger control account.

b Calculate the original total of trade payables before the correction of errors.

## Answer

**Adjusted purchases ledger control account for June**

| | $ | | $ |
|---|---|---|---|
| Purchases returns | 190 | Balance b/d | 2480 |
| Contra item | 340 | Cash entered twice | 1890 |
| Balance c/d | 3840 | | |
| | 4370 | | 4370 |
| | | Balance b/d | 3840 |

**Adjusted schedule of trade payables balances at end of June original balances**

| | $ |
|---|---|
| Original balances | ? |
| *Less* transposition error | (900) |
| Omission of purchases returns | (190) |
| Double payments | 1890 |
| Balance as per control account | 3840 |

By working backwards we can see the original balance was $3040 (= $3840 – $1890 + $190 + $900).

➤ Now try Question 3.

# 13.8 Advantages and limitations of using control accounts

## 13.8.1 Advantages of using control accounts as part of a control system

**1** Control accounts act as a check on the accuracy of all the postings made to the personal ledgers and this checks the reliability of the ledger accounts.
**2** They enable some errors in ledgers to be located quickly.
**3** If a trial balance does not balance, the control accounts may indicate which personal ledger(s) contain the error(s).
**4** Total amounts owed by trade receivables and total amounts owing to trade payables can be ascertained quickly, enabling a trial balance and/or a statement of financial position to be prepared quickly.
**5** They may be used to give responsibility to staff by making them responsible for sections of the ledger.
**6** They may be used as a check as to the honesty of staff. Control accounts should be prepared by a member of staff who is not involved in the maintenance of the ledger(s) being checked.

## 13.8.2 Limitations of using control accounts as part of a control system

The main limitation of using control accounts as a means of verifying the accuracy of the personal ledgers rests on the fact that not all errors in the ledgers will be revealed by the preparation of a control account.

Within the ledger there could be compensating errors, plus errors of reversal, omission, original entry and commission. See Chapter 10 for the details of how these errors can arise.

## Self-test questions

**14** Why might a business maintain control accounts?
**15** Give an example of a business that would not maintain a sales ledger control account.
**16** How often would a business prepare control accounts?
**17** In which control account would you expect to find purchases returns?
**18** In which control account would you expect to find bad debts?
**19** In which control account would you expect to find a provision for doubtful debts?
**20** Explain one advantage of maintaining control accounts.
**21** Explain how a debit balance might arise in a purchases ledger account.
**22** Explain how a credit balance might arise in a sales ledger account.
**23** 'Set-offs' are always found on the ____________ side of a sales ledger control account.

➤ **Now try Question 4.**

## Chapter summary

- Control accounts help find errors in the two personal ledgers quickly.
- A control account will be prepared for each personal ledger each month.
- Any transaction that is entered in a sales ledger will appear in the sales ledger control account.
- Any transaction that is entered in a purchases ledger will be entered in the purchases ledger control account.
- Credit balances in a sales ledger are trade payables and should be treated as current liabilities.
- Debit balances in a purchases ledger are trade receivables and should be treated as current assets.
- Provision for doubtful debts does not appear in a sales ledger control account.
- Transfers from one ledger to another are entered in both control accounts.
- These 'set-offs' are credited to the sales ledger control account and debited to the purchases ledger control account.

# 14 Statements of financial position

## Content

**1.1 The accounting cycle**

- Apply the accounting equation

**1.2 Accounting for non-current assets**

- Understand the distinction between and treatment of capital and revenue incomes and expenditure

**1.4 Preparation of financial statements**

1.4.2 Sole traders

- Prepare an income statement and statement of financial position for a sole trader from full or incomplete accounting records

**By the end of this chapter you should be able to:**

- prepare a statement of financial position using the appropriate classification for assets and liabilities
- list assets using the 'reverse order of liquidity'
- calculate the business capital for a sole trader
- classify business expenses into capital expenditure and revenue expenditure
- use the accounting equation to solve some accounting problems

## 14.1 Statements of financial position

Some statements of financial position are very complicated and need a great deal of experience and technical know-how to read, understand and interpret. Do not let this put you off. Everything appears daunting when you first meet it. Like all areas of study, accounting has its own jargon.

**Assets** are resources that are owned by an organisation. They are used to help the organisation survive and function.

**Liabilities** represent the debts owed by an organisation.

**Assets** used in a business could include premises, machinery, vehicles, computers, etc. Assets used in a tennis club might include the tennis courts, rollers, etc.

The **liabilities** owed by a business could include a mortgage, and money owed to the suppliers of goods and services. For example, the liabilities of a local garage may include money owed to the Honda motor company for spare parts; to the supplier of electricity; to the supplier of office stationery, etc. The liabilities of a tennis club could include money owed to a local garage for repairs to the equipment; money owed to the suppliers of tennis balls; money owed to the ground staff for wages not yet paid, etc.

A **statement of financial position** simply lists all the assets that are owned by the organisation and lists all the liabilities that are owed at one moment in time. A statement of financial position can be prepared for a business, a club or any other organisation; you can even draw up your own personal statement showing your financial position.

The only difference between your personal statement of financial position and that of, say, Microsoft is the types of assets owned and the magnitude of the figures used.

From now on we will make most of our references to businesses.

➤ Now try Questions 1 and 2.

**Trade debtors** are people (or organisations) that owe money to a business; they are customers that have not yet paid for the goods or services provided. Collectively, a group of trade debtors is known as **trade receivables**.

**Trade creditors** are people (or organisations) that the business owes money to; they have supplied goods for resale that the business has received but as yet has not paid for. Collectively, a group of trade creditors is known as **trade payables**.

**Inventory** is the term used to describe goods purchased by a business that have not yet been sold. The term also describes raw materials, components and partly finished goods (work in progress) held by a manufacturing business.

## Self-test questions

1 Define the term 'asset'.
2 What is meant by the term 'liability'?
3 Give an example of a liability typically found on the statement of financial position for a restaurant.
4 What is meant by the term 'trade creditor'?
5 What is meant by the term 'trade receivables'?

# 14.2 Capital

Statements of financial position are presented in two main ways. Here we use what is known as the **horizontal layout**. Later, we will use a **vertical layout**.

The horizontal layout lists the assets of a business on the left of the page. It lists the liabilities opposite the assets on the right of the page.

## Example

A statement of financial position for Rollo's general store might begin like this:

| | $ | | $ |
|---|---|---|---|
| Premises | 45 000 | Mortgage on premises | 25 000 |
| Van | 16 000 | Bank loan owed on van | 12 000 |
| Shop fittings | 18 000 | Trade payables | 890 |
| Inventory | 1 670 | | |
| Trade receivables | 140 | | |
| Bank balance | 900 | | |

All statements of financial position must 'balance'. This means that the total of assets held must equal the total of liabilities.

It is fairly obvious that Rollo's statement of financial position as shown above does not balance. To make it balance we need to insert a *missing figure* on the liabilities side. If we include $43 820 as a liability, the two sides would add to the same total of $81 710.

What is this missing figure? What does it represent?

Rollo's business is worth $43 820. The business has assets totalling $81 710, while the business debts amount to $37 890. If Rollo decided to stop trading he would sell his assets, settle his debts and take $43 820 out of the business.

Another way of expressing the difference between the value of the business assets and its liabilities is by using the term **net assets**; that is, all assets less all external liabilities.

Here, $43 820 is the amount the business 'owes' the owner. It is the amount Rollo has tied up (invested) in the business, on the date the statement of financial position was drawn up. This is Rollo's **capital**.

**Capital** is the term used to describe how much a business is worth. It represents how much is invested in the business by the owner(s).

**Note**

This assumes that the business assets could be sold for the value shown in the statement of financial position. In reality the assets may be sold for more or less than the values shown in the statement; we will consider this at a later stage in your studies.

**Example**

If we include the capital figure that we previously calculated, Rollo's statement of financial position will 'balance' and look like this:

| | $ | | $ |
|---|---|---|---|
| **ASSETS** | | **LIABILITIES** | |
| Premises | 45 000 | Mortgage on premises | 25 000 |
| Van | 16 000 | Bank loan owed on van | 12 000 |
| Shop fittings | 18 000 | Trade payables | 890 |
| Inventory | 1 670 | | |
| Trade receivables | 140 | **CAPITAL** | 43 820 |
| Bank balance | 900 | | |
| **Total assets** | 81 710 | **Total capital and liabilities** | 81 710 |

A statement of financial position will always balance because the **capital** figure is always the 'missing figure'.

What does Rollo's statement of financial position show us?

- It shows us what Rollo's business is worth.
- It shows us the resources (assets) that are in use in Rollo's business.
- It shows us who has provided the funds to acquire those resources.
- It shows Rollo's capital.

The funds that have financed the acquisition of the assets used in the business have been provided by:

- the mortgage provider
- the bank providing the finance for the loan to purchase the van
- the trade payables
- Rollo himself.

Notice that capital is a liability. Initially this concept is quite difficult to come to terms with. Capital is what the business 'owes' the proprietor.

**Self-test questions**

6 Explain what is meant by the term 'capital'.
7 Explain the reason that a statement of financial position will always 'balance'.
8 Why is capital usually shown in a statement of financial position as a liability?

**Current assets** are cash or assets that will be changed into cash in the near future. Examples of current assets might include inventory; trade receivables; bank balances; cash in the till.

**Liquid** is the term used to describe how easily an asset can be turned into cash.

**Non-current assets** will be used by the business for more than one year.

Spending on non-current assets is known as **capital expenditure**; spending on the everyday running costs of a business is known as **revenue expenditure**.

## 14.3 The layout of a statement of financial position

A statement of financial position is made up of two sections: assets and liabilities.

**Assets** are classified in a statement of financial position according to how long they are likely to be used in the business, and how liquid they are.

Inventory is more **liquid** than premises. Inventory can be turned into cash much more quickly than premises. Think about how long it would take to sell a property.

Machinery is less liquid than receivables. It is generally easier to obtain money from debtors than it is to obtain money from selling surplus machinery.

**Non-current assets** may be tangible (that is, they have a physical presence) or they may be intangible and cannot be seen or touched. Tangible and intangible non-current assets should be shown separately. The name of your favourite cola or sports wear would appear as an intangible non-current asset on the statement of financial position of the owner.

**Non-current liabilities** are debts owed by a business which fall due for repayment after more than one year. Examples of non-current liabilities might include a bank loan that needs to be repaid in four years' time. A 25-year loan would fall under this heading (except in its final year!)

**Current liabilities** are debts owed by a business that are due to be repaid within one year. Examples of current liabilities might include suppliers who are owed money for goods supplied (trade creditors, collectively trade payables); or money owed to a landlord for overdue rent.

- Examples of tangible non-current assets might include business premises; factory machinery; delivery vehicles.
- Examples of intangible non-current assets might include goodwill, patents, copyrights, etc.

**Liabilities** are classified according to the time allowed by the creditor to settle the debt. In reality many **current liabilities** need to be paid much more quickly than one year; for example, a supplier of goods is unlikely to allow a business 365 days before the debt is settled.

**Self-test questions**

9 What is the term used to describe how easily an asset can be turned into cash?
10 In each pair of assets identify the most liquid:
  a premises or vehicles
  b inventory or plant and machinery
  c trade receivables or land and buildings.
11 A general store receives $200 from the sale of a display cabinet that is no longer used. Is this an example of capital income or revenue income or capital expenditure or revenue expenditure?
12 A food store purchases a cash register for use in the store. Is this an example of capital income or revenue income or capital expenditure or revenue expenditure?
13 Which are most liquid, non-current assets or current assets?
14 Explain the main difference between a non-current liability and a current liability.

## 14.4 The accounting equation

The accounting equation recognises that the assets owned by a business are always equal to the claims against the business.

One side of the accounting equation shows, in monetary terms, the assets that are owned by an organisation. The other side of the equation shows how these resources have been financed with funds provided by the owner and others.

A statement of financial position is the formal way of showing the accounting equation:

**Formula**

Non-current assets + Current assets = Non-current liabilities + Current liabilities + Capital

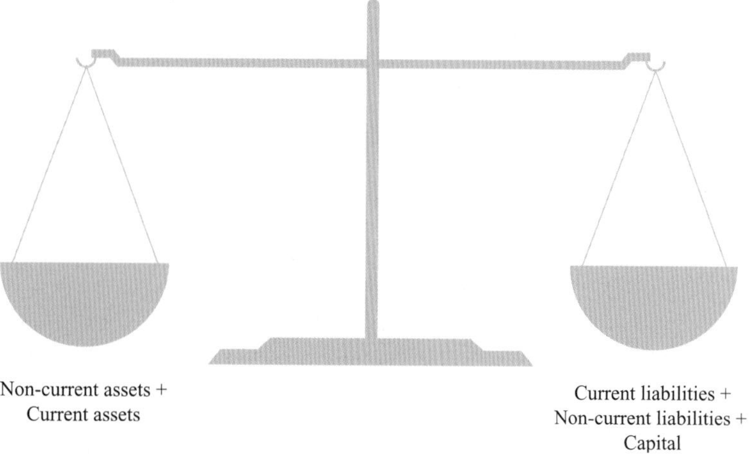


**Figure 14.1** The accounting equation

If we know four of the parts that make up the accounting equation then we should be able to find out a 'missing' part by completing the equation.

➤ Now try Questions 3 and 4.

If we use the asset classifications outlined above to Rollo's statement of financial position, it will look like this:

**Example**

| | $ | $ | Comment |
|---|---|---|---|
| **ASSETS** | | | |
| **Non-current assets** | | | |
| Premises | | 45 000 | *Normally used for many years* |
| Shop fittings | | 18 000 | *Normally used for, say, ten years* |
| Van | | 16 000 | *Normally in use for, say, four or five years* |
| | | 79 000 | |
| **Current assets** | | | |
| Inventory | 1 670 | | *Should become cash in the next few months* |
| Trade receivables | 140 | | *Should settle their debts within 30 days* |
| Bank balance | 900 | 2 710 | *Almost as good as cash* |
| **Total assets** | | 81 710 | |

The order in which assets appear under their headings is known as the **reverse order of liquidity**. This means that the most liquid of the assets appears last while the least liquid appears first.

If we classify Rollo's liabilities, the right side of his statement of financial position would look like this:

| Comment | | $ | $ |
|---|---|---|---|
| | **CAPITAL AND LIABILITIES** | | |
| *Capital is normally the first item to appear.* | **Capital** | | 43 820 |
| | **Non-current liabilities** | | |
| *Mortgage is generally owed for a long time period, as is money borrowed to purchase a vehicle. However, both of these would be classified as current liabilities in the final year of the debt.* | Mortgage on premises | 25 000 | |
| | Bank loan to purchase van | 12 000 | 37 000 |
| | **Current liabilities** | | |
| *Suppliers will normally expect payment within 30 days of the debt being incurred.* | Trade payables | | 890 |
| | **Total capital and liabilities** | | 81 710 |

Assets are recorded on statements of financial position at their **original cost**.

This does initially cause a problem for some students of accounting. The reason for valuing assets at cost is quite simple. Cost is the only *objective* valuation that can be applied to the assets that are owned.

Business transactions are normally recorded over a 12-month period. This is known as the business's **financial year**. The process is then repeated for each subsequent year.

We can now put the two sides of Rollo's completed statement of financial position together:

**Example**

**Rollo's general store**
**Statement of financial position at 31 March 2015**

| | $ | $ | | $ | $ |
|---|---|---|---|---|---|
| **ASSETS** | | | **CAPITAL AND LIABILITIES** | | |
| **Non-current assets** | | | **Capital** | | 43 820 |
| Premises at cost | | 45 000 | **Non-current liabilities** | | |
| Shop fittings at cost | | 18 000 | Mortgage | 25 000 | |
| Van at cost | | 16 000 | Loan for van | 12 000 | 37 000 |
| | | 79 000 | | | |
| **Current assets** | | | **Current liabilities** | | |
| Inventory | 1 670 | | Trade payables | | 890 |
| Trade receivables | 140 | | | | |
| Bank balance | 900 | 2 710 | | | |
| **Total assets** | | 81 710 | **Total capital and liabilities** | | 81 710 |

This layout is based on the accounting equation.

In recent years there has been a move to present statements of financial position using a vertical format. The total assets of the business are shown in the top section of the vertical statement of financial position and the capital and total liabilities of the business are shown under the total assets.

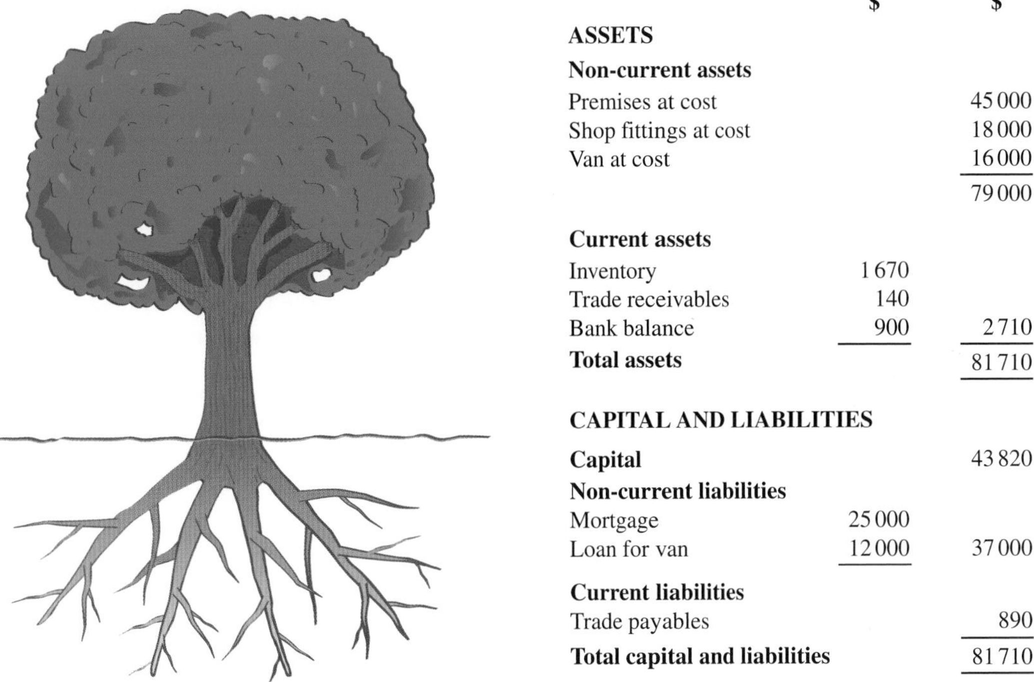

| | $ | $ |
|---|---|---|
| **ASSETS** | | |
| **Non-current assets** | | |
| Premises at cost | | 45 000 |
| Shop fittings at cost | | 18 000 |
| Van at cost | | 16 000 |
| | | 79 000 |
| **Current assets** | | |
| Inventory | 1 670 | |
| Trade receivables | 140 | |
| Bank balance | 900 | 2 710 |
| **Total assets** | | 81 710 |
| **CAPITAL AND LIABILITIES** | | |
| **Capital** | | 43 820 |
| **Non-current liabilities** | | |
| Mortgage | 25 000 | |
| Loan for van | 12 000 | 37 000 |
| **Current liabilities** | | |
| Trade payables | | 890 |
| **Total capital and liabilities** | | 81 710 |

**Figure 14.2** Statement of financial position in the vertical format

## Self-test questions

**15** What is meant by the reverse order of liquidity?
**16** In a statement of financial position, inventory appears before vehicles. True/False?
**17** In a statement of financial position, premises appears before machinery. True/False?
**18** Financial years always end on 31 December. True/False?
**19** A financial year can run from 15 January 2014 until 27 October 2014. True/False?
**20** A financial year can run from 1 February 2014 until 31 January 2015. True/False?
**21** Why does the accounting equation always balance?
**22** What is the main difference between a non-current asset and a current asset?
**23** In which part of a vertically presented statement of financial position would you expect to find trade receivables?
**24** Can we prepare a statement of financial position on 29 April?
**25** Explain why non-current assets are valued at cost in a statement of financial position.
**26** Give an example of a liability typically found in a retail shop selling DVDs.
**27** Why must a statement of financial position always balance?
**28** What is the difference between a non-current liability and a current liability?
**29** Why is capital shown as a liability in a statement of financial position?
**30** Could a business have a financial year which runs from 19 June until 30 May the following year?
**31** Explain how one type of business can include a delivery van as a current asset on its statement of financial position, and yet another type of business includes a similar delivery van as a non-current asset.
**32** Explain the circumstances that could result in a long-term bank loan being shown in a statement of financial position as a current liability.

➤ Now try Questions 5 and 6.

## Chapter summary

- A statement of financial position is prepared on one day and it shows the assets being used by a business on that day.
- Liabilities represent the indebtedness of the business to people or organisations outside the business on that day.
- Capital represents the indebtedness of the business to the owner of the business.
- A statement of financial position must always balance because of the accounting equation.
- The assets of a business must always equal the liabilities.
- Liabilities include the owner's capital.
- The term net assets is another way of saying 'all assets less all external liabilities'.
- Capital is what the business is worth.
- Net assets always equal the owner's capital.
- Capital represents the amount that the business 'owes' the owner.
- The 'top' part of a vertically presented statement of financial position must equal the 'lower' part.

# 15 Profits

## Content

### 1.4 Preparation of financial statements

1.4.2 Sole traders

- Prepare an income statement and statement of financial position for a sole trader from full or incomplete accounting records

**By the end of this chapter you should be able to:**

- explain the terms 'profit', 'loss' and 'drawings'
- calculate the net assets held by a business
- determine 'retained profits' by comparing net assets from two statements of financial position
- adjust retained profits for capital introduced and drawings to determine trading profit.

We cannot tell whether a business is profitable by analysing a statement of financial position; after all, it can only tell us what the business has in the way of assets and liabilities at one particular time.

Many teachers and textbooks have said that a statement of financial position is rather like a photograph – it only captures a moment. A statement of financial position only shows the state of affairs of the business at the time when the statement was prepared.

However, over a financial year it is likely that the financial position of a business will change. Assets may increase or decrease. Liabilities may increase or decrease. Many of the changes will take place due to business activity.

If a business is profitable, one would expect that the assets owned by the business would increase, unless the owner of the business takes more cash and/or goods from the business than the **profits** warrant. If a business is unprofitable one would expect that the business assets would decrease over time.

**Profit** is the excess of income over expenditure. A **loss** occurs when expenditure exceeds income.

Profits increase the **net assets** of a business unless profits are taken from the business by the owner.

**Net assets** of a business are all assets less all external liabilities:

Non-current assets + Current assets – (Non-current liabilities + Current liabilities)

Or:

Net assets = Capital

(Check this by referring to the accounting equation.)

The converse is also true. That is, if there is an increase in the net assets then this must be due to the business being profitable. The only exception to this rule would be if extra assets were introduced into the business from outside or if liabilities were paid off by using money obtained from outside the business. An example of this would be if the owner of the business injected more money into the business or if more assets were introduced into the business from another source.

How can we calculate the profits made by a business?

## 15.1 Calculating profits

**Worked example**

Barker Animal Foods had the following assets and liabilities at 1 January 2014:

non-current assets $270 000; current assets $21 000; trade payables $5000.

One year later on 1 January 2015 the business had the following assets and liabilities:

non-current assets $290 000; current assets $27 000; trade payables $8000.

During the year there were no withdrawals or injections of money or assets by the owner.

**Required**

Calculate the profit earned by Barker Animal Foods for the year ended 31 December 2014.

### Answer

| | | $ |
|---|---|---|
| **Barker Animal Foods net assets at 1 January 2014** | **Non-current assets** | 270 000 |
| | **Current assets** | 21 000 |
| | | 291 000 |
| | *Less* **Current liabilities** | 5 000 |
| | **Capital** (net assets) | 286 000 |
| **Barker Animal Foods net assets at 1 January 2015** | **Non-current assets** | 290 000 |
| | **Current assets** | 27 000 |
| | | 317 000 |
| | *Less* **Current liabilities** | 8 000 |
| | **Capital** (net assets) | 309 000 |

The net assets (capital) of the business increased by $23 000 ($309 000 – $286 000) during the year. This is the profit that Barker Animal Foods made during the year. It has to be profit since we were told that no money or assets had been introduced or withdrawn during the year.

**Retained profits** are profits that are kept in a business for expansion purposes. They increase the net assets of a business. They are sometimes said to be 'ploughed back'.

**Self-test questions**

1 Define the term 'profit'.
2 Define the term 'loss'.
3 Could the owner of a business prepare a statement of financial position on 9 December or 23 June or today?
4 Explain what * represents in the following equation:
Assets * Liabilities = Capital
5 Profit = Income – expenditure. True/False?
6 Capital = Non-current assets + Current assets – All external liabilities. True/False?
7 Retained profits are the profits held by the business's bankers as security on a loan. True/False?
8 Explain what is meant by the term 'ploughed back'.

## 15.2 Capital introduced and withdrawn from a business

It is unrealistic to think that money or assets would not be injected into a business if this was necessary to safeguard the business or in order to expand the business.

It is also unrealistic to imagine that the owner of a business would not withdraw some cash or resources from the business in order to pay for various items of private household expenditure during the year. This cash and/or resources taken from the business is termed **drawings**.

**Drawings** is the term used to describe the withdrawal of resources (cash or goods) from a business by the owner for private use outside the business.

It is also unrealistic to imagine that Pusmeena, who owns a garage, would send her car to another garage for servicing or for repairs. The value of servicing or repairing Pusmeena's car in her own garage is drawings.

In order to calculate business profits, it is important that we only consider transactions that involve the business:

- Money received from an inheritance and paid into the business bank account should not be included in any calculations to determine profits.
- Cash taken from the business and used to buy food for the family should not be used in our calculation of profits.
- A cheque for $85 drawn on the business bank account to pay for a repair to the family television set is not part of the calculation.

### Worked example

Anjni has been in business for a number of years. At 1 March 2014 her business assets and liabilities were as follows:

non-current assets at cost $40 000; current assets $10 000; current liabilities $5000.

One year later, on 28 February 2015, her business assets and liabilities were:

non-current assets $45 000; current assets $9000; and current liabilities $6000.

During the year she withdrew cash from the business $14 500 for private use.

**Required**

Calculate Anjni's business profits for the year ended 28 February 2015.

### Answer

| | $ |
|---|---|
| Anjni's net assets at 1 March 2014 ($40 000 + $10 000 – $5 000) | 45 000 |
| Anjni's net assets at 28 February 2015 | 48 000 |
| Increase in net assets over the year *(profits ploughed back into the business)* | 3 000 |

| | $ |
|---|---|
| Increase in net assets over the year | 3 000 |
| Drawings *(profits withdrawn during the year)* | 14 500 |
| Business profit earned during the year | 17 500 |

**Worked example**

Chang had business net assets on 1 August 2013 of $16 000. On 31 July 2014 his business net assets stood at $45 000. During the year his Uncle Hua died and left Chang a legacy of $20 000. The legacy was paid into Chang's business bank account.

**Required**

Calculate the profit that Chang's business made for the year ended 31 July 2014.

## Answer

| | $ |
|---|---|
| Chang's net assets at 1 August 2013 | 16 000 |
| Chang's net assets at 31 July 2014 | 45 000 |
| Increase in net assets over the year | 29 000 |

Some of the increase in net assets is due to Uncle Hua's legacy. This has to be disregarded if we wish to determine the profits generated by the business, so:

| | $ |
|---|---|
| Increase in net assets over the year | 29 000 |
| *Less* Capital introduced | 20 000 |
| Business profit earned during the year | 9 000 |

**Worked example**

Rahila has been in business for a number of years. On 1 February 2014 her capital stood at $30 500. At 31 January 2015 her business statement of financial position showed the following:

non-current assets $45 000; current assets $18 000; non-current liabilities $20 000; current liabilities $7000.

During the year she paid into the business bank account a cash gift of $10 000 from her grandmother. Her drawings for the year amounted to $21 000.

**Required**

Calculate the profit or loss made by the business for the year ended 31 January 2015.

## Answer

| | $ |
|---|---|
| Rahila's net assets (capital) at 1 February 2014 | 30 500 |
| Rahila's net assets (capital) at 31 January 2015 | 36 000 |
| Increase in net assets over the year | 5 500 |
| *Add* Drawings | 21 000 |
| | 26 500 |
| *Less* Capital introduced | 10 000 |
| Business profit for the year ended 31 January 2015 | 16 500 |

## Worked example

Helen's statement of financial position at 1 May 2014 showed:

non-current assets $16000; current assets $4000; current liabilities $3500; capital $16500.

On 30 April 2015 her statement of financial position showed:

non-current assets $30000; current assets $5000; current liabilities $6000 and a non-current liability $20000.

During the year Helen paid into the business bank account a legacy of $18000. Her drawings for the year amounted to $14000.

**Required**

Calculate the profit or loss made by Helen's business for the year ended 30 April 2015.

## Answer

| | $ | |
|---|---|---|
| Helen's net assets at 1 May 2014 | 16500 | |
| Helen's net assets at 30 April 2015 | 9000 | |
| Decrease in net assets over the year | (7500) | *Negative numbers are* |
| *Add* Drawings for the year | 14000 | *often shown in brackets.* |
| | 6500 | |
| *Less* Capital introduced | 18000 | |
| Loss made by Helen's business during the year | (11500) | |

## Self-test questions

9 Explain what is meant by the term 'net assets'.
10 What is the connection (if any) between capital and net assets?
11 Non-current assets $7000; current assets $3000; current liabilities $2000. Calculate net assets.
12 Non-current assets $100000; current assets $20000; non-current liabilities $40000; current liabilities $9000. Calculate capital.
13 What is meant by the term 'drawings'?
14 The owner of a clothing business takes some clothes for his son from goods in the store. What is the term used to describe this transaction?
15 Give an example of drawings that the proprietor of an electrical goods store could make.
16 Is it possible to make drawings that exceed the profit earned in a year?
17 Explain what is meant by 'capital introduced'.

➤ Now try Question 1.

## Chapter summary

- Profit can be calculated quickly and accurately by deducting total net assets held by a business at the end of a financial year from the total of net assets held at the start of the year.
- Adjustments to the difference calculated have to be made by 'adding back' drawings and eliminating any capital introduced during the year.

# 16 The trading account

**Content**

**1.2 Accounting for non-current assets**

- Understand the distinction between and treatment of capital and revenue incomes and expenditure

**1.4 Preparation of financial statements**

1.4.2 Sole traders

- Prepare an income statement and statement of financial position for a sole trader from full or incomplete accounting records

**By the end of this chapter you should be able to:**

- prepare the trading account of an income statement
- distinguish between capital and revenue expenditures
- distinguish between capital and revenue incomes
- calculate cost of sales and determine gross profit
- adjust a trading account for sales returns and purchases returns
- make the necessary entry in a trading account to record carriage inwards.

**Financial statements** (or **final accounts**) is the term often used to describe the income statement and statement of financial position produced by the owner of a business at the financial year end. (Technically, the statement of financial position is not an account, as you will discover later.)

An **income statement** is a statement that calculates the profit that a business has made for a period of time (usually a financial year).

**Capital expenditure** is spending on non-current assets or the improvement of non-current assets.

**Revenue expenditure** is spending on everyday expenses.

**Capital receipts** are derived from transactions that are not the usual activities of the business.

**Revenue receipts** are incomes derived from the 'usual' activities of the business.

A full set of **financial statements** is usually produced at the end of the financial year. This enables the owner of the business to see:

- if the business has been running profitably during the year
- the assets and liabilities that the business owns at the end of the year.

## 16.1 Income statements

An **income statement** details the incomes and expenditures incurred by the business during a set period of time (usually a financial year).

Although, as we have seen, profits and losses can be calculated accurately and fairly quickly by using the 'net asset' method, managers or owners of a business generally need to know more than just the profit figure in isolation.

An income statement is divided into two sections:

- Section 1 shows the results of trading and calculates the gross profit.
- Section 2 shows the profit (or loss) after all business expenses have been taken from the gross profit. Previously referred to as net profit, this is now referred to as **profit (before tax) for the year**.

Profits are generally calculated over a financial year but they could be calculated for any time period. Many business owners calculate their profits halfway through the year as well as at their financial year end in order to plot the progress of their business. Financial statements will be produced at any time they might be required by the owner or managers of a business.

Although the net asset method of calculating the profit of a business does calculate the profit *easily* and *accurately*, it does have a major drawback. It does not give us any details of how the profit (or loss) was arrived at.

The details of how a profit has been earned or why a loss has been incurred are important to both the owner and any external providers of finance.

- The owner will probably wish to make greater profits in the future.
- Lenders will wish to see that their investment is safe and that any interest due or repayments due will be able to be met by the business.

The term **revenue** is used in an income statement to describe the total of all revenue receipts.

➤ Now try Question 1.

The details of how profits are arrived at are shown in an income statement.

**Self-test questions**

1 The owner of a business will generally produce two statements at the end of a financial year. Name the two statements.
2 Which statement details the incomes and expenditures of the business?
3 Which statement lists the assets and liabilities of the business?
4 An income statement calculates profits more accurately than using the 'net asset' method. True/False?
5 Explain why the owner of a business might prefer to determine the profits made by his business by using an income statement rather than relying on a 'net asset' calculation.
6 Why is it important to classify expenses into capital expenditure and revenue expenditure?
7 Give an example of capital expenditure that could be incurred by a food shop.
8 Explain what is meant by the term 'revenue expenditure'.

## 16.2 The trading account of an income statement

**Gross profit** is revenue generated by selling goods, less the cost of the same goods.

The value of goods bought for resale is called **purchases**.

The income from goods that are sold is called **sales**.

➤ Now try Question 2.

The trading account of an income statement calculates the gross profit that a business has made by buying and selling its goods during a particular period of time.

The trading account shows how much it cost to buy the goods that are sold and how much they were sold for. The goods in question are the goods that the business buys and sells in its everyday activities.

A simple trading account compares the **purchases** and **sales** for a financial period. The difference between the two is the gross profit earned for the period.

The trading account is generally prepared to show the gross profit earned during a financial year. However, it could be prepared for any time period, for example a week, a month, two months or 123 days.

**Note**

- Income statements are prepared for a *period of time*.
- The statements of financial position we prepared earlier were prepared *at one moment in time*.

**Worked example**

Bernadette owns a business selling magazines and books. She is able to give you the following information relating to her business for the year ended 31 December 2014:

| | $ |
|---|---|
| Purchases of magazines and books | 32 500 |
| Purchase of cash register | 840 |
| Sales of magazines and books | 65 800 |
| Sales of shop fittings | 1 200 |

**Required**

Prepare a trading account for the year ended 31 December 2014.

## Answer

**Bernadette**
**Trading account for the year ended 31 December 2014**

| | $ |
|---|---|
| Revenue | 65 800 |
| Purchases | 32 500 |
| Gross profit | 33 300 |

**Note**

- The figures included in extract from the income statement are figures for a year, the heading tells us this.
- The purchase of the cash register has not been included – it is capital expenditure.
- The sales of shop fittings has not been included – it is a capital receipt.
- Purchases are revenue expenditure. They are part of the everyday costs associated with running Bernadette's business.
- Sales are revenue receipts. These receipts are from Bernadette's normal trading activities.
- The gross profit is found by deducting the value of purchases from the revenue generated by the sales.

The trading account of the income statement is prepared by using the total value of purchases (an example of **revenue expenditure**) and sales (an example of a **revenue receipt**).

### Self-test questions

9 Capital receipts are included in the trading account of the income statement. True/False?
10 Capital expenditure is included in a trading account. True/False?
11 A restaurant would include the purchase of a new cooker in the trading account of an income statement. True/False?
12 A vehicle repair business would include electricity charges in the trading account of an income statement. True/False?
13 How is the cost of goods available for sale calculated?
14 Gross profit is calculated by taking the cost of purchases from the revenue generated by making sales. True/False?
15 In what way is 'gross profit' different to 'profit for the year'?
16 The trading account of an income statement is prepared to calculate __________.
17 The selling price of goods is deducted from the __________ gained from the selling of those same goods to calculate gross profit.

## 16.3 The treatment of inventories

The preparation of the trading account is so simple; there has to be a complication! There always is!

As you will appreciate, very few businesses sell all the goods that they purchase each day. At the end of every day there will be goods left on the shelves, in display cabinets, and in the warehouse.

Generally, there will be goods left unsold at the end of any financial year. The last millisecond of the last day of the financial year is (almost) the same time as the first millisecond of the new financial year.

So, the inventory value at the end of one financial year is the inventory value at the start of the following financial year.

- Inventory at 30 November 2014 is inventory at 1 December 2014.
- The inventory held by a business at 31 May 2015 is the inventory held on 1 June 2015.

Unsold goods need to be valued.

The inventory held at the start of a financial year is sometimes referred to as **opening inventory**. The inventory held one year later at the end of the financial year is sometimes referred to as **closing inventory**.

**Cost of sales** is deducted from net sales to calculate the gross profit earned by a business:

Cost of sales = Opening inventory + Purchases – Closing inventory

What effect will opening and closing inventory values have on the trading account of an income statement?

We need to calculate the value of the goods that have actually been sold during the year, since not all purchases will be sold during the year of purchase.

**Worked example**

Baldeep has a market stall selling spices. She provides the following information:

- inventory of spices at 1 September 2013: $345
- purchases of spices for the year ended 31 August 2014: $18450
- sales of spices for the year ended 31 August 2014: $42750
- inventory of spices at 31 August 2014: $400.

**Required**

Prepare the trading account for the year ended 31 August 2014.

## Workings

We first have to find the value of the spices that Baldeep sold during the year.

| | $ | | |
|---|---|---|---|
| *Baldeep started the year with* | 345 | *worth of spices* | |
| *She bought a further* | 18450 | *worth of spices* | |
| *So she could have sold* | 18795 | *worth* | *... but she didn't ... she had* |
| *... some left. She had* | 400 | *worth left* | |
| *So she must have sold* | 18395 | *worth of spices.* | |

How much did she sell these spices for? $42750

Her gross profit for the year was $24355.

Talk yourself through this example a few times. It is important that you understand the process that you have gone through.

The actual trading account should be presented like this:

## Answer

**Baldeep**

**Trading account for the year ended 31 August 2014**

| | $ | $ |
|---|---|---|
| Revenue | | 42750 |
| *Less* Cost of sales | | |
| Inventory 1 September 2013 | 345 | |
| Purchases | 18450 | |
| | 18795 | |
| *Less* Inventory 31 August 2014 | 400 | 18395 |
| Gross profit | | 24355 |

**Note**

- Opening inventories are added to purchases.
- Closing inventories are deducted from goods available for sale to calculate cost of sales.

The description for $18395 is 'cost of sales'.

$18395 is the cost price of the spices Baldeep sold during the year for $ 42750.

Notice the use of two columns. After a few times using this technique you will see that it makes the calculation of gross profit much clearer.

**Self-test questions**

**18** Opening inventory must always be less than closing inventory. True/False?
**19** Inventory held at close of business on 31 July cost $13000. It will be sold for $20000. What is the value of inventory at start of business 1 August?
**20** In the first year of trading purchases cost $100000, closing inventory valued at cost amounted to $20000. What is the cost of sales?
**21** Identify two types of goods that a furniture manufacturer would include as closing inventory.
**22** Is it possible for some items held as opening inventory to be held as closing inventory?
**23** Closing inventory at 31 July 2014 is the same as opening inventory at 1 August 2014. True or false?
**24** What effect does closing inventory have on cost of sales?
**25** Purchases = Cost of sales – Opening inventory + Closing inventory. True/False?

## 16.4 The valuation of inventories

**Realisable value** is selling price.

**Net realisable value** is selling price less any expenses incurred by the business to get the goods into a saleable condition.

At the end of a financial year a trader will physically count the items purchased for resale that remain unsold in the business. The items will be listed and each category will be given a value.

At the moment we shall value our inventories at the lower of cost price and **net realisable value**. This is the overriding principle that must be used. At a later stage we consider the implications of this basic rule.

The use of net realisable value can cause a problem for many students.

**Tip** 

Make sure that you understand how to calculate net realisable value.

**Worked example**

The following information is available regarding the goods remaining unsold in Obika's business at 28 February 2014:

| Product | Cost per unit<br>$ | Selling price per unit<br>$ |
|---|---|---|
| Arkers | 12 | 31 |
| Bodins | 23 | 22 |
| Clorfs | 6 | 14 |
| Dynps | 42 | 40 |
| Edlivs | 17 | 15 |

**Required**

a State the value of each unit held as inventory.

b Calculate the total value of inventory held at 28 February 2014.

## Answer

➤ Now try Question 3.

a Arkers $12; Bodins $22; Clorfs $6; Dynps $40; Edlivs $15

b $95

**Remember**

- If closing inventory is *overvalued* then gross profit will be *overstated*.
- If gross profit is *overstated* then the profit for the year is *overstated*.
- If closing inventory is *understated* then gross profit will be *understated*.
- If gross profit is *understated* then the profit for the year is *understated*.

**Self-test questions**

**26** Inventories are goods that have been bought for resale that have not yet been sold at the financial year end. True/False?

**27** Goods held at the end of a financial year cost $450; they can currently be purchased for $500; they have a resale value of $700. What is the value of closing inventory?

**28** A damaged article held at the end of a financial year cost $40; after repairs costing $14 it can be sold for $55. What is the value of the article for inventory purposes?

**29** Gross profit is $50 000. Closing inventory was valued at $3000. It has been discovered that closing inventory should have been valued at $2000. What is the correct gross profit?

## 16.5 The treatment of returned goods

**Sales returns** are goods that have been returned by the customer. They are also known as **returns in** or **returns inwards**.

**Purchases returns** are goods that the business sends back to the supplier. They are also known as **returns out** or **returns outwards**.

Even in businesses that are extremely well run, some goods are returned by customers.

The way that these **sales returns** are treated in the income statement seems fairly obvious: the total value of sales returns is deducted from the total value of sales for the year.

No matter how good and how careful suppliers are, there will inevitably be occasions when a business has to return goods. Again, our treatment of any purchases returns seems to be fairly obvious: the total value of **purchases returns** is deducted from the total value of purchases for the year.

**Worked example**

The following information for the year ended 31 August 2014 relates to the business of Beebee:

inventory at 1 September 2013 $1200; inventory at 31 August 2014 $1500; purchases $48 000; sales $72 380; sales returns $180; purchases returns $360.

**Required**

Prepare the trading account for the year ended 31 August 2014.

### Answer

**Beebee**

**Trading account for the year ended 31 August 2014**

| | $ | $ | $ |
|---|---|---|---|
| Revenue | | | 72 380 |
| *Less* Sales returns | | | 180 |
| | | | 72 200 |
| *Less* Cost of sales | | | |
| Inventory 1 September 2013 | | 1 200 | |
| Purchases | 48 000 | | |
| *Less* Purchases returns | 360 | 47 640 | |
| | | 48 840 | |
| *Less* Inventory 31 August 2014 | | 1 500 | 47 340 |
| Gross profit | | | 24 860 |

Once again, notice the way that the calculation to find the 'net' purchases figure has been set back from the second column. Accountants often use 'extra' columns so that the main column does not get too confused.

**Self-test questions**

**30** Explain the effect that the inclusion of sales returns has on the gross profit of a business.

**31** The inclusion of purchases returns in a trading account has the effect of increasing/decreasing gross profit. (Delete the incorrect word.)

**32** Returns that occur in the last week of a financial year can be ignored. They can be included in the following year's financial statements. True/False?

## 16.6 The treatment of expenses incurred in the carriage of goods

**Carriage inwards** is an expense incurred when a supplier charges for delivery on the goods purchased.

**Carriage outwards** is also an expense which a business incurs when it pays for delivery of goods to a customer. It is sometimes referred to as **carriage on sales**.

**Carriage inwards** makes the goods that are purchased more expensive. It is added to the goods that appear as purchases in the trading account of the income statement.

**Carriage outwards** is an expense that is dealt with in Chapter 17.

**Worked example**

Benji owns a store. The following figures relate to the year ended 30 September 2014:

inventory at 1 October 2013 $5300; inventory at 30 September 2014 $4900; purchases $124 600; sales $314 000; returns inward $930; purchases returns $2100; carriage inwards $1750.

**Required**

Prepare the trading account for the year ended 30 September 2014.

## Answer

**Benji**

**Trading account for the year ended 30 September 2014**

| | $ | $ | $ |
|---|---|---|---|
| Revenue | | | 314 000 |
| *Less* Sales returns | | | 930 |
| | | | 313 070 |
| *Less* Cost of sales | | | |
| Inventory 1 October 2013 | | 5 300 | |
| Purchases | 124 600 | | |
| *Less* Purchases returns | 2 100 | | |
| | 122 500 | | |
| Carriage inwards | 1 750 | 124 250 | |
| | | 129 550 | |
| *Less* Inventory 30 September 2014 | | 4 900 | 124 650 |
| Gross profit | | | 188 420 |

This example shows the most complicated form that a trading account can take. To make a more difficult example you could only be asked to use larger numbers!

Notice once more the use of three columns. This has enabled us to get one figure for the total cost of net purchases ($124 250) without lots of calculations in the main columns.

When you attempt the questions below you may find it helpful to refer to Benji's trading account to get a good layout. Do not worry about this. You will soon start to remember where to enter the various items.

### Self-test questions

**33** State how the value of goods available for sale is calculated.
**34** State what is meant by cost of sales.
**35** Another name for returns inwards is purchases returns. True/False?
**36** Purchases returns are also known as returns outwards. True/False?
**37** Carriage inwards is deducted from sales revenue. True/False?
**38** Carriage outwards is added to purchases. True/False?
**39** Sales $37 980; sales returns $356; purchases returns $299. What is the value of net sales?
**40** Purchases $217 845; sales returns $377; purchases returns $652. What is the value of net purchases?
**41** Carriage inwards will increase/decrease the value of purchases/sales. (Circle the correct answer.)

➤ Now try Questions 4 and 5.

## Chapter summary

- The trading account is used to calculate gross profit by deducting sales at cost price from sales revenue.
- Closing inventories are deducted from goods available for sale to give cost of sales.
- Opening inventories are added to purchases to give goods available for sale.
- Inventories are valued at cost or net realisable value, whichever is the lower.
- Goods that customers return are known as returns inwards or returns in or sales returns.
- Sales returns are deducted from sales to find the net sales.
- Goods returned to a supplier are known as returns outwards or returns out or purchases returns.
- Purchases returns are deducted from purchases to find the net purchases.
- Both carriage inwards and carriage outwards are expenses incurred by a business.
- Carriage inwards is a charge made by a supplier for the delivery of goods.
- Carriage inwards appears in the trading account as an addition to purchases, making them more expensive.
- Carriage outwards is borne by a business supplying goods to a customer.
- Carriage outwards is also an expense but it is not used in the trading account.
- Carriage outwards appears in the profit and loss account of an income statement as an expense.

# 17 The profit and loss account

## Content

**1.4 Preparation of financial statements**

1.4.2 sole traders

- Prepare an income statement and statement of financial position for a sole trade from full or incomplete accounting records

**By the end of this chapter you should be able to:**

- prepare the profit and loss account of an income statement
- explain how accounting statements are used for stewardship and management purposes
- combine the trading account and profit and loss account of an income statement
- include the expense of carriage outwards in a profit and loss account.

If your weekly income does not cover your weekly expenditure, what do you do? You draw some money from your savings (if you have any) or you may borrow sufficient money to tide you over until your income is enough to cover your spending.

The same principle applies to someone in business. If the business is unprofitable, the owner may have to inject some of his or her savings into the business or borrow money to help the business to survive.

We have just seen how to calculate the **gross profit**. Put simply, the gross profit is the difference between the cost of goods sold by a business and the amount that the goods have been sold for.

Clearly there are expenses that have to be paid out of this gross profit in order that the firm can continue in business. **Profit for the year** is calculated by deducting all expenses incurred by the business from the gross profit that it has earned through buying and selling its goods during a financial year.

### Example

During April Didi buys 1000 DVDs for $4000 and she sells them all for $6990. She has made a gross profit of $2990 on the sales. However, she will have incurred some expenses in selling the DVDs, and they could have included:

- rent paid for the use of a market stall
- transport costs to get the DVDs to the stall
- wages of any sales assistants
- money paid to purchase wrapping materials, etc.

When all other expenses incurred in making the sales have been taken into account the result is profit for the month.

Therefore, if Didi paid the following expenses:

- rent of the stall $400
- wages to her assistant $880
- for wrapping materials $34
- electricity to light the stall $61,

her profit for the month would be $1615:

Gross profit $2990 – Expenses $1375 ($400 + $880 + $34 + $61) = $1615

## 17.1 The uses of accounting information

Financial statements are produced for two purposes:

- to show the providers of finance that their funds are safe and are being used wisely by the manager or owner of the business in question
- to enable the managers or owner of a business to gauge how well the business has performed and to provide information that might highlight areas in which improvements can be made in the way that the business is run.

The first is called the **stewardship function** of accounting, and the second is the **management function**.

The managers or owner of a business often use other people's money (from banks, relatives, etc.) to help provide some of the finance necessary to enable the business to operate.

A bank manager would not be able to say whether a profit of $12765 would give him confidence that the money provided by his bank is secure and being used wisely. The profit figure in isolation does not show how the gross profit of the business is being used. It does not answer the question of how much is the business spending on wages, rent, insurance, etc.

The managers of a business will wish to improve the performance of the business. A profit figure alone will not highlight areas of good practice or identify any problem areas that need to be improved. Details of all expenditure might show that a business is paying a high rent or has a large amount of vehicle expenses. If these could be reduced, then profits would rise.

How could the business reduce rent paid and spend less on vehicle expenses?

Answers could include:

- moving to smaller premises (if present premises are too large)
- moving to 'out-of-town' premises (provided customers would not be lost)
- using diesel vehicles
- charging delivery to some customers.

**Self-test questions**

1. Explain the difference between the stewardship function and the management function of using accounting information.
2. Identify two types of person that would use accounting information for stewardship purposes.
3. Identify two types of person that would use accounting information for management purposes.

## 17.2 The profit and loss account

The profit and loss account of an income statement shows how much profit is left after all business expenses have been deducted from the gross profit earned from trading.

**Worked example**

Vitaly owns and runs a general store. In the year ended 31 March 2015 he made a gross profit of $21 500. During the same year he incurred the following expenditure:

| | $ |
|---|---:|
| Rent | 750 |
| Wages | 8 000 |
| Insurance | 400 |
| Purchase of new weighing scales | 2 340 |
| Motor expenses | 1 100 |
| Light and heating expenses | 500 |
| Stationery and advertising | 250 |
| Bank charges | 135 |
| Purchase of a new delivery van | 15 600 |
| General expenses | 185 |
| Money spent on family holiday | 2 300 |

**Required**

Prepare the profit and loss account for the year ended 31 March 2015.

### Answer

**Vitaly**
**Profit and loss account for the year ended 31 March 2015**

| | $ | $ |
|---|---:|---:|
| Gross profit | | 21 500 |
| *Less* Expenses | | |
| Rent | 750 | |
| Wages | 8 000 | |
| Insurance | 400 | |
| Motor expenses | 1 100 | |
| Light and heating expenses | 500 | |
| Stationery and advertising | 250 | |
| Bank charges | 135 | |
| General expenses | 185 | 11 320 |
| Profit for the year | | 10 180 |

**Note**

- The weighing scales and the delivery van have not been included because they are both examples of capital expenditure. They will appear on Vitaly's statement of financial position.
- The money spent on the holiday has not been included since this is not a business expense. An income statement only includes business expenses.
- The money spent on the family holiday is drawings since the transaction had gone through the records of the business.

## 17.3 The 'complete' income statement

It is usual for businesses to combine the profit and loss account with the trading account to give one income statement.

**Worked example**

Danielle is a trader buying and reselling furniture. She supplies the following information relating to the year ended 31 May 2015:

| | $ |
|---|---|
| Inventory 1 June 2014 | 27268 |
| Inventory 31 May 2015 | 28420 |
| Purchases | 481690 |
| Sales | 748381 |
| Wages | 132471 |
| Rent and local taxes | 26402 |
| Advertising and insurance | 8327 |
| Motor expenses | 10513 |
| Office expenses | 12468 |
| Lighting and heating expenses | 11235 |

**Required**

Prepare an income statement for the year ended 31 May 2015.

### Answer

**Danielle**

**Income statement for the year ended 31 May 2015**

| | $ | $ |
|---|---|---|
| Revenue | | 748381 |
| *Less* Cost of sales | | |
| Inventory 1 June 2014 | 27268 | |
| Purchases | 481690 | |
| | 508958 | |
| *Less* Inventory 31 May 2015 | 28420 | 480538 |
| Gross profit | | 267843 |
| *Less* Expenses | | |
| Wages | 132471 | |
| Rent and local taxes | 26402 | |
| Advertising and insurance | 8327 | |
| Motor expenses | 10513 | |
| Office expenses | 12468 | |
| Light and heat | 11235 | 201416 |
| Profit for the year | | 66427 |

The trading account determined the gross profit of $267843.

The profit and loss account shows what is left of the gross profit when all expenses for the year have been taken into account, in other words the profit for the year.

## 17.4 The treatment of the expense of carriage outwards

**Carriage outwards** is an expense borne by the business. It is sometimes referred to as **carriage on sales**. It is included in the *profit and loss account* with all other expenses incurred by the business.

**Tip** 

This should help you in your revision:
Carriage **In**wards → Trad**IN**g account
Carriage **O**utwards → Pr**O**fit and l**O**ss account

➤ Now try Questions 1 and 2.

### Self-test questions

4 Why is it important to distinguish between capital and revenue expenditure?

5 In what way is gross profit different to profit (before tax) for the year?

6 Complete the following equations:
 a Gross profit – Revenue expenditure = ?
 b Gross profit – Profit for the year = ?
 c Profit for the year + Revenue expenditure = ?

7 One reason that the managers of a business prepare financial statements is to determine the areas of the business that need to be improved. This is an example of the stewardship/management function of accounting. (Correct the sentence.)

8 A business charges customers carriage outwards in order to appear more profitable. True/False?

### Chapter summary

- Providers of finance use financial statements to see if the funds they have provided are being used wisely. This is the stewardship use of accounting.
- Managers use the financial statements to see where improvements to the business can be made and to see which parts of the business are being run efficiently.
- The profit and loss account provides the detail of how gross profit has been utilised in the paying of the business's expenses.
- It lists all revenue expenditure incurred by a business and revenue incomes earned.
- The total of all the revenue expenditure is deducted from gross profit to give the profit for the year.
- Carriage inwards is added to purchases in the trading account, while carriage outwards is included as an expense in the profit and loss account of an income statement.

# 18 Irrecoverable debts and provision for doubtful debts

**Content**

**1.4 Preparation of financial statements**

1.4.1 Adjustments to financial statements
- Calculate the adjustments needed for irrecoverable debts and doubtful debts

**By the end of this chapter you should be able to:**
- write off individual debts that cannot be settled
- make provision for likely doubtful debts
- prepare a provision for doubtful debts account
- calculate an annual provision based on past experience of doubtful debts and on an age profile of individual debtors
- record the recovery of money from a debtor who was regarded as a bad debt some years ago.

In the business world of today a large proportion of all business is conducted on credit. A business that deals with credit customers always runs the risk that some of those customers may not honour their debt.

## 18.1 Irrecoverable or bad debts

If it is known that a debtor will not or cannot pay his or her debt, we cannot leave the debit balance in the debtor's account.

If we did:
- the total amount of trade receivables would be overstated
- the current assets would be overstated
- the total assets would be overstated
- capital would be overstated.

Once we are certain that a debtor is unable to pay, the debt must be written off. This is done by debiting a **bad debts** account in the general ledger and crediting the debtor's account in the sales ledger.

An irrecoverable or a **bad debt** occurs when a debtor cannot pay the amount that is owed.

**Worked example**

The following accounts appear in Nobel's sales ledger:

| Dr | Moussa | | Cr |
|---|---|---|---|
| | $ | | |
| Balance b/d | 143 | | |

| Dr | Cindy | | Cr |
|---|---|---|---|
| | $ | | |
| Balance b/d | 619 | | |

| Dr | Rett | | Cr |
|---|---|---|---|
| | $ | | |
| Balance b/d | 51 | | |

| Dr | Sandie | | Cr |
|---|---|---|---|
| | $ | | |
| Balance b/d | 430 | | |

| Dr | Deck | | Cr |
|---|---|---|---|
| | $ | | |
| Balance b/d | 628 | | |

| Dr | Tina | | Cr |
|---|---|---|---|
| | $ | | |
| Balance b/d | 92 | | |

It has been revealed that Moussa and Tina are unable to pay their debts and Nobel has decided to write them off at the year ended 31 December 2014.

**Required**

Show the necessary entries to record the transactions.

## Answer

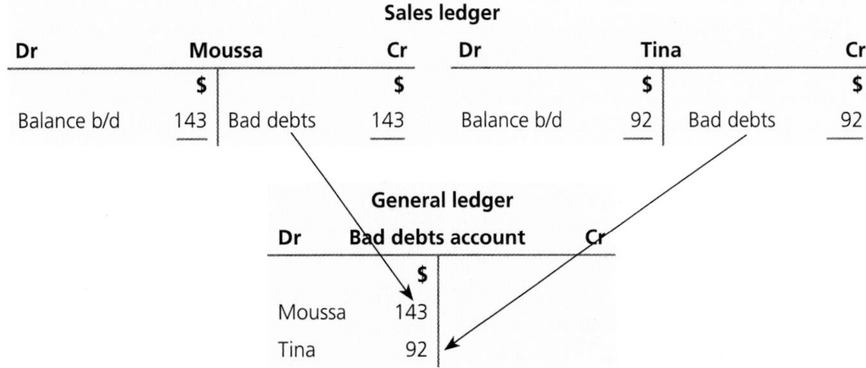

**Sales ledger**

| Dr | Moussa | | Cr | Dr | Tina | | Cr |
|---|---|---|---|---|---|---|---|
| | $ | | $ | | $ | | $ |
| Balance b/d | 143 | Bad debts | 143 | Balance b/d | 92 | Bad debts | 92 |

**General ledger**

| Dr | Bad debts account | | Cr |
|---|---|---|---|
| | $ | | |
| Moussa | 143 | | |
| Tina | 92 | | |

Any entries in the double-entry system must first be entered in a book of prime entry.

We should use the general journal to record the transfer of each debtor to the bad debts account *before* recording the entries in the general ledger.

The general journal entries would show:

| | Dr | Cr |
|---|---|---|
| | $ | $ |
| Bad debts account: | 143 | |
| Moussa | | 143 |
| Writing off Moussa's debt (irrecoverable) to the bad debts account | | |
| Bad debts account: | 92 | |
| Tina | | 92 |
| Writing off Tina's debt (irrecoverable) to the bad debts account | | |

At the end of the financial year, the bad debts account is totalled and closed by transferring the amount to the income statement as a revenue expense.

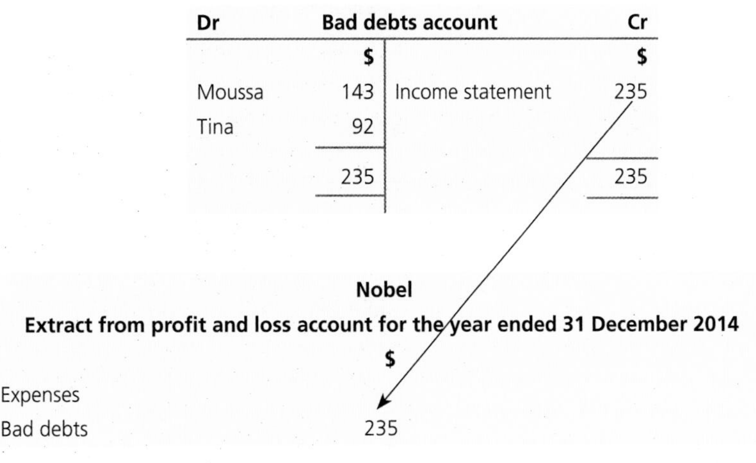

| Dr | Bad debts account | | Cr |
|---|---|---|---|
| | $ | | $ |
| Moussa | 143 | Income statement | 235 |
| Tina | 92 | | |
| | 235 | | 235 |

**Nobel**

**Extract from profit and loss account for the year ended 31 December 2014**

| | $ |
|---|---|
| Expenses | |
| Bad debts | 235 |

## 18.2 Provision for doubtful debts

This is sometimes called a **provision for bad debts**.

As we have seen, individual debts that cannot be paid are transferred to a bad debts account.

As well as actual bad debts there is always the risk that other debtors *may not* pay. Those who might not pay are called **doubtful debtors**.

An estimate of amounts owed by those credit customers who might be unable to pay their debt is made.

A prudent businessman or woman should not anticipate possible profits but will make provision for likely losses. (See the concept of prudence in Chapter 7.)

It therefore seems to be sensible to make provision for debtors where there is a strong possibility that they will not be able to settle their debt. Remember the definition of a provision: 'an amount set aside out of profits for a known expense, the amount of which is uncertain'.

When we provide for doubtful debts we know that some debtors may not pay but we are not sure who they will be. Therefore we do not know the exact amount of the provision.

How do we calculate the amount to be provided?

We can:

- examine the sales ledger and try to identify the individual debtors who are most likely to default on payment
- take a percentage of total trade receivables based on experience of bad debts written off in previous years
- prepare an age profile of trade receivables and base the provision on the age of each outstanding amount.

### 18.2.1 Calculation of the provision based on past experience

**Worked example**

Digby has estimated that each year around two per cent of his debtors fail to pay.

At 31 October 2014, his trade receivables amounted to $31 900.

He wishes to make provision for doubtful debts at the rate of two per cent.

**Required**

a Calculate the amount of provision for doubtful debts at 31 October 2014.

b Prepare an extract from the statement of financial position at that date, showing the details.

#### Answer

a The provision for doubtful debts is $638 ($31 900 × 2%).

b

**Extract from statement of financial position at 31 October 2014**

| | $ | $ |
|---|---|---|
| **Current assets** | | |
| Trade receivables | 31 900 | |
| *Less* Provision for doubtful debts | (638) | 31 262 |

### 18.2.2 Calculation of the provision based on an age profile of individual debtors

**Worked example**

Deirdre provided the following age profile of her trade receivables at 31 May 2015. The percentage of debtors proving to be bad has been gained from over 20 years' experience in her business.

| Time outstanding | 0–1 month | 1–3 months | 3–6 months | 6 months–1 year | over 1 year |
|---|---|---|---|---|---|
| Amounts owed | $120 000 | $3 000 | $400 | $300 | $1 100 |
| Provision for doubtful debts | 1% | 3% | 5% | 20% | 50% |

**Required**

a Calculate the amount of provision for doubtful debts at 31 May 2015.

b Prepare an extract from the statement of financial position at that date.

#### Workings

| | $ |
|---|---|
| 120 000 × 1% | = 1 200 |
| 3000 × 3% | = 90 |
| 400 × 5% | = 20 |
| 300 × 20% | = 60 |
| 1100 × 50% | = 550 |
| | 1920 |

#### Answer

a The provision for doubtful debts is $1920.

b **Extract from statement of financial position at 31 May 2015**

| | $ | $ |
|---|---|---|
| **Current assets** | | |
| Trade receivables | 124 800 | |
| *Less* Provision for doubtful debts | (1 920) | 122 880 |

**Note**

It was doubtful whether Digby would receive $31 900 from his debtors. From past experience he feels that $31 262 will be a more accurate figure. The creation of the provision has allowed him to be prudent.

It was also doubtful whether Deirdre would receive $124 800 from her debtors. She feels that $122 880 is a more accurate figure. She has been prudent in creating a provision for doubtful debts.

## 18.3 The ledger accounts recording provision for doubtful debts

In which ledger would the provision for doubtful debts be found? It is not a person, so the provision for doubtful debts account would be found in the general ledger.

Once a provision for doubtful debts account has been opened in the general ledger it stays open from one financial year to the next. Adjustments will be made each year to the balance in the provision for doubtful debts account and a corresponding entry made in the income statement with the adjustments either increasing gross profit or decreasing it.

**Worked example**

Lew has decided to create a provision for doubtful debts account at two per cent of trade receivables outstanding at the financial year end on 30 June each year. Trade receivables outstanding at 30 June 2014 was $36 700.

**Required**

Prepare:

a a provision for doubtful debts account at 30 June 2014

b an extract from the income statement for the year ended 30 June 2014 showing relevant details

c an extract from the statement of financial position at 30 June 2014.

## Answer

a

| Dr | | Provision for doubtful debts account | | | Cr |
|---|---|---|---|---|---|
| | | | | | $ |
| | | | 30 June 2014 | Income statement | 734 |

b

**Extract from income statement for the year ended 30 June 2014**

| | $ |
|---|---|
| Expenses | |
| Provision for doubtful debts | 734 |

c

**Extract from statement of financial position at 30 June 2014**

| | $ | $ |
|---|---|---|
| **Current assets** | | |
| Trade receivables | 36 700 | |
| *Less* Provision for doubtful debts | (734) | 35 966 |

**Worked example**

At the financial year end 30 June 2015 Lew had outstanding trade receivables amounting to $41 300. He continues to maintain his provision for doubtful debts account at two per cent per annum based on trade receivables outstanding at his year end.

**Required**

Prepare:

a a provision for doubtful debts account at 30 June 2015

b an extract from the income statement for the year ended 30 June 2015 showing relevant details

c an extract from the statement of financial position at 30 June 2015.

## Answer

a

| Dr | | Provision for doubtful debts account | | | Cr |
|---|---|---|---|---|---|
| | | $ | | | $ |
| 30 June 2014 | Balance c/d | 734 | 30 June 2014 | Income statement | 734 |
| | | | 1 July 2014 | Balance b/d | 734 |
| 30 June 2015 | Balance c/d | 826 | 30 June 2015 | Income statement | 92 |
| | | 826 | | | 826 |
| | | | 1 July 2015 | Balance b/d | 826 |

b

**Extract from income statement for the year ended 30 June 2015**

| | $ |
|---|---|
| Expenses | |
| Provision for doubtful debts | 92 |

c

**Extract from statement of financial position at 30 June 2015**

| | $ | $ |
|---|---|---|
| Current assets | | |
| Trade receivables | 41 300 | |
| *Less* Provision for doubtful debts | 826 | 40 474 |

**Note**

- The amount entered on the income statement is only the increase in the provision.
- It is the amount needed to 'top up' the account to the required level.

➤ Now try Questions 1 and 2.

In each example and question used so far there has been an increase in the provision for doubtful debts. A decrease in the provision now needs to be considered.

## 18.4 Decreasing a provision for doubtful debts

**Worked example**

Bernie maintains a provision for doubtful debts account. His provisions for the last three years are listed:

| Year ended 30 April | 2013 | 2014 | 2015 |
|---|---|---|---|
| | $ | $ | $ |
| Provision for doubtful debts | 250 | 340 | 270 |

**Required**

Prepare for each of the three years

a a provision for doubtful debts account

b an extract from an income statement showing the adjustment to the provision account.

### Answer

a

**Dr — Provision for doubtful debts account — Cr**

| | | $ | | | $ |
|---|---|---|---|---|---|
| 30 April 2013 | Balance c/d | 250 | 30 April 2013 | Income statement | 250 |
| | | | 1 May 2013 | Balance b/d | 250* |
| 30 April 2014 | Balance c/d | 340 | 30 April 2014 | Income statement | 90 |
| | | 340 | | | 340 |
| 30 April 2015 | Income statement | 70 | 1 May 2014 | Balance b/d | 340* |
| 30 April 2015 | Balance c/d | 270 | | | |
| | | 340 | | | 340 |
| | | | 1 May 2015 | | 270* |

* The balance brought down is always equal to the amount of provision needed.

b

**Bernie**

**Extract from income statement for the year ended 30 April 2013**

| | $ |
|---|---|
| *Less* Expenses | |
| Provision for doubtful debts | 250 |

**Bernie**

**Extract from income statement for the year ended 30 April 2014**

| | $ |
|---|---|
| *Less* Expenses | |
| Provision for doubtful debts | 90 |

**Bernie**

**Extract from income statement for the year ended 30 April 2015**

| | $ | |
|---|---|---|
| Gross profit | | |
| *Plus* reduction in provision for doubtful debts | 70 | *(added to gross profit)* |

## Example

Mussa Green makes a provision for doubtful debts based on one per cent of trade receivables outstanding at the financial year end.

The following table shows the entries in the books of account for each of the first five years in business:

| | Trade receivables outstanding | Provision | Income statement entry | Statement of financial position detail | |
|---|---|---|---|---|---|
| End of year | $ | $ | $ | $ | $ |
| 1 | 10 000 | 100 | 100 expense | 10 000 | |
| | | | | (100) | 9 900 |
| 2 | 12 000 | 120 | 20 expense | 12 000 | |
| | | | | (120) | 11 880 |
| 3 | 16 000 | 160 | 40 expense | 16 000 | |
| | | | | (160) | 15 840 |
| 4 | 14 000 | 140 | 20 'income' | 14 000 | |
| | | | | (140) | 13 860 |
| 5 | 18 000 | 180 | 40 expense | 18 000 | |
| | | | | (180) | 17 820 |

➤ Now try Question 3.

To summarise:

- The amount needed to *increase* the provision for doubtful debts is entered as an expense on the income statement.
- The amount needed to *decrease* the provision for doubtful debts is entered as an 'income' on the income statement.

## 18.5 Recovery of bad debts

Sometimes a debtor, whose debt has been written off as a bad debt in an earlier year, may subsequently be able to settle his or her previously outstanding debt.

The simple treatment is as follows:

| | |
|---|---|
| Debit cash book | Credit bad debt recovered account |

Then at the financial year end:

| | |
|---|---|
| Debit bad debt recovered account | Entry on income statement. |

If a question does not require ledger accounts, the result of the transactions above can be recorded in the financial statements as:

- an increase in profit, and
- an increase in cash.

**Example**

Hassan owed Bill $237 five years ago. At that time Bill wrote Hassan's debt off as bad.

| Dr | Hassan | | Cr |
|---|---|---|---|
| | $ | | $ |
| Balance b/d | 237 | Bad debts | 237 |

| Dr | Bad debts account | | Cr |
|---|---|---|---|
| | $ | | $ |
| Hassan | 237 | Income statement | 237 |

Hassan has set up in business again and is now able to pay the $237 that was previously written off.

Hassan should be reinstated as a debtor as he is about to repay the debt. This fact should be recorded in Bill's books of account.

This is important to Hassan since he may require credit facilities from Bill in the future. The fact that he has repaid his debt may be taken into consideration by Bill.

| Dr | Hassan | | Cr |
|---|---|---|---|
| | $ | | |
| Bad debt recovered | 237 | | |

| Dr | Bad debt recovered account | | Cr |
|---|---|---|---|
| | | | $ |
| | | Hassan | 237 |

Hassan has now been reinstated.

Hassan is then credited with the payment made to Bill.

| Dr | Hassan | | Cr |
|---|---|---|---|
| | $ | | |
| Bad debt recovered | 237 | Cash | 237 |

| Dr | Bad debt recovered account | | Cr |
|---|---|---|---|
| | | | $ |
| Income statement | 237 | Hassan | 237 |

## Self-test questions

1 Define the term 'debtor'.
2 Explain the connection between debtors and trade receivables.
3 Fill in the gaps with 'debited', 'credited', 'income' or 'expense'.
  a When a bad debt is written off, the debtor's account is ____________ and the bad debts account is ____________.
  b When the provision for doubtful debts is increased, the provision account is ____________ and the amount is entered in the income statement as an ____________.
4 In which ledger would you find the bad debts account?
5 Name the three methods that a trader may use to calculate the amount needed for the provision for doubtful debts.
6 In which ledger would you find the provision for doubtful debts account?

➤ Now try Questions 4–6.

## Chapter summary

- The amount owed by individual debtors who will definitely not pay their debts is written off to the income statement.
- A provision for doubtful debts is created to take account of credit customers who may not pay their debts. Any increase in the provision is entered as an expense in the income statement (thus decreasing profit for the year) and any decrease in the provision is entered as an addition to gross profit (thus increasing profit for the year).
- Bad debts recovered are added to gross profit in the income statement (increasing profit for the year) or are used to reduce any bad debts written off in the current year and debited to the cash book.

# 19 Depreciation of non-current assets

**Content**

**1.2 Accounting for non-current assets**

- Understand the causes of depreciation
- Understand the purpose of accounting for depreciation and the application of relevant accounting concepts in respect of non-current assets
- Calculate depreciation using the reducing balance, straight-line and revaluation methods
- Evaluate the most appropriate method of calculating depreciation
- Prepare ledger accounts and journal entries for non-current assets, depreciation and disposal (including entries for part exchange)
- Calculate the profit or loss on disposal of a non-current asset
- Record the effect of providing for depreciation in the income statement and statement of financial position

**1.4 Preparation of financial statement**

1.4.1 Adjustments to financial statements

- Calculate the adjustments needed for depreciation

**By the end of this chapter you should be able to:**

- describe the factors that affect the life of a non-current asset
- calculate the annual depreciation charge using:
  - the straight-line method
  - the reducing balance method
  - the revaluation method
- calculate the profit or loss on disposal of non-current assets
- record the disposal of a non-current asset in the general ledger
- record the allowance made for a 'trade-in'
- understand the connection between depreciation and cash.

## 19.1 Non-current assets and depreciation

**Depreciation** is the apportioning of the cost of a non-current asset over its useful economic life.

A business purchases resources to be used in the generation of profits. Some of the resources are used up in one time period.

- Goods purchased for resale will be used in one time period.
- Petrol purchased for a delivery vehicle will be used in one time period.
- The work provided by staff is used in one time period.

Each of the expenses described here can be classified as **revenue expenditure**. The benefits derived from revenue expenditure will be earned in the year and the expense is entered in the income statement for the year in question.

Other resources will be used over a number of time periods. These are **non-current assets**. Just like the resources listed above, a non-current asset is an item that has been purchased by a business in order to generate profits for the business. However, a non-current asset will be used by the business *for more than one financial year*. Non-current assets will yield benefits to the business over a prolonged period of time.

- Premises will, generally, be used for more than one time period.
- A delivery van will, generally, be used for more than one time period.
- Machinery will, generally, be used for more than one time period.

Expenditure on non-current assets, such as those items listed here, is classified as **capital expenditure**. Since the benefits derived from capital expenditure will continue to be earned over a number of years it seems sensible to charge part of the cost of the non-current assets over those years.

Revenues and expenses are recorded in **nominal accounts** in the general ledger. Non-current assets are recorded in **real accounts** in the general ledger.

**Finite life** means a limited life span.

All non-current assets (except land) have a **finite life**. The UK Companies Act 1985 says that all assets with a finite life should be depreciated.

- A machine will eventually cease to produce the goods for which it was purchased.
- A delivery vehicle will eventually cease to be useful for the delivery of goods.

**Infinite life** means an unlimited life span.

Of course, land should not be depreciated, because land has an **infinite life**.

So, the total cost of a non-current asset is never charged to the income statement for the year in which it was purchased. The cost is spread over all the years that it is used in order to reflect in the income statement the cost of using the asset in that particular financial year.

When a non-current asset is purchased and later sold, the amount that is not recovered is called **depreciation**.

**Worked example**

Donna purchased a non-current asset for $20 000. She sold it three years later for $2 000.

**Required**

Calculate the cost of using the asset (the amount of depreciation) for the three years.

### Answer

The cost of using the non-current asset (i.e. the depreciation) is $18 000 ($20 000 – $2 000).

---

This means that the actual depreciation can only be accurately calculated when the non-current asset is no longer being used.

The annual depreciation charge is therefore an estimate made based on experience.

If we know the cost and can make an estimate of how long the non-current asset will be useful and how much it might be worth at the end of its life, we can calculate the amount of depreciation that will take place over the lifetime of the non-current asset.

We need to apportion this lifetime cost into each of the years that the non-current asset was used.

## 19.2 Factors that affect the useful life of a non-current asset

When determining the useful life of a non-current asset the following factors should be considered:

- physical deterioration based on expected wear and tear: this will depend on the type of use that the asset is employed in, how well the asset is maintained and how well any repairs are carried out
- economic factors such as the necessary output and the potential capacity of the asset
- the introduction of new technology making the asset obsolete
- obsolescence due to a change in demand for the product the asset produces
- a change in demand which makes the asset incapable of producing the quantity (or quality) of product required
- the age of the asset

- legal or other limits placed on the asset; for example, when an asset is acquired under a leasing agreement the lessor may place restrictions on the use of the asset.

There are many methods of dividing the lifetime depreciation charge. We shall consider the following three methods:

- straight-line method (also known as equal instalment method)
- reducing balance method
- revaluation method.

When a method of calculating the provision for depreciation has been decided upon, it should be used consistently so that the results shown in the financial statements of different years can be compared.

**Self-test questions**

1 Identify two factors that cause a non-current asset to depreciate.
2 Explain the term 'finite'.
3 In which type of account would you expect to find non-current assets?
4 In which ledger would you expect to find the machinery account?
5 A second-hand vehicle is purchased. Because the previous owner charged depreciation on the vehicle, the new owner does not need to. True/False?

## 19.3 The straight-line method of depreciating non-current assets

The straight-line method requires that the same amount is charged annually to the income statement over the lifetime of a non-current asset.

To calculate depreciation using the straight-line method it is therefore necessary to consider:

- the cost of the non-current asset
- the estimated life of the non-current asset
- the estimated **residual value** or scrap value.

The **cost of an asset** is the purchase price including any taxes plus any other costs directly attributable to bring the asset to the location and condition ready for use.

**Attributable costs** that are included as part of cost would include:

- delivery and handling charges
- professional fees charged by solicitors, architects, site engineers, etc.
- making ready the site where the asset is to be used
- any costs involved in assembling and testing the asset.

**Residual (scrap) value** is the amount that a non-current asset can be sold for at the end of its useful life.

**Formula**

$$\text{Annual depreciation charge} = \frac{\text{Cost of non-current asset} - \text{Any residual value}}{\text{Estimate of number of years' use}}$$

If we know the life of an asset we can easily calculate the annual rate of depreciation.

- If an asset has an expected life of ten years, the annual rate of depreciation would be ten per cent (100 per cent divided by ten years).
- If an asset has an expected life of 50 years, the annual rate of depreciation would be two per cent (100 per cent divided by 50 years).
- If an asset has an expected life of two years, the annual rate of depreciation would be 50 per cent (100 per cent divided by two years).

**Worked example**

A computer is purchased for $2300. Its useful life is expected to be two years, after which it will be replaced. It is expected that it will have a trade-in value of $100.

**Required**

Calculate the annual depreciation charge using the straight-line method.

## Answer

Annual depreciation charge = $1100.

### Workings

$$\frac{\text{Cost of computer} - \text{Residual value}}{\text{Estimated years of use}} = \frac{\$2200 - \$100}{2}$$

A **provision** is an amount set aside out of profits for a known expense, the amount of which cannot be calculated with substantial accuracy.

**Carrying amount** is the cost of a non-current asset shown in the general ledger (and therefore the statement of financial position) less the total depreciation charged to date. Carrying amount is also often termed **net book value (NBV)**.

The depreciation account is found in the general ledger.

I know that my car is depreciating (a known expense) but I cannot tell you exactly the amount of annual depreciation. I will only be able to give you an accurate figure in the future when I change my car.

We have just seen how to calculate depreciation. How is the charge entered in the double-entry system?

Entry on the income statement — Credit provision for depreciation account

### Worked example

Tanya purchases a delivery van for $18000 on 1 January 2011. She will use the van for four years, after which she estimates she will be able to sell the van for $6000.

Tanya's financial year end is 31 December.

**Required**

Prepare:

a the delivery van account
b the provision for depreciation account
c the income statement extracts to record the necessary entries
d the statement of financial position extracts for the four years.

## Answer

a

| Dr | | Delivery van account | | | Cr |
|---|---|---|---|---|---|
| | | $ | | | |
| 1 Jan 2011 | Bank | 18000 | | | |

b

| Dr | | | Provision for depreciation on delivery van account | | Cr |
|---|---|---|---|---|---|
| | | $ | | | $ |
| 31 Dec 2011 | Balance c/d | 3000 | 31 Dec 2011 | Income statement | 3000 |
| | | 3000 | | | 3000 |
| | | | 1 Jan 2012 | Balance b/d | 3000 |
| 31 Dec 2012 | Balance c/d | 6000 | 31 Dec 2012 | Income statement | 3000 |
| | | 6000 | | | 6000 |
| | | | 1 Jan 2013 | Balance b/d | 6000 |
| 31 Dec 2013 | Balance c/d | 9000 | 31 Dec 2013 | Income statement | 3000 |
| | | 9000 | | | 9000 |
| | | | 1 Jan 2014 | Balance b/d | 9000 |
| 31 Dec 2014 | Balance c/d | 12000 | 31 Dec 2014 | Income statement | 3000 |
| | | 12000 | | | 12000 |
| | | | 1 Jan 2015 | Balance b/d | 12000 |

c **Extract from income statement for the year ended 31 December 2011**

| | $ |
|---|---|
| *Less* Expenses | |
| Provision for depreciation of delivery van | 3000 |

**Extract from income statement for the year ended 31 December 2012**

| | $ |
|---|---|
| *Less* Expenses | |
| Provision for depreciation of delivery van | 3000 |

**Extract from income statement for the year ended 31 December 2013**

| | $ |
|---|---|
| *Less* Expenses | |
| Provision for depreciation of delivery van | 3000 |

**Extract from income statement for the year ended 31 December 2014**

| | $ |
|---|---|
| *Less* Expenses | |
| Provision for depreciation of delivery van | 3000 |

d **Extract from statement of financial position at 31 December 2011**

| | $ |
|---|---|
| **Non-current asset** | |
| Delivery van at cost | 18000 |
| *Less* Depreciation to date | 3000 |
| | 15000 |

**Extract from statement of financial position at 31 December 2012**

| | $ |
|---|---|
| **Non-current asset** | |
| Delivery van at cost | 18000 |
| *Less* Depreciation to date | 6000 |
| | 12000 |

**Extract from statement of financial position at 31 December 2013**

| | $ |
|---|---|
| **Non-current asset** | |
| Delivery van at cost | 18000 |
| *Less* Depreciation to date | 9000 |
| | 9000 |

**Extract from statement of financial position at 31 December 2014**

| | $ |
|---|---|
| **Non-current asset** | |
| Delivery van at cost | 18000 |
| *Less* Depreciation to date | 12000 |
| | 6000 |

Note the following:

- the double entries – entry in the income statement; credit provision account
- the equal instalments in each year's income statement
- the delivery van is entered in the statement of financial position at cost
- the accumulated depreciation is taken from the non-current asset in the statement of financial position
- the total shown at the end of each year in the statement of financial position for the delivery van is the carrying amount.

➤ **Now try Question 1.**

## 19.4 The reducing balance method of depreciating non-current assets

A fixed percentage is applied to the cost of the non-current asset in the first year of ownership. The same percentage is applied in subsequent years to the carrying amount of the asset.

**Worked example**

A vehicle was purchased for $18 000 on 1 January 2012. Depreciation is to be provided at the rate of 40 per cent per annum using the reducing balance method.

**Required**

a Calculate the annual charge for depreciation in the years ended 31 December 2012, 2013 and 2014.

b Prepare journal entries for the years 2013 and 2014 to show the entries in the double-entry system.

### Answer

a

| | | *Workings* |
|---|---|---|
| Year 2012 | $7 200 | *($18 000 x 40%)* |
| Year 2013 | $4 320 | *($18 000 – $7 200) x 40%* |
| Year 2014 | $2 592 | *($18 000 – $7200 – $4320) x 40%* |

b Journal entries for the year ended 31 December 2013:

| | Dr | Cr |
|---|---|---|
| | $ | $ |
| Income statement | 4 320 | |
| Provision for depreciation of vehicles | | 4 320 |
| Depreciation charge for vehicles for the year ended 31 December 2013 | | |

Journal entries for the year ended 31 December 2014:

| | Dr | Cr |
|---|---|---|
| | $ | $ |
| Income statement | 2 592 | |
| Provision for depreciation of vehicles | | 2 592 |
| Depreciation charge for vehicles for the year ended 31 December 2014 | | |

The provision for depreciation account will look very similar no matter which method is used; only the annual charge entered in the income statement will change.

**Worked example**

Steig Wallander purchased a machine on 1 January 2012 for $64 000.

Depreciation is to be charged at 20 per cent per annum using the reducing balance method.

Steig's financial year end is 31 December.

**Required**

Prepare:

a a machinery account

b a provision for depreciation of machinery account

c income statement extracts to record the necessary entries

d extracts from the statements of financial position for the three years 2012, 2013 and 2014.

## Answer

a

| Dr | | Machinery account | | | Cr |
|---|---|---|---|---|---|
| | | $ | | | |
| 1 Jan 2012 | Bank | 64 000 | | | |

b

| Dr | | Provision for depreciation of machinery account | | | Cr |
|---|---|---|---|---|---|
| | | $ | | | $ |
| 31 Dec 2012 | Balance c/d | 12 800 | 31 Dec 2012 | Income statement | 12 800 |
| | | 12 800 | | | 12 800 |
| | | | 1 Jan 2013 | Balance b/d | 12 800 |
| 31 Dec 2013 | Balance c/d | 23 040 | 31 Dec 2013 | Income statement | 10 240 |
| | | 23 040 | | | 23 040 |
| | | | 1 Jan 2014 | Balance b/d | 23 040 |
| 31 Dec 2014 | Balance c/d | 31 232 | 31 Dec 2014 | Income statement | 8 192 |
| | | 31 232 | | | 31 232 |
| | | | 1 Jan 2015 | Balance b/d | 31 232 |

c

**Extract from income statement for the year ended 31 December 2012**

| | $ |
|---|---|
| Gross profit | |
| *Less* Expenses | |
| Provision for depreciation of machinery | 12 800 |

**Extract from income statement for the year ended 31 December 2013**

| | $ |
|---|---|
| Gross profit | |
| *Less* Expenses | |
| Provision for depreciation of machinery | 10 240 |

**Extract from income statement for the year ended 31 December 2014**

| | $ |
|---|---|
| Gross profit | |
| *Less* Expenses | |
| Provision for depreciation of machinery | 8 192 |

d

**Extract from statement of financial position at 31 December 2012**

| **Non-current asset** | $ |
|---|---|
| Machinery at cost | 64 000 |
| *Less* Depreciation to date | 12 800 |
| | 51 200 |

**Extract from statement of financial position at 31 December 2013**

| | $ |
|---|---|
| **Non-current asset** | |
| Machinery at cost | 64 000 |
| *Less* Depreciation to date | 23 040 |
| | 40 960 |

**Extract from statement of financial position at 31 December 2014**

| | $ |
|---|---|
| **Non-current asset** | |
| Machinery at cost | 64 000 |
| *Less* Depreciation to date | 31 232 |
| | 32 768 |

**Self-test questions**

6 A reducing balance method of providing for depreciation of non-current assets is more accurate than the straight-line method. True/False?

7 What are the double entries to record the provision for depreciation using a reducing balance method?

➤ Now try Question 2.

## 19.5 The revaluation method of depreciating non-current assets

**Loose tools** is the term used to describe small items of non-current assets that have a life expectancy greater than one year, but individually are owned for a much shorter period due to breakages, being misplaced or being stolen. They are also individually of much lower value than the non-current assets already encountered in your studies.

The revaluation method is generally used where the asset is made up of many small items.

An example could be the small tools that are used on a regular basis in a large auto repair business or in an engineering works. Clearly, it would be inappropriate to use either of the two methods of providing for depreciation previously described on a hammer that cost $4.50 or on a pair of wire cutters costing $4.75.

You can imagine the amount of time that would be taken up if each small tool was entered in the general ledger and depreciated separately at the end of each year.

Individually, these items are small and might seem to be insignificant, but they are non-current assets because they are to be used for more than one financial year.

In order to calculate the depreciation provision in such cases, the following calculation is necessary:

Value placed on the items at the start of the financial year

*plus* any purchases of more items during the year

*less* the value placed on the items at the end of the year

*equals* depreciation for the year.

**Worked example**

The managers of Redjor Engineering Works valued loose tools on 1 January 2014 at $2190. During the year more tools costing $930 were purchased.

On 31 December 2014 the managers valued loose tools at $2400.

**Required**

Calculate the depreciation of loose tools for the year ended 31 December 2014.

### Answer

| | $ |
|---|---|
| Value of loose tools at 1 January 2014 | 2 190 |
| *Plus* Additions during the year | 930 |
| | 3 120 |
| *Less* Value of loose tools at 31 December 2014 | 2 400 |
| Depreciation for the year | 720 |

The depreciation would be shown in a manufacturing account (see Chapter 32) since the tools will be used in the factory.

The value at the end of the year of $2400 is shown as the carrying amount for the non-current asset on the statement of financial position at 31 December 2014.

## 19.6 The sale or disposal of non-current assets

You will have noticed that the word 'expected' has been used quite freely in the discussion so far. The owner of a business tries to guess how many years a non-current asset will be used. He or she will try to guess how much cash will be received when the asset is sold when it is no longer of any use.

When an asset is sold it is highly unlikely that the sum received will be the same as the carrying amount. It is likely that a profit or loss based on the carrying amount will arise.

**Worked example**

A machine which cost $32 000 five years ago has been sold for $14 000. The accumulated (total) depreciation to date was $15 000.

**Required**

Calculate the profit or loss arising from the disposal of the machine.

### Answer

| | $ | |
|---|---|---|
| Machine at cost | 32 000 | *The cost of the machine* |
| Depreciation to date | (15 000) | *less depreciation to date* |
| Carrying amount | 17 000 | *gives the net value recorded in the ledger.* |
| Sale proceeds | 14 000 | *The cash received from the sale* |
| Loss on disposal | 3 000 | *is less than the value shown in the ledger, hence the loss on disposal.* |

**Worked example**

A machine which cost $18 000 ten years ago has been sold for $1 500. The accumulated (total) depreciation to date was $17 000.

**Required**

Calculate the profit or loss on disposal.

## Answer

**Tip** 

If you are asked for a calculation, you may use the method shown above or you may choose to show an account to record the disposal (a disposal account). However, if you are asked for a disposal account, you *must* show your answer in account format.

| | $ | |
|---|---|---|
| Machine at cost | 18000 | *The cost of the machine* |
| Depreciation to date | (17000) | *less depreciation to date* |
| Carrying amount | 1000 | *gives the net value recorded in the ledger.* |
| Sale proceeds | 1500 | *The cash received from the sale* |
| Profit on disposal | 500 | *is more than the value shown in the ledger, hence the profit on disposal* |

## 19.7 The ledger accounts used to record the disposal of non-current assets

The following procedure should be followed when ledger accounts are required to record the disposal of a non-current asset.

| | | |
|---|---|---|
| 1 | Open an account in the general ledger headed 'disposal account'. | |
| 2 | Debit the disposal account with the cost of the asset. | Credit the asset account. |
| 3 | Debit the provision for depreciation account. | Credit the disposal account. |
| 4 | Debit the cash account with the cash received for sale. | Credit the disposal account. |
| 5 | Debit the disposal account with loss on disposal. *OR* | Credit the disposal account with profit. |

**Worked example**

Mmasekgoa provides the following information from her general ledger:

| Dr | Machinery account | | Cr |
|---|---|---|---|
| | $ | | |
| 1 April 2013 Balance b/d | 66000 | | |

| Dr | Provision for depreciation of machinery account | | Cr |
|---|---|---|---|
| | | | $ |
| | | 1 April 2013 Balance b/d | 43000 |

In January 2014 Mmasekgoa sold a machine for $3000 cash. She has entered the cash received in the cash book but has made no other entries in the ledger.

The machine had cost $18000 some years ago. The accumulated depreciation relating to the machine amounted to $16500.

**Required**

Prepare the machinery disposal account to record the sale of the machine.

## Answer

| Dr | Disposal of machinery account | | Cr |
|---|---|---|---|
| | $ | | $ |
| Machinery | 18000 | Provision for depreciation of machinery | 16500 |
| Income statement (profit) | 1500 | Cash | 3000 |
| | 19500 | | 19500 |

## Answer

**General journal**

| | Dr | Cr |
|---|---|---|
| | $ | $ |
| Disposal of machinery account | 18000 | |
| Machinery account | | 18000 |
| Transfer of machinery to disposal account | | |
| Provision for depreciation of machinery account | 16500 | |
| Disposal of machinery account | | 16500 |
| Depreciation relating to the machine being sold transferred to disposal account | | |
| Cash account* | 3000 | |
| Disposal account | | 3000 |
| Cash received for sale of machine | | |
| Disposal of machinery account | 1500 | |
| Income statement | | 1500 |
| Profit on disposal of machine transferred to income statement | | |

* Cash entries should not really be shown in the general journal. The cash book is the book of prime entry that is used for all transactions using cash. However, you may have to show cash entries in an answer requiring general journal entries.

➤ Now try Question 3.

## 19.8 The treatment of a 'trade-in'

Sometimes when a non-current asset is replaced, the 'old' asset is traded in and an allowance is made by the supplier of the 'new' asset.

I recently purchased a new car for $14000. The garage took my 'old' car in part exchange. They made an allowance on my 'old' car of $6500. I paid $7500 cash for the new car. The garage actually bought my old car from me for $6500 – this, together with my payment of $7500, made up the total purchase price.

**Worked example**

Alessandro purchased a delivery van registration number DQ13 WDA costing $19000. The new van replaced vehicle B19 JJH, which cost $11500 a number of years ago. The accumulated depreciation on B19 JJH amounted to $9000.

The garage gave an allowance of $2750 on B19 JJH; the balance due was paid by cheque.

**Required**

Prepare the ledger accounts to record the purchase of the new van.

## Answer

**Van B19 JJH account**

| Dr | | Cr | |
|---|---|---|---|
| | $ | | $ |
| Balance b/d | 11500 | Disposal | 11500 |

**Provision for depreciation on van B19 JJH account**

| Dr | | Cr | |
|---|---|---|---|
| | $ | | $ |
| Disposal | 9000 | Balance b/d | 9000 |

**B19 JJH Disposal account**

| Dr | | Cr | |
|---|---|---|---|
| | $ | | $ |
| Van | 11500 | Depreciation | 9000 |
| Income statement | 250 | Van DQ03 WDA | 2750 |
| | 11750 | | 11750 |

**Van DQ13 WDA account**

| Dr | | Cr | |
|---|---|---|---|
| | $ | | |
| Disposal | 2750 | | |
| Bank | 16250 | | |

**Note**

The procedure is very similar to that used when a non-current asset is purchased for cash only. The only difference is that the new non-current asset is debited with any allowance being made by the supplier and the disposal account is credited with the allowance.

## 19.9 The connection between cash and providing for depreciation

There is no direct connection between providing depreciation on non-current assets in the income statement and providing cash to replace the asset when it is no longer of use.

A person does not visit the business every weekend asking for cash to pay for the use of each non-current asset being used!

Depreciation is a **non-cash expense**.

Cash flows out of a business when a non-current asset is purchased; the annual depreciation charge is that cost being spread over the lifetime of the asset.

A second-hand car was purchased for $2750 in January 2012 for cash. It is kept for four years.

- The cash outflow took place in January 2012.
- No further cash outflows have taken place (apart from the usual running costs) but the car will be depreciated in each year of its use.

In the case of a business, there is an indirect influence that depreciation has on cash flows.

Depreciation is entered in the income statement. This non-cash expense reduces profits for each year of ownership. The reduction in profit may cause the owner of the business to withdraw less money from the business for personal use; thus conserving more cash within the business.

**Example**

Tomaz's business earns an annual profit of around $45 000. His drawings average $20 000 per year.

Tomaz purchases a new machine for the business costing $80 000. The machine is expected to be used for four years before it needs to be replaced.

When depreciation on the new machine (using the straight-line method) is included in the income statement, annual profits are reduced to $25 000.

Tomaz may well reduce his cash drawings in recognition of the business's reduced profitability.

## Self-test questions

8 Define depreciation.

9 What is a provision?

10 Fill in the following gaps.
   a Non-current assets are shown on the ____________ side of real accounts in the general ledger.
   b All assets with a ____________ life should be depreciated.
   c Only the asset of ____________ has an infinite life.

11 Name two methods of calculating annual depreciation.

12 What are the book-keeping entries required to record the annual charge for depreciation?

13 What is meant by the term 'accumulated depreciation'?

14 What is meant by the term 'carrying amount'?

15 An asset with a carrying amount of $4000 is sold for $3800. Calculate the profit or loss on disposal.

➤ **Now try Questions 4–6.**

## Chapter summary

- Depreciation is provided on all non-current assets except land.
- Depreciation represents the use of a non-current asset during each year of ownership.
- The accruals concept is being applied when depreciation is charged to the income statement.
- Three methods of calculating the annual charge for depreciation are the straight-line method, the reducing balance method and the revaluation method.
- Whichever method is used by a business, the provision for depreciation account in the general ledger will look similar; the only difference will be the annual charge.

# 20 The valuation of inventories

**Content**

**1.4 Preparation of financial statements**

1.4.1 Adjustments to financial statements
- Calculate the adjustments needed for inventory

**2.1 Costing for materials and labour**
- Calculate the value of closing inventory using the FIFO and AVCO methods (perpetual and periodic)
- Understand the different characteristics, and the appropriateness, of using FIFO, AVCO and LIFO
- Demonstrate the effect of different methods of valuing inventory of material on profit

**By the end of this chapter you should be able to:**
- value closing inventories using the principle of 'cost or net realisable value'
- understand the three methods that may be used to value closing inventories
- outline the advantages and disadvantages of using each method of valuation
- comment on the effect that the choice of method would have on reported profits and on the value of net assets
- understand the difference between using a perpetual method and a periodic method of valuation
- apply relevant accounting concepts to inventory valuation
- calculate the value of inventory when a physical check is conducted some time after the financial year end.

## 20.1 The use of cost or net realisable value

In Chapter 16 we considered the valuation of inventories. We said that the overriding principle that should be used at all times is that inventory should be valued at the lower of cost or net realisable value.

'IAS 2 Inventories' states that cost should include:

- costs of purchase
- conversion costs
- any other costs incurred in bringing the inventories to their present location and condition.

A warehouse storing unsold goods – inventory

The standard defines net realisable value as the estimated selling price in the ordinary course of business less estimated costs of completion and all estimated costs to be incurred in marketing, selling and distributing the items.

**Worked example**

Thea sells one type of vacuum cleaner. They cost $80 each to purchase. At 31 March 2015 Thea has 14 cleaners as inventory. The cleaners normally sell for $120 each. Thea has one damaged cleaner remaining. She intends to have the cleaner repaired at a cost of $35. It can then be sold for $100.

**Required**

Calculate the value of Thea's closing inventory at 31 March 2015.

## Answer

Thea's inventory should be valued at $1 105.

### Workings

| | $ | $ |
|---|---|---|
| 13 cleaners at $80 each | | 1 040 |
| 1 damaged cleaner: | | |
| Selling price | 100 | |
| *Less* Repair costs | 35 | 65 |
| | | 1 105 |

Up to now we have valued most inventory at cost and net realisable value. It looks fairly straightforward, but consider the following example.

**Example**

Jitesh sells only one product, a 'sedrit'. He provides the following information:

| Purchases of sedrits | | Sales of sedrits | |
|---|---|---|---|
| January | 2 at $10 each | May | 4 at $30 each |
| April | 3 at $15 each | December | 3 at $35 each |
| November | 4 at $20 each | | |

In total Jitesh purchased nine sedrits. He has sold seven. Therefore he has two sedrits remaining as inventory at 31 December. How should he value the two sedrits remaining?

He should value them at cost!

Should he choose to value them at $10 each; or $15 each; or $20 each; or one at $10 the other at $15; or …?

You can see that there are many combinations that we could choose when valuing Jitesh's closing inventory.

So valuing inventory at cost is not quite as simple as it first seems. The total purchases figure for the year is $145 and the total sales revenue for the year is $225. We could prepare the trading account of an income statement if we could decide on a method by which we could value the closing inventory.

In the example used above, it might be fairly straightforward to identify the actual units of sedrits that had been sold and hence identify the two remaining in the business. However, if we had many hundreds of items available for sale this would be almost impossible.

Most businesses will be unable to identify with any precision the actual items that they have remaining as inventory at the end of their financial year and even if they could it would be a huge task to go back through purchase invoices to determine the price paid for each item.

The valuation of inventories is therefore a matter of expediency rather than strict accuracy.

In the valuation of closing inventory, we do not trace through the actual units that have been sold; rather we identify certain items that are deemed to be sold and therefore certain items that are deemed to remain.

The methods listed in the following section are most frequently used to identify the goods deemed to have been issued either to a final customer or to another department within the same business.

## 20.2 Methods of valuing inventory

### 20.2.1 First-in first-out method of valuing inventory (FIFO)

As the name suggests, this method *assumes* that the first goods received by the business will be the first ones to be delivered to the final customer or the department requisitioning the goods. It assumes that goods have been used in the order in which they were purchased. Therefore, any remaining inventory will be valued as if it were the latest goods purchased.

Remember this is only an assumption.

FIFO, like the methods below, is a method of *valuing inventory*. It is not necessarily the way that goods are actually issued. Goods may be issued in any way that best suits a particular business, regardless of when goods were received.

**Example**

A garage mechanic requires a battery to fit into the car he is working on. The store keeper in the parts department will issue the first battery he can lay his hands on; he will not waste time seeking out the first one bought in to give to the mechanic.

Questions requiring detailed calculations of valuing inventory using LIFO will not be discussed in this book.

### 20.2.2 Last-in first-out method of valuing inventory (LIFO)

This method *assumes* that the last goods to be purchased are the first ones to be issued to the final customer or requisitioning department. This means that the valuation of inventory will begin using the value of the earliest goods purchased.

### 20.2.3 Weighted average cost method of valuing inventory (AVCO)

The average cost of goods held is recalculated each time a new delivery of goods is received. Issues are then priced out at this weighted average cost.

## 20.3 Perpetual and periodic ways of valuing closing inventory

Some businesses keep extremely detailed records of the goods that they hold. Every transaction affecting the purchases and sales of goods is recorded in great detail.

The value of the inventory held is then recalculated after each transaction. (The inventory records look rather like a bank statement.)

The method of recalculating the value of goods held after each transaction is known as the **perpetual method**.

This method is used by businesses that need to cost their work out to customers very carefully. It is also used in major supermarkets. Each time a transaction is 'scanned' at the check-out the bar code is read and the inventory records are updated electronically to record the sale (issue). Each time a delivery arrives in the warehouse the goods received will be 'scanned' and the inventory records will be updated with the receipt of the goods.

Other less sophisticated businesses may simply value their inventory once at the financial year end. The owner of your local store or restaurant will probably value inventory at close of business on the last day of the financial year. They will list all items remaining unsold on the last day of the financial year; they will then assign a value to each category of goods held, and the total value of all goods gives the closing inventory figure to be used in the year end financial statements.

This is known as a **periodic method** of inventory valuation.

Let us now examine the results given when we use a *perpetual* method of inventory valuation.

## Worked example

During the month of February the following receipts and issues of the component SMH/19 took place:

| | Receipts of SMH/19 | Issues of SMH/19 |
|---|---|---|
| 2 February | 8 @ $10 | |
| 7 February | | 6 |
| 9 February | 9 @ $11 | |
| 16 February | | 10 |
| 24 February | 7 @ $12 | |
| 27 February | | 6 |

**Required**

Calculate the value of closing inventory of component SMH/19 using the first-in first-out method of valuation (FIFO).

### Answer

The value of closing inventory using the FIFO method of issue is $24.00.

| Date | Receipts | Issues | Balance | |
|---|---|---|---|---|
| 2 February | 8 @ $10 | | $80.00 | (8 @ $10) |
| 7 February | | 6 | $20.00 | (2 @ $10) |
| 9 February | 9 @ $11 | | $119.00 | (2 @ $10; 9 @ $11) |
| 16 February | | 10 | $11.00 | (1 @ $11) |
| 24 February | 7 @ $12 | | $95.00 | (1 @ $11; 7 @$12) |
| 27 February | | 6 | $24.00 | (2 @ $12) |

## Worked example

Use the same data for February shown above.

**Required**

Calculate the value of closing inventory of component SMH/19 using the weighted average cost method (AVCO).

## Answer

The value of closing inventory of component SMH/19 using the weighted average cost (AVCO) method is $23.70.

| Date | Receipts | Issues | Balance | |
|---|---|---|---|---|
| 2 February | 8 @ $10 | | $80.00 | (8 @ $10) |
| 7 February | | 6 | $20.00 | (2 @ $10) |
| 9 February | 9 @ $11 | | $119.00 | (Average cost $119.00/11 = $10.82) |
| 16 February | | 10 | $10.82 | ($10.82 x 1) |
| 24 February | 7 @ $12 | | $94.82 | (Average cost $94.82/8 = $11.85) |
| 27 February | | 6 | $23.70 | ($11.85 x 2) |

Check each of the methods shown above. They are an important element of your studies and you will need to know them well.

## 20.4 The effect of inventory valuation on reported profit and net assets

Since each method gives a different closing inventory figure, it follows that different gross profits will be revealed by using different methods of valuation.

Imagine that component SMH/19 has been sold for $20 per unit.

What would be the gross profit for each method of issue?

**Tip**

If the value of closing inventory is altered, reported profits will also change:

- *Increase* the value of closing inventory and you *increase* reported profit.
- *Decrease* the value of closing inventory and you *decrease* reported profit.

Note that FIFO reveals the highest profits; LIFO reveals the lowest profits; while AVCO gives a profit figure between the two extremes. (However, do note that this is the case only where purchase prices are rising over the period under review.)

| | FIFO | | AVCO | |
|---|---|---|---|---|
| | $ | $ | $ | $ |
| Sales | | 440.00 | | 440.00 |
| *Less* Cost of sales | | | | |
| Opening inventory | 0 | | 0 | |
| Purchases | 263.00 | | 263.00 | |
| | 263.00 | | 263.00 | |
| *Less* closing inventory | 24.00 | 239.00 | 23.70 | 239.30 |
| Gross profit | | 201.00 | | 200.70 |

The level of profits revealed in a set of financial statements always depends on the way the inventory has been valued.

The value of closing inventory also has an effect on the net assets of a business. A high valuation gives higher net assets and therefore a higher capital figure.

A low valuation gives a lower net asset value and a lower capital figure.

## 20.5 Perpetual or periodic?

Twenty-four SMH/19 components were purchased during February and 22 were issued, so at the end of the month there were two remaining. Using FIFO we assume that the first components were the first ones to be issued. The two components that are remaining as inventory are deemed to be from the last ones purchased. Closing inventory is therefore deemed to consist of two from the last batch purchased. Closing inventory is valued at $24.00 (2 x $12).

We have arrived at the same figure that we calculated using the perpetual method – coincidence? No, FIFO will give the same result whether you use the perpetual or the periodic method.

Unfortunately there is no shorter version of calculating closing inventory when an average price is taken for issuing goods.

Should you use the periodic method or the perpetual method? Always use the method you find easiest. Use the method you are most comfortable using. Since the periodic method is, I think, easier I would use it every time for FIFO – *unless* a question specifically requires you to show the perpetual method in detail.

➤ Now try Questions 1 and 2.

# 20.6 Advantages and disadvantages of using FIFO, LIFO and AVCO

## 20.6.1 Advantages of using FIFO

- Most people feel that it is intuitively the right method to use, since it seems to follow the natural way that goods are generally issued, i.e. in the order in which they are received.
- Inventory values are easily calculated.
- Issue prices are based on prices actually paid for purchases of goods.
- Closing inventory is based on prices most recently paid.
- It is a method that is acceptable for the purposes of the Companies Act 1985 and IAS 2.

## 20.6.2 Disadvantages of using FIFO

Remember that you will not need to provide 'detailed calculations' using the LIFO method.

- Because it feels right intuitively many people feel that this is actually the way goods are issued.
- Issues from inventory are not at the most recent prices and this may have an adverse effect on pricing policy.
- In times of rising prices FIFO values inventory at higher prices than other methods. This lowers the value of cost of sales and thus increases reported profits (advantageous if the business is to be sold). However, this can be regarded as being contrary to the concept of prudence.

## 20.6.3 Advantages of using LIFO

- The value of closing inventory is based on prices actually paid for the goods.
- Valuation of closing inventory is easy to calculate.
- Issues from stores are valued at most recent prices.
- In times of rising prices LIFO values inventory at lower prices than other methods. This reduces reported profits.

## 20.6.4 Disadvantages of using LIFO

- LIFO is less realistic than FIFO since it assumes that most recently acquired goods will be issued before older goods.
- The most recent prices are not used for inventory valuation purposes.
- LIFO is not accepted by international accounting standards (IAS 2).

## 20.6.5 Advantages of using AVCO

- Issues of goods are made at a weighted average price. This recognises that all issues from stores have equal value and equal importance to the business.
- Variations in issue prices are minimised.
- AVCO allows the comparison of reported profits to be made on a more realistic basis, since any marked changes in the price of inventory issues are ironed out.
- Because the average price used for issues is weighted towards the most recent purchases, the value of closing inventory will be fairly close to the latest prices paid for purchases.
- AVCO is acceptable to the Companies Act 1985 and international accounting standards (IAS 2).

### 20.6.6 Disadvantages of using AVCO

- AVCO requires a new calculation each time a purchase of goods is made. This makes it rather more difficult to calculate than the other two methods.
- The prices charged for issues of inventory will not generally agree with the prices paid to purchase the goods.

## 20.7 Accounting concepts and inventory valuation

You will need to decide which concepts to use when valuing inventory.

- Clearly, the **cost concept** is adhered to.
- The principle of **consistency** is important since results obtained from the financial statements must be able to be used for comparative purposes.
- The concept of **prudence** should be adhered to so that profits are not overstated – this means that the lower of cost and net realisable value should be applied when valuing inventories.
- The **accruals concept** is used when considering repair costs or delivery charges, etc. to be deducted from selling price to determine net realisable value.

IAS 2 states that:

- inventory should be valued at the total of the lower of cost and net realisable value of the separate items of inventory. (It allows the grouping of similar items.)
- FIFO and AVCO are acceptable bases for valuing inventory. LIFO and replacement cost are not acceptable
- inventories include finished goods and work in progress.

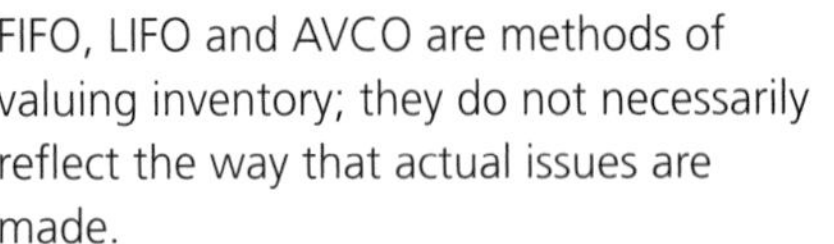

FIFO, LIFO and AVCO are methods of valuing inventory; they do not necessarily reflect the way that actual issues are made.

## 20.8 Inventory reconciliations

The value of inventory that appears as a current asset on a statement of financial position of a business is the result of a physical count and valuation. Although many businesses use a perpetual method of valuing their inventory by the use of bar code technology, the computerised valuation that results from this is invariably incorrect.

How can this be? Computers never make errors! They are much more efficient than people!

It is true that computers can be much faster than we are. They can be more accurate than some of us. So why use a physical means of checking closing inventory?

The computer relies on accurate inputs by receiving departments of a business – no problem. It also relies on accurate records for issues and this is where the problem arises.

Consider your local supermarket. Most goods sold in the store do get scanned and the inventory records are immediately updated, but what of the goods that are stolen and damaged?

None of these 'issues' will be recognised by the computer. This is why a physical check is important to gain an accurate closing inventory figure to complete the financial statements.

One final problem: sometimes it is not possible to make an inventory check immediately after the close of business on the final day of the financial year. Staff may be absent on the day. It may be too big a job to complete in that one day.

Adjustments need to be made to the figures arrived at if the inventory valuation was made after the financial year end in order to determine the actual figure at the appropriate date.

**Goods sent on sale or return** remain the property of the 'sender' until the customer indicates that a sale has taken place.

**Worked example**

Gomez was unable to conduct his annual inventory check on 31 March 2015, his financial year end. However, he was able to complete it on 6 April 2015. The goods held had a value of $8430 on that date.

Gomez provides the following information on transactions that took place between 1 April and 6 April 2015:

goods purchased $450; sales made $600; goods returned by Gomez to suppliers $90; faulty goods returned by customers $120

A mark up of 20 per cent is earned by Gomez on all his sales.

**Required**

Calculate the value of inventory at 31 March 2015.

## Answer

**Gomez**

**Calculation of inventory held at 31 March 2015**

| | **$** | |
|---|---|---|
| Inventory at 6 April 2014 | 8430 | |
| *Less* Net purchases | (360) | ($450 – $90) |
| *Add* Net sales | 400 | ($600 – $120 = $480 ÷ 1.2) |
| Inventory at 31 March 2014 | 8470 | |

**Note**

- The purchases and sales figures are net of returns.
- Inventory is always valued at cost (or net realisable value) so the profit margin included in the net sales figure must be removed.
- Purchases are deducted from the inventory valuation at 6 April since they were not with Gomez at the 31 March. Sales have been added back since Gomez did have these goods at the end of March.

➤ Now try Question 3.

**Self-test questions**

1 Which methods used to value inventory are acceptable under IAS 2?
2 Which methods are acceptable for the purposes of the Companies Act 1985?
3 A greengrocer must always use FIFO as a method of valuing his closing inventory. True/False?
4 Which accounting standard deals with inventory?
5 Which method of inventory valuation uses the most recent prices paid to purchase the goods?
6 In times of rising prices, which method reveals profits earlier than other methods?
7 The closing inventory figure shown on a statement of financial position is always determined by a physical count / computer printout. (Delete the incorrect answer.)
8 Financial year end 31 May. The inventory valuation is conducted on 10 June.
   a How should goods purchased on 7 June be treated?
   b How should sales returns received on 5 June be treated?
9 Borgia sends Mungo some goods on sale or return. Who includes these goods as part of their inventory?
10 If inventory has been overvalued, what effect has this had on reported profits?
11 If inventory has been undervalued, this will __________ reported profits.

➤ Now try Questions 4–6.

## Chapter summary

- FIFO, LIFO and AVCO are methods of valuing inventory.
- Although you should be aware of the characteristics of using LIFO you are not required to be able to calculate the value of closing inventory using the LIFO method of valuation.
- FIFO, LIFO and AVCO are methods of valuing inventory; they do not necessarily determine the order in which goods are actually issued.
- FIFO may be calculated using either a perpetual method or a periodic method. If the method to be used is not stipulated, then use the periodic method. It is quicker and easier, and you are less likely to make an error.
- There is no right or wrong method of valuing inventory but some methods are more acceptable than others.
- The method chosen will determine the level of reported profit.
- If an inventory valuation is made some time after the financial year end a statement showing the necessary adjustment must be prepared to determine the value of inventory held at the financial year end.

# 21 Financial statements

**Content**

**1.4 Preparation of financial statements**

1.4.2 Sole traders

- Prepare an income statement and statement of financial position for a sole trader from full or incomplete accounting records

**By the end of this chapter you should be able to:**

- prepare a 'full set' of financial statements
- understand the relationship between all the parts of financial statements.

## 21.1 Financial statements

**Financial statements** is the term applied to the income statement and the statement of financial position. A 'full set' of financial statements is generally produced at the end of each financial year (although they can be prepared at any time that managers or owners require them).

A 'full set' of **financial statements** enables the owner and managers of a business to see:

- if the business has been profitable
- the assets and liabilities that the business has at the end of the financial year.

**Worked example**

Eduardo provides the following information relating to his shop. All the figures in the list relate to the year ended 28 February 2015, except the inventory figure and the capital figure. These two figures are the value of the inventory at the start of the year and Eduardo's capital at the start of the year.

| | $ |
|---|---|
| Premises | 80000 |
| Fixtures | 14200 |
| Vehicle | 8700 |
| Purchases | 211640 |
| Sales | 408830 |
| Inventory at 1 March 2014 | 26480 |
| Wages | 152610 |
| Light and heating expenses | 8420 |
| Motor expenses | 3170 |
| Drawings | 18500 |
| Advertising | 860 |
| Insurance | 1540 |
| General expenses | 3950 |
| Trade receivables | 1340 |
| Trade payables | 7140 |
| Bank balance | 2790 |
| Capital at 1 March 2014 | 118230 |

Inventory at 28 February 2015 was valued at $24560.

**Required**

Prepare a statement of financial position at 28 February 2015 and an income statement for the year ended 28 February 2015.

## Answer

**Eduardo**

**Statement of financial position at 28 February 2015**

| | $ | $ |
|---|---|---|
| **ASSETS** | | |
| **Non-current assets** | | |
| Premises | | 80 000 |
| Fixtures | | 14 200 |
| Vehicle | | 8 700 |
| | | 102 900 |
| **Current assets** | | |
| Inventory | 24 560 | |
| Trade receivables | 1 340 | |
| Bank balance | 2 790 | 28 690 |
| **Total assets** | | 131 590 |
| **CAPITAL AND LIABILITIES** | | |
| Capital (balancing figure) | | 124450 |
| **Current liabilities** | | |
| Trade payables | | 7 140 |
| **Total capital and liabilities** | | 131 590 |

When you have studied a topic, ask yourself this question:
'Could I explain what I have just learned to a friend who is not an accountant?'
If the answer is 'Yes, I think I could', then you do understand the topic.
If the answer is 'I don't think I could', then further work is required on your part.

We have calculated the capital figure (net assets) at the date of the statement of financial position.

The list provided by Eduardo tells us that one year earlier his capital (net assets) was $118 230.

Eduardo's business has $6 220 more net assets at the end of the financial year than at the start of the year. These assets have been provided by the profits retained in the business over the year.

| | $ |
|---|---|
| Net assets at 28 February 2015 | 124 450 |
| *Less* Net assets 1 March 2014 | 118 230 |
| Profit retained in business | 6 220 |

But, Eduardo has been withdrawing profits all through the year in order to finance his life outside the business. He has been making **drawings** during the year.

These profits (drawings) taken from the business need to be added to the retained profits to tell us the total profit generated by the business during the year.

| | $ |
|---|---|
| Profit retained in the business | 6 220 |
| Profit withdrawn by Eduardo (drawings) | 18 500 |
| Total business profit for the year ended 28 February 2014 | 24 720 |

This calculation does not provide us with the details that may be required for **management** and **stewardship** reasons. Therefore, we must prepare a detailed income statement for the year.

Always give a full heading. Do not abbreviate any part of the heading. State the date in full, for example '31 March 2014' not '31/03/14'. Always use the business name in the heading.

**Eduardo**

**Income statement for the year ended 28 February 2015**

| | **$** | **$** |
|---|---|---|
| Revenue | | 408 830 |
| *Less* Cost of sales | | |
| Inventory 1 March 2014 | 26 480 | |
| Purchases | 211 640 | |
| | 238 120 | |
| *Less* Inventory 28 February 2015 | 24 560 | 213 560 |
| Gross profit | | 195 270 |
| *Less* Expenses | | |
| Wages | 152 610 | |
| Light and heating expenses | 8 420 | |
| Motor expenses | 3 170 | |
| Advertising | 860 | |
| Insurance | 1 540 | |
| General expenses | 3 950 | 170 550 |
| Profit for the year | | 24 720 |

You should now be aware that if a business is making profits the net assets of a business will increase provided those profits are reinvested ('ploughed back') and are not withdrawn from the business.

You should also be aware that if the business was running at a loss the net assets would reduce. Spend a little time running through this in your mind. It is quite sensible. If you do not spend all of your income, the surplus must show up in your net assets.

## 21.2 Preparation of financial statements

Now for a small change in the presentation of the work that has already been covered. Accountants generally present financial statements in a set order. You should now be reasonably confident on the preparation of the statements that make up financial statements.

The income statement is usually presented before the statement of financial position.

To help in the preparation of an income statement and a statement of financial position, you may find it useful to go down the list of information and indicate alongside where each item will be used.

**Example**

| | |
|---|---|
| Purchases | *Trading account* |
| Sales | *Trading account* |
| Wages | *Profit and loss account* |
| Drawings | *Statement of financial position* |
| Machinery | *Statement of financial position* |
| Mortgage on premises | *Statement of financial position* |
| Carriage inwards | *Trading account* |
| Carriage outwards | *Profit and loss account* |

**Worked example**

Emeli owns and runs a vehicle repair garage. She supplies the following information for the year ended 31 May 2015:

| | $ |
|---|---|
| Premises | 180 000 |
| Break-down recovery truck | 24 000 |
| Office furniture | 8 000 |
| Trade receivables | 3 450 |
| Trade payables | 1 673 |
| Inventory at 1 June 2014 | 945 |
| Purchases | 48 620 |
| Sales | 92 431 |
| Wages and general expenses | 23 789 |
| Local taxes | 872 |
| Insurance | 2 150 |
| Advertising | 450 |
| Stationery | 357 |
| Mortgage on premises | 160 000 |
| Drawings | 15 750 |
| Bank balance | 849 |
| Capital at 1 June 2014 | 55 128 |

Emeli has valued her inventory at 31 May 2015 at $1 045.

**Required**

Prepare an income statement for the year ended 31 May 2015 and a statement of financial position at 31 May 2015.

## Answer

**Emeli**

**Income statement for the year ended 31 May 2015**

| | $ | $ |
|---|---|---|
| Revenue | | 92 431 |
| *Less* Cost of sales | | |
| Inventory 1 June 2014 | 945 | |
| Purchases | 48 620 | |
| | 49 565 | |
| *Less* Inventory 31 May 2015 | 1 045 | 48 520 |
| Gross profit | | 43 911 |
| *Less* Expenses | | |
| Wages | 23 789 | |
| Local taxes | 872 | |
| Insurance | 2 150 | |
| Advertising | 450 | |
| Stationery | 357 | 27 618 |
| Profit for the year | | 16 293 |

**Emeli**
**Statement of financial position at 31 May 2015**

| | $ | $ |
|---|---|---|
| **ASSETS** | | |
| **Non-current assets** | | |
| Premises | | 180000 |
| Breakdown truck | | 24000 |
| Office furniture | | 8000 |
| | | 212000 |
| **Current assets** | | |
| Inventory | 1045 | |
| Trade receivables | 3450 | |
| Bank balance | 849 | 5344 |
| **Total assets** | | 217344 |
| **CAPITAL AND LIABILITIES** | | |
| **Capital** (balancing figure) | | 55671 |
| **Non-current liabilities** | | |
| Mortgage on premises | | 160000 |
| **Current liabilities** | | |
| Trade payables | | 1673 |
| **Total capital and liabilities** | | 217344 |

If you are asked to *calculate* profit, use the 'net asset' method; it is much quicker (and you will probably have insufficient information to use any other method).

If you are asked to *prepare* an income statement, then that is precisely what you must show!

We can check to see whether or not we have arrived at the correct figure for Emeli's profit. In Chapter 15 we used the net asset method of calculating profit. We shall use it to check the profit for the year that we have calculated by preparing an income statement.

| | $ |
|---|---|
| Closing capital 31 May 2015 | 55671 |
| *Less* Opening capital 1 June 2014 | 55128 |
| Profits retained in Emeli's business | 543 |
| *Plus* drawings | 15750 |
| Total profits generated by the business | 16293 |

These details are an important source of information so they are usually incorporated into the statement of financial position. From now on we shall include them in any statement of financial position that we prepare.

## 21.3 Capital in the statement of financial position

Talk yourself through this new layout until you remember it.

The way that the information is presented on the statement of financial position is as follows:

| | $ | |
|---|---|---|
| Opening capital | 55128 | *The worth of the business at the start of the year* |
| *Add* Profit for the year | 16293 | *The increase in worth over the year* |
| | 71421 | |
| *Less* Drawings | 15750 | *The decrease in worth during the year because of drawings of profits* |
| Closing capital | 55671 | *The worth of the business at the end of the year* |

**Worked example**

Drew has been trading as a flower seller for some years. The following information relates to his financial year end 31 August 2014:

| | $ |
|---|---|
| Purchases | 58400 |
| Sales | 97260 |
| Inventory 1 September 2013 | 230 |
| General expenses | 4260 |
| Rent and local taxes | 5500 |
| Light and heating expenses | 2300 |
| Stationery and wrapping materials | 8700 |
| Fixtures and fittings | 3400 |
| Vehicle | 7500 |
| Trade receivables | 85 |
| Trade payables | 432 |
| Drawings | 13200 |
| Cash in hand | 87 |
| Balance at bank | 990 |
| Capital 1 September 2013 | 6960 |

The inventory at 31 August 2014 has been valued at $210.

**Required**

Prepare an income statement for the year ended 31 August 2014 and a statement of financial position at that date.

## Answer

**Drew**

**Income statement for the year ended 31 August 2014**

| | $ | $ |
|---|---|---|
| Revenue | | 97260 |
| *Less* Cost of sales | | |
| Inventory 1 September 2013 | 230 | |
| Purchases | 58400 | |
| | 58630 | |
| Inventory 31 August 2014 | 210 | 58420 |
| Gross profit | | 38840 |
| *Less* Expenses | | |
| General expenses | 4260 | |
| Rent and local taxes | 5500 | |
| Light and heating expenses | 2300 | |
| Stationery and wrapping materials | 8700 | 20760 |
| Profit for the year | | 18080 |

**Drew**

**Statement of financial position at 31 August 2014**

| | $ | $ |
|---|---|---|
| **ASSETS** | | |
| **Non-current assets** | | |
| Fixtures and fittings | | 3400 |
| Vehicle | | 7500 |
| | | 10900 |

| | | |
|---|---|---|
| **Current assets** | | |
| Inventory | 210 | |
| Trade receivables | 85 | |
| Balance at bank | 990 | |
| Cash in hand | 87 | 1 372 |
| **Total assets** | | 12 272 |
| | | |
| **CAPITAL AND LIABILITIES** | | |
| **Capital** | | |
| Opening balance | | 6 960 |
| *Add* Profit for the year | | 18 080 |
| | | 25 040 |
| *Less* Drawings | | 13 200 |
| | | 11 840 |
| **Current liabilities** | | |
| Trade payables | | 432 |
| **Total capital and liabilities** | | 12 272 |

➤ Now try Question 1.

Accounting students are frequently asked to correct errors and then to work on a draft profit to arrive at a corrected profit for the period. Make sure you gets lots of practice in this.

## 21.4 The effect that the correction of errors has on financial statements

Any errors occurring in the double-entry system will generally have an effect on:

- profit
- assets
- liabilities *or*
- a combination of any of the three.

Errors that affect the profit of a business will also affect the statement of financial position in that profit affects the owner's capital.

**Worked example**

The following accounts contain errors:

- office equipment account
- sales account
- wages account
- sales returns account
- Horace's account – a trade receivable account.

**Required**

Complete the table showing changes to profit for the year and a statement of financial position when corrections are made.

| Account | Profit | Statement of financial position |
|---|---|---|
| Office equipment account | | |
| Sales account | | |
| Wages account | | |
| Sales returns account | | |
| Horace's account | | |

## Answer

| Account | Profit | Statement of financial position |
|---|---|---|
| Office equipment account | No change | Change to assets |
| Sales account | Change | Change to capital (because of change to profit) |
| Wages account | Change | Change to capital (because of change to profit) |
| Sales returns account | Change | Change to capital (because of change to profit) |
| Horace's account | No change | Change to trade receivables |

After any errors are discovered:

- the journal should be used to effect the changes that are necessary
- the ledger accounts should be corrected
- profit for the period should be adjusted
- changes to items on the statement of financial position should be made.

### Worked example

The trial balance of Divya Talwar failed to balance on 31 March 2015. The difference was entered in a suspense account. A set of draft financial statements was prepared before the errors were discovered. The draft profit for the year was $27 864.

The following errors were discovered:

1 The purchases journal had been overcast by $100.

2 A payment made to M. Dhillon $121 had been posted to the incorrect side of her account.

3 Fixtures purchased for $2340 had been entered in the purchases journal.

4 Goods sold on credit to B. Irfan $97 had been completely omitted from the books of account.

5 An insurance payment for $430 had been correctly entered in the cash book but had not been entered in the insurance account.

**Required**

Prepare:

a general journal entries to correct the errors

b a suspense account showing the correction of appropriate errors

c a statement showing the corrected profit for the year.

## Answer

a

**General journal**

| | Dr | Cr |
|---|---|---|
| | **$** | **$** |
| Suspense account | 100 | |
| Purchases account | | 100 |
| Correction of error: Purchases book overcast by $100 | | |
| M.Dhillon | 242 | |
| Suspense account | | 242 |
| Correction of error: Payment of $121 posted to the incorrect side of Dhillon's account | | |
| Fixtures account | 2 340 | |
| Purchases account | | 2 340 |
| Correction of error: Fittings incorrectly entered in Purchases account | | |

| | | |
|---|---|---|
| B. Irfan | 97 | |
| Sales account | | 97 |
| Correction of error: Sale of goods to Irfan omitted from ledgers | | |
| Insurance account | 430 | |
| Suspense account | | 430 |
| Correction of error: Insurance premium omitted from insurance account | | |

b

| Dr | Suspense account | | Cr |
|---|---|---|---|
| | $ | | $ |
| Purchases account | 100 | M.Dhillon | 242 |
| Trial balance difference* | 572 | Insurance account | 430 |
| | 672 | | 672 |

* The amount of the difference on the trial balance was not given in the question. The $572 must be assumed to be the amount necessary to make the suspense account balance after all the errors have been corrected.

c

**Statement of corrected profit**

| | $ |
|---|---|
| Profit as per draft accounts | 27864 |
| 1 Decrease in purchases | 100 |
| 3 Decrease in purchases | 2340 |
| 4 Increase in sales | 97 |
| 5 Increase in insurance | (430) |
| Corrected profit for the year | 29971 |

- Error 2 does not affect the profit for the year. It would, however, affect the total of trade payables which appears on the statement of financial position. It would reduce current liabilities.
- Error 3 will also decrease profit by the amount of depreciation provided for on the fixtures purchased.

If a transaction has no effect on the answer to a problem, say so. If you do not, no-one will know whether you have omitted the transaction because this is the correct treatment or because you do not know what the effect is.

When correcting a draft profit for the year, remember that:

- any expense account that is debited in the journal will reduce draft profit for the year
- any expense account that is credited in the journal will increase draft profit for the year.

**Notes**

- Always use headings.
- Always give a precise narrative to each journal entry.
- You may have to calculate the trial balance difference to enter in the suspense account.
- Identify any items you have not used in the statement of adjusted profit.

## Self-test questions

1 Why is it important to make the distinction between capital and revenue expenditure?
2 Which statement would you prepare to calculate gross profit?
3 Give an example of a revenue receipt for a restaurant.
4 Which statement would you prepare to calculate net assets?
5 Explain what is meant by the term 'capital receipts'.
6 Which statement would you prepare to calculate the capital of a business?
7 Give two reasons why the owner of a business would prepare financial statements.
8 How is carriage inwards treated in an income statement?
9 In what way is gross profit different to profit for the year?
10 Why are assets shown on a statement of financial position at cost?
11 Define 'drawings'.
12 Sales – Cost of sales – Expenses = ?
13 Closing capital – Opening capital + Drawings = ?
14 List three items that could be classified as current liabilities.
15 Would an error in the purchases returns account affect profit for the year?

➤ **Now try Question 2.**

## Chapter summary

- Financial statements comprise an income statement and a statement of financial position. They are interconnected.
- An income statement contains two accounts, as the name implies: a trading account and a profit and loss account.
- An income statement calculates gross profit and profit for the year.
- The trading account is used to calculate gross profit by deducting the sales at cost price from the sales figure.
- The profit and loss account lists and totals all revenue expenditure incurred during the financial year.
- Total expenditure is deducted from gross profit to determine profit for the period.
- Income statements provide the details for (a) the stewardship function and (b) the management function of accounting.
- The profit for the year is transferred from the income statement to the capital account shown in the statement of financial position.

# 22 Incomplete records

**Content**

**1.4 Preparation of financial statements**

1.4.2 Sole traders

- Prepare an income statement and statement of financial position for a sole trader from full or incomplete records

**By the end of this chapter, you should be able to:**

- calculate the profit or loss earned by a cash-based business
- prepare a 'full set' of financial statements for a cash-based business
- calculate the amount of cash missing from a business
- calculate the amount of inventory missing from a business.

There are two main types of organisation that may not keep a full set of double-entry records: small cash-based businesses, and clubs and societies.

Make sure you know about both types of organisation. They both rely on similar skills and techniques in order to prepare a full set of financial statements.

In this chapter we turn our attention to small cash-based businesses.

## 22.1 Small cash-based businesses

Much of the work of any professional accountant is taken up with the preparation of the financial statements of small businesses. Because many of these carry on their business on a cash basis, they will not keep a full set of ledgers in which to record their business transactions.

Remember that a sales ledger will contain the accounts of all credit customers. Since the vast majority of the customers of small businesses pay cash, there is no need to open accounts for them.

Also many (if not all) of the purchases of goods for resale and the services consumed will be paid for by using cash or by writing cheques.

The main book for the recording of transactions for these small businesses will be a cash book in which all transactions using cash or cheques will be recorded. The information contained in the cash book will be supplemented by bank statements, till rolls and by invoices and receipts.

The task that is faced in this situation is to build up a more complete picture of the financial transactions that have taken place during the financial year than the one that is shown by the cash book on its own.

There are two main types of questions on this topic:

- those where you are required to calculate the business's profit or loss
- those where you are required to prepare an income statement for the business.

It is important that you are able to recognise each type of question.

## 22.2 Calculation of the profit or loss of a cash-based business

Tip 

The key to recognising what is required is found in the wording. This type of question will always ask you to *calculate* the profit or loss for the business.

There are five stages to calculate the profit or loss for a business. You have already used them in Chapter 15. You will use a shortened version in Chapter 33.

- Stage 1: Calculate the opening capital (net assets) of the business either by listing the assets and then deducting the liabilities or by preparing a statement of affairs.
- Stage 2: Calculate the closing capital (net assets).
- Stage 3: Deduct the opening capital from the closing capital. This will indicate the profit or loss retained in the business.
- Stage 4: Some profits may have been taken out of the business during the year in the form of cash and/or goods (or services) as drawings. These **drawings** (profits) have to be added to the retained profits.
- Stage 5: Deduct capital introduced. Sometimes the proprietor of a business may inject new capital into the business. This extra capital will increase the assets owned by the business at the end of the year: in turn this will increase the figure we have calculated as retained profit (it could reduce the figure calculated as a retained loss). Obviously, the amount of capital introduced is not an increase in the net assets earned by the business so it must be disregarded in our calculation – hence Stage 5: deduct capital introduced.

We can summarise these stages as follows:

| | |
|---|---|
| | Closing capital |
| *Deduct* | Opening capital |
| Retained profit | xxxxxxxxxxxx |
| *Add* | Drawings |
| | xxxxxxxxxxxx |
| *Deduct* | Capital introduced |
| Profit (loss) for the year | xxxxxxxxxxxx |

**Worked example**

At 1 January 2014 Gaston had the following assets and liabilities:

vehicle at valuation $2400; equipment at valuation $5400; inventory $670; trade receivables $45; bank balance $1730; trade payables $260.

At 31 December 2014 he had the following assets and liabilities:

vehicles at valuation $12400; equipment at valuation $4860; inventory $590; trade receivables $55; bank balance $2540; trade payables $180.

During the year Gaston withdrew $16750 cash from the business for his household expenses. He also withdrew goods to the value of $1230 for personal use.

**Required**

Calculate the business profit or loss for the year ended 31 December 2014.

Tip  

Note the wording of what is required: the key word is 'calculate'.

Tip  

Always show your workings – they can help you find any errors in your calculations.

### Answer

| | $ | |
|---|---|---|
| Closing capital | 20265 | (12400 + 4860 + 590 + 55 + 2540 – 180) |
| *Less* Opening capital | 9985 | (2400 + 5400 + 670 + 45 + 1730 – 260) |
| Retained profits | 10280 | |
| *Add* Drawings | 17980 | (16750 + 1230) |
| Profit for the year ended 31 December 2014 | 28260 | |

**Worked example**

Dreyfus supplies the following information relating to his business:

| | at 31 March 2015 | at 30 April 2014 |
|---|---|---|
| | **$** | **$** |
| Premises at cost | 60000 | 60000 |
| Machinery at valuation | 32400 | 36000 |
| Vehicles at valuation | 11340 | 12600 |
| Inventory | 2120 | 1650 |
| Trade receivables | 120 | 135 |
| Trade payables | 430 | 470 |
| Bank balance | 3560 | 1450 |

During the year ended 31 March 2015 Dreyfus made drawings of $23700. In February 2015 he inherited a legacy of $7800 from a relative; he paid this sum into the business bank account.

**Required**

Calculate the business profit or loss for the year ended 31 March 2015.

## Answer

| | $ |
|---|---|
| Closing capital | 109110 |
| *Less* Opening capital | 111365 |
| Retained profits | (2255) |
| *Add* Drawings | 23700 |
| | 21445 |
| *Less* Capital introduced | 7800 |
| Profit for the year ended 31 March 2015 | 13645 |

**Workings**

Closing capital = $60000 + $32400 + $11340 + $2120 + $120 + $3560 − $430

= $109110

Opening capital = $60000 + $36000 + $12600 + $1650 + $135 + $1450 − $470

= $111365

➤ Now try Questions 1 and 2.

## 22.3 Preparation of financial statements of a cash-based business

We have seen how we can calculate the profit or loss by comparing closing and opening capital values. In real life this is usually not sufficient to satisfy the tax authorities. This government department generally requires more detailed records to be kept.

The records do not have to be a full set of double-entry records – there is no statutory requirement that sole traders or partnerships should maintain a full set of accounting records.

However, to satisfy the authorities, most traders do keep a record of all cash and bank transactions. They also keep all source documents received and copies of those sent. The source documents would include: purchases invoices, copies of sales invoices, bank statements, cheque book counterfoils, paying in counterfoils, till rolls, invoices from the utilities (gas, electricity, water), etc. The source documents are records of all monies received and paid out.

These source documents will:

- help us build up a picture of the financial transactions that have taken place throughout the financial year
- verify the receipts and payments made.

Whenever you are asked to prepare an income statement and a statement of financial position, you will need to follow the procedures outlined below. So we must examine our task very carefully.

In order to be able to use this second method it is essential that we have the following information to hand:

- valuations of assets and liabilities at the start of the financial year
- totals of trade receivables and trade payables at the start of the financial year
- accrued expenses at the start of the year
- prepayments made at the start of the financial year
- payments made by trade receivables during the financial year
- payments made to trade payables during the financial year
- cash payments made during the financial year
- cash receipts during the financial year
- valuations of assets and liabilities at the end of the financial year
- totals of trade receivables and trade payables at the end of the financial year
- accrued expenses (payables) at the end of the financial year
- prepayments (receivables) made at the end of the financial year.

Learn these five stages – they are very important.

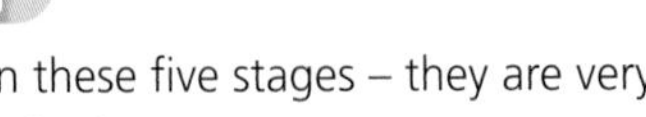

There are five stages involved in the preparation of the financial statements from a set of records that are incomplete.

- Stage 1: Prepare an opening statement of affairs. You may have to calculate the capital (net assets) figure if it is not provided for you.
- Stage 2: Compile a summary of bank transactions.
- Stage 3: Compile a summary of cash transactions.
- Stage 4: Construct adjustment accounts (some teachers call these 'control accounts').
- Stage 5: Prepare the financial statements by using all the information gained from Stages 1, 2, 3 and 4.

It is essential to follow these stages methodically each time you are asked to produce a set of financial statements from incomplete records.

The stage that gives most people a problem is Stage 4.

Stage 4 is necessary because most of the records kept by traders who keep less than a full set of books of account are records of cash spent to acquire the necessary resources to carry on business or records of cash when it is received.

As accountants, we must be aware of and apply the **accruals concept** – the payment to acquire a resource is not the same as the use of that resource.

Consider this example:

**Example**

Rohan receives $120 on 15 February 2015 for a sale of goods that took place on 21 December 2014.

Cash was recorded in February – the profit was earned in December (application of the realisation concept, which is part of the accruals concept).

The electricity meter was read on 28 July for electricity used in May, June and July. The invoice for electricity used was received on 13 August and the amount was paid (very late!) on 12 October.

Electricity (a resource) was used in May, June and July, so the expense is recorded then – even though the payment was not made until October.

---

Stage 4 sounds very complicated, but if we rely on first principles that we learned earlier it should be simplified.

- Rely on your knowledge of double entry.
- Rely on using 'T' accounts.

We will concentrate on Stage 4 since this is the stage that seems to cause most problems.

**Worked example**

Saleem Zain does not keep full accounting records. He is able to provide the following information for the year ended 28 February 2015:

**Summarised bank account**

| | $ | | $ |
|---|---|---|---|
| Balance 1 March 2014 | 1 456 | Payments to trade payables | 43 675 |
| Receipts from trade receivables | 86 494 | General expenses | 24 911 |
| | | Purchase of non-current asset | 17 500 |
| | | Balance 28 February 2015 | 1 864 |
| | 87 950 | | 87 950 |

**Additional information**

| | at 28 February 2015 | at 1 March 2014 |
|---|---|---|
| | $ | $ |
| Trade receivables | 918 | 752 |
| Trade payables | 633 | 857 |
| Inventory | 2 779 | 2 152 |

**Required**

Prepare the trading account for the year ended 28 February 2015.

## Workings

We need to prepare an adjustment account in order to determine the amount of sales for the year. (Remember that this may be different to the cash paid to the trade receivables during the year.)

We also need to construct a similar account to determine the amount of the purchases for the year.

Note that 'missing figures' for sales and purchases in the following accounts are italicised.

To avoid making an error with your receivables and payables always put the closing balances under the account totals and 'bring them up into the account':

- Receivables (debtors) on the debit *under the account*
- Payables (creditors) on the credit *under the account*

**Trade receivables account**

| | $ | | $ |
|---|---|---|---|
| Balance b/d | 752 | Cash received | 86494 |
| *Sales* | *86660* | Balance c/d | 918 |
| | 87412 | | 87412 |
| Balance b/d | 918 | | |

**Trade payables account**

| | $ | | $ |
|---|---|---|---|
| Cash paid | 43675 | Balance b/d | 857 |
| Balance c/d | 633 | *Purchases* | *43451* |
| | 44308 | | 44308 |
| | | Balance b/d | 633 |

## Answer

**Saleem Zain**

**Trading account for the year ended 28 February 2015**

| | $ | $ |
|---|---|---|
| Revenue | | 86660 |
| *Less* Cost of sales | | |
| Inventory 1 March 2014 | 2152 | |
| Purchases | 43451 | |
| | 45603 | |
| Inventory 28 February 2015 | (2779) | 42824 |
| Gross profit | | 43836 |

➤ Now try Question 3.

We can use the same approach to determine the amount of any expenses to be entered to the income statement if we know the cash paid and the amount of any accruals and prepayments outstanding at the end of the financial year.

**Worked example**

Harry Cary does not keep a full set of accounting records but he is able to provide the following information for the year ended 31 July 2015:

| | $ |
|---|---|
| Amounts paid for staff wages | 21387 |
| Amounts paid to landlord for rent | 3400 |
| Amounts paid for electricity | 2162 |
| Amounts paid for insurances | 3467 |

**Additional information**

| | at 31 July 2015 | at 1 August 2014 |
|---|---|---|
| **Amounts owed** | $ | $ |
| for staff wages | 297 | 212 |
| for rent | 136 | 118 |
| for electricity | 48 | 167 |
| **Amount paid in advance** for insurances | 346 | 196 |

**Required**

Calculate the amounts to be included in the income statement for the year ended 31 July 2015.

## Answer

| | |
|---|---|
| Wages | $21472 |
| Rent | $3418 |
| Electricity | $2043 |
| Insurances | $3317 |

Notice that the balances have been brought down. Remember, this is important!

## Workings

Use the same procedure that was used to determine sales and purchases earlier.

**Wages account**

| | $ | | $ |
|---|---|---|---|
| Cash | 21 387 | Balance b/d 1 August 2014 | 212 |
| Balance c/d 31 July 2015 | 297 | *Income statement* | *21 472* |
| | 21 684 | | 21 684 |
| | | Balance b/d 1 August 2015 | 297 |

**Rent account**

| | $ | | $ |
|---|---|---|---|
| Cash | 3 400 | Balance b/d 1 August 2014 | 118 |
| Balance c/d 31 July 2015 | 136 | *Income statement* | *3 418* |
| | 3 536 | | 3 536 |
| | | Balance b/d 1 August 2015 | 136 |

**Electricity account**

| | $ | | $ |
|---|---|---|---|
| Cash | 2 162 | Balance b/d 1 August 2014 | 167 |
| Balance c/d 31 July 2015 | 48 | *Income statement* | *2 043* |
| | 2 210 | | 2 210 |
| | | Balance b/d 1 August 2015 | 48 |

**Insurances account**

| | $ | | $ |
|---|---|---|---|
| Balance b/d 1 August 2014 | 196 | *Income statement* | *3 317* |
| Cash | 3 467 | Balance c/d 31 July 2015 | 346 |
| | 3 663 | | 3 663 |
| Balance b/d 1 August 2015 | 346 | | |

➤ **Now try Question 4.**

We shall now work through an example that incorporates the techniques outlined above using the five stages outlined at the start of this section.

**Worked example**

Roger Guillaume owns a shop selling flowers. He does not maintain proper books of account. He provides the following information for the year ended 30 April 2015:

**Summarised bank account**

| | $ | | $ |
|---|---|---|---|
| Balance 1 May 2014 | 1 793 | Payments to creditors | 22 497 |
| Takings banked | 74 887 | Local taxes | 2 430 |
| | | Rent | 2 800 |
| | | Other expenses | 20 075 |
| | | Drawings | 8 409 |
| | | Purchase of vehicle | 17 000 |
| | | Balance 30 April 2015 | 3 469 |
| | 76 680 | | 76 680 |

All takings were paid into the bank account with the exception of the following:

| | |
|---|---|
| Wages | $14 280 |
| Drawings | $12 000 |

**Additional information**

| | at 30 April 2015 | at 1 May 2014 |
|---|---|---|
| | $ | $ |
| **Assets and liabilities** | | |
| Inventory | 164 | 212 |
| Trade receivables | 130 | 48 |
| Trade payables | 328 | 467 |
| Cash in hand | 237 | 142 |
| Local taxes paid in advance | 1 340 | 1 080 |
| Rent owed | 120 | 102 |
| Fixtures at valuation | 648 | 720 |
| Vehicles at valuation | 16 500 | 4 200 |

**Required**

Prepare an income statement for the year ended 30 April 2015 and a statement of financial position at that date.

## Workings

Note that because we are asked for the *preparation* of a set of financial statements, we must go carefully and methodically through each of the five stages outlined earlier.

If we are asked for a *calculation* of the profit or loss, we could have used the much quicker net asset (capital) method.

Both methods will give us the same profit figure but the net asset method will not give us the same amount of detail that a full set of financial statements will.

Stage 1 is part of your workings *but* do write the figures down neatly as well as quickly.

### Stage 1

Prepare an opening statement of affairs. Do not be concerned with categories of assets and liabilities. At this point in your studies, you should be able to do this almost as quickly as you can write the items down.

**Statement of affairs at 1 May 2014**

| | | $ | $ | |
|---|---|---|---|---|
| **Assets** | Inventory | | 212 | |
| | Trade receivables | | 48 | |
| | Local taxes paid in advance | | 1 080 | |
| | Cash | | 142 | |
| | Local taxes paid in advance | | 1 080 | |
| | Fixtures | | 720 | |
| | Vehicles | | 4 200 | |
| *Don't forget ...* | Bank balance | | 1 793 | |
| | | | 8 195 | |
| **Liabilities** | Trade payables | (467) | | |
| | Rent owed | (102) | | |
| | | | (569) | |
| | Net assets | | 7 626 | *This is also Roger's capital.* |

Do not just key the assets and liabilities into your calculator. You will not be able to find the error if you make one. Write the items down as part of your answer before you key the amounts in.

Note that the assets have been written down in the order that they have appeared in the question. No attempt has been made to categorise them. The question did not ask you to prepare an opening statement of financial position.

Do take care to include the bank balance if it is not included in the list of assets and liabilities given.

### Stages 2 and 3

Compile summarised cash and/or bank accounts. A bank summary has been provided for us, but we do need to prepare a cash summary.

**Cash account**

| | $ | | $ |
|---|---|---|---|
| Balance 1 May 2014 (from list of assets) | 142 | Takings banked (from bank summary) | 74 887 |
| *Total takings for year (missing figure)* | *101 262* | Wages paid | 14 280 |
| | | Drawings | 12 000 |
| | | Balance 30 April 2015 (from list of closing balances) | 237 |
| | 101 404 | | 101 404 |

### Stage 4

Construct adjustment accounts. You may be uncertain how many adjustment accounts to use, on which accounts to open and which items do not need to be adjusted. Then open an account for every item listed in your statement of affairs.

Inventory will be adjusted in Stage 5 in the trading account of the income statement; we have adjusted our cash figures in Stage 2; bank has been adjusted for us in the question.

Open an adjustment account for each of: trade receivables; local taxes fixtures; trade payables; and finally rent.

Do each adjustment in turn. Open a 'T' account for each.

1 Enter the opening balance (debit for an asset credit for a liability).
2 Enter the closing balance under your 'T' account.
3 Take the closing balance up diagonally into the body of the account.
4 From the bank or cash account, debit cash paid.
5 From the bank or cash account, credit cash received.
6 and 7 Total the account.
8 Calculate the *missing figure* to be posted to the income statement.

Let us prepare the adjustment accounts. Numbers are given in the first two accounts as a guide to the order in which the entries are made.

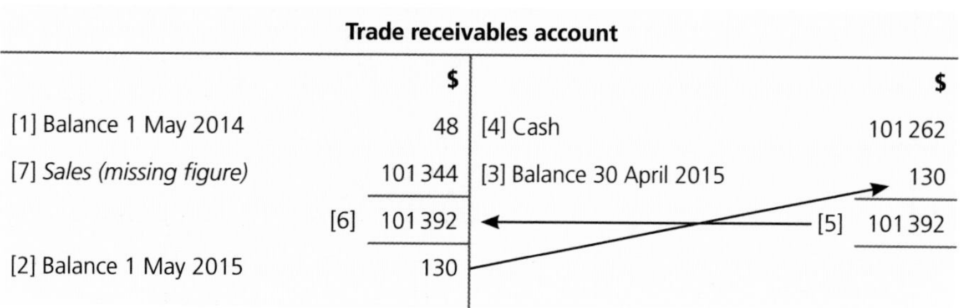

**Trade receivables account**

| | $ | | $ |
|---|---|---|---|
| [1] Balance 1 May 2014 | 48 | [4] Cash | 101 262 |
| [7] *Sales (missing figure)* | 101 344 | [3] Balance 30 April 2015 | 130 |
| | [6] 101 392 | | [5] 101 392 |
| [2] Balance 1 May 2015 | 130 | | |

Tip 

Show all your workings, no matter how trivial they seem to be. They are useful in finding any error in compiling your financial statements.

**Local taxes account**

| | | $ | | | $ |
|---|---|---|---|---|---|
| [1] Balance 1 May 2014 | | 1 080 | [7] *Inc stat (missing figure)* | | *2 170* |
| [4] Cash | | 2 430 | [3] Balance 30 April 2015 | | 1 340 |
| | [5] | 3 510 | | [6] | 3 510 |
| [2] Balance 1 May 2015 | | 1 340 | | | |

**Fixtures account**

| | $ | | $ |
|---|---|---|---|
| Balance 1 May 2014 | 720 | *Inc stat (missing figure – depreciation)* | *72* |
| | | Balance 30 April 2015 | 648 |
| | 720 | | 720 |
| Balance 1 May 2015 | 648 | | |

**Vehicles account**

| | $ | | $ |
|---|---|---|---|
| Balance 1 May 2014 | 4 200 | *Inc stat (missing figure – depreciation)* | *4 700* |
| Cash | 17 000 | Balance 30 April 2015 | 16 500 |
| | 21 200 | | 21 200 |
| Balance 1 May 2015 | 16 500 | | |

**Trade payables account**

| | $ | | $ |
|---|---|---|---|
| Cash | 22 497 | Balance 1 May 2014 | 467 |
| Balance 30 April 2015 | 328 | *Purchases (missing figure)* | *22 358* |
| | 22 825 | | 22 825 |
| | | Balance 1 May 2015 | 328 |

**Rent account**

| | $ | | $ |
|---|---|---|---|
| Cash | 2 800 | Balance 1 May 2014 | 102 |
| Balance 30 April 2015 | 120 | *Inc stat ( missing figure)* | *2 818* |
| | 2 920 | | 2 920 |
| | | Balance 1 May 2015 | 120 |

Generally at this point you will not have reached your goal unless you were specifically asked to prepare the opening statement of affairs or one or two of the adjustment accounts in detail. Here we were asked to prepare an income statement and a statement of financial position and as yet we have not done that. All that we have done is the preparatory work – we have got all our information ready for the final part of the answer.

An accountant in practice would call all the workings that we have done so far 'working papers'.

## Stage 5

It is now time for Stage 5, where we bring all our workings together to prepare the financial statements.

## Answer

**Roger Guillaume**

**Income statement for the year ended 30 April 2015**

| | $ | $ |
|---|---|---|
| Revenue | | 101 344 |
| *Less* Cost of sales | | |
| Inventory at 1 May 2014 | 212 | |
| Purchases | 22 358 | |
| | 22 570 | |

| | | |
|---|---|---|
| Inventory at 30 April 2015 | (164) | 22 406 |
| Gross profit | | 78 938 |
| *Less* Expenses | | |
| Local taxes | 2 170 | |
| Rent | 2 818 | |
| Wages | 14 280 | |
| Other expenses | 20 075 | |
| Depreciation – Fixtures | 72 | |
| Vehicles | 4 700 | 44 115 |
| Profit for the year | | 34 823 |

**Roger Guillaume**

**Statement of financial position at 30 April 2015**

| | **$** | **$** |
|---|---|---|
| **ASSETS** | | |
| **Non-current assets** | | |
| Fixtures at valuation | | 648 |
| Vehicles at valuation | | 16 500 |
| | | 17 148 |
| **Current assets** | | |
| Inventory | 164 | |
| Trade receivables | 130 | |
| Other receivables (local taxes) | 1 340 | |
| Bank balance | 3 469 | |
| Cash | 237 | 5 340 |
| **Total assets** | | 22 488 |
| | | |
| **CAPITAL AND LIABILITIES** | | |
| **Capital** | | |
| Opening balance | | 7 626 |
| *Add* Profit for the year | | 34 823 |
| | | 42 449 |
| *Less* Drawings | | 20 409 |
| | | 22 040 |
| | | |
| **Current liabilities** | | |
| Trade payables | 328 | |
| Other payables (rent) | 120 | 448 |
| **Total capital and liabilities** | | 22 488 |

## 22.4 Calculation of missing cash

You may be told that cash has been stolen during the course of the year; your task is to calculate the amount of cash that is missing.

The procedure involves working out what the cash position would have been, had the theft not occurred and comparing that position with the actual position.

**Worked example**

Adele owns a general store. At 1 January 2014 her cash in hand was $167. At the end of the year on 31 December 2014 cash in hand was $143. Her till rolls show her takings to be $53788. During the year she banked $21894 after taking $13600 cash for private use and paying wages $17840.

Adele believes that some cash has been stolen in a burglary in the last week of December.

**Required**

Calculate the amount of cash stolen.

## Answer

**Cash account**

| | $ | | $ |
|---|---|---|---|
| Cash in hand 1 January 2014 | 167 | Cash banked | 21894 |
| Takings | 53788 | Drawings | 13600 |
| | | Wages | 17840 |
| | | *Cash stolen (missing figure)* | *478* |
| | | Cash in hand 31 December 2014 | 143 |
| | 53955 | | 53955 |

Note that the question asked for a calculation, not for an account. The answer has been given in account form as this fits in with the workings used throughout the chapter, but the same result could have been gained by other means.

There are a variety of ways of arriving at the correct answer. Each would be acceptable. However, do show full workings if you choose another method of arriving at your answer.

## 22.5 Calculation of missing inventory

To calculate the value of inventory that has gone missing during a financial year a trading account from the income statement that uses *actual figures* is compared to the figures that ought to have applied.

**Worked example**

Gary owns a hairdressing salon. Several boxes of 'Hairglo', an expensive hair product, have been stolen. Gary is unsure of the value of the stolen goods. He provides the following information for the year ended 30 April 2015:

- inventory of Hairglo at 1 May 2014 $210
- inventory of Hairglo at 30 April 2015 $70
- purchases of Hairglo during the year ended 30 April 2015 $4690
- sales of Hairglo during the year $7080.

Hairglo carries a uniform mark-up of 50 per cent.

**Required**

Calculate the value of the missing inventory.

## Answer

| | Actual figures are: | | They should be: | |
|---|---|---|---|---|
| | $ | $ | $ | $ |
| Revenue | | 7 080 | | 7 080 |
| *Less* Cost of sales | | | | |
| Inventory at 1 May 2014 | 210 | | 210 | |
| Purchases | 4 690 | | 4 690 | |
| | 4 900 | | 4 900 | |
| Inventory 30 April 2015 | 70 | | 180 | 4 720 |
| Stolen goods (*missing figure*) | *110* | 4 720 | | |
| Gross profit | | 2 360 | | 2 360 |

Note the closing inventory $70 appears as a current asset on the statement of financial position. The mark-up percentage was used to calculate the gross profit.

The stolen inventory of Hairglo, $110, must appear as an expense on the income statement to complete the double entry.

### Self-test questions

1 A statement of affairs is the same as a ____________.
2 Total assets – Total liabilities = ____________.
3 Opening capital + Profit for year – Drawings = ____________.
4 Closing capital – Opening capital = ____________.
5 Profits retained in the business + Drawings = ____________.
6 Profits retained in the business ____________ Drawings ____________ Capital introduced = Profit for year.
7 Opening balance in a vehicles account is $23 000. No purchases or sales of vehicles take place over the year. The closing balance is $18 000. What does the difference in balances represent?
8 Cash paid to credit suppliers during the year is credited to the trade payables adjustment account. True/False?
9 Cash received from credit customers during the year is credited to the trade receivables adjustment account. True/False?
10 Sole traders are required by law to keep a full set of double-entry books. True/False?

➤ Now try Questions 5–8.

### Chapter summary

- Profit for the year can be calculated by comparing net assets at the start of a period (usually a year) with net assets at the end of the period.
- This is a very accurate way of determining profit but it has the major drawback that it does not show all the financial details of exactly how this profit was earned. This detail is essential for stewardship and management purposes.
- If a set of financial statements is to be prepared, then the five-step approach must be adopted:
  1 Prepare an opening statement of affairs.
  2 Compile a summary of bank transactions.
  3 Compile a summary of cash transactions.
  4 Construct adjustment accounts.
  5 Prepare financial statements.

# 23 Partnership accounting

**Content**

**1.4 Preparation of financial statements**

1.4.3 Partnerships

- Prepare an income statement, appropriation account and statement of financial position for a partnership from full or incomplete accounting records
- Prepare capital and current accounts

**By the end of this chapter, you should be able to:**

- discuss the differences between being a sole trader and being in a partnership
- outline the advantages and disadvantages of both forms of business ownership
- prepare partnership income statements and incorporate partners' salaries, interest on capital and interest on drawings
- prepare partners' capital and current accounts.

## 23.1 Sole traders

Up to now we have concentrated much of our studies on the books of account and financial statements of the simplest form of business organisation – that is, the sole trader.

Although being a sole trader does have many advantages, many people form partnerships.

**Table 23.1** Advantages and disadvantages of being a sole trader

| Advantages | Disadvantages |
|---|---|
| The sole trader has complete control over how the business is run, so success or failure is dependent on the trader. | The sole trader has unlimited liability for the debts of the business. |
| The business can be established with the minimum of legal formalities. | Being a sole trader may involve long hours of work. |
| The financial results of the business do not need to be divulged to other members of the general public. | Illness or other reasons that cause absence may affect the running of the business. |
| | There is no-one with whom to share problems or ideas. |
| | It may be difficult to raise extra finance when it is needed. |

Expansion of a business usually involves raising extra finance. Raising the necessary finance is very difficult without involving other people. This generally means that a sole trader is faced with the choice of converting the business into either a partnership or a limited liability company.

We will deal with limited companies in Chapter 25.

## 23.2 Partnership accounting

The UK Partnership Act of 1890 defines a **partnership** as 'the relationship which subsists between persons carrying on business with a view of profit'.

Forming a partnership overcomes some of the disadvantages associated with being in business as a sole trader.

**Table 23.2** Advantages and disadvantages of being in partnership

| Advantages | Disadvantages |
|---|---|
| Access to more capital. | Partners have less independence than sole traders. Decisions have to be agreed by all partners. So, a partner's ideas for development of the business may be frustrated by other partner(s). |
| Partners can share the workload. | The number of partners is limited to 20 (at least as far as we are concerned). There are exceptions to this limit, e.g. firms of solicitors, accountants, etc. |
| Partners can pool ideas and share problems. | Partners have unlimited liability for the debts of the business. |

You can tell this is a partnership business by the use of two partners' names.

It is usual for a partnership to have a written partnership agreement (although it is possible that the agreement could be a verbal one); this will reduce the possibility of any disputes arising.

The agreement usually covers:

- the duties of the individual partners
- the amount of capital to be subscribed by each of the partners
- the ways that profits are to be shared
- the financial arrangements if there are any changes to the structure of the partnership.

If there is no agreement, the Partnership Act of 1890 lays down the following rules which must apply:

- Partners should contribute equal amounts of capital.
- No partner should be entitled to interest on capital.
- No partner is entitled to a salary.
- No partner is to be charged interest on drawings.
- Residual profits or losses are to be shared equally.
- Any loan made to the partnership by a partner will carry interest at the rate of five per cent per annum.

**Tip**

If no details of the way profits are to be shared are given, you must assume that no partnership agreement exists and so the Partnership Act of 1890 applies.

**Self-test questions**

1 A sole trader has limited liability. True/False?
2 Partners have unlimited liability. True/False?
3 Explain two advantages of being in partnership.
4 Give the date of the Partnership Act that governs the basic rules that apply if a partnership does not have a partnership agreement.
5 List four rules that apply if a partnership does not have a partnership agreement.

## 23.3 Partnership income statements

The internal financial statements for all businesses are prepared in much the same way in most respects. It is only after the calculation of profit for the year that a change may take place.

When you prepared the financial statements of a sole trader, the profit (or loss) was entered in the trader's capital account.

The profit (or loss) earned by a partnership has to be shared between the partners in accordance with any agreement (or according to the Act if there is no agreement).

How profits (or losses) are distributed is shown in detail in the final section of the income statement.

The **appropriation account** shows how profits (or losses) are shared between partners.

**Residual profits (or losses)** are the profits (or losses) that remain once all appropriations of profits for the year have been allocated to the partners.

Partners usually agree to share profits in ways that will reflect:

- the workload of each partner
- the amount of capital invested in the business by each partner
- the risk-taking element of being in business.

Partners, like all entrepreneurs, receive a share of profits, the profit division is shown in the **appropriation account** under the following headings:

- salaries
- interest on capital
- share of **residual profits**.

**Self-test questions**

6 Explain the term 'appropriation'.
7 Why is an appropriation account included in an income statement for a partnership?
8 Explain the term 'residual profit'.

### 23.3.1 Partners' salaries

**Worked example**

Antoine and Burcu are in partnership, sharing residual profits in the ratio of 2:1 respectively.

The profit (before tax) for the year ended 31 July 2014 was $36 450.

**Required**

Prepare an appropriation account for the year ended 31 July 2014.

#### Answer

**Antoine and Burcu**
**Appropriation account for the year ended 31 July 2014**

| | $ | $ |
|---|---|---|
| Profit for the year | | 36 450 |
| Share of profit – Antoine | (24 300) | |
| Burcu | (12 150) | (36 450) |

Note that negative numbers are sometimes shown in brackets.

If a partner is entitled to a partnership salary, this is taken from the profit for the year before the residual profit shares are calculated.

**Worked example**

Conserva and Divya are in partnership, sharing residual profits in the ratio 3:2 respectively after crediting Divya with a partnership salary of $4 200.

The profit for the year ended 31 December 2014 was $29 460.

**Required**

Prepare an appropriation account for the year ended 31 December 2014.

## Answer

**Conserva and Divya**

**Appropriation account for the year ended 31 December 2014**

| | | $ | $ |
|---|---|---|---|
| Profit for the year | | | 29460 |
| *Less* Salary – Divya | | | (4200) |
| | | | 25260 |
| Share of profit – | Conserva | (15156) | |
| | Divya | (10104) | (25260) |

**Note**

- Divya's salary is deducted before the sharing of residual profits.
- Divya's share of profits is $14304. (She does not earn a salary in the same way that employees earn a salary, she is a part owner of the business and as such she earns profits no matter how they are described.)

## 23.3.2 Interest on partners' capital account balances

**Worked example**

Enriques and Faraz are in partnership. They maintain fixed capital accounts, the balances of which are $30000 and $20000 respectively. Their partnership agreement provides that profits and losses are shared 2:1 after interest on capital is provided at eight per cent per annum. The profit for the year ended 31 March 2015 was $32269.

**Required**

Prepare an appropriation account for the year ended 31 March 2015.

## Answer

**Enriques and Faraz**

**Appropriation account for the year ended 31 March 2015**

| | $ | $ |
|---|---|---|
| Profit for the year | | 32269 |
| *Less* Interest on capital – Enriques | (2400) | |
| Faraz | (1600) | (4000) |
| | | 28269 |
| Share of profit – Enriques | (18846) | |
| Faraz | (9423) | (28269) |

Note the use of the 'inset' to show clearly the individual appropriations and the total appropriations.

- Enriques' share of the profit is $21246 (interest $2400 plus $18846 share of residual profit).
- Faraz's share of the profit is $11023.

## Worked example

Gervais and Harpreet are in partnership. They maintain fixed capital accounts at $50 000 and $32 000 respectively. The profit for the year ended 31 August 2014 was $47 632.

The partnership agreement provides that Harpreet be credited with a partnership salary of $3750 per annum; that interest at the rate of seven per cent per annum be credited on partners' capital account balances; and that residual profits be shared in the ratio 4:1 respectively.

**Required**

Prepare an appropriation account for the year ended 31 August 2014.

## Answer

**Gervais and Harpreet**

**Appropriation account for the year ended 31 August 2014**

| | $ | $ |
|---|---|---|
| Profit for the year | | 47 632 |
| *Less* Salary – Harpreet | | (3750) |
| | | 43 882 |
| *Less* Interest on capital – Gervais | (3 500) | |
| Harpreet | (2 240) | (5 740) |
| | | 38 142 |
| Share of profit – Gervais | (30 514) | |
| Harpreet | (7 628) | (38 142) |

➤ Now try Questions 1–3.

Note that the residual profit shares have been rounded.

**Tip**

If figures do not divide exactly, quickly check that you have not overlooked an entry somewhere. If nothing has been missed, then 'round' your figures.

## Self-test questions

9 Explain why a partner may be entitled to a partnership salary.

10 Interest on capital is paid to a partnership by the business's bankers. True/False?

11 Profit for the year is $40 000, partners' salaries are £12 000 and interest on capital is $16 000. Calculate the amount of residual profits.

12 A partner works as a sales assistant in the partnership store. Explain how his partnership salary should be shown in an income statement.

### 23.3.3 Interest on partners' drawings

Some partnership agreements provide that partners will be charged interest on any drawings made during the financial year. This is supposed to deter partners from drawing cash from the business in the early part of the financial year.

We say 'supposed' since, if a partner needs to draw cash from the business, an interest charge is hardly likely to act as a deterrent.

## Worked example

The partnership agreement of Arbuthnot and Beebee provides that interest be charged on drawings at five per cent per annum. The business year end is 31 December.

During the year the partners made drawings as follows:

| | Arbuthnot | Beebee |
|---|---|---|
| | $ | $ |
| 31 March | 3000 | 2000 |
| 30 June | 5000 | 6500 |
| 30 September | 4300 | 5600 |
| 31 December | 7900 | 4000 |

**Required**

Calculate the amount of interest on drawings to be charged to each partner for the year.

## Answer

Arbuthnot will be charged £291.25 interest on drawings.

Beebee will be charged $307.50 interest on drawings.

### Workings

Arbuthnot

$3000 × 5% × ¾ year = $112.50

$5000 × 5% × ½ year = $125.00

$4300 × 5% × ¼ year = $53.75

Beebee

$2000 × 5% × ¾ year = $75.00

$6500 × 5% × ½ year = $162.50

$5600 × 5% × ¼ year = $70.00

Note that no interest has been charged for drawings made on the last day of the year.

The entries in the partnership account:

- add the interest on drawings to the profit for the year in the appropriation section of an income statement
- debit the partners' current accounts with the interest charged on their drawings.

The debit entry in the partners' current accounts has the effect of increasing the amount withdrawn during the year. It is in effect an additional amount of drawings.

The amount of interest on drawings will be given, so you will not be required to calculate the amounts to be charged to each partner.

**Worked example**

Goctay and Hanif are in partnership. They supply the following information for the year ended 31 August 2014:

- The partnership agreement provides that Goctay be credited with a partnership salary of $5600; that partners be credited with interest on capital of eight per cent per annum; that partners be charged interest on their drawings at five per cent per annum; and that residual profits be shared equally.
- Goctay's fixed capital account stands at $42000, while Hanif's fixed capital account stands at $50000.
- The profit for the year before appropriations was $56934.
- During the year Goctay made drawings of $32900 and Hanif's drawings were $21750.
- Interest on drawings was calculated at $348 for Goctay and $180 for Hanif.

**Required**

Prepare an appropriation account for the year ended 31 August 2014.

## Answer

**Goctay and Hanif**

**Appropriation account for the year ended 31 August 2014**

| | $ | $ |
|---|---|---|
| Profit for the year | | 56934 |
| *Add* Interest on drawings – Goctay | 348 | |
| Hanif | 180 | 528 |
| | | 57462 |
| *Less* Salary – Goctay | | (5600) |
| | | 51862 |
| *Less* Interest on capital – Goctay | (3360) | |
| Hanif | (4000) | (7360) |
| | | 44502 |
| Share of profit – Goctay | (22251) | |
| Hanif | (22251) | (44502) |

➤ Now try Question 4.

## 23.4 Partnership capital and current accounts

**Partners' capital accounts** show deliberate injections of capital into the business; plus any goodwill adjustments; plus any profits or losses arising on a revaluation of assets (generally on the admission or the retirement of a partner).

**Partners' current accounts** record entries relating to each partner's share of the profits of the business in the current year. The current account would also be used to adjust for any errors made in the profit share in previous years.

A statement of financial position for a partnership differs from that of a sole trader in that, since there is more than one owner, there must be more than one capital account, showing the financial commitment of each partner to the business.

Indeed, the capital employed in the business is usually divided into **partners' capital accounts** and **partners' current accounts**.

Capital accounts may change each year if current accounts are not maintained and they would resemble the capital accounts that you have already prepared in your studies. It is more usual for partnerships to maintain fixed capital accounts. However, questions sometimes state that only capital accounts are maintained.

**Worked example**

The appropriation account for the year ended 30 June 2015 of Tayyiba and Adnan is shown:

| | $ | $ |
|---|---|---|
| Profit for the year | | 34745 |
| *Less* Salary – Tayyiba | | (6000) |
| | | 28745 |
| Interest on capital – Tayyiba | (2400) | |
| Adnan | (3000) | (5400) |
| | | 23345 |
| Share of profit – Tayyiba | (9338) | |
| Adnan | (14007) | (23345) |

- The capital account balances at 1 July 2014 were $40000 and $50000 respectively.
- Drawings for the year were Tayyiba $22350 and Adnan $26850.

**Required**

Prepare the capital accounts of Tayyiba and Adnan at 30 June 2015.

## Answer

**Capital accounts**

| | Tayyiba | Adnan | | Tayyiba | Adnan |
|---|---|---|---|---|---|
| | $ | $ | | $ | $ |
| Drawings | 22 350 | 26 850 | Balance b/d | 40 000 | 50 000 |
| Balance c/d | 35 388 | 40 157 | Salary | 6 000 | |
| | | | Interest on capital | 2 400 | 3 000 |
| | | | Share of profit | 9 338 | 14 007 |
| | 57 738 | 67 007 | | 57 738 | 67 007 |
| | | | Balances b/d | 35 388 | 40 157 |

If you are asked to prepare capital accounts, you must produce the information *in account form* as shown above. If you are asked for a calculation, or are not asked specifically for 'accounts', then a 'calculation' approach is acceptable.

The use of the accounts will save space in an answer so in many ways it is preferable to draw up the ledger accounts and merely insert the totals of the ledger accounts in the statement of financial position.

So, in the above example, the statement of financial position might be drawn up only showing:

**Tayyiba and Adnan**

**Extract from statement of financial position at 30 June 2015**

| | $ | $ |
|---|---|---|
| **Capital accounts** | | |
| Tayyiba | 35 388 | |
| Adnan | 40 157 | 75 545 |

Notice that a columnar layout has been used. This saves time and space. Do try it. It may be difficult the first time or two that you use it but it does mean that you do not have to repeat the descriptions used in each account.

The capital accounts would generally be shown on the statement of financial position of the partnership as follows:

**Tayyiba and Adnan**

**Extract from statement of financial position at 30 June 2015**

| | Tayyiba | Adnan | |
|---|---|---|---|
| | $ | $ | $ |
| **Capital accounts** | | | |
| Opening balance | 40 000 | 50 000 | |
| *Add* Salary | 6 000 | | |
| Interest on capital | 2 400 | 3 000 | |
| Share of profit | 9 338 | 14 007 | |
| | 57 738 | 67 007 | |
| *Less* Drawings | 22 350 | 26 850 | |
| | 35 388 | 40 157 | 75 545 |

Both the accounts showing adjustments to capital and the 'vertical' layout used above give the same result.

It is more usual for a partnership to maintain fixed capital accounts and show all appropriations in the partnership current accounts.

All entries relating to profits earned and profits withdrawn are entered in the current accounts.

**Worked example**

Tawanda and Jacob are in partnership. They provide the following information for the year ended 31 August 2014:

| | Tawanda | Jacob |
|---|---|---|
| | $ | $ |
| Capital account balances 1 September 2013 | 30 000 | 45 000 |
| Current account balances 1 September 2013 | 1 542 Cr | 238 Cr |
| Drawings for the year were | 20 653 | 16 234 |
| Interest to be charged on drawings | 541 | 452 |

An extract from the appropriation account shows:

| | $ |
|---|---|
| Salary – Tawanda | 4800 |
| Interest on capital – Tawanda | 2100 |
| Jacob | 3150 |
| Share of residual profits – Tawanda | 18000 |
| Jacob | 9000 |

**Required**

Prepare detailed capital accounts and current accounts for the partnership at 31 August 2014.

## Answer

**Capital accounts**

| | Tawanda | Jacob | | Tawanda | Jacob |
|---|---|---|---|---|---|
| | $ | $ | | $ | $ |
| | | | Balances b/d | 30000 | 45000 |

**Current accounts**

| | Tawanda | Jacob | | Tawanda | Jacob |
|---|---|---|---|---|---|
| | $ | $ | | $ | $ |
| Drawings | 20653 | 16234 | Balances b/d | 1542 | 238 |
| Interest on drawings | 541 | 452 | Salary | 4800 | |
| | | | Interest on capital | 2100 | 3150 |
| | | | Share of profits | 18000 | 9000 |
| Balance c/d | 5248 | | Balance c/d | | 4298 |
| | 26442 | 16686 | | 26442 | 16686 |
| Balance b/d | | 4298 | Balance b/d | 5248 | |

The capital accounts have remained 'fixed' and the profits earned and profits withdrawn from the business (drawings) and interest on drawings are recorded in the current accounts.

It is, of course, possible that a partner may withdraw more profits from the business than they have earned. In such a case the partner's current account will show a debit balance.

### Worked example

Vikram and Walter provide the following information for their partnership for the year ended 30 April 2015:

| | Vikram | Walter |
|---|---|---|
| | $ | $ |
| Current account balances | 164 Cr | 298 Cr |
| Interest on capital for the year | 500 | 700 |
| Share of residual profits | 25300 | 12650 |
| Drawings for the year | 20000 | 15000 |
| Interest on drawings | 270 | 460 |

**Required**

Prepare:

a an appropriation account for the year ended 30 April 2015

b current accounts at 30 April 2015.

## Answer

a

**Vikram and Walter**

**Appropriation account for the year ended 30 April 2015**

| | $ | $ |
|---|---|---|
| Profit for the year | | *38420** |
| *Add* Interest on drawings – Vikram | 270 | |
| Walter | 460 | 730 |
| | | 39150 |
| *Less* Interest on capital – Vikram | (500) | |
| Walter | (700) | (1200) |
| | | 37950 |
| Share of profits – Vikram | (25300) | |
| Walter | (12650) | (37950) |

*Missing figure

b

**Current accounts**

| | Vikram | Walter | | Vikram | Walter |
|---|---|---|---|---|---|
| Drawings | 20000 | 15000 | Balances b/d | 164 | 298 |
| Interest on drawings | 270 | 460 | Interest on capital | 500 | 700 |
| | | | Share of profits | 25300 | 12650 |
| Balance c/d | 5694 | | Balance c/d | | 1812 |
| | 25964 | 15460 | | 25964 | 15460 |
| Balance b/d | | 1812 | Balance b/d | 5694 | |

## Self-test questions

**13** Partners have unlimited liability. True/False?

**14** Explain two advantages of being in partnership.

**15** Give the date of the Partnership Act.

**16** List four financial rules to be applied if a partnership does not have a partnership agreement.

**17** Interest on drawings cannot be charged if partners are entitled to interest on capital. True/False?

**18** Give an example of an entry in a partner's capital account.

**19** Give two examples of debit entries in a partner's current account.

**20** Give two examples of credit entries in a partner's current account.

➤ Now try Questions 5 and 6.

## Chapter summary

- A partnership exists when two or more people are jointly engaged in business with the aim of making profits.
- A partnership should have a partnership agreement.
- If there is no agreement, the Partnership Act 1890 lays down the rules by which the partnership is governed.
- Financial statements contain an appropriation account that shows how profits and losses are shared between the partners.
- Partnerships can maintain fixed or fluctuating capital accounts.
- Most partnerships maintain fixed capital accounts. In such cases all appropriations of profits are entered in current accounts.
- Entries in partnership capital accounts involve only capital transactions.

# 24 Partnership accounting – structural changes

**Content**

**1.4 Preparation of financial statements**

1.4.3 Partnerships

- Prepare capital and current accounts to record changes required in respect of goodwill and revaluation of assets on the introduction of a new partner, retirement of an existing partner and the dissolution of a partnership

**By the end of this chapter you should be able to:**

- account for the admission of a new partner
- account for the retirement of a partner
- understand the term 'goodwill'; how it is valued and the factors that may contribute to its establishment
- make entries in the books of account to record adjustments to partners' capital accounts when:
  - a goodwill account is maintained
  - goodwill is written out of the books
- make the necessary adjustments in the books of account to record a change in the profit sharing ratio
- suggest reasons why a partnership might be dissolved
- use a realisation account to aid the dissolution process
- record the effects that the purchase of assets by a limited company have on the books of account of a partnership
- close the partnership books of account.

## 24.1 Changes in partnerships

During the lifetime of any business there could well be changes in the ownership of that business. For example, Conserva, a sole trader, may decide that she no longer wishes to trade as a farmer and she sells her business to Jami on 31 July.

The ownership of a partnership could change for any of these reasons:

- Partners may decide to terminate the partnership.
- Partners may decide to admit another partner.
- Partners may decide to alter their profit sharing ratios.

When there is any kind of change to the structure of a partnership the treatment is the same; one business ceases to exist at the date of the change and immediately after the date of the change a new business comes into being.

**Example**

1 When Arturo and Batista admitted Carlos as a partner on 1 April 2014 there were two businesses involved:

| Up to 31 March 2014 | From 1 April 2014 |
|---|---|
| Owners are Arturo and Batista. | Owners are Arturo, Batista and Carlos. |

2 When Iain retired from the partnership of Iain, Jing and Kris on 30 September 2014 there were two businesses involved:

| Up to 30 September 2014 | From 1 October 2014 |
|---|---|
| Owners are Iain, Jing and Kris. | Owners are Jing and Kris. |

3 Deirdre and Englebert were in partnership sharing profits and losses equally. When they changed their profit sharing ratio to 3:2 on 30 June 2014 there were two businesses involved:

| Up to 30 June 2014 | From 1 July 2014 |
|---|---|
| Owners are Deirdre and Englebert. (profit share equal) | Owners are Deirdre and Englebert. (profit share 3:2) |
| different profit share = different business | |

**Tip**

When there is a structural change to a partnership, treat the information relating to the business before the change separately from the information relating to the business after the change.

## 24.1.1 The admission of a new partner

**Worked example**

Adele and Gaynor are in partnership, sharing profits and losses equally. Their financial year end is 31 December. They admit Chin as a partner on 1 July 2014. They all agree that Adele, Gaynor and Chin will share profits 3:2:1 respectively.

The profit for the year ended 31 December 2014 was $40000. The profit accrued evenly throughout the year.

**Required**

Prepare the appropriation accounts for the year ended 31 December 2014.

### Answer

Remember that we are dealing with two businesses.

| Up to 30 June 2014 | From 1 July 2014 |
|---|---|
| Owners were Adele and Gaynor. | Owners are Adele, Gaynor and Chin. |

So:

**Adele and Gaynor**

**Appropriation account for the six months ended 30 June 2014**

| | $ | $ |
|---|---|---|
| Profit for the six months | | 20000 |
| Profit share – Adele | (10000) | |
| Gaynor | (10000) | (20000) |

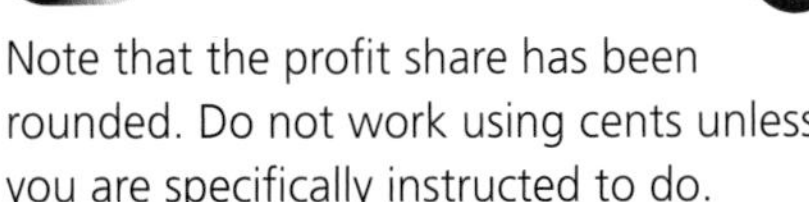

Note that the profit share has been rounded. Do not work using cents unless you are specifically instructed to do.

**Adele, Gaynor and Chin**

**Appropriation account for the six months ended 31 December 2014**

| | $ | $ |
|---|---|---|
| Profit for the six months | | 20000 |
| Profit share – Adele | (10000) | |
| Gaynor | (6667) | |
| Chin | (3333) | (20000) |

The worked example shown was fairly straightforward.

However, common sense would tell us that Adele and Gaynor would not simply have allowed Chin to become a partner without her contributing some capital to the business.

Common sense would also suggest that Adele and Gaynor would have considered the value of their business assets before allowing Chin to become a part owner of those business assets.

Imagine that your grandparents have been in business for 40 years. Their business assets are recorded on the business statement of financial position as follows:

| | $ |
|---|---|
| Premises at cost | 18500 |
| Equipment at cost | 5500 |
| Other assets at cost | 2000 |
| | 26000 |
| Capital – Grandfather | 11000 |
| Grandmother | 15000 |
| | 26000 |

*Remember that we value assets at cost, not at what they could be sold for – the 'going concern' concept.*

Now imagine that your grandparents admit William Fox as a partner into their business. They ask him to provide $20000 capital. He agrees and enters the business.

What would the statement of financial position look like now?

| | $ |
|---|---|
| Premises at cost | 18500 |
| Equipment at cost | 5500 |
| Other assets at cost | 22000 |
| | 46000 |
| Capital – Grandfather | 11000 |
| Grandmother | 15000 |
| William Fox | 20000 |
| | 46000 |

*Simple!*

*Your grandparents would not agree to what has taken place! Remember that they have been in business for 40 years. How much must the premises be worth now? Surely they are worth more than the carrying amount shown?*

Can you see your likely future inheritance disappearing into William Fox's pocket?

In fact, what needs to happen when any kind of structural change takes place is that the business assets have to be revalued. The increase in value (or decrease in value) belongs to the *original* partners.

## Worked example

Mikael and Jeanette have been in partnership for many years, sharing profits and losses equally. The financial year end for the business is 31 December. They decide to admit Kiri into the partnership with effect from 1 May 2015. Kiri will pay $25 000 capital into the business bank account. The partnership statement of financial position at 30 April 2015 was as follows:

**Mikael and Jeanette**

**Statement of financial position at 30 April 2015**

| | $ | $ |
|---|---|---|
| **ASSETS** | | |
| **Non-current assets** | | |
| Premises at cost | | 28 000 |
| Vehicles at cost | | 16 000 |
| | | 44 000 |
| **Current assets** | | |
| Inventory | 3 500 | |
| Trade receivables | 4 300 | |
| Bank | 1 560 | 9 360 |
| **Total assets** | | 53 360 |
| | | |
| **CAPITAL AND LIABILITIES** | | |
| **Capital accounts** – Mikael | | 25 000 |
| Jeanette | | 25 000 |
| | | 50 000 |
| **Current liabilities** | | |
| Trade payables | | 3 360 |
| **Total capital and liabilities** | | 53 360 |

Over the years property prices have risen. The premises were valued $70 000 at the end of April 2015.

**Required**

Prepare a statement of financial position at 1 May 2015 after the admission of Kiri as a partner.

## Answer

**Mikael, Jeanette and Kiri**

**Statement of financial position at 1 May 2015**

| | $ | $ |
|---|---|---|
| **ASSETS** | | |
| **Non-current assets** | | |
| Premises at valuation | | 70 000 |
| Equipment at cost | | 16 000 |
| | | 86 000 |
| **Current assets** | | |
| Inventory | 3 500 | |
| Trade receivables | 4 300 | |
| Bank balance | 26 560 | 34 360 |
| **Total assets** | | 120 360 |

| | | |
|---|---|---|
| **CAPITAL AND LIABILITIES** | | |
| **Capital accounts –** Mikael | | 46 000 |
| Jeanette | | 46 000 |
| Kiri | | 25 000 |
| | | 117 000 |
| **Current liabilities** | | |
| Trade payables | | 3 360 |
| **Total capital and liabilities** | | 120 360 |

The rise in the value of the premises has taken place while Mikael and Jeanette have been the only proprietors, so any profits (because of property inflation) belong to them.

The increase in the value of the premises did not occur when Kiri was a partner, so she should not benefit. As they are equal partners, the increase has been divided equally between Mikael and Jeanette.

➤ **Now try Question 1.**

It is more usual to find a statement of financial position showing details of all assets and liabilities. When a structural change takes place in such instances we use an account to record any changes to the values of assets and liabilities shown on the statement of financial position and hence to calculate the profit or loss resulting from the changes in value.

A temporary account is opened and it is only used to record adjustments to the account balances from the ledgers shown on the statement of financial position.

This is how the temporary account works:

**Worked example**

Xandra and Aziz are in partnership, sharing profits and losses in the ratio 4:3 respectively. They admit Liana as a partner on 1 August 2014. She pays $35 000 to the partnership as her capital.

The partnership statement of financial position at 31 July 2014 was:

**Xandra and Aziz**
**Statement of financial position at 31 July 2014**

| | | $ | $ |
|---|---|---|---|
| **ASSETS** | | | |
| **Non-current assets** | | | |
| Premises at cost | | | 48 000 |
| Equipment at cost | | | 12 000 |
| Vehicle at cost | | | 15 000 |
| | | | 75 000 |
| **Current assets** | | | |
| Inventory | | 2 400 | |
| Trade receivables | | 1 750 | |
| Bank balance | | 2 200 | 6 350 |
| **Total assets** | | | 81 350 |
| **CAPITAL AND LIABILITIES** | | | |
| **Capital accounts –** | Xandra | 40 000 | |
| | Aziz | 30 000 | 70 000 |
| **Current accounts –** | Xandra | 3 410 | |
| | Aziz | 5 150 | 8 560 |
| | | | 78 560 |
| **Current liabilities** | | | |
| Trade payables | | | 2 790 |
| **Total capital and liabilities** | | | 81 350 |

It was agreed that the assets on 31 July 2014 be valued as follows:

| | $ |
|---|---|
| Premises | 100 000 |
| Equipment | 4 500 |
| Vehicle | 6 000 |
| Inventory | 2 000 |
| Trade receivables | 1 650 |

**Required**

Prepare a statement of financial position at 1 August 2014 after the admission of Liana as a partner.

## Workings

An account is opened for each asset that is to be revalued:

**Premises account**

| | $ | | $ |
|---|---|---|---|
| Bal b/d | 48 000 | | |
| Revaluation | 52 000 | Bal c/d | 100 000 |
| | 100 000 | | 100 000 |
| Bal b/d | 100 000 | | |

**Equipment account**

| | $ | | $ |
|---|---|---|---|
| Bal b/d | 12 000 | Revaluation | 7 500 |
| | | Bal c/d | 4 500 |
| | 12 000 | | 12 000 |
| Bal b/d | 4 500 | | |

**Vehicle account**

| | $ | | $ |
|---|---|---|---|
| Bal b/d | 15 000 | Revaluation | 9 000 |
| | | Bal c/d | 6 000 |
| | 15 000 | | 15 000 |
| Bal b/d | 6 000 | | |

**Inventory account**

| | $ | | $ |
|---|---|---|---|
| Bal b/d | 2 400 | Revaluation | 400 |
| | | Bal c/d | 2 000 |
| | 2 400 | | 2 400 |
| Bal b/d | 2 000 | | |

**Trade receivables account**

| | $ | | $ |
|---|---|---|---|
| Bal b/d | 1 750 | Revaluation | 100 |
| | | Bal c/d | 1 650 |
| | 1 750 | | 1 750 |
| Bal b/d | 1 650 | | |

A revaluation account is used to adjust the asset accounts and to calculate any profit or loss on revaluation. The profit or loss is transferred to the existing partners' capital accounts *before* the new partner is admitted.

**Revaluation account**

| | $ | | $ |
|---|---|---|---|
| Equipment | 7 500 | Premises | 52 000 |
| Vehicle | 9 000 | | |
| Stock | 400 | | |
| Trade receivables | 100 | | |
| Capital – | | | |
| Xandra | 20 000 | | |
| Aziz | 15 000 | | |
| | 52 000 | | 52 000 |

**Capital – Xandra**

| | $ | | $ |
|---|---|---|---|
| | | Bal b/d | 40 000 |
| Bal c/d | 60 000 | Revaln a/c | 20 000 |
| | 60 000 | | 60 000 |
| | | Bal b/d | 60 000 |

**Capital – Aziz**

| | $ | | $ |
|---|---|---|---|
| | | Bal b/d | 30 000 |
| Bal c/d | 45 000 | Revaln a/c | 15 000 |
| | 45 000 | | 45 000 |
| | | Bal b/d | 45 000 |

## Answer

**Xandra, Aziz and Liana**

**Statement of financial position at 1 August 2014**

| | | $ | $ |
|---|---|---|---|
| **ASSETS** | | | |
| **Non-current assets** | | | |
| Premises at valuation | | | 100 000 |
| Equipment at valuation | | | 4 500 |
| Vehicle at valuation | | | 6 000 |
| | | | 110 500 |
| **Current assets** | | | |
| Inventory | | 2 000 | |
| Trade receivables | | 1 650 | |
| Bank balance | | 37 200 | 40 850 |
| **Total assets** | | | 151 350 |
| **CAPITAL AND LIABILITIES** | | | |
| **Capital accounts –** | Xandra | 60 000 | |
| | Aziz | 45 000 | |
| | Liana | 35 000 | 140 000 |
| **Current accounts –** | Xandra | 3 410 | |
| | Aziz | 5 150 | 8 560 |
| | | | 148 560 |
| **Current liabilities** | | | |
| Trade payables | | | 2 790 |
| **Total capital and liabilities** | | | 151 350 |

Note that the changes to the capital structure of the business are entered in the partners' capital accounts. The current accounts have not been used. The current accounts will only change when trading profits or losses are shared between partners or as partners make drawings.

Notice also that the non-current assets are now labelled 'at valuation' since they do not now appear 'at cost'.

➤ **Now try Question 2.**

When you get used to making adjustments to the partnership statement of financial position because of a structural change you may find that you do not have to open an account for each asset and liability. However, it will be safer for you to always open a revaluation account to 'collect' the changes that have been implemented.

## 24.2 Goodwill

**Goodwill** is the cost of acquiring a business less the total value of the assets and liabilities that have been purchased.

**Goodwill** is an intangible asset. It cannot be seen; it has no physical presence, unlike tangible assets like premises or machinery or vehicles.

When a successful business is sold the vendor will generally price the business at a price greater than the total of the net assets being sold.

**Example**

The statement of financial position of a local restaurant owned by Terri is shown:

| | $ | $ |
|---|---|---|
| **ASSETS** | | |
| **Non-current assets** | | |
| Equipment | | 34 000 |
| Fixtures and fittings | | 8 400 |
| | | 42 400 |
| **Current assets** | | |
| Inventory | 840 | |
| Bank balance | 2 345 | |
| Cash in hand | 455 | 3 640 |
| **Total assets** | | 46 040 |
| **CAPITAL AND LIABILITIES** | | |
| **Capital** – Terri | | 44 620 |
| **Current liabilities** | | |
| Trade payables | | 1 420 |
| **Total capital and liabilities** | | 46 040 |

**Tip**

Goodwill is not sold; it is only purchased. The seller makes a profit; the purchaser buys all the net assets including goodwill.

Terri decided to sell her business. She advertised it at $90 000. Hua bought the business for $90 000.

Two points emerge:

- Terri sold her business at a profit of $48 180. (She would not sell the bank balance or cash in hand.) She sold non-current assets $42 400, inventory $840 less current liabilities $1 420 for $90 000.
- Hua purchased the business net assets for $90 000. He has purchased net tangible assets for $41 820 and an intangible asset (goodwill) for $48 180.

We have already said that when there is a structural change to a partnership the change involves two businesses:

- the business that existed before the change
- the business that comes into existence *because* of the change.

When a new partner is admitted to a partnership we have already seen that the assets need to be revalued. We also need to place a value on the intangible asset goodwill.

## 24.2.1 The valuation of goodwill

We cannot give a definitive method that can be used in every type of business when goodwill has to be valued. If a business were being purchased, then goodwill would represent how much would be paid in excess of the value of the net assets being purchased. We have already seen this when Terri sold her restaurant to Hua in the example used above.

How can we value goodwill when there is a structural change to a partnership, when no-one is actually purchasing the business?

The value placed on goodwill has to be acceptable to the partners in the 'old' partnership as well as being acceptable to the 'new' partner(s).

The following are the most commonly used methods of determining the value of goodwill.

Goodwill is valued at a multiple of the:

- average profits generated over the past few years
- average weekly sales generated over the past financial year
- average of gross fees earned over a number of years
- super profits earned by the business.

## 1 A multiple of average profits generated over the past few years

**Worked example**

It has been agreed that goodwill be valued at two years' purchase of the average profits taken over the past five years. Profits for the past five years were:

| Year | $ |
|---|---|
| 1 | 12 450 |
| 2 | 12 560 |
| 3 | 14 890 |
| 4 | 8 450 |
| 5 | 11 650 |

**Required**

Calculate the value to be placed on goodwill.

### Answer

Goodwill is valued at \$24 000.

### Workings

Total profits for five years = \$12 450 + \$12 560 + \$14 890 + \$8 450 + \$11 650

= \$60 000

$$\text{Goodwill valued} = \frac{\text{Total profits for five years}}{5} \times 2$$

$$= \frac{\$60\,000}{5} \times 2$$

$$= \$24\,000$$

## 2 A multiple of average weekly sales generated over the past financial year

**Worked example**

It has been agreed that goodwill be valued at four weeks' purchase of average weekly sales over the past financial year. Last year's annual sales were \$322 400.

**Required**

Calculate the value to be placed on goodwill.

### Answer

Goodwill is valued at \$24 800.

### Workings

$$\frac{\$322\,400}{52} \times 4 = \$6\,200 \times 4 = \$24\,800$$

### 3 A multiple of an average of the gross fees earned over a number of years

This method is used by many professional businesses, such as accountants, doctors, lawyers, veterinary surgeons, etc., when a partner retires or a new partner enters the business.

**Worked example**

It has been agreed that goodwill be valued at two years' purchase of average gross fees over the past four years. Fees for the past four years were:

| Year | $ |
|---|---|
| 1 | 98 000 |
| 2 | 77 000 |
| 3 | 72 000 |
| 4 | 69 000 |

**Required**

Calculate the value to be placed on goodwill.

## Answer

Goodwill is valued at $158 000.

### Workings

$98 000 + $77 000 + $72 000 + $69 000 = $316 000

$$\frac{\$316\,000}{4} \times 2 = \$79\,000 \times 2 = \$158\,000$$

### 4 A multiple of super profits earned by the business

**Opportunity cost** is the cost of making a decision in terms of the benefit lost by not using a resource in the next best alternative.

Super profits are calculated using the principle of **opportunity cost**.

**Worked example**

Dirgen, a property developer, has $50 000 capital invested in his business. If he were working for another property developer he could earn $23 000 salary per annum. His business is currently earning profits of $38 000.

**Required**

Calculate the amount of super profits earned by Dirgen's business.

## Answer

Super profits earned were $12 500.

### Workings

| | $ |
|---|---|
| If Dirgen worked for another property developer he could earn: | 23 000 |
| If Dirgen invested his capital outside his business he could earn (say) five per cent | 2 500 |
| | 25 500 |

By carrying on as a self-employed property developer, he earns $12 500 more than he would earn using his capital and talents in the next best alternative.

**Worked example**

Homer owns and runs a small car repair business. Profits for the past few years have averaged $18000. Homer has $14000 capital invested in his business. He could earn $12000 as a car mechanic working locally. He currently earns five per cent per annum on a savings account at a local bank. Goodwill is to be valued at three years super profits.

**Required**

Calculate the value to be placed on goodwill.

### Answer

Goodwill is valued at $15900.

### Workings

| | |
|---|---|
| Earnings as mechanic | $12000 |
| Interest on capital ($14000) invested in bank | $700 |
| | $12700 |

($18000 – $12700) × 3 = $5300 × 3 = $15900

### 24.2.2 Factors that contribute to the establishment of goodwill

The factors that determine the value of goodwill placed on a business vary. They include:

- a good reputation because of the quality of a product
- a good reputation because of good service
- a good reputation for the helpfulness of staff
- good after sales service
- a prominent physical position of premises
- popularity among customers.

No doubt you can think of one or two other factors that might contribute to the establishment of goodwill.

So, why might you pay $30000 more than the net asset value placed on a business in order to purchase it?

- You cannot purchase a good reputation – you could destroy that overnight.
- You cannot buy popularity.
- You certainly cannot purchase customers.

The reason why you might pay the 'extra' $30000 is because you can see the prospect of earning high profits in the future – you can envisage yourself earning lots of profits.

## 24.3 Adjustments to partners' capital accounts to record goodwill

A payment for goodwill is paid by the purchaser of a business in order to gain access to future profits that may be generated by that business. Let us see the two methods of dealing with goodwill when a partner is *admitted into* a business.

### 24.3.1 Adjustments made with a goodwill account

**Worked example**

Issmail and Gudrun are in partnership, selling cleaning materials. They travel from house to house selling their products to people in their homes. They share profits and losses in the ratio 3:1 respectively. Their statement of financial position at 31 August 2014 showed:

**Issmail and Gudrun**

**Statement of financial position at 31 August 2014**

| | | $ |
|---|---|---|
| **ASSETS** | | |
| **Current assets** | | |
| Bank balance | | 370 |
| **Total assets** | | 370 |
| **CAPITAL** | | |
| **Capital accounts** – | Issmail | 200 |
| | Gudrun | 170 |
| **Total capital** | | 370 |

Issmail and Gudrun admit Lucrezia to the partnership with effect from 1 September 2014. Lucrezia contributes $2000 as her capital. They agree that goodwill be valued at $8000.

**Required**

Prepare a statement of financial position at 1 September 2014 immediately after Lucrezia was admitted to the partnership.

## Answer

**Issmail, Gudrun and Lucrezia**

**Extract from statement of financial position at 1 September 2014**

| | | $ |
|---|---|---|
| **ASSETS** | | |
| **Non-current assets** | | |
| Goodwill | | 8000 |
| **Current assets** | | |
| Bank balance | | 2370 |
| **Total assets** | | 10370 |
| **CAPITAL** | | |
| **Capital accounts** – | Issmail | 6200 |
| | Gudrun | 2170 |
| | Lucrezia | 2000 |
| **Total capital** | | 10370 |

## Workings

Notice that a new asset has appeared on the statement of financial position, a non-current asset (intangible) that has built up over the years while Issmail and Gudrun have been in business as partners. The two original partners have been responsible for creating the goodwill through their personality, products, after sales service, etc., so it is only their capital accounts that have been credited in the profit sharing ratios.

The book-keeping entries to record the introduction of goodwill into the partnership books would look like this:

**Capital – Issmail**

| | $ | | $ |
|---|---|---|---|
| | | Balance b/d | 200 |
| Bal c/d | 6200 | Goodwill | 6000 |
| | 6200 | | 6200 |
| | | Balance b/d | 6200 |

**Capital – Gudrun**

| | $ | | $ |
|---|---|---|---|
| | | Balance b/d | 170 |
| Bal c/d | 2170 | Goodwill | 2000 |
| | 2170 | | 2170 |
| | | Balance b/d | 2170 |

**Goodwill account**

| | $ | |
|---|---|---|
| Capital – Issmail | 6 000 | |
| Capital – Gudrun | 2 000 | |

➤ **Now try Question 3.**

Goodwill only appears in a statement of financial position when it is purchased. If you see the asset on any statement of financial position, you can say with some certainty that

- either the ownership has changed recently
- or the business has recently purchased another business.

This applies no matter what type of business statement of financial position you are examining.

**Inherent goodwill** is the goodwill that has been generated internally. It has not been purchased. It is the goodwill that is enjoyed by a business while it is still ongoing.

**Inherent goodwill** is not entered in the books of account so it is never shown on a statement of financial position.

Well established businesses like Royal Dutch Shell Petroleum plc or McDonald's enjoy much inherent goodwill but this will not be shown on their statements of financial position. Both these businesses are going concerns.

The going concern concept tells us that assets should be shown at cost price, not at what they would fetch if sold. Neither Shell nor McDonald's is due to be sold in the next few days, so as a going concern neither would show inherent goodwill on their statement of financial position.

Goodwill can appear in the books of any business when it is purchased.

## 24.3.2 Adjustments made when no goodwill account is introduced

We have considered scenarios where a goodwill account remains in the business books of account after a new partner is admitted. On other occasions, goodwill is written off immediately after purchase.

**Worked example**

Adhaf and Shavay are in partnership, sharing profits and losses equally. They provide the following information:

**Adhaf and Shavay**
**Extract from statement of financial position at 31 July 2014**

| | | $ |
|---|---|---|
| **ASSETS** | | |
| **Current assets** | | |
| Bank balance | | 6 500 |
| **Total assets** | | 6 500 |
| **CAPITAL** | | |
| **Capital accounts** – Adhaf | | 3 500 |
| | Shavay | 3 000 |
| **Total capital** | | 6 500 |

They admit Paris as a partner with effect from 1 August 2014. Paris pays $5000 into the partnership bank account as her capital. They agree that goodwill be valued at $18 000 and that the account will not appear in the statement of financial position. They further agree to share future profits and losses 3:2:1 respectively.

**Required**

Prepare a statement of financial position at 1 August 2014 after the admission of Paris as a partner.

## Answer

**Adhaf, Shavay and Paris**
**Extract from statement of financial position at 1 August 2014**

| | $ |
|---|---|
| **ASSETS** | |
| **Current assets** | |
| Bank balance | 11 500 |
| **Total assets** | 11 500 |
| **CAPITAL** | |
| **Capital accounts** – Adhaf | 3 500 |
| Shavay | 6 000 |
| Paris | 2 000 |
| **Total capital** | 11 500 |

## Workings

The book-keeping entries showing the above transactions are:

**Bank**

| | $ | | $ |
|---|---|---|---|
| Balance b/d | 6500 | | |
| Capital – Paris (3) | 5000 | | |

**Capital – Adhaf**

| | $ | | $ |
|---|---|---|---|
| Goodwill (4) | 9 000 | Balance b/d | 3 500 |
| Balance c/d | 3 500 | Goodwill (1) | 9 000 |
| | 12 500 | | 12 500 |
| | | Balance b/d | 3 500 |

**Capital – Shavay**

| | $ | | $ |
|---|---|---|---|
| Goodwill (5) | 6 000 | Balance b/d | 3 000 |
| Balance c/d | 6 000 | Goodwill (2) | 9 000 |
| | 12 000 | | 12 000 |
| | | Balance b/d | 6 000 |

**Capital – Paris**

| | $ | | $ |
|---|---|---|---|
| Goodwill (6) | 3 000 | Bank (3) | 5 000 |
| Balance c/d | 2 000 | | |
| | 5 000 | | 5 000 |
| | | Balance b/d | 2 000 |

**Goodwill account**

| | | $ | | | $ |
|---|---|---|---|---|---|
| Capitals – | Adhaf (1) | 9 000 | Capitals – | Adhaf (4) | 9 000 |
| | Shavay (2) | 9 000 | | Shavay (5) | 6 000 |
| | | | | Paris (6) | 3 000 |
| | | 18 000 | | | 18 000 |

Numbers in brackets have been placed next to each entry so that you can trace each entry individually to each account.

➤ Now try Question 4.

Notice that the goodwill account has disappeared and is not shown in the final statement of financial position.

Clearly it is very unusual for a business to have a bank balance as its only asset. The above examples were used to highlight the way goodwill is treated when it does not remain in the books of account.

Let us put together a more detailed scenario – a situation where the assets are revalued and a value is placed on goodwill.

**Worked example**

Lopata, Djilali and Beauregard are in partnership, sharing profits and losses in the ratio 3:2:1 respectively. They provide the following information:

**Lopata, Djilali and Beauregard**
**Statement of financial position at 31 May 2015**

| | | $ |
|---|---|---|
| **ASSETS** | | |
| **Non-current assets** at cost | | 26 000 |
| **Current assets** | | 9000 |
| **Total assets** | | 35 000 |
| | | |
| **CAPITAL AND LIABILITIES** | | |
| **Capital accounts –** | Lopata | 10 000 |
| | Djilali | 15 000 |
| | Beauregard | 8 000 |
| | | 33 000 |
| **Current liabilities** | | 2 000 |
| **Total capital and liabilities** | | 35 000 |

They agree that Chantile be admitted as a partner with effect from 1 June 2015. Profits and losses in future will be shared equally. They further agree that non-current assets be valued at $28 000 and that goodwill be valued at $10 000. Goodwill should not remain in the business books of account.

Chantile is to pay $5000 into the business bank account as capital.

**Required**

Prepare:

a a revaluation account

b an intangible assets account

c capital accounts for each partner

d a statement of financial position at 1 June 2015 after the admission of Chantile as a partner.

## Answer

a

**Revaluation account**

| | | $ | | $ |
|---|---|---|---|---|
| Cap – | Lopata | 6 000 | Non-current assets | 2 000 |
| | Djilali | 4 000 | Goodwill | 10 000 |
| | Beauregard | 2 000 | | |
| | | 12 000 | | 12 000 |

b

**Goodwill account**

| | $ | | $ |
|---|---|---|---|
| Revaluation a/c | 10 000 | Capital – Lopata | 2 500 |
| | | Djilali | 2 500 |
| | | Beauregard | 2 500 |
| | | Chantile | 2 500 |
| | 10 000 | | 10 000 |

c

**Capital accounts**

| | Lopata | Djilali | Beauregard | Chantile | | Lopata | Djilali | Beauregard | Chantile |
|---|---|---|---|---|---|---|---|---|---|
| | $000 | $000 | $000 | $000 | | $000 | $000 | $000 | $000 |
| Goodwill | 2.5 | 2.5 | 2.5 | 2.5 | Balances b/d | 10 | 15 | 8 | |
| Balances c/d | 13.5 | 16.5 | 7.5 | 2.5 | Revaluation a/c | 6 | 4 | 2 | |
| | | | | | Bank | | | | 5 |
| | 16 | 19 | 10 | 5 | | 16 | 19 | 10 | 5 |
| | | | | | Balances b/d | 13.5 | 16.5 | 7.5 | 2.5 |

d

**Lopata, Djilali, Beauregard and Chantile**

**Statement of financial position at 1 June 2015 (after the admission of Chantile)**

| | | $ |
|---|---|---|
| **ASSETS** | | |
| **Non-current assets** at valuation | | 28 000 |
| **Current assets** | | 14 000 |
| **Total assets** | | 42 000 |
| | | |
| **CAPITAL AND LIABILITIES** | | |
| **Capital accounts –** | Lopata | 13 500 |
| | Djilali | 16 500 |
| | Beauregard | 7 500 |
| | Chantile | 2 500 |
| | | 40 000 |
| | | |
| **Current liabilities** | | 2 000 |
| **Total capital and liabilities** | | 42 000 |

Write figures out in full. Many students make errors when they forget that they are using thousands and put a figure as, say, $13.5 when it should say $13 500. Careless mistakes cost! Check your work carefully.

Note the use of columnar capital accounts; this technique saves a little time. Four partners have been involved in the partnership to show that the techniques do not change when a question has more than three partners. Questions usually have two or three partners.

Note the heading too. All accounting statements need a heading, including the name of the business.

➤ Now try Question 5.

If we consider a more detailed statement of financial position, we will see that the principles for dealing with the introduction of another partner are just the same as those already used.

Remember that we collect all the detailed changes to assets and liabilities in the revaluation account.

**Worked example**

Gwok and Dimitri are in partnership, sharing profits and losses in the ratio 3:2 respectively. The following information is provided:

**Gwok and Dimitri**

**Statement of financial position at 30 June 2014**

| | | $ | $ |
|---|---|---|---|
| **ASSETS** | | | |
| **Non-current assets** | | | |
| Premises at cost | | | 45 000 |
| Equipment at cost | | | 23 000 |
| Vehicles at cost | | | 17 000 |
| | | | 85 000 |
| **Current assets** | | | |
| Inventory | | 11 000 | |
| Trade receivables | | 4 500 | |
| Bank balance | | 1 500 | 17 000 |
| **Total assets** | | | 102 000 |
| | | | |
| **CAPITAL AND LIABILITIES** | | | |
| **Capital accounts –** | Gwok | | 60 000 |
| | Dimitri | | 40 000 |
| | | | 100 000 |

| | |
|---|---|
| **Current liabilities** | |
| Trade payables | 2 000 |
| **Total capital and liabilities** | 102 000 |

Antoinette was admitted to the partnership on 1 July 2014. It was agreed that she paid $30 000 into the business bank account as her capital and share of the goodwill.

It was agreed that the assets of the business be valued at:

| | $ |
|---|---|
| Premises | 80 000 |
| Equipment | 15 000 |
| Vehicles | 8 000 |
| Inventory | 10 800 |
| Trade receivables | 4 400 |
| Goodwill | 40 000 |

It was further agreed that in future profits and losses be shared equally and that goodwill should not remain in the books of account.

**Required**

Prepare:

a a revaluation account

b a goodwill account

c partners' capital accounts

d a statement of financial position at 1 July 2014 after the admission of Antoinette as a partner.

## Answer

a

**Revaluation account**

| | $ | | $ |
|---|---|---|---|
| Equipment | 8 000 | Premises | 35 000 |
| Vehicles | 9 000 | Goodwill | 40 000 |
| Inventory | 200 | | |
| Trade receivables | 100 | | |
| Capital – Gwok | 34 620 | | |
| Dimitri | 23 080 | | |
| | 75 000 | | 75 000 |

b

**Goodwill account**

| | $ | | $ |
|---|---|---|---|
| Revaluation account | 40 000 | Capital – Gwok | 13 334 |
| | | Dimitri | 13 333 |
| | | Antoinette | 13 333 |
| | 40 000 | | 40 000 |

c

**Capital accounts**

| | Gwok | Dimitri | Antoinette | | Gwok | Dimitri | Antoinette |
|---|---|---|---|---|---|---|---|
| | $ | $ | $ | | $ | $ | $ |
| Goodwill | 13 334 | 13 333 | 13 333 | Balances b/d | 60 000 | 40 000 | |
| | | | | Revaluation a/c | 34 620 | 23 080 | |
| Balances c/d | 81 286 | 49 747 | 16 667 | Bank | | | 30 000 |
| | 94 620 | 63 080 | 30 000 | | 94 620 | 63 080 | 30 000 |
| | | | | Balances b/d | 81 286 | 49 747 | 16 667 |

d

**Gwok, Dimitri and Antoinette**

**Statement of financial position at 1 July 2014**

| | $ | $ |
|---|---|---|
| **ASSETS** | | |
| **Non-current assets** | | |
| Premises at valuation | | 80 000 |
| Equipment at valuation | | 15 000 |
| Vehicles at valuation | | 8 000 |
| | | 103 000 |
| **Current assets** | | |
| Inventory | 10 800 | |
| Trade receivables | 4 400 | |
| Bank balance | 31 500 | 46 700 |
| **Total assets** | | 149 700 |
| **CAPITAL AND LIABILITIES** | | |
| **Capital accounts** – Gwok | | 81 286 |
| Dimitri | | 49 747 |
| Antoinette | | 16 667 |
| | | 147 700 |
| **Current liabilities** | | |
| Trade payables | | 2 000 |
| **Total capital and liabilities** | | 149 700 |

➤ **Now try Question 6.**

## 24.4 The retirement of a partner

We have dealt with the admission of a new partner in some detail. The same principles regarding a valuation of the business apply when a partner *leaves* a partnership. The business assets (and liabilities) need to be examined in order to determine whether they reflect the true worth of the business.

**Example**

Imagine that you have been a partner in a business for many, many years and the following is the summarised statement of financial position:

| | $ | |
|---|---|---|
| **ASSETS** | | |
| **Non-current assets** at cost | 12 000 | *These non-current assets include your premises that were purchased many years ago. Property prices in general have risen over your years of ownership and these premises could now be sold for, say, $80 000!* |
| **Current assets** | 8 000 | |
| **Total assets** | 20 000 | |
| **Capital** | | *Would you settle for a payout of $10 000 – your worth (capital) shown on the statement of financial position? I think not!* |
| Capital – You | 10 000 | |
| Your partner | 10 000 | |
| **Total capital** | 20 000 | |

You would have the business assets valued so that you could retire (or perhaps start a new business) and receive the true value of your worth represented by the net assets of the business.

## Worked example

Gerard, Sylvestre and Jean are in partnership, sharing profits and losses in the ratio 3:2:1 respectively. They supply the following information:

**Gerard, Sylvestre and Jean**

**Statement of financial position at 30 September 2014**

| | $ | $ |
|---|---|---|
| **ASSETS** | | |
| **Non-current assets at cost** | | 45 000 |
| **Current assets** | | |
| Inventory | 4 300 | |
| Trade receivables | 3 700 | |
| Bank balance | 4 000 | 12 000 |
| **Total assets** | | 57 000 |
| | | |
| **CAPITAL AND LIABILITIES** | | |
| **Capital accounts** – Gerard | | 20 000 |
| Sylvestre | | 15 000 |
| Jean | | 14 000 |
| | | 49 000 |
| **Current liabilities** | | 8 000 |
| **Total capital and liabilities** | | 57 000 |

Jean has decided to retire with effect from close of business on 30 September 2014.

The partners have agreed that:

- non-current assets be valued at $100 000
- inventory be valued at $4 000
- trade receivables be valued at $3 000
- goodwill be valued at $12 000 and that goodwill should not appear in the business books of account.
- Any amount due to Jean would be paid from the business bank account (assume that overdraft facilities have been agreed with the business bank).
- In the future Gerard and Sylvestre will share profits and losses equally.

**Required**

Prepare:

a a revaluation account

b a goodwill account

c partners' capital accounts

d a statement of financial position at 30 September 2014 after the retirement of Jean.

## Answer

a

**Revaluation account**

| | $ | | $ |
|---|---|---|---|
| Inventory | 300 | Non-current assets | 55 000 |
| Receivables | 700 | Goodwill | 12 000 |
| Capital – G | 33 000 | | |
| Capital – S | 22 000 | | |
| Capital – J | 11 000 | | |
| | 67 000 | | 67 000 |

b

**Goodwill account**

| | $ | | $ |
|---|---|---|---|
| Revaluation account | 12 000 | Capital – G | 6 000 |
| | | Capital – S | 6 000 |
| | 12 000 | | 12 000 |

c

**Capital accounts**

| | Gerard | Sylvestre | Jean | | Gerard | Sylvestre | Jean |
|---|---|---|---|---|---|---|---|
| | $ | $ | $ | | $ | $ | $ |
| Bank | | | 25 000 | Balances b/d | 20 000 | 15 000 | 14 000 |
| Goodwill | 6 000 | 6 000 | | Revaluation | 33 000 | 22 000 | 11 000 |
| Balances c/d | 47 000 | 31 000 | | | | | |
| | 53 000 | 37 000 | 25 000 | | 53 000 | 37 000 | 25 000 |
| | | | | Balances b/d | 47 000 | 31 000 | |

d

**Gerard and Sylvestre**
**Statement of financial position at 30 September 2014**

| | $ | $ |
|---|---|---|
| **ASSETS** | | |
| **Non-current assets at valuation** | | 100 000 |
| **Current assets** | | |
| Inventory | 4 000 | |
| Trade receivables | 3 000 | 7 000 |
| **Total assets** | | 107 000 |
| | | |
| **CAPITAL AND LIABILITIES** | | |
| **Capital accounts –** Gerard | | 47 000 |
| Sylvestre | | 31 000 |
| | | 78 000 |
| **Current liabilities** | | |
| Trade payables | 8 000 | |
| Bank overdraft | 21 000 | 29 000 |
| **Total capital and liabilities** | | 107 000 |

### Workings

Note the question is dealt with in two parts because it involves two businesses:

| Up to midnight 30 September 2014 | From a microsecond after midnight 1 October 2014 |
|---|---|
| Owners were Gerard, Sylvestre, Jean. | Owners are Gerard and Sylvestre. |

We credited the capital accounts with the increase in the value of the net assets in order that Jean can receive his just dues before his retirement. After all, he has presided over the increase in the value of the assets as well as contributing to the value of the goodwill of the business.

We debited the two capital accounts (there are only two partners, Gerard and Sylvestre, in this 'new' business) with the writing off of the asset of goodwill. Notice that when we wrote off the goodwill there were only two partners in the 'new' business – Jean is now no longer involved in the running of the business.

## 24.5 Methods of paying a partner when they leave a partnership

This can pose problems to a partnership. A retiring partner could have a considerable amount standing to the credit of their capital (and current) account. If a large sum were to be paid out the withdrawal could deprive the business of a great deal of liquid resources. How can the problem be resolved?

- The retiring partner's capital account balance could be transferred to a loan account and an amount could be paid each year to the partner who had retired.
- A new partner could join the business and the payment made by the new partner could be used to pay off the 'old' partner.
- The cash to pay off the 'old' partner could be borrowed from a bank or other financial institution.
- Remaining partners could inject sufficient further capital into the business, allowing the payment to be made.
- An investment could be made, which, on maturity, would pay for the retirement.

## 24.6 A change to the profit sharing ratio

Any change to the profit sharing ratios must be treated in much the same way as other structural changes.

View the change as that involving two separate distinct businesses. The 'first' business must be valued in order that the 'old' owners can be credited with any increase in the value of their business.

If a goodwill account is not to be maintained in the books of account of the 'new' business then it must be deleted and the 'new' partners debited in their profit sharing ratios.

**Worked example**

Juan and José are in partnership, sharing profits and losses in the ratio 3:1 respectively. From 1 January 2015 they agree to share profits and losses equally.

Their summarised statement of financial position at 31 December 2014 showed:

**Juan and José**
**Statement of financial position at 31 December 2014**

| | $ |
|---|---|
| **ASSETS** | |
| **Non-current assets** | 48 000 |
| **Current assets** | 12 000 |
| **Total assets** | 60 000 |
| | |
| **CAPITAL AND LIABILITIES** | |
| **Capital accounts –** Juan | 30 000 |
| José | 22 000 |
| | 52 000 |
| **Current liabilities** | 8 000 |
| **Total capital and liabilities** | 60 000 |

The partners agreed that non-current assets be valued at $70000 and that goodwill be valued at $28000. They further agreed that a goodwill account would not be maintained in the business books of account.

**Required**

Prepare a statement of financial position at 31 December 2014 after the change to the new profit sharing ratios has been implemented.

## Answer

**Juan and José**

**Statement of financial position at 31 December 2014**

| | | $ | |
|---|---|---|---|
| **ASSETS** | | | |
| **Non-current assets** | | 70000 | |
| **Current assets** | | 12000 | |
| **Total assets** | | 82000 | |
| | | | |
| **CAPITAL AND LIABILITIES** | | | |
| **Capital accounts –** | Juan | 53500 | ($30000 + $37500 – $14000) |
| | José | 20500 | ($22000 + $12500 – $14000) |
| | | 74000 | |
| **Current liabilities** | | 8000 | |
| **Total capital and liabilities** | | 82000 | |

**Self-test questions**

1 Identify two types of structural change to a partnership.
2 Explain why it is necessary to revalue the assets of a partnership when a structural change takes place.
3 Define the term 'goodwill'.
4 Explain one method of placing a value on goodwill.
5 Goodwill is the purchase of existing customers. True/False?
6 Non-current assets $30000; current liabilities $8000; purchase price $50000. What is the value placed on goodwill?
7 Explain the term 'inherent goodwill'.
8 Explain how inherent goodwill should be shown on a statement of financial position.

## 24.7 Partnership dissolution

A partnership may be dissolved, that is, it may cease to be a partnership, under the following circumstances:

- on the death of a partner
- on the retirement of a partner
- when a partner is declared bankrupt
- by mutual agreement of the partners.

## 24.8 Realisation accounts

When a partnership is dissolved, the assets of the business are disposed of and any liabilities are then settled. The order of settling any debts (liabilities) is as follows:

**1** trade and other payables (creditors)

**2** partners' loan accounts
**3** partners' capital accounts

The assets can be disposed of in a variety of ways:
- Some assets may be sold for cash.
- Some assets may be taken over by one or more of the partners.
- Some assets may be sold to a limited company.

As we saw in Chapter 2, all entries in books of account must first be entered in a book of prime entry. We use the journal as the book of prime entry when a business closes down. This is the sixth and final use of the journal.

We have also used the journal to help us when revising complex topics.

The way we tackle the closing down of a partnership is by preparing a **realisation account**.

On the debit side of the account, we find the assets that are disposed of and any expenses incurred in the dissolution. On the credit side, we find what the assets realised (what they have been sold for).

**Tip** 

The most common error made by students is to enter the amount raised by the sale of the assets in the debit side of the realisation account. Make sure that it is the carrying amount of the assets that you enter on the debit side.

**Realisation account**

| | |
|---|---|
| The carrying amount of the assets | The proceeds from the sales of the assets shown opposite |
| Costs of the dissolution | Other incomes or benefits |
| Discounts allowed | Discounts received |
| Profit on dissolution | Loss on dissolution |

Unless you are told differently, assume that the partnership will collect any outstanding monies from receivables (debtors) and pay off outstanding payables (creditors). Try to think what you would be doing in the circumstances when a partnership is dissolved.
- All the assets to be disposed of are entered on the debit side of the realisation account.
- All the proceeds are entered on the credit side.

Any *profit* resulting from the disposal of the assets will appear on the debit side of the realisation account. It is posted from here to the credit side of the partners' capital accounts in their profit sharing ratios.

Any *loss* will be shown on the credit side of the realisation account and it will be posted to the debit side of the partners' capital accounts in their profit sharing ratios.

If any partner takes over any of the partnership assets, treat this as a 'sale' to that partner. Credit the realisation account with the agreed value of the asset(s) to be taken over by the partner and debit the respective capital account.

**Example**

A partner, Josie, takes over the inventory of the partnership.

| | |
|---|---|
| **Debit** Josie's capital account with the agreed value of the inventory | **Credit** Realisation account |

A partner, Hernan, takes a business-owned vehicle at an agreed valuation of $3500.

| | |
|---|---|
| **Debit** Hernan's capital account $3500 | **Credit** Realisation account $3500 |

## Worked example

Wu and Xian are in partnership, sharing profits and losses in the ratio 2:1 respectively. They agree to dissolve the partnership on 30 November 2014. They provide the following information:

**Wu and Xian**
**Statement of financial position at 30 November 2014**

| | $ | $ |
|---|---|---|
| **ASSETS** | | |
| **Non-current assets** | | 80 000 |
| **Other current assets** | 17 000 | |
| Bank | 3 000 | 20 000 |
| **Total assets** | | 100 000 |
| | | |
| **CAPITAL AND LIABILITIES** | | |
| **Capital accounts** – Wu | | 50 000 |
| Xian | | 36 000 |
| | | 86 000 |
| | | |
| **Current liabilities** | | 14 000 |
| **Total capital and liabilities** | | 100 000 |

- The current liabilities were paid their due amounts.
- The non-current assets were sold for $100 000 cash.
- The current assets realised $15 000.

**Required**

Prepare:

a a bank account
b a realisation account
c partners' capital accounts.

## Answer

a

**Bank account**

| | $ | | $ |
|---|---|---|---|
| Balance | 3 000 | Current liabilities | 14 000 |
| Realisation – Non-current assets | 100 000 | Wu – Capital account | 62 000 |
| Current assets | 15 000 | Xian – Capital account | 42 000 |
| | 118 000 | | 118 000 |

b

**Realisation account**

| | $ | | $ |
|---|---|---|---|
| Non-current assets | 80 000 | bank (non-current assets) | 100 000 |
| Current assets | 17 000 | bank (current assets) | 15 000 |
| Capital accounts – Wu | 12 000 | | |
| Xian | 6 000 | | |
| | 115 000 | | 115 000 |

c

**Capital accounts**

| | Wu | Xian | | Wu | Xian |
|---|---|---|---|---|---|
| | $ | $ | | $ | $ |
| Bank | 62 000 | 42 000 | Balance b/d | 50 000 | 36 000 |
| | | | Realisation account | 12 000 | 6 000 |
| | 62 000 | 42 000 | | 62 000 | 42 000 |

**Tip**

You may find the preparation of journal entries to be a very useful revision aid. If you journalise any complex answer or an exercise that your teacher has gone through in class, you should find it easier to revise the order in which the processes involved took place when you return to the example some weeks or months later.

## Workings

In order to show the sequence of the entries shown above, the entries have been journalised:

| | Dr<br>$ | Cr<br>$ |
|---|---|---|
| Current liabilities | 14 000 | |
| Bank account | | 14 000 |
| Paying current liabilities | | |
| Realisation account | 80 000 | |
| Non-current assets | | 80 000 |
| Clearing the non-current assets from the partnership books of account | | |
| Realisation account | 17 000 | |
| Current assets | | 17 000 |
| Clearing current assets from the partnership books of account | | |
| Bank account | 100 000 | |
| Realisation account | | 100 000 |
| Sale of non-current assets for cash | | |
| Bank account | 15 000 | |
| Realisation account | | 15 000 |
| Sale of current assets for cash | | |
| Realisation account | 12 000 | |
| Capital account – Wu | | 12 000 |
| Wu's share of profits on realisation | | |
| Realisation account | 6 000 | |
| Capital account – Xian | | 6 000 |
| Xian's share of profit on realisation | | |
| Capital account – Wu | 62 000 | |
| Bank account | | 62 000 |
| Payment from partnership bank account to clear the balance on Wu's capital account | | |
| Capital account – Xian | 42 000 | |
| Bank account | | 42 000 |
| Payment from partnership bank account to clear the balance on Xian's capital account | | |

**Note**

- Do not attempt to share any balance left in the bank account in any pre-determined ratio. The bank account is used to clear any outstanding balances left on the partners' capital accounts.
- At the end of this type of exercise there should be no outstanding balances anywhere in your answer.

## Worked example

Rollo and Johann are in partnership, sharing profits and losses 3:2 respectively. They agree to dissolve their partnership on 28 February 2015. They provide the following information:

**Rollo and Johann**

**Statement of financial position 28 February 2015**

| | $ | $ |
|---|---|---|
| **ASSETS** | | |
| **Non-current assets** | | 40 000 |
| **Other current assets** | 8 000 | |
| Bank | 2 000 | 10 000 |
| **Total assets** | | 50 000 |
| | | |
| **CAPITAL AND LIABILITIES** | | |
| **Capital accounts** – Rollo | | 25 000 |
| Johann | | 19 000 |
| | | 44 000 |
| | | |
| **Current liabilities** | | 6 000 |
| **Total capital and liabilities** | | 50 000 |

- The non-current assets were taken over by Rollo at an agreed value of $36 000.
- The current assets realised $7 000 cash.
- The current liabilities were settled at the value shown in the business books of account.

**Required**

Prepare:

a a realisation account

b a bank account

c partners' capital accounts.

## Answer

a

**Realisation account**

| | $ | | $ |
|---|---|---|---|
| Non-current assets | 40 000 | Capital – Rollo | 36 000 |
| Current assets | 8 000 | Bank | 7 000 |
| | | Capital – Rollo | 3 000 |
| | | Johann | 2 000 |
| | 48 000 | | 48 000 |

b

**Bank account**

| | $ | | $ |
|---|---|---|---|
| Balance b/d | 2 000 | Current liabilities | 6 000 |
| Realisation account | 7 000 | Capital account – Johann | 17 000 |
| Capital account – Rollo | 14 000 | | |
| | 23 000 | | 23 000 |

c

**Capital accounts**

| | Rollo | Johann | | Rollo | Johann |
|---|---|---|---|---|---|
| | $ | $ | | $ | $ |
| Realisation account | 36 000 | | Balances b/d | 25 000 | 19 000 |
| Realisation account | 3 000 | 2 000 | Bank | 14 000 | |
| Bank | | 17 000 | | | |
| | 39 000 | 19 000 | | 39 000 | 19 000 |

### Workings

Again, to show the sequence of events, here are the journal entries:

| | Dr | Cr |
|---|---|---|
| | $ | $ |
| Current liabilities | 6000 | |
| Bank account | | 6000 |
| Paying off current liabilities | | |
| Realisation account | 40000 | |
| Non-current assets | | 40000 |
| Closing down non-current asset accounts | | |
| Realisation account | 8000 | |
| Current assets | | 8000 |
| Closing down current asset accounts | | |
| Capital account – Rollo | 36000 | |
| Realisation account | | 36000 |
| Rollo 'buys' non-current assets from the partnership. | | |
| Bank account | 7000 | |
| Realisation account | | 7000 |
| Sale of current assets | | |
| Bank account | 14000 | |
| Capital account – Rollo | | 14000 |
| Rollo pays off the deficit on his capital account. | | |
| Capital account – Johann | 17000 | |
| Bank account | | 17000 |
| Johann withdraws sufficient cash to clear the amount the partnership owes him. | | |

Clearly, there are times when receivables do not all pay the amounts that they owe to the business when a partnership is wound up. This may be because there may be some bad debts or because the partnership offers cash discounts in order to get the cash in quickly.

Similarly, there may be times when a partnership is able to benefit from cash discounts available from trade payables.

Any discounts allowed to receivables is debited to the realisation account (as would any debtors who proved to be bad). Any discounts received from payables is credited to the realisation account. The actual cash received from receivables is debited to the partnership bank account and the cash paid to payables is credited to the bank account.

**Worked example**

Aslam, Brannen and Chesney decide to dissolve their partnership on 30 April 2015. At that date trade receivables amounted to $7450 and trade payables totalled $3950.

Debtors (receivables) paid $7250 in settlement and creditors (payables) accepted $3800 in settlement.

**Required**

Prepare the following accounts to record the transactions:

a a realisation account

b a bank account

c total trade receivables account

d total trade payables account.

## Answer

a

**Realisation account**

| | $ | | $ |
|---|---|---|---|
| Total trade receivables account | 200 | Total trade payables account | 150 |

b

**Bank account**

| | $ | | $ |
|---|---|---|---|
| Total trade receivables account | 7 250 | Total trade payables account | 3 800 |

c

**Total trade receivables account**

| | $ | | $ |
|---|---|---|---|
| Balance b/d | 7 450 | Bank account | 7 250 |
| | | Realisation account | 200 |
| | 7 450 | | 7 450 |

d

**Total trade payables account**

| | $ | | $ |
|---|---|---|---|
| Bank account | 3 800 | Balance b/d | 3 950 |
| Realisation account | 150 | | |
| | 3 950 | | 3 950 |

Winding up a partnership will inevitably incur costs. These costs may be to advertise various assets to be sold; there may be costs paid to a lawyer who will tie up and formalise the legal side of the dissolution. Any costs involved should be:

debited to the realisation account … and … credited to the bank account.

Finally, remember to settle any partnership loans after you have dealt with receivables and payables – very straightforward:

Debit Loan account Credit Bank account

**Worked example**

Yoko and Cesc were in partnership, sharing profits and losses equally. They agreed to dissolve their partnership on 31 July 2015. They provide the following information:

**Yoko and Cesc**
**Statement of financial position at 31 July 2015**

| | $ | $ |
|---|---|---|
| **ASSETS** | | |
| **Non-current assets** | | 40 000 |
| **Current assets** | | |
| Inventory | 9 000 | |
| Trade receivables | 4 000 | |
| Bank balance | 2 000 | 15 000 |
| **Total assets** | | 55 000 |

| CAPITAL AND LIABILITIES | |
|---|---|
| **Capital accounts** – Yoko | 25 000 |
| Cesc | 20 000 |
| | 45 000 |
| **Non-current liabilities** | |
| Loan from Cesc | 2 000 |
| **Current liabilities** | |
| Trade payables | 8 000 |
| **Total capital and liabilities** | 55 000 |

- Non-current assets were sold for $58 000 cash.
- Inventory was taken over by Yoko at an agreed valuation of $7700.
- Trade receivables paid $3800 in settlement.
- Trade payables were paid $7500 in settlement.
- The costs incurred during the dissolution amounted to $3400.

**Required**

Prepare:

a a realisation account

b a bank account

c partners' capital accounts.

## Answer

a

**Realisation account**

| | $ | | $ |
|---|---|---|---|
| Discounts allowed | 200 | Discounts received | 500 |
| Non-current assets | 40 000 | Bank (non-current assets) | 58 000 |
| Inventory | 9 000 | Capital account – Yoko (inventory) | 7 700 |
| Bank (costs) | 3 400 | | |
| Profit on realisation – Yoko | 6 800 | | |
| Cesc | 6 800 | | |
| | 66 200 | | 66 200 |

b

**Bank account**

| | $ | | $ |
|---|---|---|---|
| Balance b/d | 2 000 | Loan – Cesc | 2 000 |
| Trade receivables | 3 800 | Trade payables | 7 500 |
| Realisation account (non-current assets) | 58 000 | Realisation account (costs) | 3 400 |
| | | Capital accounts – Yoko | 24 100 |
| | | Cesc | 26 800 |
| | 63 800 | | 63 800 |

c

**Capital accounts**

| | Yoko | Cesc | | Yoko | Cesc |
|---|---|---|---|---|---|
| | $ | $ | | $ | $ |
| Realisation account | 7 700 | | Balances b/d | 25 000 | 20 000 |
| Bank | 24 100 | 26 800 | Realisation account | 6 800 | 6 800 |
| | 31 800 | 26 800 | | 31 800 | 26 800 |

## Self-test questions

9 Under what circumstances might a partnership be dissolved?

10 A partnership is dissolved.
   a Which account should be debited if a partner takes over the inventory of the business?
   b Which account should be credited if a partner takes over one of the business vehicles?

11 After dissolution a partner has a debit balance on his capital account. Will he pay or receive cash from the partnership bank account?

12 From the following list identify the items that could be found on the debit side of a realisation account:
- bank balance
- discounts allowed
- discounts received
- dissolution costs
- inventory
- non-current assets
- partners' capital account balances
- partners' current account balances.

13 Identify from the list the items that could be found on the credit side of a realisation account.

➤ Now try Questions 7 and 8.

# 24.9 Assets taken over by a limited company

So far, all assets of the business have either been taken over by a partner or have been sold for cash. We must now consider the situation where some of the assets are sold to a limited company. The limited company could settle the deal by paying in any of the following combinations:

- cash
- cash and shares
- cash and debentures
- debentures and shares
- cash, debentures and shares.

## Worked example

Karl and Burcu were in partnership, sharing profits and losses in the ratio 2:1 respectively. They agreed to sell their business to Tontong Ltd. The purchase consideration was $100 000, being made up of $20 000 cash and 50 000 ordinary shares of $1 each. The partners agreed that the shares be distributed in the profit sharing ratios. The following information immediately prior to the takeover is provided:

| | | $ |
|---|---|---|
| **Net assets** | | 82 000 |
| **Capital accounts** – Karl | | 50 000 |
| | Burcu | 32 000 |
| | | 82 000 |

**Required**

Prepare ledger accounts to close the books of account.

## Answer

**Realisation account**

| | $ | | $ |
|---|---|---|---|
| Net assets | 82 000 | Tontong Ltd | 100 000 |
| Capital accounts (profit on realisation) – Karl | 12 000 | | |
| Burcu | 6 000 | | |
| | 100 000 | | 100 000 |

**Tontong Ltd**

| | $ | | $ |
|---|---|---|---|
| Realisation account | 100 000 | Bank | 20 000 |
| | | Capital (Shares) – Karl | 53 333 |
| | | Burcu | 26 667 |
| | 100 000 | | 100 000 |

**Bank account**

| | $ | | $ |
|---|---|---|---|
| Tontong Ltd | 20 000 | Capital accounts – Karl | 8 667 |
| | | Burcu | 11 333 |
| | 20 000 | | 20 000 |

**Capital accounts**

| | Karl | Burcu | | Karl | Burcu |
|---|---|---|---|---|---|
| | $ | $ | | $ | $ |
| Ordinary shares in Tontong Ltd | 53 333 | 26 667 | Balances b/d | 50 000 | 32 000 |
| Bank | 8 667 | 11 333 | Realisation account | 12 000 | 6 000 |
| | 62 000 | 38 000 | | 62 000 | 38 000 |

## Workings

Here are journal entries so that you can follow the chronology of the entries:

| | Dr | Cr |
|---|---|---|
| | $ | $ |
| Realisation account | 82 000 | |
| Net assets | | 82 000 |
| This closes down the asset accounts. | | |
| Tontong Ltd | 100 000 | |
| Realisation account | | 100 000 |
| Purchase consideration agreed between the partners and Tontong Ltd | | |
| Realisation account | 18 000 | |
| Capital – Karl | | 12 000 |
| Burcu | | 6 000 |
| Profit on realisation credited to partners in their profit sharing ratios | | |
| Bank account | 20 000 | |
| Tontong Ltd | | 20 000 |
| Cash paid by Tontong Ltd | | |
| Capital accounts – Karl | 53 333 | |
| Burcu | 26 667 | |
| Tontong Ltd | | 80 000 |
| Shares given to partners in the agreed ratios – note that the ordinary shares are distributed in value terms not in nominal values. | | |

The shares must be worth $1.60 each ($80 000 ÷ 50 000) to the partners.

| | | |
|---|---|---|
| Capital accounts – Karl | 8 667 | |
| Burcu | 11 333 | |
| Bank | | 20 000 |
| Cash is withdrawn from the bank account to balance the capital accounts. | | |

Talk yourself through this example a couple of times. It is much easier than you think. The point at which most students go wrong is when the ordinary shares have to be shared between the partners – simply divide the balance (of share value to be distributed) remaining in the purchasing company's account by the ratios given in the question.

**Worked example**

Umberto and Claudius are in partnership, sharing profits and losses in the ratio 3:2 respectively. They sell their business to Dorken Ltd for an agreed purchase consideration of $200 000. The purchase consideration is made up as follows:

| | |
|---|---|
| Cash | $40 000 |
| 6% debentures | $50 000 |
| 30 000 ordinary shares of $1 each | |

Remember that those $1 shares may be worth more (or less) than the $1 nominal value. So how much they are worth per share? $3.67 each.

It was agreed that the partners would distribute the debentures in the last agreed capital account ratios and that the ordinary shares would be divided according to the profit and loss sharing ratio.

The partnership statement of financial position immediately prior to the takeover showed:

| | $ |
|---|---|
| **Net assets** | 120 000 |
| **Capital accounts** – Umberto | 80 000 |
| Claudius | 40 000 |
| | 120 000 |

**Required**

Prepare ledger accounts to close the books of account.

## Answer

**Realisation account**

| | $ | | $ |
|---|---|---|---|
| Net assets | 120 000 | Dorken Ltd | 200 000 |
| Capital accounts – Umberto | 48 000 | | |
| Claudius | 32 000 | | |
| | 200 000 | | 200 000 |

**Dorken Ltd**

| | $ | | $ |
|---|---|---|---|
| Realisation account | 200 000 | Bank | 40 000 |
| | | Capital accounts – Debentures | 50 000 |
| | | Capital accounts – Ordinary shares | 110 000 |
| | 200 000 | | 200 000 |

**Bank account**

| | $ | | $ |
|---|---|---|---|
| Dorken Ltd | 40 000 | Capital accounts – Umberto | 28 667 |
| | | Claudius | 11 333 |
| | 40 000 | | 40 000 |

**Capital accounts**

| | Umberto | Claudius | | Umberto | Claudius |
|---|---|---|---|---|---|
| | $ | $ | | $ | $ |
| Dorken Ltd (debentures) | 33 333 | 16 667 | Balances b/d | 80 000 | 40 000 |
| Dorken Ltd (ordinary shares) | 66 000 | 44 000 | Realisation account | 48 000 | 32 000 |
| Bank account (to balance) | 28 667 | 11 333 | | | |
| | 128 000 | 72 000 | | 128 000 | 72 000 |

## Workings

Journal entries (as a revision aid):

| | Dr | Cr |
|---|---|---|
| | $ | $ |
| Realisation account | 120 000 | |
| Net assets account | | 120 000 |
| Dorken Ltd | 200 000 | |
| Realisation account | | 200 000 |
| Realisation account | 48 000 | |
| Realisation account | 32 000 | |
| Capital accounts – Umberto | | 48 000 |
| Claudius | | 32 000 |
| Bank account | 40 000 | |
| Dorken Ltd | | 40 000 |
| Capital accounts – Umberto | 33 333 | |
| Claudius | 16 667 | |
| Dorken Ltd (debentures) | | 50 000 |
| Capital accounts – Umberto | 66 000 | |
| Claudius | 44 000 | |
| Dorken Ltd (ordinary shares) | | 110 000 |
| Capital accounts – Umberto | 28 667 | |
| Claudius | 11 333 | |
| Bank account | | 28 667 |
| Bank account | | 11 333 |

As a point of interest, the entries in the ledger of Dorken Ltd would show:

- bank account reduced by $40 000
- debentures increased by $50 000
- ordinary share capital increased by $30 000
- share premium account increased by $80 000
- net tangible assets increased by $120 000
- goodwill $80 000 (Dorken paid $200 000 for $120 000 of tangible assets.)

➤ Now try Questions 9 and 10.

## Self-test questions

**14** Explain the circumstances when a partnership would be dissolved.

**15** Explain how a loss on realisation should be treated.

**16** A and B share profits and losses in the ratio 2:1. Profit on realisation is $24 000; balance at bank is $9000. Explain how the profit and bank balance are shared between A and B.

**17** Purchase consideration $84 000, made up of $12 000 cash; $50 000 seven per cent debentures and 20 000 ordinary shares of $1 each. What is the value of one ordinary share?

## Chapter summary

- When a structural change takes place to a partnership:
  - two separate sets of financial statements must be prepared – one set before the change takes place and a further set after the change has been implemented
  - the business assets must be valued (including goodwill if appropriate)
  - any change to the value of assets 'belongs' to the 'old' partners
  - if goodwill has to be written off this is done in the profit sharing ratios of the 'new' partners.
- A partnership is dissolved
  - on the death of a partner
  - on the retirement of a partner
  - when a partner is declared bankrupt
  - by mutual agreement of the partners.
- The debts of a partnership should be settled in the following order:
  - payables
  - partners' loan accounts
  - partners' capital accounts.
- When a partnership is wound up, assets are transferred to the debit of a realisation account. The realisation account is credited with the 'selling' price of each asset. The profit or loss on realisation is calculated. The profit (or loss) is then apportioned to the partners in their profit sharing ratios.

# 25 The financial statements of limited companies

**Content**

**1.4 Preparation of financial statements**

1.4.4 Limited companies

- Prepare an income statement, statement of financial position and simple cash flows for a limited company from full or incomplete accounting records
- Describe the distinction between capital and revenue reserves
- Explain the different types of shares a company may issue
- Prepare ledger accounts to record the issue of the different types of shares, including bonus and rights issues
- Prepare a statement of changes in equity

**By the end of this chapter you should be able to:**

- explain the characteristics of a limited company
- make a comparison between partnerships, private limited companies and public limited companies
- prepare the income statement of a limited company suitable for internal use
- prepare a statement of changes in equity
- prepare a simple cash flow statement
- identify and explain the different components of a statement of financial position of a limited company
- explain the term 'reserves'
- distinguish between revenue and capital reserves
- show the effect of an issue of shares at a premium on the statement of financial position of a limited company
- show how the revaluation of non-current assets will affect a statement of financial position
- show the effect on a statement of financial position of a rights issue of shares and a bonus issue of shares.

## 25.1 Limited companies

A **limited company** is an organisation that has a legal identity that is separate from that of its owners. The owners of a limited company are called **shareholders** (or members); their liability is limited to the amount that they have agreed to pay the company for their shares.

A **limited company** can be a very small business or a giant multinational business with branches and/or subsidiary companies trading throughout the world.

The majority of businesses are **sole traders** or **partnerships**. The major drawback of these two types of business is that their owner(s) have unlimited liability.

As we have seen, a sole trader is responsible for all debts incurred by him or her in the course of running the business. For example, if Moona, a sole trader, runs up business debts of $25 000, she may have to settle these debts from her private savings or she may have to sell her house or car to clear the debts. Moona has unlimited liability.

Similarly, if the business partnership of Clint and Dyke has debts of $30 000, both partners are 'jointly and severally responsible' for the debts of the business and between them they may have to raise the money privately to pay off the amount that is owed. Clint and Dyke have unlimited liability.

However, Blinva plc (public limited company) has debts of $345 000. Jemma, a shareholder in the company (she owns 500 ordinary shares of $1 each), could not be asked to contribute further funds in order to help pay off the debts of the company. She could lose her investment but that is all she would lose. Her personal possessions are safe. Jemma has limited liability.

So, unlimited liability means that the owners of a business have responsibility for all the debts incurred by their business.

In the vast majority of cases, unlimited liability is of little significance. However, if a business is making losses on a regular basis then the continuous existence of the business may well be in doubt. So a major drawback of being a sole trader or a partner in a business is unlimited liability for the owners.

As a consequence of unlimited liability there is another major drawback for unlimited businesses. There are fewer opportunities to find extra capital that may be necessary for an expansion programme. Prospective investors may not wish to take the risk of losing their private assets as well as their investment.

## 25.2 Partnerships and private limited companies

**Table 25.1** The main features of partnerships and private limited companies

| Partnership | Private limited company (Ltd) |
|---|---|
| Two to 20 partners | At least one member, no maximum |
| Unlimited liability of partners | Limited liability of shareholders |
| Profits credited to partners' current accounts according to partnership agreement | Profits distributed by dividends |
| No tax on business profits* | Corporation tax charged on company profits |
| Partners run the business | Shareholders delegate running of the business to directors |

* Partnerships are not taxed on their business profits. Individual partners pay tax on their earnings as partners.

**Self-test questions**

1 Explain why the owners of a partnership might turn their business into a private limited company.
2 What is meant by 'limited liability'?
3 Directors are the owners of a limited company. True/False?
4 Explain why shareholders appoint directors to run a limited company.

## 25.3 Private limited companies and public limited companies

**Authorised share capital** identifies the amount of share capital that a company is allowed to issue in accordance with its memorandum and articles of association.

**Table 25.2** The main features of private limited companies and public limited companies

| Private limited company | Public limited company |
|---|---|
| 'Ltd' appears after company name | 'plc' appears after company name |
| Minimum of one shareholder to the limit of authorised share capital and at least one director | Minimum of two shareholders to the limit of authorised share capital and at least two directors |
| Share trading restricted | No restriction to share trading |
| No stock market listing | Usually listed on recognised stock market |

Private limited companies do not sell their shares to the general public, so if a private limited company wishes to raise additional finance through a share issue, the directors must find other individuals who might be willing to invest in the company. This is why many private limited companies are often family businesses with members of the family or close friends of the family owning all the shares.

On the other hand, if the directors of a public limited company wish to raise additional finance, the directors may well advertise the fact in the financial sections of daily newspapers in order that the public at large may subscribe to the offer.

The advantages of limited liability status and the ability to raise large amounts of finance are offset by certain legal obligations:

- Annual financial statements must be audited by professionally qualified personnel. (This is not the case with partnerships or with sole traders.)
- Annual returns must be completed and filed with the Registrar of Companies. These returns may be inspected by the general public. The financial statements included as part of the annual return lack much of the detail that could be used by a competitor.
- Companies are usually regulated by government legislation and/or agencies.
- Copies of the company's annual audited financial statements must be sent to each shareholder and debenture holder.

## 25.4 Financial statements

All business organisations produce financial statements for two main purposes.

Financial statements are produced:

- for *management* purposes: the financial statements are used by management to highlight areas of good practice and to find areas within the business that could benefit from improvement
- for *stewardship* reasons: the financial statements show the providers of finance how the funds that they provided are being used. Are the funds being used wisely or is the finance being squandered?

Under the stewardship umbrella we also find the need to provide accounts that comply with:

- governmental requirements
- accounting standards
- stock exchange regulations
- tax legislation.

We have seen that the financial statements prepared for all business organisations are broadly similar. Apart from the heading, a set of financial statements prepared for a limited company would look similar to a set of financial statements prepared for a sole trader.

Figure 25.1 shows the potential users of the financial statements prepared for a limited company.

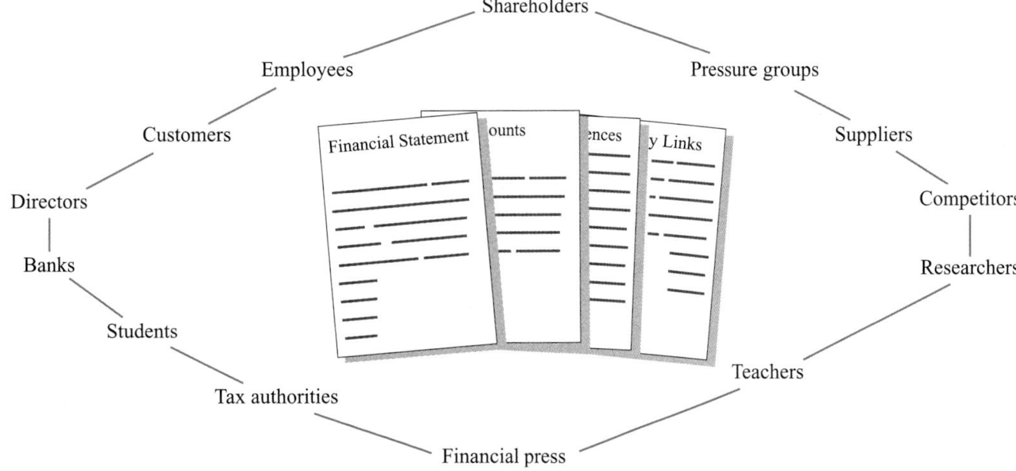


**Figure 25.1** The users of the financial statements of a limited company

**Self-test questions**

5 Identify the difference between a private limited company and a public limited company.
6 Private limited companies can have their shares quoted on a recognised stock market. True/False?
7 A private limited company could have 35 shareholders. True/False?
8 Private limited companies cannot sell their goods in another country. True/False?
9 Private limited companies can only issue shares to relatives. True/False?
10 Which type of businesses file their annual financial statements with the Registrar of Companies?
11 Only profitable companies must file their annual financial statements with the Registrar of Companies. True/False?

## 25.5 The income statement of a limited company

**Income statements** identify gross profit and profit for the year.

**Revenue** comprises the receipts from the sales of goods and/or services by a company.

**Overheads** are the expenses incurred by a company during the financial year.

**Profit from operations** is the profit earned by a company before deducting finance costs and taxation.

**Finance costs** comprise interest paid on all debt.

**Dividends** are the rewards paid to shareholders out of profits earned by a limited company. The dividends are paid to individual shareholders in proportion to the number of shares they own. Dividends are paid annually, but most limited companies will pay **interim dividends** part way through their financial year.

**Ordinary dividends** are variable in nature. The dividend will vary according to the level of profits earned by a company.

**Preference dividends** are normally a fixed amount. Generally, half of the total dividend is paid as an interim dividend, the balance being paid at the year end.

**Debenture interest** is paid to debenture holders (investors) who have loaned money to a company. The interest is usually paid in two equal instalments during the year.

These definitions are expanded in Section 25.7 of this chapter where shares and debentures are discussed more fully.

Here is an example of an income statement of a limited company:

**Example**

**Nedert Ltd**

**Income statement for the year ended 31 December 2014**

| | **$000** | **$000** | |
|---|---|---|---|
| Revenue | | 3434 | |
| *Less* Cost of sales | | | |
| Inventory 1 January 2014 | 632 | | *Looks similar to 'other' financial statements so far, doesn't it?* |
| Purchases | 1578 | | |
| | 2210 | | |
| Inventory 31 December 2014 | (711) | 1499 | |
| Gross profit | | 1935 | |
| *Less* Expenses | | | |
| Wages | (451) | | |
| Other general expenses | (349) | | |
| Depreciation | (56) | (856) | |
| Profit from operations | | 1079 | |
| Finance costs (debenture interest) | | (25) | *Here is where there are changes.* |
| Profit before tax | | 1054 | |
| Tax | | (223) | |
| Profit for the year attributable to equity holders | | 831 | |

 Tip 

Learn the layout for a set of financial statements for a limited company. You already know most of it. So concentrate on the lower third – the parts after the profit from operations has been calculated.

Why is it important to identify the profit from operations?

Consider this simple example:

**Example**

Kris is a sole trader. His wealthy father set him up in business a number of years ago by providing all the necessary finance. His business earns a gross profit of $100 000 per annum.

Kate is a sole trader. She is in the same business sector as Kris. Their businesses are a similar size. Kate has no wealthy relatives and she borrowed money from a bank to help finance her business. Her business also earns a gross profit of $100 000 per annum.

Kris's business expenses for the year are $60 000. Kate's business expenses for the year are $70 000, of which $20 000 is interest payments to the bank.

Which of the two business owners runs a more efficient business?

Kris's profit from operations for the year is $40 000 while Kate's is $50 000.

If Kate's parents had given her the necessary finance for her business, her profits would have been the greater of the two. She appears to be running a more efficient business.

After the deduction of interest payable from the profit from operations we have profit before taxation.

One other point is that it is usual to group certain types of expenses together. The reason for this is that it makes the production of published accounts easier. We will consider published accounts in Chapter 34 in the A-level section of the book.

**Worked example**

The directors of Treadle plc provide the following information at 31 October 2014:

| | $ |
|---|---|
| Sales | 956 230 |
| Purchases | 438 920 |
| Inventory 1 November 2013 | 43 310 |
| Inventory 31 October 2014 | 41 760 |
| Directors' fees | 106 900 |
| Salaries – sales personnel | 54 970 |
| administrative | 67 830 |
| Depreciation – delivery vehicles | 54 000 |
| premises | 20 000 |
| Other expenses – selling and distribution | 31 140 |
| administrative | 34 800 |
| Audit fees | 23 000 |
| Debenture interest | 40 000 |
| Corporation taxation | 21 000 |

**Required**

Prepare an income statement for the year ended 31 October 2014.

## Answer

**Treadle plc**

**Income statement for the year ended 31 October 2014**

| | $ | $ |
|---|---|---|
| Revenue | | 956 230 |
| *Less* Cost of sales | | |
| Inventory 1 November 2013 | 43 310 | |
| Purchases | 438 920 | |
| | 482 230 | |
| Inventory 31 October 2014 | (41 760 ) | 440 470 |
| Gross profit | | 515 760 |
| Overheads: | | |
| Selling and distribution costs | | |
| Salaries | (54 970) | |
| Directors' fees | (106 900) | |
| Other expenses | (31 140) | |
| Audit fees | (23 000) | |
| Depreciation – delivery vehicles | (54 000) | (270 010) |
| Administrative expenses | | |
| Salaries | (67 830) | |
| Other expenses | (34 800) | |
| Depreciation – premises | (20 000) | (122 630) |
| Profit from operations | | 123 120 |
| Finance costs | | (40 000) |
| Profit before tax | | 83 120 |
| Corporation tax | | (21 000) |
| Profit for the year attributable to equity holders | | 62 120 |

## 25.6 Statements of changes in equity

A **statement of changes in equity** details changes that have taken place in share capital and reserves during the financial year.

**Revenue reserves** are profits that are retained within the company.

International Accounting Standards (see Chapter 36) require that limited companies show how the shareholders' (the owners') stake in the company has changed over the course of the financial year.

The income statement concludes with the profit for the year. Standards require that a **statement of changes in equity** is prepared. This provides the link between the income statement and the statement of financial position by showing changes to permanent share capital and reserves (equity).

Dividends are the part of the profits of a company that are paid to the shareholders (owners). Any part of the profit that is not paid out to the shareholders as dividends is retained within the company as a **revenue reserve**.

The portion of profit retained in the company is sometimes said to be 'ploughed back', and are described on the statement of financial position as retained earnings.

All profits (after taxation and preference dividends) belong to the ordinary shareholders so the amount of profit retained within the company will, generally, have a positive effect on the price of second-hand shares in the (stock) market.

### Worked example

The following information is available at 31 March 2015 for Evahline plc:

| | $000 |
|---|---|
| Profit before tax | 746 |
| Tax | 218 |
| Ordinary dividends paid | 146 |
| Preference dividends paid | 70 |
| Retained earnings at 1 April 2014 | 814 |

**Required**

Prepare:

a an extract from the income statement for the year ended 31 March 2015

b an extract from a statement showing changes in equity.

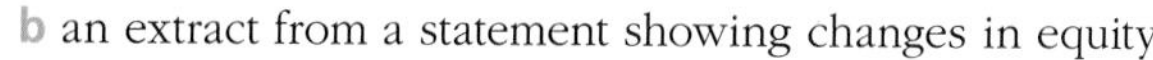

**Tip**

Be careful when using millions and thousands – many errors are caused when decimal points are put in the wrong place. For example:

| Correct ✓ | Wrong ✗ |
|---|---|
| $000 | $000 |
| 30 | 30000 |
| 1.6 | 1600 |

Errors like this can be expensive!
If you are not confident, then write the figures in full, for example:

| $ |
|---|
| 30000 |
| 1600 |

## Answer

a

**Evahline plc**

**Extract from income statement for the year ended 31 March 2015**

| | $000 |
|---|---|
| Profit before tax | 746 |
| Tax | 218 |
| Profit for the year attributable to equity holders | 528 |

b

**Evahline plc**

**Extract from statement of changes in equity**

| **Retained earnings** | **$000** |
|---|---|
| Balance at 1 April 2014 | 814 |
| Profit for the year | 528 |
| | 1342 |
| Dividends paid | (146) |
| Balance at 31 March 2015 | 1196 |

Preference dividends will have been included as part of the finance costs.

A statement of changes in equity shows details of changes that have taken place to any of the components of a limited company's equity. Changes to permanent share capital and any changes to the reserves held by a company are shown.

**Issued share capital** is the amount of share capital that has actually been issued by a company. The issued share capital can never exceed the authorised share capital.

### Worked example

An extract from the statement of financial position of Tantang plc shows the following details:

| | $000 |
|---|---|
| **EQUITY AND LIABILITIES** | |
| **Equity** | |
| Issued share capital | 2500 |
| Share premium | 500 |
| Revaluation reserve | 1000 |
| General reserve | 750 |
| Retained earnings | 1876 |

During the year ended 31 December 2014 the following changes to equity took place:
1000000 ordinary shares of $1 each were issued at a price of $2.50 each.
Non-current assets currently valued at $850000 were revalued at $1000000.

A transfer of $50 000 was made from retained earnings to the general reserve.
The profit for the year ended 31 December 2014 was $638 160.
Ordinary dividends paid were $125 000.

**Required**

Prepare a statement of changes in equity for the year ended 31 December 2014.

## Answer

**Statement of changes in equity for the year ended 31 December 2014**

| | Share capital | Share premium | Revaluation reserve | General reserve | Retained earnings | Total |
|---|---|---|---|---|---|---|
| | $000 | $000 | $000 | $000 | $000 | $000 |
| Balance at start of the year | 2 500 | 500 | 1 000 | 750 | 1 876 | 6 626 |
| Share issue | 1 000 | 1 500 | | | | 2 500 |
| Revaluation | | | 150 | | | 150 |
| Transfer to general reserve | | | | 50 | (50) | 0 |
| Profit for the year | | | | | 638.16 | 638.16 |
| Dividends paid | | | | | (125) | (125) |
| Balance at end of the year | 3 500 | 2 000 | 1 150 | 800 | 2 339.16 | 9 789.16 |

You can see that the statement has been adjusted to reflect the new value of each component making up equity capital.

### Worked example

The following information is provided for the year ended 31 December 2014 for Dohoma plc:

| | $000 |
|---|---|
| Revenue | 3 160 |
| Purchases | 211 |
| Inventory at 1 January 2014 | 87 |
| at 31 December 2014 | 91 |
| Salaries and general expenses | 531 |
| Directors' fees | 312 |
| Rent and local taxes | 80 |
| Depreciation of delivery vehicles | 75 |
| Salaries of sales assistants | 612 |
| Advertising | 147 |
| Ordinary share dividend paid | 200 |
| Preference share dividend paid | 180 |
| Tax | 312 |
| Depreciation – office equipment | 28 |
| Debenture interest | 50 |
| Retained earnings at 1 January 2014 | 4 106 |

**Required**

Prepare:

a an income statement for the year ended 31 December 2014

b a statement showing changes in equity for the year ended 31 December 2014.

## Answer

a

**Dohoma plc**
**Income statement for the year ended 31 December 2014**

| | **$000** | **$000** |
|---|---|---|
| Revenue | | 3 160 |
| *Less* Cost of sales | | |
| Inventory at 1 January 2014 | 87 | |
| Purchases | 211 | |
| | 298 | |
| Inventory at 31 December 2014 | (91) | 207 |
| Gross profit | | 2 953 |
| Selling and distribution costs | | |
| Salaries | (612) | |
| Advertising | (147) | |
| Depreciation – delivery van | (75) | (834) |
| Administrative expenses | | |
| Salaries and general expenses | (531) | |
| Directors' fees | (312) | |
| Rent and local taxes | (80) | |
| Depreciation – office equipment | (28) | (951) |
| Profit from operations | | 1 168 |
| Finance costs | | (230) |
| Profit before tax | | 938 |
| Tax | | (312) |
| Profit for the year attributable to equity holders | | 626 |

b **Extract from statement of changes in equity for the year ended 31 December 2014**

| | **$000** |
|---|---|
| **Retained earnings** | |
| Balance at 1 January 2014 | 4 106 |
| Profit for the year | 626 |
| | 4 732 |
| Dividends paid | (200) |
| Balance at 31 December 2014 | 4 532 |

Note the way that the expenses are categorised. You should be able to tell quite easily which expense goes under which heading.

Make sure that you use the correct labels as they are crucial in the financial statements:

- cost of sales
- gross profit
- profit from operations
- profit before tax
- profit for the year attributable to equity holders.

**Self-test questions**

12 What is the term used to describe a dividend that is paid part way through a financial year?
13 A limited company must always pay an interim dividend. True/False?
14 Ordinary dividends must be greater than preference dividends. True/False?
15 A public limited company could have 3500 shareholders. True/False?
16 Explain to a potential investor the difference between the return on debentures and the return on ordinary shares.
17 Ordinary shareholders must own a minimum of 100 shares in order to have a vote at a company's AGM. True/False?
18 Profit from operations is only earned by privately owned hospitals and clinics. True/False?
19 What expenses might be found under the heading of financial costs?
20 Name two sets of people who should receive the annual financial statements of a limited company.
21 What is shown in a statement of changes in equity?
22 Explain why dividends paid are shown in a statement of changes in equity.
23 Finance costs and tax paid are shown as deductions in a statement of changes in equity. True/False?

➤ Now try Question 1.

# 25.7 The statement of financial position of a limited company (including types of share capital)

**Authorised share capital** identifies the amount of share capital that a company is allowed to issue in accordance with its memorandum and articles of association.

**Issued share capital** is the amount of share capital that has actually been issued by a company. The issued share capital can never exceed the authorised share capital.

**Called-up share capital** is the amount of issued share capital that the shareholders have been asked to pay to date. It may be less than the value of the issued share capital.

**Paid-up capital** is the amount of share capital that appears on the statement of financial position and is the amount of cash that the company has actually received from the shareholders.

## 25.7.1 Capital structure

A limited company raises capital in order to provide finance for the purchase of non-current assets (and initially to provide working capital). It raises capital in a variety of ways.

A company can:

- issue shares
- issue debentures
- borrow from financial institutions.

The statement of financial position of a limited company is very similar to the statements of financial position that you have already prepared many times before. But there are some important differences in layout and in the accounting terms used.

The 'top' section of a statement of financial position for sole traders and partnerships might look like this:

| | $ | |
|---|---|---|
| **ASSETS** | | |
| **Non-current assets** | 100 | |
| **Current assets** | 30 | *Figures are included for* |
| **Total assets** | 130 | *illustrative purposes only* |

**Tip**

Show the authorised share capital at the start of the lower section of the statement of financial position; rule it off, but do not add it to the remainder of the section.

It is only the 'lower part' of the statement that looks different.

| Sole trader | $ | Partnership | $ | $ |
|---|---|---|---|---|
| | | | | |
| **CAPITAL AND LIABILITIES** | | **CAPITAL AND LIABILITIES** | | |
| **Capital** | 70 | **Capital accounts** - Doe | | 40 |
| **Non-current liabilities** | 50 | Ray | | 25 |
| | | | | 65 |
| **Current Liabilities** | 10 | **Current Accounts** - Doe | 3 | |
| **Total capital and liabilities** | 130 | Ray | 2 | 5 |
| | | **Non-current liabilities** | | 50 |
| | | **Current liabilities** | | 10 |
| | | **Total capital and liabilities** | | 130 |

**Equity** is made up of the ordinary share capital, permanent preference share capital and reserves of a limited company.

The lower part of the statement of financial position of a limited company might look like this:

| | $ |
|---|---|
| **EQUITY AND LIABILITIES** | |
| **Equity** | |
| Ordinary shares of $1 each | 35 |
| 6% preference shares of $0.50 each | 25 |
| Reserves | 10 |
| | 70 |
| **Non-current liabilities** | 50 |
| **Current liabilities** | 10 |
| **Total equity and liabilities** | 130 |

We will now look in detail at the *lower* section of a statement of financial position for a limited company.

The section should be headed 'Equity'.

Share capital can have ordinary and preference shares. Each should be described fully, for example:

| | $m |
|---|---|
| **Equity** | |
| Ordinary shares of $1 each | 50.00 |
| 7% preference shares of $1 each | 1.00 |

The extract from the statement of financial position shows that the **nominal value** of each class of share is $1. It shows that 50 million ordinary shares have actually been issued and 1 million preference shares have actually been issued.

Any ordinary dividend to be paid will be expressed as a percentage of the nominal value or as an amount per share. So a dividend may be declared as five per cent (i.e. five per cent of $1 nominal value) or as an amount of, say, 6.3 cents (i.e. the holder of 100 shares would receive $6.30 as a dividend).

The preference shareholder will receive a dividend of seven per cent (i.e. 7 cents for every $1 share held).

## 25.7.2 Ordinary shares

**Nominal value**, also known as the **par value**, is the face value of shares. Once the shares have been issued their market price can rise or fall. Any change in the market price is not reflected in the company's books of account.

Ordinary shares are the most common type of share. The holders of ordinary shares are part owners of the company. At meetings in which voting is required, each shareholder can cast one vote for each share they own, so the shareholders can appoint directors and can influence policies that directors and managers wish to follow. They may receive a variable dividend in years when the company is profitable (and has sufficient cash resources). They may receive interim dividends during the year and a final dividend shortly after the financial year end.

**Liquidation** is a legal procedure applied to a limited company when it is unable to discharge its liabilities.

### 25.7.3 Preference shares

Preference shareholders are entitled to a fixed dividend (if profits and cash are available). The percentage is calculated on the nominal value of the shares. In the event of **liquidation**, the preference shareholders are entitled to be repaid the nominal value of their shares before the ordinary shares are repaid.

Preference shares may be **cumulative** or **non-cumulative**.

- The dividends due on cumulative preference shares will accumulate if the company is unable to pay a dividend in any particular year – for example if six per cent cumulative preference shares have not received a dividend for three years, the holders would receive 24 per cent dividend in year 4 if sufficient profits were made and the cash was available. Most preference shares are cumulative.
- If the preference shares are non-cumulative, any dividends not paid are forfeit.

We must also distinguish between **participating preference shares** and **redeemable preference shares**:

- If a company's profits exceed a predetermined level, participating preference shares receive an additional dividend, above the normal percentage that they would usually receive.
- Redeemable preference shares may be bought back by the company on a specified date. The date is shown on the statement of financial position or as a note to the statement.

### 25.7.4 Debentures

Do not show debentures as part of equity. They should always be shown on a statement of financial position as a non-current liability.

**Debentures** are *not* shares; they are bonds recording a long-term loan to a company. The document is evidence of the loan and the holder is entitled to a fixed rate of interest each year. Debentures may be repayable at some future date or they may be irredeemable – that is, the holder will only be repaid if the company goes into liquidation.

Some debentures have the loan secured against specific non-current assets or against all the company's assets. These are known at **mortgage debentures**.

If the company is wound up or fails to pay the interest due, the holders of mortgage debentures can sell the assets of the company and recoup any outstanding amounts.

### 25.7.5 Characteristics of long-term finance available to limited companies

**Table 25.3** Ordinary shares, preference shares and debentures

| Ordinary shares | Preference shares | Debentures |
|---|---|---|
| Shares | Shares | Long-term loans (payables) |
| Part owner of company | Not owners | Not owners |
| Voting rights | (Usually) no voting rights | No voting rights |
| Paid out last in case of liquidation | Paid out before ordinary shareholders in case of liquidation | Paid out before preference shareholders in case of liquidation |
| Dividends | Dividends | Interest |
| Variable dividend | Fixed dividend | Fixed rate of interest |
| Part of equity capital | Part of equity capital (unless they are redeemable) | Not part of equity capital |

## 25.8 Reserves

The profits of any business belong to the owners. The profit earned by a sole trader or by partners belongs to them (the owners). The profit earned by a limited company also belongs to the owners – that is, the ordinary shareholders.

In the case of a sole trader or partnership, some profits may be taken out of a business by the owners as drawings. In the case of a limited company, some of the profits may be paid to the shareholders as dividends. The profit that remains in the business increases the capital structure of the business.

**Example**

| | Sole trader | Partnership | Limited company |
|---|---|---|---|
| **Profit $26 000** | Drawings $12 000 | Drawings, say $8 000 and $4 000 | Dividends $12 000 |
| **Retained profits** | $14 000<br>Part of capital account | $14 000<br>Part of capital or current accounts | $14 000<br>Part of equity as revenue reserve |

**Self-test questions**

**24** Name two ways in which a limited company can raise finance.
**25** Give another term used for the nominal value of a share.
**26** Name two components of the equity of a limited company.
**27** The two types of shares that pay a fixed dividend are preference and debentures. True/False?
**28** What does the term 'cumulative' mean when applied to a preference share?
**29** Authorised share capital is one of the terms applied to the shares issued by a limited company. True/False?

## 25.8.1 Retained earnings (profits)

Share capital and reserves show how much a company is worth. They show how the assets have been financed – do you remember the accounting equation?

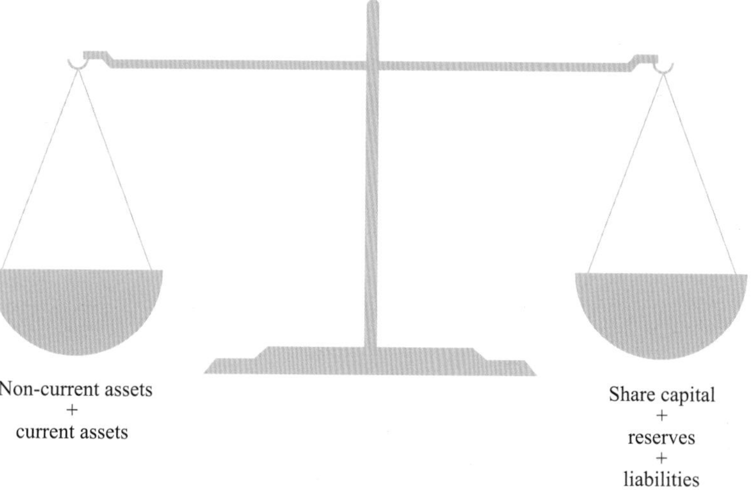


**Figure 25.2** The accounting equation

**Tip**

Do not say that reserves are cash. Some of the profits will already have been used to replace non-current and other assets.

**Revenue reserves** are profits that are retained in a company to strengthen its financial position. They are 'normal' trading profits that have been retained ('ploughed back') in the company. They are added to the retained earnings from previous years in a statement of changes in equity.

Reserves are profits. Retained earnings are a major source of finance for all successful businesses.

There are two types of reserves: **revenue reserves** and **capital reserves**.

## 25.8.2 Revenue reserves

Revenue reserves are the most flexible form of reserve. If in the future the revenue reserves are found to be excessive or are unnecessary they can be added back to current profits and used for dividend purposes.

The revenue reserves can either be set aside for a specific purpose like the expansion of the company or replacement of non-current assets or, more generally, in order to strengthen the financial position of the company.

The main revenue reserves that you might encounter are:

- retained earnings
- general reserve (less commonly seen in practice nowadays)
- non-current asset replacement reserve.

**Capital reserves** arise from capital transactions and adjustments to the capital structure of the company.

### 25.8.3 Capital reserves

Since **capital reserves** do not arise through 'normal' trading activities, they are not available for the payment of cash dividends. Any distribution to shareholders of these reserves will take the form of bonus shares.

The three main capital reserves that you might encounter are:

- share premium account
- revaluation reserve
- capital redemption reserve.

**Tip** 

A share premium account only arises when the company issues the shares. If Margaretha sells her $1 shares in Placton plc to Ncube for more than the nominal value (or the price that she paid for them), there is no share premium. This is a private financial transaction and will not be recorded in the company's books of account. (Margaretha's name will be taken out of the company share register and Ncube's name will be included.)

## 25.9 The issue of shares and the share premium account

A share premium account arises when a company issues shares at any price that is greater than the nominal value of the shares.

The book-keeping entries are fairly straightforward.

**Worked example**

Premsha plc offers 100 000 ordinary shares of 50 cents each for sale at $1.50 each. All monies were received on application.

**Required**

Prepare the ledger accounts to record the share issue.

### Answer

**Ordinary share capital account**

| | | | $ |
|---|---|---|---|
| | | Bank | 50 000 |

**Bank account**

| | $ | | |
|---|---|---|---|
| Ordinary share capital and share premium | 150 000 | | |

**Share premium account**

| | | | $ |
|---|---|---|---|
| | | Bank | 100 000 |

More often than not the ledger accounts will not be required, although you may be asked to show the effect on the company statement of financial position.

Changes to a statement of financial position:

| | $ |
|---|---|
| **Current assets** | |
| Bank | +150 000 |
| **Equity** | |
| Ordinary shares of 50 cents each | +50 000 |
| Share premium account | +100 000 |

A share premium account may be used to:

- pay up unissued shares to issue as bonus shares
- write off preliminary expenses (expenses incurred in the formation of a company)
- write off any expenses incurred in an issue of shares
- provide any premium payable on the redemption of shares or debentures.

**Worked example**

The summarised statement of financial position for Capdo Ltd at 31 October 2014 is shown:

**Capdo Ltd**

**Statement of financial position at 31 October 2014**

| | $ | $ |
|---|---|---|
| **ASSETS** | | |
| **Non-current assets** | | 17 000 |
| Other **current assets** | 10 000 | |
| Bank balance | 2 000 | 12 000 |
| **Total assets** | | 29 000 |
| | | |
| **EQUITY AND LIABILITIES** | | |
| **Equity** | | |
| Ordinary shares of $0.10 | | 10 000 |
| Retained earnings | | 11 000 |
| | | 21 000 |
| | | |
| **Current liabilities** | | 8 000 |
| **Total equity and liabilities** | | 29 000 |

On 1 November 2014 a further 200 000 ordinary shares were issued at a price of $0.50 each.

**Required**

Prepare a summarised statement of financial position at 1 November 2014 after the share issue.

## Answer

**Capdo Ltd**

**Summarised statement of financial position at 1 November 2014**

| | $ | $ |
|---|---|---|
| **ASSETS** | | |
| **Non-current assets** | | 17 000 |
| Other **current assets** | 10 000 | |
| Bank balance *($2000 + $100 000)* | 102 000 | 112 000 |
| **Total assets** | | 129 000 |
| | | |
| **EQUITY AND LIABILITIES** | | |
| **Equity** | | |
| Ordinary shares of $0.10 each | | 30 000 |
| Share premium *(200 000 X $0.40)* | | 80 000 |
| Retained earnings | | 11 000 |
| | | 121 000 |
| **Current liabilities** | | 8 000 |
| **Total equity and liabilities** | | 129 000 |

➤ Now try Question 2.

A **revaluation reserve** is created when non-current assets are revalued in order to reflect an increase in the value. It ensures that the statement of financial position shows the permanent increase in value.

## 25.10 Revaluation reserves

Once again the book-keeping entries are fairly straightforward.

**Worked example**

A summarised statement of financial position of Kato plc is shown:

**Kato plc**
**Summarised statement of financial position at 31 December 2014**

| | $000 |
|---|---|
| **ASSETS** | |
| **Non-current assets** at cost | 40 000 |
| **Current assets** | 12 000 |
| **Total assets** | 52 000 |
| **EQUITY AND LIABILITIES** | |
| **Equity** | |
| Ordinary shares | 25 000 |
| Retained earnings | 23 000 |
| | 48 000 |
| **Current liabilities** | 4 000 |
| **Total equity and liabilities** | 52 000 |

The directors of the company revalue the non-current assets on 31 December 2014 at $51 000 000.

**Required**

Prepare a summarised statement of financial position at 31 December 2014 after revaluation of the non-current assets.

### Answer

**Kato plc**
**Summarised statement of financial position at 31 December 2014**

| | $000 | |
|---|---|---|
| **ASSETS** | | |
| **Non-current assets** at valuation | 51 000 | *(increase of $11 000 000)* |
| **Current assets** | 12 000 | |
| **Total assets** | 63 000 | |
| **EQUITY AND LIABILITIES** | | |
| **Equity** | | |
| Ordinary shares | 25 000 | |
| Revaluation reserve | 11 000 | |
| Retained earnings | 23 000 | |
| | 59 000 | |
| **Current liabilities** | 4 000 | |
| **Total equity and liabilities** | 63 000 | |

The book-keeping entries would be:

**Non-current assets account**

| | $ | | |
|---|---|---|---|
| Balance | 40 000 000 | | |
| Revaluation reserve | 11 000 000 | | |

**Revaluation reserve account**

| | | | $ |
|---|---|---|---|
| | | Non-current assets | 11 000 000 |

If the non-current asset to be revalued has been depreciated, then any depreciation needs to be written off.

**Worked example**

The ledger of Heret plc shows the following accounts:

**Premises account**

| | $ | | |
|---|---|---|---|
| | 200 000 | | |

**Provision for depreciation of premises account**

| | | | $ |
|---|---|---|---|
| | | | 120 000 |

The directors revalue the premises at $350 000.

**Required**

Prepare:

a book-keeping entries to record the revaluation of premises

b journal entries to record the revaluation.

## Answer

a

**Premises account**

| | $ | | |
|---|---|---|---|
| Bal b/d | 200 000 | | |
| Revaluation reserve | 150 000 | | |

**Provision for depreciation of premises account**

| | $ | | $ |
|---|---|---|---|
| Revaluation reserve | 120 000 | Bal b/d | 120 000 |

**Revaluation reserve**

| | | | $ |
|---|---|---|---|
| | | Premises | 150 000 |
| | | Depreciation | 120 000 |

b

**General journal**

| | $ | $ |
|---|---|---|
| Premises account | 150 000 | |
| Provision for depreciation of premises account | 120 000 | |
| Revaluation reserve | | 270 000 |
| Revaluation of premises to a value of $350 000 | | |

A revaluation reserve may be used to pay up unissued shares to issue as bonus shares.

## 25.11 Increases and reductions of share capital

A limited company may alter its share capital if empowered to do so by its articles of association. The company may:

- increase its authorised share capital, for example increase authorised share capital from 500 000 ordinary shares of $0.50 to 1000 000 ordinary shares of $0.50
- consolidate and divide all or part of its share capital into shares of a greater value than its existing share capital, for example 500 000 ordinary shares of $0.50 each made into 250 000 ordinary shares of $1.00 each

The words 'stocks' and 'shares' are generally interchangeable. **Stock** is made up of bundles of shares that may be traded in fractional amounts. **Shares** may only be traded in bundles of $1. So stock could be traded for $78.90 or $23.45; whereas shares can only be traded in multiples of $1.

- convert all or part of the share capital into shares of a lower nominal value, for example 100 000 ordinary shares of $1.00 made into 400 000 ordinary shares of $0.25 each
- cancel shares that have not yet been taken up
- convert paid up shares into stock
- reconvert stock into shares.

## 25.12 Rights issues and bonus issues of shares

Right issues and bonus issues of shares are frequently confused by students. This is an important topic, so make sure you are clear about this distinction.

**Table 25.4** The characteristics of a rights issue and a bonus issue

| Rights issue | Bonus issue (scrip issue) |
|---|---|
| Issue is offered to existing shareholders | Issued is offered to existing shareholders |
| Issue based on present holding | Issue based on present holding |
| The control of the company does not change; it remains with the existing shareholders | The control of the company does not change; it remains with the existing shareholders |
| Specified price is usually cheaper than present market price since the company saves on widely advertising the issue and preparing a full prospectus | No charge to shareholders |
| If shareholder does not wish to exercise his or her right, it may be sold to a third party | |

### 25.12.1 A rights issue of shares

A company can issue more shares if it needs to raise more capital. A rights issue of shares is a much cheaper way of raising capital than an issue of shares to the general public. A rights issue is an invitation to existing shareholders to subscribe for more shares. A rights issue entitles existing shareholders to apply for a specified number of shares based on their existing shareholding.

**Worked example**

The summarised statement of financial position of Ardele plc is shown:

| | $000 |
|---|---|
| **Total assets** | 2 925 |
| **EQUITY** | |
| Ordinary shares of $0.50 each | 2 500 |
| Retained earnings | 425 |
| **Total equity** | 2 925 |

The company made a rights issue of one new share for every four shares already held at a price of $1.25. All shareholders took up their rights and monies due were paid.

**Required**

a Redraft the statement of financial position after the rights issue has been completed.

b Gahir owns 500 ordinary shares in Ardele plc. After the rights issue has been completed, calculate:

 i the total number of ordinary shares owned by Gahir

 ii the price paid by Gahir for her new shares.

## Answer

a

| Ardele plc | |
|---|---|
| **Statement of financial position after the rights issue** | |
| | **$** |
| **Total assets** | 4487 500 |
| **EQUITY** | |
| Ordinary shares of $0.50 each | 3 125 000 |
| Share premium | 937 500 |
| Retained earnings | 425 000 |
| **Total equity** | 4487 500 |

b Gahir now owns 625 ordinary shares. She paid $156.25 for the new shares.

Shareholders who do not wish to exercise their rights may sell their rights. The effect of a rights issue on a statement of financial position is exactly the same as the effects of a 'normal' issue to the general public.

## 25.12.2 A bonus issue of shares

Bonus shares are issued when the directors of a company feel that the ordinary share capital account does not adequately reflect the net asset base of the company.

Consider two scenarios for the same limited company:

| **Statement of financial position many years ago** | | **Statement of financial position today** | |
|---|---|---|---|
| | **$** | | **$** |
| **Total assets** | 800 | **Total assets** | 25 000 |
| **EQUITY** | | **EQUITY** | |
| Ordinary share capital | 800 | Ordinary share capital | 800 |
| | | Reserves | 24 200 |
| | | **Total equity** | 25 000 |

You can see that over the years the ordinary share capital has remained unchanged, whereas the asset base of the company has increased with retained revenue reserves and capital reserves.

The directors may redress this imbalance, if the shareholders agree, by transferring some of the balances on reserve accounts to the ordinary share capital account.

Again, the process is fairly straightforward:

| **Debit** the reserve(s) account | **Credit** the share capital account |
|---|---|

**Worked example**

The following summarised statement of financial position is given for Blazet plc:

| | **$** |
|---|---|
| **Total assets** | 13 000 |
| **EQUITY** | |
| Ordinary share capital | 4 000 |
| Share premium account | 2 000 |
| Retained earnings | 7 000 |
| **Total equity** | 13 000 |

A bonus issue is made on the basis of one new share for every share already held.

It is the directors' policy to maintain reserves in their most flexible form.

**Required**

Prepare a summarised statement of financial position after the bonus issue has been completed.

## Answer

**Tip** 

The information relating to 'maintaining the reserves in their most flexible form' means that capital reserves should be used before using revenue reserves for an issue of bonus shares, since capital reserves have a much more restricted use than revenue reserves.

**Blazet plc**

**Summarised statement of financial position after completion of the bonus issue**

| | $ |
|---|---|
| **Total assets** | 13000 |
| **EQUITY** | |
| Ordinary share capital | 8000 |
| Retained earnings | 5000 |
| **Total equity** | 13000 |

Notice that the share premium account has been fully used and the remainder of the issue has come from the retained earnings.

**Self-test questions**

**30** Another name for a rights issue is a bonus issue. True/False?
**31** Both a rights issue and a bonus issue of shares are offered only to existing shareholders. True/False?
**32** Explain one difference between a rights issue and a bonus issue of shares.
**33** Why is the price quoted for a rights issue of shares generally lower than the current market price?
**34** What does the term 'maintaining reserves in their most flexible form' mean?
**35** Explain the difference between revenue reserves and capital reserves.
**36** Shares issued through a rights issue are more valuable to a shareholder than shares given in a bonus issue. True/False?
**37** Identify one revenue reserve.
**38** Identify one capital reserve.
**39** Explain how the reserves identified in your previous two answers were created.
**40** Explain the main difference between a rights issue of shares and a bonus issue of shares.
**41** Companies may reduce their capital if the value of their shares falls on the stock market. True/False?
**42** Bonus shares can be issued out of revenue reserves. True/False?
**43** Bonus shares can be issued out of capital reserves. True/False?

➤ Now try Questions 3–5.

# 25.13 Other headings used in the statements of financial position of a limited company

## 25.13.1 Non-current assets

Non-current assets should be shown under three headings:

- **Intangible non-current assets:** these are non-physical assets such as goodwill, the ownership of a patent, a licence, a trade mark, etc.

- **Tangible non-current assets:** these are assets that can be seen and touched – examples would include land and buildings, plant and machinery, fixtures and fittings, vehicles, etc.
- **Investments**, like other assets, should be valued at cost. (Remember that these investments are long term, i.e. invested for more than one year. If the investment was for less than one year then it would be classified as a current asset.)

### 25.13.2 Provisions, reserves and liabilities

At this point it may be as well to highlight the differences between provision, reserves and liabilities.

- **Provision**: amounts set aside out of profits for a known expense, the amount of which is uncertain.
- **Reserves**: any other amount set aside out of profits.
- **Liabilities**: amounts owed that can be determined with substantial accuracy.

### 25.13.3 Liabilities

Liabilities are classified according to when payment is due.

- **Non-current liabilities** fall due for repayment in more than one financial year. These could include debentures, mortgages, long-term bank loans.
- **Current liabilities** would include trade payables and other payables (e.g. current taxation due, accrued expenses, etc).

**Self-test questions**

**44** Gross profit $30 000; administrative expenses $10 000; interest payable $8 000. Calculate profit from operations and profit before tax.
**45** A reserve is money saved by a limited company for use in times of financial hardship. True/False?
**46** Give one example of a revenue reserve and one example of a capital reserve.
**47** Give an example of an intangible non-current asset.
**48** Land is an example of a tangible non-current asset. True/False?
**49** How should redeemable preference shares due for repayment in 20 years' time be classified in the statement of financial position?
**50** How should seven per cent debentures due to be redeemed in five months' time be classified?

## 25.14 Statements of cash flows

The **income statement** of a business concentrates on the determination of profits or losses, since profits should ensure the long-term survival of the business.

A **statement of financial position** concentrates on the state of affairs of the business. A statement of financial position prepared at the start of a financial year shows the state of affairs of a business on the first day of the financial year. A statement of financial position prepared one year later shows the position on the last day of the financial year. What has gone on during the year? The income statement bridges the gap from one important perspective – profits.

A **statement of cash flows** bridges the gap from the equally important perspective of liquidity. A statement of cash flows concentrates on **cash**. It reveals information that is not disclosed overtly in the income statement and statement of financial position. This concentration on liquidity is very important, since the inability to generate cash resources is the biggest single reason for many businesses going into liquidation.

**Cash** is money in notes and coins and deposits that are repayable on demand.

These three statements, taken together, show summaries of most of the financial information required by the users of accounting information.

The statement of cash flows takes information from a variety of sources to show an overall picture of the monies flowing into and out of the business during the financial year. The statement concentrates on liquidity and may explain why, for example, a business may need a bank overdraft in a year when profits were buoyant.

Even though small companies, sole traders and partnerships do not have to produce a statement of cash flows, they may find that it is in their best interests to prepare one.

### 25.14.1 Cash flows and profits

**Cash equivalents** are short-term highly liquid investments that are convertible into cash without notice. They have less than three months to run when acquired. Overdrafts repayable in less than three months are deducted from cash equivalents.

Changes in cash held by a business over the period of a year are not the same as the profits generated by the business over the year. A business could have a positive bank balance at the start of a year, make a profit over the year, yet end the year with a bank overdraft. A business could improve its bank balance over the course of a year, yet have incurred a loss. How can this be so?

**Example**

Here are four examples of transactions undertaken by a business and the resulting effects on profits and cash.

| | | Profit | Cash |
|---|---|---|---|
| 1 | Purchase of goods for resale for cash $200 | No effect | Reduce $200 |
| 2 | Purchase of goods for resale on credit $300 | No effect | No effect |
| 3 | Sale of goods (which cost $150) for cash for $400 | Increase $250 | Increase $400 |
| 4 | Sale of goods (which cost $250) on credit $600 | Increase $350 | No effect |

Some examples of transactions that will reduce cash balances in a business but that would not affect profits:

| Sole trader | Limited company |
|---|---|
| Drawings | |
| | Dividends |
| Capital expenditure | Capital expenditure |
| Withdrawals of capital | |
| Repayments of loans | Repayment of loans |
| | Repayment of debentures |
| | Payment of taxation |

Some examples of transactions that would increase the cash balances but that would not affect profits:

| Sole trader | Limited company |
|---|---|
| Capital introduced | |
| | Issue of shares and/or debentures |
| Sale of non-current assets | Sale of non-current assets |
| | Tax refunds |

Some examples of transactions that would reduce profits (or increase losses) in a business but that would not affect cash:

| Sole trader | Limited company |
|---|---|
| Increase in provision for depreciation | Increase in provision for depreciation |
| Increase in provision for doubtful debts | Increase in provision for doubtful debts |
| Loss on sale of non-current assets | Loss on sale of non-current assets |

Some examples of transactions that would increase profits (or decrease losses) in business but that would not affect cash:

| Sole trader | Limited company |
|---|---|
| Decrease in provision for depreciation | Decrease in provision for depreciation |
| Decrease in provision for doubtful debts | Decrease in provision for doubtful debts |
| Profit on sale of non-current assets | Profit on sale of non-current assets |

It is important that you understand the clear distinction between cash flows and profits.

## 25.15 The calculations

In examination questions, information will generally be given in the form of two statements of financial position: one prepared at the beginning of a financial year and one prepared at the end of the financial year. This is known as the **indirect method** of preparing a statement of cash flows.

The technique used to find cash flows is to compare the two sets of information and calculate any changes that have taken place over the year.

**Worked example**

The following statements of financial position are given:

**Nohinar plc**
**Statements of financial position**

| | at 31 March 2015 | | at 31 March 2014 | |
|---|---|---|---|---|
| | $000 | $000 | $000 | $000 |
| **ASSETS** | | | | |
| **Non-current assets** | | | | |
| Premises | 11 377 | | 7 065 | |
| *Less* Depreciation | (3 967) | 7 410 | (3 112) | 3 953 |
| Machinery at cost | 4 413 | | 3 789 | |
| *Less* Depreciation | (1 736) | 2 677 | (1 351) | 2 438 |
| Vehicles at cost | 1 657 | | 1 657 | |
| *Less* Depreciation | (1 176) | 481 | (763) | 894 |
| | | 10 568 | | 7 285 |
| **Current assets** | | | | |
| Inventory | | 918 | | 734 |
| Trade receivables | | 323 | | 330 |
| Cash and cash equivalents | | 145 | | 112 |
| | | 1 386 | | 1 176 |
| **Total assets** | | 11 954 | | 8 461 |
| **EQUITY AND LIABILITIES** | | | | |
| **Equity** | | | | |
| Ordinary shares | | 3 850 | | 2 570 |
| Share premium | | 2 375 | | 1 735 |
| Retained earnings | | 4 739 | | 3 235 |
| | | 10 964 | | 7 540 |
| **Current liabilities** | | | | |
| Trade payables | | 338 | | 312 |
| Tax liabilities | | 652 | | 609 |
| | | 990 | | 921 |
| **Total equity and liabilities** | | 11 954 | | 8 461 |

**Note**

- No interim dividends have been paid during the year.
- There have been no disposals of non-current assets during the year.

**Required**

Prepare a statement identifying cash inflows and outflows during the year ended 31 March 2015.

## Workings

Each calculation is done in turn, identifying the cash inflow or cash outflow. We are going to systematically consider each item and compare the figures from the statement of financial position at the start of the year and the figures from the statement at the end of the year. Any difference between the two figures will be because of a movement of cash (with one notable exception). Thus we will identify any cash inflows or outflows. The summary appears at the end when all the calculations have been completed.

**Premises** on the first day of the financial year cost $7 065 000; on the last day of the financial year the figure had risen to $11 377 000. Nohinar plc must have purchased additional premises during the year at a cost of $4 312 000. The purchase of these additional premises must have entailed cash being spent by Nohinar.

Cash outflow $4 312 000

The next item on our way down the statements of financial position is **depreciation of premises**. To help clarify the treatment of depreciation, consider the following example:

### Example

Ragesh is a trader who deals only in cash transactions. During one particular week, Ragesh drives his van to a local manufacturer and purchases sports shoes costing $400; he sells them during the week for $600.

He prepares an income statement for the week:

| | $ |
|---|---|
| Sales | 600 |
| *Less* Purchases | (400) |
| Fuel costs for van | (35) |
| Profit for the week | 165 |

His cash position would show:

| | $ |
|---|---|
| Income from sales | 600 |
| *Less* Payment for sports shoes | (400) |
| Payment for fuel | (35) |
| Cash inflow for the week | 165 |

Ragesh's cash inflow and his profit for the week are the same! However, as a student of accounting, you are able to explain to Ragesh that the 'matching' concept requires him to include the value placed on the use of assets used to generate profit. He should include in his income statement an amount for the use of his van (i.e. depreciation on his van). You suggest $20.

His redrafted income statement now shows:

| | $ |
|---|---|
| Sales | 600 |
| *Less* Purchases | (400) |
| Fuel costs for van | (35) |
| Depreciation of van | (20) |
| Profit for the week | 145 |

Ragesh's profit for the week no longer matches his cash flow. How can we reconcile the two figures?

We can do that by adding the depreciation charge to the profit figure calculated in the income statement:

Profit $145 + Depreciation of van $20 = $165

which agrees with the cash inflow figure.

---

**Worked example *continued***

So, in order to calculate any cash flows for the year, depreciation charges should be added to the profit for the year (or deducted from any loss for the year).

**Depreciation of premises** at the start of the year was $3 112 000; at the end of the year it is $3 967 000. The charge for the year was $855 000.

Although this is not really a cash inflow, it is treated as though it were, just as we did with Ragesh.

Cash inflow: $855 000

The depreciation charge to the income statement for the other two non-current assets should be treated in the same way. Add to cash inflow:

Depreciation of vehicles: $413 000

Depreciation of machinery: $385 000

**Machinery** purchased during the year amounted to $624 000. Would this cause cash to flow into the business or to flow out of the business? It is a cash outflow.

Cash outflow: $624 000

There has been no change in the **value of vehicles** held by the business over the financial year. So, as far as we can tell from the two statements of financial position, no purchases or sales of vehicles have taken place.

During the financial year **inventories** have increased by $184 000. In order to increase inventories a cash outflow needed to take place.

Cash outflow: $184 000

**Trade receivables** at the start of the financial year were $330 000. At the end of the financial year the amount owed was $323 000, so trade receivables have fallen by $7000. This is because of a net cash inflow.

Cash inflow: $7 000

The next item, **cash and cash equivalents**, is overlooked at the moment, because we are trying to amass information to explain why there is a change in the balance over the financial year.

**Trade payables** at the start of the financial year were owed $312 000. One year later, they were owed $338 000. They have increased by $26 000. This increase in trade payables can be used to finance the company's activities and is therefore treated as an inflow of cash.

Cash inflow: $26 000

We can see that at the end of the financial year Nohinar plc owed the **tax** authorities $652 000. This amount has been entered in the company's income statement for the year – it has reduced this year's retained earnings but it will not be paid to the tax authorities for some time yet (this is why it appears as a current liability). It has reduced the profit for the year but it has not as yet become a cash outflow. This amount needs to be added back to the profit as a cash inflow.

Cash inflow: $652 000

In last year's calculation of cash flows the same adjustment for **taxation** was made. But last year's tax owed will have been paid in the year under review, so:

Cash outflow: $609 000

The **ordinary share capital** has increased by $1280 000. The company has made a further issue of ordinary shares during the year, bringing cash into the business.

Cash inflow: $1 280 000

The **share premium** has increased by $640 000. The new issue of shares has clearly been issued at a premium of 50 cents on their nominal value. More cash flowing into the business:

Cash inflow: $640 000

Finally, **retained earnings** increased by $1504 000, the amount of unappropriated profit ploughed back into the company.

Cash inflow: $1 504 000

A summary of all the differences would look like this:

## Answer

| **Cash inflows** | | **Cash outflows** | |
|---|---|---|---|
| | **$000** | | **$000** |
| Depreciation– premises | 855 | Purchase of premises | 4312 |
| machinery | 385 | machinery | 624 |
| vehicles | 413 | Increase in inventory | 184 |
| Decrease in trade receivables | 7 | Tax paid | 609 |
| Increase in trade payables | 26 | | |
| Tax owed | 652 | | |
| Share issue | 1 280 | | |
| Premium on share issue | 640 | | |
| Profit | 1 504 | | |
| | 5762 | | 5729 |

So you can see that according to our calculations Nohinar plc received $33 000 ($5762 000 – $5729 000) more cash than it spent during the year.

This should be reflected in the cash and cash equivalent balances held by the company at the end of the financial year compared to those it held at the start of the financial year.

| | **$000** |
|---|---|
| Net increase/(decrease) in cash and cash equivalents | 33 |
| Cash and cash equivalents at beginning of the year | 112 |
| Cash and cash equivalents at the end of the year | 145 |

## Self-test questions

51 Cash flows show details of how profits have been earned. True/False?
52 Legally, sole traders must prepare a statement of cash flows. True/False?
53 In year 1 a business has a provision for depreciation of $200. In year 2 the provision is increased to $240. What is the cash flow resulting from the change in provision?
54 Non-current assets cost $50 000; they have an estimated life of ten years. Depreciation is provided at $5000 per annum. How much cash is set aside as depreciation in order to replace the assets in the future? Explain how the cash flow of a business is affected.
55 A sole trader makes drawings during a year of $8900. How would these drawings be shown on a cash flow statement?
56 Which of the following transactions would result in a flow of cash into a business?
  a Purchase of a machine
  b Sale of a vehicle
  c Increase in inventories
  d Increase in payables
  e Capital introduced into a business.

➤ Now try Questions 6 and 7.

## Chapter summary

- Companies must send a copy of the financial statements to all shareholders and debenture holders. The published financial statements are produced in an abridged format in order to protect the company.
- A limited company has a legal identity separate from that of its members.
- Shareholders have limited liability. They may receive dividends if the company is profitable and it has sufficient cash to pay the dividend.
- Directors of a company are not its owners. They run the company on behalf of the shareholders.
- Companies raise capital by issuing shares and debentures. Debentures are not part of the share capital.
- A share premium account is created when a company issues shares for a price that is greater than the nominal value.
- When non-current assets are revalued at a price that is higher than the carrying amount, a revaluation reserve is created.
- A share premium account and a revaluation reserve are both capital reserves.
- Profits are retained within the company in the form of reserves.
- Revenue reserves are trading profits that have been 'ploughed back' into the company and may be used to pay dividends. Capital reserves arise through capital profits and may not be used to issue dividends.
- Assets should be classified as tangible, intangible and investments.
- Liabilities are classified into those that fall due in less than one year and those that are due to be paid in more than a year.
- A bonus issue of shares may be made from either capital or revenue reserves.
- If a company wishes to maintain its reserves in the most flexible form, it should issue bonus shares from capital reserves before using revenue reserves.
- Statements of cash flows are prepared to show differences in cash and cash equivalents that have taken place over a year that are not evident in the preparation of other parts of financial statements.
- All movements of cash are shown in the statement.
- Non-cash flows are not shown in the statement.

# 26 Company financing

**Content**
**1.4 Preparation of financial statements**
1.4.4 Limited companies

**By the end of this chapter, you should be able to:**
- identify short-term internal and external sources of finance available to businesses
- identify long-term internal and external sources of finance
- describe the various methods of raising finance
- understand the appropriateness of use for each method.

## 26.1 Sources of finance

Finance is vitally important to the survival and growth of all businesses. We have already seen that limited companies raise finance by issuing shares and debentures. There are other forms of finance available to limited companies: some sources are used for short-term financing while other forms are used for long-term financing. Finance can be generated from within the business or it can be provided by external parties.

**Table 26.1** Sources of finance available to limited companies

| | Internal sources of finance | External sources of finance |
|---|---|---|
| Short-term financing | Cash management<br>Credit control<br>Inventory management | Bank overdrafts<br>Short-term bank loans<br>Factoring and invoice discounting<br>Sale of unused non-current assets<br>Hire purchase<br>Trade and other payables |
| Long-term financing | Retained earnings | Share capital<br>Loan capital – debentures<br>Convertible loan stock<br>Long-term bank loans<br>Leasing<br>Sale and leaseback |

## 26.2 Short-term internal financing

Short-term internal financing is also known as **management of working capital**, that is, managing the elements that make up current assets. Efficient management of the components of current assets means that limited companies will need to borrow less to finance their day-to-day operations. If a company is inefficient in its working capital management, it may have to borrow short term to finance inventory, trade receivables and cash needs.

Stock exchange traders assessing sources of finance

## 26.2.1 Cash management

Companies must have sufficient **cash** to carry on their daily activities yet not hold too much cash. (Cash is an idle asset that does not earn anything.)

Managers should prepare cash budgets in order to predict the cash necessary for the business to function effectively (see Chapter 44). If a cash budget shows that the cash requirements are insufficient to allow the business to function effectively then the managers will have to borrow in the short term.

## 26.2.2 Credit control

Credit control is the term often used to describe management of trade receivables. It is important for managers to ensure that receivables pay on time and in full. Managers must ensure that any expansion of credit sales does not result in:

- too great an increase in extra administrative costs
- a lengthening of the collection period.

They must also ensure that prospective credit customers have a sound credit rating.

## 26.2.3 Inventory management

The holding of inventory is necessary to ensure that demand for the finished product is always met on time. It also acts as a protection against any shortages of raw materials or components and any price increases. Management of inventories can be achieved by applying an 'economic order quantity' (EOQ) model and employing 'just in time' (JIT) techniques. Much profit and cash is tied up in excessive holdings of inventory. EOQ is a method of finding the optimal order level to minimise costs of holding inventory. JIT means that raw materials inventory is delivered just before it is needed. This again means that holding large amounts of inventory is unnecessary and that inventory holding costs are kept to a minimum.

## 26.3 Short-term external financing

If a business is not generating enough cash through normal trading activities, then it may have to borrow through a bank overdraft or short-term bank loan.

### 26.3.1 Bank overdrafts

A bank overdraft facility is a good way to overcome the irregular cash flows experienced by many businesses. It is in the best interests of managers to agree an overdraft limit in case they need to use this source of finance. This is wise because the interest rate charged on an unauthorised overdraft is usually much higher than if an agreement had been reached before the overdraft is required.

The rates of interest charged on overdrafts tend to be greater than those charged on longer term borrowings. This is why businesses are only likely to use overdrafts in the short term (although many businesses have a permanent overdraft facility).

Providers of overdrafts do not require **collateral** on the loan and therefore the level of risk for the provider is greater than that incurred with a loan. This is why the rate of interest charged is greater than that charged on a loan.

**Collateral** is used to guarantee the repayment of a loan. Often collateral will be the title deeds to land or business premises.

### 26.3.2 Bank loans

Bank loans tend to have a repayment period of a longer term than that of a bank overdraft. Overdraft facilities are dependent on the management of a business convincing the bank that cash shortages are of a temporary nature. Loans tend to require some more tangible form of security. They are often secured on some specific asset. The loan is taken out for an agreed length of time. The repayments are usually for an agreed amount on specified intervals during the period of the loan.

Even though a bank may hold the title to non-current assets as collateral, the loan does not give the bank any say or rights in the everyday running of the business.

### 26.3.3 Factoring and invoice discounting

Trade receivables are assets and may be used to raise finance.

**Debt factoring** involves the sales ledger being administered by a debt factoring company. The debt factoring company buys the business's debts, at a discount, paying the creditor an advance based on the total amount to be collected. The debt factoring company then collects the debts when they fall due. The debt factoring company charges a fee based on the volume of credit sales and also charges interest on any advance payments made. Debt factoring has often been seen negatively by suppliers and customers of the business, since control of the customer database is lost.

**Invoice discounting** involves using trade receivables as security on an advance. The credit control function is not contracted out as it is with factoring. So the database of credit customers remains with the creditor.

Both factoring and invoice discounting are methods of collecting money owed as quickly as possible.

## 26.4 Other ways of raising short-term finance

There are other ways that a business can conserve or increase working capital in the short term.

### 26.4.1 Unused non-current assets

A business may sell any non-current assets that are not likely to be used in the foreseeable future. This will clearly increase cash balances.

### 26.4.2 Hire purchase

A business may purchase non-current assets using a hire purchase agreement. This means that the cost of the asset is spread over several time periods. Although ownership of the asset rests with the hire purchase company until the final payment is made, the purchaser will show the asset on their statement of financial position. (This is an application of substance over form.) The amount still outstanding on the agreement will be shown as a creditor.

### 26.4.3 Trade and other payables

Trade and other payables provide short-term finance. However, this form of financing must be used with caution. If payables feel that their credit terms are being abused, they may revert to requiring their supplies of goods and services being purchased on a cash basis only or that any beneficial credit facilities are withdrawn.

## 26.5 Long-term internal financing – retained earnings

This is probably the most important source of financing for any business. This means that the business is self-financing. If a business has to rely on injections of external finance then it is vulnerable, as these sources might eventually dry up. The retained earnings show up on a statement of financial position as revenue reserves.

## 26.6 Long-term external financing

Apart from retained earnings in the form of revenue reserves, there are two main ways of raising large sums of new external long-term finance available to a limited company. These are by issuing share capital and borrowing loan capital.

### 26.6.1 Share capital

There are three main methods of raising capital available to a public limited company. These are:

- by a rights issue of shares, which is an issue to existing shareholders in some proportion to their existing holding
- by a public issue, which requires new shareholders to purchase the shares
- by placing, which involves underwriters making shares available to financial institutions of their choosing. This method is often used by companies coming to the market for the first time.

All these share issues provide finance that can be used in whatever way the directors feel is appropriate to the needs of the company.

We discussed the different types of shares more fully in Chapter 25 'The financial statements of limited companies'.

### 26.6.2 Loan capital

Loan capital is long-term borrowing. This may be from banks or other financial institutions (see Section 26.3.2).

Many companies raise additional finance by issuing debentures. A debenture is acknowledgement of a loan to a company. The loan is generally secured against the company's assets.

The lenders are paid a fixed rate of interest whether the company is profitable or not; interest is paid half-yearly and is a charge against profits, unlike dividends. As has already been stressed, debenture holders are not owners of a company. They are shown on a statement of financial position as non-current liabilities (that is, until they have less than a year before being repaid).

### 26.6.3 Convertible loan stock

The holders of convertible loan stock will be paid a fixed rate of interest, generally at a lower rate than on debentures. Additionally, the holders have the right to exchange their stock into shares at some future date.

## 26.7 Other ways of raising long-term finance

There are other ways of raising long-term finance.

### 26.7.1 Leasing

A business may lease non-current assets rather than purchase them. Once again, this action will conserve cash in the short term. However, the business does not own the asset. The rental charges are shown in the income statement as an expense.

### 26.7.2 Sale and leaseback

This involves a business selling non-current assets to a leasing company and then leasing them for continued use within the business. A cash sum is released immediately and rental payments are made for future use of the asset.

**Self-test questions**

1 Explain two reasons why a company might need to raise finance.
2 A company wishes to purchase more land in order to extend its manufacturing base. The finance director believes that he should negotiate an overdraft facility with the company's bankers. Do you consider his action to be reasonable?
3 'Debentures' is another name for preference shares. True/False?
4 Identify two problems that might occur if a company embarks on a marketing policy that is aimed at doubling sales revenue.
5 Explain the difference between a bank overdraft and a bank loan.
6 Explain how a company might benefit from issuing ordinary shares rather than issuing debentures.
7 Explain how company directors might be able to predict the need for additional finance in the future.

**Chapter summary**

- Sources of finance are important for the survival and growth of a company.
- Companies can raise finance using internal or external means.
- Some forms of finance are used for short-term commitments; it is appropriate to use short-term finance, for example working capital management, overdrafts, etc.
- In other cases where long-term investment in, say, non-current assets is planned then long-term finance is essential, for example a share issue.

# 27 Interpretation and analysis of financial data

## Content

### 1.5 Analysis and communication of accounting information to stakeholders

- Identify and discuss the differing requirements for information of user groups including: management, employees, potential investors, creditors, government, public and environmental bodies; and communicate information required by these different stakeholder groups
- Calculate key accounting ratios to measure profitability, liquidity and efficiency
- Use ratios to evaluate and comment on the profitability, liquidity and efficiency of an organisation
- Identify and discuss the limitations of accounting information

**By the end of this chapter you should be able to:**

- identify the users of financial information and be aware of the information they would find useful
- explain why ratios are used as a performance indicator
- calculate and interpret profitability ratios
- calculate and interpret liquidity ratios
- assess the advantages of using ratios as a performance indicator
- identify the limitations of using accounting information as a performance indicator.

Financial statements are prepared to convey information to management and the other users of accounts.

The financial statements provide us with much financial information but in order to use this information we must be able to analyse and interpret it. Figures cannot be used in isolation because they can sometimes be misleading.

A woman earns $20 000 per year. Is this a good annual income? It depends on whether she lives in Zimbabwe, Singapore, Australia or the USA. The income is given as an absolute figure, and we need to be able to put it in context in order to understand it.

The same is true about accounting information. Financial statements use absolute numbers. We need to place the figures in context.

A business makes a profit of $45 000 for the year ended 31 March 2015. Has the business had a good year?

If the business under review was Raana's general store in the high street, what would your answer be? I guess your answer would be different if the business was CitiBank.

Profits provide only one facet of business activity. Profits are important; they ensure the long-term survival of a business.

The other main facet of business activity is the ability to generate cash. Cash is so important for the day-to-day survival of the business. If a business has insufficient cash then it might be unable to pay staff wages; it might be unable to pay the providers of the utilities; it might be unable to pay its creditors. All of these people are likely to withdraw resources if the business does not pay its debts.

So two key areas of performance evaluation of a business are: profitability and liquidity.

## 27.1 Users of financial information

As we saw in Chapter 25, there are many different interested parties in the performance of a business, as shown in Figure 27.1.

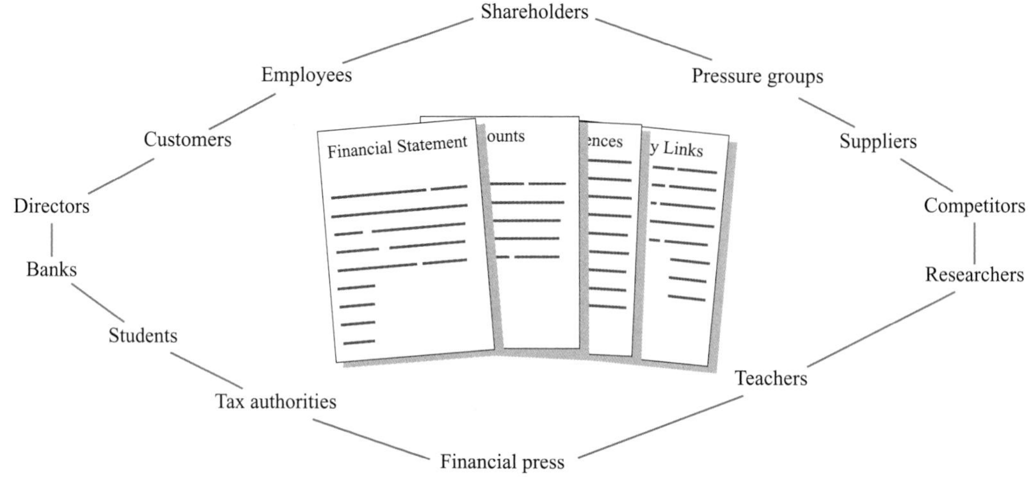


**Figure 27.1** The users of the financial statements of a limited company

What are these different groups of people interested in? With the odd exception, all are probably interested in the survival of the business. The exceptions might include competitors and environmental groups.

Survival of the business will depend on the business's ability to generate:

- profits – profitability
- cash – liquidity.

Profits are necessary for the long-term survival of the business and cash is needed for its day-to-day running, in other words its short-term survival.

## 27.2 Requirements of users

The published financial statements of limited companies must satisfy the requirements of the Companies Acts, international accounting standards and the Stock Exchange. The statements are also used in various ways by other user groups.

**Table 27.1** The requirements for information of different groups of users

| User | Use |
|---|---|
| Managers | As an aid to general decision making; also in order to make decisions regarding planning and control of the business |
| Employees | For wage negotiations and to gauge their job security |
| Existing shareholders | To make decisions about the adequacy of return on their investment and whether or not to sell or increase investment in the company |
| Potential shareholders | To make a decision on whether or not to invest in the business (based on the information in the statements) |
| Providers of finance | To know whether or not the business is able to service loans and, at term, to repay them |
| Suppliers and customers | May wish long-term survival to ensure a sound and lasting trading partnership |
| General public | To gain information regarding the business's attitude towards environmental issues, etc. |
| Government agencies | For tax purposes and to ensure that the business conforms to Acts of Parliament that may be relevant, e.g. long-term planning |
| Financial press | To comment and report on various business issues and activities |

Analysing business data

Users of financial information will look at the published financial statements of limited companies. However, the results obtained from a set of financial statements cannot be viewed in isolation; and the information may not be in a form that is required by the users. The data must be put into a useful form.

It is desirable to compare performance over a period of four or five years. If the time period reviewed is too short then it would be difficult to identify any trends. If the time period is too long then much of the earlier information will be out of date.

## 27.3 Methods of arranging data for analysis purposes

There are four main methods of arranging the data into a form that can be used by a person or organisation that wishes to analyse the results of a business.

1 **Horizontal analysis** makes a line-by-line comparison of each year's results, revealing trends in the raw data.

**Example**

| | 2012 | 2013 | 2014 |
|---|---|---|---|
| | $000 | $000 | $000 |
| Sales | 2 176 | 2 581 | 2 667 |

This may be done using percentage changes:

| % | % | % |
|---|---|---|
| 8.8* | 18.6 | 3.3 |

* Assuming sales in 2011 of $2000 000.

2 **Trend analysis** uses a base level of 100 for the first year of analysis. Each subsequent year is then related to the base level of 100.

**Example**

Using same data as example 1 on previous page:

| 2012 | 2013 | 2014 |
|---|---|---|
| 108.8 | 129.05 | 133.35 |

3 **Vertical analysis** requires each component of a part of the financial statements to be expressed as a percentage of the total.

**Example**

| | 2012 | 2013 | 2014 |
|---|---|---|---|
| Current assets – Inventory | 25 | 28 | 24 |
| Trade receivables | 54 | 48 | 52 |
| Cash and cash equivalents | 21 | 24 | 24 |
| | 100 | 100 | 100 |

**Ratio** is the term applied to the results of calculations used to compare the performance of businesses. It is a generic term applied to results expressed in:

- true ratios, e.g. a current ratio might be 4:1
- percentages, e.g. a gross margin might be 58 per cent
- time, e.g. a trade receivables turnover might be 32 days.

4 **Ratio analysis:** To be useful, ratio analysis must be put into context. Ratios must not be used in isolation.

**Example**

Anders scores 28 in an accounting test. Has he done well? We cannot tell; we need to put the result in context.

- If the maximum mark available was 30, then he has done well.
- If the maximum mark was 100, he has not done too well.
- If the rest of the class scored more than 60 marks, then Anders has a poor score. However, if the rest of the class scored below 20 marks, he has done well.

**Tip**

Questions on interpretation and analysis generally require performance evaluation using ratio analysis. Learn the following ratio formulae and what they reveal.

## 27.4 Performance evaluation

How would the users of accounting information decide whether the profitability and/or the liquidity of a business is acceptable?

The answer is: the same way that you decide whether the state of your earnings is acceptable or not.

- You compare your earnings this year with your earnings last year.
- You compare your earnings with those of your friends.
- You compare your earnings with the national average.
- You might even compare your earnings with what you planned to earn.

The users of accounting information follow similar procedures to the ones that you might use.

Managers will ask: 'Is the business performing better (or worse) than the figures produced in budgets or forecasts?'

They and other users ask:

- 'Is the business performing better (or worse) than last year?' They compare previous results with the current year's results.

- 'Is the business performing better (or worse) than similar businesses?' They compare the results of businesses in the same industrial sector.
- 'Is the business performing better (or worse) than the figures available for national publicly quoted companies in the same business sector?' They compare the results with those available for quoted companies, published as national statistics.

## 27.5 Why use ratios?

Annual raw data is converted into ratios for the following reasons:

- Amounts expressed in isolation are meaningless; they need to be put into some context.
- Conversion into ratios helps in the analysis of the current year's performance.
- It allows identification of trends by comparing results over a number of years.
- It means that trends may be extrapolated to make decisions that will influence future performance.
- It allows comparisons to be made with other similar businesses.

The most common ratios may be classified into:

- profitability ratios
- liquidity ratios
- efficiency ratios
- investment (or stock exchange ratios).

Although we will group ratios under these four major headings, you will not usually be asked to categorise your answers in this way.

In order to calculate and explain the ratios, we will use the following financial statements of Oyan Magenta, a public limited company, for the years 2015 and 2014. Even though the figures relate to a limited company, the principles would apply equally as well to the financial results of a sole trader or a partnership.

**Example**

**Oyan Magenta plc**

**Income statement for the year ended 31 March**

| | **2015** | | **2014** | |
|---|---|---|---|---|
| | **$000** | **$000** | **$000** | **$000** |
| Revenue | | 2 600 | | 2 000 |
| *Less* Cost of sales | | | | |
| Inventories | 110 | | 90 | |
| Purchases | 1 460 | | 1 240 | |
| | 1 570 | | 1 330 | |
| Inventories | (120) | 1 450 | (110) | 1 220 |
| Gross profit | | 1 150 | | 780 |
| *Less* Selling and distribution costs | (310) | | (140) | |
| Administration expenses | (340) | (650) | (180) | (320) |
| Profit from operations | | 500 | | 460 |
| Finance costs (debenture interest and preference dividend) | | (46) | | (22) |
| Profit before tax | | 454 | | 438 |
| Tax | | (145) | | (151) |
| Profit for the year attributable to equity holders | | 309 | | 287 |

**Oyan Magenta plc**

**Statements of financial position**

| | at 31 March 2015 | | at 31 March 2014 | |
|---|---|---|---|---|
| | **$000** | **$000** | **$000** | **$000** |
| **ASSETS** | | | | |
| **Non-current assets** at carrying amount | | 3063 | | 1800 |
| **Current assets** | | | | |
| Inventories | 120 | | 110 | |
| Trade receivables | 240 | | 220 | |
| Cash and cash equivalents | 140 | 500 | 570 | 900 |
| **Total assets** | | 3563 | | 2700 |
| **EQUITY AND LIABILITIES** | | | | |
| **Equity** | | | | |
| Ordinary shares of $1 | | 1500 | | 1500 |
| 6% preference shares | | 100 | | 100 |
| Retained earnings | | 849 | | 595 |
| | | 2449 | | 2195 |
| **Non-current liabilities** | | | | |
| 8% debentures | | 800 | | 200 |
| **Current liabilities** | | | | |
| Trade payables | | 169 | | 154 |
| Taxation | | 145 | | 151 |
| | | 314 | | 305 |
| **Total liabilities** | | 1114 | | 505 |
| **Total equity and liabilities** | | 3563 | | 2700 |

**Oyan Magenta plc**

**Extract from statement of changes in equity for the year ended 31 March 2015**

| | **$000** |
|---|---|
| **Retained earnings** | |
| Balance 1 April 2014 | 595 |
| Profit for the year | 309 |
| | 904 |
| Dividends paid | (55) |
| Balance 31 March 2015 | 849 |

## 27.6 Profitability ratios

### 27.6.1 Return on capital employed (ROCE)

This ratio is often known as the **primary ratio**. It is the measure of how effectively the managers of the business are using the capital employed in the business.

Capital employed can be calculated by using:

- total assets less current liabilities, or
- issued equity capital and reserves plus long-term loan capital.

There are a variety of ways of calculating the capital employed. We could use:

- opening capital employed

- closing capital employed
- or an average of opening and closing capital employed.

It is important that you use the same method each time. Choose the method you feel most comfortable with.

To enable your answer to be checked, always state the formula that you use. This principle applies to all ratio calculations.

Generally, ROCE (as well as inventory turnover, trade receivables turnover and trade payables turnover) uses average figures. However, on occasion it is impossible to calculate an average figure, so closing figures are used.

It is important that the same method of calculating is used each year (consistency) in order that results may be compared either with previous years or with other similar businesses.

Profit for the year to be used is profit from operations (i.e. profit before interest and tax). This enables us to make comparisons between businesses with different levels of borrowings.

**Formula**

$$\text{ROCE} = \frac{\text{Profit for the year before interest and tax}}{\text{Capital employed}} \times 100$$

Always state the formula that you use when calculating any ratio.

| **2015** | **2014** |
|---|---|
| $\frac{500 \times 100}{3249} = 15.39\%$ | $\frac{460 \times 100}{2395} = 19.21\%$ |

This tells us that for every $100 invested in the business in 2013 the business earned $19.21; a year later the business earned $15.39 for every $100 invested – a worse result.

Could the capital be used elsewhere to earn a greater return? Compare this ratio with the return in similar businesses.

Certainly, there has been a deterioration since 2014.

## 27.6.2 Gross margin

This ration is also known as the **gross profit percentage**.

**Formula**

$$\text{Gross margin} = \frac{\text{Gross profit}}{\text{Revenue}} \times 100$$

| **2015** | **2014** |
|---|---|
| $\frac{1150 \times 100}{2600} = 44.23\%$ | $\frac{780 \times 100}{2000} = 39\%$ |

This shows that for every $100 of sales, the margin was $39.00 in 2014; that is, every $100 of sales earned the business $39.00 of gross profit. It then improved to $44.23 in 2015.

The margin will vary from business to business. Businesses with a rapid turnover of inventory will generally have a lower margin than a business with a slower inventory turnover.

The change identified might be due to a decrease in the cost of goods sold while maintaining selling price or it may be due to a slight increase in the selling price while the cost of goods sold has reduced.

## 27.6.3 Mark up

Mark up is calculated as follows:

**Formula**

$$\text{Mark up} = \frac{\text{Gross profit}}{\text{Cost of sales}} \times 100$$

| 2015 | 2014 |
|---|---|
| $\frac{1\,150 \times 100}{1450} = 79.31\%$ | $\frac{780 \times 100}{1\,220} = 63.93\%$ |

**Tip**

An increase in the volume of sales will not affect mark up or margin. These ratios will remain constant. Changes in selling price and/or changes in purchasing price will affect both these ratios.

This means that for every $100 of goods purchased the price has been increased to a selling price of $163.93 in 2014 and $179.31 in the following year.

Students are advised not to use both the margin and mark up in any analysis they undertake because of the similarity in the data used.

## 27.6.4 Profit margin

**Formula**

$$\text{Profit margin} = \frac{\text{Profit for the year (after interest)}}{\text{Revenue}} \times 100$$

| 2015 | 2014 |
|---|---|
| $\frac{454 \times 100}{2600} = 17.46\%$ | $\frac{438 \times 100}{2000} = 21.90\%$ |

This shows that, in 2014, out of every $100 sales, the business earned $21.90 after all operating costs and cost of sales had been covered. This amount fell to $17.46 the following year. We can look at this from another angle.

## 27.6.5 Expenses to revenue ratio

**Formula**

$$\text{Expenses to revenue ratio} = \frac{\text{Expenses}}{\text{Revenue}} \times 100$$

| 2015 | 2014 |
|---|---|
| $\frac{696 \times 100}{2600} = 26.77\%$ | $\frac{342 \times 100}{2000} = 17.1\%$ |

This ratio tells us that in 2014 the business expenses were $17.10 out of every $100 of goods sold. In 2015 this amount spent on expenses rose to $26.77. This begs the question: is the business losing control as far as expenses are concerned?

There is also the **operating expenses to revenue ratio**, which excludes finance charges.

Operating expenses to revenue

$$= \frac{\text{Operating expenses}}{\text{Revenue}} \times 100$$

| 2015 | 2014 |
|---|---|
| $\frac{650 \times 100}{2600} = 25\%$ | $\frac{320 \times 100}{2000} = 16\%$ |

In absolute terms, expenses have more than doubled yet sales have only increased by 600/2000, i.e. 30 per cent. We can perhaps see why this has happened by examining the details of the expenses shown in the income statement.

In 2014 selling and distribution expenses accounted for $7 of each $100 of sales revenue generated; in 2015 it rose to $11.92.

In 2014 administration costs amounted to $9 in every $100 of sales revenue generated; in 2014 it rose to $13.08.

## 27.7 Liquidity ratios

In the above analysis we have simply considered the available information. You must try to develop this technique.

**Solvency** is the ability of a business to settle its debts when they require payment.

Liquidity ratios assess the ability of a business to pay its short-term liabilities as they fall due. Liquidity is important since a business has not only to pay its trade payables but its employees and other providers of resources too. Although creditors are grouped on a statement of financial position under headings that indicate payment within 12 months and payments due after 12 months, in reality many creditors require payment in a much shorter time.

Long-term investors are mainly interested in the **solvency** of the business – they require that the business will survive into the foreseeable future (or at least until their debt can be settled).

Although solvency means an excess of assets over liabilities, many assets are difficult to dispose of and so many users of accounts are more interested in the liquidity position of the business. They wish to examine and analyse the components of working capital in detail.

### 27.7.1 Current ratio

There is *no ideal current ratio* that suits all businesses.

This ratio is also known as the working capital ratio.

The ratio shows how many times the current assets are covering the current liabilities. It is usually expressed as a 'times' ratio, that is, the right-hand term should be expressed as unity so the ratio should be expressed as 'something':1. Generally, the ratio should be in excess of unity (i.e. greater than 1:1), although many businesses prosper with a ratio which is less than this.

Once again we should be looking for trends when we consider the **current ratio**. If a series of results shows that the current ratio has been declining over a number of years, this may mean that the business might have some difficulties in meeting its short-term obligations in the future.

If the series shows that the current ratio is increasing each year, this could be an indication that the business is tying up an increasing proportion of its resources in inventory, receivables and cash and cash equivalent balances, i.e. non-productive assets instead of the resources being invested in non-current assets that will earn profits.

Many analysts consider that a reasonable current ratio should fall between 1.5:1 and 2:1, although it is dangerous to be too dogmatic about this. The ratio will depend on the type of business and the direction of any trend.

**Formula**

$$\text{Current ratio} = \frac{\text{Current assets}}{\text{Current liabilities}}$$

| **2015** | **2014** |
|---|---|
| $\frac{500}{314} = 1.59{:}1$ | $\frac{900}{305} = 2.95{:}1$ |

The current ratio has fallen by around 46 per cent (1.36/2.95). It appears that in 2014 too many resources were tied up in unproductive assets and it appears that in 2015 this was more under control.

Obviously, the greater the number of years' results that are available, the easier it is to identify and confirm a trend.

### 27.7.2 The liquid ratio

This ratio is also known as the **acid test ratio** or the **quick ratio**.

Once again we should be looking for trends when considering this ratio. Liquid assets are current assets and a definition of current assets is that they are assets that are cash or will be cash in the near future. The least liquid of the current assets is inventory. The liquid ratio tests the ability of the business to cover its current liabilities with its current assets other than inventories.

**Formula**

$$\text{Liquid ratio} = \frac{\text{Current assets} - \text{Inventory}}{\text{Current liabilities}}$$

| **2015** | **2014** |
|---|---|
| $\frac{380}{314} = 1.21:1$ | $\frac{790}{305} = 2.59:1$ |

The ratio for 2014 seems rather high, so rather too many resources are tied up in a liquid form not earning profits.

The ratio improved in 2015. The business is still able to cover every \$1 owed with \$1.21 of liquid assets.

Once again, it is impossible to say what is an acceptable level of ratio – some businesses, for example some supermarkets, perform satisfactorily with a liquid ratio of less than 0.5:1.

## 27.8 Efficiency ratios

### 27.8.1 Non-current asset turnover

Non-current assets are the wealth generators of a business, acquired to generate sales revenue and hence profits. A high level of non-current assets should generate a high level of sales. The ratio is a measure of the efficient use of non-current assets. It indicates how much \$1 investment in non-current assets is able to generate in terms of sales. The higher the non-current asset turnover ratio, the greater is the recovery of the investment in those non-current assets.

An increase in the ratio year on year indicates a more efficient use of non-current assets.

A fall in the ratio might indicate:

- less efficient use of the assets
- purchase of more non-current assets
- revaluation of the assets.

**Formula**

$$\text{Non-current asset turnover} = \frac{\text{Net revenue}}{\text{Total carrying amount of non-current assets}}$$

| **2015** | **2014** |
|---|---|
| $\frac{2600}{3063} = 0.85$ times | $\frac{2000}{1800} = 1.11$ times |

There has been less efficient use of non-current assets in 2015. In 2014 each $1 invested earned $1.11. Investment in non-current assets increased by more than 70 per cent. However, the sales revenue only increased by 30 per cent. There is no indication when the extra assets were purchased. The increase may be greater in the future when a full year's revenue will be earned.

## 27.8.2 Trade receivables turnover

This ratio is also known as **debtors turnover** or **average collection period**. It calculates how long, on average, it takes a business to collect its debts.

Generally, the longer a debt is outstanding, the more likely it is that the debt will prove to be irrecoverable. It is also advisable to have a shorter debt collection period than the trade payables turnover.

A question might not identify cash and credit sales; in such cases it is acceptable to use the total sales figure given. It is essential that the same basis is used when making comparisons.

**Formula**

$$\text{Trade receivables turnover} = \frac{\text{Trade receivables}}{\text{Credit sales}} \times 365 \text{ days}$$

| **2015** | **2014** |
|---|---|
| $\frac{240}{2600} \times 365 = 34$ days | $\frac{220}{2000} \times 365 = 41$ days |

Note the rounding of the answer. In 2014 the actual figure calculated was 40.15 days (that is, 40 days 3 hours 36 minutes!). We always round to the next full day.

Remember that the calculation will give us an average collection time. It uses all trade receivables – this may mask the fact that one significant debtor is a very poor payer while the other debtors pay promptly.

Thirty days' credit is a reasonable yardstick to use. So, using this measure, in 2014 debts were outstanding for 41 days – perhaps a little too long. There was an improvement in 2015 when debts were collected in 34 days – a week faster.

### 27.8.3 Trade payables turnover

This is also known as **creditors turnover** or **average payment period**.

It measures the average time a business takes to pay its trade payables.

**Formula**

$$\text{Trade payables turnover} = \frac{\text{Trade payables}}{\text{Credit purchases}} \times 365 \text{ days}$$

| 2015 | 2014 |
|---|---|
| $\frac{169}{1\,460} \times 365 = 43$ days | $\frac{154}{1\,240} \times 365 = 46$ days |

In 2014 the business was paying its trade payables on average in 46 days; a year later it was paying in 43 days.

The 3-day reduction does need investigation.

A comparison of the receivable collection days and the payables payment days shows that, in both years, the trade payables are on average being paid more slowly than cash is being received from the trade receivables. This is a good policy. However, care must be taken to ensure that suppliers are not antagonised by being paid too slowly.

### 27.8.4 Inventory turnover

In every 'bundle' of inventory held by a business there is an element of profit and there is cash tied up in the goods. It is essential that this cash is released and that profits are earned as quickly as possible. So the more often inventory can be 'turned over'(sold), the better it is for the business.

**Formula**

$$\text{Inventory turnover} = \frac{\text{Average inventory held}}{\text{Cost of sales}} \times 365 \text{ days}$$

| 2015 | 2014 |
|---|---|
| $\frac{115 \times 365}{1\,450} = 29$ days (28.95) | $\frac{100 \times 365}{1\,220} = 30$ days (29.92) |

This shows that in 2015 Oyan Magenta sold the inventory held one day faster than in 2014.

### 27.8.5 Rate of inventory turnover

**Formula**

$$\text{Rate of inventory turnover} = \frac{\text{Cost of sales}}{\text{Average inventory held during the year}}$$

| 2015 | 2014 |
|---|---|
| $\frac{1\,450}{115} = 12.61$ times | $\frac{1\,220}{100} = 12.2$ times |

This shows that in 2014 the company sold the goods held as inventory approximately 12 times during the year; its inventory turnover was faster in 2015.

## 27.9 Limitations of using accounting information to assess performance

- The results are based on the use of historic cost because it is objective. However, some results may be misleading if results are compared over a long period. For example, the value of assets shown on a statement of financial position from a number of years ago is unlikely to be the same as the market value today.
- Emphasis is placed on past results. Past results are not a totally reliable indicator of future results. If your football team has won its past six matches, there is no guarantee that it will win its seventh game.
- Published accounts only give an overview – perhaps disguising inefficient sections of a business. The return on capital employed may be 27 per cent; however, on closer scrutiny, we might find that one section of the business is earning a return on capital of 50 per cent and the other section earns a return of just 4 per cent.
- Financial statements only show the monetary aspects of a business. They do not show the strengths and weaknesses of individual managers or members of staff. They do not show staff welfare. Some businesses are very successful and pay top wages but have workers who hate going to work each day.
- It is extremely difficult to compare like with like between two businesses. They have:
  - different sites
  - different management teams
  - different staff
  - different customers, etc.
- The external environment faced by the business may change. The changes may have an immediate effect or the result of the changes may only be felt after a time lag. A devaluation of a currency may cause imported materials to rise in price, but if the business carries large inventories and issues those items using the FIFO method of issue, increased costs may not be incorporated into product costs for some time.
- Different organisations have different structures; different methods of financing their operation; different expense and revenue patterns. They may use different accounting policies, techniques, methods of measuring; and they may apply different conventions. No matter how similar businesses appear to be from the outside, all businesses are different.
- The financial statements of a business are prepared on a particular date. A statement of financial position on that date may well be unrepresentative of the usual position of the business. A fancy goods business may well have low inventories after a public holiday rush. The rest of the year it may carry large inventories.
- Ratios only show the results of business activity. They do not indicate the causes of good or bad results.

Avoid making assumptions where there is no evidence in the question. If you do make an assumption, make this known. It is important that you do so.

Business renting premises vs Business owning premises

*(include notional rent of premises for the second business)*

Business employing management team vs. Business run by owner

*(include notional manager's salary for the second business)*

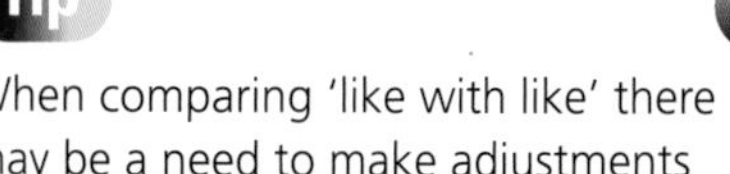

When comparing 'like with like' there may be a need to make adjustments to the figures given. Notional rents and management salaries may need to be included in one set of comparative figures.

Always state the formulae you have used. The person checking your calculation may have based his or her result on one formula; you may have obtained your results by using an alternative (equally correct) formula. No-one will know this if you do not state the formula used.

➤ Now try Questions 1 and 2.

## Self-test questions

1 Why are results converted into ratios?
2 What do profitability ratios tell us?
3 Give an example of a profitability ratio.
4 What do liquidity ratios tell us?
5 Give an example of a liquidity ratio.
6 Give the formula for calculating the profit margin.
7 Give the formula for calculating inventory turnover.
8 How is average inventory calculated?
9 Bima makes a gross profit ratio of 54 per cent. Is this good or bad?
10 Mary's average collection period is 42 days; her average payment period is 19 days. Explain whether or not this is a good or a bad policy.
11 Identify two limitations of using ratios as an evaluation of performance.

## Chapter summary

- Ratios are used as a method of performance evaluation. 'Ratios' is the generic term used for true ratios, percentages and other measures.
- Ratios are only useful if comparisons are made either with other organisations in the same line of business or with previous years' results – i.e. trend analysis.
- Ratios can be divided into profitability ratios, liquidity ratios and efficiency ratios.
- It is necessary to learn the formulae for ratios and produce these before calculating the figures.

# 28 Absorption (total) costing

## Content

**2.1 Costing for materials and labour**

- Understand the need to account for material and labour costs
- Identify and calculate fixed costs, variable costs, semi-variable costs and stepped costs
- Identify the elements of direct and indirect materials and labour
- Calculate labour costs using different methods of remuneration including bonus schemes

**2.2 Traditional costing methods**

- Understand the application of traditional costing methods

2.2.1 Absorption costing

- Allocate and apportion overhead expenditure between production and service departments
- Calculate overhead absorption rates
- Calculate and explain the causes of under absorption and over absorption of overheads
- Identify and explain the uses and limitations of absorption costing

**By the end of this chapter, you should be able to:**

- classify various types of cost according to their reaction to changes in levels of business activity
- calculate the pay due to workers using differing wage systems
- prepare a statement using absorption costing techniques
- explain the uses of absorption costing
- select appropriate bases of apportioning overheads
- prepare a statement to apportion overheads to individual departments
- apportion service department costs to production departments
- select and use appropriate absorption rates for overheads and use these in pricing policy
- explain how an over absorption and under absorption of overheads affect the financial statements of a business
- identify limitations of using absorption costing techniques
- explain the use of absorption costing as a basis for inventory valuation.

Tip

Practise defining terms on a regular basis. Remembering them is not as difficult as it first seems. When you have a spare moment between lessons, or waiting for a friend, go over definitions in your head. Remember that a definition is an explanation of a term; it is not an example. However, if you find it difficult to express yourself precisely, an example may help to clarify your thoughts and persuade the reader or listener that you know exactly what the term means.

## 28.1 Types of cost

Here we define some of the terms commonly used when dealing with any system of costing. It is important that you learn the terms used by cost accountants.

### 28.1.1 Fixed costs

Fixed costs do not change with levels of business activity. They are sometimes called **period costs** as they are time based. Examples would include supervisors' wages, factory rent, etc. In the long run, fixed costs may change: supervisory staff may get a pay rise; the landlord may increase the rent to be paid for the use of the factory.

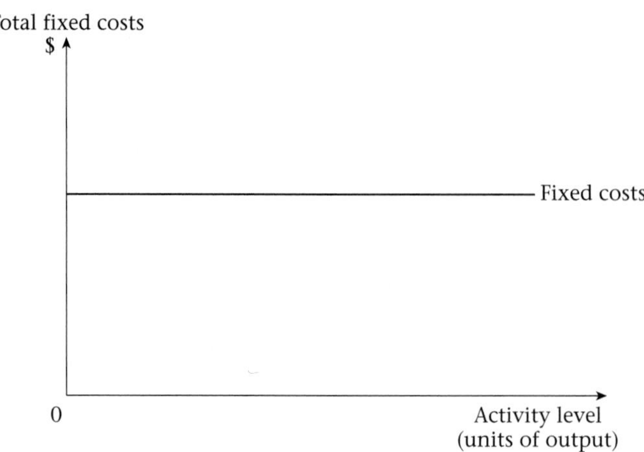


**Figure 28.1** Total fixed costs

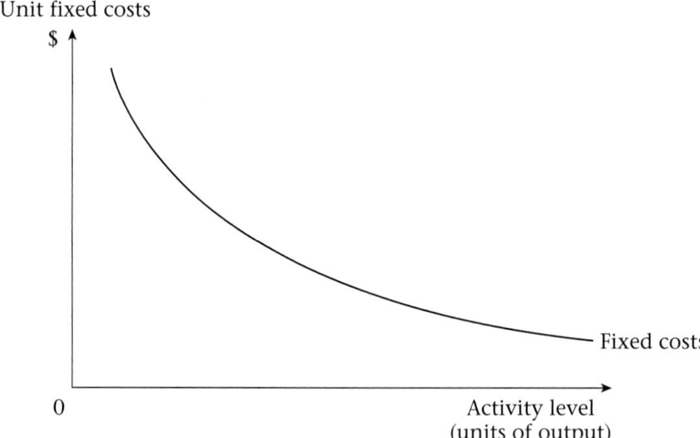


**Figure 28.2** Unit fixed costs

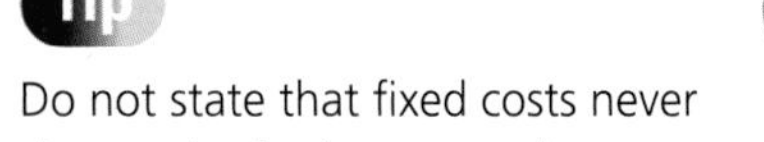

Tip

Do not state that fixed costs never change. In the long term they may.

## 28.1.2 Variable costs

Variable costs vary in direct proportion to levels of activity. For example, if production is 10 000 units and each unit of direct material costs \$8.50, the total variable material costs would be \$85 000. If production rises to 11 000 units, the total variable material costs would rise to \$93 500. If production fell to 9000 units, the total variable material costs would fall to \$76 500.

Other examples of variable costs would include:

- direct labour costs, when workers are paid using piece work rates (in questions on this topic, direct labour costs are generally treated as variable costs)
- royalties.

You will recognise this classification as those items that make up **prime cost** in the preparation of a manufacturing account (see Chapter 32).

Short-term decision making is mainly concerned with accounting for variable costs.

**Cost centres** are usually determined by the type of business being considered. A cost centre may be a department, a machine or a person to whom costs can be associated. In your college or a large retailer, the primary cost centre might be each department. In a garage, the cost centres might be the repair department, the sales department or the parts department.

**Cost unit** is a unit of a product (or service) to which costs can be attributed – a unit which absorbs the cost centre's overhead costs. Cost units in a college might be students, while in the garage repairs department the cost unit might be each car being worked on. It could be a vehicle in a factory producing motor vehicles. In a passenger transport business, a cost unit might be a passenger mile.

**Direct costs** are defined by the Chartered Institute of Management Accountants (CIMA) as 'expenditure which can be economically identified with a specific saleable cost unit'. Direct costs can be directly attributed to a unit of production, so direct costs are always variable costs. The cost of the paper that this book is printed on is an example of a **direct materials cost**. The wages of a hairdresser styling your hair is an example of a **direct labour cost**.

**Direct expenses** are any other costs that can be specifically identified with the finished product (or service). Royalties payable to the inventor of a process or design of a product is an example of a direct expense; another example might be the costs of hiring equipment needed for a specific job.

**Direct materials costs** and **direct labour costs** can be specifically identified with the finished product (or service).

**Prime cost** is the total of all the direct costs:

Prime cost = Direct material costs + Direct labour costs + Direct expenses

**Indirect costs** are items of expenditure that cannot easily be identified with a specific saleable cost unit.

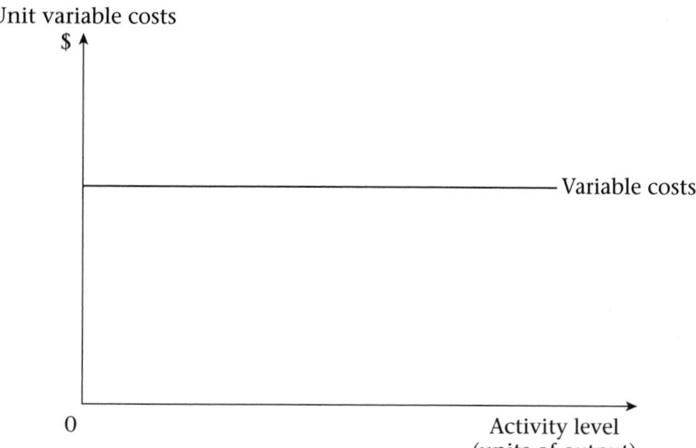


**Figure 28.3** Unit variable costs

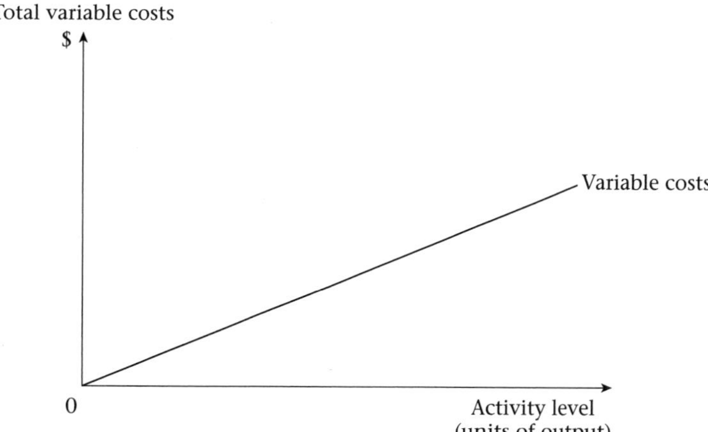


**Figure 28.4** Total variable costs

## 28.1.3 Semi-variable costs

These are costs that cannot be classified as either fixed costs or variable costs because they contain an element of both.

An example of a semi-variable cost is the charge for consumption of electricity. The standing charge is a fixed cost – it is charged at a fixed rate that is not dependent on the amount of electricity used. The variable cost part is based on the number of units consumed during the period.

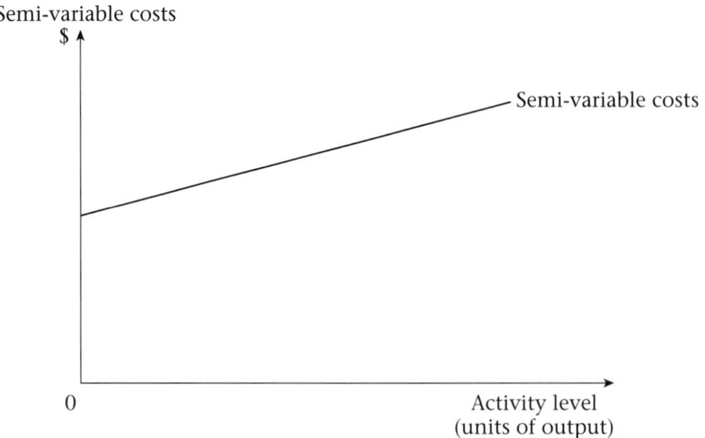


**Figure 28.5** Semi-variable costs

## 28.1.4 Stepped costs

Stepped costs remain fixed until a certain level of business activity is reached. When production exceeds this level, additional fixed costs may be incurred. The cost then rises to a higher fixed level. Costs remain at this level until the next level of activity requiring a change is reached.

An example of a stepped cost is the salaries of quality controllers. One quality controller can inspect 200 units of production per week. If output is 200 units, one quality controller must be employed. If output rises to 210 units per week, two controllers must be employed. If output rises to 410 units per week, three quality controllers must be employed.

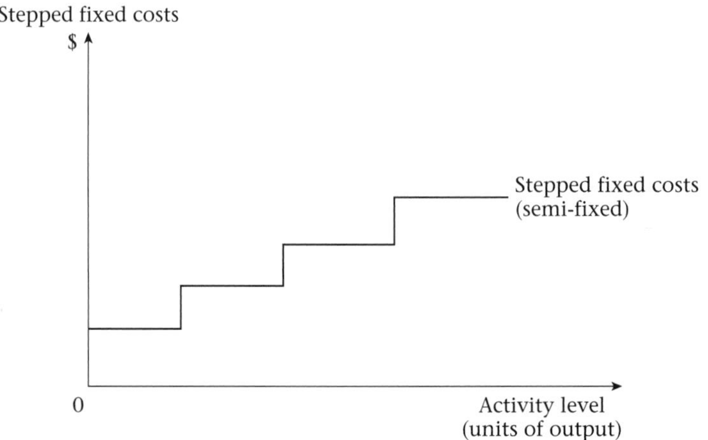


**Figure 28.6** Stepped fixed costs

## 28.1.5 Sunk costs

When a decision has to be made about a future business opportunity, managers need to estimate the likely future costs of the project and the revenue that is likely to be generated. Some costs of the project may already have been incurred, for example, market research costs or the cost of a machine purchased a number of years ago. These historic costs cannot influence a decision that is about to be taken.

Fixed costs are sometimes referred to as sunk costs since a business is committed to paying these costs whatever level of activity is achieved. Decisions made now or to be made in the future cannot affect these costs so they should be disregarded when preparing a budget on which a decision will be based.

### 28.1.6 Total costs

The total cost of production is made up by adding all the costs incurred in producing each product. Total cost is used in a variety of ways, which can be seen in some of the following chapters.

### 28.1.7 Unit costs

Unit costs are those that can easily be identified and so allocated to a specific unit, for example material costs, labour costs and other direct costs. When it is not possible to identify material costs to a specific unit, the costs will be allocated by using first-in first-out (FIFO) or weighted average cost (AVCO) methods of issue (see Chapter 20 for a detailed explanation of these methods).

Labour costs are generally much simpler to allocate to specific units.

The cost of each individual unit of production can be calculated by dividing the total costs attributed to it by the number of units actually produced. Any partly completed units (work in progress) are converted into their equivalent number of completed units.

**Self-test questions**

1 Identify a direct cost incurred in the manufacture of a pair of shoes.
2 Identify an indirect cost incurred in their manufacture.
3 Identify a direct cost incurred in the manufacture of the bread you may have eaten yesterday.
4 Identify an indirect cost incurred in their manufacture.
5 Identify a sunk cost incurred by your school or college.
6 Number of units produced 200. Total costs involved in their production $7500. Calculate the cost per unit.

## 28.2 Wage systems

The cost of employing staff who work directly on the production process is known as a **direct labour cost.** The remuneration of staff who work in a factory to support the direct labour is known as an indirect labour cost. Examples of support staff are cleaners and maintenance engineers, etc.

Direct labour costs form part of prime cost while indirect labour costs are part of the factory overheads.

Wage costs represent the income of workers and form a significant part of the running costs of a business.

A wage system may:

- have an effect on staff motivation
- affect the relationship that exists between managers and other staff
- influence staff turnover
- guide the efficiency of the organisation by affecting productivity.

There are three main methods of calculating labour remuneration:

1 time based remuneration
2 piece-work remuneration
3 bonus schemes.

### 28.2.1 Time rates

The number of hours worked is multiplied by the agreed wage rate.

**Example**

Production workers are paid $6.00 per hour for a 40-hour working week.

Each employee is paid $240.00 per week (40 × $6.00).

---

Any hours worked over the agreed contractual requirements are generally paid at overtime rates. This is an extra payment above the agreed hourly rate. It could be at 'time and a half', that is one-and-a-half times the hourly rate, or 'double time', that is twice the hourly rate. Overtime is an overhead cost unless it is at the request of a customer in order to speed up the completion of a job. In such cases the overtime becomes part of direct wages. The calculation is relatively straightforward and employees can calculate for themselves how much their wage will be each week.

A criticism of this form of remuneration is that it can lead to staff only doing a minimum level of work during their normal contractual hours so that they have to complete extra work at overtime rates.

### 28.2.2 High day rates

High day rates may be introduced to overcome the disadvantage of time work, where if higher than normal or expected performance is consistently achieved, higher than agreed hourly rates of pay will be paid. The system is designed to attract well qualified staff that will benefit themselves and the business with higher productivity.

**Worked example**

Time rate employees are paid $5.00 per hour for a 40-hour working week. Normal output is 20 units per hour.

High day rate employees are paid $6.00 per hour for a 40-hour working week. They produce 25 units per hour.

**Required**

Calculate the unit costs for each type of employee.

#### Answer

Time rate workers: 40 hours × 20 units = weekly output 800 units

So each unit costs $0.25 ($200 ÷ 800 units).

High day rate workers: 40 hours × 25 units = weekly output 1000 units

So each unit costs $0.24 ($240 ÷ 1000 units).

---

### 28.2.3 Piece work

Piece work involves workers being paid an agreed amount for each complete unit or batch of units that they produce.

**Worked example**

A worker is paid $10.00 for every batch of eight units produced. A worker produces 184 units in one particular week.

**Required**

Calculate the wages earned by the worker for her week's work.

### Answer

She will be paid $230.00 for her week's work.

---

Some workers resent the use of straight piece work to calculate their weekly income since they cannot guarantee their 'take home pay'. To overcome this problem many businesses guarantee workers a minimum weekly wage.

## 28.2.4 Premium bonus schemes

The principle behind the use of these schemes is to encourage workers to save time in the production process.

If a job normally takes six hours to complete and a worker completes the task in five hours, the worker has saved one hour. The worker would be rewarded for their efficiency: they would receive their normal time-based rate plus the premium bonus.

## 28.2.5 The Halsey scheme

This scheme involves an extra reward for the worker based on half the time the worker has saved the business.

**Worked example**

40 hours are allowed per week to complete a job. A worker takes only 35 hours. His rate of pay is $7.50 per hour.

**Required**

Calculate the worker's pay for the week.

### Answer

The worker's pay for the week is $318.75 (= Time rate $300.00 (40 hours × $7.50) + $18.75 (½ of 5 hours × $7.50)).

---

## 28.2.6 The Halsey-Weir scheme

This scheme is similar in operation to the Halsey scheme. However, the extra reward is based on 30 per cent of the time saved by the worker.

**Worked example**

36 hours are allowed to complete a job. A worker takes only 32 hours. Her rate of pay is $6.00 per hour.

**Required**

Calculate the worker's pay for the week.

### Answer

The worker's pay for the week is $223.20.

Time rate $216.00 (36 hours × $6.00) + $7.20 (30% of 4 hours × $6.00)

---

### 28.2.7 The Rowan scheme

The reward in this type of scheme is based on the relationship between the time actually taken to complete the job and the time originally allowed for the job.

The relationship is then used to calculate a proportion of the time saved. So if it is thought that a job will take 12 hours and it is completed in 10 hours the bonus will be based on 10/12ths of the hourly rate of pay for two hours of saved time.

**Worked example**

14 hours are allowed to complete a job. A worker completes the task in only 11 hours. The rate of pay is $8.00 per hour.

**Required**

Calculate the worker's pay for the job.

#### Answer

The worker's pay = $130.86

Time rate $112.00 (14 × $8.00) + $18.86 (rounded) (11/14ths of 3 × $8.00)

## 28.3 Absorption costing statements

It is of vital importance that a business is able to calculate what each product or service (or group of products or services) has cost to make or provide. This is necessary so that the business can fix a selling price in order to recover the costs incurred in operating the business and provide profits to ensure the survival of the business.

Absorption costing determines the total cost of production. (In fact it is sometimes called **total costing**.)

This means that all costs incurred in the production of the product are absorbed into the cost of production.

**Worked example**

The following information is available for the month of January 2015 for Chaudhry and Son, a manufacturing business. The business produces one product, a 'higle'. Production for January 2015 was 1000 higles and the costs involved were:

| | $ |
|---|---|
| Direct labour costs | 78 000 |
| Direct material costs | 56 000 |
| Indirect labour costs | 34 000 |
| Indirect material costs | 17 000 |
| Other indirect costs | 26 000 |
| Selling and distribution costs | 46 000 |
| Administration expenses | 62 000 |
| Manufacturing royalties | 2 000 |
| Depreciation of factory machinery | 14 000 |

**Required**

a Prepare an absorption costing statement for the month of January 2015.

b Calculate the cost of producing one higle, using an absorption costing basis.

## Answer

a **Absorption costing statement for January 2015**

| | $ |
|---|---|
| Direct materials | 56 000 |
| Direct labour | 78 000 |
| Royalties | 2 000 |
| **Prime cost** | 136 000 |
| Indirect materials | 17 000 |
| Indirect labour | 34 000 |
| Other indirect costs | 26 000 |
| Depreciation | 14 000 |
| Total production cost | 227 000 |
| Selling and distribution costs | 46 000 |
| Administration costs | 62 000 |
| Total cost | 335 000 |

b On an absorption costing basis, each higle has cost \$335.00 (= \$335 000 ÷ 1000).

# 28.4 Uses of absorption costing

The total cost of producing goods is necessary when calculating a selling price. It is also necessary for long-term planning, since total revenue must cover both direct costs and overheads.

## 28.4.1 Calculation of profit when selling price is fixed

If the selling price of higles is fixed at \$500.00 per unit, the profit on the sale of each higle is \$165.00 (\$500 – \$335).

## 28.4.2 Calculating the selling price when a predetermined level of profit is required

If Chaudhry and Son wishes to achieve a profit of \$70.00 on the sale of each higle, the selling price has to be \$405.00 per unit (\$335 + \$70).
If Chaudhry and Son requires a profit margin of 25 per cent:

- Profit on sales = 25 per cent (the same as 33.3 per cent on cost of sales)
- Cost of sales = \$335 000
- 33.3 per cent of \$335 000 = \$111 667
- So the profit margin is \$111 667.

| | |
|---|---|
| Total cost of producing higles | \$335 000 |
| Profit | \$111 667 |
| Selling price | \$446 667 or \$446.67 per unit (\$446 667 ÷ 1 000) |

➤ Now try Questions 1–3.

**Allocation of costs** is the term used to describe the process of charging whole items of expenditure to a cost centre or a cost unit. The costs are easily identified as deriving from the cost centre.

# 28.5 Overheads

The examples that we have considered so far have only considered one product. All overheads have simply been added to the prime cost of the product to arrive at the total cost. The overheads have been absorbed into the total cost of the product.

In the 'real world' (and generally in exam questions) things are rarely so simple.

Some costs are not easily allocated to a cost centre, yet the cost centre may have benefited from the service provided. For example, the cost of rent or local taxes

**Apportionment of overheads** is the process by which some overhead costs are charged to cost centres on some rational basis because they cannot be directly attributed to a particular cost centre.

When all overhead costs have been apportioned to a cost centre, the total has to be charged to specific units of production. This process is known as **absorption**.

applies to the business as a whole; each cost centre should bear some part of the total cost of providing the services.

Cost centres that are actively involved in the production process will be allocated, mainly, with direct costs – there is no need for apportionment in such cases but they should also be charged with other appropriate indirect costs.

These are usually costs which apply to the business as a whole. They need to be apportioned on some equitable basis. Apportionment will be based on managers' perception of the benefits that each individual cost centre receives from the provision of the service.

Consider the following scenario.

## Example

Ivor Fillin sets up in business manufacturing toothbrushes. He employs Harry Sheen to help in the manufacturing process. Ivor rents two units on a local industrial estate.

Ivor can very easily prepare an absorption costing statement since all the costs go towards manufacturing the toothbrushes. He can use the statement to calculate his profits and he can even use it to work out his pricing strategy.

After a couple of successful years, Harry, by now a skilled brush maker, suggests that they should diversify into also producing hairbrushes. Ivor agrees that this would be an excellent idea. In the smaller of the two rented units, Ivor continues to produce toothbrushes, while in the larger unit Harry produces hairbrushes.

How would Ivor determine the costs involved in producing the two different types of brushes?

He can easily allocate the direct costs to each product, since labour costs, and material costs, are unique to each product.

The problem arises when rent, local taxes, utility charges and other overheads have to be charged to the two products. These are costs that apply to the business as a whole. They need to be apportioned in some equitable manner.

**Table 28.1 Bases of apportioning indirect costs**

| Overhead | Basis of apportionment to cost centres |
|---|---|
| Rent | Floor area of cost centre |
| Local taxes | Floor area of cost centre |
| Insurance | Value of items being insured |
| Heating and lighting | Volume of cost centre (if this is not available then floor area may be used) |
| Depreciation | Cost or book value of the asset in cost centre |
| Canteen | Numbers of personnel in each cost centre |
| Personnel | Numbers of personnel in each cost centre |

## Worked example

The directors of the Beckmond Engineering Company provide the following information for the month of February.

The following budgeted overheads cannot be allocated to the two departments run by the company:

| | $ |
|---|---|
| Rent | 375 000 |
| Local taxes | 90 000 |
| Power | 300 000 |
| Supervisory wages | 96 000 |
| Depreciation of factory machinery | 150 000 |

**Additional information**

| | |
|---|---|
| Total factory area is 240 000 m² | Department A occupies 60 000 m²<br>Department B occupies 180 000 m² |
| Power used in each department | Department A 60 000 kWh<br>Department B 40 000 kWh |
| Cost of machinery in each department | Department A $300 000<br>Department B $600 000 |
| Staff employed in each department | Department A 30 workers<br>Department B 10 workers |

**Required**

Prepare an overhead analysis sheet for February.

### Answer

| Overhead | Total cost $ | Basis of apportionment | Dept A $ | Dept B $ |
|---|---|---|---|---|
| Rent | 375 000 | Floor area | 93 750 | 281 250 |
| Local taxes | 90 000 | Floor area | 22 500 | 67 500 |
| Power | 300 000 | kWh | 180 000 | 120 000 |
| Supervisory wages | 96 000 | Number of workers | 72 000 | 24 000 |
| Depreciation of machinery | 150 000 | Cost of machinery | 50 000 | 100 000 |
| | 1 011 000 | | 418 250 | 592 750 |

➤ **Now try Question 4.**

## 28.6 Transfer of service department costs

A canteen provides a service to all other departments.

Departments that provide services for the production department, and hence other cost centres, clearly are not involved directly in the production of finished products. They cannot recoup their costs by incorporating them into the selling price of their product or service. Yet their costs must be recovered by the business.

The estimated costs of service departments must be apportioned to each production department. This means that each production department will recover its own overheads and some of the overheads incurred by the service department.

Service departments in effect charge the other cost centres in the business for the services that they provide for them.

Sometimes service departments keep detailed records of work completed in each department. In such cases these costs can be allocated to the appropriate department.

This is often the case in a reprographics department of a college or school. Each department will be charged for the photocopying they are responsible for.

Examples of service departments include:

- canteen
- stores
- maintenance
- personnel.

**Worked example**

Thierity Ltd has three production departments. The company operates a staff canteen for all staff. The following budgeted cost information is given *after* all costs have been allocated or apportioned to the appropriate department.

| | $ |
|---|---|
| Department D | 412 000 |
| Department E | 346 000 |
| Department F | 110 000 |
| Canteen | 63 000 |

**Required**

Prepare a table showing the apportionment of canteen overheads to the production departments.

## Answer

| Overhead | Total $ | Basis of apportionment | Dept D $ | Dept E $ | Dept F $ | Canteen $ |
|---|---|---|---|---|---|---|
| Total | 931 000 | | 412 000 | 346 000 | 110 000 | 63 000 |
| Canteen | | ? | 30 000 | 24 000 | 9 000 | (63 000) |
| | 931 000 | | 442 000 | 370 000 | 119 000 | |

**Note**

Can you guess how the canteen costs have been apportioned? What information was missing in the question?

The information that was missing was the numbers of people working in each department. There were ten workers in Department D; eight in Department E; three in Department F.

Do not worry – the information will be given in any question you need to answer.

➤ Now try Question 5.

## 28.7 Reciprocal services

The picture becomes a little more complicated when **reciprocal services** are provided. **Reciprocal services** is the term used when a department provides a service for another department and receives a service from the same department.

For example, the canteen provides a service for all staff including the maintenance engineers; the maintenance engineers keep the canteen equipment in good working order as well as servicing equipment and machinery in all other departments.

Questions will normally only have two service departments as a maximum.

We will use the **elimination method** (sometimes referred to as the 'simplified method') to apportion costs incurred by service departments.

### Worked example

The cost accountant of Oxian Ltd provides the following information on budgeted total departmental costs after all costs have been allocated or apportioned:

| | Production departments | | | Service departments | |
|---|---|---|---|---|---|
| | M | N | P | Q | R |
| | $ | $ | $ | $ | $ |
| Total costs | 45 000 | 60 000 | 20 000 | 10 000 | 12 000 |

The service departments' costs are to be apportioned as follows:

| | | | | | |
|---|---|---|---|---|---|
| Department Q | 40% | 30% | 20% | – | 10% |
| Department R | 20% | 10% | 30% | 40% | – |

**Required**

Prepare a statement to show how the costs of the service departments are reapportioned between the production departments.

## Answer

| | Production departments | | | Service departments | |
|---|---|---|---|---|---|
| | M | N | P | Q | R |
| | $ | $ | $ | $ | $ |
| Total costs | 45000 | 60000 | 20000 | 10000 | 12000 |
| Apportionment of Dept R costs | 2400 | 1200 | 3600 | 4800 | (12000) |
| | 47400 | 61200 | 23600 | 14800 | |

**Note**

- Department R has now been eliminated.
- Always start with the service department with the greater costs.

| | | | | | |
|---|---|---|---|---|---|
| From above: | 47400 | 61200 | 23600 | 14800 | |
| Apportionment of Dept Q costs | 5920 | 4440 | 2960 | (14800) | 1480 |
| | 53320 | 65640 | 26560 | | 1480 |

This method ignores the amount left over for Department R.

Strictly speaking, this method is slightly inaccurate, but the estimated overheads themselves might be inaccurate since they are after all 'estimates'. Also, the method of apportioning overheads is only a matter of convention and none of the methods that could have been used can claim to be perfectly accurate. In most cases the figure remaining when the process is completed will be insignificant.

➤ Now try Question 6.

## 28.8 The absorption of overheads

After the overheads have been apportioned to the appropriate cost centres we need to calculate the amount of the overhead to be included into the cost of each unit passing through the cost centre.

The amount of each cost centre's overheads that needs to be absorbed (added) to each unit of production is termed the **overhead absorption rate** (OAR).

There are a number of different methods of calculating the overhead absorption rate.

### 28.8.1 Direct labour hour rate

**Direct labour hours per unit** is the number of hours (or part of an hour) that a worker would take to produce one unit of output.

When a particular department is labour intensive and there is little machinery used or machine costs are low, the overhead absorption rate may be calculated using the man hours required to complete each unit of production.

**Worked example**

Stemods Ltd manufactures two products: 'culas' and 'ginars'.

The budgeted production for each product for October is shown:

| | Units | Direct labour hours per unit |
|---|---|---|
| Cula | 10000 | 2 |
| Ginar | 8000 | 1.5 |

Budgeted overheads for October are expected to be $75 840.

**Required**

Calculate:

a the overhead absorption rate for each product using the direct labour hour method
b the total amount of overheads absorbed by each product if budgets are met.

## Answer

Total direct labour hours = 20 000 + 12 000 = 32 000

Labour hour overhead absorption rate = $\frac{\$75\,840}{32\,000}$ = $2.37 per hour

a Overhead absorption rate for each unit: cula = $4.74 (2 hours × $2.37)
ginar = $3.56 (1½ hours × $2.37)

b If the budgets are met, then the total overheads will be absorbed as follows:

| | $ | |
|---|---|---|
| 10 000 units of cula will absorb | 47 400 | (10 000 × $4.74) |
| 8 000 units of ginar will absorb | 28 440 | (8 000 × $3.555) |
| Total overheads absorbed | 75 840 | |

➤ Now try Question 7.

You may find that the two subtotals calculated above are referred to as the **overhead recovery rates**. So, in the month of October the total overheads $75 840 will be recovered by culas $47 400 and by ginars $28 440.

**Machine hours** relates to the number of hours a machine will be used in the production of one unit of output.

### 28.8.2 Machine hour rate

This method is appropriate when production methods are capital intensive or machine costs are relatively high. The overhead absorption rate will take into account the number of machine hours required to produce each unit of output.

**Worked example**

Tryndra Ltd manufactures 'dertins' and 'ghilos'. The budgeted production for each product for February is shown:

| | Units | Machine hours per unit |
|---|---|---|
| Dertin | 4 000 | 0.5 |
| Ghilo | 20 000 | 0.25 |

Budgeted overheads for February are expected to be $66 780.

**Required**

Calculate:

a the overhead absorption rate using the direct machine hour method
b the total amount of overheads absorbed by each product if budgets are met.

## Answer

Total machine hours: 2 000 + 5 000 = 7 000

Machine hour overhead absorption rate = $\frac{\$66\,780}{7\,000}$ = $9.54 per hour

a Overhead absorption rate: dertin = 0.5 × $9.54 = $4.77
ghilo = 0.25 × $9.54 = $2.39

b If the budgets are met, the total overheads will be absorbed as follows:

| | $ | |
|---|---|---|
| 4000 units of dertin will absorb | 19080 | (4000 × $4.77) |
| 20000 units of ghilo will absorb | 47700 | (20000 × $2.385) |
| | 66780 | |

The total overheads in February will be recovered partly by sales of dertin ($19080) and partly by sales of ghilos ($47700).

➤ Now try Question 8.

There are four other possible ways of calculating the overhead recovery rate.

### 28.8.3 Direct labour cost rate

The estimated overheads are expressed as a proportion of the estimated cost of direct wages. The weakness of this method is that overheads will, in the main, accrue on a time basis whereas wages often accrue in a more complex way depending on the method of rewarding labour. For example, payment of wages may be based on some kind of piecework or a premium bonus method.

**Worked example**

Total overheads for April are estimated to be $283992. Total direct labour costs are estimated to be $151060.

**Required**

Calculate the overhead recovery rate for April using the direct labour cost method.

#### Answer

$$\text{Overhead recovery rate} = \frac{\$283992}{\$151060} = \$1.88 \text{ per } \$1 \text{ of direct labour cost.}$$

### 28.8.4 Direct material cost rate

This is a similar method to the direct labour cost method. The total cost of materials is used as the denominator in the calculation. The method's main weakness is that it assumes that time taken to process materials bears some kind of relationship to its cost. So high value materials will attract more overheads than cheaper materials, regardless of the time taken to process them.

**Worked example**

Total overheads for December are estimated to be $1954170. Total material costs are estimated to be $502350.

**Required**

Calculate the overhead recovery rate for December using the direct material cost method.

#### Answer

$$\text{Overhead recovery rate} = \frac{\$1954170}{\$502350} = \$3.89 \text{ per } \$1 \text{ of direct materials used}$$

### 28.8.5 Prime cost rate

This method uses prime cost as the denominator. The method has the same weaknesses as the direct labour cost method and the direct material cost method.

**Worked example**

Total overheads for July are estimated to be \$1355 500. Prime cost is estimated to be \$412 000.

**Required**

Calculate the overhead recovery rate for July using the prime cost method.

#### Answer

$$\text{Overhead recovery rate} = \frac{\$1355\,500}{\$412\,000} = \$3.29 \text{ per } \$1 \text{ of prime cost}$$

### 28.8.6 Unit produced rate (cost unit rate)

The total overheads allocated and apportioned to production are divided by the estimated number of units produced; so the overheads are spread over the goods produced. The method can only realistically be used if the business manufactures only one type of product.

**Worked example**

Total overheads for May are estimated to be \$15 500. The total number of units produced is estimated to be 14 500.

**Required**

Calculate the overhead recovery rate for May using the cost unit method.

#### Answer

$$\text{Overhead recovery rate} = \frac{\$15\,500}{14\,500} = \$1.07 \text{ per unit}$$

## 28.9 Products passing through several departments

So far, we have considered products that are produced in one department only. Some jobs pass through several departments before completion. As a job passes through a department, it attracts a proportion of the overheads of that department. When it passes to the next department, it will attract a proportion of the overheads of the second department and so on until it is complete.

Job ——► Prime costs ——► Proportion of overheads from Department 1 ——► Proportion of overheads from Department 2 ——► etc.

——► Total cost of product + Mark up = Selling price

**Figure 28.7** Products passing through departments

**Worked example**

Yves Pichot manufactures 'desirs'. Each desir passes through two departments on its path to completion.

Information for each department is given:

| | Department 1 | Department 2 |
|---|---|---|
| Budgeted total overheads | $40 320 | $18 864 |
| Budgeted total labour hours worked | 4800 | 900 |
| Budgeted total machine hours worked | 300 | 3600 |

A desir spends four hours passing through Department 1 and three hours passing through Department 2 before completion.

**Required**

a Calculate the overhead absorption rate for a desir for each department using:

i labour hours

ii machine hours.

b State which method of overhead recovery should be used in the two departments. Give reasons for your answer.

c Calculate the total overheads to be absorbed by one unit of desir if budgets are met.

### Answer

a

| Department 1: | OAR using labour hours = $8.40 ($40 320 ÷ 4800)<br>OAR using machine hours = $134.40 ($40 320 ÷ 300) |
|---|---|
| Department 2: | OAR using labour hours = $20.96 ($18 864 ÷ 900)<br>OAR using machine hours = $5.24 ($18 864 ÷ 3600) |

b Since Department 1 is labour intensive, labour hours should be chosen as the method of overhead recovery. Machine hours should be chosen for Department 2 since it is capital intensive.

c A desir takes four hours in Department 1, so $33.60 needs to be absorbed.

A desir takes three hours in Department 2, so $15.72 needs to be absorbed.

Total overheads to be absorbed by a desir: $49.32 ($33.60 + $15.72) if budgets are met.

➤ Now try Question 9.

## 28.10 Over absorption and under absorption of overheads

Overhead recovery rates are based on predictions of future levels of activity and predicted (budgeted) levels of overhead expenditure.

If the actual level of activity is equal to that budgeted, and actual expenditure on overheads is equal to budgeted expenditure, then the expenditure on overheads will be recovered exactly.

If the actual level of activity is less than the budgeted level, and spending on overheads is equal to the predicted level, then the actual overheads will not be recovered. There will be an **under recovery of overheads**.

If the actual level of activity is equal to the level that was budgeted, but the actual spending on overheads is greater than the budgeted amount, then this too will mean an under recovery of overheads.

If the actual level of activity is higher than the budgeted level, and actual spending on overheads is equal to that budgeted, then the overheads will be more than recovered. There will be an **over recovery of overheads**.

If activity levels are the same as those budgeted, but actual spending is less than that budgeted, then this too will mean less spending on overheads. There will be an over recovery of overheads.

Any under recovery of overheads is *debited* to the costing income statement.

Any over recovery of overheads is *credited* to the costing income statement.

**Worked example**

Bartasil Ltd manufactures 'kityos'. The directors budget for overhead expenditure of $25 000 each month. This figure is based on an output of 5000 kityos. The overhead absorption rate is $5.00 per unit.

The following information is given:

| | Actual output | Actual expenditure on overheads |
|---|---|---|
| | Units | $ |
| January | 5 000 | 24 000 |
| February | 4 900 | 25 000 |
| March | 5 100 | 25 000 |
| April | 5 000 | 25 100 |
| May | 5 100 | 28 050 |
| June | 5 100 | 26 000 |

**Required**

Calculate the over or under recovery rate for each of the six months.

### Answer

| | Actual expenditure on overheads | Overheads recovered | Over/under recovery | |
|---|---|---|---|---|
| | $ | $ | $ | |
| January | 24 000 | 25 000 | 1 000 | over recovery |
| February | 25 000 | 24 500 | 500 | under recovery |
| March | 25 000 | 25 500 | 500 | over recovery |
| April | 25 100 | 25 000 | 100 | under recovery |
| May | 28 050 | 25 500 | 2 550 | under recovery |
| June | 26 000 | 25 500 | 500 | under recovery |

## 28.11 Other overheads

The other costs incurred by a business must also be recovered if the business is to survive in the long term.

- Selling and distribution costs must be recovered.
- Administration costs must be recovered.
- Finance charges must be recovered.

These costs are recovered through the mark-up added to the goods before they are sold to the final customer.

These costs are treated as period costs and as such are entered in the income statement as we have done on previous occasions in this book.

## 28.12 Problems associated with the use of absorption costing

Overhead absorption rates must be updated on a regular basis. They are derived from budgeted information and are therefore subject to change.

Management decision making relies heavily on the provision of accurate information; the information provided by absorption costing may be inaccurate, since it relies on budgeted information.

## 28.13 Absorption costing and IAS 2

IAS 2 Inventories requires that the value of inventories, reported in the published financial statements of limited companies, includes the costs of converting the raw materials used into finished goods.

All 'normal' production costs will be included in the total cost of the product.

Occasionally there may be 'unusual' items of expenditure incurred during production. These might include idle time losses or exceptional wastage due to unforeseen circumstances. These should be excluded in the valuation.

Other overheads may be included if management deems it prudent to do so. Examples might include overheads incurred by the accounts department or the personnel department if either has a direct input into the running of the production department.

Managers can use whatever basis they like when producing financial statements for internal management use, since IAS 2 does not apply.

### Self-test questions

7 Give an alternative name for absorption costing.
8 Identify one use of absorption costing.
9 Identify one example of a cost centre.
10 Identify one example of a cost unit.
11 Tick the appropriate box to indicate whether the expense should be allocated or apportioned to the appropriate cost centre:

| Overhead | Allocate | Apportion |
|---|---|---|
| Direct wages | ✓ | |
| Heating and lighting | | |
| Direct materials | | |
| Insurances | | |
| Cost of running the canteen | | |

12 What does the abbreviation OAR stand for?
13 Explain what is meant by the term 'reciprocal service departments'.
14 Identify two methods of calculating an overhead absorption rate other than by using a direct labour hour method.
15 Budgeted overheads are \$23 600; actual overheads are \$24 000; and actual activity is equal to budgeted activity. Does this result in an over or under absorption of overheads?
16 Budgeted overheads are equal to actual overheads and actual activity is 23 000 units of production compared to budgeted activity of 25 000 units. Does this result in an over or under absorption of overheads?

➤ Now try Questions 10 and 11.

## Chapter summary

- Allocation of expenditure is used when the cost is incurred for a specific cost centre.
- Expenditure that cannot be allocated is apportioned to the cost centres, using some equitable basis.
- Service costs are apportioned to production cost centres.
- In the case of reciprocal services, costs should be apportioned by the elimination method.
- The overheads of cost centres are charged to cost units by using calculated overhead absorption rates.
- Overhead absorption rates are generally based on direct labour hours if the operation is labour intensive, or on direct machine hours if the operation is capital intensive.
- Higher than budgeted activity and/or lower than budgeted overhead expenditure will result in an over recovery of overheads.
- Lower than budgeted activity and/or higher than budgeted overhead expenditure will result in an under recovery of overheads.

# 29 Marginal costing

## Content

### 2.2 Traditional costing methods

2.2.2 Marginal costing
- Understand the application of marginal costing
- Calculate the contribution of a product
- Prepare a break-even chart
- Calculate the break-even point, contribution to sales ratio and margin of safety
- Explain the use and limitations of break-even charts
- Prepare a statement reconciling the reported profit using marginal costing and absorption costing
- Identify the uses and limitations of marginal costing
- Calculate the effect of limiting factors on production

2.2.3 Cost-volume-profit analysis
- Identify and explain the advantages and limitations of cost-volume-profit analysis
- Evaluate and interpret cost-volume-profit data and its value as a support for management decision making
- Apply costing concepts to make business decisions and recommendations using supporting data

**By the end of this chapter you should be able to:**
- prepare a marginal costing statement
- use marginal costing for decision making in respect of 'make or buy' decisions, acceptance or rejection of additional work, price setting, optimum use of scarce resources
- calculate break even
- prepare a break-even graph.

**Marginal costing** is defined by CIMA as 'the cost of one unit of a product or service which would be avoided if that unit were not produced or provided'.

**Variable costs** vary with levels of activity within the business.

**Fixed costs** do not vary with levels of business activity.

**Semi-variable costs** cannot be classified as either fixed costs or variable costs since they contain an element of both.

## 29.1 Marginal costing

**Marginal costing** is a decision-making technique used by management accountants. It is based on the extra costs incurred and the extra revenue generated by the production and sale of an additional unit of output.

Marginal costing makes a clear distinction between fixed and variable costs. When using marginal costing, no attempt is made to allocate or apportion any fixed costs incurred by cost centres or cost units.

**Formula**

$$\text{Total variable cost of sales} = \text{Variable production cost} + \text{Variable selling and distribution cost} + \text{Variable administrative cost}$$

When used in a marginal cost statement or marginal cost calculation, **variable cost** is total variable cost of sales.

We saw in Chapter 28 that the total cost of a product was made up of variable costs plus fixed costs.

We also know that fixed costs or period costs are not affected by changes in the number of units produced. Therefore, if the number of units produced is increased, then only the variable cost part of total cost would increase.

**Marginal costs** are the costs that are incurred when one extra unit is produced above the planned level.

**Marginal revenues** are the revenues earned by the sale of one extra unit.

**Marginal costs** usually comprise extra material costs, extra direct wage costs, extra direct expenditure, other extra variable costs in selling and distributing the product and any extra administration costs that arise when there is an increase in the level of production.

By definition, an increase in production (that is an increase in business activity) will not increase fixed costs – they will remain unchanged.

**Contribution** is the difference between selling price and total variable costs. Contribution should more properly be termed 'contribution towards fixed costs and profit', since once fixed costs are all covered, contribution becomes profit.

## Example

| Output in units | Fixed costs | Variable costs | Total costs | Marginal costs per unit |
|---|---|---|---|---|
| | $ | $ | $ | $ |
| 100 | 5000 | 1000 | 6000 | |
| 101 | 5000 | 1010 | 6010 | 10 |
| 102 | 5000 | 1020 | 6020 | 10 |
| 103 | 5000 | 1030 | 6030 | 10 |

- Note the variable costs change in line with the level of production.
- The fixed costs have not changed with the increase in the level of production.
- The variable costs are the marginal costs (in this simple example).

## Worked example

| | | $ |
|---|---|---|
| The selling price of a unit of VX/32 is | | 100 |
| Variable costs per unit – direct materials | | 27 |
| | direct labour | 32 |
| | royalties | 8 |
| Fixed costs per unit | | 17 |

**Required**

Calculate the contribution made by the sale of one unit of VX/29.

### Answer

Contribution per unit = Selling price per unit – Variable costs per unit

= $100 – $67 ($27 + $32 + $8)

= $33

## Self-test questions

1 What is meant by the term 'marginal'?

2 Total cost = $3500. After producing one more unit of production, total cost rises to $3510. What is the marginal cost?

3 Contribution is the amount that a single unit of a product can be sold for. True/False?

4 Fixed costs + Profit = ?

## 29.2 Marginal cost statements

Marginal cost statements offer an alternative layout to the traditional income statements already encountered.

Marginal cost statements emphasise fixed and variable costs separately and so emphasise the total fixed costs incurred by the business.

**Worked example**

Rault Ltd is a manufacturing business. The following information relates to the year ended 31 May 2015:

| | $ |
|---|---|
| Direct materials | 120 000 |
| Direct wages | 360 000 |
| Variable factory overhead expenses | 60 000 |
| Fixed factory overhead expenses | 110 000 |
| Variable selling and distribution expenses | 56 000 |
| Fixed selling and distribution expenses | 45 000 |
| Variable administrative expenses | 16 000 |
| Fixed administrative expenses | 38 000 |
| Total sales revenue | 950 000 |

**Required**

Prepare a marginal cost statement for the year ended 31 May 2015.

### Answer

**Rault Ltd**

**Marginal cost statement for the year ended 31 May 2015**

| | | $ | $ |
|---|---|---|---|
| Revenue | | | 950 000 |
| *Less* | Variable costs | | |
| | Direct materials | (120 000) | |
| | Direct wages | (360 000) | |
| | Factory expenses | (60 000) | |
| | Selling and distribution expenses | (56 000) | |
| | Administrative expenses | (16 000) | (612 000) |
| Total contribution | | | 338 000 |
| *Less* | Fixed costs | | |
| | Factory overheads | (110 000) | |
| | Selling and distribution overhead | (45 000) | |
| | Administrative overhead | (38 000) | (193 000) |
| Profit for the year | | | 145 000 |

**Worked example**

Emam produces a single product. The following information relates to the production and sales of the product in October:

| Costs and revenues per unit | | $ |
|---|---|---|
| Sales revenue | | 70 |
| Costs – | direct materials | 15 |
| | direct labour | 12 |
| | royalties | 5 |
| | fixed costs | 20 |

Production and sales = 1000 units.

**Required**

Prepare a marginal cost statement for October, showing the total contribution and profit.

## Answer

**Emam**

**Marginal cost statement for the month of October**

| | | $ | $ |
|---|---|---|---|
| Revenue | | | 70 000 |
| *Less* | Direct materials | (15 000) | |
| | Direct labour | (12 000) | |
| | Royalties | (5 000) | (32 000) |
| Contribution | | | 38 000 |
| *Less* Fixed costs | | | (20 000) |
| Profit for the month | | | 18 000 |

**Worked example**

The data are the same as in the above worked example but 1001 units are produced and sold.

**Required**

Prepare an income statement for October, showing the total contribution and profit.

## Answer

**Emam**

**Income statement for the month of October**

| | | $ | $ |
|---|---|---|---|
| Revenue | | | 70 070 |
| *Less* | Direct materials | (15 015) | |
| | Direct labour | (12 012) | |
| | Royalties | (5 005) | (32 032) |
| Contribution | | | 38 038 |
| *Less* Fixed costs | | | (20 000) |
| Profit for the month | | | 18 038 |

**Note**

- The total contribution has risen by the contribution of the extra unit produced and sold.
- The fixed costs have not risen even though the activity rate has risen.
- The profit has risen by the amount of the contribution gained from the sale of the one extra unit.

Marginal costing splits total costs into its two main elements – fixed costs and variable costs.

The identification of contribution is essential in this type of problem.

**Self-test questions**

5 What is the difference between a marginal cost statement and an income statement?
6 How would total contribution be calculated?
7 Give two examples of direct costs that might be used in a marginal cost statement.
8 Give two examples of fixed costs that might appear in a marginal cost statement.

➤ Now try Question 1.

## 29.3 The uses of marginal costing

Marginal costing is used whenever a business is:

- costing 'special' or 'one off' opportunities
- deciding whether to make or buy a product
- choosing between competing alternative actions
- employing a penetration or destroyer pricing strategy
- calculating the break-even level of output.

All of these circumstances tend to be short-term decisions.

### 29.3.1 'Special' or 'one off' business opportunities

**Worked example**

The Troncell Manufacturing Company is based in Malaysia. It manufactures one product, 'troncells'. The following information is available for a production level of 5000 troncells:

| Costs and revenues per unit | $ |
|---|---|
| Selling price | 45 |
| Direct materials | 12 |
| Direct labour | 19 |
| Royalties | 1 |
| Fixed costs | 8 |

There is spare capacity in the factory. A retailer in the USA has indicated that she would be willing to purchase 200 troncells but only if the price to her was $35 each.

**Required**

Advise the management of Troncell whether they should accept the order.

## Answer

The order should be accepted. The order will make a positive contribution of $600 ($3 per unit).

### Workings

Contribution = Selling price per unit – Marginal costs per unit

= $35 – $32

= $3 per troncell

**Note**

- The special order has no need to cover the fixed costs since they have already been absorbed into the 'normal' selling price.
- The American contract has no need to cover the fixed costs again.
- The contract is providing the manufacturer with an extra (marginal) contribution.

We can check to see if the acceptance of the American contract does make the business more profitable by preparing marginal cost statements:

| Non-acceptance of the order | | | Acceptance of the order | | |
|---|---|---|---|---|---|
| | $ | $ | | $ | $ |
| Revenue | | 225 000 | Revenue | | 232 000 |
| Direct materials | (60 000) | | Direct materials | (62 400) | |
| Direct labour | (95 000) | | Direct labour | (98 800) | |
| Royalties | (5 000) | (160 000) | Royalties | (5 200) | (166 400) |
| Contribution | | 65 000 | | | 65 600 |
| Fixed costs | | (40 000) | Fixed costs | | (40 000) |
| Profit | | 25 000 | Profit | | 25 600 |

**Note**

- The fixed costs have not changed with the increased level of production.
- The profit has increased by the amount of the total contribution earned by accepting the order from America.

## 29.3.2 Conditions that must apply if an order priced on marginal costing techniques is to be accepted

Care must be taken when accepting an order based on marginal costing principles.

- There must be spare production capacity in the business.
- The order must not displace other business. (If it does, then the revenue lost also becomes a marginal cost.)
- There must be clear separation of existing customers from customers receiving the order priced at marginal cost. (Existing customers are likely to be unaware of the cheaper price charged to the customer receiving the goods at the lower price.)
- The customer receiving the goods should not be in a position to sell the goods to other customers at a price lower than the regular price.
- The customer receiving the order priced using marginal costing must be aware that the price quoted is for that one order only – the price charged should not set a precedent so that the 'cheaper price' is demanded for future orders.

- Care must be taken to ensure that competitors do not match the price for their regular customers, thus starting a price war in which all producers will suffer from lower prices.

A manufacturing business must cover all costs incurred in running the business. A business cannot survive by costing all its production at marginal cost. If it did, then none of the fixed costs would be covered (absorbed).

So, generally, any 'special' order which results in a positive contribution should be accepted.

### 29.3.3 Acceptance of an order that will result in a negative contribution

A special order that yields a negative contribution may be accepted under the following conditions:

- in order to retain a highly skilled workforce
- in order to maintain machinery in good condition, i.e. if failure to use the machinery would result in its deterioration
- in order to stimulate further orders (at the 'normal price' in the future)
- for altruistic reasons, i.e. because it is a worthwhile thing to do, for example providing a product at less than full cost for disabled children.

**Self-test questions**

9 Marginal costing can only be used when a business is considering whether or not to undertake a 'one off' contract. True/False?

10 Outline two conditions that must apply when a special price based on marginal costing techniques is accepted by a business.

11 Outline two reasons why the manager of a business might accept an order even when the order yields a negative contribution.

➤ Now try Questions 2 and 3.

## 29.4 'Make or buy' decisions

A business may have the opportunity to purchase the product that it currently manufactures itself.

In order to arrive at a decision whether or not to purchase the product, rather than make it, the managers should consider the marginal costs and revenues.

**Worked example**

Achim Droblin manufactures sweatshirts in Mauritius for sale to sports retailers. The estimated costs and revenues for the next financial year are given:

**Costs and revenues per unit, based on production and sales of 140 000 sweatshirts**

| | $ | |
|---|---|---|
| Selling price | 12 | |
| Direct materials | 2 | |
| Direct labour | 3 | |
| Fixed costs | 4 | |
| Total production cost | 9 | |
| Profit per sweat shirt | 3 | Total profit $420 000 |

A manufacturer in India has indicated that the sweatshirts could be supplied to Achim at a total cost of only $7 each. Achim has calculated that if existing selling price is maintained then profits will rise to $5 per sweatshirt and total profits will rise to $700 000 next year – an increase in profits of $280 000.

**Required**

Advise Achim whether, on financial grounds, he should accept the offer from the Indian manufacturer.

## Answer

Achim should not accept the offer. If he did, he would be worse off next year than if he continued to manufacture the sweatshirts himself. Profits would fall to only $140 000.

### Workings

Contribution per unit if he continues to manufacture himself = $7.00

(Selling price $12.00 – Marginal (variable costs) $5.00 ($2.00 + $3.00))

Contribution per unit if he purchases from India = $5.00

(Selling price $12.00 – Marginal (variable cost) $7.00).

Marginal costing statements show the positions clearly:

| **Make** | | | **Buy** | |
|---|---|---|---|---|
| | **$** | **$** | | **$** |
| Revenue | | 1 680 000 | Revenue | 1 680 000 |
| Direct materials | (280 000) | | | |
| Direct labour | (420 000) | (700 000) | Purchase price | (980 000) |
| Contribution | | 980 000 | Contribution | 700 000 |
| *Less* Fixed costs | | 560 000 | *Less* Fixed costs | 560 000 |
| Profit | | 420 000 | Profit | 140 000 |

**Note**

It has been assumed that any resources released by accepting the offer from India could not be used elsewhere by Achim.

If the manufacturing space could be sublet to another manufacturer, the income received would be a source of marginal revenue and should be added to the sales revenue as extra income.

If extra costs had to be incurred in transporting the goods to the USA, this would have represented a further marginal cost.

If extra costs were incurred keeping the manufacturing area safe and/or secure, these costs would also represent marginal costs and would have to be included in Achim's calculations.

**Worked example**

Achim is faced with the same details given above. However, he can sublet his manufacturing area at a rental of $200 000.

**Required**

Advise Achim whether, on financial grounds, he should accept the offer from India.

## Answer

He should not accept the offer.

With the rental income, the total contribution would rise to $900 000 (original contribution $700 000 + rental income $200 000), which is still less than the $980 000 contribution he would earn by continuing to manufacture the sweatshirts himself. Profit would fall to $340 000 compared to $420 000.

**Worked example**

Achim is faced with the same details as given in the original example. But Achim has to employ a security firm to keep the factory premises secure from vandals. This will cost $120 000 per year and additional maintenance costs of $100 000.

**Required**

Advise Achim whether, on financial grounds, he should accept the offer from India.

### Answer

Achim should not accept the Indian offer.

The contribution would only be $480 000 compared to the original contribution of $980 000.

➤ Now try Question 4.

Although in each case the contribution is positive, the new contribution would be less than the contribution earned if Achim continued to manufacture the sweatshirts.

## 29.5 Making a choice between competing courses of action

The managers of a business may have to consider a choice between two or more competing strategies that would incur the same level of fixed costs. If this is the case, then only the marginal costs need to be considered. The strategy that provides the greatest contribution should be the one adopted.

**Worked example**

Marsha Knit starts a small furniture manufacturing business. She is only able to produce one type of product. She needs to choose whether to produce tables, chairs or cupboards.

She provides the following predicted information:

| Predicted production and sales | Tables<br>500<br>$ | Chairs<br>500<br>$ | Cupboards<br>500<br>$ |
|---|---|---|---|
| Selling price per unit | 400 | 120 | 380 |
| Direct material costs per unit | 80 | 13 | 70 |
| Direct labour costs per unit | 70 | 67 | 110 |
| Total fixed costs | 50 000 | 50 000 | 50 000 |

**Required**

Advise Marsha which product she should manufacture.

### Answer

Marsha should produce tables.

Each table produced will give a positive contribution of $250, compared to a contribution of $40 per chair and $200 per cupboard.

➤ Now try Question 5.

Check your answer by preparing marginal cost statements for each type of furniture.

## 29.6 Choosing the most profitable production pattern when only a limited amount of a factor of production is available

**Factors of production** are resources that are needed in the process of manufacturing a product or in providing a service; for example, land, labour, finance and capital equipment.

A business may be faced by a short-term shortage of one or more **factors of production** necessary to continue the manufacturing process. There could be a temporary shortage of skilled labour; there could be a temporary shortage of direct materials or a temporary shortage of storage space. Any shortage of a particular resource will limit the business's ability to maximise profits.

A scarce resource is sometimes referred to as a **key factor** or a **limiting factor**.

It is essential that the managers of a business utilise the scarce resources available in a way that will yield the maximum return to the business.

### Worked example

The Laville Company manufactures four products. The products use the same type of materials and skilled labour. The following information is given:

| | Product | | | |
|---|---|---|---|---|
| | P | Q | R | S |
| Selling price per unit ($) | 200 | 300 | 100 | 400 |
| Maximum demand for product (units) | 1 000 | 800 | 1 200 | 900 |
| Material usage per unit (kg) | 7 | 12 | 4 | 15 |
| Labour hours per unit | 3 | 4 | 2 | 6 |

Materials cost $10.00 per kilogram; labour costs $15.00 per hour.

**Required**

Prepare a statement showing the level of production for each product that would maximise the profits for the Laville Company if:

a only 25 000 kilograms of materials are available

b only 10 000 labour hours are available.

### Answer

| | P | Q | R | S |
|---|---|---|---|---|
| **Contribution earned by each product** | **$** | **$** | **$** | **$** |
| Selling price per unit | 200 | 300 | 100 | 400 |
| Marginal costs per unit | 115 | 180 | 70 | 240 |
| Contribution per unit | 85 | 120 | 30 | 160 |

a

| Contribution per kilogram of material used | $12.14 | $10.00 | $7.50 | $10.67 |
|---|---|---|---|---|
| Ranking | 1 | 3 | 4 | 2 |

You can see that the Laville Company should produce as many of product P as possible. If there are still materials available, it should produce as many of product S as possible; then product Q and finally product R.

If Laville could produce all products:

| they would produce | 1 000 | 800 | 1 200 | 900 |
|---|---|---|---|---|
| this would use | 7 000 kg | 9 600 kg | 4 800 kg | 13 500 kg |

Since this is not possible:

| they should produce | 1 000 | 375 | nil | 900 |
|---|---|---|---|---|
| this would use | 7 000 kg | 4 500 kg | nil | 13 500 kg |

This combination of products will maximise profits while only using 25 000 kilograms of materials.

b

| Contribution per hour of labour used | $28.33 | $30.00 | $15.00 | $26.67 |
|---|---|---|---|---|
| Ranking | 2 | 1 | 4 | 3 |

You can see that the Laville Company should produce as many units of product Q as possible; then produce as many units of product P as possible; then product S and finally product R.

If Laville could produce all products:

| they would produce | 1 000 | 800 | 1 200 | 900 |
|---|---|---|---|---|
| this would use | 3000 hrs | 3200 hrs | 2400 hrs | 5400 hrs |

Since this is not possible:

| they should produce | 1 000 | 800 | nil | 633 |
|---|---|---|---|---|
| this would use | 3000 hrs | 3200 hrs | nil | 3798 hrs |

This production pattern would maximise profits while only using 9998 hours of scarce labour. (The company has to produce only 633 of product S since the next unit would be only two-thirds complete!)

**Self-test questions**

12 Explain the term 'key factor'.
13 Give an example of a key factor.
14 Would the shortage of a component used in the production of computers be classified as a key factor?
15 A key factor should be used to produce the product that gives the highest profit. True/False?.

➤ **Now try Question 6.**

## 29.7 Penetration or destroyer pricing

This strategy may be employed by the managers of a business when they wish to gain a foothold in a market in which a number of firms are already well established. They decide to cost their product using only marginal costs.

They can do this because their existing customers will already be covering (absorbing) the fixed costs incurred by the business.

**Example**

A Japanese business manufactures electrical generators. The generators retail in Japan at $273 per unit. The cost of producing one generator is:

| | $ |
|---|---|
| Components | 56 |
| Labour costs | 112 |
| Fixed costs | 32 |
| Total costs | 200 |
| Profit | 73 |
| Selling price in Japan | 273 |

The managers wish to penetrate the Scandinavian market.

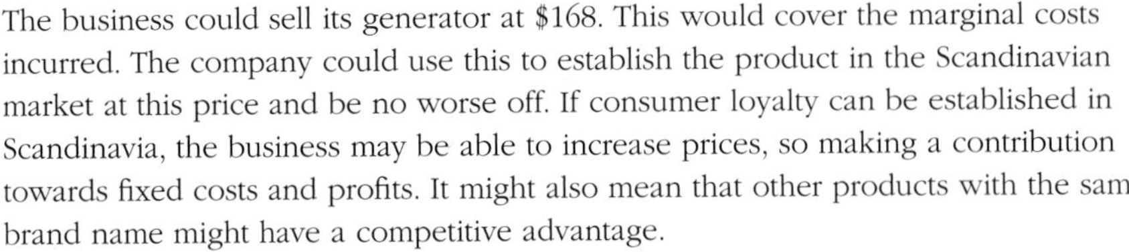
The business could sell its generator at $168. This would cover the marginal costs incurred. The company could use this to establish the product in the Scandinavian market at this price and be no worse off. If consumer loyalty can be established in Scandinavia, the business may be able to increase prices, so making a contribution towards fixed costs and profits. It might also mean that other products with the same brand name might have a competitive advantage.

## 29.8 Cost-volume-profit analysis

The **break-even point** is the level of sales revenue and units sold at which a business makes neither a profit nor a loss. Alternatively, it is the point where contribution equals fixed costs.

**Margin of safety** is the difference between actual sales achieved or forecast as achievable and the break-even level of sales. The margin indicates to management how far sales can fall before the business will move out of profit and into a loss-making situation.

This is often called **break-even analysis**.

Cost-volume-profit analysis is an important topic; it is worth spending some time mastering the three methods of determining the **break-even point**.

### 29.8.1 The unit contribution method

This is probably the easiest method to use if the figures are readily available. The method should always be used unless a question specifically asks you to use another method.

If the contribution per unit can be calculated easily, then it should be quite simple to determine how many of those units must be sold to cover the total fixed costs incurred.

**Formula**

$$\text{Break-even point} = \frac{\text{Total fixed costs}}{\text{Contribution per unit}} = \text{Number of units required to be sold}$$

Note that it is *total* fixed costs that are used.

**Worked example**

**Tip**

If the answer that you arrive at is very low and very unlikely, then you may have used fixed cost per unit rather than total fixed cost.

The following information is given for the production and sales of 50 000 'pimkles':

| | $ |
|---|---|
| Selling price per unit | 30 |
| Direct material costs per unit | 8 |
| Direct labour costs per unit | 9 |
| Fixed costs per unit | 5 |

**Required**

Calculate:

a the break-even point for pimkles

b the break-even sales revenue necessary to break even

c the margin of safety.

### Answer

a $\text{Break-even point} = \frac{\text{Total fixed costs}}{\text{Contribution per unit}} = \frac{\$250\,000}{\$13} = 19\,231$ pimkles

b Break-even sales revenue = 19 231 × $30 = $576 930

c Margin of safety = 30 769 pimkles (50 000 – 19 231)

Sometimes information is not given in the precise way that we would like. We may need to get it into a form that we would prefer.

## Worked example

The following information is given for the production and sales of 2450 'hupers':

| | $ |
|---|---:|
| Total direct material costs | 56 350 |
| Total direct labour costs | 41 650 |
| Total fixed costs | 54 000 |
| Total sales revenue | 183 750 |

**Required**

Calculate:

a the break-even point for hupers

b the margin of safety.

### Workings

The information given uses total costs and total revenue. The break-even calculation using this formula uses *total* fixed cost and contribution *per unit*. So it is necessary that we work out the contribution per unit to use in our calculation.

| | $ | |
|---|---:|---|
| Direct material costs per unit | 23 | ($56 350 ÷ 2 450) |
| Direct labour costs per unit | 17 | ($41 650 ÷ 2 450) |
| Total variable costs | 40 | |
| Sales revenue per unit | 75 | ($183 750 ÷ 2 450) |
| Contribution per unit | 35 | ($75 – $40) |

### Answer

a Break-even point $= \dfrac{\text{Total fixed costs}}{\text{Contribution per unit}} = \dfrac{\$54\,000}{\$35} = 1\,543$ hupers

b Margin of safety = Achievable sales – Break-even sales level

= 2450 – 1543

= 907 hupers

**Note**

The exact answer for break even is 1542.857 hupers, but we always round up since it is usually impossible to sell part of the unit that we are concerned with.

## Worked example

The following information is given for the production and sales of 1 500 'dorcs':

| | $ |
|---|---:|
| Direct material costs per unit | 8.00 |
| Direct labour costs per unit | 13.00 |
| Fixed costs per unit | 7.50 |
| Selling price per unit | 40.00 |

**Required**

Calculate:

a the break-even point for dorcs

b the margin of safety.

### Workings

*Total* fixed costs must be used but contribution *per unit* is required when using this formula.

Total fixed costs = \$11 250 (\$7.50 × 1 500)

Contribution per unit = Selling price per unit – Variable costs per unit
= \$40 – \$13 and \$8
= \$19

## Answer

a Break-even = $\frac{\text{Total fixed costs}}{\text{Contribution per unit}} = \frac{\$11\,250}{\$19}$ = 593 dorcs (actually 592.105)

b Margin of safety = Achievable sales – Break-even level of sales
= 1 500 – 593
= 907 dorcs

If the break-even level of sales revenue is required, then the break-even volume is multiplied by the selling price per unit.

Total sales revenue required in order for hupers to break even was \$115 725 (1 543 × \$750).

Total sales revenue required in order for dorcs to break even was \$23 720 (593 × \$40).

Break-even analysis can be used to determine the level of production and sales revenue that would be required in order to achieve a particular level of profit.

This information is useful to managers when planning the future activities of a business.

**Tip**

Always start your calculations with the formula.

**Formula**

Units to be sold to reach target profit = $\frac{\text{Total fixed costs + Profit required}}{\text{Contribution per unit}}$

**Worked example**

Tanzeel requires a profit of \$80 000. He supplies the following information:

| | \$ |
|---|---|
| Selling price per unit | 56.00 |
| Variable costs per unit | 32.00 |
| Total fixed costs | 60 000 |

**Required**

Calculate the number of units that need to be sold in order to achieve a profit of \$80 000.

## Answer

Units to be sold = $\frac{\text{Total fixed costs + target profit}}{\text{Contribution per unit}}$

$= \frac{\$60\,000 + \$80\,000}{\$56 - \$32}$

$= \frac{\$140\,000}{\$24}$

= 5834 units (rounded from 5833.33)

The major drawback with using the above method of determining break even is that it will only work for a single product. Obviously, different products will have different cost patterns and therefore different contributions to different fixed costs. In order to overcome this problem, the following method can be used. However, the method about to be described will not calculate the number of units to be sold in order to break even.

## 29.8.2 The contribution to sales method

This is sometimes called the **profit/volume method**. This method is used when:

- there are a number of products being manufactured and sold
- a marginal costing statement is given
- the variable cost per unit and the selling price per unit are not available or would be extremely difficult to calculate.

**Formula**

$$\text{Contribution to sales (c/s) ratio} = \frac{\text{Total contribution}}{\text{Total sales revenue}}$$

$$\text{Break even} = \frac{\text{Total fixed costs}}{\text{Contribution/sales (c/s) ratio}}$$

Provided that the selling price per unit and the marginal costs per unit do not change, the contribution/sales ratio will remain fixed.

A simple illustration demonstrates this:

**Example**

| | 1 unit | 2 units | 3 units | 10 units | 1000 units | |
|---|---|---|---|---|---|---|
| Sales at $4 per unit | 4 | 8 | 12 | 40 | 4 000 | |
| Marginal costs $3 per unit | 3 | 6 | 9 | 30 | 3 000 | |
| Contribution | 1 | 2 | 3 | 10 | 1 000 | |
| $\frac{\text{Contribution}}{\text{Sales}} \times 100$ | $\frac{1}{4} \times 100$ | $\frac{2}{8} \times 100$ | $\frac{3}{12} \times 100$ | $\frac{10}{40} \times 100$ | $\frac{1000}{4000} \times 100$ | *... which are all 25%* |

We can use this information to calculate break even and the total sales revenue needed to achieve a particular level of profits.

**Example**

**Ben Chan plc**

**Marginal cost statement for the year ended 31 August 2014**

| | $ |
|---|---|
| Sales | 358 700 |
| Variable costs | (126 300) |
| Total contribution | 232 400 |
| Fixed costs | (150 000) |
| Profit | 82 400 |

$$\text{C/S ratio} = \frac{\text{Contribution}}{\text{Sales}} = \frac{\$232\,400}{\$358\,700} = 64.8\% \text{ or } 0.648$$

$$\text{Break-even point} = \frac{\text{Total fixed costs}}{\text{Contribution/sales ratio}} = \frac{\$150\,000}{0.648} = \$231\,482 \text{ sales revenue}$$

This method gives the break-even level of **sales revenue**.

Worked example

The following information relates to Gorki Ltd:

**Marginal cost statement for the year ended 30 November 2014**

| | $ |
|---|---|
| Sales | 400000 |
| *Less* Variable costs | 190000 |
| Contribution | 210000 |
| Fixed costs | 140000 |
| Profit | 70000 |

**Required**

Calculate the sales revenue necessary to give Gorki Ltd a profit of $90000.

## Answer

$$\text{Contribution to sales ratio} = \frac{\$210000}{\$400000} \times 100 = 52.5\% \ (0.525)$$

$$\text{Sales volume required to give } \$90000 \text{ profit} = \frac{\text{Fixed costs} + \$90000}{\text{Contribution/sales ratio}}$$

$$\text{Sales volume required} = \frac{\$140000 + \$90000}{52.5\%} = \frac{\$230000}{0.525} = \$438096$$

So sales have to increase by $38096 from the current level of $400000.

➤ Now try Question 7.

## 29.8.3 The graphical method of determining break-even

Do not use this method unless you are specifically asked for a graph.

When drawing your graph, work methodically.

Build up the graph in stages – each stage is important.

The accuracy of your graph and the results you can read from it will depend on the amount of care you take.

Worked example

They following information is given for the production of 100000 tables:

| | | $ |
|---|---|---|
| Selling price per table | | 25 |
| Costs per unit – | Wood | 4 |
| | Direct wages | 7 |
| | Variable manufacturing overhead | 3 |
| | Fixed manufacturing overhead | 4 |
| | Variable sales overhead | 1 |
| | Fixed sales overhead | 2 |

Graphs are a visual aid. They must be accurate and easy to read.

**Required**

Prepare a break-even graph for tables, showing the break-even point and the margin of safety.

## Workings

### Stage 1

The horizontal axis of your graph is used to show the sales output in units.
The vertical axis of your graph is used to show costs and revenues.
Where the two axes meet is called the origin and denotes zero for both axes. It should be marked 0.

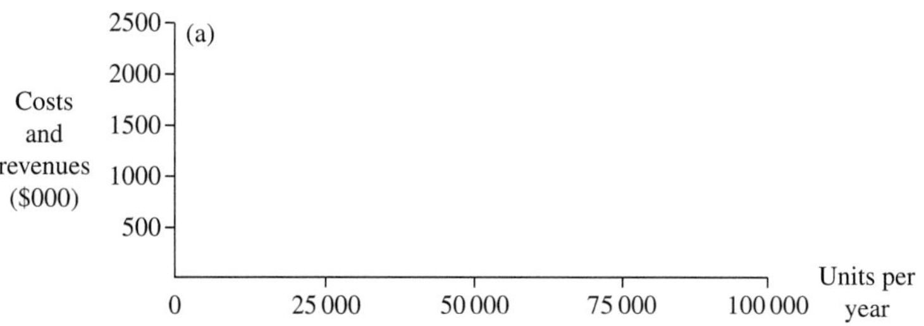


It is important to remember that the data must be scaled evenly, otherwise the graph that you draw will be distorted and will give inaccurate results.

### Stage 2

Always give your graph a heading.

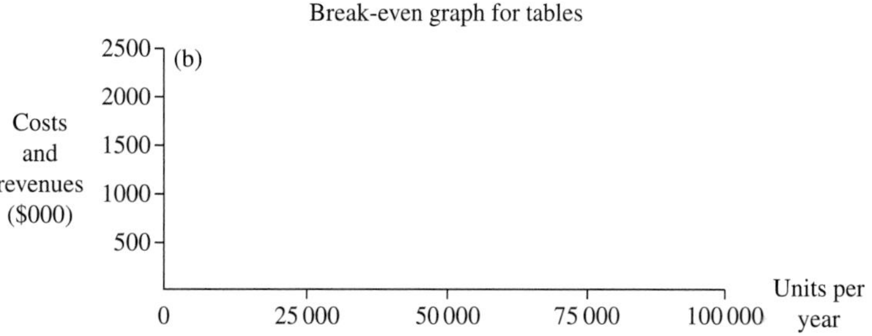


### Stage 3

Draw in the fixed costs.

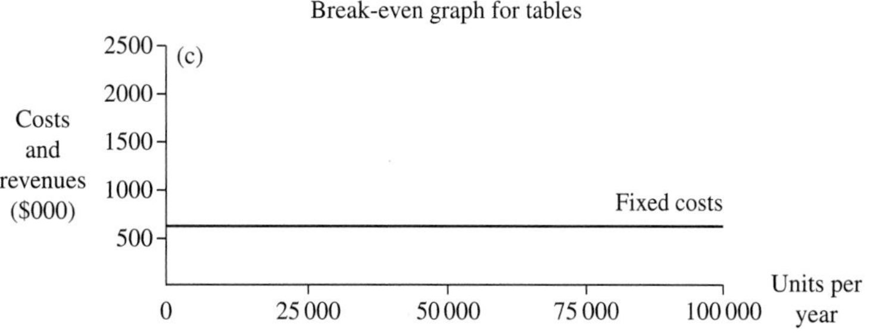


### Stage 4

In order to plot the variable costs, you need to do a few calculations.

The variable costs are $15 per table (Wood costs + direct wages + variable manufacturing overheads + variable sales overhead).

| **Sales output** | **0** | **10 000** | **60 000** |
|---|---|---|---|
| | **$** | **$** | **$** |
| Variable costs ($15 per unit) | 0 | 150 000 | 900 000 |
| Fixed costs | 600 000 | 600 000 | 600 000 |
| Totals costs | 600 000 | 750 000 | 1 500 000 |

We now mark with an *x* the point that indicates 0 on the horizontal axis and 600 000 on the vertical axis.

We then put an $x$ on the point that indicates 10 000 on the horizontal axis and 750 000 on the vertical axis.

We then put an $x$ on the point that indicates 60 000 on the horizontal axis and 1 500 000 on the vertical axis.

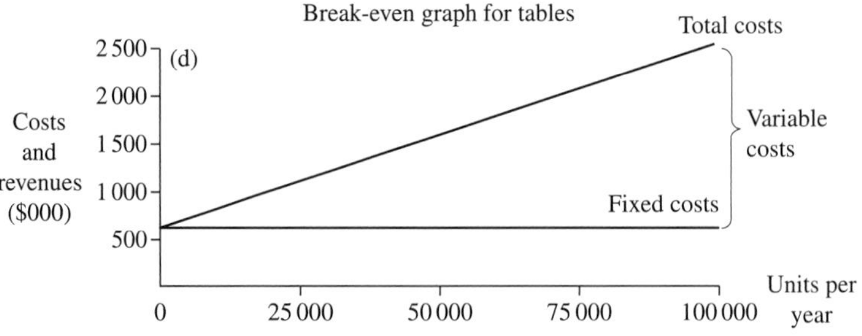


We now have in place the total cost curve.

Remember to label each curve after you have finished drawing it.

### Stage 5

Draw in the sales revenue curve.

The complete graph should look like this:

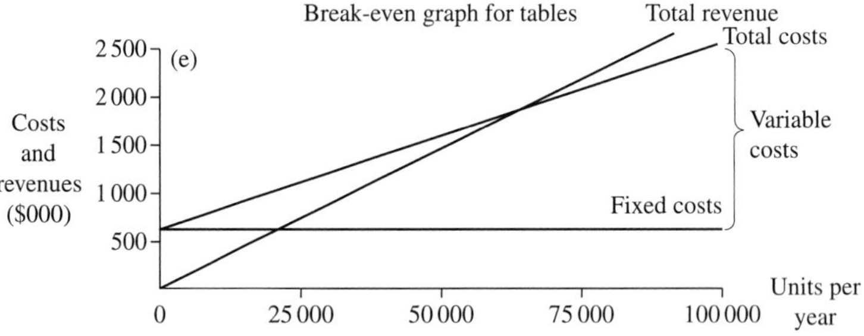


### Stage 6

Mark on your graph the break-even point and indicate the margin of safety.

### Answer

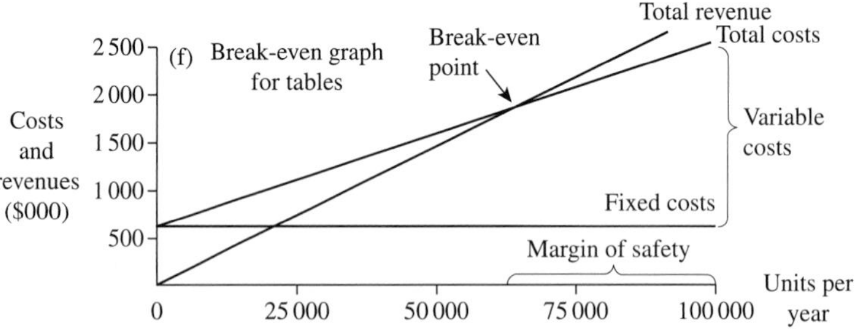


You will notice that fixed costs have been drawn in as a line that is parallel to the horizontal (sales volume) axis of the graph.

➤ Now try Question 8.

An alternative way to construct a graph draws the fixed costs line parallel to the variable cost line – this is known as a **contribution graph**.

## 29.8.4 Limitations of break-even charts

- There is an assumption that all data behave in a linear manner:
  - Fixed costs are assumed to remain fixed regardless of circumstances.
  - Selling price is assumed to remain constant in all circumstances.

- The break-even chart assumes that the only factor affecting costs and sales revenues is sales volume. Costs and revenues may be affected by:
  - increases in output
  - changes in economic climate
  - changes in technology, etc.
- It is assumed that the cost mix remains constant but businesses change their capital-labour mix over time or as circumstances may dictate.
- There is an assumption that all production is sold.
- The charts generally apply to only one product.

### 29.8.5 Profit/volume graphs

Another problem associated with break-even charts is that they do not show clearly the actual amount of profit (or loss) at each level of sales. To see the profit or loss, the gap between the total sales revenue line and the total cost line must be measured.

A profit/volume graph solves this problem. The graph shows how profits change as the volume of sales changes.

Profit-volume graph

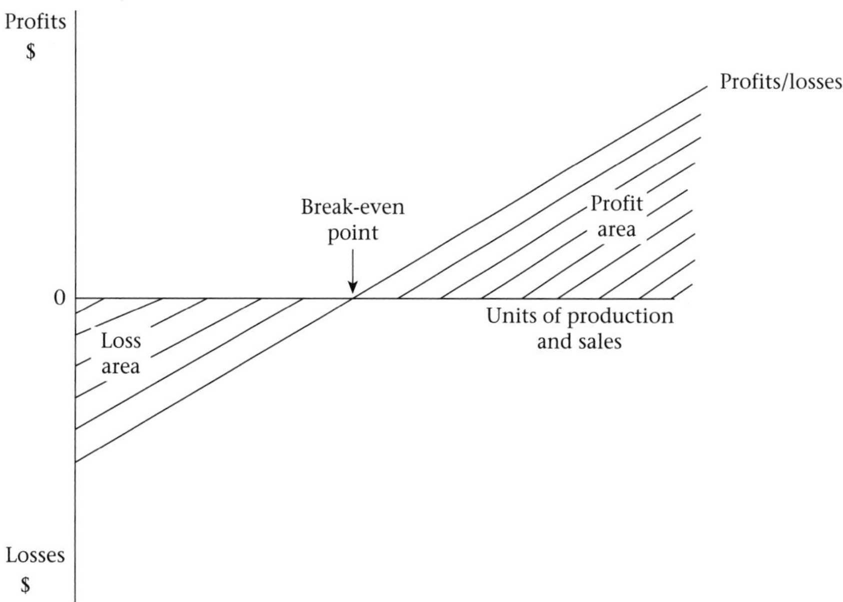


**Figure 29.1** Profit/volume graph

## 29.9 The value of cost-profit-volume (CPV) analysis as an aid to decision making

CPV analysis:

- is a useful tool in short-term decision making
- examines the relationship that exists between sales volume, sales revenue, costs and profits
- shows how costs behave at varying levels of output
- can be used in 'what if' analysis
- can help to provide answers to questions on the likely outcome when a particular course of action is followed by management, for example the effect on profit if more goods were sold at a reduced price.

Graphs:

- depict CPV in a form that helps most people understand the information shown quickly and more effectively (but do remember that for decision-making purposes the use of calculations is much more accurate)

- show clearly the break-even point
- identify the margin of safety
- show visually and clearly the impact that changes in sales volume has on profits.

## 29.10 Sensitivity analysis

All forecasts are predictions of future outcomes. Forecasts of profitability are based on the accuracy of the predictions of future costs and future revenues.

**Example**

Planned sales of 'diorth' are 5000 units at $20 per unit.

Variable costs are predicted to be $5 per unit.

Fixed costs are estimated to be $52 000.

A forecast income statement based on this information shows:

| | $ | $ |
|---|---|---|
| Sales (5000 × $20) | | 100 000 |
| Variable costs (5000 × $5) | (25 000) | |
| Fixed costs | (52 000) | (77 000) |
| Profit | | 23 000 |

$$\text{Break-even point} = \frac{\text{Total fixed cost}}{\text{Contribution per unit}} = \frac{52\,000}{\$15} = 3\,467 \text{ units}$$

A loss would be incurred if planned sales volume fell below 3 467 units.

A loss would result if:

- sales volume fell by 30.66 per cent $= \dfrac{(1533 \text{ margin of safety} \times 100)}{(5000 \text{ predicted sales volume})}$
- selling price fell by 23 per cent $= \dfrac{(\$23\,000 \times 100)}{(\$100\,000)}$
- variable costs rose by 92 per cent $= \dfrac{(\$23\,000 \times 100)}{(\$25\,000)}$
- fixed costs rose by 44.23 per cent $= \dfrac{(\$23\,000 \times 100)}{(52\,000)}$

## 29.11 Marginal costing and IAS 2

Inventories should not be valued using marginal costing techniques.

IAS 2 Inventories states that inventories should be valued at the lower of cost and net realisable value (see Chapters 16 and 20). It states that costs should include costs of purchase, costs of conversion and other costs incurred in bringing the inventories to their present location and condition.

Costs of conversion include fixed and variable manufacturing overheads. Since marginal costing principles ignore fixed costs, it is evident that marginal costs cannot be used as a basis for inventory valuation.

## Self-test questions

16 State the formula used to calculate the break-even point using the unit contribution method.
17 Explain when the contribution/sales method would be used to find the break-even point.
18 Another name for break-even is margin of safety. True/False?
19 Break-even output = 7 500 units; total production = 10 000 units. What is the margin of safety in units?
20 A graph should be used where possible to find the break-even point since it is the most accurate of the methods. True/False?
21 Give another name for break-even analysis.
22 Explain the term 'sensitivity analysis'.
23 Inventories cannot be valued using marginal cost techniques. True/False?

➤ **Now try Questions 9–14.**

## Chapter summary

- Marginal means 'one extra'.
- Marginal costing is a decision-making technique.
- Contribution is an important concept in using marginal costing techniques.
- You should be able to calculate contribution and use it in arriving at decisions.
- Contribution towards fixed costs and profit is the difference between selling price and variable costs.
- Questions often deal with acceptance or rejection of a special order at less than the price charged to 'regular' customers.
- 'Make or buy' decisions can be determined by comparing contributions for the alternatives.
- Choices between different products having the same level of fixed costs can be made by comparing the relevant contributions.
- When there is a shortage of a factor of production, the factor must be used to give the greatest contribution for each unit of the 'key factor' used.
- Both the unit contribution method and the contribution/sales methods of determining break even are important topics.
- The break-even point is the lowest level of sales or units sold at which total revenue received by a business is equal to the total costs of the business.
- Margin of safety is the difference between the actual sales achieved or forecast as achievable and the break-even level of sales.
- Target profit is found by adding the target profit to the fixed costs and dividing by the contribution per unit or the contribution/sales ratio.
- Finding the break-even point by graphical means is useful, but it is time consuming and so may not be required in a question. However, you should be able to extract data from a graph.
- Forecast profit is dependent on the accuracy of predicted data. Sensitivity analysis considers the degree of change necessary in the data that will result in a loss arising.

# 30 Unit, job and batch costing

**Content**

**2.2 Traditional costing methods**

2.2.3 Cost-volume-profit analysis

- Prepare costing statements using unit, job and batch costing principles
- Apply costing concepts to make business decisions and recommendations using supporting data

**By the end of this chapter, you should be able to:**

- identify and describe the types of business that would use unit, job and batch costing systems
- value simple work in progress inventory.

At this point in your studies, you need to concentrate only on job, unit and batch costing.

A method of costing is designed to meet the needs of the business using it.

There are two main types of collecting financial information to be used when costing products or services. These are:

- job costing
- process costing.

Managers adapt these two main types to suit the individual requirements of their business. The system they employ will depend on the type of production process in their factory and the type of good or service being provided. The adaptations will have a number of names, including batch costing and contract costing.

Absorption costing can be used in any business. The principles of cost allocation and apportionment are still applied. The type of costing system used will depend on the type of business being considered.

Business activity generally falls into one of two categories:

- businesses whose production process is a continuous operation
- those that deal with **specific orders**.

## 30.1 Unit costing

**Continuous operation costing** is used in organisations where goods or services are produced using a sequence of continuous or repetitive operations or processes. This type of costing is used to find the cost of a single unit of production or single unit of providing a service. This is an example of **unit costing**.

## 30.2 Job costing

A **job** is work carried out by a business for a customer who has placed an order for specific work to be done.

Job costing is used where each product or service is different from the provision of other products. It is used by businesses that produce specialised or made to order outputs, where **jobs** are tailored to the specific requirements of an individual customer as a result of a special order. The system is employed where goods or services are provided on a 'one off' basis, as opposed to being mass produced.

In organisations that produce a wide range of products or jobs and where each order is unique, the cost of each order must be separately calculated. Each job will require differing amounts of labour, materials and overheads spent on it. Because of this, separate costing records are kept for each job, detailing all the costs incurred in completing the job and identifying the profit or loss for the job.

The job is a cost centre to which all the costs are charged.

The costing details may also be used to cost similar future jobs and to form the basis of preparing future quotations for jobs being considered.

It is therefore an appropriate costing system for businesses whose work consists of separate jobs, for example installers of air conditioning units, specialist building contractors, specialist home decorators, architects and tailors.

**Worked example**

The following information relates to a business using a system of absorption costing:

| Department | Budgeted overheads | Absorption base |
|---|---|---|
| Machine shop | $18000 | 4000 machine hours |
| Assembly shop | $10500 | 3000 labour hours |
| Paint shop | $5000 | 2500 labour hours |

An order is placed for job A/341 with a selling price of $9000.

The following information relates to job A/341:

| | |
|---|---|
| Direct materials costs | $3450 |
| Direct labour costs – machine shop | 60 hours at $5.00 per hour |
| assembly shop | 240 hours at $4.00 per hour |
| paint shop | 40 hours at $4.50 per hour |

Time booked in the machine shop for the job is 120 machine hours.

Administration and selling overheads are calculated at 20 per cent of factory cost.

**Required**

Calculate the cost of job A/341 and the profit made on the job.

## Answer

Overhead absorption rates (OAR):

Machine shop: $\frac{\$18000}{4000} = \$4.50$ per machine hour

Assembly shop: $\frac{\$10500}{3000} = \$3.50$ per labour hour

Paint shop: $\frac{\$5000}{2500} = \$2.00$ per labour hour

**Costings for Job A/341**

| | $ | $ |
|---|---|---|
| Direct materials | | 3450 |
| Direct wages – machine shop | 300 | |
| assembly shop | 960 | |
| paint shop | 180 | 1440 |
| Prime cost | | 4890 |

| | | |
|---|---|---|
| Factory overheads – machine shop (120 × $4.50) | 540 | |
| assembly shop (240 × $3.50) | 840 | |
| paint shop (40 × $2.00) | 80 | 1460 |
| Factory cost | | 6350 |
| Administration and selling overheads | | 1270 |
| Total cost | | 7620 |
| Selling price | | 9000 |
| Profit | | 1380 |

**Self-test questions**

1 What is meant by the term 'job'?
2 Identify a business that is likely to employ a system of job costing.
3 Ali runs a mobile DJ business. He will cost out each booking using job costing techniques. True/False?

➤ Now try Questions 1–3.

## 30.3 Batch costing

A **cost accumulation system** is a system that relies on all the individual elements of cost being added together.

Batch costing is used where a quantity of identical items is manufactured as a batch; the identical items are manufactured and treated as one individual job for costing purposes. This could be because a customer orders a quantity of identical items, for example a builder of houses requires a woodworking business to make identical roof timbers or uniform kitchen cupboards. The woodworker would use a system of batch costing.

Costing a batch is very similar to costing a job, and the same procedures are followed. But the whole batch is treated as one separate identifiable job.

Costs are recorded against each batch and the final total production cost for the whole batch is divided by the number of good individual units produced to get the production cost per article.

It is ideally suited to the costing requirements of mass-production industries where identical items are manufactured. Such items keep their individual identity as separate units, even though there may be several common, distinct stages in arriving at the end result.

Examples of industries employing batch costing techniques would include a business producing components for a car manufacturer or a business making microchips for an electrical goods manufacturer.

When the batch is completed, the total cost of the batch is divided by the number of goods completed to determine the cost per unit.

Where manufactured goods have some common characteristics and also have some individual characteristics, the **cost accumulation system** may be a combination of both the job costing and process costing systems. For example, production of furniture, footwear and clothing involves the production of batches that are variations of a single design and therefore require a sequence of standardised operations.

Consider a business making women's dresses. Each unit may have the same basic design and require the same operation but the remaining operations may differ. Some dresses may require pockets, others no pockets, other dresses may require higher quality materials. The cost of a dress will therefore consist of the basic pattern plus additional costs. The product cost will consist of the average cost of the common operation to achieve the 'basic' dress plus the specific costs of the additional changes. The final product cost consists of a combination of process costing techniques and job costing techniques. This system is referred to as **operation costing** or **batch costing**.

**Self-test questions**

4 Explain the term 'batch'.
5 Identify an industry that would employ a system of batch costing.
6 A custom car company adapts production cars into racing cars. It would use a system of batch costing. True/False?
7 A manufacturer of television remote controls would use a system of batch costing. True/False?

➤ Now try Question 4.

## 30.4 Calculation of the value of inventory

When using unit, job or batch costing principles, closing inventory is valued according to the principle of taking the lower of cost and net realisable value (see Chapter 20). This is usually fairly straightforward when raw materials or finished goods are considered. However, it would be rather unusual if there were no partly completed goods remaining as inventory at the end of a period. The costs incurred during the period are for all the goods passing through the factory: those that are complete and those that have yet to be completed. The units that are partly completed have to be converted into the equivalent number of completed units.

**Worked example**

The following information is given for January:

Total production costs amount to \$29 440. By the end of January, 12 000 units had been completed and 1000 were partly finished. It is decided that these partly finished goods are 80 per cent complete.

At 31 January, 1 500 completed units were held as inventory.

**Required**

Calculate the value of closing inventory.

### Answer

$$\text{Cost per unit} = \frac{\$29\,440}{12\,000 + 800} = \$2.30$$

Closing inventory = \$3 450.00 (1500 complete units at \$2.30 each)

\$1 840.00 (80 per cent of 1 000 units at \$2.30 each)

Total value of closing inventory \$5 290.00

➤ Now try Question 5.

## Self-test questions

8 Job costing is a type of process costing. True/False?

9 Which of the following industries is likely to use a system of batch costing – a producer of breakfast cereals; a house builder; a potato chip manufacturer?

10 Linas installs swimming pools using the customer's specification. What type of costing system is Linas likely to use?

11 What does the term 'OAR' stand for?

12 Nine thousand units of a product are 30 per cent complete. What is the equivalent number of complete units?

## Chapter summary

- Specific order costing is used when production is designed to meet a specific customer's requirements.
- It is also used in the preparation of quotations for an individual job.
- Batch costing is used in production processes where many identical items are produced and it would be difficult or not cost effective to calculate the cost of each individual item.
- The cost of partly finished goods is converted into the equivalent number of completed units.

# 31 Business planning

## Content

### 2.3 The application of accounting to business planning

- Understand the benefit to business planning by the use of accounting data
- Explain the need for a business to plan for the future
- Explain why organisations prepare budgets and the benefits they bring to the planning process
- Explain the advantages and disadvantages of budgetary control, including financial and non-financial factors

**By the end of this chapter you should be able to:**

- explain why the managers of a business prepare budgets
- describe some of the benefits of preparing budgets
- describe some of the limitations of budgeting
- explain what is meant by the term 'budgetary control'.

A **forecast** is a prediction of what is *likely* to occur in the future.

A **budget** is a short-term financial plan. It is defined by CIMA as 'a plan expressed in money'. A budget details what *should* occur.

## 31.1 Budgets

We have already said that accounting fulfils two purposes: the stewardship function and the management function.

The management function can be broken down into:

- planning
- coordinating
- communicating
- decision making
- controlling.

Planning can be divided according to the time horizon under review:

- **long-term planning** (sometimes referred to as strategic or corporate planning)
  - Management identifies the current position of the business by using all the accounting data at their disposal. This is the starting point for their future strategies.
  - After taking into account this position they try to analyze the circumstances that the business is likely to encounter in the period of the plan. For example likely demand for the product; influence on the product from competitors; availability of resources.
  - Finally managers must decide on strategies to implement the strategic plan.
- **short-term planning** (sometimes referred to as operational planning).
  - Operational plans, using monetary terms, are known as budgets. Such budgets aid the functions of management outlined above. In addition, budgets can have a motivating influence on managers and once implemented may be used as an evaluative tool by comparing actual results with those outlined in the budget.
  - The budgets produced by a business are 'plans expressed in money'. The budgets show what management hope to achieve in a future time period in terms of overall plans and individual departmental plans.
  - The individual budgets are intertwined with each other – they depend on each other and influence each other. There is a need to ensure that the individual budgets are not contradictory or in conflict.

Because of the interdependency and the coordination of the budgets, managers must communicate with each other when preparing budgets – they must also communicate the plans to staff below and management above.

The nature of forecasting means that decisions have to be made. If profits are to increase then decisions must be made regarding sales and production levels, etc.

Budgets will be compared with actual results. Remedial action can then be taken when actual results are worse than budgeted results. In cases where actual results are better than those budgeted, examples of good practice may be identified and repeated elsewhere in the organisation.

## 31.2 The benefits of budgeting

- The preparation of individual budgets means that planning must take place. Plans need to be prepared in a coordinated way and this requires communication throughout all levels of the business.
- The budgeting process defines areas of responsibility and targets to be achieved by different personnel.
- Budgets can act as a motivating influence at all levels, although this is usually only true when all staff are involved in the preparation of budgets. If budgets are imposed on staff who have had little or no involvement in their development they can have a negative effect on morale and lead to staff feeling demotivated.
- Budgets are a major part of the overall strategic plan of the business and so individual departmental and personal goals are more likely to be an integral part of the 'bigger picture'.
- Budgets generally lead to a more efficient use of resources at the disposal of the business – leading to a better control of costs.

## 31.3 Limitations of budgeting

- Budgets are only as good as the data being used. If data are inaccurate, the budget will be of little use. Should one departmental budget be too optimistic or too pessimistic this will have a knock-on effect on other associated budgets.
- Budgets might become an overriding goal. This could lead to a misuse of resources or incorrect decisions being made.
- Budgets might act as a demotivator if they are imposed rather than negotiated.
- Budgets might be based on plans that can be easily achieved – so making departments/managers appear to be more efficient than they really are. There is also a possibility that this could lead to complacency and/or underperformance.
- Budgets might lead to departmental rivalry.
- Smaller businesses may find that they experience only limited benefits from what can be a lengthy, complicated procedure to implement.
- While budgets are being prepared, any limiting factors need to be identified and taken into account.

### Self-test questions

1 A budget is an accounting term used to describe a forecast. True/False?
2 Explain the term 'budget'.
3 Who would generally prepare the budgets for a business?
4 Outline two advantages that managers of a business would hope to achieve by preparing budgets.
5 Outline two drawbacks of budgeting that might be encountered by managers.
6 The Companies Act 1985 requires that all limited companies must prepare budgets and distribute them to all shareholders. True/False?

## 31.4 Budgetary control

Budgetary control delegates financial planning to managers. It evaluates their performance by continuously comparing actual results achieved by their departments against those set in the budget.

The characteristics of a system of budgetary control include the following:

- A clear definition of each manager's role.
- Once budgets have been approved, individual managers are responsible for the implementation of their departmental budget outcomes.
- Departmental budgets are action plans for each area of responsibility. Any deviations from set budgets must be approved by the senior management team.
- Performance is constantly monitored and compared to the agreed budget and in cases where budget targets are not met, corrective action is taken. Unexplained variations from budgets must be investigated and, where possible, departmental performance modified to reflect the agreed budget outcomes.

## 31.5 Advantages and disadvantages of using a system of budgetary control

The advantages and disadvantages of implementing a system of budgetary control are generally those outlined above in Sections 31.2 and 31.3. Budgeting and budgetary control systems involve a set of complex procedures which can prove to be expensive to set up. So it seems to be a matter of common sense that the benefits that accrue must outweigh the cost of installing such procedures.

Further consideration of budgeting is covered in Chapter 44.

### Self-test questions

7 Explain the difference between a forecast and a budget.

8 Only large public companies use a system of budgetary control. True/False?

9 Explain how a system of budgetary control might demotivate a departmental manager.

10 Identify how poor outcomes in a sales department budget might affect other departmental budgets.

### Chapter summary

- Budgets help managers to
  - plan
  - coordinate
  - communicate
  - make appropriate decisions and
  - control.
- Budgeting generally means that resources are allocated and used in a more efficient manner.
- Budgets are only as good as the data that they are derived from and care must be taken to ensure that they do not become the overriding goal of the business. They are one of the tools for use by managers.
- Budgetary control delegates financial planning to managers and it is used as a way of assessing departmental outcomes.

# AS Level examination-style questions

## Examination-style questions

**1** The following information relates to the business of Moussa:

| | at 31 July 2015 | at 31 July 2014 | at 31 July 2013 |
|---|---|---|---|
| | $ | $ | $ |
| Bank balance | 800 | 1 100 | 1 000 |
| Bank loan repayable in 2023 | 30 000 | | |
| Inventories | 7 000 | 6 500 | 6 000 |
| Machinery | 65 000 | 65 000 | 48 000 |
| Premises | 70 000 | 50 000 | 50 000 |
| Trade payables | 2 700 | 2 600 | 2 500 |
| Trade receivables | 3 800 | 4 200 | 4 000 |
| Vehicles | 12 000 | 10 000 | 10 000 |

**Required**

**a** Calculate the profit or loss for the years ended 31 July 2014 and 31 July 2015. [7]

**b** Prepare a statement of financial position at 31 July 2015. [10]

**c** Explain why it might be in Moussa's best interests to prepare a detailed income statement showing his profit or loss for the year. [7]

**d** Identify three pieces of additional information that Moussa would need in order to prepare a detailed financial statements. [6]

[Total: 30]

**2** The following selected information relates to Mendoza plc at 30 April 2014:

| | $ |
|---|---|
| Issued ordinary shares of $1 each | 200 000 |
| Issued 6% preference shares of $1 each | 75 000 |
| 4% debentures | 50 000 |
| 8% bank loan repayable 2023 | 100 000 |
| Premises at cost | 350 000 |
| Equipment at cost | 110 000 |
| Provision for depreciation – premises | 49 000 |
| – equipment | 70 400 |
| General reserve | 62 000 |
| Share premium | 30 000 |
| Retained earnings | 88 600 |
| Inventory | 85 000 |

The following transactions took place during the year ended 30 April 2015:

| | $ |
|---|---|
| Purchases | 400 000 |
| Sales | 600 000 |
| Purchases returns | 8 000 |
| Sales returns | 12 000 |
| Wages | 60 000 |
| Other expenses | 75 000 |

Additional information at 30 April 2015:

- Inventory was valued at $91 000.
- Trade receivables were $61 000.
- Trade payables were $43 000.
- Bank balance was $251 700.
- Accrued wages amounted to $2700.
- Prepaid expenses were $3300.
- It was decided that debts of $3000 should be written off as bad.
- Loan and debenture interest for the year were paid in full on 30 April 2015.
- The provision for doubtful debts was to be 2.5% of trade receivables.
- Depreciation on premises was two per cent straight line.
- Depreciation on equipment was 40% reducing (diminishing) balance.
- A further 40 000 ordinary shares were issued at a premium of $0.50 in April 2015.
- A dividend of 7% was paid on all ordinary shares in issue at the end of February 2015.
- The preference dividend was paid in full.
- $20 000 was transferred to the General Reserve.
- A provision of $6000 for taxation due is to be made.

**Required**

**a** Prepare an income statement for the year ended 30 April 2015. [10]

**b** Prepare a statement of changes in equity for the year ended 30 April 2015. [10]

**c** Prepare the statement of financial position at 30 April 2015. [10]

[Total: 30]

**3** Hang, Ivan and Atiya are in partnership, sharing profits 2:1:1 respectively. Their partnership agreement provided that:

- interest at 4% per annum be allowed on capital account balances at the start of each financial year
- Hang be allowed an annual salary of $21 000.

The partners maintain only capital accounts. The balances on 1 August 2014 were:

| | $ |
|---|---|
| Hang | 80 000 |
| Ivan | 50 000 |
| Atiya | 40 000 |

Drawings for the year to 31 July 2015:

| | $ |
|---|---|
| Hang | 28 000 |
| Ivan | 45 000 |
| Atiya | 35 000 |

The profit for the year ended 31 July 2015 was calculated at $96 000, and it accrued evenly throughout the year. Hang retired from the business on 30 January 2015. The partners agreed that:

- goodwill be valued at $48 000 but would not be shown in the books of account
- Hang was to take from the business $35 000 in cash and a vehicle (carrying amount $10 200) at an agreed value of $7400
- any balance on Hang's capital account was to be regarded as a loan with interest at 7% per annum.

After Hang's retirement it was agreed that:

- Ivan and Atiya share profits and losses 2:1 respectively
- interest on capital accounts be credited at 4% on balances at the start of the year
- Ivan be credited with a salary of $12 000 per annum.

Ivan paid off the partnership debt to Hang on 31 July 2015 from private funds.

**Required**

Prepare:

**a** the appropriation account for the year ended 31 July 2015 [12]

**b** capital accounts for the year ended 31 July 2015 [15]

**c** a loan account for Hang. [3]

[Total: 30]

4 The Ikhet manufacturing company has loose tools valued at $12 980 on 1 February 2012. During the year tools costing $1780 were purchased. At 31 January 2013 loose tools were valued at $10 740.

**Required**

**a** Calculate the depreciation of loose tools for the year ended 31 January 2013. [3]

**Additional information**

The company sold some out-of-date equipment that had cost $30 000. It had been depreciated at 50% per annum using the reducing balance method.

It was sold after three years of use for $3700.

**Required**

**b** Prepare a disposal account for the equipment. [4]

**c** Explain how a provision for depreciation affects a statement of financial position [2]

**d** Explain the connection between cash and making a provision for depreciation. [6]

[Total: 15]

5 The following information is given for Bajpan plc:

| | at 28 February 2015 | at 28 February 2014 |
|---|---|---|
| | $ | $ |
| Sales (credit) | 1 100 000 | 900 000 |
| Purchases (credit) | 524 000 | 537 000 |
| Opening inventory | 50 000 | 42 000 |
| Closing inventory | 52 000 | 50 000 |
| Trade receivables | 102 000 | 85 000 |
| Cash and cash equivalents | 1 000 | 4 000 |
| Trade payables | 44 500 | 60 000 |

**Required**

**a** Calculate the following ratios (show the formulae used).

- **i** current ratio [2]
- **ii** liquid ratio [2]
- **iii** trade receivables turnover [2]
- **iv** trade payables turnover [2]
- **v** rate of inventory turnover. [2]

**b** Comment on the current and efficiency ratios. [5]

[Total: 15]

6 Break-even analysis has been described as a useful tool for the accountant.

**Required**

**a** **i** Define the break-even point. [2]

**ii** Define the margin of safety. [2]

The following figures have been extracted from Katerina's books of account for the month of April 2010:

| | $ | $ |
|---|---|---|
| Sales | | 460 000 |
| Total variable costs | 299 000 | |
| Total fixed costs | 90 000 | 389 000 |
| Profit | | 71 000 |

**Required**

**b** Calculate Katerina's contribution as a percentage of sales (c/s ratio). [4]

**c** Calculate Katerina's break-even point. [3]

**d** Calculate the sales in dollars necessary to make a profit of $100 000. [4]

**e** Calculate the profit or loss if sales for the month are $375 000. [4]

**f** If the original sales prices are reduced by 5% but costs do not change, calculate the value of sales needed to achieve a profit of $80 000. [11]

[Total: 30]

*(Cambridge International AS and A Level Accounting 9706, Paper 22 Q3, May/June 2010)*

7 The following is the draft statement of financial position of Marshall Klingsman, a sole trader, at 30 April 2011.

**Statement of financial position at 30 April 2011**

| | $ | $ |
|---|---|---|
| **ASSETS** | | |
| **Non-current assets** | | |
| Buildings at valuation | | 300 000 |
| Equipment at book value | | 540 000 |
| Motor vehicles at book value | | 330 000 |
| | | 1 170 000 |
| **Current assets** | | |
| Inventories | 70 000 | |
| Trade receivables | 19 000 | |
| Other receivables | 2000 | |
| Cash and cash equivalents | 4000 | 95 000 |
| **Total assets** | | 1 265 000 |
| **CAPITAL AND LIABILITIES** | | |
| **Capital** | | |
| Opening balance | | 1 000 000 |
| Add Profit for the year | | 80 000 |
| | | 1 080 000 |
| Less Drawings | | 75 000 |
| | | 1 005 000 |
| **Non-current liabilities** | | |
| Loan | | 200 000 |
| **Current liabilities** | | |
| Trade payables | 57 000 | |
| Other payables | 3000 | 60 000 |
| **Total capital and liabilities** | | 1 265 000 |

**Additional information:**

After preparation of the draft statement of financial position the following errors were found.

1. Goods in inventory at 30 April 2011, valued at cost $15 000, were found to be damaged. The estimated net realisable value is $8 000.
2. Loan interest of 4% per annum had been omitted from the accounts.
3. No provision for depreciation on equipment had been made for the year. Depreciation should have been provided at 5% per annum using the reducing balance method.
4. Motor vehicles are depreciated by 10% per annum. During the year vehicle repairs of $10 000 had been incorrectly debited to the motor vehicles account.
5. On 28 April 2011 a credit customer, who owed $3600, was declared bankrupt. It was decided to write off this amount in full. No record of this has been made in the accounts.

**Required**

a Prepare a statement to show the corrected profit for the year ended 30 April 2011. [9]

b Prepare the corrected statement of financial position at 30 April 2011. [7]

c i Explain **two** differences between cost and net realisable value.

ii Discuss the accounting treatment of the damaged inventory in item 1. [4]

d Using your answers to **a** and **b** calculate the following ratios to **two** decimal places:

i current ratio [2]

ii liquid ratio (acid test). [2]

e State **four** ways in which Klingsman could improve his working capital. [4]

f Explain why the liquid ratio (acid test) is a more reliable indicator of liquidity than the current ratio. [2]

[Total: 30]

*(Adapted from Cambridge International AS and A Level Accounting 9706, Paper 23 Q1, May/June 2011)*

8 An extract from the statement of financial position of Bach Ltd at 1 January 2012 is shown below:

| | Cost | Accumulated depreciation | Net book value |
|---|---|---|---|
| **Non-current assets** | **$** | **$** | **$** |
| Machinery | 138 600 | 52 200 | 86 400 |

During 2012 the following transactions took place for machinery.

**Disposals**

| Date | Machinery reference | Year of purchase | Initial cost | Disposal proceeds |
|---|---|---|---|---|
| | | | $ | $ |
| 26 March | M12 | 2009 | 14 000 | 7 100 |
| 17 August | M18 | 2008 | 8 000 | 1 320 |
| 13 December | M20 | 2007 | 9 600 | 850 |

**Additions**

| Date | Machinery reference | Cost |
|---|---|---|
| | | $ |
| 20 April | M27 | 11 500 |
| 25 October | M31 | 16 200 |

All receipts and payments for these transactions are processed through the business bank account.

All of the remaining machinery at 31 December 2012 was purchased after 2008.

Depreciation on the factory premises is charged on a straight line basis based on a 50 year life, with no residual value.

Depreciation on machinery is charged on a straight line basis based on a five year life and an estimated residual value of 10% of the original cost.
It is the company policy to charge a full year's depreciation in the year of purchase but none in the year of disposal.

**Required**

a Prepare the following ledger accounts for the year ended 31 December 2012.
   i Machinery account [5]
   ii Provision for depreciation of machinery account [6]
   iii Machinery disposals account. [6]

b Identify **two** alternative methods of providing for depreciation. [2]

c State **three** causes of depreciation. [3]

Total: [22]

*(Adapted from Cambridge International AS and A Level Accounting 9706, Paper 21 Q2 a-c, May/June 2013)*

9 Airlie Limited manufactures one product. The following information is available for the production of one unit of product for the year ending 30 June 2014.

| | $ |
|---|---|
| Selling price | 32.00 |
| Direct materials | 6.50 |
| Direct labour | 8.50 |
| Fixed factory overheads | 5.00 |
| Variable factory overheads | 3.00 |
| Fixed selling and administration overheads | 3.50 |
| Variable selling and administration overheads | 2.50 |

The budgeted output is 18000 units per year, which represents 75% of total production capacity.

**Required**

a Calculate the breakeven point in units. [5]

b Calculate the breakeven point as a percentage of capacity. [3]

c Prepare a marginal cost statement to show Airlie Limited's budgeted total profit for the year ending 30 June 2014 based on the budgeted output of 18000 units. [3]

**Additional information**

1 The directors are considering purchasing additional machinery at a cost of $45 000.

2 This will increase capacity by 10%.

3 The machinery will be written off over five years, with an estimated residual value of $5000.

4 The directors plan to reduce the selling price by 12.5% and this will increase demand by 50%.

5 Fixed selling and administration overheads will increase by 10%.

**Required**

d Calculate the revised breakeven point in units. [5]

e Calculate the revised breakeven point as a percentage of capacity. [3]

f Prepare a marginal cost statement to show Airlie Limited's revised total profit for the year ending 30 June 2014 if the machinery is purchased. [4]

g Advise the directors whether they should go ahead with their plans. Give reasons for your answer. [7]

[Total: 30]

*(Adapted from Cambridge International AS and A Level Accounting 9706, Paper 21 Q3, May/June 2014)*

10 Asif operates a delivery service and does not keep proper accounting records. He provided the following information for the year ended 30 June 2014.

| | $ |
|---|---|
| Cash in hand at 1July 2013 | 3270 |
| Cash in hand at 30 June 2014 | 2349 |
| Cash receipts and payments: | |
| Vehicle repairs | 2400 |
| Fuel payments for vehicles | 14301 |
| Driver's wages | 4748 |
| Rent of a garage | 1600 |
| Sundry expenses | 2972 |
| Drawings | 11450 |
| Receipts from sale of old vehicle | 1300 |
| Cash stolen by Asif's driver | 430 |
| Cash received from customers | ? |

**Required**

a Prepare Asif's cash account for the year ended 30 June 2014. [7]

**Additional information**

| | $ |
|---|---|
| Trade receivables at 1 July 2013 | 3766 |
| Trade receivables at 30 June 2014 | 2863 |
| Bad debts written off during the year ended 30 June 2014 | 1648 |

**Required**

b Calculate Asif's revenue figure for the year ended 30 June 2014. [5]

**Additional information**

1 The vehicle which had been sold was purchased in May 2012 for $6200. Asif's policy is to depreciate the vehicles at 50% per annum using the reducing balance method. A full year's depreciation is charged in the year of acquisition. No depreciation is charged in the year of disposal.

2 At 30 June 2014 driver's wages of $200 were owing and garage rent of $400 was prepaid.

**Required**

c Prepare Asif's income statement for the year ended 30 June 2014. [12]

**Additional information**

Asif is considering introducing a system of credit control.

**Required**

d Explain the benefits this may bring to the business. [4]

e State **two** ratios that Asif could use to measure the profitability of his business. [2]

[Total: 30]

*(Adapted from Cambridge International AS and A Level Accounting 9706, Paper 23 Q1, October/November 2014)*

**11** Lance, a trader, has provided the following balances at 30 November 2014 after the preparation of the income statement for the year.

| | $000 |
|---|---|
| Profit for the year | 30 |
| Non-current assets – at cost | 500 |
| – accumulated depreciation | 200 |
| Accrued expenses | 20 |
| Cash in hand | 10 |
| Bank overdraft | 25 |
| Inventory | 80 |
| Trade payables | 35 |
| Trade receivables | 50 |
| Bank loan (2020) | 40 |
| Opening capital | 310 |
| Drawings | 20 |

a Prepare the statement of financial position at 30 November 2014. [8]

b Calculate, stating the formula used, the following ratios correct to two decimal places. [4]

| Ratio | Formula | Calculation |
|---|---|---|
| Current | | |
| Liquid (acid test) | | |

**Additional information**

| Ratio | 2013 | 2012 |
|---|---|---|
| Current | 2.30:1 | 2.0:1 |
| Liquid (acid test) | 1.0:1 | 1.40:1 |

**Required**

c Evaluate the change in Lance's liquidity position over the three years. [8]

**Additional information**

Lance has provided the following forecast for December 2014:

1 Sales are expected to be $75 000 of which 30% will be on a cash basis and the remainder payable the month after sale. All trade receivables outstanding at 30 November 2014 were expected to pay in full during December 2014.

2 Purchases are expected to be $45 000 of which 40% will be cash and the remainder payable the month after purchase. All trade payables at 30 November 2014 were expected to be paid in full during December 2014.

3 Business expenses of $12 500 will be paid in the month incurred.

4 Depreciation on non-current assets will be $9 500 per month.

5 A loan of $25 000 will be negotiated with the bank and interest at 6% per annum will be paid on a monthly basis from December 2014 onwards.

**Required**

d Complete the following cash budget for December 2014. [10]

**Lance**

**Cash budget for December 2014**

| | $ |
|---|---|
| Receipts | |
| Payments | |
| Net cash flow | |
| Opening balance | |
| Closing balance | |

[Total: 30]

*(Adapted from Cambridge International AS and A Level Accounting 9706, Paper 23 Q2, October/November 2014)*

**12** Kim owns and runs a small retail business. She supplies the following information for the year ended 30 September 2015:

All purchases and sales are on credit.

| | at 30 September 2015 | at 1 October 2014 |
|---|---|---|
| | $ | $ |
| Trade receivables | 27000 | 16000 |
| Trade payables | 12000 | 14000 |

During the year ended 30 September 2015 customers paid Kim $590000 and were allowed discounts of $10000. Suppliers were paid $374000 and allowed discounts of $12000.

During the year bad debts written off amounted to $2000 and transfers from the purchases ledger to the sales ledger amounted to $9000.

At 1 October 2014 inventories were valued at $12000 they increased by $3000 during the year to 30 September 2015.

Operating expenses other than those derived from the control accounts for the year ended 30 September 2015 amounted to $99000.

**Required**

**a** Prepare a sales ledger control account. [6]

**b** Prepare a purchases ledger control account. [4]

**c** Prepare an income statement for the year ended 30 September 2015. [6]

**d** State one advantage and one limitation of maintaining control accounts. [2]

**e** Calculate the following ratios for Kim's business:

- **i** gross profit margin [1]
- **ii** profit margin [1]
- **iii** rate of inventory turnover [1]
- **iv** expenses to revenue. [1]

For the year ended 30 September 2014 Kim calculated the following ratios:

| | |
|---|---|
| Gross profit margin | 29.6% |
| Profit margin | 14.7% |
| Rate of inventory turnover | 24 times |
| Expenses to revenue | 16.4% |

**Required**

**f** Assess the performance of Kim's business in respect of profitability. [8]

[Total: 30]

# 32 Manufacturing accounts

## Content

### 1.1 Preparation of financial statements

1.1.1 Manufacturing businesses

- Prepare a manufacturing account, including profit on transfer from factory to finished inventory
- Account for manufacturing profit and the elimination of unrealised profit from unsold inventory

**By the end of this chapter you should be able to:**

- prepare the financial statements for a manufacturing business
- calculate provision for unrealised profit
- show relevant entries in an income statement
- show the treatment of the provision of unrealised profit in a statement of financial position.

So far we have prepared the financial statements of traders – businessmen and women who have bought finished goods and sold them on to the final customer. Most of the businesses that you come into contact with in everyday life fall into the category of trading organisations. The common factor is that retail outlets buy their products from a manufacturer and sell them on.

We have already produced many income statements. Now, we need to prepare the financial statements of businesses that make goods that are sold to retailers, who then sell them to members of the general public – in other words, manufacturing businesses.

These business organisations prepare **manufacturing accounts** as part of their internal financial statements. A manufacturing account shows the costs of running and maintaining the factory in which a final product is made.

A manufacturing business will also trade by selling its finished product to wholesalers or retailers, so it will prepare a **trading account** in its income statement as well as a manufacturing account.

A manufacturer that produces clothes

## 32.1 Prime costs

**Direct costs** are defined by the Chartered Institute of Management Accountants (CIMA) as 'expenditure which can be economically identified with a specific saleable cost unit'.

**Indirect costs** are factory expenses that are not directly identifiable with the final product.

**Overheads** are described by CIMA as 'expenditure on labour, materials or services which cannot be economically identified with a specific saleable cost'.

**Royalties** are payments made to the inventor of a product or a process or an idea. The royalty is often a percentage of the revenue earned by the user.

Prime costs are **direct costs**. Examples of direct costs include purchases of direct materials and direct labour charges. The purchase of wood and paint to make a table and the wages of the person who assembled the parts of the table are direct costs.

Examples of **indirect costs** include factory rent, local taxes paid for the factory and depreciation of factory machinery.

A manufacturing account is split into two main sections showing separately **prime costs** and **overheads**.

The prime cost section shows all the direct expenses incurred in production. The expenses can be *directly* and clearly traced to the particular product being produced. For example, in every pair of trousers that you buy you can see the cloth used, the thread, buttons and zip. You also know that someone has stitched the pieces together; they have worked *directly* on the trousers – their wages are a direct cost. The other main direct cost is the payment of **royalties**.

The overheads section includes all other revenue expenditure for a factory that is not part of prime cost.

### Example

Hinge & Co. is a manufacturer of cotton clothes and it has the following expenses:

- sales staff wages
- purchases of cotton
- office heating and lighting expenses
- cotton dyes
- managers' salaries
- rent of canteen
- weaving machine operatives' wages.

Among the above expenses, purchases of cotton, cotton dyes and weaving machine operatives' wages can be used to prepare the prime cost section of its manufacturing account. All of these expenses can be easily traced to the final product.

---

The prime cost section of a manufacturing account would contain all the resources used in the manufacturing process:

- purchases of raw materials
- direct wages
- royalties
- any other direct costs.

The raw materials used in the manufacturing process are not necessarily the raw materials purchased, so we have to make an adjustment to the raw material purchase figure in order to find how many of the raw material purchases were actually used during the year.

### Worked example

Ralph Shoemaker makes footwear. The following information relates to the year ended 31 March 2015:

- inventory of leather at 1 April 2014 $4790
- purchases of leather during the year $50 790
- inventory of leather at 31 March 2015 $3640.

**Required**

Calculate the value of leather used to make shoes during the year ended 31 March 2015.

## Answer

| | $ |
|---|---:|
| Inventory 1 April 2014 | 4790 |
| Purchases of leather | 50790 |
| | 55580 |
| *Less* Inventory 31 March 2015 | (3640) |
| Leather used in production | 51940 |

A prime cost section can now be prepared.

### Worked example

Shavay makes cakes for sale to hotels and restaurants. She provides the following information for the year ended 30 April 2015:

- inventory of materials at 1 May 2014 $376
- inventory of materials at 30 April 2015 $297
- purchases of materials during the year $58748
- direct wages $27380; other wages $16492.

**Required**

Prepare a statement showing the prime costs for the year ended 30 April 2015.

## Answer

**Shavay**

**Statement showing prime costs for the year ended 30 April 2015**

| | $ |
|---|---:|
| Inventory of raw materials 1 May 2014 | 376 |
| Purchases of raw materials | 58748 |
| | 59124 |
| *Less* Inventory of raw materials 30 April 2015 | (297) |
| Cost of raw materials used | 58827 |
| Direct wages | 27380 |
| Prime cost | 86207 |

**Note**

Only the direct wages have been included. Prime cost only lists the resources directly used in the production of the cakes, i.e. the flour, butter, sugar, etc, plus the wages of the people who actually work directly on producing the cakes – the people who mix the ingredients, bake the cakes and decorate them.

Office workers' wages or sales assistants' wages are not included – these people do not work in the factory.

### Self-test questions

1 Name two businesses that would prepare a manufacturing account.
2 Identify two costs that would be included in the calculation of prime cost.
3 The sales managers' wages are included as part of prime cost. True/False?

➤ Now try Question 1.

## 32.2 The overhead expenses

Factory **overheads** are the expenses incurred in running the factory that cannot be easily traced to the product.

**Worked example**

The following list has been prepared by Bhooni Beech, a manufacturer of garden furniture:

- Purchases of timber
- Rent of workshop
- Office manager's wages
- Delivery van expenses
- Wood glue
- Depreciation of power saws, planes, etc.
- Wages of assembly workers
- Screws and nails
- Bhooni's drawings
- Factory power

**Required**

Identify which are prime costs and which are overheads.

### Answer

Purchases of timber, screws and nails, wood glue and wages of assembly workers can all be identified as prime costs. Rent of workshop, depreciation of power saws, planes, etc and factory power are all overheads.

**Note**

Office manager's wages would appear in the profit and loss account of the income statement, as would delivery van expenses. Bhooni's drawings would be deducted from her capital on the statement of financial position.

## 32.3 The manufacturing account

Initially, you might find it helpful to label the items PC (prime cost) or OH (overhead).

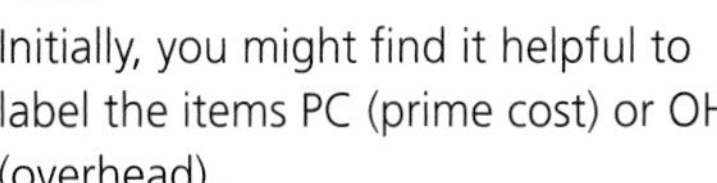

Let us put the prime cost section and the factory overheads together.

**Worked example**

The factory manager of Fawcett Products has supplied the following information for the year ended 30 November 2014:

| | $ |
|---|---|
| Inventory of raw materials 1 December 2013 | 90 000 |
| Inventory of raw materials 30 November 2014 | 80 000 |
| Purchases of raw materials | 390 000 |
| Manufacturing wages | 212 000 |
| Manufacturing royalties | 15 000 |
| Supervisor's wages | 27 000 |
| Factory rent | 120 000 |
| Factory insurance | 30 000 |
| Depreciation of machinery | 17 500 |

**Required**

Prepare a manufacturing account for the year ended 30 November 2014.

## Answer

**Fawcett Products**

**Manufacturing account for the year ended 30 November 2014**

| | $ | $ |
|---|---|---|
| **Cost of material consumed** | | |
| Inventory of raw materials 1 December 2013 | | 90 000 |
| Purchases of raw materials | | 390 000 |
| | | 480 000 |
| *Less* Inventory of raw materials 30 November 2014 | | (80 000) |
| | | 400 000 |
| Manufacturing wages | | 212 000 |
| Royalties | | 15 000 |
| **Prime cost** | | 627 000 |
| ***Add* Factory overheads** | | |
| Supervisor's wages | 27 000 | |
| Factory rent | 120 000 | |
| Factory insurance | 30 000 | |
| Depreciation – machinery | 17 500 | 194 500 |
| **Production cost of goods completed** | | 821 500 |

**Note**

- The most common mistake you can make when preparing a manufacturing account is to deduct the total overheads from the prime cost. Remember, we are calculating the total cost of manufacturing a product.
- Always label the prime cost and the cost of manufacture – these labels help to show the high standard of your work.

In Chapter 16 we saw that carriage inwards was included on the trading account of an income statement. Carriage inwards always makes purchases more expensive. A manufacturing business is no exception. Carriage inwards is added to the purchases (of raw materials) in the manufacturing account.

### Worked example

The following balances have been extracted at 31 December 2014 from the books of Atul Patel, a manufacturer of kitchen furniture:

| | $000 |
|---|---|
| Purchases of raw materials | 2 470 |
| Manufacturing wages | 1 380 |
| Manufacturing royalties | 37 |
| Supervisory wages | 87 |
| Carriage inwards | 3 |
| Factory rent | 60 |
| Factory power | 30 |
| Other factory overheads | 27 |
| Depreciation of machinery | 42 |
| Depreciation of office equipment | 13 |
| Inventory of raw materials 1 January 2014 | 89 |
| Inventory of raw materials 31 December 2014 | 111 |

**Required**

Prepare a manufacturing account for the year ended 31 December 2014, showing prime cost and cost of manufacture.

## Answer

**Atul Patel**

**Manufacturing account for the year ended 31 December 2014**

| | $000 | $000 |
|---|---|---|
| **Cost of material consumed** | | |
| Inventory of raw materials 1 January 2014 | | 89 |
| Purchases of raw materials | 2470 | |
| Carriage inwards | 3 | 2473 |
| | | 2562 |
| *Less* Inventory of raw materials 31 December 2014 | | (111) |
| | | 2451 |
| Manufacturing wages | | 1380 |
| Royalties | | 37 |
| **Prime cost** | | 3868 |
| ***Add* Factory overheads** | | |
| Supervisory wages | 87 | |
| Factory rent | 60 | |
| Factory power | 30 | |
| Other factory overheads | 27 | |
| Depreciation – machinery | 42 | 246 |
| **Production cost of goods completed** | | 4114 |

**Note**

Office equipment is not used in the factory – it is an office expense and so should be entered in the profit and loss account of an income statement. Machinery is always used in the factory, hence its inclusion in the manufacturing account.

**Self-test questions**

4 Identify two expenses incurred by a manufacturing business that would be included as factory overheads.
5 A factory produces rice noodles. Which section of a manufacturing account would you expect to find the wages of the owner's personal assistant?
6 Repairs to manufacturing machinery is a prime cost. True/False?

## 32.4 The treatment of inventories in a manufacturing business

In any manufacturing business there are always three kinds of inventory:

- **raw materials**: As yet these resources are in the factory in the condition in which they were bought – they have not entered the manufacturing process. Examples of inventories of raw materials from previous examples would include flour, butter, leather, DVD components, wood, etc.
- **work in progress**: These are partly finished goods; goods that are still undergoing part of the manufacturing process – cakes waiting to be decorated; partly finished

shoes; DVD players short of a few components; kitchen furniture without doors and handles, etc.
- **finished goods**: These are goods that have completed the journey through the manufacturing process and are waiting to be sold or despatched to a customer.

Each type of inventory appears in a different part of the financial statements. They appear in chronological order in the financial statements, i.e. the manufacturing account and the trading account of the income statement.

Inventories are current assets and are shown in the statement of financial position. In the case of a manufacturing business, the three types of inventory held have to be identified.

We have just seen how to treat inventories of raw materials.

You have already worked with inventory of finished goods – in the trading account of an income statement (a business usually trades with finished goods).

Work in progress still has to go through the remainder of the manufacturing process before it becomes a finished product, so it should appear in the manufacturing account. Work in progress appears after the cost of manufacture has been calculated.

The treatment is the same as for all types of inventories. We add the value of work in progress at the start of the period and deduct the value of work in progress at the end of the period.

There are two ways of doing this; both are acceptable and are equally regarded. Here is an example that illustrates both methods.

## Worked example

Berti Logg is a manufacturer. He provides the following information for the year ended 31 July 2014:

| | $ |
|---|---|
| Cost of manufacture | 217 432 |
| Work in progress 1 August 2013 | 4 698 |
| Work in progress 31 July 2014 | 3 481 |

**Required**

Calculate total production costs for the year ended 31 July 2014 for Berti.

## Answer

**Method 1**

| | $ |
|---|---|
| Cost of manufacture | 217 432 |
| *Add* Work in progress 1 August 2013 | 4 698 |
| (Subtotal) | 222 130 |
| *Less* Work in progress 31 July 2014 | (3 481) |
| **Production cost of goods completed** | 218 649 |

**Method 2**

| | $ | $ |
|---|---|---|
| Cost of manufacture | | 217 432 |
| *Add* Work in progress 1 August 2013 | 4 698 | |
| *Less* Work in progress 31 July 2014 | (3 481) | 1 217 |
| **Production cost of goods completed** | | 218 649 |

You can see that both methods give exactly the same total production costs.

Choose one method and always use it. In the following examples, we use Method 1 (it is usually considered to be easier).

## Worked example

Laurel Choo is a manufacturer. She provides the following information for the year ended 28 February 2015:

| | $ |
|---|---|
| Inventories at 1 March 2014: | |
| Raw materials | 16 500 |
| Work in progress | 18 200 |
| Finished goods | 20 600 |
| Purchases of raw materials | 237 300 |
| Manufacturing wages | 458 900 |
| Office salaries | 186 200 |
| Factory supervisor's wages | 17 800 |
| Carriage inwards | 1 500 |
| Rent and local taxes: | |
| Factory | 14 900 |
| Office | 7 200 |
| Depreciation: | |
| Machinery | 90 000 |
| Office equipment | 21 000 |
| Royalties | 7 500 |
| Other indirect expenses: | |
| Factory | 32 600 |
| Office | 28 400 |
| Sales | 1 000 000 |
| Inventories 28 February 2015: | |
| Raw materials | 16 000 |
| Work in progress | 19 400 |
| Finished goods | 21 350 |

**Required**

Prepare:

a a manufacturing account for the year ended 28 February 2015

b a trading account for the year ended 28 February 2015

c an extract from a statement of financial position at 28 February 2015 showing how inventories would appear.

## Answer

a

**Laurel Choo**

**Manufacturing account for the year ended 28 February 2015**

| | **$** | **$** |
|---|---|---|
| Cost of material consumed | | |
| Inventory of raw materials 1 March 2014 | 16 500 | |
| Purchases of raw materials | 237 300 | |
| Carriage inward | 1 500 | |
| | 255 300 | |
| *Less* Inventory of raw materials 28 February 2015 | 16 000 | 239 300 |
| Manufacturing wages | | 458 900 |
| Royalties | | 7 500 |
| **Prime cost** | | 705 700 |
| ***Add* Factory overheads** | | |
| Supervisor's wages | 17 800 | |
| Rent and local taxes | 14 900 | |
| Other indirect expenses | 32 600 | |
| Depreciation – machinery | 90 000 | 155 300 |
| **Manufacturing cost** | | 861 000 |
| *Add* Work in progress 1 March 2014 | | 18 200 |
| | | 879 200 |
| *Less* Work in progress 28 February 2015 | | (19 400) |
| **Total production cost** | | 859 800 |

b

**Laurel Choo**

**Trading account for the year ended 28 February 2015**

| | **$** | **$** |
|---|---|---|
| Revenue | | 1 000 000 |
| Less costs of sales | | |
| Opening inventory of finished goods | 20 600 | |
| Production cost of goods completed | 859 800 | |
| | 880 400 | |
| Less closing inventory of finished goods | (21 350) | 859 050 |
| Gross profit | | 140 950 |

c

**Laurel Choo**

**Extract from statement of financial position at 28 February 2015**

| | **$** |
|---|---|
| Current assets | |
| Inventories – Raw materials | 16 000 |
| Work in progress | 19 400 |
| Finished goods | 21 350 |

## Worked example

Mike Tong is a manufacturer. He provides the following information for the year ended 31 May 2015:

| | $ |
|---|---|
| Sales | 2913502 |
| Inventories at 1 June 2014: | |
| Raw materials | 49780 |
| Work in progress | 23640 |
| Finished goods | 40210 |
| Purchases of raw materials | 846289 |
| Direct wages | 750199 |
| Supervisors' wages | 68720 |
| Indirect wages | 187442 |
| Royalties | 19000 |
| Carriage inwards | 4612 |
| Carriage outwards | 5218 |
| Rent and local taxes – factory | 48700 |
| office | 21300 |
| Insurance – factory | 19170 |
| office | 10830 |
| Heat and light – factory | 4260 |
| office | 1830 |
| Factory power | 17282 |
| Other production expenses | 5671 |
| Depreciation – factory equipment | 48000 |
| office equipment | 12000 |
| Inventories at 31 May 2015: | |
| Raw materials | 48340 |
| Work in progress | 20119 |
| Finished goods | 38461 |

**Required**

Prepare:

a a manufacturing account for the year ended 31 May 2015

b a trading account for the year ended 31 May 2015.

## Answer

a

**Mike Tong**

**Manufacturing account for the year ended 31 May 2015**

| | $ | $ |
|---|---|---|
| Cost of material consumed | | |
| Inventory of raw materials 1 June 2014 | 49780 | |
| Purchases of raw materials | 846289 | |
| Carriage inwards | 4612 | |
| | 900681 | |
| *Less* Inventory of raw materials 31 May 2015 | 48340 | 852341 |
| Direct wages | | 750199 |
| Royalties | | 19000 |
| **Prime cost** | | 1621540 |
| *Add* Factory overheads: | | |
| Indirect wages | 187442 | |
| Supervisors' wages | 68720 | |
| Rent and local taxes | 48700 | |
| Insurance | 19170 | |
| Heating and lighting expenses | 4260 | |
| Power | 17282 | |
| Other indirect expenses | 5671 | |
| Depreciation | 48000 | 399245 |
| | | 2020785 |
| *Add* Work in progress 1 June 2014 | | 23640 |
| | | 2044425 |
| *Less* Work in progress 31 May 2015 | | (20119) |
| Production cost of goods completed | | 2024306 |

b

**Mike Tong**

**Trading account for the year ended 31 May 2015**

| | $ | $ |
|---|---|---|
| Revenue | | 2913502 |
| Less cost of sales | | |
| Inventory of finished goods 1 June 2014 | 40210 | |
| Production cost of goods completed | 2024306 | |
| | 2064516 | |
| *Less* Inventory of finished goods 31 May 2015 | 38461 | 2026055 |
| Gross profit | | 887447 |

➤ **Now try Question 2.**

## 32.5 Manufacturing profit

Sometimes the managers of a business will wish to gauge how efficiently their factory is operating. They compare the price that the goods cost to produce in their factory with the cost of purchasing the same goods from an 'outside' supplier. If it would be cheaper to purchase the goods externally then it may be in the best interest of the business to cease manufacturing and purchase the goods. (But see marginal costing in Chapter 29.)

When the managers of a business transfer the total production cost to the trading account, gross profit is found by deducting the cost of sales (cost of goods sold or COGS) from sales revenue. This method does have a flaw – there is no indication of how profitable the factory is.

Gross profit in a manufacturing business is derived in two ways:

- by manufacturing efficiently
- by selling the goods at a price that is higher than the production cost.

We can determine the factory manufacturing profit by finding the difference between the cost of production and the cost of purchasing the goods externally.

Let us look at the manufacturing accounts of Laurel Choo and Mike Tong produced in Section 32.4 above.

**Worked example**

The same number of goods made in Laurel's factory could be purchased by Laurel's buying department for $900 000.

**Required**

Prepare:

a a summarised manufacturing account for the year ended 28 February 2015 showing the manufacturing profit

b the trading account for the year ended 28 February 2015.

## Answer

a

**Laurel**

**Summarised manufacturing account for the year ended 28 February 2015**

| | **$** |
|---|---|
| Prime cost | 705 700 |
| *Add* Overheads | 155 300 |
| *Add* Work in progress 1 March 2014 | 18 200 |
| | 879 200 |
| *Less* Work in progress 28 February 2015 | (19 400) |
| Production cost of goods completed | 859 800 |
| Manufacturing profit | 40 200 |
| Transfer price to income statement | 900 000 |

b

**Laurel**

**Trading account for the year ended 28 February 2015**

| | **$** | **$** |
|---|---|---|
| Revenue | | 1 000 000 |
| Less cost of sales | | |
| Inventory of finished goods 1 March 2014 | 20 600 | |
| Transfer price of manufactured goods | 900 000 | |
| | 920 600 | |
| *Less* Inventory of finished goods on 28 February 2015 | 21 350 | 899 250 |
| Gross profit on trading | | 100 750 |
| Gross profit from manufacturing | | 40 200 |
| Total gross profit | | 140 950 |

## Worked example

Mike Tong's buying department could purchase the same number of goods made in his factory for $2.5 million.

**Required**

Prepare:

a a summarised manufacturing account for the year ended 31 May 2015

b the trading account for the year ended 31 May 2015.

## Answer

a

**Mike Tong**

**Summarised manufacturing account for the year ended 31 May 2015**

| | $ |
|---|---|
| Prime cost | 1621540 |
| *Add* Overheads | 399245 |
| | 2020785 |
| *Add* Work in progress 1 June 2014 | 23640 |
| | 2044425 |
| *Less* Work in progress 31 May 2015 | (20119) |
| Production cost of goods completed | 2024306 |
| Factory profit | 475694 |
| Transfer price to income statement | 2500000 |

b

**Mike Tong**

**Trading account for the year ended 31 May 2015**

| | $ | $ |
|---|---|---|
| Revenue | | 2913502 |
| *Less* Cost of sales | | |
| Inventory of finished goods 1 June 2014 | 40210 | |
| Transfer price of manufactured goods | 2500000 | |
| | 2540210 | |
| *Less* Inventory of finished goods on 31 May 2015 | (38461) | 2501749 |
| Gross profit on trading | | 411753 |
| Gross profit on manufacturing | | 475694 |
| Total gross profit | | 887447 |

It is usual in questions to add a percentage to the total production costs in order to arrive at the transfer price.

**Worked example**

Olga Stravinska is a manufacturer. The following information relates to her business at 31 October 2014:

Production cost of goods completed $348 700; inventory of finished goods at 1 November 2013 $37 498; inventory of finished goods at 31 October 2014 $39 613; sales for the year $598 136

Olga transfers goods from her factory to the trading account at cost plus 20 per cent.

**Required**

Prepare:

a an extract from the manufacturing account

b the trading account for the year ended 31 October 2014, showing manufacturing profit and the transfer price of the goods manufactured.

## Answer

a

**Olga Stravinska**

**Extract from manufacturing account for the year ended 31 October 2014**

| | $ | |
|---|---|---|
| Production cost of goods completed | 348 700 | |
| Factory profit | 69 740 | ($348 700 × 20%) |
| Transfer price | 418 440 | |

b

**Olga Stravinska**

**Trading account for the year ended 31 October 2014**

| | $ | $ |
|---|---|---|
| Revenue | | 598 136 |
| Cost of sales | | |
| Inventory of finished goods 1 November 2013 | 37 498 | |
| Transfer price of manufactured goods | 418 440 | |
| | 455 938 | |
| *Less* Inventory of finished goods on 31 October 2014 | 39 613 | 416 325 |
| Gross profit on trading | | 181 811 |
| Gross profit from manufacturing | | 69 740 |
| Total gross profit | | 251 551 |

➤ Now try Questions 3 and 4.

## 32.6 Provision for unrealised profit

We have seen in Chapter 16 that the overriding principle that governs all inventory valuations is that all goods should be valued at the lower of cost or net realisable value (because it is prudent).

This does not pose a problem with raw materials or work in progress. It can cause a problem with finished goods, however.

Finished goods are stored in a warehouse ready for sale or ready to be despatched to a customer. In all probability, some of these finished goods will be left unsold at the end of the financial year. How should these goods be valued?

There is no problem if the finished goods are passed to the warehouse at their cost price. Like raw materials and work in progress, the finished goods would be valued at cost (or their realisable value if this was lower than cost).

A problem does arise when finished goods are passed from the factory at cost price plus a profit margin.

We stated above that inventories should be valued at cost (if cost is less than net realisable value) – not at cost and some factory profit.

If goods are valued at cost plus some factory profit we need to get rid of the factory profit because it has not yet been earned – we need to find the cost price of the goods.

**Worked example**

Mougli Godin manufactures printed circuits. He passes the goods from his factory at cost plus 25 per cent. At his financial year end his inventory of finished goods is valued at $250 000.

**Required**

Calculate the cost price of Mougli's closing inventory to be entered in the business statement of financial position.

### Answer

The cost price of the closing inventory of finished goods is $200 000.

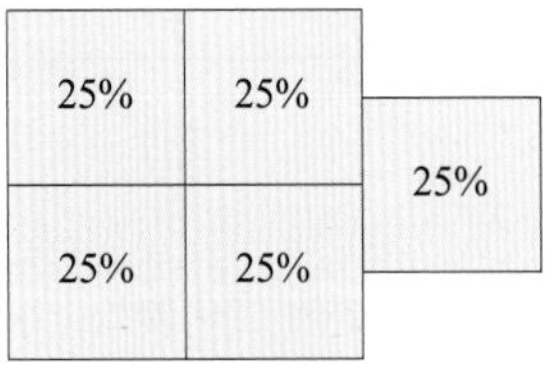

25% 25%
25% 25% 25% = 125% of cost = $250 000

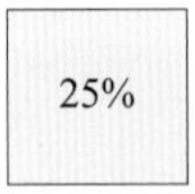

25% 25%
25% 25% + 25% = $250 000

**So**

$$\frac{100}{125} \text{ of } \$250\,000 + \frac{25}{125} \text{ of } \$250\,000 = \$250\,000$$

$$\$200\,000 + \$50\,000 = \$250\,000$$

**Worked example**

Siobhan O'Riley manufactures generators. The finished generators are transferred to an income statement at cost price plus ten per cent. At her financial year end Siobhan's inventory of finished goods is valued at $385 000.

**Required**

Calculate the cost price of Siobhan's closing inventory of finished goods as it would be shown in a statement of financial position drawn up at the end of the financial year.

## Answer

The closing inventory of finished generators should be valued at $350 000.

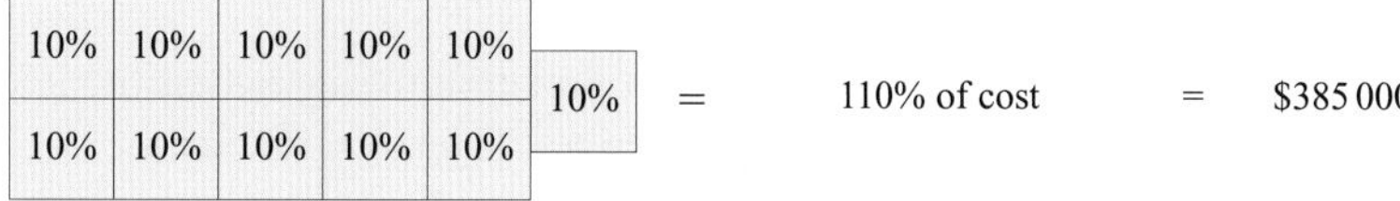


10% 10% 10% 10% 10% / 10% 10% 10% 10% 10% + 10% = $385 000

So

$\frac{100}{110}$ of $385 000 + $\frac{10}{110}$ of $385 000 = $385 000

$350 000 + $35 000 = $385 000

➤ Now try Question 5.

Both methods used to calculate the cost price or the profit element are quite difficult, so it is worth practising them.

This is an important topic, which you are very likely to meet, and many students find it difficult.

If the value of inventory is increased by the profit element, then the gross profit and hence the profit for the year will be increased by the same amount.

The closing inventory of finished goods has yet to be sold, so we are anticipating the earning of profit that has not yet been realised.

The concept of prudence tells us that we should not do this. We need to remove the profit element from our financial statements. We do this by creating a provision for **unrealised profit**.

In Chapters 18 and 19 we saw how to deal with provisions for depreciation and provisions for doubtful debts.

We now need to make a provision for the profits 'tied up' in the inventories, profit that is as yet unrealised.

All provision accounts look similar.

| Dr | | Provision for ?!???!!! account | | | Cr |
|---|---|---|---|---|---|
| | | $ | | | $ |
| | | | Start of year | Balance b/d | 2 000 |
| End of year | Balance c/d | 2 150 | End of year | Income statement | 150 |
| | | 2 150 | | | 2 150 |
| | | | Start of following year | Balance b/d | 2 150 |

The ?!???!!! could be depreciation, doubtful debts or unrealised profits.

The balance on a provision for unrealised profit account is shown in the statement of financial position as a deduction from the closing inventory of finished goods, thus ensuring that the inventory appears in the statement of financial position at cost price. The amount shown in the provision account described as 'income statement' ($150) is deducted from the gross profit on manufacturing in the income statement.

**Worked example**

Paquito plc transfers manufactured goods to its income statement at cost plus 30 per cent. The balance brought down in the provision for unrealised profit account at 1 April 2014 is $1 300. Inventory of finished goods is valued at $6 500 on 31 March 2015.

**Required**

Prepare a provision for unrealised profit account showing clearly the amount to be transferred to the income statement.

## Answer

**Provision for unrealised profit account**

| Dr | | | | | Cr | |
|---|---|---|---|---|---|---|
| | | $ | | | $ | |
| | | | 1 Apr 2014 | Balance b/d | 1 300 | |
| 31 Mar 2015 | Balance c/d | 1 500 | 31 Mar 2015 | Income statement | 200 | *Missing figure to be deducted from GP on manufacture in income statement* |
| | | 1 500 | | | 1 500 | |
| | | | 1 Apr 2015 | Balance b/d | 1 500 | ($6500 × 30 ÷ 130) |

Questions often ask you to prepare the whole of the provision account (including the calculation of the opening balance). If you can calculate the closing balance in the question above, the opening balance should pose no problem.

**Worked example**

Celine marks up the goods manufactured in her factory by 35 per cent to transfer them to an income statement. Her inventory of finished goods on 1 March 2014 was $9 450. Her inventory of finished goods one year later on 28 February 2015 was $9 720.

**Required**

Prepare a provision for unrealised profit account for the year ended 28 February 2015.

## Answer

**Provision for unrealised profit account**

| Dr | | | | | Cr | |
|---|---|---|---|---|---|---|
| | | $ | | | $ | |
| | | | 1 Mar 2014 | Balance b/d | 2 450 | ($9450 × 35% ÷ 135%) |
| 28 Feb 2015 | Balance c/d | 2 520 | 28 Feb 2015 | Income statement | 70 | *Missing income statement figure* |
| | | 2 520 | | | 2 520 | |
| | | | 1 Mar 2015 | Balance b/d | 2 520 | ($9720 × 35% ÷ 135%) |

**Worked example**

Bertoli manufactures washing machines. They are transferred to an income statement at cost plus 60 per cent. The inventory of finished washing machines at 1 June 2013 was $57 600; at 31 May 2014 it was $60 160.

**Required**

Prepare a provision for unrealised profit showing the amount to be transferred to an income statement for the year ended 31 May 2014.

## Answer

**Provision for unrealised profit account**

| Dr | | | | | Cr | |
|---|---|---|---|---|---|---|
| | | $ | | | $ | |
| | | | 1 Jun 2013 | Balance b/d | 21 600 | ($57 600 × 60% ÷ 160%) |
| 31 May 2014 | Balance c/d | 22 560 | 31 May 2014 | Income statement | 960 | *Missing figure* |
| | | 22 560 | | | 22 560 | |
| | | | 1 Jun 2014 | Balance b/d | 22 560 | ($60160 × 60% ÷ 160%) |

Like all provision accounts, it is possible that the provision at the end of the financial year could be less than the provision brought down at the start of the financial year. In such cases, the amount transferred to an income statement would be added to the gross profit on manufacture shown in the income statement.

**Worked example**

Chin manufactures woks. The finished woks are transferred to her income statement at cost price plus 50 per cent. The inventory of finished woks at 1 November 2013 was $4 500. The inventory of finished woks at 31 October 2014 was $3 900.

**Required**

Prepare a provision for unrealised profit showing clearly the amount to be transferred to an income statement for the year ended 31 October 2014.

## Answer

**Provision for unrealised profit account**

| | Dr | | | | | Cr | |
|---|---|---|---|---|---|---|---|
| | | | $ | | | $ | |
| *Missing figure added to GP* | 31 Oct 2014 | Income statement | 200 | 1 Nov 2013 | Balance b/d | 1 500 | ($4500 × 50% ÷ 150%) |
| | 31 Oct 2014 | Balance c/d | 1 300 | | | | |
| | | | 1 500 | | | 1 500 | |
| | | | | 1 Nov 2014 | Balance b/d | 1 300 | ($3 900 × 50% ÷ 150%) |

➤ Now try Question 6.

## 32.7 The inclusion of unrealised profit in financial statements

Finally, let us see how the relevant figures are dealt with in an income statement.

**Worked example**

Matisse manufactures lawnmowers. He transfers finished goods from the factory to his income statement at cost plus 30 per cent. He provides the following information for the financial year ended 30 September 2014:

| | $ |
|---|---|
| Total production at cost price | 76 500 |
| Inventory of finished goods 1 October 2013 | 6 045 |
| Inventory of finished goods 30 September 2014 | 6 864 |
| Sales for the year ended 30 September 2014 | 210 000 |

**Required**

a Calculate the transfer price of goods manufactured for inclusion in an income statement for the year ended 30 September 2014.

b Prepare an income statement for the year ended 30 September 2014 showing the transfer.

c Prepare a provision for unrealised profit account for the year.

d Prepare an extract from an income statement for the year ended 30 September 2014 showing total gross profit and the treatment of the provision for unrealised profit.

e Prepare an extract from a statement of financial position at 30 September 2014 showing how the inventory of finished goods is treated.

### Answer

a Transfer price is $99 450: production cost $76 500 plus $22 950 ($76 500 × 30%).

b

**Matisse**

**Extract from income statement for the year ended 30 September 2014**

| | $ | | $ |
|---|---|---|---|
| Revenue | | | 210 000 |
| Less cost of sales | | | |
| Inventory at 1 October 2013 | 6 045 | | |
| Production cost of goods completed | 99 450 | ($76 500 × 130%) | |
| | 105 495 | | |
| *Less* inventory at 30 September 2014 | 6 864 | | 98 631 |
| Gross profit on trading | | | 111 369 |

c

**Dr — Provision for unrealised profit account — Cr**

| | | $ | | | $ | |
|---|---|---|---|---|---|---|
| | | | 1 Oct 2013 | Balance b/d | 1 395 | ($6045 × 30% ÷ 130%) |
| 30 Sept 2014 | Balance c/d | 1 584 | 30 Sept 2014 | Income statement | 189 | *Missing figure* |
| | | 1 584 | | | 1 584 | |
| | | | 1 Oct 2014 | Balance b/d | 1 584 | ($6864 × 30% ÷ 130%) |

d

**Matisse**

**Extract from income statement for the year ended 30 September 2014**

| | $ | $ |
|---|---|---|
| Gross profit on trading | | 111 369 |
| Gross profit on manufacturing (from part a) | 22 950 | |
| *Less* Provision for unrealised profit | (189) | 22 761 |
| Total gross profit | | 134 130 |

e

**Matisse**

**Extract from statement of financial position at 30 September 2014**

| Current assets | $ | $ |
|---|---|---|
| Inventory of finished goods | 6 864 | |
| *Less* Provision for unrealised profit | 1 584 | 5 280 |

**Worked example**

Rawstric manufactures bedroom furniture. He transfers finished goods from his factory to his income statement at cost plus 70 per cent. He provides the following information for the year ended 31 December 2014:

| | $ |
|---|---|
| Sales for the year ended 31 December 2014 | 974 000 |
| Total production at cost price | 476 400 |
| Inventory of finished goods 1 January 2014 | 10 540 |
| Inventory of finished goods 31 December 2014 | 15 980 |

**Required**

a Calculate the transfer price of goods manufactured for inclusion in an income statement.

b Prepare an extract from the income statement for the year ended 31 December 2014.

c Prepare a provision for unrealised profit account for the year.

d Prepare an extract from the income statement for the year ended 31 December 2014 showing total gross profit and the treatment of the provision for unrealised profit.

e Prepare an extract from a statement of financial position at 31 December 2014 to show how the inventory of finished goods is treated.

## Answer

a Transfer price $809 880: production cost $476 400 plus $333 480 ($476 400 × 70%).

b

**Rawstric**

**Extract from income statement for the year ended 31 December 2014**

| | $ | $ |
|---|---|---|
| Revenue | | 974 000 |
| Cost of sales | | |
| Inventory at 1 January 2014 | 10 540 | |
| Production cost of goods completed | 809 880 | |
| | 802 420 | |
| Inventory at 31 December 2014 | (15 980) | 804 440 |
| Gross profit | | 169 560 |

c

| Dr | | Provision for unrealised profit account | | | Cr | |
|---|---|---|---|---|---|---|
| | | $ | | | $ | |
| | | | 1 Jan 2014 | Balance b/d | 4340 | ($10540 × 70% ÷ 170%) |
| 31 Dec 2014 | Balance c/d | 6580 | 31 Dec 2014 | Income statement | 2240 | |
| | | 6580 | | | 6580 | |
| | | | 1 Jan 2015 | Balance b/d | 6580 | ($15980 × 70% ÷ 170%) |

d

**Rawstric**
**Extract from income statement for the year ended 31 December 2014**

| | $ | $ |
|---|---|---|
| Gross profit on trading | | 169560 |
| Gross profit on manufacturing | 333480 | |
| *Less* Provision for unrealised profit | (2240) | 331240 |
| Total gross profit | | 500800 |

e

**Rawstric**
**Extract from statement of financial position at 31 December 2014**

| **Current assets** | $ | $ |
|---|---|---|
| Inventory of finished goods | 15980 | |
| *Less* Provision for unrealised profit | (6580) | 9400 |

## Self-test questions

7 Name two businesses that would prepare manufacturing accounts.
8 Identify two costs that would be included in the calculation of prime cost.
9 Identify two costs that would be included as factory overheads.
10 Name the three types of inventory generally held by a manufacturing business.
11 Define the term 'direct costs'.
12 Give an example of a direct cost for a car manufacturer.
13 Define 'indirect costs'.
14 Give an example of an indirect cost for a manufacturer of sports shoes.
15 Why might a manufacturing business transfer goods to an income statement at a price exceeding total production cost?
16 Why is there a need to make provision for unrealised profit?
17 Name the two types of gross profit usually earned in a manufacturing business.
18 From which type of inventory is the provision for unrealised profit deducted in a statement of financial position of a manufacturing business?

➤ **Now try Questions 7–9.**

## Chapter summary

- Businesses that produce goods prepare a manufacturing account as part of their internal financial statements.
- A manufacturing account lists all the costs involved in running a factory.
- A manufacturing account is split into a section showing prime costs and a second section listing the factory overheads.
- Two types of inventory are included in a manufacturing account: raw materials and partly finished goods.
- Goods are often transferred from a manufacturing account to an income statement inclusive of a factory profit.
- A provision account must be opened to eradicate the unrealised profit from the financial statements.

# 33 Clubs and societies

**Content**

**1.1 preparation of financial statements**

1.1.2 Not for profit organisations

- Prepare financial statements, including a trading account, an income and expenditure account and a statement of financial position
- Understand the need for the purpose of financial statements for not for profit organisations

**By the end of this chapter, you should be able to:**

- use the correct terminology employed in the financial statements of clubs and societies
- calculate the surplus or deficit incurred by a club or society
- prepare a 'full set' of financial statements for a club or society
- incorporate additional activities into financial statements
- understand the treatment of life membership subscriptions, entrance fees and donations.

There are two main types of organisation that may not keep a full set of double-entry records. They are:

- clubs and societies
- small cash-based businesses.

It is essential that you know about both types of organisation; both feature frequently in questions.

Both types rely on similar skills and techniques in order to prepare a full set of financial statements.

In this chapter we consider the financial statements of clubs and societies; the financial statements of cash-based businesses that do not keep a 'full set' of financial records have been dealt with in Chapter 22.

The principles involved in calculating the surplus or deficit for a club or society are the same as those used in Chapters 15 and 22.

**Note**

For ease of reference, both clubs and societies are referred to in this chapter as 'clubs'.

The financial statements of a club use different terms.

## 33.1 Changes in terminology

There are a number of superficial changes made to some of the headings used when preparing financial statements.

- The revenue statement of a club is not called an income statement. It is headed **Income and expenditure account**.
- Any profit made by a club is called an **excess of income over expenditure**. It is often shortened to **surplus**. Similarly, any loss made by a club is called an **excess of expenditure over income**, sometimes shortened to **deficit**.
- The capital account of a club is known as the **accumulated fund**.
- The summarised cash book may be called a **receipts and payments account**.

### 33.1.1 Receipts and payment account

Clubs and societies require a different form of financial statement to those of a commercial organisation.

The main function of a club or society is not to trade. Its existence is to provide facilities for members or to provide an opportunity for people to meet and further their common interest.

Often the members of a club have little or no knowledge of accounting or book-keeping and because of this many club treasurers present a 'receipts and payments account' to the club's annual general meeting as a set of financial statements.

A receipts and payments account does not show the members:

- the true financial position of the club
- any accrued expenses or any prepayments made
- the asset base of the club or by how much the assets have depreciated during the year
- any liabilities that are outstanding at the year end.

To present a more complete picture of the club's financial activities and position, an income and expenditure account and a statement of financial position should be prepared.

### 33.1.2 Income and expenditure account

An income and expenditure account is prepared using the accruals concept (see Chapter 9), and so:

- all incomes and expenditures for the period under review are recorded
- it includes all expenditures accrued and as yet unpaid for the period
- it includes all incomes due that have not yet been received
- it includes non-cash expenses such as depreciation
- the completed income and expenditure account will reveal a surplus or deficit for the period
- it shows whether the club is generating sufficient income to pay for members' activities.

Any profit made by a club is called an excess of income over expenditure. It is often shortened to 'surplus'. Any loss made by a club is called an excess of expenditure over income, sometimes shortened to 'deficit'.

### 33.1.3 Statement of financial position

The statement of financial position of a club is very similar to that of a sole trader; non-current assets and liabilities are identified, as are the current assets and liabilities. The major difference is in the heading of what would be the capital account for a business.

The capital account of a club is known as the accumulated fund.

## 33.2 Calculation of financial results for clubs and societies

In this type of organisation there is generally no ledger.

To calculate the surplus or deficit for a club requires a comparison of the net assets at the start of the period with the net assets at the end of the period. Exactly the same technique is used as in Chapter 14. Can you remember how you calculated the profit or loss for a business using the net asset method?

There are four stages to this procedure.

- **Stage 1:** calculate the opening accumulated fund (net assets) of the club either by:
  - listing the assets and then deducting the liabilities, or
  - preparing a statement of affairs.
- **Stage 2:** calculate the closing accumulated fund (net assets).
- **Stage 3:** deduct the opening accumulated fund from the closing accumulated fund. This will indicate the surplus or deficit earned by the club during the year.

- **Stage 4:** deduct any 'extra' funds introduced. Sometimes the club may receive a donation or a legacy that has to be treated as a capital receipt. This extra injection of funds will increase the assets owned by the club at the end of the year. In turn this will increase the figure we have calculated as a surplus (it could reduce the figure calculated as a deficit). Obviously the amount of the donation or legacy is not an increase in net assets 'earned' by the activities of the club so it must be disregarded in our calculation – hence Stage 4: deduct any 'extra' funds 'introduced'.

We can summarise these stages as follows:

| | |
|---|---|
| | Closing accumulated fund |
| *Deduct* | Opening accumulated fund |
| | xxxxxxxxxxxx |
| *Deduct* | Funds 'introduced' |
| Surplus (deficit) for the year | xxxxxxxxxxxxxxx |

**Worked example**

Hightown Tennis Club had the following assets and liabilities at 1 January 2014:

nets $112; inventory of tennis balls $26; amount owed to supplier of tennis balls $72; inventory of fertiliser $54; line paint $8; balance at bank $136

At 31 December 2014 the club assets and liabilities were:

nets $80; inventory of tennis balls $20; inventory of fertiliser $48; balance at bank $207

In this type of question, you will always be asked to *calculate* the surplus or deficit.

**Required**

Calculate the surplus or deficit for the year ended 31 December 2014.

## Answer

| | $ | |
|---|---|---|
| Closing net assets (accumulated fund) | 355 | (80 + 20 + 48 + 207) |
| Opening net assets (accumulated fund) | 264 | (112 + 26 + 54 + 8 +136 – 72) |
| Surplus for the year | 91 | |

## 33.3 Preparation of financial statements for clubs and societies

When asked to prepare a set of financial statements, we need to go carefully through the following four stages:

- **Stage 1:** prepare an opening statement of affairs.
- **Stage 2:** compile a summarised receipts and payments account and a summarised bank account.
- **Stage 3:** construct adjustment accounts.
- **Stage 4:** prepare the financial statements.

Stage 3 is the stage that will take up much of our time since this is the area that seems to cause most problems.

The summarised receipts and payments account and the summarised bank (Stage 2) are generally given in the question.

## 33.4 Additional activities

A **statement of affairs** is exactly the same as a statement of financial position.

Many clubs organise activities that are not the core activity of the club. These activities are useful in

- raising additional funds, which means that subscriptions may be lower than if additional activities were not undertaken
- keeping members interested at times when major club activities are quiet – a cricket club may organise 'out of season' activities, for example social events during the 'out of season' months.

For each ancillary activity the club treasurer should calculate whether the activity is profitable or not and include the profit or loss in the income and expenditure account.

### 33.4.1 Snack bar (café) trading account

If a club has a snack bar, in order to raise additional funds for the club, a trading account should be prepared. The profit or loss generated should be transferred to the income and expenditure account.

The trading account prepared is no different to any of the trading account of an income statement that you have produced on a regular basis during your studies.

You may have to do an adjustment account in order to determine the amount of the purchases to use in the trading account.

**Worked example**

The treasurer of the Apes Rugby Club provides the following information for the year ended 31 May 2015 for a snack bar operated by the club:

- 1 June 2014: amount owed to supplier of fruit juices and snacks $213
- 31 May 2015: amount owed to supplier of fruit juices and snacks $186
- snack bar sales for the year $27759
- amounts paid to the supplier of fruit juices and snacks during the year $14621
- inventory of fruit juices and snacks 1 June 2014: $165
- inventory of fruit juices and snacks 31 May 2015: $191.

The key to recognising this type of question, on financial statements, is found in the words used. You must read the 'required' instruction very carefully. The key word here is *prepare*.

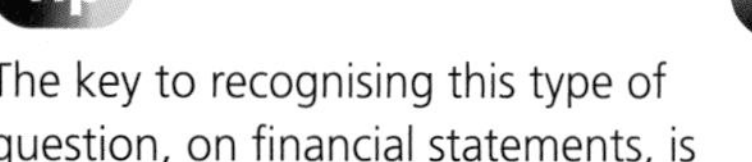

**Required**

Prepare a snack bar trading account for the year ended 31 May 2015.

## Answer

**Apes Rugby Club**

**Snack bar trading account for the year ended 31 May 2015**

| | | $ | $ |
|---|---|---|---|
| Revenue | | | 27759 |
| *Less* Cost of sales | | | |
| | Inventory 1 June 2014 | 165 | |
| | Purchases | 14594 | |
| | | 14759 | |
| | Inventory 31 May 2015 | (191) | 14568 |
| **Snack bar profit** *(to income and expenditure account)* | | | 13191 |

**Workings**

**Trade payables account**

| | | $ | | | $ |
|---|---|---|---|---|---|
| 31 May 2015 | Cash | 14621 | 1 June 2014 | Balance b/d | 213 |
| 31 May 2015 | Balance c/d | 186 | 31 May 2015 | *Café trading account (missing figure)* | *14594* |
| | | 14807 | | | 14807 |
| | | | 1 June 2015 | Balance b/d | 186 |

## 33.4.2 Dinner dances, treasure hunts, family games nights, etc.

These activities are often used as fund raisers. A trading account should be prepared for each of these activities and the profit or loss generated should be transferred to the income and expenditure account.

It is important to prepare these 'extra' revenue accounts so that members are able to identify one figure (profit or loss) relating to the activity. This helps members to decide whether or not the activities should continue in the future. Clearly, if the activity is unprofitable, it is likely that the members will wish to discontinue the activity.

**Worked example**

The following receipts and payments account for the year ended 31 October 2014 has been prepared by the treasurer of the Dantong Gardening Club:

An **honorarium** is a payment made to a club official to cover expenses and time spent on club activities.

| | $ | | $ |
|---|---|---|---|
| Bank balance 1 November 2013 | 146 | Payments to seed supplier | 407 |
| Seed sales | 612 | Purchase of gardening equipment | 2842 |
| Subscriptions received | 5040 | Meeting room rent | 750 |
| Show entry fees | 326 | Secretary's honorarium | 100 |
| Annual dinner dance ticket sales | 2250 | Speakers' expenses | 240 |
| Equipment hire | 420 | Bank charges | 28 |
| | | Advertising | 126 |
| | | Insurances | 348 |
| | | Postages and telephone | 142 |
| | | Dinner dance expenses | 1874 |
| | | Printing for dinner dance | 128 |
| | | Show prizes | 247 |
| | | Show expenses | 148 |
| | | Balance at bank 31 October 2014 | 1414 |
| | 8794 | | 8794 |

The following additional information is available:

| | at 31 October 2014 | at 1 November 2013 |
|---|---|---|
| **Assets and liabilities** | $ | $ |
| Equipment at valuation | 3000 | 840 |
| Amounts owed for seed purchases | 84 | 128 |
| Amount owed for printing for dinner dance | 75 | 62 |
| Prepayment for insurance | 206 | 112 |
| Subscriptions paid in advance | 135 | 360 |
| Subscriptions owing at financial year end | 225 | 180 |

**Required**

Prepare an income and expenditure account for the year ended 31 October 2014 and a statement of financial position at that date.

## Answer

**Stage 1:** prepare an opening statement of affairs

| | $ | $ |
|---|---|---|
| Assets | | |
| Equipment | 840 | |
| Prepayment – insurance | 112 | |
| Subscriptions owing | 180 | |
| Bank balance | 146 | 1278 |
| Liabilities | | |
| Payables – seed merchants | (128) | |
| Printing | (62) | |
| Subscriptions paid in advance | (360) | (550) |
| Accumulated fund | | 728 |

*Subscriptions owing – members who owe the club money are receivables (debtors).*

*Subscriptions in advance – payables (creditors).*

**Stage 2:** compile a receipts and payments account and/or bank account – it has been provided for us.

**Stage 3:** construct adjustment accounts. This is the important stage. Use one account for each item in Stage 1.

**Equipment account**

| | | $ | | | $ |
|---|---|---|---|---|---|
| 1 November 2013 | Balance b/d | 840 | 31 October 2014 | *Income and expenditure account (missing figure)* | *682* |
| 31 October 2014 | Bank | 2842 | 31 October 2014 | Balance c/d | 3000 |
| | | 3682 | | | 3682 |
| 1 November 2014 | Balance b/d | 3000 | | | |

**Insurance account**

| | | $ | | | $ |
|---|---|---|---|---|---|
| 1 November 2013 | Balance b/d | 112 | 31 October 2014 | *Income and expenditure account (missing figure)* | *254* |
| 31 October 2014 | Bank | 348 | 31 October 2014 | Balance c/d | 206 |
| | | 460 | | | 460 |
| 1 November 2014 | Balance b/d | 206 | | | |

**Seeds account**

| | | $ | | | $ |
|---|---|---|---|---|---|
| 31 October 2014 | Bank | 407 | 1 November 2013 | Balance b/d | 128 |
| 31 October 2014 | Balance | 84 | 31 October 2014 | *Income and expenditure account missing figure)* | *363* |
| | | 491 | | | 491 |
| | | | 1 November 2014 | Balance | 84 |

**Printing account**

| | | $ | | | $ |
|---|---|---|---|---|---|
| 31 October 2014 | Bank | 128 | 1 November 2013 | Balance | 62 |
| 31 October 2014 | Balance c/d | 75 | 1 November 2014 | *Income and expenditure account (missing figure)* | *141* |
| | | 203 | | | 203 |
| | | | 1 November 2014 | Balance | 75 |

Put yourself in the position of a club treasurer.

The next adjustment account is the one that seems to cause the most problems. It is the subscriptions account.

- Amounts owed by people (including members) or organisations are **receivables (debit balances)**.
- Subscriptions owing (or in arrears) at the end of the year are **receivables (debit balances)**.

At the end of any year there may be some members of a club who have paid their subscriptions for the following year. He or she will be a creditor of the club.

- Amounts owed to people (including members) or organisations are **payables (credit balances)**.
- Subscriptions paid in advance at the end of the year are **payables (credit balances)**.

Monies received during the year from members are debited in the cash book. We need to complete the double entry in the subscriptions (adjustment) account.

Tip

Subscriptions accounts are also often asked for as a short question.

It will be shown as a debit in the receipts and payments account (the cash book summary). We complete the double entry by *crediting* the subscriptions account.

You will make fewer errors if you use the technique outlined earlier in Chapter 9. Put your closing balances below the account and then bring them back into the account.

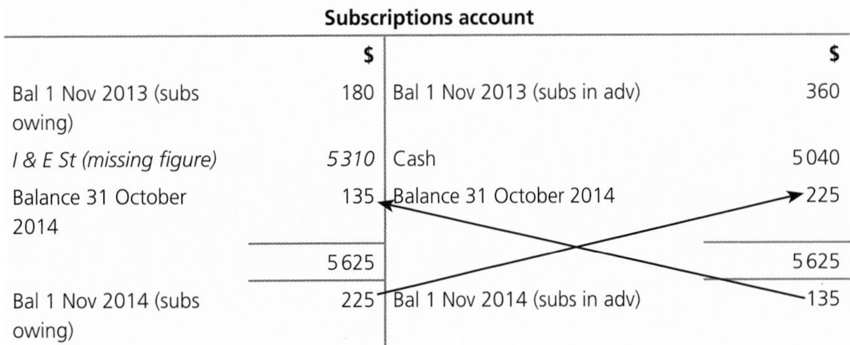

**Subscriptions account**

| | $ | | $ |
|---|---|---|---|
| Bal 1 Nov 2013 (subs owing) | 180 | Bal 1 Nov 2013 (subs in adv) | 360 |
| *I & E St (missing figure)* | *5310* | Cash | 5040 |
| Balance 31 October 2014 | 135 | Balance 31 October 2014 | 225 |
| | 5625 | | 5625 |
| Bal 1 Nov 2014 (subs owing) | 225 | Bal 1 Nov 2014 (subs in adv) | 135 |

As you can see, there is quite a bit of work involved just for the figure of $5310 for subscriptions.

**Stage 4:** prepare an income and expenditure account.

**Dantong Gardening Club**

**Income and expenditure account for the year ended 31 October 2014**

| | $ | $ | |
|---|---|---|---|
| Income | | | |
| Subscriptions | 5310 | | |
| Profit on seed sales | 249 | | (612 – 363) |
| Profit on dinner dance | 235 | | (2250 – 1874 – 141) |
| Equipment hire | 420 | 6214 | |
| Expenditure | | | |
| Loss on show | 69 | | (326 – 395) |
| Rent | 750 | | |
| Secretary's honorarium | 100 | | |
| Speakers' expenses | 240 | | |
| Bank charges | 28 | | |

Show your adjustment accounts neatly; the person reading your work may have to refer to them to understand your method.

| | | |
|---|---|---|
| Advertising | 126 | |
| Insurance | 254 | |
| Postages and telephone | 142 | |
| Depreciation of equipment | 682 | 2391 |
| Excess of income over expenditure | | 3823 |

**Dantong Gardening club**

**Statement of financial position at 31 October 2014**

| | $ | $ |
|---|---|---|
| **ASSETS** | | |
| **Non-current assets** | | |
| Equipment at valuation | | 3000 |
| **Current assets** | | |
| Bank balance | 1414 | |
| Trade receivable – Insurance | 206 | |
| Subscriptions | 225 | 1845 |
| **Total assets** | | 4845 |
| **CAPITAL AND LIABILITIES** | | |
| **Accumulated fund** | | |
| Opening balance | | 728 |
| *Add* Surplus | | 3823 |
| | | 4551 |
| **Current liabilities** | | |
| Payables – seeds | 84 | |
| printing | 75 | |
| Subscriptions in advance | 135 | 294 |
| **Total capital and liabilities** | | 4845 |

➤ Now try Questions 1–3.

**Note**

Each of the additional activities, i.e. sales of seeds, the dinner dance and the show, has been 'netted' to reveal whether the activity has been beneficial to the club or whether it has drained resources from the club.

The workings have been shown to help you. Do show your workings, but show them separately, outside the main body of your answer.

Notice also the change in the terms used: income and expenditure account, excess of income over expenditure and accumulated fund.

In practice many clubs write off any subscriptions not paid by the end of the club's financial year, since if a member has not paid their subscription by the end of the year there is a strong likelihood that the membership has lapsed.

If you are expected to take this line of action, this will be made clear in the question.

**Worked example**

During the year ended 30 June 2014 cash received for subscriptions to the Dropkick Rugby Club amounted to $1860.

At 1 July 2013 subscriptions paid in advance amounted to $140; at 30 June 2014 subscriptions paid in advance were $80.

At 30 June 2014 subscriptions totalling $60 remained unpaid.

It is club policy to write off any subscriptions that remain unpaid at the financial year end.

**Required**

Prepare a subscriptions account for the year ended 30 June 2014.

## Answer

**Subscriptions account**

| | $ | | $ | |
|---|---|---|---|---|
| *I & E St* | *1 980* | Balance b/d | 140 | *$1980 is shown as income on I & E Statement* |
| Balance c/d | 80 | Cash | 1 860 | |
| | | I & E St (subs w/o) | 60 | *$60 is shown as an expense on I & E Statement* |
| | 2 060 | | 2 060 | |
| | | Balance b/d | 80 | |

## 33.5 Income from other sources

Some clubs gain income from other sources.

### 33.5.1 Life membership

This is a lump sum paid by a member. It entitles the member to use the club's facilities for the rest of his or her life without any further payment. Money received from the member is debited to the bank account and credited to a life membership fund.

The balance on the life membership fund is credited to the income and expenditure account in equal annual instalments over a period that has been agreed by the club committee.

The balance on the life membership fund is shown on the statement of financial position as a non-current liability.

**Worked example**

The Old Jacks Bowling Club operates a life membership scheme. The life membership subscription is $350. The balance standing on the life membership fund at 30 September 2013 was $2940.

During the year ended 30 September 2014 five members took out life membership, paying $1750. The club transfers ten per cent of the balance standing in the life membership fund at the end of each financial year to the income and expenditure account.

**Required**

Prepare a life membership fund for the year ended 30 September 2014.

## Answer

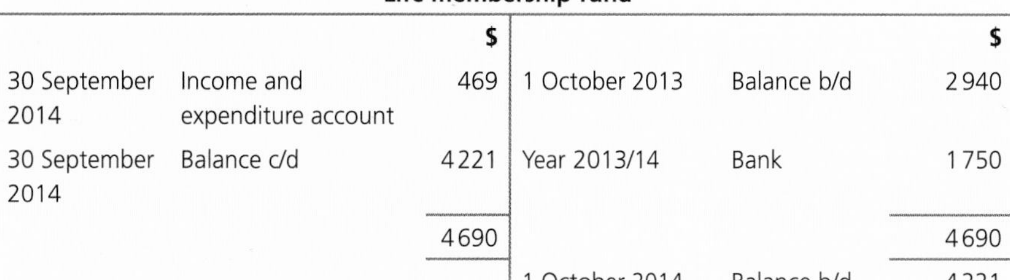

**Life membership fund**

| | | $ | | | $ |
|---|---|---|---|---|---|
| 30 September 2014 | Income and expenditure account | 469 | 1 October 2013 | Balance b/d | 2 940 |
| 30 September 2014 | Balance c/d | 4 221 | Year 2013/14 | Bank | 1 750 |
| | | 4 690 | | | 4 690 |
| | | | 1 October 2014 | Balance b/d | 4 221 |

**Tip**

A life membership payment is a 'one off' payment and is received by the club when the payment is made. The annual transfers to the club income and expenditure account are merely transfers in the club's books of account. The amount transferred does not increase the cash inflow that year.

**Note**

- $469 is shown as an income on the income and expenditure account.
- $4221 is shown as a non-current liability in the statement of financial position.

### 33.5.2 Entrance fees paid by new members

In their first year of membership, members may be charged an entrance fee in addition to the normal annual subscription. Generally these entry fees are regarded as revenue income and are credited to the income and expenditure account. However, some clubs treat this form of income as a capital income and in these cases they would be added to the accumulated fund.

### 33.5.3 Donations

Another source of income is in the form of donations. Small donations should be treated as revenue income. However, if a large donation is received it should be treated as a capital receipt.

If a club receives a large donation (or legacy) that has been given for a particular purpose it should be credited to a special trust fund and a special bank account should be opened. This avoids the money being used for general club expenditure.

The trust fund should be debited each year with the amount of the annual expenditure on the special purpose; the debit entry is in the income and expenditure account. The entries are similar to those used in a life membership fund account.

**Worked example**

On 1 January 2014 the Stumps Cricket Club received a donation of $50000 to build a new pavilion. In August 2014, Chang, a builder, was paid $3874 after laying the foundations. In September 2014 another building firm, Chou, was paid $4751 for work done.

**Required**

Prepare the necessary accounts to record the transactions.

**Tip** 

Label your workings so that people can see which figure you have been calculating.

### Answer

**Bank – building account**

| | $ | | $ |
|---|---|---|---|
| [1] Building fund | 50000 | [4] Chang | 3874 |
| | | [5] Chou | 4751 |
| | | Balance c/d | 41375 |
| | 50000 | | 50000 |
| Balance b/d | 41375 | | |

**Trust fund – pavilion**

| | $ | | $ |
|---|---|---|---|
| [6] Income and expenditure a/c | 8625 | [1] Bank | 50000 |
| Balance c/d | 41375 | | |
| | 50000 | | 50000 |
| | | Balance b/d | 41375 |

**Pavilion account**

| | $ | | |
|---|---|---|---|
| [2] Chang | 3874 | | |
| [3] Chou | 4751 | | |

**Chang**

| | $ | | $ |
|---|---|---|---|
| [4] Bank | 3874 | [2] Pavilion | 3874 |

**Chou**

| | $ | | $ |
|---|---|---|---|
| [5] Bank | 4751 | [3] Pavilion | 4751 |

The numbers refer to the sequence of events. There will be an 'extra' income in the income and expenditure account for the year.

## Self-test questions

1 What is the name given to the summarised cash book of a club?
2 Name two additional activities that might be organised by a club.
3 Why would a club organise additional activities?
4 Give one advantage that a club will obtain by running a life membership scheme.
5 Give one disadvantage of running a life membership scheme.
6 How would entrance fees be treated in the financial statements accounts of a club?
7 What is the name of the capital account of a club?
8 Subscriptions in arrears is a current asset. True/False?
9 Subscriptions paid in advance is a current asset. True/False?
10 Equipment at valuation at the beginning of a year $3400; equipment at valuation at the end of a year $2700. There have been no additions or disposals during the year. What has caused the $700 difference?

➤ **Now try Questions 4–8.**

## Chapter summary

- There is a change in some of the headings used when preparing the financial statements of clubs and societies.
- Income statement becomes 'income and expenditure account'.
- Profit becomes 'excess of income over expenditure' or 'surplus'.
- Loss becomes 'excess of expenditure over income' or 'deficit'.
- Capital becomes 'accumulated fund'.
- Any additional activities should be netted to appear as one figure on the income and expenditure account.
- Life membership, entrance fees and donations are generally treated as capital receipts.

# 34 Published financial statements of limited companies

**➔ Content**

**1.1 Preparation of financial statements**

1.1.3 Limited companies

- Understand the nature and purpose of the financial statements of limited companies, and the regulatory framework in which they operate

**By the end of this chapter you should be able to:**

- identify and comment on the main disclosure requirements associated with the published annual reports of limited companies, including:
  - income statement
  - statement of financial position
  - statement of cash flows
  - statement of changes in equity
  - directors' report
  - auditors' report.

## 34.1 Statutory accounts and the corporate report

We saw in Chapter 25 that the owners of a limited company are the shareholders. We have also said that directors conduct the everyday management of a limited company. Control of a limited company is therefore separate from the ownership. The UK Companies Act 1985 requires the directors to report regularly to the shareholders on the way that they have managed the company on the shareholders' behalf. (This is an example of the stewardship function of accounting.)

The **annual accounts** must be approved by the board of directors and signed by one of the directors on behalf of the board before they are filed.

The Act requires that five documents must be published annually (these are known as the **statutory accounts**). The statutory accounts are produced in accordance with company law and must be filed with the Registrar of Companies.
The documents that make up the statutory accounts are:

- an income statement
- a statement of financial position
- a statement of cash flows
- a directors' report
- an auditor's report.

The **annual return** is filed with the Registrar of Companies and may be examined by any member of the general public.

Legislation requires every company to send a copy of the **corporate report** to:

- every shareholder
- every debenture holder
- all other persons entitled to receive copies.

The financial statements must be sent not less than 21 days before the Annual General Meeting (AGM).

**True** means that all the transactions reported in the income statement have taken place and assets recorded in the statement of financial position actually exist and are valued appropriately. **Fair** implies that all transactions conform to generally accepted accounting rules.

In addition to the statutory accounts, the corporate report will contain notes to the accounts and a statement of the accounting policies that have been applied in the preparation of the accounts.

The Companies Act 1985 requires that the financial statements give a **true** and **fair** view of the financial state of the company during the time period covered by the statements.

Directors are responsible for ensuring that the provisions of the Companies Act 1985 are adhered to. The directors must also ensure that the financial statements are prepared in accordance with International Accounting Standards (IAS) (see Chapter 36).

The directors must ensure that the company's accounting records contain:

- details of all transactions involving money
- a record of all the company's assets and liabilities, including details of inventories held at the financial year end.

The directors must also ensure that the records:

- show and explain the company's financial transactions
- disclose the financial position of the company with reasonable accuracy
- enable the directors to be confident that the income statement and the statement of financial position show a true and fair view of the company's financial position.

Tip 

At this stage it is important to stress that:

- you will not be required to have a detailed knowledge of the standards
- you should know the IAS number and a broad outline of what the standard covers, for example IAS 36 'Impairment of assets'.

You will now be required to have 'an understanding of the disclosure standards adopted by quoted companies' and 'a basic knowledge of [certain] standards and how these standards relate to topics'.

IAS 1 details how a company's financial statements should be presented. This is intended to ensure comparability with previous accounting periods and with other businesses. Details of the standards used in the preparation of the statutory accounts and the corporate report are given in Chapter 36.

The compliance to the Companies Acts and the international standards should ensure that the information contained in the published accounts is presented fairly and without bias. IAS 1 requires that all companies must make a statement in the notes to the accounts stating that the accounts do comply with the standards. Any departure from applying standards must be noted and reasons for such deviation explained. (A departure from the application of standards may be necessary in order to achieve a fair presentation.)

Standards have been introduced to provide a framework for the production of accounting information in order to reduce the subjective elements that could be evident if company directors had free licence to produce accounting information in a format of their own choosing. The standards help to increase the uniformity in presentation. So, the standards are the 'ground rules' that apply to the preparation of the published accounts of limited companies and to the audit of those accounts. This ensures that the standards that apply in Canberra are the same as those applied in Canton.

## 34.2 The published financial statements of limited companies

The **financial statements** that a limited company produces are used by the directors and managers for decision-making purposes. They contain much useful detail. If those same accounts were published in this form, competitors might gain access to information that could be used to undermine the company.

So, although legally the shareholders, lenders and others must be sent a copy of the financial statements, the law protects the company by allowing it to publish an 'abridged' version that contains much less detail.

The financial statements that are published are incorporated into an annual report.

IAS 1 states that a complete set of financial statements must include:

- an income statement
- a statement of financial position
- a statement of cash flows
- a statement of changes in equity
- notes on accounting policies and explanatory notes on items in the statements.

In addition, financial statements will include:

- a statement from the chairman
- a directors' report
- an auditors' report.

You may obtain copies of company reports by writing to the registered office of the company or you may visit the company website. Try:

www.manutd.com
www.vodafone.com

### 34.2.1 Notes on accounting policies

The notes on accounting policies will explain the accounting policies used to prepare the accounting statements and will show details of the figures published in the income statement, the statement of financial position and statement of cash flows. They will cover items such as: turnover, depreciation policy, treatment of goodwill, etc.

### 34.2.2 The chairman's statement

The statement from the chairman will give a brief review of the company's progress over the past year. It may indicate future developments in the company while evaluating current developments (see Chapter 37).

### 34.2.3 The directors' report

The directors' report will consist of a review of the period covered by the financial statements, commenting on results and dividend policies. It will outline company employment policy, paying particular attention to equal opportunities and policies on the employment of people with disabilities. It provides a list of directors and their interest in the company, together with any share options. The report itemises political and charitable donations, health and safety policy, and provides an insight into future developments for the company (see Chapter 37).

### 34.2.4 The auditors' report

The auditors' report is a legal requirement. The report sets out the respective responsibilities of directors and auditors. The report makes a statement on the basis of the audit opinion (how the audit was planned and conducted) and then gives the auditors' opinion stating whether the financial statements present a 'true and fair view' of the company's activities over the financial period covered by the financial statements (see Chapter 37).

## Self-test questions

1 What is the difference between statutory accounts and the annual report and accounts?
2 Private limited companies do not have to file their statutory accounts with the Registrar of Companies. True/False?
3 Directors own a company. True/False?
4 Shareholders own a company. True/False?
5 Directors run a company for the shareholders. True/False?
6 Auditors run a company for the tax authorities. True/False?
7 A shareholder could be a director of a limited company. True/False?
8 Name two public limited companies.
9 Name the components of a complete set of financial statements.
10 Explain why the published income statement of a limited company does not have to give all the details of every expense incurred during the accounting period.
11 Identify three items that must be disclosed in an income statement for a limited company.

## Chapter summary

- The owners of a limited company are the shareholders.
- The shareholders elect directors to run the company on a day-to-day basis.
- The directors are responsible for applying the Companies Acts and accounting standards in the keeping and preparation of the company's records.

# 35 IAS 7 Statements of cash flows

**Content**

**1.1 Preparation of financial statements**

1.1.3 Limited companies

- Prepare an income statement, statement of financial position and statement of cash flows for a limited company in line with the relevant international accounting standards

**By the end of this chapter you should be able to:**

- prepare a statement of cash flows using the IAS 7 format
- use the headings required by IAS 7
- explain the purposes of preparing a statement of cash flows
- calculate all the cash flows associated with depreciation and disposal of non-current assets
- explain the effect that an issue of bonus shares has on cash flows
- explain the effect that a revaluation of non-current assets has on cash flows
- reconcile net cash flows with movements in net debt

## 35.1 International accounting standards (IAS)

Nowadays limited companies must prepare financial statements that adhere to the UK Companies Act 1985 as amended by the UK Companies Act 1989 and to international accounting standards.

You do not need a detailed knowledge of any of the IASs with the exception of IAS 7 'Statement of cash flows'.

All but the smallest limited companies are required to prepare a statement of cash flows using the format dictated in IAS 7. This ensures that businesses report their cash generation and cash absorption in a way that makes the statements comparable with other businesses.

## 35.2 Uses of statements of cash flows

What are the uses of a statement of cash flows?

- Because a standard format is used, significant components of cash flows can be identified.
- The statement highlights and concentrates on cash inflows and cash outflows. Liquidity is important for the short-term survival of all businesses; this is of great interest to creditors, shareholders, workers, etc.
- The statement provides information that enables users to assess the efficiency (or inefficiency) of how cash and cash equivalents have been used during the financial period.
- The statement explains why profits and losses are different from changes in cash and cash equivalents.
- The statement shows sources of internal financing and the extent to which the business has relied on external financing.

- It reveals information that is not disclosed in the income statement. This helps in financial planning.
- It provides information that helps to assess the liquidity, viability and financial adaptability of the business.
- It allows comparisons to be made year on year or inter-firm. This is facilitated by the prescribed format. (But do remember, when making comparisons, that the statement is a historical document. The statement is prepared using figures from the previous financial year.)
- It helps provide information that will assist in the projection of future cash flows.

➤ Now try Question 1.

## 35.3 Transactions that result in cash inflows and cash outflows

IAS 7 requires that companies prepare a statement of cash flows in the format described in the standard. A statement of cash flows should be included with the other published financial statements.

The standard requires an adjustment to profit from operations in order to calculate the cash flow generated from operating activities.

So, the statement of cash flows should include all inflows and outflows from the business involving cash. Any transactions that do not involve cash should not appear in the statement.

**Table 35.1** Examples of transactions that result in cash inflows and cash outflows

| Cash inflows | Cash outflows |
|---|---|
| Profits | Losses |
| Interest received | Interest paid |
| Investment income received | |
| Dividends received | Dividends paid |
| Tax refund | Taxation paid |
| Sale of non-current assets | Purchase of non-current assets |
| Decrease in inventory | Increase in inventory |
| Decrease in trade receivables | Increase in trade receivables |
| Increase in trade payables | Decrease in trade payables |
| Increase in share capital | Redemption of share capital |
| Increase in debentures | Redemption of debentures |
| Increase in long term loans | Repayment of long-term loans |

Tip 

It is important that you memorise the headings and use them each time you prepare a statement of cash flows using the IAS 7 format.

Tip 

Some students learn the headings by remembering the capital letters of the first words as 'OIF' or by using a mnemonic such as 'Ostriches Invade France'.

**Operating activities** are the cash effects of transactions that do not fall under either of the headings 'investing activities' or 'financing activities'.

## 35.4 The IAS 7 headings

IAS 7 'Statement of cash flows' requires that cash flows should be analysed under three headings:

- operating activities
- investing activities
- financing activities.

The standard provides a template using the three headings.

### 35.4.1 Operating activities

Cash flows from **operating activities** are the cash inflows and outflows resulting from operating or trading activities. They are the main revenue producing activities of the company.

Using the indirect method of preparing a statement of cash flows means that we have to adjust the profit (or loss) for the year since this figure has been calculated using the accruals basis of preparation.

**Amortisation** is the writing off of part (or all) of the cost of an intangible asset such as goodwill. It is similar to the depreciation charged on a tangible non-current asset.

The calculation is done using the profit from operations (that is, profit for the year before deduction of tax and interest). So, the operating cash flows section of the statement contains the following adjustments:

- add depreciation for the year (and any **amortisation** of goodwill)
- add losses on sales of non-current assets
- deduct profits on sales of non-current assets
- add decrease in inventory (or deduct decrease in inventory)
- add decrease in trade receivables (or deduct increase in trade receivables)
- add increase in trade payables (or deduct decrease in trade payables).

These adjustments to the profit from operations gives the cash (used in)/from operations. Two further adjustments are necessary:

- deduct interest paid during the year
- deduct taxation paid during the year.

The result is the net cash (used in)/from operating activities.

### 35.4.2 Investing activities

**Investing activities** are inflows and outflows of cash resulting from the acquisition and disposal of non-current assets (but not cash equivalents) and investments.

- Cash inflows include receipts from the sale or disposal of all types of non-current assets.
- Cash outflows include payments to acquire all types of non-current assets.

### 35.4.3 Financing activities

**Financing activities** are activities that change the equity capital or long-term borrowing structure of the company. They are the result of receipts from and payments to external providers of finance.

- Cash inflows include receipts from share issues or issues of debentures; also receipts from other long-term borrowings (but not overdrafts).
- Cash outflows include dividends paid and payments to redeem shares and the repayment of long-term loans.

There are a number of difficult areas involved in the preparation of a statement of cash flows.

## 35.5 Calculation of profit from operations

Profit from operations is the profit for the year calculated before tax and interest.

**Worked example**

The following information is given for the year ended 31 July 2014 for Schmidt plc:

| | $000 |
|---|---|
| Profit before tax (interest paid $60) | 212 |
| Tax liability | 70 |

**Required**

Prepare an extract from the income statement showing clearly the profit from operations, profit before tax and the profit for the year.

### Answer

**Schmidt plc**
**Extract from income statement for the year ended 31 July 2014**

| | $000 |
|---|---|
| Profit from operations | 272 |
| Interest paid | (60) |
| Profit before tax | 212 |
| Tax | (70) |
| Profit for the year | 142 |

It is often the case that no income statement extract is given in the question; it has to be reconstructed from the available information.

**Worked example**

The following extracts are taken from the statements of financial position of Ocset plc at 31 December:

| | 2014 | 2013 |
|---|---|---|
| | $000 | $000 |
| **Current liabilities** | | |
| Tax liability | (120) | (168) |
| **Equity** | | |
| Ordinary shares | 2 500 | 2 500 |
| General reserve | 400 | 350 |
| Retained earnings | 1 662 | 1 346 |

During the year ended 31 December 2014, debenture interest paid amounted to $78 000. Dividends amounting to $150 000 were paid.

**Required**

Calculate the profit from operations for the year ended 31 December 2014.

## Answer

| | $000 | $000 |
|---|---|---|
| Increase in retained earnings over the year | | 316 |
| *Add* Provision for taxation | 120 | |
| Debenture interest paid | 78 | |
| Transfer to general reserve | 50 | |
| Dividends paid | 150 | 398 |
| Profit from operations | | 714 |

Extracts from the financial statements would have shown:

**Extract from income statement for the year ended 31 December 2014**

| | $000 |
|---|---|
| Profit from operations | 714 |
| *Less* Debenture interest | (78) |
| | 636 |
| Tax | (120) |
| Profit for the year | 516 |

**Extract from statement of changes in equity**

| | $000 |
|---|---|
| **Retained earnings** | |
| Balance at 1 January 2014 | 1 346 |
| Profit for the year | 516 |
| | 1 862 |
| Dividends paid | (150) |
| Transfer to general reserve | (50) |
| Balance at 31 December 2014 | 1 662 |
| **General reserve** | |
| Balance at 1 January 2014 | 350 |
| Transfer for the year | 50 |
| Balance at 31 December 2014 | 400 |

➤ Now try Question 2.

## 35.6 Calculation of cash flows created by depreciation of non-current assets

In some cases the calculation of cash flows created by the provision of depreciation of non-current assets is straightforward. It involves comparing the accumulated depreciation at the start of the financial year with the accumulated depreciation at the end of the year.

The resulting amount should then be added to the profit from operations.

**Worked example**

The following extracts have been taken from the statements of financial position of Beta and Bigga plc:

| | 31 July 2014 | | 31 July 2013 | |
|---|---|---|---|---|
| | **$000** | **$000** | **$000** | **$000** |
| **ASSETS** | | | | |
| **Non-current assets** | | | | |
| Premises | 2 500 | | 2 500 | |
| *Less* Accumulated depreciation | (1 850) | 650 | (1 800) | 700 |
| Machinery | 1 830 | | 1830 | |
| *Less* Accumulated depreciation | (1 281) | 549 | (1 098) | 732 |
| Office equipment | 611 | | 611 | |
| *Less* Accumulated depreciation | (369) | 242 | (308) | 303 |
| Vehicles | 1 100 | | 1100 | |
| *Less* Accumulated depreciation | (855) | 245 | (630) | 470 |

**Required**

Calculate:

a the provision for depreciation for the year ended 31 July 2014 for each non-current asset

b the amount to be included in the statement of cash flows for the year ended 31 July 2014.

### Answer

a

| | | $ |
|---|---|---|
| Provision for depreciation – | premises | 50 000 |
| | machinery | 183 000 |
| | office equipment | 61 000 |
| | vehicles | 225 000 |

b The amount to be added to the profit from operations under the heading of 'operating activities' is $519 000.

➤ Now try Question 3.

## 35.7 Calculation of cash flows resulting from the disposal of non-current assets (derecognition)

**Worked example**

The following is an extract from the statements of financial position of Nepps plc at 30 April:

| | 2015 | 2014 |
|---|---|---|
| | $000 | $000 |
| **Non-current assets** at cost | 2 573 | 2 332 |
| *Less* Depreciation | (1 238) | (1 021) |
| | 1 335 | 1 311 |

During the year ended 30 April 2015, non-current assets which had cost $720 000 were sold for $274 000. The assets sold had been depreciated by $433 000.

**Required**

Identify any cash flows resulting from the sale of non-current assets.

### Workings

Using 'T' accounts, we can gain a complete picture of the transactions involved in the problem.

Journal entries are given to help you with the timing of each entry:

**Non-current assets account**

| | $ | | $ |
|---|---|---|---|
| 1 May 2014 Balance b/d | 2 332 | Disposal | 720 |
| *Missing figure* | | 30 April 2015 Balance c/d | 2 573 |
| | 3 293 | | 3 293 |
| 1 May 2015 Balance b/d | 2 573 | | |

**Provision for depreciation of non-current assets account**

| | $ | | $ |
|---|---|---|---|
| Disposal | 433 | 1 May 2015 Balance b/d | 1 021 |
| 30 April 2015 Balance c/d | 1 238 | *Missing figure* | |
| | 1 671 | | 1 671 |
| | | 1 May 2015 Balance b/d | 1 238 |

**Disposal of non-current assets account**

| | $ | | $ |
|---|---|---|---|
| Non-current assets | 720 | Depreciation of non-current assets | 433 |
| | | Bank | 274 |
| | | Income statement | 13 |
| | 720 | | 720 |

Journal entries showing the 'timing' of each entry:

| | Dr | Cr |
|---|---|---|
| | $ | $ |
| Disposal of non-current assets account | 720000 | |
| Non-current assets account | | 720000 |
| Non-current assets are removed from the non-current assets account and are entered in a disposal account. | | |
| Provision for depreciation of non-current assets account | 433000 | |
| Disposal of non-current assets account | | 433000 |
| Depreciation 'belonging' to the asset is taken from the provision for depreciation account and entered in the disposal account. | | |
| Bank account (not shown) | 274000 | |
| Disposal of non-current assets account | | 274000 |
| The cash inflow is entered in the disposal account. | | |

At this point we need to insert a 'missing' figure of $13000:

| | $ | $ |
|---|---|---|
| Income statement | 13000 | |
| Disposal of non-current assets account | | 13000 |

The 'loss' incurred on disposal is entered in the income statement. It is *not* cash but it has been entered in the income statement as an extra expense – it reduces profit but $13000 is *not* cash – there has been no movement of cash.

Enter the closing balances given in the question. Enter them underneath the account and take them back diagonally into the account.

Add the non-current asset account and the depreciation account. They will not add unless you put in the two missing figures. The missing figure in the non-current account must either be a revaluation or the purchase of further non-current assets. A revaluation has not been mentioned, so the missing figure must be non-current assets purchased during the year: a cash outflow of $961000.

To make the provision for depreciation account balance, this year's charge to the income statement must be inserted: $650000 is the amount to be entered in the account and in the income statement.

The profit is reduced by $650000 but *no* cash has moved in or out of the business.

Both the loss on disposal $13000 and the depreciation for the year of $650000 have reduced profit but there has been *no* movement of cash.

Both have to be added back to the profit from operations to arrive at the actual cash flow generated by the company, just like the depreciation charge on Ragesh's van in the example in Chapter 25.15.

**Answer**

Cash 'inflows': loss $13000 and depreciation $650000; cash outflow: $961000.

➤ Now try Questions 4 and 5.

## 35.8 Treatment of a revaluation of non-current assets

A revaluation of non-current assets will clearly have an impact on the statement of financial position of a company. The non-current assets will increase in value, as will the equity of the company. However, since such a revaluation merely involves book entries there will be no movement in cash, so there will be no entry in a statement of cash flows.

Both revaluations of non-current assets and bonus issues of shares give many students problems. Students often include them when answering questions on statements of cash flow. Do not be one of these students!

## 35.9 Treatment of a bonus issue of shares

Such transactions will impact on the statement of financial position of a limited company but will not cause any movements in cash resources. The book entries to record the issue of bonus shares will not be shown in a statement of cash flows.

Remember that statements of cash flows are historic documents, that is, they relate to a past time period. Do not confuse a statement of cash flows with a cash flow forecast, which should more properly be known as a cash budget. Statements of cash flows do not try to determine future cash flows. However, detailed knowledge of specific sources of cash receipts and the uses of cash outflows made may have some use in the assessment of future inflows and outflows of cash.

## 35.10 Reasons why a business might prepare a statement of cash flows

- It may be a statutory requirement.
- Together with the income statement and the statement of financial position it helps to give a fuller picture of the financial activities of the business.
- It is one of the statements that 'bridges the gap' between the dates of statements of financial position.
- Cash flows are an objective measure.

You have now seen how the constituent parts of cash flows are calculated.

Questions usually ask for a statement of cash flows prepared in accordance with IAS 7. Here is a worked example to show you where your calculated figures fit into such a statement.

**Worked example**

The directors of Yukita plc provide the following statements of financial position at 31 May:

| | 31 May 2015 | 31 May 2014 |
|---|---|---|
| | $000 | $000 |
| **ASSETS** | | |
| **Non-current assets** (Note 1) | | |
| Land and buildings | 23 970 | 18 125 |
| Machinery | 1 990 | 3 370 |
| Vehicles | 950 | 1 050 |
| Investments | 6 000 | 5 050 |
| | 32 910 | 27 685 |
| **Current assets** | | |
| Inventories | 2 000 | 1 730 |
| Trade receivables | 850 | 550 |
| Cash and cash equivalents | 283 | 278 |
| | 3 133 | 2 558 |
| **Total assets** | 36 043 | 30 243 |

| | 31 May 2015 | 31 May 2014 |
|---|---|---|
| | $000 | $000 |
| **EQUITY AND LIABILITIES** | | |
| **Equity** | | |
| Ordinary shares | 12 600 | 12 100 |
| Share premium | 6 150 | 4 650 |
| Revaluation reserve | 3 200 | - |
| Retained earnings (note 2) | 11 298 | 10 906 |
| | 33 248 | 27 656 |
| **Non-current liabilities** | | |
| 8% debenture stock (repayable 2045) | 1 200 | 1 200 |
| **Current liabilities** | | |
| Trade payables | (1 175) | (1 007) |
| Tax liabilities | (420) | (380) |
| | (1 595) | (1 387) |
| **Total liabilities** | (2 795) | (2 587) |
| **Total equity and liabilities** | 36 043 | 30 243 |

**Notes to the statements of financial position:**

**Note 1 Non-current assets**

| | 31 May 2015 | 31 May 2014 |
|---|---|---|
| | $000 | $000 |
| **Land and buildings** | | |
| Cost | 31 020 | 27 815 |
| Revaluation | 3 200 | |
| Depreciation to date | (10 250) | (9 600) |
| Carrying amount | 23 970 | 18 215 |
| **Machinery** | | |
| Cost | ? | 6 500 |
| Depreciation to date | ? | (3 130) |
| Carrying amount | ? | 3 370 |
| **Vehicles** | | |
| Cost | 1 750 | 1 650 |
| Depreciation to date | (800) | (600) |
| Carrying amount | 950 | 1 050 |

During the year ended 31 May 2015 machinery which had originally cost $1200 000 was sold for $750 000. The depreciation charge on this machinery up to 31 May 2014 was $480 000. No additions to machinery were made during the year ended 31 May 2015.

There were no disposals of land, buildings or vehicles during the year ended 31 May 2015.

**Note 2**

The summarised income statement for the year ended 31 May 2015 was as follows (a changes in equity statement has not been used):

| | $000 |
|---|---|
| Profit for the year before tax | 1 112 |
| Provision for corporation tax | (420) |
| | 692 |
| Dividends paid | (300) |
| Increase in retained earnings for the year | 392 |

**Required**

Prepare a statement of cash flows for the year ended 31 May 2015 using the IAS 7 format.

## Workings

(mf = missing figure)

**Land and buildings account**

| $000 | $000 |
|---|---|
| 27 815 | |
| 3 200 | |
| *mf* 3 205 | 34 220 |
| 34 220 | 34 220 |
| 34 220 | |

**Depreciation account**

| $000 | $000 |
|---|---|
| | 9 600 |
| 10 250 | *mf* 650 |
| 10 250 | 10 250 |
| | 10 250 |

**Cash flows**

| $000 | $000 |
|---|---|
| 650 | (3 205) |

**Revaluation reserve**

| | $000 |
|---|---|
| | 3 200 |

**Machinery account**

| $000 | $000 |
|---|---|
| 6 500 | 1 200 |
| | 5 300 |
| 6 500 | 6 500 |
| 5 300 | |

**Depreciation account**

| $000 | $000 |
|---|---|
| 480 | 3 130 |
| 3 310 | *mf* 660 |
| 3 790 | 3 790 |
| | 3 310 |

**Cash flows**

| $000 | |
|---|---|
| 750 | |
| 660 | |

**Disposal of machinery account**

| $000 | $000 |
|---|---|
| 1 200 | 480 |
| 30 | 750 |
| 1 230 | 1 230 |

**Cash flows**

| | $000 |
|---|---|
| | (30) |

Carrying amount at year end = $5 300 000 – Depreciation = $1 990 000

So, balance on depreciation account at year end = $3 310 000.

**Vehicles account**

| $000 | $000 |
|---|---|
| 1 650 | |
| *mf* 100 | 1 750 |
| 1 750 | 1 750 |
| 1 750 | |

**Depreciation account**

| $000 | $000 |
|---|---|
| | 600 |
| 800 | *mf* 200 |
| 800 | 800 |
| | 800 |

**Cash flows**

| $000 | $000 |
|---|---|
| 200 | (100) |

**Investments account**

| $000 | $000 |
|---|---|
| 5 050 | |
| *mf* 950 | 6 000 |
| 6 000 | 6 000 |
| 6 000 | |

**Cash flows**

| | $000 |
|---|---|
| | (950) |

| | Cash flows | |
|---|---|---|
| | $000 | $000 |
| Increase in inventories | | (270) |
| Increase in trade receivables | | (300) |
| Increase in trade payables | 168 | |
| Taxation (last year's tax liability paid in this year) | | (380) |
| Dividends paid | | (300) |
| Debenture interest (You might have to deduct debenture interest. The interest figure might be given in the question, or you may have to calculate it, as in this example.) 8% of $1 200 000 = $96 000 | | (96) |
| Increase in share capital | 500 | |
| Increase in share premium | 1 500 | |
| Revaluation reserve | No movement of cash | |
| **Profit from operations** | | |
| (Profit before tax + Interest $1 112 000 + $96 000) | 1 208 | |
| The difference in the total of these cash flows should equal the change in cash and cash equivalents over the year. | | |
| **Totals** | **5 636** | **5 631** |
| Change in cash and cash equivalents over the year $5 000 | | |
| Change in cash flows $5636 000 – $5631 000 = ($5 000) | | |
| Increase in cash and cash equivalents during the year | 5 | |

We now have all the necessary information required to prepare a statement of cash flows. Take the figures from your workings and insert them under the correct headings.

## Answer

**Yukita plc**
**Statement of cash flows for the year ended 31 May 2015**

| | $000 | $000 |
|---|---|---|
| **Cash flows (used in)/from operating activities** | | |
| Profit from operations | | 1 208 |
| Adjustments for | | |
| Depreciation charges – land and buildings | 650 | |
| machinery | 660 | |
| vehicles | 200 | 1510 |
| Profit on disposal of machinery | | (30) |
| Increase in inventories | | (270) |
| Increase in trade receivables | | (300) |
| Increase in trade payables | | 168 |
| Cash (used in) from operations | | 2 286 |
| Interest paid (during the year) | | (96) |
| Income tax paid (during the year) | | (380) |
| Net cash (used in) from operating activities | | 1810 |
| **Cash flows from investing activities** | | |
| Purchases of non-current assets | (3 305) | |
| Proceeds from sale of non-current assets | 750 | |
| Purchases of investments | (950) | |
| Net cash (used in)/ from investing activities | | (3 505) |

| **Cash flows from financing activities** | | |
|---|---|---|
| Proceeds from issue of share capital | 2 000 | |
| Dividends paid | (300) | |
| Cash (used in) from financing activities | | 1 700 |
| Net increase/decrease in cash and cash equivalents | | (5) |
| Cash and cash equivalents at beginning of year | | 278 |
| Cash and cash equivalents at end of year | | 283 |

## 35.11 Reconciliation of net cash to movement in net debt

**Net debt** is the borrowings of a company less cash and liquid resources.

This part of a statement of cash flows shows how increases or decreases in the components of a company's debt have influenced the increase/decrease in cash generated during the year.

**Worked example**

The following information relates to Fagus plc:

| | 31 May 2015 | 31 May 2014 |
|---|---|---|
| | $000 | $000 |
| Cash and cash equivalents | 144 | 81 |
| 6% debentures | (150) | (300) |

**Required**

Prepare a reconciliation of net cash flow to movement in net debt.

### Answer

**Reconciliation of net cash flow to movement in net debt for the year ended 31 May 2015**

| | $000 |
|---|---|
| Increase in cash in the period | 63 |
| Cash used to repurchase debentures | 150 |
| Change in net debt | 213 |
| Net debt at 1 June 2014 | (219) |
| Net debt at 31 May 2015 | (6) |

**Note**

Net increase in cash and cash equivalents during the year ended 31 May 2015: $63 000.

Net debt is borrowings less cash and cash equivalents.

Debentures – Cash 1 June 2014 ($300 000 – $81 000 = $219 000)

31 May 2015 ($150 000 – $144 000 = $6 000)

An increase in cash resources of $63 000, coupled with a reduction of $150 000 in debenture debt, accounts for the improvement of $213 000 in the net debt.

➤ Now try Question 6.

## Self-test questions

1 All businesses must prepare a statement of cash flows. True/False?
2 Statements of cash flows calculate the profits earned by a business. True/False?
3 State two reasons why a business might prepare a statement of cash flows.
4 Explain why depreciation is added to profit from operations when calculating cash flows.
5 Explain how a profit on the disposal of a non-current asset is treated in a statement of cash flows.
6 Explain how a loss on the disposal of a non-current asset is treated in a statement of cash flows.
7 Land and buildings have been revalued from $120000 to $250000. Under which heading would this transaction be shown in a statement of cash flows?
8 Proposed final ordinary dividend $31000; interim dividend paid $12000. Under which heading should dividends be shown in a statement of cash flows? How much should be shown in this case?
9 A company that makes losses does not have to produce a statement of cash flows until it becomes profitable. True/False?
10 At the start of a year a company has cash resources totalling $67000. It has debentures of $360000. At the end of the year, cash resources amount to $80000 after repurchasing $50000 of the debentures.
   a How much has the cash and cash equivalents increased/decreased over the year?
   b Calculate the net debt at the start of the year.
   c Calculate the net debt at the end of the year.
   d Prepare a statement reconciling net cash to the movement in net debt.

➤ Now try Questions 7–10.

## Chapter summary

- All limited companies (except small companies) must prepare and present a statement of cash flows.
- IAS 7 requires that statements of cash flows must be prepared using a standard format.
- All movements of cash are shown in the statement.
- Non-cash flows are not shown in the statement (i.e. issues of bonus shares and revaluations of non-current assets).
- Net debt is borrowings less cash and cash equivalents.

# 36 International accounting standards

## Content

### 1.1 Preparation of financial statements

1.1.4 International Accounting standards

- Explain and apply the main provisions of each of the following international Accounting standards (IAS):
  - IAS 1 Presentation of financial statements
  - IAS 2 Inventories (not long-term contracts)
  - IAS 7 Statement of cash flows
  - IAS 8 Accounting policies
  - IAS 10 Events after reporting period
  - IAS16 Property, plant and equipment
  - IAS 36 Impairment of assets
  - IAS 37 Provisions, contingent liabilities and contingent assets
  - IAS 38 Intangible assets
- Explain the need for an ethical framework in accounting

**By the end of this chapter you should be able to:**

- demonstrate knowledge of the following international accounting standards:
  - IAS 1 Presentation of financial statements
  - IAS 2 Inventories
  - IAS 7 Statement of cash flows
  - IAS 8 Accounting policies
  - IAS 10 Events after the reporting period
  - IAS 16 Property, plant and equipment
  - IAS 36 Impairment of assets
  - IAS 37 Provisions, contingent liabilities and contingent assets
  - IAS 38 Intangible assets.
- understand the non-financial aspect of decision making
- identify a number of social costs and ethical considerations
- discuss the conflict of profitability versus social responsibility and identify areas of such conflict.

## 36.1 International accounting standards

Limited companies must prepare their financial statements within a regulatory framework. This framework consists of:

- the UK Companies Act 1985 as amended by the UK Companies Act 1989
- international accounting standards (International Accounting Standards and International Financial Reporting Standards)
- regulation required by the London Stock Exchange (these will not be discussed here as they are not necessary for your course).

Why is there a need to have standards?

The standards seek to:

- resolve areas of difference in the preparation and presentation of accounting information
- recommend disclosure of accounting bases
- identify any departure from the standards
- improve existing disclosure requirements.

International Accounting Standards (IAS) are gradually being replaced with International Financial Reporting Standards (IFRS).

Although it is not, as yet, mandatory for the financial statements of private limited companies to be prepared in accordance with the IASs, it seems inevitable that, in time, the standards will apply to all limited companies. Consequently, in this book appropriate standards have been applied to the preparation of the financial statements of all limited companies.

The Companies Act 1989 introduced a requirement that the financial statements of companies must be prepared in accordance with the standards in force and that any material deviations from these standards should be identified and reasons given for any such deviation.

Although the adherence to international accounting standards is not embodied in law, the Companies Act 1989 requires that directors of a company using the standards to prepare the company's financial statements must state that they are doing so.

In 1989 'Framework for the preparation of financial statements' was issued by the International Standards Committee. It sets out the underlying principles for the preparation and presentation of financial statements.

The Framework states that:

> '... financial statements ... provide information about the financial position, performance and changes in financial position of an entity ...'

It can be assumed that all financial statements have been prepared using two concepts that you came across in Chapter 7:

- The accruals concept (or matching concept). This records the value of the resources used by the business and the benefits derived from the use of those resources in the financial year of use and not when cash is paid or received.
- The going concern concept. This concept means that unless we have knowledge to the contrary, we assume that the company will continue to trade in its present form for the foreseeable future.

Financial statements should be useful to all the people who use the statements. The Framework identifies four characteristics of financial statements that are meant to ensure their usefulness to the users:

- Understandability. Information should be capable of being understood by people with a reasonable knowledge of business and accounting. This may require 'study with reasonable diligence on behalf of the user'.
- Relevance. The statements must contain information that is able to influence the decisions of users and, if it is provided in time, influence those decisions.
- Reliability. The statements must contain information that can be relied on as a faithful representation of the substance of what has taken place. The information should be unbiased, prudent, completely free from material errors and record the effect of a transaction (accurate representation; substance over form).
- Comparability. The users of financial statements must be confident that they can compare data from one time period to another. This is achieved by the financial statements being prepared on a consistent basis and ensuring that accounting policies used in the preparation of the financial statements are disclosed. This will enable users to identify and evaluate differences and similarities.

The Framework states that if the four characteristics are present in the preparation of financial statements then, under normal circumstances, the statements will show a true and fair view of the financial position.

There are a number of concepts (see Chapter 7) which form the major influences in preparing the financial statements:

- Business entity. Only the expenses and revenues relating to the business are recorded in the business books of account. Transactions involving the private affairs of the owner(s) or directors should not be included in the business books of account.
- Materiality. If the inclusion or exclusion of information would mislead the users of financial statements then that information is material. This concept recognises that some types of expenditure are less important in a business context than others – so absolute precision is not always essential.
- Prudence. This requires that revenues and profits are only included in the accounts when they are realised or where their realisation is reasonably certain. The concept

Directors ensure that standards are applied to their preparation of a company's financial statements.

does allow for provisions to be made for known expenses or losses when they become known (characteristic of reliability).

- Consistency. This requires that once a method of treating information has been established the method should be used in subsequent years' accounts. If information is treated differently each year then inter-year results cannot be easily compared and trends determined (characteristic of comparability).
- Historical cost. This is an objective valuation. Values based on what any asset(s) might be sold for if the business were to liquidate are irrelevant to the business's ability to generate profits or cash.
- Duality. The assets of a business are always equal to the liabilities of the business. So, every financial transaction has a double impact on the financial records of the business.

You will need 'an understanding of the disclosure standards adopted by quoted companies'. You will also need 'a basic knowledge of ... standards and how these standards relate' to other topics in your accounting studies.

However, remember that you do not need a detailed knowledge of any of the IASs with the exception of IAS 7 Statement of cash flows. In each instance you should know the number and the heading, for example IAS 2 Inventories.

## 36.2 IAS 1 Presentation of financial statements

The standard sets out the ground rules of how financial statements should be presented. Adherence to the standard means that comparisons can be made with previous accounting periods and with other companies.

The standard identifies five components that make up a complete set of financial statements. These are:

- an income statement
- a statement of changes in equity
- a statement of financial position
- a statement of cash flows
- a statement of accounting policies and explanatory notes to the accounts.

The standard requires that the financial statements should contain an explicit and unreserved statement that they comply with international standards. This should mean that the statements achieve a fair presentation.

The standard requires that the statements comply with accounting concepts.

In order to facilitate comparison, there is a requirement that the figures from previous periods must be published.

The name of the company should be given, along with the time period covered by the financial statements.

### 36.2.1 The income statement

Although much of the detail of all expenses does not need to be shown in the income statement of a company, certain items must be disclosed:

- revenue
- finance costs
- tax expense
- profit (or loss) for the period attributable to equity holders.

In reality, you would be required to show more detail. Indeed, more information is needed to make the income statement understandable.

An income statement prepared in answer to an examination question is likely to require more detail than that prescribed by the standard.

**Worked example**

The following information is available for Sonuk plc for the year ended 31 August 2014:

| | $000 |
|---|---|
| Administrative expenses | 173 |
| Debenture interest paid | 28 |
| Distribution costs | 158 |
| Ordinary dividends paid | 48 |
| Inventories – 1 September 2013 | 32 |
| 31 August 2014 | 28 |
| Purchases | 243 |
| Retained earnings at 1 September 2013 | 623 |
| Revaluation reserve at 1 September 2013 | 470 |
| Sales | 900 |
| Sales returns | 12 |

The directors wish to make a provision for corporation tax of $69 000.

**Required**

Prepare an income statement for the year ended 31 August 2014.

## Answer

**Sonuk plc**

**Income statement for the year ended 31 August 2014**

| | $000 | |
|---|---|---|
| Revenue | 888 | *Sales less sales returns* |
| Cost of sales | (247) | *Opening inventory plus purchases less closing inventory* |
| Gross profit | 641 | |
| Distribution costs | (158) | *Warehouse costs plus cost of getting goods to customers* |
| Administrative expenses | (173) | *Costs of maintaining and running the offices* |
| Profit from operations | 310 | |
| Finance costs | (28) | *Interest paid* |
| Profit before tax | 282 | |
| Tax | (69) | |
| Profit for the year | 213 | |

### 36.2.2 Statement of changes in equity

IAS 1 requires that a statement of changes in equity is included as part of the financial statements.

This statement shows the changes that have affected the shareholders' stake in the company.

**Worked example**

Use the same information given in the previous worked example.

**Additional information**

During the year ended 31 August 2014 non-current assets have been revalued from a cost price of $340 000 to a value of $450 000.

**Required**

Prepare a statement showing the changes in equity for the year ended 31 August 2014.

## Answer

**Extract from statement of changes in equity**

| | $000 |
|---|---|
| **Retained earnings** | |
| Balance at 1 September 2013 | 623 |
| Profit for the year | 213 |
| | 836 |
| Dividends paid | (48) |
| Balance at 31 August 2014 | 788 |
| **Revaluation reserve** | |
| Balance at 1 September 2013 | 470 |
| Revaluation of non-current assets | 110 |
| Balance at 31 August 2014 | 580 |

IAS 1 allows an alternative layout to that shown above.

### 36.2.3 A statement of recognised gains and losses

A statement of recognised gains and losses shows the total of the changes in equity and the individual changes that make up the total change.

**Example**

Using the same information provided previously for Sonuk plc, the statement would appear as follows:

**Sonuk plc**

**Statement of recognised gains and losses for the year ended 31 August 2014**

| | $000 |
|---|---|
| Gains/(losses) on revaluation of non-current assets | 110 |
| **Net income recognised directly in equity** | 110 |
| Profit/(loss) for the year | 165 |
| **Total recognised gain for the year** | 275 |

### 36.2.4 The statement of financial position

IAS 1 states the items that must be shown as a minimum in the statement of financial position. These include:

- intangible assets
- property, plant and equipment
- investment property
- financial assets
- investments
- inventories
- trade and other receivables
- cash and cash equivalents
- trade and other payables
- provisions
- financial liabilities

- tax liabilities
- issued capital
- reserves.

## Current assets and non-current assets

Current assets comprise:

- cash and cash equivalents
- assets that will be disposed of within the next normal operating cycle (usually the next financial year); examples are inventories, trade receivables and cash and cash equivalents.

All other assets are classified as non-current assets.

## Current liabilities and non-current liabilities

Current liabilities comprise liabilities that are expected to be settled within the next normal operating cycle (usually the next financial year); examples are trade payables, tax liabilities and bank overdrafts (shown as negative cash and cash equivalents).

All other liabilities are non-current liabilities.

## Equity

The following details must be shown either as part of the statement of financial position or in the notes to the financial statements:

- the number of shares issued and fully paid
- the number of shares issued and not fully paid
- the par value of the shares.

All shares of a permanent nature are classified as equity. So equity comprises ordinary share and preference shares. However, redeemable preference shares are not part of equity capital.

## 36.2.5 Reserves

A list of all the reserves created is shown either on the face of the statement of financial position or as a note to the financial statements. If the detailed list of reserves is shown as a note, then the total of all reserves is shown on the face of the statement of financial position.

**Worked example**

The directors of Nivlan plc provide the following information at 31 July 2014:

| | $000 |
|---|---|
| Cash and cash equivalents | 142 |
| Goodwill | 150 |
| Inventories at 31 July 2014 | 896 |
| Issued share capital | 3000 |
| Property, plant and equipment | 8760 |
| Retained earnings | 2298 |
| Revaluation reserve | 1500 |
| Share premium account | 1000 |
| Trade and other payables | 587 |
| Trade and other receivables | 779 |
| 9% debentures (repayable 2028) | 2000 |

The directors have made a provision for corporation tax of $342000.

**Required**

Prepare a statement of financial position at 31 July 2014.

## Answer

**Nivlan plc**
**Statement of financial position at 31 July 2014**

| | $000 | $000 |
|---|---|---|
| **ASSETS** | | |
| **Non-current assets** | | |
| Goodwill | 150 | |
| Property, plant and equipment | 8760 | 8910 |
| **Current assets** | | |
| Inventories | 896 | |
| Trade and other receivables | 779 | |
| Cash and cash equivalents | 142 | 1817 |
| **Total assets** | | 10727 |
| **EQUITY AND LIABILITIES** | | |
| **Equity** | | |
| Issued share capital | | 3000 |
| Share premium account | | 1000 |
| Revaluation reserve | | 1500 |
| Retained earnings | | 2298 |
| | | 7798 |
| **Non-current liabilities** | | |
| 9% debentures (2027) | | 2000 |
| **Current liabilities** | | |
| Trade and other payables | 587 | |
| Tax liability | 342 | 929 |
| **Total equity and liabilities** | | 10727 |

## 36.2.6 Dividends

Dividends are distributions to shareholders of profits earned by a limited company. Dividends are paid annually but most limited companies will pay an interim dividend approximately halfway through their financial year.

Interim dividends are based on the profits earned during the financial year. The final dividend is based on the reported profits for the full year.

Since directors do not have the authority to pay dividends without the approval of the owners of the company (i.e. the shareholders), the final dividend can only be proposed after the financial year end. Shareholder approval should occur two or three months later at the company annual general meeting.

Only dividends actually paid during a financial year can be recorded in the financial statements.

**Worked example**

The following information is available for Engary plc for the financial year ended 31 December 2014:

| | |
|---|---|
| January 2014 | Directors propose a final dividend of $34 000 on ordinary shares based on reported profits for the year ended 31 December 2013 |
| March 2014 | Shareholders approve the final dividend for the year ended 31 December 2013 |
| May 2014 | Final dividend of $34 000 for the year ended 31 December 2013 paid to shareholders |
| August 2014 | Interim dividend of $19 000 paid to shareholders based on reported profits for the half year ended 30 June 2014 |
| January 2015 | Directors propose a final dividend of $41 000 based on reported profits for the year ended 31 December 2014 |

**Required**

Prepare a statement detailing the total entry in the financial statements for the year ended 31 December 2014 for dividends.

## Answer

**Dividend entry in financial statements for the year ended 31 December 2014**

| | $ |
|---|---|
| Final dividend for year ended 31 December 2013 | 34 000 |
| Interim dividend for half year ended 30 June 2014 | 19 000 |
| Total entry for dividends | 53 000 |

The details of dividends paid during the financial year are shown in a note to the published accounts. The above information for Engary plc would be shown as follows:

**Example**

**Dividends**

| | $ |
|---|---|
| Equity dividends on ordinary shares | |
| Amounts recognised during the year: | |
| Final dividend for the year ended 31 December 2013 of 3.4 cents | 34 000 |
| Interim dividend for the year ended 31 December 2014 of 1.9 cents | 19 000 |
| | 53 000 |
| Proposed final dividend for the year ended 31 December 2014 of 4.1 cents | 41 000 |

The proposed final dividend is subject to approval by shareholders at the annual general meeting and accordingly has not been included as a liability in the financial statements.

The financial statements must contain a directors' report and an auditors' report.

### 36.2.7 The directors' report

The report contains:

- a statement of the principal activities of the company
- a review of performance over the preceding year

- a review of likely future developments
- the names of directors and their shareholdings
- details of dividends
- differences between book value (carrying amount) and market value of land and buildings
- political and charitable donations
- a statement on employees and employment policies (i.e. equal opportunities policy; policy with regard to people with disabilities; and health and safety of employees)
- policy of opportunities and participation of employees
- suppliers' payment policy.

### 36.2.8 The auditors' report

This report contains three sections:

- Respective responsibilities of directors and auditors. The directors' responsibilities are to prepare the annual report and financial statements in accordance with the law and international reporting standards.
- Basis of audit opinion. The audit should be conducted in accordance with international accounting standards. The auditors should obtain all the information and explanations that are necessary to provide sufficient evidence to allow them to assure the shareholders that the financial statements are free from material misstatement.
- Opinion. This is the auditors' view of the financial statements and their opinion as to whether they give a true and fair view, in accordance with international financial reporting standards and international accounting standards, of the state of the company's affairs and of its profit/loss for the period covered by the audit.

The auditors' report should also give an opinion as to whether or not the financial statements have been properly prepared in accordance with the Companies Act 1985.

### 36.2.9 Notes to the financial statements

IAS 1 requires that notes to the financial statements be included. These notes:

- give additional detail to items that may be summarised in the main body of the financial statements
- provide additional information to help the users understand the financial statements
- are also used to explain the particular treatment of items contained in the main body, that is, the bases used in the preparation (see Section 36.5).

## 36.3 IAS 2 Inventories

Inventories are defined as:

- goods or other assets purchased for resale
- consumable stores
- raw materials and components purchased for incorporation into products for sale
- products and services in intermediate stages of completion
- finished goods.

Cost of purchase comprises the purchase price including import taxes, transport and handling **costs** and any other costs that are directly attributable to the goods.

Costs of conversion comprise:

- costs that can be specifically attributed to units of production, for example direct labour, other direct expenses and subcontracted work
- **production overheads**
- any other overheads.

The standard states that inventory should be valued at 'the lower of cost and **net realisable value'** of separate items of inventory or of groups of similar items.

> **Cost** is defined as 'expenditure which has been incurred in the normal course of business in bringing the product or service to its present location and condition'.

> **Production overheads** are expenditures on materials, labour or services for production purposes based on the normal level of activity, taking one year with another.

> **Net realisable value** is the actual or estimated selling price (net of trade discount but before any cash discount that may be allowed) less all further costs to completion and all marketing, selling and distribution costs.

Inventories should be categorised in a statement of financial position as:

- raw materials
- work in progress *or*
- finished goods.

The standard accepts valuations using:

- the first-in first-out method (FIFO)
- the weighted average cost method (AVCO)
- the standard cost if it bears a reasonable relationship to actual costs obtained during the period.

The standard does not accept:

- the last-in first-out method (LIFO)
- the **base cost**
- the replacement cost (unless it provides the best measure of net realisable value and that this is lower than cost).

**Base cost** is 'the calculation of the cost of inventories on the basis that a fixed unit value is ascribed to a predetermined number of units of inventory ...'

## 36.4 IAS 7 Statements of cash flows

This topic was dealt with in detail in Chapter 35.

## 36.5 IAS 8 Accounting policies, changes in accounting estimates, and errors

IAS 1 requires companies to include details of specific accounting policies used in the preparation of financial statements. IAS 8 gives more detail. It defines accounting policies as:

> '... the specific principles, bases, conventions, rules and practices applied ... in preparing and presenting financial statements'.

The principles are the concepts that you have already learned. They apply to all the financial statements that you have prepared in your studies so far. They are the going concern concept, the accruals concept, prudence, consistency and materiality.

The bases are the individual methods of treatment used when applying accounting principles to particular situations, for example the application of cost value or net realisable value to certain items of inventory.

Accounting bases are selected by directors, for example method of selecting and applying the methods of depreciation to be used in preparing the financial statements.

Where an accounting policy is given in a standard, that policy must be applied. If there is no standard to provide guidance, the directors must use their judgement in selecting a policy to follow, bearing in mind that any information provided in the financial statements should be relevant and reliable.

Accounting policies should be applied consistently in similar situations.

IAS 8 also deals with the effect of errors on financial statements.

Once a material error is discovered, it should be corrected in the next set of financial statements by adjusting the comparative figures.

## 36.6 IAS 10 Events after the reporting period

These are events that occur after the reporting period but before the financial statements are authorised for issue. The events may be:

- adjusting events – this is evidence that certain conditions arose at or before the end of the reporting period that have not been taken into account in the financial statements. If the financial implications are material, then changes should be made in the financial accounts before they are authorised. An example is where a customer that owed a material debt at the financial year end becomes insolvent after the end of the financial year. It would be necessary to make a change to the amount recorded as trade receivables
- non-adjusting events – these arise after the end of the reporting period and no adjustments to the financial statements are necessary. However, if they are material, they should be disclosed by way of a note to the accounts. An example would be a large purchase of non-current assets.

Proposed dividends at the financial year end are non-adjusting events and so are not recorded as a current liability on the statement of financial position. They are recorded as a note to the accounts. See the example of Engary plc in Section 36.2.5.

## 36.7 IAS 16 Property, plant and equipment

**Property, plant and equipment (PPE)** comprises all non-current tangible assets from which economic benefits flow. They are held for more than one time period for use in the production process or the supply of goods and services. Examples would include land and buildings, plant and machinery, office equipment, vehicles, etc.

**Carrying amount** is the amount shown on the statement of financial position after the deduction of accumulated depreciation or impairment losses.

**Depreciation** is the apportioning of the cost or valuation of an asset over its useful economic life.

**Fair value** is the amount for which an asset could be exchanged between knowledgeable, willing parties in an 'arm's length' transaction.

The objective of the standard is to ensure that accounting principles regarding non-current assets are applied consistently and that the company's treatment of the assets is understood by the users of the financial statements.

**Property, plant and equipment (PPE)** should initially be valued at cost in the statement of financial position. Cost includes expenditure directly attributable to bringing the asset into a usable condition. Costs could include import duties, delivery charges, the costs of preparing the site and other installation costs.

After acquisition of PPE, the company must show the **carrying amount** of the assets at either:

- cost less accumulated **depreciation** and impairment losses *or*
- revaluation based on fair value less subsequent depreciation and impairment losses (see Section 36.8)

**Fair values** based on the revaluation model for land and buildings would generally be based on market value calculated by professional valuers. In the case of plant and equipment, the fair value would usually be based on market value.

### 36.7.1 Depreciation

The object of providing depreciation is to reflect the cost of using an asset.

The depreciation for a financial period is shown in the income statement and should reflect the cost of using the asset over the financial period under review. It should reflect the pattern in which the economic benefits derived from the asset are consumed.

When determining the useful life of an asset, several factors should be taken into account:

- the expected use of the asset
- the expected wear and tear on the asset
- economic and technical obsolescence
- legal or similar restraints.

**Residual value** is the amount that the company expects to obtain for an asset less any disposal costs at the end of its useful life.

Depreciation policy is not affected by repairs and/or maintenance. However, the **residual value** and the useful life of the asset need to be reviewed on an annual basis to determine if any change should be made in the depreciation policy.

Generally, land and buildings should be treated separately since land is not depreciated; it has an infinite economic life, unlike other non-current assets, which have a finite economic life. Note that leasehold land *does* have a finite life (the duration of the lease), and therefore should be depreciated.

A variety of methods can be used to calculate the annual depreciation charge. The three that you will find most useful are:

- the straight-line method, which charges a constant annual amount over the life of the asset
- the reducing balance method, which charges a decreasing annual amount over the life of the asset
- the revaluation method, which charges the difference between the value of an asset at the end of a year and the value at the start of the year plus any additions to the asset during the year.

When the pattern of use of an asset is uncertain, the straight-line method is usually adopted.

Changing the basis of calculating the annual charge is permissible only when the new method gives a fairer representation of the use of the asset. The change must be documented in a note to the financial statements. Any change to methods must be a permanent change. The method chosen should reflect, as closely as possible, the way that the assets benefits are consumed.

**Derecognition** occurs when an asset is disposed of or is incapable of yielding any further economic benefits.

**Derecognition** means that the asset will no longer be recognised on the statement of financial position. If the asset is sold then the profit or loss on disposal is shown in the income statement.

For each asset, the financial statements must show (generally in the notes to the financial statements):

- the basis for determining the carrying amount
- the depreciation method used
- the duration of the useful economic life or the rates of charging depreciation
- the carrying amount
- accumulated depreciation and impairment losses at the start and end of the accounting period
- a reconciliation of the carrying amount at the start and end of the accounting period that shows:
  - additions
  - disposals
  - revaluations
  - impairment losses
  - depreciation.

## 36.8 IAS 36 Impairment of assets

**Recoverable amount** is the higher of an asset's fair value (the amount for which the asset could be sold less selling costs) and its value in use (calculated by discounting all the future cash flows generated by using the asset).

Impairment applies to nearly all non-current assets.

Impairment occurs when the recoverable amount is less than the asset's carrying amount (the value shown in the statement of financial position after deduction of accumulated depreciation).

The value of assets shown on the statement of financial position needs to be reviewed at each statement of financial position date to determine if there is any indication of impairment.

Evidence of impairment could be:

- a significant fall in the market value of the asset
- a significant fall in the value of an asset due to a change in technology
- a significant fall in the value of an asset due to an economic downturn

- a significant fall in the value of an asset due to it being damaged, resulting in the asset's fair value falling or its future cash-generating ability falling
- a significant fall in the value of an asset due to a restructuring of the business.

An impairment loss is recognised when the recoverable amount is less than the carrying amount. The amount of the loss is to be shown in the income statement.

## 36.9 IAS 37 Provisions, contingent liabilities and contingent assets

A **provision** is an amount set aside out of profits for a known expense, the amount of which is uncertain.

A **contingent liability** is a potential liability which exists when the statement of financial position is drawn up, the full extent of which is uncertain.

A **contingent asset** is a potential asset which exists when the statement of financial position is drawn up. The inflow of economic benefit is uncertain.

The standard seeks to ensure that there is sufficient information given to enable the users of the financial statements to understand the effects of **provisions**, **contingent liabilities** and **contingent assets**.

Provisions are to be recognised as a liability in the financial statements if the company has an obligation because of a past event and it is *probable* that the obligation requires settlement (i.e. a more than 50 per cent chance of occurrence). It is also necessary that a reliable estimate of the amount of the liability can be made.

A note to the financial statements should detail the provisions.

Contingent liabilities are *possible* obligations (i.e. a less than 50 per cent chance of occurrence). If the liability is possible, the contingent liability should be disclosed as a note to the financial statements, but no disclosure is necessary in the main body of the statements. If there is only a remote chance of the occurrence then no reference needs to be made in either the financial statement or the notes.

Contingent assets are *possible* assets arising from past events and it is possible that economic benefit could accrue in the future.

If there is a *probable* economic benefit in the future deriving from the past event, then a note to the financial statements should be made. If the future economic benefits are only possible or remote, no reference needs to be made.

## 36.10 IAS 38 Intangible assets

**Goodwill** is the difference between the fair value of the assets and liabilities acquired in the combination and the cost of acquisition. Goodwill must be tested annually for impairment.

IFRS 3 'Business combinations' deals with goodwill.

Intangible assets do not have physical substance. They are identifiable and are controlled by the company. They include licences, quotas, patents, copyrights, franchises, trademarks, etc. **Goodwill** is not covered in this standard.

Intangible assets are either purchased or internally generated. Internally generated assets cannot be recognised in the financial statements.

Like PPE, intangible assets are initially shown at cost in the statement of financial position. After acquisition they can be shown at:

- cost less accumulated depreciation and impairment losses
- revaluation based on fair value less subsequent amortisation and impairment losses.

Revaluations are to be made regularly to ensure that the carrying value does not differ materially from the fair value at the date of the statement of financial position.

Any increase in value should be recognised in the statement of changes in equity and shown as part of any revaluation reserve.

Any reduction in value will be recognised as an expense in the income statement.

An intangible asset with a finite life is amortised over its useful economic life, whereas an intangible asset with an infinite life is not amortised.

**Research and development** is the exploration of new scientific methods of manufacturing, and using the results to produce an end product. The research can be:

- pure research, where no end result was foreseen when the research was first undertaken; the main aim was to further knowledge in the field
- applied research, directed towards a practical application, for example a cure for cancer.

Development is the application of knowledge gained from research to produce or improve a product or process before it is marketed commercially.

IAS 38 requires that a distinction is made between revenue expenditure and capital expenditure on research.

Revenue expenditure is entered in the income statement, while capital expenditure on non-current assets is recorded as non-current assets and they are depreciated over their useful life.

Development costs are treated as an expense in the income statement when they are incurred, or they may be capitalised as an intangible asset if the directors can demonstrate that they can establish the result as an asset that can be used or sold.

**Self-test questions**

1 Why is there a need for international accounting standards?
2 What does IAS 7 deal with?
3 Which standard deals with depreciation of non-current assets?
4 What does IAS 2 deal with?
5 Which standard deals with the treatment of research and development costs?
6 Which standard deals with intangible non-current assets?
7 Which standard says that financial statements should be understandable?
8 Which objective in the preparation of financial statements is missing: relevance; comparability; understandability?
9 What is the overriding principle in the valuation of inventories?
10 What are the six components of a complete set of financial statements?

## 36.11 Social responsibility

In recent years, managers of businesses of all sizes have had to consider the impact of their business decisions on stakeholders. This impact affects:

- staff working in the business
- people outside the business, for example customers, suppliers and others that use or rely on the business
- the local, national and international environment.

### 36.11.1 Non-financial aspects of accounting

Traditionally, financial statements were prepared for management and stewardship purposes and concentrated on purely monetary aspects of the business. However, consideration of the non-financial aspects of running and controlling a business have become increasingly more important, since business activity affects all our lives in one way or another.

### 36.11.2 Social awareness

Consumers and society at large are becoming increasingly aware of the environmental damage that is often a by-product of business activity and the danger of depleting non-renewable resources.

Social networking sites on the internet mean that we are constantly updated on business issues that affect our everyday lives.

As a result of this, business managers are under pressure to show that they are:

- aware of and accepting of their social responsibilities
- manufacturing products with an appreciation of more than just financial considerations.

Profitability is now just one factor considered by managers. Today, consideration must also be given to the impact that a business has on others. We are all consumers, some of us are employees and we all live in a global environment that is influenced to a greater or lesser degree by the business world.

A business may be profitable but what of its 'hidden costs'? In pursuing profitability what are the costs to people outside the organisation as well as those employed within the business?

## 36.11.3 Social costs

The social costs of carrying out business activity include:

- stress in the workplace, such as fears about job security, introduction of new technologies, etc.
- pollution in the workplace, such as dust, fumes, noise, etc.
- pollution of the local surroundings of the workplace, for example noise, traffic congestion, etc.

The business activity may also have an impact nationally in the form of pollution and damage to rivers and air quality and even globally, for example through pollution which contributes to global warming.

## 36.11.4 Social costs versus profitability

Cynics among us would say that managers do not care about the impact that their business has on others so long as sufficient profits are earned. However, social issues can affect profitability adversely.

If the workforce are stressed or unhappy because of environmental issues inside or outside the workplace they are less likely to work at full capacity and so their productivity will suffer. There may be high staff turnover and/or absenteeism. Replacement staff may need to be trained thus increasing recruitment and training costs.

If the environment close to the business is poor, new staff might be difficult to recruit; product sales in the locality could be affected. Both these factors could attract adverse publicity.

Bad publicity via global social network sites might affect not only a business's national sales, but in the case of larger organisations, could affect worldwide sales too.

If consumers unite in opposition against a producer or supplier and cease to use a product, inevitably sales and therefore profits will suffer. Managers that ignore such reactions from pressure groups do so at their peril.

The major problem that managers face when trying to evaluate the consequences of following a particular line of action is that it is difficult to put a monetary value on the issues discussed above. As accountants, we have already stated in Chapter 7 that when preparing the accounting statements we do not include items that cannot be measured in monetary terms (the money measurement concept).

## 36.11.5 Some areas of concern

If a factory closes we can calculate the savings in variable costs and in the longer term the savings in fixed costs. In such a case we can measure any redundancy and pension payments due. But how do we put a value on the distress caused to an office worker or factory floor worker?

When a business purchases a new IT system the cost of purchase is very obvious. The time and effort saved by staff can be quantified and costed. But what of the cost to workers who have been made redundant? What price can be put on frustration or the feeling of threat felt by employees who find the operation of the system difficult?

A supermarket relocates to an out-of-town shopping mall. How do we value the convenience that many consumers will experience by being able to get all their shopping at one outlet? And how do we balance this against the cost and convenience to your grandparents who can no longer shop locally because shops have had to close because they were less competitively priced than the supermarket?

There are no easy answers to any of these questions but it is vital that business managers take such issues into consideration when making long-term decisions so that the profitability of the business is not adversely affected.

Do not lose focus when answering questions on social issues. Many students feel strongly about issues covered under this topic heading and as a result become distracted in their answers. You can avoid this by planning your answer carefully.

## Self-test questions

**11** Identify two social issues affecting staff that a manager might consider.
**12** Social responsibility issues do not apply to sole traders who do not employ any workers. True/False?
**13** Multinational organisations do not need to take social costs into consideration since they are extremely powerful. Do you agree?
**14** 'Profits are more important than members of staff.' Outline a case to refute such a statement.

➤ **Now try Questions 1–5.**

## Chapter summary

- International accounting standards provide the basic ground rules by which all accounting records are produced.
- It is important that you know the number and title of each standard.
- You need not know the content of each standard by heart – just ensure that you understand the broad outlines.
- The general principles of each standard must be understood so that you can apply them to a variety of business problems.
- Social responsibility is an important area that business managers should be aware of since it affects the perception of stakeholders and thus impacts on profitability.

# 37 The role of the auditor and directors

**Content**

**1.1 Preparation of financial statements**

1.1.5 Auditing and stewardship of limited companies
- Explain the role of the auditor
- Explain and discuss the role of directors and their responsibilities to shareholders (stewardship)
- Discuss the importance of a true and fair view in respect of financial statements.

**By the end of this chapter you should be able to:**
- discuss the role of the auditor
- discuss the auditor's basis of opinion
- identify the records that require to be audited
- explain the connection between shareholders, directors and auditors
- understand what is meant by the term 'true and fair view'
- discuss the role of directors.

## 37.1 The role of an auditor

**Auditors** examine the financial records and financial statements of a business. An audit is carried out by staff headed by a qualified accountant.

**External auditors** are independent of the business. In the case of limited companies external auditors are appointed by the shareholders.

**Internal auditors** are staff members who scrutinise the internal controls of the business.

### 37.1.1 Auditing

Auditing is normally associated with the accounts of limited companies. It is compulsory that larger limited companies have their financial statements audited by **external auditors**.

However, tax authorities or a business's bank may request sight of audited financial statements of non-incorporated businesses.

An external auditor investigates whether or not the business has kept adequate records, that financial statements are consistent with the records from which they are prepared and that financial statements prepared by management give a true and fair view of the business's state of affairs. The auditor verifies that transactions have actually taken place and that they have been recorded in the books of account accurately.

The audit provides the users of financial statements with an assurance that the statements provided to them can be relied upon.

### 37.1.2 The auditor's opinion

If, in the auditor's opinion, adequate records have not been kept of the company's financial statements or the auditable part of its directors' report is not in agreement with the company's records and returns, the auditor will issue a qualified opinion to the report.

A qualified report will raise points that the auditor considers have not been dealt with correctly by the directors in their preparation of the financial statements.

Where such points are not of a serious nature, the report might state '…with the exception of … the financial statements do show a true and fair view …' If, however, the auditor is of the opinion that there has been a serious breach the statement will state that 'the financial statements do not show a true and fair view'.

The auditor's report has three main sections:

1 Responsibilities of directors and auditors
   a Directors are responsible for preparing the financial statements.
   b Auditors are responsible for forming an opinion on the financial statements.

2 Basis of opinion – the framework of auditing standards within which the audit was conducted, other assessments and the way in which the audit was planned and performed. If the auditor fails to obtain information and explanations necessary to support his audit then this must be reported. Any deviation from the necessary disclosure requirements must be identified.
3 Opinion – the auditor's view of the company's financial statements.

### 37.1.3 Audit requirements

The main statements that have to be audited are:

- the income statement
- the statement of financial position
- statement of cash flows
- statement of total recognised gains and losses
- reconciliation of movements in shareholders' funds
- accounting policies
- notes to the accounts.

### 37.1.4 Regulatory framework

The regulatory framework is made up of shareholders, directors and auditors:

- Shareholders are responsible for the appointment of directors and auditors.
- Directors recommend the appointment of auditors to the shareholders.

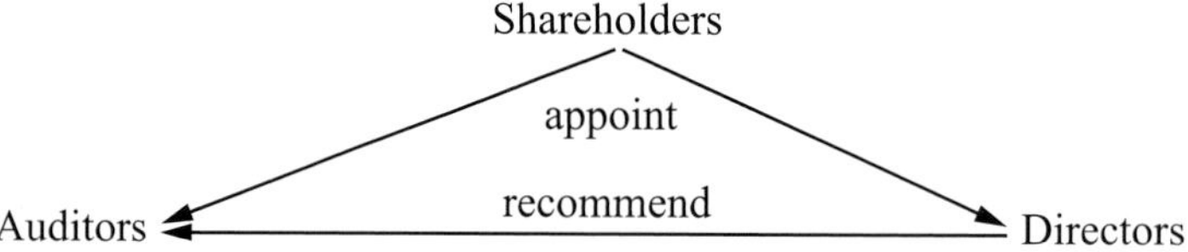


**Figure 37.1** The regulatory framework

Because of the interdependence of the three parties there is a need for rules and regulations that accountants follow in the preparation and presentation of financial statements. The sources of the regulations are the Companies Acts and the application of accounting standards.

Accounting standards are not laws. However, in the UK, the Companies Act 1985 requires that directors must state in the notes to the financial statements that international accounting standards have been applied in the preparation of the statements.

### 37.1.5 True and fair view

A true and fair view requires that the auditor must give an opinion as to whether the financial statements presented to the shareholders are truthful and unbiased.

In the UK, Section 226[2] of the Companies Act 1985 requires that 'the [statement of financial position] should give a true and fair view of the state of affairs of the company at the end of the financial year; and the [income statement] shall give a true and fair view of the profit or loss of the company for the financial year.'

The auditor must give an opinion as to whether or not the financial statements presented to the shareholders are a fair representation of the company's results. So the auditor must be satisfied that the records audited have formed a suitable basis for the preparation of the statements.

The auditor must verify that financial statements agree with company records. They must confirm that:

- results shown in income statements are truly and fairly stated
- fundamental accounting concepts have been applied
- the accounting convention followed in the preparation of financial statements is stated
- the preparation of financial statements is consistent with previous periods.

The auditor must verify that:

- assets exist and are owned by the company and are stated at amounts that are in accordance with accepted accounting policies
- all liabilities are included and stated at amounts that are in accordance with accepted accounting policies.

# 37.2 The role of directors

## 37.2.1 Directors

We saw in Chapter 17 that keeping financial records and producing financial statements has two primary functions:

1 the stewardship function
2 the management function.

Shareholders provide the capital of limited companies by the purchase of shares. In the case of public limited companies there are often many thousands of shareholders. Clearly, all these shareholders cannot run the business on a day-to-day basis, so it is the responsibility of shareholders to appoint directors to run and manage the business on their behalf. The directors of a limited company are responsible for the preparation of annual financial statements that are then used by shareholders to assess the performance of the company and the directors whom they have appointed. The directors must ensure that the provisions of the Companies Act 1985 are implemented.

Directors are paid **emoluments** as their reward for running the business.

'Divorce of ownership and control' is the term often used to describe the relationship between shareholders and directors because although shareholders are the owners of a company, it is the directors who control the day-to-day affairs of the business.

**Emoluments** are the rewards that directors receive for running a company on a daily basis. The payment takes the form of a salary, possibly profit bonuses and share options based on their performance and other benefits such as private health insurance, a company car, etc.

## 37.2.2 Directors' responsibilities

Directors have a responsibility to:

- keep proper accounting records that allow financial statements to be prepared in accordance with relevant companies legislation
- safeguard business assets
- select the accounting policies to be applied to the business books of account
- state whether international standards have been applied
- report on the state of the company's affairs
- ensure that the financial statements are signed by two members of the board of directors.

If the directors are responsible for keeping financial records and the preparation of the annual financial statements, how can shareholders be guaranteed that the records are prepared in an objective way? Shareholders appoint a team of professionally qualified accountants (auditors) to check and verify the financial statements and the transactions that led to their preparation.

**Self-test questions**

1 Auditor is another term used to describe a director. True/False?
2 Auditors appoint directors. True/False?
3 'The main role of a director is the application of the management function of accounting; while the main role of auditors is stewardship'. How true is this statement?
4 What is meant by the term 'emoluments'?
5 Identify two items that the auditor must verify.
6 In what circumstances might an auditor qualify his opinion?

## Chapter summary

- Auditors are appointed by shareholders to verify that the financial statements show a true and fair view of the state of affairs of the company.
- Auditors give an opinion as to whether or not the financial statements do show a true and fair view.
- Directors are responsible for managing a company on a day-to-day basis on behalf of the owners (the shareholders).

# 38 Business purchase and merger

**Content**

**1.2 Business purchase and merger**

- Understand the nature and purpose of the merger of different types of businesses to form a new enterprise
- Make entries in the ledger accounts to record the:
  - merger of two or more sole traders' businesses to form a partnership
  - merger of a sole trader's business with an existing partnership to form an enlarged partnership
  - acquisition of a sole trader's business or partnership by a limited company.
- Prepare income statements and statements of financial position for the newly formed business following the merger, for example the limited company acquiring the partnership
- Evaluate and discuss the advantages and disadvantages of the proposed merger

**By the end of this chapter you should be able to:**

- evaluate a business with a view to its acquisition
- prepare a statement of financial position of:
  - unincorporated businesses merging to form a partnership by combining or purchasing assets and liabilities
  - a limited company that has purchased an unincorporated business by issuing shares, debentures and by cash
  - one business purchasing the assets and liabilities of another business
  - a new company purchasing one or more existing businesses
  - a limited company acquiring shares in another limited company.

## 38.1 The benefits gained by combining businesses

**Return on investment** is the term used to describe the financial benefits that will result from investing in another business.

When the owners (or directors in the case of a limited company) decide that they wish to purchase another business they will appraise the financial benefits to be gained through the acquisition.

Financial benefits may take the form of increased profitability of the 'new' enlarged business due to:

- synergy – greater effectiveness obtained by two or more businesses joining forces than could be obtained by them acting individually as single businesses
- vertical integration – control of different stages of production or sale of a product
- the acquisition of larger, more profitable contracts
- greater geographical coverage
- greater skills coverage – a larger business may be able to attract a more skilful workforce
- perception of the 'new larger' business being more prestigious.

Other benefits may also be gained:

- An increase in market share may lead to disadvantaging a rival(s).
- The new company will be able to take advantage of internal economies of scale; these could include:
  - **technical economies** – larger businesses can often be more efficient since costs are generally not proportionate to the increase in size
  - **managerial economies** – larger businesses can generally afford specialist managers who concentrate on one or two major areas of expertise

- **financial economies** – larger businesses are generally able to raise finance more easily and they tend to have a greater variety of potential sources from which to choose
- **purchasing economies** – larger businesses are more likely to purchase materials in larger quantities and therefore take advantage of bulk discounting.

- Research and development can be undertaken more effectively by a larger business.
- Diversification is easier in a larger business; a more diverse portfolio of products will open up further markets and reduce the risks associated with a limited range of products.

You will need to be able to show the effects of the business purchase on the statement of financial position for the 'new' business.

**Self-test questions**

1 Explain the term 'synergy'.
2 Explain the difference between vertical and horizontal integration.
3 Explain why a business might wish to acquire another business.
4 Identify and explain two types of economies of scale.
5 A manufacturer of television sets starts production of microwave cookers. This is an example of diversification. True/False?

## 38.2 The amalgamation of two sole traders' businesses

A **merger** takes place when two or more businesses join together to form a new business. The term is generally applied to the agreed takeover of one limited company by another.

**Unincorporated businesses** is the term used to describe all businesses that are not limited companies.

The process here simply involves the fusing together of the two statements of financial position. This takes place after the owners of the two businesses have agreed on values for all the assets and liabilities that are to form the basis of the new partnership business.

After the assets have been valued it may be necessary for the partners to make payments or withdrawals of capital in order to achieve the required capital accounts balances that the two partners have agreed upon.

**Worked example**

Aiisha and Borak are sole traders. They agree to merge their two businesses into a partnership as from 1 January 2015.

The following information relating to the two businesses is given:

**Statements of financial position at 31 December 2014**

| | Aiisha | | Borak | |
|---|---|---|---|---|
| | $ | $ | $ | $ |
| **ASSETS** | | | | |
| **Non-current assets** | | 25 000 | | 75 000 |
| **Current assets** | | | | |
| Inventory | 3 500 | | 16 000 | |
| Trade receivables | 6 000 | | 7 000 | |
| Cash and cash equivalents | 700 | 10 200 | 1 200 | 24 200 |
| **Total assets** | | 35 200 | | 99 200 |

| | Aiisha | | Borak | |
|---|---|---|---|---|
| | $ | $ | $ | $ |
| **CAPITAL AND LIABILITIES** | | | | |
| **Capital** | | 32 700 | | 94 200 |
| **Current liabilities** | | | | |
| Trade payables | | 2 500 | | 5 000 |
| **Total capital and liabilities** | | 35 200 | | 99 200 |

The partners agree the following values for the assets to be taken over by the partnership:

| | Aiisha | Borak |
|---|---|---|
| | $ | $ |
| Non-current assets | 30 000 | 70 000 |
| Inventories | 3 000 | 15 000 |
| Trade receivables | 5 000 | 6 700 |

The partnership would assume responsibility for the current liabilities at 31 December 2014 of both sole traders.

They further agree that each partner will start in the partnership business with capital of $50 000.

The partnership bankers have agreed to provide any necessary overdraft facilities.

**Required**

Prepare a statement of financial position for the partnership as it would appear at the start of trading on 1 January 2015.

## Answer

**Aiisha and Borak**
**Statement of financial position at 1 January 2015**

| | $ | $ |
|---|---|---|
| **ASSETS** | | |
| **Non-current assets** | | 100 000 |
| **Current assets** | | |
| Inventories | 18 000 | |
| Trade receivables | 11 700 | 29 700 |
| **Total assets** | | 129 700 |
| **CAPITAL AND LIABILITIES** | | |
| **Capital accounts –** Aiisha | 50 000 | |
| Borak | 50 000 | 100 000 |
| **Current liabilities** | | |
| Trade payables | 7 500 | |
| Cash and cash equivalents (overdraft) | 22 200 | 29 700 |
| **Total capital and liabilities** | | 129 700 |

## Workings

**Capital account – Aiisha**

| | $ | | $ |
|---|---|---|---|
| Cash | 700 | Bal b/d | 32 700 |
| Bal c/d | 35 500 | Valuation | 3 500 |
| | 36 200 | | 36 200 |
| | | Bal b/d | 35 500 |
| | | Cash | 14 500 |

**Capital account – Borak**

| | $ | | $ |
|---|---|---|---|
| Cash | 1 200 | Bal b/d | 94 200 |
| Valuation | 6 300 | | |
| Bal c/d | 86 700 | | |
| | 94 200 | | 94 200 |
| Cash | 36 700 | Bal b/d | 86 700 |

➤ Now try Question 1.

## 38.3 The purchase of the business of a sole trader by a limited company

**Purchase consideration** is the agreed amount that will be paid to acquire a business.

When a sole trader's business is taken over by a limited company the **purchase consideration** may be discharged in a number of ways. The purchasing company may pay the sole trader:

- by a cash payment
- by the issue of shares
- by a combination of a share issue and a cash payment.

The purchase consideration may be:

- the same as the value of assets taken over
- less than the value of assets taken over *or*
- more than the value of assets taken over.

**Goodwill** is the cost of acquiring a business less the total value of the and liabilities that have been purchased. It is an intangible asset, that is, it is without physical substance.

Why, you might ask, would a purchaser pay more than the value of the net assets (assets less the liabilities) acquired?

The purchaser is paying for the advantage of acquiring an already established business. This advantage usually takes the form of profits greater than those that could reasonably be expected on the tangible assets taken over.

On occasions the amount paid for a business is less than the fair value of its separable (individual) net assets; this results in the purchase of **negative goodwill**. Negative goodwill is shown as a negative amount under the heading of intangible non-current assets.

When a successful business is sold, the vendor will generally set the selling price at a level greater than the value of the net assets being sold.

The cash paid by the purchaser of a business to acquire the goodwill is paid in order to gain access to future profits generated by the business taken over.

**Example**

Hovig owns a successful, busy general store. The latest summarised statement of financial position shows:

| | $ |
|---|---|
| **ASSETS** | |
| **Non-current assets** | 120 000 |
| **Current assets** (including $1000 cash) | 61 000 |
| **Total assets** | 181 000 |
| **CAPITAL AND LIABILITIES** | |
| **Capital** – Hovig | 147 000 |
| **Current liabilities** | 34 000 |
| **Total capital and liabilities** | 181 000 |

Fawzig purchases the business, paying $200 000.

Hovig has sold his business for a capital gain (profit) of $54 000 (he would not sell his cash balances).

Fawzig purchased the net assets for $200 000. She has purchased the business net tangible assets for $146 000 and the intangible asset of goodwill for $54 000.

The opening statement of financial position for Fawzig would appear as follows:

| | $ |
|---|---|
| **ASSETS** | |
| **Non-current tangible assets** | 120 000 |
| **Non-current intangible asset** | |
| Goodwill | 54 000 |

| | |
|---|---|
| **Current assets** | 60 000 |
| **Total assets** | 234 000 |
| | |
| **CAPITAL AND LIABILITIES** | |
| **Capital** | 200 000 |
| **Current liabilities** | 34 000 |
| **Total capital and liabilities** | 234 000 |

For more on goodwill, its treatment and valuation, see Section 24.2 on the structural changes in partnerships.

Although the examples used refer to unincorporated businesses, the principles apply to any business purchasing net assets at a price greater than a value of those assets to the vendor.

## Worked example

A summarised statement of financial position of Akrim shows the following position at 31 December 2014:

| | **$** |
|---|---|
| **ASSETS** | |
| **Non-current assets** | 48 000 |
| **Current assets** | 12 000 |
| **Total assets** | 60 000 |
| **CAPITAL** | 60 000 |

A summarised statement of financial position of Seabee Hay plc on the same date shows:

| | **$000** |
|---|---|
| **ASSETS** | |
| **Non-current assets** | 1 750 |
| **Current assets** | 290 |
| **Total assets** | 2 040 |
| | |
| **EQUITY AND LIABILITIES** | |
| **Equity** | |
| Ordinary shares of $1 each | 1 500 |
| Reserves | 520 |
| **Current liabilities** | 20 |
| **Total equity and liabilities** | 2 040 |

Akrim's business was purchased by Seabee Hay plc at the start of business on 1 January 2015. The purchase consideration was $100 000, made up of $35 000 cash and 30 000 ordinary shares in Seabee Hay plc.

Seabee Hay plc valued the non-current assets taken over at $75 000 and the net current assets at $10 000.

**Required**

Prepare a summarised statement of financial position for Seabee Hay plc at 1 January 2015, immediately after the acquisition of the business of Akrim.

## Answer

**Seebee Hay Ltd**
**Summarised statement of financial position at 1 January 2015**

| | | |
|---|---|---|
| **ASSETS** | | |
| **Non-current assets** | 1825 | (1750 + 75) |
| **Goodwill** | 15 | ($85000 tangible assets purchased for $100000) |
| **Current assets** | 265 | (290 – 35 + 10) |
| **Total assets** | 2105 | |
| | | |
| **EQUITY AND LIABILITIES** | | |
| **Capital and reserves** | | |
| Ordinary shares of $1 each | 1530 | ($100000 + $30000) |
| Share premium | 35 | (30000 Shares with a value of $ 65000) |
| Other reserves | 520 | |
| | 2085 | |
| **Current liabilities** | 20 | |
| **Total equity and liabilities** | 2105 | |

**Note**

Akrim has made a capital gain (profit) on the sale of his business of $40000. Akrim's 30000 ordinary shares have a value to Akrim of $65000 ($100000 purchase consideration less cash $35000) or $2.17 per share ($65000/30000).

➤ Now try Question 2.

## 38.4 The purchase of more than one business to form a new limited company

The process involved when more than one business is taken over by a limited company follows the same procedures as if only one business is involved.

**Worked example**

Sole traders, Axel and Brian, decide to form a limited company, Briaxel Ltd, that will incorporate both businesses. The company will commence trading on 1 February 2015 and will have an issued share capital of 400000 ordinary shares of $1 each to be issued at par; the shares will be divided equally between the two men. Statements of financial position for the two businesses at 31 January 2015 are shown:

**Statements of financial position at 31 January 2015**

| | Axel | Brian |
|---|---|---|
| | $ | $ |
| **ASSETS** | | |
| **Non-current assets** | | |
| Premises | 60000 | 80000 |
| Machinery | 40000 | 50000 |
| Vehicles | 12000 | 10000 |
| | 112000 | 140000 |
| **Current assets** | | |
| Inventory | 8000 | 9000 |
| Trade receivables | 6000 | 7500 |

| | | |
|---|---:|---:|
| Cash | 2000 | 1500 |
| | 16000 | 18000 |
| **Total assets** | 128000 | 158000 |
| | | |
| **CAPITAL AND LIABILITIES** | | |
| **Capital** – Axel | 124000 | |
| Brian | | 153000 |
| **Current liabilities** | | |
| Trade payables | 4000 | 5000 |
| **Total capital and liabilities** | 128000 | 158000 |

All assets held by the two sole traders will be taken over by Briaxel Ltd at the following values. The new company will assume responsibility for the payment of current liabilities.

| | Axel | Brian |
|---|---:|---:|
| | $ | $ |
| Premises | 100000 | 90000 |
| Machinery | 20000 | 20000 |
| Vehicles | 10000 | 10000 |
| Inventory | 7000 | 8000 |
| Trade receivables | 5000 | 7000 |

**Required**

Prepare a statement showing the financial position of Briaxel Ltd at the start of trading on 1 February 2015.

## Answer

**Briaxel Ltd**
**Statement of financial position at 1 February 2015**

| | $ |
|---|---:|
| **ASSETS** | |
| **Non-current assets** | |
| Goodwill | 128500 |
| Premises | 190000 |
| Machinery | 40000 |
| Vehicles | 20000 |
| | 378500 |
| **Current assets** | |
| Inventory | 15000 |
| Trade receivables | 12000 |
| Cash and cash equivalents | 3500 |
| | 30500 |
| **Total assets** | 409000 |
| | |
| **EQUITY AND LIABILITIES** | |
| **Equity** | |
| Ordinary shares of $1 each | 400000 |
| **Current liabilities** | |
| Trade payables | 9000 |
| **Total equity and liabilities** | 409000 |

You could also be asked to close the books of account for each sole trader. In such cases do not attempt to answer both parts of the question at the same time; treat each part as a separate task.

**Workings**

Goodwill calculations

'Purchase' consideration less value of Axel's net assets taken over by the company:

| | |
|---|---|
| 200 000 ordinary shares of $1 each | = $200 000 |
| ($100 000 + $20 000 + $10 000 + $7 000 + $5 000 + $2 000 – $4 000) | = $140 000 |
| Value of goodwill (Axel) | = $60 000 |

'Purchase' consideration less value of Brian's net assets taken over by the company:

| | |
|---|---|
| 200 000 ordinary shares of $1 each | = $200 000 |
| ($90 000 + $20 000 + $10 000 + $8 000 + $7 000 + $1 500 – $5 000) | = $131 500 |
| Value of goodwill (Brian) | = $68 500 |

**Worked example**

Using the information given in the previous worked example, prepare relevant accounts in the books of account of Brian to show the entries necessary to close his business.

## Answer

**Realisation account**

| | $ | | $ |
|---|---|---|---|
| Premises | 80 000 | Trade payables | 5 000 |
| Machinery | 50 000 | Briaxel Ltd | 200 000 |
| Vehicles | 10 000 | | |
| Inventory | 9 000 | | |
| Trade receivables | 7 500 | | |
| Cash | 1 500 | | |
| Profit on realisation | 47 000 | | |
| | 205 000 | | 205 000 |

**Capital account – Brian**

| | $ | | $ |
|---|---|---|---|
| Briaxel Ltd | 200 000 | Balance b/d | 153 000 |
| | | Realisation | 47 000 |
| | 200 000 | | 200 000 |

**Briaxel Ltd**

| | $ | | $ |
|---|---|---|---|
| Briaxel Ltd | 200 000 | Capital – Brian | 200 000 |

**Self-test questions**

6 Explain why two sole traders might combine their businesses and form a limited company.

7 When two sole traders form a limited company they would retain the principle of unlimited liability. True/False?

## 38.5 The purchase of a partnership by a limited company

The process involved when a limited company purchases a partnership business is similar to that employed when a sole trader's business is purchased.

Technical difficulties could be encountered when apportioning shares and debentures between partners. However, you will find that the proportions of each security to be allocated to each partner will be given in any question you are asked to answer at this level.

### Worked example

Yukio and Mussa are in partnership, sharing profits and losses in the ratio of 2:1 respectively. A statement of financial position at 31 January 2015 showed:

**Yukio and Mussa**
**Statement of financial position**
**at 31 January 2015**

| | $ |
|---|---|
| **ASSETS** | |
| **Non-current assets** | |
| Premises | 150 000 |
| Office equipment | 40 000 |
| Vehicles | 60 000 |
| | 250 000 |
| **Current assets** | |
| Inventory | 18 000 |
| Trade receivables | 6 000 |
| Bank balance | 4 000 |
| | 28 000 |
| **Total assets** | 278 000 |
| **CAPITAL AND LIABILITIES** | |
| **Capital accounts** – Yukio | 120 000 |
| Mussa | 100 000 |
| | 220 000 |
| **Non-current liabilities** | |
| Loan – Mussa | 50 000 |
| **Current liabilities** | |
| Trade payables | 8 000 |
| **Total capital and liabilities** | 278 000 |

The partnership was taken over by Sparta plc before the start of business on 1 February 2015. The purchase consideration was $400 000, consisting of:

- $30 000 cash
- $60 000 seven per cent debentures to be shared between the partners in their profit sharing ratios
- 800 000 ordinary shares of $0.25 each shared equally between the partners.

For the purposes of the takeover, the partnership assets have been valued as follows:

| | $ |
|---|---|
| Premises | 200 000 |
| Office equipment | 20 000 |
| Vehicles | 50 000 |
| Inventory | 16 000 |
| Trade receivables | 5 000 |

A statement of financial position for Sparta plc at 31 January 2015 showed:

**Sparta plc**
**Statement of financial position at 31 January 2015**

| | $000 |
|---|---|
| **ASSETS** | |
| **Non-current assets** | |
| Land and buildings | 6700 |
| Machinery | 560 |
| Vehicles | 300 |
| | 7560 |
| **Current assets** | |
| Inventory | 56 |
| Trade receivables | 34 |
| Cash and cash equivalents | 17 |
| | 107 |
| **Total assets** | 7667 |
| **EQUITY AND LIABILITIES** | |
| **Equity** | |
| Ordinary shares of $0.25 each | 4000 |
| Share premium | 1000 |
| Reserves | 2269 |
| | 7269 |
| **Non-current liabilities** | |
| 7% debentures | 350 |
| **Current liabilities** | |
| Trade payables | 48 |
| **Total equity and liabilities** | 7667 |

**Required**

a Prepare a statement of financial position for Sparta plc at 1 February 2015 immediately after the takeover of the partnership.

b Based on the purchase consideration price, calculate the value of one share held by a partner on 1 February 2015.

## Answer

a

**Sparta plc**
**Statement of financial position at 1 February 2015**

| | $000 |
|---|---|
| **ASSETS** | |
| **Non-current assets** | |
| Goodwill | 117 |
| Land and buildings | 6900 |
| Machinery | 560 |
| Office equipment | 20 |
| Vehicles | 350 |
| | 7947 |
| **Current assets** | |
| Inventory | 72 |
| Trade receivables | 39 |
| | 111 |
| **Total assets** | 8058 |

| **EQUITY AND LIABILITIES** | |
|---|---|
| **Equity** | |
| Ordinary shares of $0.25 each | 4200 |
| Share premium | 1110 |
| Other reserves | 2269 |
| | 7579 |
| **Non-current liabilities** | |
| 7% debentures | 410 |
| **Current liabilities** | |
| Trade payables | 56 |
| Cash and cash equivalents | 13 |
| | 69 |
| **Total equity and liabilities** | 8058 |

**b** $0.3875 each

$$= \frac{\text{Value of shares}}{\text{Number of shares}} = \frac{\$310\,000}{800\,000}$$

## Worked example

Using the information given in the above example, show the entries required in the partnership books of account to dissolve the partnership of Yukio and Mussa.

Remember *do not* try to close the books of account at the same time as you prepare the company's statement of financial position. Treat each part of such a question as if it were *a totally separate question*.

If you need help in remembering how to do this, turn back to Chapter 24 on structural changes to partnerships, where the dissolution of a partnership is covered in detail.

## Answer

**Realisation account**

| | $ | | $ |
|---|---|---|---|
| Premises | 150000 | Sparta plc | 400000 |
| Office equipment | 40000 | Trade payables | 8000 |
| Vehicles | 60000 | | |
| Inventory | 18000 | | |
| Trade receivables | 6000 | | |
| Capital – Yukio | 89333 | | |
| Capital – Mussa | 44667 | | |
| | 408000 | | 408000 |

**Sparta plc**

| | $ | | $ | |
|---|---|---|---|---|
| Realisation | 400000 | Cash | 30000 | |
| | | Cap – Y | 40000 | (deb) |
| | | Cap – M | 20000 | (deb) |
| | | Cap – Y | 155000 | (shares) |
| | | Cap – M | 155000 | (shares) |
| | 400000 | | 400000 | |

**Loan account – Mussa**

| | $ | | $ |
|---|---|---|---|
| Bank | 50000 | Bal b/d | 50000 |

**Capital accounts**

| | Yukio | Mussa | | Yukio | Mussa |
|---|---|---|---|---|---|
| | $ | $ | | $ | $ |
| Sparta (debs) | 40 000 | 20 000 | Bals b/d | 120 000 | 100 000 |
| Sparta (shares) | 155 000 | 155 000 | Profit on realisation | 89 333 | 44 667 |
| Bank | 14 333 | | Bank | | 30 333 |
| | 209 333 | 175 000 | | 209 333 | 175 000 |

**Bank account**

| | $ | | $ |
|---|---|---|---|
| Bal b/d | 4 000 | Loan – Mussa | 50 000 |
| Sparta plc | 30 000 | Capital – Yukio | 14 333 |
| Capital – Mussa | 30 333 | | |
| | 64 333 | | 64 333 |

## 38.6 The acquisition of one limited company by another limited company (amalgamation)

An **amalgamation** takes place when one limited company purchases the assets of another company and assumes the responsibility of paying any trade and other payables.

The assets and liabilities of the two companies are combined in the books of account.

**Worked example**

The statements of financial position at 30 April 2015 of Aravane Ltd and Borg Ltd were as follows:

| | Aravane Ltd | Borg Ltd |
|---|---|---|
| | $ | $ |
| **ASSETS** | | |
| **Non-current assets** | 565 000 | 120 000 |
| **Current assets** | 84 000 | 28 500 |
| **Total assets** | 649 000 | 148 500 |
| | | |
| **EQUITY AND LIABILITIES** | | |
| **Equity** | | |
| Ordinary shares of $1 each | 400 000 | 80 000 |
| Retained earnings | 189 000 | 50 500 |
| | 589 000 | 130 500 |
| **Current liabilities** | 60 000 | 18 000 |
| **Total equity and liabilities** | 649 000 | 148 500 |

On 1 May 2015 Aravane Ltd acquired all the assets of Borg Ltd except the bank balance ($2500) and assumed responsibility for paying the current liabilities. The purchase consideration consisted of 75 000 shares in Aravane Ltd at par, with any balance being paid in cash.

**Required**

Prepare a statement of financial position for Aravane Ltd at 1 May 2015 immediately after the acquisition of the net assets of Borg Ltd.

## Answer

**Aravane Ltd**
**Statement of financial position at 1 May 2015**

| | $ | |
|---|---|---|
| **ASSETS** | | |
| **Non-current assets** | 685 000 | ($565 000 + $120 000) |
| **Current assets** | 57 000 | ($84 000 + $26 000 – $53 000) |
| **Total assets** | 742 000 | |
| **EQUITY AND LIABILITIES** | | |
| **Equity** | | |
| Ordinary shares of $1 each | 475 000 | ($400 000 + $75 000) |
| Retained earnings | 189 000 | |
| | 664 000 | |
| **Current liabilities** | 78 000 | ($60 000 + $18 000) |
| **Total equity and liabilities** | 742 000 | |

### Workings

Net assets of Borg Ltd = $128 000 (Aravane would not purchase the bank balance of Borg). The purchase consideration was $75 000 in shares and the balance $53 000 in cash.

The retained earnings are merely a book entry in Borg's books of account, so this does not feature in the 'new' statement of financial position.

---

The assets of the company being taken over are unlikely to be taken over at the book value shown in the company's statement of financial position, as in the previous worked example.

When the purchase price is greater than the value of the net assets being taken over then the excess represents a payment for goodwill.

**Worked example**

The following statements of financial position at 31 July 2014 are given:

| | Adelaide plc | Bradford Ltd |
|---|---|---|
| | $000 | $000 |
| **ASSETS** | | |
| **Non-current assets** | | |
| Premises | 2 700 | 200 |
| Plant and machinery | 1 200 | 150 |

| | | |
|---|---|---|
| Vehicles | 800 | 70 |
| Office equipment | 400 | 80 |
| | 5 100 | 500 |
| **Current assets** | | |
| Inventory | 65 | 20 |
| Trade receivables | 17 | 8 |
| Cash and cash equivalents | 24 | 7 |
| | 106 | 35 |
| **Total assets** | 5206 | 535 |
| **EQUITY AND LIABILITIES** | | |
| **Equity** | | |
| Ordinary shares of $1 each | 4000 | 300 |
| Retained earnings | 1 194 | 229 |
| | 5 194 | 529 |
| **Current liabilities** | | |
| Trade payables | 12 | 6 |
| **Total equity and liabilities** | 5206 | 535 |

Adelaide plc took over the assets of Bradford (except the cash and cash equivalents) on 1 August 2014 at the following values:

| | **$000** |
|---|---|
| Premises | 350 |
| Plant and machinery | 75 |
| Vehicles | 40 |
| Office equipment | 50 |
| Inventory | 18 |
| Trade receivables | 6 |

Adelaide settled the payables of Bradford Ltd.

The purchase consideration was $650 000, settled by the issue of 500 000 ordinary shares of $1 in Adelaide plc at a price of $1.25 each and the balance in cash.

**Required**

Prepare a statement of financial position for Adelaide plc at 1 August 2014 immediately after the acquisition of Bradford Ltd.

## Answer

**Adelaide plc**
**Statement of financial position at 1 August 2014**

| | **$000** | |
|---|---|---|
| **ASSETS** | | |
| **Non-current assets** | | |
| Goodwill | 117 | |
| Premises | 3050 | ($2 700 + $350) |
| Plant and machinery | 1 275 | ($1 200 + $75) |
| Vehicles | 840 | ($800 + $40) |
| Office equipment | 450 | ($400 + $50) |
| | 5 732 | |

| | | |
|---|---|---|
| **Current assets** | | |
| Inventory | 83 | ($65 + $18) |
| Trade receivables | 23 | ($17 + $6) |
| | 106 | |
| **Total assets** | 5838 | |
| **EQUITY AND LIABILITIES** | | |
| **Equity** | | |
| Ordinary shares of $1 each | 4500 | ($4000 + $500) |
| Share premium | 125 | |
| Retained earnings | 1194 | |
| | 5819 | |
| **Current liabilities** | | |
| Trade payables | 12 | |
| Cash and cash equivalents | 7 | ($24 - $25 - $6) |
| | 19 | |
| **Total equity and liabilities** | 5838 | |

**Note**

The value to Adelaide plc of the assets taken over was $539000 less payables of $6000, giving a net asset value of $533000.

Goodwill is therefore valued at $117000 (purchase consideration $650000 less $533000 value of net assets taken over).

| | | |
|---|---|---|
| Purchase consideration is made up of | $500000 | ordinary shares |
| | $125000 | premium on ordinary shares |
| | $25000 | cash |
| | $650000 | |

## 38.7 The acquisition of a shareholding in one limited company by another limited company

The directors of a company may purchase shares in another company as an investment, in much the same way as they may purchase any other security that would financially benefit their business.

**Worked example**

The following summarised information is given for two limited companies at 30 November 2014:

| | Sands plc | Beach plc |
|---|---|---|
| | $000 | $000 |
| **ASSETS** | | |
| **Non-current assets** | 54000 | 760 |
| **Current assets** | 1340 | 65 |
| **Total assets** | 55340 | 825 |

| | | |
|---|---|---|
| **EQUITY** | | |
| Ordinary shares of $1 each | 25 000 | 500 |
| Retained earnings | 30 340 | 325 |
| **Total equity** | 55 340 | 825 |

Before start of business on 1 December 2014, Sands plc purchased ordinary shares in Beach plc.

**Required**

Prepare statements of financial position for both limited companies to show the effects of Sands plc purchasing at par:

a 100 000 ordinary shares in Beach plc
b 251 000 ordinary shares in Beach plc
c all the ordinary shares in Beach plc.

## Answer

In each case the statement of financial position for Beach would remain the same as shown in the question. The only change that has taken place is the change in the ownership of the ordinary shares; this change would be recorded in Beach's register of members held at the company's registered office.

In the case of Sands plc the statement of financial position would show:

| | (a) | (b) | (c) |
|---|---|---|---|
| | $000 | $000 | $000 |
| **ASSETS** | | | |
| **Non-current assets** | | | |
| Other non-current assets | 54 000 | 54 000 | 54 000 |
| Ordinary shares in Beach plc | 100 | 251 | 500 |
| **Current assets** | 1 240 | 1 089 | 840 |
| **Total assets** | 55 340 | 55 340 | 55 340 |

The equity section of the statement of financial position would remain the same in all cases:

| | $000 |
|---|---|
| **Equity** | |
| Ordinary shares of $1 each | 25 000 |
| Retained earnings | 30 340 |
| **Total equity** | 55 340 |

**Example**

The answer shown above involved a purchase price of $1 per share in Beach plc.

Consider the statements of financial position if the purchase price per ordinary share had been:

a $1.10 per share
b $1.60 per share or
c $2.10 per share.

Then the total assets section would have read:

| Price per share | $1.10 | $1.60 | $2.10 |
|---|---|---|---|
| | $000 | $000 | $000 |
| **ASSETS** | | | |
| **Non-current assets** | | | |
| Other non-current assets | 54000 | 54000.00 | 54000 |
| Ordinary shares in Beach plc | 110 | 401.60 | 1050 |
| **Current assets** | 1230 | 938.40 | 290 |
| **Total assets** | 55340 | 55340.00 | 55340 |

Once again the equity section in each scenario would not change:

| EQUITY | $000 |
|---|---|
| Ordinary shares of $1 each | 25000 |
| Retained earnings | 30340 |
| **Total equity** | 55340 |

Company A may gain control of Company B by purchasing more than 50 per cent of ordinary shares in Company B.

In such a case, company A is known as the **holding company**, while Company B is known as the **subsidiary company**. If Company A owned all of the ordinary shares in Company B, then Company B would be a **wholly owned subsidiary**.

Take the example of Beach and Sands above.

- In example (a), the investment should be recorded as a non-current asset (until the final year of holding the investment when it would be classified as a current asset).
- In example (b), Beach plc should be regarded as a subsidiary company.
- In example (c), Beach plc would be a wholly owned subsidiary of Sands plc.

## Chapter summary

- Owners generally wish to combine businesses to gain greater financial benefits (i.e. a positive return on investment).
- Sole traders may combine their businesses to achieve this.
- When a limited company acquires another business the purchase consideration may be made up of cash, debentures or shares, or any combination of the three.
- Sole traders or partnerships may combine to achieve a greater return on investment.
- Unincorporated businesses may be purchased by a limited company for the same reason.
- Limited companies acquire the share capital or a proportion of the share capital in other limited companies for the return that the investment will yield.

# 39 Consignment accounts

## → Content

**1.3 Consignment and Joint venture accounts**

- Distinguish between consignments and joint ventures and the environment in which they operate
- Prepare ledger accounts for consignment transactions including the calculation of closing inventory valuation

**By the end of this chapter you should be able to:**

- understand the terms used in the preparation of consignment accounts
- prepare ledger accounts to record the consignment of goods to an agent
- calculate the value of inventories held by an agent at the end of an accounting period.

## 39.1 Consignment accounts

A **consignor** is the owner of goods sent to an agent.

A **consignee** collects, stores and sells goods on behalf of the consignor.

A consignment is the transfer of goods from the owner (**consignor**) to an agent (**consignee**), generally in another country. The agent is paid by means of a percentage based on the sale value of the goods involved. The title to the goods remains with the consignor until they are sold.

The agent collects the money generated from the sales of the consignor's goods and deducts his expenses and commission payable. The balance is then paid to the consignor.

**Worked example**

Ankir, an exporter based in South Africa, sends goods to Sim, her agent, in Kuala Lumpur.

Ankir purchased the goods for $1 000 on 1 April. She paid freight charges of $120. Sim incurred Malaysian import duties amounting to $235 and further expenses of $65. Sim sold the goods for $2 150. He deducted his expenses and his commission of 10 per cent of sales. Sim remitted the amount due to Ankir at the end of May.

**Required**

Prepare appropriate accounts in Ankir's books of account.

### Answer

**Consignment account – Sim**

| | $ | | $ |
|---|---|---|---|
| Goods on consignment | 1 000 | Sim – sales | 2 150 |
| Bank | 120 | | |
| Sim – import duties | 235 | | |
| Sim – other expenses | 65 | | |
| Sim – commission | 215 | | |
| Profit on consignment | 515 | | |
| | 2 150 | | 2 150 |

**Goods on consignment account**

| | $ | | $ |
|---|---|---|---|
| | | Consignment account – Sim | 1000 |

**Bank account**

| | $ | | $ |
|---|---|---|---|
| Sim | 1 635 | Consignment account – Sim | 120 |

**Profit on consignment account**

| | $ | | $ |
|---|---|---|---|
| | | Consignment account – Sim | 515 |

**Sim**

| | $ | | $ |
|---|---|---|---|
| Consignment account – sales | 2 150 | Consignment account – Sim (duties) | 235 |
| | | Consignment account – Sim (exports) | 65 |
| | | Consignment account – Sim (commission) | 215 |
| | | Bank account | 1 635 |
| | 2 150 | | 2 150 |

## 39.2 Commission

If a question gives the sales on the consignment after the deduction of the commission earned by the consignee, the amount of sales before deduction of commission must be determined for inclusion in the consignment account.

**Worked example**

Gruber makes sales of $4500 net of 7.5 per cent commission.

**Required**

Calculate the amount of sales before the commission was deducted.

### Workings

7.5 per cent of the sales value gives the commission earned.

The sales value divided by 0.925 (100% – 7.5%) will give the sales net of commission.

Sales before deduction of commission $4500 ÷ 0.925 (92.5%) = $4865.

Now try these calculations to determine sales from which the commission has been deducted:

| Sales after deduction of commission | Commission earned |
|---|---|
| $ | |
| 1 890 | 10% |
| 16 840 | 3% |
| 14 260 | 31% |

## Answer

Sales of $2100, $17 360 and $20 667.

# 39.3 Valuation of inventories remaining with an agent

At the end of a financial year it is quite possible that the whole consignment will not have been sold.

Inventory valuation will include the cost price of the goods sent to the agent plus any expenses incurred to get the goods into a saleable condition (see Chapters 8 and 20). These expenses can include import duties, freight charges, landing charges, etc. However, care must be taken to ensure that this expenditure relates only to the goods remaining unsold at the financial year end.

**Example**

800 units of a product costing $2.50 each have been despatched to an agent. Duties and landing charges amounting to $600 have been paid. At the financial year end 100 units remain unsold with the agent. The inventory is valued at $325 (cost $250 + 100 × $0.75).

**Worked example**

Chang, a trader in Hong Kong, sent a consignment of 450 units of his product to Umesh, an agent in Nepal. The goods had cost Chang $68 each; he also paid freight and insurance costs amounting to $360.

At Chang's financial year end Umesh had sold 380 units for $90 each. Umesh had paid landing charges $1 800, import duties of $675 and other direct expenses of $45. Umesh is paid 5 per cent commission on sales plus 2.5 per cent del credere commission. At the financial year end Umesh sent Chang $25 000.

A **del credere agent** is an agent who guarantees payment by a customer. For this guarantee the agent is paid an additional commission.

**Required**

Prepare:

a The consignment account in Chang's books of account.

b Umesh's account.

## Answer

**Consignment account – Umesh**

| | $ | | $ |
|---|---|---|---|
| Goods on consignment | 30 600 | Umesh – sales | 34 200 |
| Bank – freight and insurance | 360 | Balance c/d | 5 208* |
| Umesh – landing charges | 1 800 | | |
| Umesh – import duties | 675 | | |
| Umesh – other expenses | 45 | | |
| Umesh – basic commission | 1 710 | | |
| Umesh – del credere commission | 855 | | |
| Consignment profit | 3 363 | | |
| | 39 408 | | 39 408 |
| Balance b/d | 5 208 | | |

* This balance is made up of 70 units of the product unsold (cost $68 + freight and insurance $0.8 + landing charges $4 + import duties $1.50 + other direct expenses $0.10 so 70 units at $74.40 per unit).

**Umesh**

| | $ | | $ |
|---|---|---|---|
| Consignment account – sales | 34200 | Consignment account – landing charges | 1800 |
| | | Consignment account – import duties | 675 |
| | | Consignment account – other expenses | 45 |
| | | Consignment account – commission | 2565 |
| | | Bank | 25000 |
| | | Balance c/d | 4115 |
| | 34200 | | 34200 |
| Balance b/d | 4115 | | |

## Self-test questions

1 Import duties are always paid by the consignor. True/False?
2 A business can only make one consignment in any one financial year. True/False?
3 Explain the difference between a consignor and a consignee.
4 Explain the difference between an agent and a consignee.
5 Explain how the value of inventory at the end of an accounting period is calculated.
6 A quantity of 500 electrical generators are shipped to an overseas agent. The agent sells 400. Import duties amount to $1 500. Calculate the import duty that relates to the remaining inventory.
7 Explain the term 'del credere commission'.

➤ **Now try Questions 1 and 2.**

## Chapter summary

- A consignment is goods sent by the owner (the consignor) to an agent who then sells them on behalf of the consignor.
- The debit side of the consignment account records all expenditures incurred by both the consignor and his agent relating to the consignment.
- If the debits are greater than the credit entries then a loss has been incurred; if the credit side is the larger then the consignment has been profitable.
- Inventories held by an agent at a year end are valued; care must be taken in the determination of the cost of these goods. Only costs relating to the unsold goods are included in this valuation.

# 40 Joint venture accounts

## Content

### 1.3 Consignment and joint venture accounts

- Distinguish between consignments and joint ventures and the environment in which they operate
- Prepare ledger accounts for joint ventures
- Calculate the profit for joint ventures

**By the end of this chapter you should be able to:**

- explain why businesses undertake a joint venture
- prepare ledger accounts to record joint venture transactions
- calculate the profit or loss generated by a joint venture by preparing a joint venture memorandum account
- share the profit or loss and record the transfer of the cash settlement between the partners to the venture.

## 40.1 Joint ventures

A **joint venture** is a form of partnership formed to undertake one particular transaction that will be mutually beneficial to the parties involved.

Two or more parties may decide to form a temporary partnership in order to engage in a business opportunity.

A trader may be involved in a number of joint ventures at any one time with the same party or with several different parties. Each party to the venture opens a joint venture account which is debited with all expenditure undertaken in pursuit of the venture, i.e. payments for goods and other expenses. The account is credited with venture receipts.

This means that the full extent of all the transactions relating to the venture cannot be found in only one set of books of account. Each party to the joint venture only records the transactions that they have undertaken.

### Worked example

Selena and Micha enter into a joint venture. They both supply materials and sell the finished products. Profits are to be shared Selena two-thirds and Micha one-third.

| | | $ |
|---|---|---|
| Materials supplied | Selena | 3400 |
| | Micha | 2900 |
| Wages paid | Selena | 800 |
| | Micha | 1150 |
| Micha paid warehouse costs | | 315 |
| Micha paid delivery costs | | 199 |
| Other selling expenses paid | Selena | 238 |
| | Micha | 307 |
| Cash received from sales | Selena | 6780 |
| | Micha | 5220 |

**Required**

Prepare the entries relating to the joint venture in the books of account of:

a Selena

b Micha.

## Answer

a Selena's books of account

| Joint venture with Micha | | | |
|---|---|---|---|
| | $ | | $ |
| Purchases (materials) | 3400 | Cash (sales) | 6780 |
| Cash (wages) | 800 | | |
| Cash (selling expenses) | 238 | | |

b Micha's books of account

| Joint venture with Selena | | | |
|---|---|---|---|
| | $ | | $ |
| Purchases (materials) | 2900 | Cash (sales) | 5220 |
| Cash (wages) | 1150 | | |
| Cash (warehouse costs) | 315 | | |
| Cash (delivery costs) | 199 | | |
| Cash (selling expenses) | 307 | | |

Deal with each party to the joint venture separately. In the example shown, we first make the entries in Selena's books of account. When these entries have been completed we then make the entries in Micha's books.

The entries shown above are entered using basic double-entry principles.

In Selena's books of account there will be a credit entry in the purchases account in her general ledger for $3400; there will be two credit entries in her cash book for $800 and $238 and a debit entry amounting to $6780.

Micha's double entry would be completed with the following cash book entries: a debit entry of $5220 and credit entries of $1150, $315, $199 and $307. There would also be a credit entry in his purchases account of $2900.

## 40.2 Memorandum joint venture accounts

At this time each party is only aware of the transactions conducted by themselves. They are probably unaware of all the transactions undertaken by the other person involved in the venture. They will not know whether or not the venture has been profitable and the amount of cash to be transferred between them to settle the arrangement.

At this point the parties involved in the joint venture will supply the information regarding their transactions to the other party.

Each party merges all the information into a memorandum account. You will recall that memorandum accounts are not part of a double-entry system; they merely provide additional useful information.

The memorandum joint venture account is in reality an income statement for the venture. The account reveals the profit or loss generated by the venture. This profit or loss can then be shared in some pre-arranged ratio and entered in the partners' individual joint venture account which is then closed by cash transfers.

Example

**Selena and Micha memorandum joint venture account**

| | | $ | | $ |
|---|---|---|---|---|
| Purchases of materials | | 6300 | Sales | 12000 |
| Wages | | 1950 | | |
| Warehouse costs | | 315 | | |
| Delivery costs | | 199 | | |
| Selling expenses | | 545 | | |
| Venture profit | | | | |
| Selena | 1794 | | | |
| Micha | 897 | 2691 | | |
| | | 12000 | | 12000 |

Now that the parties know the profit earned it can be entered in their own joint venture accounts. This will determine how much cash needs to be transferred between the parties to draw the venture to a close.

In Selena's books of account:

**Joint venture with Micha**

| | $ | | $ |
|---|---|---|---|
| Materials | 3400 | Sales | 6780 |
| Wages | 800 | | |
| Expenses | 238 | | |
| Share of profit (transferred to Selena's income statement) | 1794 | | |
| | 6232 | | |
| Cash paid to Micha | 548 | | |
| | 6780 | | 6780 |

In Micha's books of account:

**Joint venture with Selena**

| | $ | | $ |
|---|---|---|---|
| Materials | 2900 | Sales | 5220 |
| Wages | 1150 | | |
| Warehouse costs | 315 | | |
| Delivery costs | 199 | | |
| Expenses | 307 | | |
| Share of profit (transferred to Micha's income statement) | 897 | Cash received from Selena | 548 |
| | 5768 | | 5768 |

Being part of a joint venture does not guarantee that the venture will be profitable, although parties to the venture obviously wish it to be so. Should a loss arise after the venture is wound up this would be borne by the parties in the agreed 'profit' sharing ratios.

A shared loss may not altogether be what the parties would have wished but the venture may lead to a more profitable venture in the future or even increase trade in their day-to-day course of business.

## Self-test questions

1 Joint ventures can only be entered into by joint stock companies. True/False?
2 How many parties can be involved in a joint venture?
3 Explain the difference between a joint venture and a partnership.
4 A joint venture can only be entered into by people living in different countries. True/False?

➤ **Now try Question 1.**

## Chapter summary

- Joint ventures are short-term partnerships lasting for one particular business opportunity for the parties involved.
- Each party to the venture records only their own transactions involved in the venture.
- The parties concerned merge their records of the venture in a memorandum account to determine the profit (or loss) earned when the venture is completed.
- The profit (or loss) is shared between the parties in an agreed ratio.
- The profit (or loss) is entered into the joint venture accounts to calculate the cash transfers required to terminate the venture.
- The profit or loss is posted to the income statement of each of the parties.

# 41 Computerised accounting systems

## Content

### 1.4 Computerised accounting systems

- Understand the need for and be able to discuss the process of computerising the accounts of a business
- Discuss the advantages and disadvantages of introducing a computerised accounting system
- Discuss the process of computerising the business accounts
- Discuss ways in which the integrity of the accounting data can be ensured during the transfer to a computerised system

**By the end of this chapter you should be able to:**

- explain the need to computerise an accounting system
- discuss the advantages and disadvantages that occur when a computerised system is introduced into a business
- explain the process of computerising an accounting system
- describe ways that ensure the integrity of a computerised system.

## 41.1 Why computerise a system of record keeping?

The business world is becoming increasingly competitive with each passing year and changing at a pace never before seen. Businesses today are competing in a global economy and to cope with these pressures managers need to take full advantage of all aspects of information technology. It has been said that 'information is one of the most important resources' that managers have. This information includes records of the activities of all stakeholders – customers, suppliers and staff – and how the business deals with them through its activities that involve inventory, payroll, etc. Customers and suppliers expect a business to be efficient. Managers need to react to stakeholder requirements quickly and efficiently, so reaction time is of the essence. Information technology (IT) makes relevant and detailed data available at the click of a mouse.

Nearly all managers of businesses that use a double-entry system of recording financial transactions will use a computer in some, if not all, parts of their business.

As the use of computers has increased in all kinds and sizes of business, the use of handwritten entries in the accounting system has steadily decreased; paper documents have given way to onscreen documents and computer printouts.

The underlying system of accounting remains unaltered but the speed at which information is processed and made available to users has greatly increased. In any accounting system all transactions have a 'knock on effect'; all transactions are interrelated and interdependent and an efficient computerised accounting system will provide useful feedback to management and staff.

A good IT system of computerised accounting will allow all levels of management to:

- create plans
- put those plans into practice
- control activities
- evaluate outcomes so that adjustments to the business can be made and any errors can be rectified quickly.

A computerised accounting system provides managers with instant and up-to-date reliable information in real time that can be used to plan and control the business, allowing prompt decision making. Information obtained from the computerised accounting system can be used to help guide and control business policy.

## 41.2 Spreadsheets

A spreadsheet is a table of cells (boxes) arranged in rows and columns in which text and figures are entered. The computer works out any calculations that need to be made. Managers and staff at all levels can use spreadsheets for a variety of tasks.

The major advantage of using a spreadsheet is that if any figures are adjusted all other figures affected are changed automatically. For example, 'What would happen to all other parts of the business if sales were to increase by seven per cent?' Changing this one variable would stimulate automatic recalculation of changes in all related areas.

## 41.3 Benefits to staff of using a computerised accounting system

### 41.3.1 Senior managers

Senior managers use the accounting information for strategic planning purposes. They will use the system to access regular updated trial balances, income statements and statements of financial position, enabling them to see whether strategic plans are on track or if adjustments need to be made. They can also make use of budgeting programs which allow them to consider 'what if …' changes to strategy.

A computerised system with its automatic updating of all records means that all general ledger accounts show the current position, enabling managers to judge whether strategic goals are being achieved. If they are not then modifications to strategy can take place very quickly.

Quick access to general ledger accounts makes changes to asset management (both non-current and liquid) more appropriate in a fast-changing economic climate. The progress of individual projects is easily monitored. Senior management can use spreadsheets to prepare strategic budgets and to prepare income statements and statements of financial position, etc.

### 41.3.2 Middle managers

**Middle managers** use the computerised accounting system to control the business and ensure that the business as a whole is achieving the goals that will contribute to and help achieve overall strategic goals. They will use the system to monitor receivables and inventories and to gain up-to-date information regarding all aspects of human resource management, including payroll and vacation times. All aspects of the businesses bank account is readily available, including receipts from customers and payments to settle payables. Information regarding the computerised accounting system's compliance with IASs can be programmed into the system. Spreadsheets can be used for monitoring cash flow forecasts, enabling overdraft facilities to be arranged if necessary, while payroll issues can also be resolved by use of spreadsheets.

### 41.3.3 Administrative staff

Administrative staff will use a computerised system to record all accounting methods used and to enable instant scrutiny of any part of the accounting system. Spreadsheets can be used to produce invoices, calculate costs and prepare customer quotes, etc.

## 41.4 Advantages of introducing a computerised accounting system

- **Speed**: Data entry into the system can be carried out much more quickly than if done manually. One entry can be processed into a multitude of different areas. For example one entry can be made that will simultaneously update a customer's account, sales account in the general (nominal) ledger and inventory records.
- **Accuracy**: Provided that the original entry is correct there are fewer areas where an error can be made since only one entry is necessary to provide the data that is replicated throughout the system.
- **Automatic document production**: Fast and accurate invoices and credit notes are produced and processed in the appropriate sections of the system.
- **Availability of information**: Accounting records are automatically updated once information is keyed in. This information is then readily available to anyone within the organisation who requires it.
- **Taxation returns**: Information required by tax authorities is available at the touch of a button.
- **Legibility**: Data are always legible, whether shown on screen or as a printout. This reduces the possibility of errors caused by poor handwriting.
- **Efficiency**: Time saved may mean that staff resources can be put to better use in other areas of the business.
- **Staff motivation**: Since staff require training to acquire the necessary skills to use a computerised accounting system, their career and promotion prospects are enhanced, both within their current role and for future employment. Some staff may benefit from increased responsibility, job satisfaction and pay.

## 41.5 Disadvantages of introducing a computerised accounting system

- **Hardware costs**: The initial costs of installing a computerised accounting system can be expensive. Once the decision has been made to install a system, the hardware will inevitably need to be updated and replaced on a regular basis, leading to further costs.
- **Software costs**: Accounting software needs to be kept up to date. Investment in software therefore requires a long-term financial commitment.
- **Staff training**: Staff will need training to use the software and training updates each time the system is modified.
- **Opposition from staff**: Some staff may feel demotivated at the prospect of using a computerised system. Other members of staff may fear that the introduction of a new system will lead to staff redundancies, which could include them. Changing to a computerised system can cause disruption in the workplace and changes to existing working practices may make staff feel uneasy.
- **Inputting errors**: Staff can become complacent because inputting into the system becomes more repetitive and therefore they may lose concentration which can lead to input errors.
- **Damage to health**: There are many cases of reported health hazards to staff working long hours at a computer terminal. The health issues range from repetitive strain injuries through to backache and headaches.

- **Back-up requirements**: All work entered into the computerised accounting system must be backed up regularly in case there is a failure of the system. Much work has to be printed out on paper as a back-up, so hard copies might require further expenditure on secure storage facilities.
- **Security breaches**: There is always a danger that computer hackers might try to breach the security of the accounting system while others may try to gain access to hard copy. Some might argue that a computerised system makes staff fraud simpler to achieve. A computer system that communicates with outside agencies such as customers, suppliers and government agencies means there is always the danger of infection from software viruses. Robust anti-virus protection and firewalls will need to be put in place to protect sensitive and important data.

## 41.6 Computerising the records

### 41.6.1 Accounting packages

Small or medium-sized businesses may purchase an 'off-the-shelf' accounting package to aid the recording of transactions particular to their own business needs. The complexity of such packages varies according to the individual needs of the business, with some being used to carry out functions such as invoicing or complete payroll activities. Others are used to provide management with instant reports of the state of the business.

Larger, more complex businesses will require bespoke packages 'tailored' to their own individual business needs.

Whatever accounting package is chosen, all are designed to be easy to use. They are also integrated, which means that the input of one transaction is recorded simultaneously in all the appropriate accounting records. For example, when the receipt of an invoice from a supplier is keyed into the system, all ledger entries are made instantly:

- the supplier's account in the purchases ledger is credited
- the purchases account in the general ledger is debited
- inventory records show an increase in goods held.

When the supplier is paid:

- the bank account is credited
- the supplier's account is debited.

### 41.6.2 Moving from a manual to a computerised system

When a computerised accounting system is first installed great care must be taken to ensure that the transition from manual records to computer records is smooth and accurate. The opening entries in the computerised system should be double checked by different members of staff. The check can take the form of, say, a manually prepared control account which is then compared with a printout; clearly the two should match. Similarly, a manually prepared trial balance can be compared to a trial balance extracted from the computer.

A system of protective devices (firewalls, virus protection, etc.) must also be introduced into the system.

Each member of staff should have a unique password allowing access to their area(s) of responsibility within the system.

## Self-test questions

1 Explain two disadvantages of using a computerised accounting system to record financial transactions.
2 Explain two advantages of using a computerised accounting package to prepare a production budget.
3 Outline advantages to members of staff who will be required to use a computerised accounting system.
4 A spreadsheet can only be used in very large businesses. True/False?
5 Explain what is meant by the term 'what if'.
6 Explain how a middle manager might use a spreadsheet.

➤ Now try Questions 1 and 2.

## Chapter summary

- Computerised accounting packages are increasingly being used by business, both large and small, to achieve the efficiency and effectiveness required by the modern business world.
- The advantages of using a system include speed, accuracy and the ability to produce detailed information about the state of the business at the touch of a button. The disadvantages include cost, both in terms of investment in hardware and software and also in terms of staff training and the impact on staff that the introduction of such a system may have on morale.
- The change from a manual system to a computerised system should be smooth and methodical, to reduce the possibility of errors being introduced into the system.
- Care must be taken to ensure the safety of information stored electronically by the use of appropriate virus protection software and use of staff passwords.

# 42 Investment and other ratios

## Content

### 1.5 Analysis and communication of accounting information

- Understand the need for the analysis of financial data to aid decision making by potential investors in a business
- Calculate the following ratios:
  - working capital cycle (in days)
  - net working assets to revenue (sales)
  - income gearing
  - gearing ratio
  - earnings per share
  - price earnings ratio
  - dividend yield
  - dividend cover
  - dividend per share
- Analyse and evaluate the results of the ratios and draw conclusions
- Make appropriate recommendations to potential investors on the basis of the analysis undertaken
- Evaluate the interrelationships between ratios

**By the end of this chapter you should be able to:**

- understand the reasons for converting financial information into ratios
- be aware of the need and use that potential investors have for the stock exchange (investment) ratios
- calculate and comment on:
  - the working capital cycle
  - net working assets to sales ratio
  - income gearing
  - gearing ratio
- calculate and comment on the investment ratios:
  - earnings per share (EPS)
  - price earnings ratio (P/E)
  - dividend yield
  - dividend cover
  - dividend paid per share.

Shareholders, generally, have invested in a limited company to gain a return on their investment. They are also interested in the market value of their shares.

Before ordinary shareholders are able to receive any return on their investment, the providers of long-term loans (debenture holders) and preference shareholders need to be rewarded.

- Debenture holders must receive their interest, however profitable or unprofitable the company has been.
- The preference shareholders are entitled to dividends (provided there are sufficient profits) before ordinary shareholders.

Information from the financial statements of Oyan Magenta from Chapter 27 is given. Data in the following sections will be based on this information:

**Oyan Magenta & Co.**
**Statements of financial position**

| | at 31 March 2015 | | at 31 March 2014 | |
|---|---|---|---|---|
| | **$000** | **$000** | **$000** | **$000** |
| **ASSETS** | | | | |
| **Non-current assets** at carrying amount | | 3063 | | 1800 |
| **Current assets:** | | | | |
| Inventories | 120 | | 110 | |
| Trade receivables | 240 | | 220 | |
| Cash and cash equivalents | 140 | 500 | 570 | 900 |
| **Total assets** | | 3563 | | 2700 |
| **EQUITY AND LIABILITIES** | | | | |
| **Equity** | | | | |
| Ordinary shares of $1 | | 1500 | | 1500 |
| 6% Preference shares | | 100 | | 100 |
| Retained earnings | | 849 | | 595 |
| | | 2449 | | 2195 |
| **Non-current liabilities** | | | | |
| 8% debentures | | 800 | | 200 |
| **Current liabilities** | | | | |
| Trade payables | | 169 | | 154 |
| Taxation | | 145 | | 151 |
| | | 314 | | 305 |
| **Total equity and liabilities** | | 3563 | | 2700 |

**Extract from statement of changes in equity for the year ended 31 March 2015**

| | **$000** |
|---|---|
| **Retained earnings** | |
| Balance 1 April 2014 | 595 |
| Profit for the year | 309 |
| | 904 |
| Dividends paid | (55) |
| Balance 31 March 2015 | 849 |

## Additional information

| | **2015** | **2014** |
|---|---|---|
| | **$** | **$** |
| Profit for the year after tax and preference dividends | 309000 | 287000 |
| Debenture interest paid during the year | 40000 | 16000 |
| Market price per share | 1.70 | 1.50 |
| **Dividends paid during the year** | | |
| Preference shares | 6000 | 6000 |
| Ordinary shares | 55000 | 48000 |

## Results from Chapter 27

| | 2015 | 2014 |
|---|---|---|
| Sales | $2600000 | $2000000 |
| Profit from operations | $500000 | $460000 |
| Trade receivables turnover | 34 days | 41 days |
| Trade payables turnover | 43 days | 46 days |
| Inventory turnover | 29 days | 30 days |

## 42.1 Working capital cycle

This ratio calculates the time taken between a business making payment for goods received and the receipt of cash from customers for the sale of the goods. The shorter the time between the business laying out cash for the purchase of goods and the collection of cash for the sales of the goods, the better for the business, since less finance from other sources is needed.

**Formula**

**Working capital cycle = Trade receivables turnover + Inventory turnover − Trade payables turnover**

| **2015** | **2014** |
|---|---|
| 34 + 29 − 43 = 20 days | 41 + 30 − 46 = 25 days |

In both years the ratios seem acceptable. There has been a slight improvement of the situation. Although receivables and inventory turnovers are moving in the right direction, for some reason the company is paying its payables some 3 days faster! The shorter the cycle, the lower the value of working capital needed to be financed from other sources.

The cycle can be shortened by:

- reducing levels of inventories held
- speeding up collection of monies from receivables
- delaying payment to payables.

## 42.2 Net working assets to sales

This calculation shows the proportion of sales revenue that is tied up in the less liquid net current assets; in other words, the value of the net working assets that is not immediately available for use in the business.

**Formula**

**Net working assets = Inventories + Trade receivables − Trade payables**

$$\text{Net working assets to revenue (sales)} = \frac{\text{Inventories + Trade receivables − Trade payables}}{\text{Sales}} \times 100$$

**2015**

$$\frac{120 + 240 - 169}{2600} \times 100 = 7.35\%$$

**2014**

$$\frac{110 + 220 - 154}{2000} \times 100 = 8.8\%$$

This shows that the proportion of net current assets held in a non-cash form is low. There has been a slight improvement over the two years under consideration.

## 42.3 Income gearing

Income gearing shows the ratio of interest paid on borrowings expressed as a percentage of profit from operations.

**Formula**

$$\text{Income gearing} = \frac{\text{Interest charges}}{\text{Profit from operations}} \times 100$$

**2015**

$$\frac{40\,000}{500\,000} \times 100 = 8\%$$

**2014**

$$\frac{16\,000}{460\,000} \times 100 = 3.48\%$$

Both ratios are low – interest is easily covered by profits. However, in the second year the income gearing has increased by more than half due to the increased debenture interest. Debentures have risen from $200 000 to $800 000, so a full year's interest next year will be $64 000, which could increase the income gearing even more.

## 42.4 Gearing ratio

**Gearing** is the relationship that exists between fixed cost capital and total capital.

The ordinary shareholders' return may be at risk if the company's capital is provided mainly by debenture holders and preference shareholders.

The degree of risk is measured by the gearing ratio.

So:

**Formula**

$$\text{Gearing ratio} = \frac{\text{Fixed cost capital}}{\text{Total capital}} = \frac{\text{Non-current liabilities + Issued preference share capital}}{\text{Non-current liabilities + Issued preference shares + Issued ordinary shares + All reserves}}$$

**2015**

$$\frac{800 + 100}{800 + 100 + 1500 + 849} = \frac{900 \times 100}{3249} = 27.7\%$$

**2014**

$$\frac{200 + 100}{200 + 100 + 1500 + 595} = \frac{300 \times 100}{2395} = 12.5\%$$

The gearing of a company is said to be:
- **high** when the ratio is more than 50 per cent
- **neutral** when the ratio is 50 per cent
- **low** when the ratio is less than 50 per cent.

High geared means:
- high borrowing
- high debt
- high risk

while low geared means:
- low borrowing
- low debt
- low risk.

In the first year, 2014, 12.5 per cent of total capital employed was provided by people other than ordinary shareholders. In the second year, 2015, the company became more highly geared: 27.7 per cent of capital employed was provided by people other than the ordinary shareholders. The company became more highly geared but on our measure it remained a low-geared company; 72.3 per cent of capital employed was provided by the ordinary shareholders.

Investment in a highly geared company is more of a risk than an investment in a low-geared company because if the company is unable to service its long-term liabilities then it may be forced into liquidation by those long-term investors.

It follows that a highly geared company may find it difficult to borrow further funds because of the inherent risk. Banks may also be reluctant to lend to highly geared companies since they may feel that the ordinary shareholders should be prepared to finance their own company rather than rely on 'outsiders'.

# 42.5 Investment ratios

Investment ratios are primarily of interest to those who are contemplating an investment in a business by purchasing ordinary shares.

**Earnings** are profit for the year after taxation and preference dividends; that is, earnings that belong totally to the ordinary shareholders.

The calculation uses the *numbers* of ordinary shares issued, not the value. So \$2 000 000 ordinary shares of 25 cents each would use 8 000 000 as the denominator in the calculation.

## 42.5.1 Earnings per share

In year 2014: Earnings are \$309 000 profit for the year after taxation and preference dividends, that is, profits available for ordinary shareholders

In year 2015 : Earnings are \$319 000 profit for the year after taxation and preference dividends, that is, profits available for ordinary shareholders

**Formula**

$$\text{Earnings per share} = \frac{\text{Profit after taxation and preference dividends in cents}}{\text{Number of ordinary shares}}$$

| 2015 | 2014 |
|---|---|
| $\frac{30\,900\,000}{1\,500\,000} = 20.6$ cents | $\frac{28\,700\,000}{1\,500\,000} = 19.1$ cents |

The earnings per share (EPS) increased in the second year. It improved by 1.5 cents per share.

## 42.5.2 Price earnings ratio

The price earnings (P/E) ratio relates the market price of the share to the earnings per share. It represents the number of years' earnings that investors are prepared to pay to purchase one of the company's shares.

The higher the P/E ratio, the greater the confidence investors have in the future of the company.

**Formula**

$$\text{Price earnings ratio} = \frac{\text{Market price per share}}{\text{Earnings per share}}$$

| 2015 | 2014 |
|---|---|
| $\frac{\$1.70}{20.6 \text{ cents}} = 8.25$ | $\frac{\$1.50}{19.1 \text{ cents}} = 7.85$ |

Investors are more confident at 31 March 2015 than they were a year earlier. They are paying 8.25 times the earnings to acquire shares in Oyan Magenta plc.

Since the ratio compares current market price with earnings per share, an increase in market price will increase the ratio. Demand for shares is dependent on investors' perception of the company's future performance. An increase in demand for the shares will generally cause an increase in the share price. A high P/E ratio will indicate expected future growth (or an overvalued share). A low P/E ratio indicates expected poor performance in the future (or an undervalued share).

### 42.5.3 Dividend yield

Shareholders invest in a company in order to gain a return (dividends) on their investment (they also hope that the market price of the share will rise so that if they sell their holding they will make a capital profit – a capital gain).

The dividend yield expresses the actual dividend received by the shareholder as a percentage of the market price of the share. It shows the actual percentage return an investor can expect based on the current market price of the shares.

**Formula**

$$\text{Dividend yield} = \frac{\text{Dividend paid and proposed}}{\text{Market price of share}}$$

| **2015** | **2014** |
|---|---|
| $\frac{55\,000 \times 100}{2\,550\,000} = 2.16\%$ | $\frac{48\,000 \times 100}{2\,250\,000} = 2.13\%$ |

The dividend yield is still low but has increased slightly in the second year.

Another version of the formula is:

**Formula**

$$\text{Declared rate of dividend} \times \frac{\text{Nominal value of ordinary shares}}{\text{Market price of ordinary shares}}$$

### 42.5.4 Dividend cover

This ratio indicates how likely it is that the company can continue to pay its current rate of ordinary share dividend in the future.

A high figure is good since it suggests that the company should be able to maintain dividends to ordinary shareholders at the current level even if profits fall. It may indicate that the directors operate a conservative dividend policy and that much of the profits are being reinvested in the company.

Low dividend cover may indicate a reckless dividend policy and that a small reduction in company profits may have an adverse effect on dividends in future.

**Formula**

$$\text{Dividend cover} = \frac{\text{Profits available to pay ordinary dividends}}{\text{Ordinary dividend paid}}$$

| **2015** | **2014** |
|---|---|
| $\frac{309\,000}{55\,000} = 5.62$ times | $\frac{287\,000}{48\,000} = 5.98$ times |

Both are quite high but the second year shows a slight deterioration. Although profits have increased (7.7 per cent), the dividend paid has increased by a greater percentage (14.6 per cent). Is this a sign of a change in dividend policy?

### 42.5.5 Dividend paid per share

This indicates how much dividend was paid for each ordinary share held.

**Formula**

$$\text{Dividend per share} = \frac{\text{Ordinary dividend paid}}{\text{Number of issued ordinary shares}}$$

Always indicate whether the answer to your calculations is a percentage (%) or numbers of days, cents, times, etc. If you do not, you are not showing work to your best potential.

| **2015** | **2014** |
|---|---|
| $\frac{55\,000}{1\,500\,000} = 3.67$ cents | $\frac{48\,000}{1\,500\,000} = 3.2$ cents |

The amount of dividend received per share by each ordinary shareholder improved by 14.7 per cent to 3.67 cents per share held.

**Self-test questions**

1 How is the working capital cycle calculated?
2 Gearing shows how much long-term finance a limited company needs. True/False?
3 Sales ÷ Number of shares = Earnings per share. True/False?
4 A limited company has issued ordinary share capital \$100 000; preference shares \$50 000; reserves \$120 000; debentures \$70 000. This company is highly geared.
True/False?
5 A limited company has an issued ordinary capital of \$200 000. Each share was issued a number of years ago for \$0.25. The total dividend paid for the year is \$56 000. The current market price is \$0.70 per share. Calculate the dividend yield.
6 What is meant by an investment ratio?

➤ Now try Questions 1–5.

**Chapter summary**

- There are ratios to be considered in addition to those met in Chapter 27. They are:
  - the working capital cycle, which gives an indication of the time taken between paying for goods and receiving cash from the sales of those goods
  - the net working assets to sales ratio, which shows net current assets other than cash as a proportion of sales revenue
  - income gearing, which shows the ratio of interest paid as a percentage of profit from operations
  - gearing ratio, which indicates how reliant a business is on outside finance.
- The investment ratios are mainly used by potential investors to determine whether an investment should be made in the company. They are:
  - earnings per share – the amount of profit attributable to each ordinary share
  - price earnings ratio – the number of years' earnings that an investor is prepared to pay to purchase one share
  - dividend yield – what the dividends received by the shareholder are, expressed as a percentage of the price paid for the share
  - dividend cover – how many times the current dividend could have been paid out of profit
  - dividend paid per share – the actual dividend paid on one ordinary share held.

# 43 Activity based costing

**➔ Content**

**2.1 Activity based costing (ABC)**

- Understand and discuss the application of activity based costing and identify and explain its uses and limitations
- Use ABC to apportion overheads; calculate the total cost of a unit; calculate the value of inventory; demonstrate the effect of different methods of overhead absorption on profit
- Apply ABC costing techniques to make business decisions and recommendations using supporting data

**By the end of the chapter you should be able to:**

- define the terms used in an activity based costing system
- allocate appropriate overheads to cost drivers
- calculate activity cost driver rates
- absorb direct and indirect costs into a product
- calculate a selling price after the absorption of all costs
- identify the advantages and disadvantages of using an activity based costing system.

## 43.1 Activity as a basis for apportioning overheads

The use of the absorption methods already considered in Chapter 28 assumes that all factory overheads are linked to that particular method of absorption. However, closer examination of the causes of activities that cause costs will allow a more accurate method of absorption.

CIMA defines **activity based costing** as 'cost attribution to cost units on the basis of benefit received from indirect activities (i.e. overheads that cannot be allocated to a particular product or process.)'

Activity based costing is an attempt to absorb factory overhead costs more accurately than the alternative methods of absorption that use labour hours or machine hours as a basis.

Each activity that drives (generates) the cost is analysed in detail. The cost incurred is then absorbed according to the number of times the activity is performed in the time period under review.

**Cost drivers** are activities undertaken in each department; they are activities that are part of the process of making a product.

If a number of overheads are incurred it follows that a number of absorption rates will need to be calculated.

The costs of running each department are analysed and each separate activity (or **cost driver**) is totalled into **cost pools**. Cost pools can attract the cost of an activity that 'bridges' a number of different departments. The number of times that each activity is performed is totalled.

**Cost pools** are accounts that collect the costs incurred by each activity.

The cost of each activity can then be calculated:

$$\frac{\text{Cost of activity}}{\text{Number of times that activity is performed}}$$

The result can then be determined if a product requires multiple performances.

## 43.2 Stages in using an activity based costing system

The stages of an activity based costing system are:

1 Record and classify all costs
2 Identify the activities producing the overhead cost
3 Identify cost drivers
4 Apportion appropriate overheads to the cost drivers
5 Calculate the cost driver rate
6 Absorb both indirect and direct costs into the product or service.

**Worked example**

Biolop incurred the following costs:

| | $ |
|---|---|
| Machinery set-up | 7452 |
| Ordering costs | 6000 |
| Quality control | 1972 |
| Selling expenses | 7225 |

Product selling price is based on cost plus 30 per cent.

**Additional information**

| | Product A | Product B | Product C |
|---|---|---|---|
| Direct materials | $10000 | $3000 | $9000 |
| Direct labour | $12000 | $15000 | $4000 |
| Number of machine set-ups | 30 | 16 | 8 |
| Number of purchase orders | 3000 | 1000 | 2000 |
| Number of quality inspections | 20 | 18 | 30 |
| Number of sales | 4000 | 3500 | 1000 |
| Number of products produced | 5000 | 3000 | 900 |

**Required**

Calculate:

a The activity-cost driver rate
b Overheads per product
c Total cost per product
d Selling price for each product.

### Answer

a

| Activity | Machine set-ups | Ordering | Quality control | Selling expenses |
|---|---|---|---|---|
| Cost ($) | 7452 | 6000 | 1972 | 7225 |
| Cost driver | 54 | 6000 | 68 | 8500 |
| Cost driver rate | $138.00 | $1.00 | $29.00 | $0.85 |

b

| | Machine set-ups | Ordering | Quality control | Selling expenses |
|---|---|---|---|---|
| A | 30 × $138 = $4140 | 3000 × $1 = $3000 | 20 × $29 = $580 | 4000 × $0.85 = $3400 |
| B | 16 × $138 = $2208 | 1000 × $1 = $1000 | 18 × $29 = $522 | 3500 × $0.85 = $2975 |
| C | 8 × $138 = $1104 | 2000 × $1 = $2000 | 30 × $29 = $870 | 1000 × $0.85 = $850 |

Total overheads:

**A** $11 120 ($4 140 + $3 000 + $580 + $3 400)

**B** $6705 ($2 208 + $1 000 + $522 + $2975)

**C** $4824 ($1 104 + $2 000 + $870 + $850)

c

| | Product A | Product B | Product C |
|---|---|---|---|
| | $ | $ | $ |
| Allocated direct costs – | | | |
| materials | 10 000 | 3 000 | 9 000 |
| labour | 12 000 | 15 000 | 4 000 |
| Apportioned overheads | 11 120 | 6 705 | 4 824 |
| Total cost | 33 120 | 24 705 | 17 824 |

d The selling price can be determined by using the total costs from (c) or by using the unit costs.

Using **total costs** $33 120 × 1.3 (mark-up) = $43 056 for 5000 units of A

Selling price per unit of product A = $8.61 ($43 056 ÷ 5000)

Total costs $24 705 × 1.3 = $32 117 for 3000 units of B

Selling price per unit of product B = $10.71 ($32 117 ÷ 3000)

Total costs $17 824 × 1.3 = $23 171 for 900 units of product C

Selling price per unit of product C = $25.75 ($23 171 ÷ 900)

Using **unit costs** for each product:

| | Product A | Product B | Product C |
|---|---|---|---|
| | $ | $ | $ |
| Direct materials | 2.00 | 1.00 | 10.00 |
| Direct labour | 2.40 | 5.00 | 4.44 |
| Prime cost | 4.40 | 6.00 | 14.44 |
| Overheads | 2.22 | 2.24 | 5.36 |
| Total cost per unit | 6.62 | 8.24 | 19.80 |
| Mark-up | 1.99 | 2.47 | 5.94 |
| Selling price per unit | 8.61 | 10.71 | 25.74 |

## 43.3 Advantages of using an activity based costing system

A system of activity based costing allows managers to:

- provide more accurate costing information
- identify where and understand how overheads arise
- set bench marks for planning and control purposes
- improve performance by replicating good practice identified in one department across other departments
- help in the preparation of estimates and quotes for other work
- identify individual products or services that are unprofitable or overpriced.

## 43.4 Limitations of applying an activity based system of apportioning overheads

Some of the limitations of an activity based cost system are that some overhead costs cannot be assigned to a cost pool, for example the CEO's salary or factory depreciation. Implementing a system of ABC is also a costly process because of its complexity.

### Self-test questions

1 Explain the difference between allocating costs and apportioning costs.
2 A business produces 850 units of a product. Allocated direct costs – materials \$10 000; labour \$2000; apportioned overheads \$1175. Calculate the cost of producing one unit of the product.
3 The allocation of overheads using labour hours is a much more accurate method of apportioning overheads than using machine hours. Do you agree?
4 ABC method of apportioning overheads stands for 'A Better Cost method' of apportioning overheads. True/False?
5 Cost drivers and cost pools are different descriptions for the same activity. True/False?
6 Cost of ordering materials \$400; number of purchase orders 200. Calculate the cost driver rate per order.

➤ Now try Question 1.

### Chapter summary

- ABC allocates costs according to how those costs are actually consumed.
- It is argued that ABC allocates costs in a more accurate way by identifying the activities that drive each overhead.
- Cost drivers measure the use of each overhead in shared activities.
- ABC links cost recovery to cost behaviour.
- When the activity cost driver rate is calculated the rate can then be allocated more accurately.

# 44 Budgeting and budgetary control

## Content

### 2.2 Budgeting and budgetary control

- Understand the need for and benefits of a budgetary control system to an organisation
- Discuss the advantages and disadvantages of a budgetary control system to an organisation
- Prepare the following budgets: sales; production; purchases; labour; trade receivables; trade payables; cash; master budget
- Recognise the effect of limiting factors on the preparation of budgets
- Prepare a flexed budget statement
- Identify and explain the causes of differences between actual and flexed budgets
- Make business decisions and recommendations using supporting data
- Discuss the behavioural aspects of budgeting

**By the end of this chapter you should be able to:**

- understand the need for budgeting
- explain the benefits of budgets and budgetary control
- explain the limitations of budgeting and budgetary control
- prepare: sales budgets; production budgets; purchases budgets; labour budgets; trade receivables budgets; trade payables budgets; cash budgets; master budgets (budgeted income statements and budgeted statements of financial position)
- explain the need to flex a budget
- prepare a flexed budget statement
- calculate variances that arise when actual performance data is available.

## 44.1 Sales budgets

The sales budget is generally the first budget to be prepared, because most businesses are sales led. It shows predicted sales and the revenues that are expected to be generated from the sales for the budget period.

Once the sales budget has been drawn up, the other budgets can be prepared using the information from the sales budget. If the sales budget is inaccurate, these inaccuracies will filter through and make the other budgets inaccurate too.

The sales budget will be based on sales forecasts for the budget period.

Sales budgets are difficult to prepare because there are so many variables that are out of the control of the managers who will prepare the budget.

These variables could include:

- actions of potential customers – e.g. customers changing to or from other suppliers
- actions of competitors – e.g. competitors increasing or decreasing their price and/or output
- the state of the economy – e.g. cycles of 'boom' and 'bust'
- government action – e.g. changes in levels of taxation; changes in government spending; imposition of trade sanctions.

**Worked example**

Zaid produces one type of machine, the ZT/103. The expected sales for the machine for the three months ending 31 March are:

| | January | February | March |
|---|---|---|---|
| Budgeted sales | 10 | 12 | 13 |
| Expected selling price per machine | $2 100 | $2 100 | $2 150 |

**Required**

Prepare a sales budget for the three months ending 31 March.

### Answer

**Sales budget for the three months ending 31 March**

| | January | February | March |
|---|---|---|---|
| Budgeted sales | 10 | 12 | 13 |
| Budgeted sales revenue | $21 000 | $25 200 | $27 950 |

## 44.2 Production budgets

A production budget is prepared to determine whether the levels of production necessary to satisfy the anticipated level of sales are attainable. The budget shows the quantities of finished goods that must be produced to meet expected sales plus any increase in inventory levels that might be required.

**Worked example**

Zaid is expected to have an opening inventory of five ZT/103 machines on 1 January. He requires a closing inventory of six machines at 31 March.

**Required**

Prepare a production budget based on the budgeted sales used in the previous worked example. Zaid requires an even production flow throughout the three months.

### Answer

The total production for the three months is found by using the following calculation:

| | |
|---|---|
| Budgeted sales (10 + 12 + 13) | 35 |
| *Plus* Budgeted closing inventory | 6 |
| Total production needed to meet budgeted sales and closing inventory | 41 |
| *Less* Budgeted opening inventory | 5 |
| Budgeted production over the three months | 36 |

**Note**

The calculation has been used to determine the budgeted production for a period of three months. The same calculation could be used to determine the budgeted production for a month, six months, a year, etc.

An even production flow means that Zaid will have to produce 12 machines per month. The production budget will look like this:

**Production budget for the three months ending 31 March**

| | January | February | March |
|---|---|---|---|
| Budgeted sales | 10 | 12 | 13 |
| *Plus* Budgeted closing inventory | 7 | 7 | 6 |
| Total production needed | 17 | 19 | 19 |
| *Less* Budgeted opening inventory | 5 | 7 | 7 |
| Budgeted production | 12 | 12 | 12 |

## 44.3 Purchases budgets

A purchases budget is required to determine the quantities of purchases required, either for resale or, in the case of a manufacturing business, for use in the production process. The method to be used is similar to that used to compile a production budget.

**Worked example**

Danst Ltd has the following budget for sales of 'limts':

| | February | March | April |
|---|---|---|---|
| Budgeted sales (units) | 120 | 140 | 160 |

The opening inventory on 1 February is expected to be 26 units of limts and the closing inventory at 30 April is expected to be 41 units of limts.

**Required**

Calculate the number of limts to be purchased over the three months ending 30 April.

### Answer

| | Units |
|---|---|
| Budgeted sales (120 + 140 + 160) | 420 |
| *Plus* Budgeted closing inventory | 41 |
| Total purchases needed to meet budgeted sales and closing inventory | 461 |
| *Less* Budgeted opening inventory | 26 |
| Budgeted purchases of goods for resale | 435 |

Danst will need to purchase 435 units in total during February, March and April. If an even amount of purchases were required each month throughout the year, then 145 units (435 divided by 3) would be purchased each month. Therefore, using the figures that we now know, the budget would look like this:

**Purchases budget for the three months ending 30 April**

| | February | March | April |
|---|---|---|---|
| Budgeted sales | 120 | 140 | 160 |
| *Plus* Budgeted closing inventory | | | 41 |
| Total purchases needed | | | 201 |
| *Less* Budgeted opening inventory | | | |
| Budgeted purchases of limts required for resale | 145 | 145 | 145 |

We can now fill in the gaps (we hope!) by working back through the months:

| | February | March | April |
|---|---|---|---|
| Budgeted sales | 120 | 140 | 160 |
| *Plus* Budgeted closing inventory | *51* | *56* | 41 |
| Total purchases needed | *171* | *196* | 201 |
| *Less* Budgeted opening inventory | 26 | *51* | *56* |
| Budgeted purchases of limts required for resale | 145 | 145 | 145 |

It is not usually necessary to have an equal flow of purchases each month. However, it might be necessary to have a specified number of units held as inventory at the start of each month.

The method of calculation for this type of budget is the same as that used in the previous example.

**Worked example**

Borga & Co. supply the following budgeted sales figures:

| | July | August | September | October |
|---|---|---|---|---|
| Budgeted sales (units) | 40 | 72 | 92 | 96 |

It is the manager's policy to maintain inventory levels at 25 per cent of the following month's budgeted sales.

**Required**

Prepare a purchases budget for the three months ending 30 September.

## Answer

We can calculate the opening inventory each month from what we know:

| July | August | September |
|---|---|---|
| 10 units (25% of 40) | 18 units (25% of 72) | 23 (25% of 92) |

We also know that the budgeted closing inventory at the end of September (i.e. the opening inventory on 1 October) should be 24 (25% of 96).

We can now put into our budget the figures that we know:

**Purchases budget for the three months ending 30 September**

| | July | August | September |
|---|---|---|---|
| Budgeted sales (units) | 40 | 72 | 92 |
| *Plus* Budgeted closing inventory | 18 | 23 | 24 |
| Total purchases needed | | | |
| *Less* Budgeted opening inventory | 10 | 18 | 23 |
| Budgeted purchases of goods needed for resale | | | |

And now we just need to fill in the gaps:

| | July | August | September |
|---|---|---|---|
| Budgeted sales (units) | 40 | 72 | 92 |
| *Plus* Budgeted closing inventory | 18 | 23 | 24 |
| Total purchases needed | *58* | *95* | *116* |
| *Less* Budgeted opening inventory | 10 | 18 | 23 |
| Budgeted purchases of goods needed for resale | *48* | *77* | *93* |

➤ Now try Question 1.

If each unit of purchases costs $2.00, the budget in terms of $s spent would show.

| | July | August | September |
|---|---|---|---|
| Budgeted sales | 80 | 144 | 184 |
| *Plus* Budgeted closing inventory | 36 | 46 | 48 |
| Total purchases needed | 116 | 190 | 242 |
| *Less* Budgeted opening inventory | 20 | 36 | 46 |
| Budgeted purchases of goods needed for resale | 96 | 154 | 186 |

## 44.4 Labour budgets

A labour budget is prepared to determine the business's need for planned labour in the budget period. It can be prepared to show:

- the number of labour hours required
- the number of workers required
- the cost of hiring the required number of workers.

**Worked example**

Cerise has produced the following production budget for the three months ending 31 August:

| | June | July | August |
|---|---|---|---|
| Planned production in units | 4000 | 5000 | 3500 |

Each unit of production requires four hours of labour. Each worker works 40 hours per week. Cerise has 100 workers.

**Required**

Prepare a labour budget for the three months ending 31 August (assume four weeks in each month).

### Answer

**Labour budget for the three months ending 31 August**

| | June | July | August |
|---|---|---|---|
| Hours presently available | 16000 | 16000 | 16000 |
| Labour requirement (hours) | 16000 | 20000 | 14000 |
| Surplus hours | – | – | 2000 |
| Shortfall in hours | – | 4000 | – |
| Workers presently available | 100 | 100 | 100 |
| Workers required | 100 | 125 | 87.5 |
| Surplus labour | – | – | 12.5 |
| Labour shortfall | – | 25 | – |

The budget shows that in July Cerise has a shortage of workers required to meet production targets. She will have to hire 25 full time workers.

In August she has labour surplus to requirements so 12 full time workers will need to be laid off and one member of staff will have to have his/her hours cut and work part time. Alternatively staff may be moved to another part of the business if this is possible.

## 44.5 Trade receivables budgets

The trade receivables budget forecasts the amounts that will be owed to a business by credit customers at the end of each month.

This budget is closely linked to the production budget, the sales budget and the cash budget. It will take into account the length of credit period that is allowed on customers' balances that are outstanding.

**Worked example**

The managers of Chin Ltd provide the following budgeted information for the three months ending 31 March:

| | | $ |
|---|---|---|
| 1 January amounts owed by credit customers | | 30 000 |
| Budgeted credit sales for | January | 40 000 |
| | February | 50 000 |
| | March | 60 000 |
| Cash sales for | January | 12 000 |
| | February | 10 000 |
| | March | 14 000 |

All credit customers are expected to settle their debts in the month following the sale of goods. They are allowed, and will take, five per cent cash discount.

**Required**

Prepare a trade receivables budget for the three months ending 31 March.

### Answer

**Trade receivables budget for the three months ending 31 March**

| | January | February | March |
|---|---|---|---|
| | $ | $ | $ |
| Balance brought forward | 30 000 | 40 000 | 50 000 |
| Credit sales | 40 000 | 50 000 | 60 000 |
| | 70 000 | 90 000 | 110 000 |
| Cash received from credit customers | (28 500) | (38 000) | (47 500) |
| Discount allowed | (1 500) | (2 000) | (2 500) |
| Balance carried forward | 40 000 | 50 000 | 60 000 |

**Note**

Cash sales have not been included. Cash customers do not have an account in the sales ledger. Cash customers are never trade receivables. The cash received from cash sales will be recorded in a cash budget (see below).

**Worked example**

The managers of Novotny Ltd provide the following information for the three months ending 30 November:

| | | $ | |
|---|---|---|---|
| Budgeted credit sales | July | 33 000 | |
| | August | 27 000 | |
| 31 August amount owed by credit customers | | 38 000 | *(receivables from July $11 000; receivables from August $27 000)* |
| Budgeted credit sales | September | 30 000 | |
| | October | 39 000 | |
| | November | 36 000 | |

Two-thirds of credit customers are expected to settle their debts in the month following receipt of the goods; the remainder will settle two months after receipt.

**Required**

Prepare a trade receivables budget for the three months ending 30 November.

## Answer

**Trade receivables budget for the three months ending 30 November**

| | September | | October | | November | |
|---|---|---|---|---|---|---|
| | $ | | $ | | $ | |
| Balance brought forward | 38 000 | | 39 000 | | 49 000 | |
| Credit sales | 30 000 | | 39 000 | | 36 000 | |
| | 68 000 | | 78 000 | | 85 000 | |
| Cash received | (18 000) | (Aug) | (20 000) | (Sept) | (26 000) | (Oct) |
| Cash received | (11 000) | (July) | (9 000) | (Aug) | (10 000) | (Sept) |
| Balance carried forward | 39 000 | | 49 000 | | 49 000 | |

➤ Now try Question 2.

## 44.6 Trade payables budgets

The trade payables budget forecasts the amounts that will be owed to trade creditors at the end of each month (whether suppliers of components or raw materials in the case of a manufacturing business, or suppliers of goods for resale in the case of a retailing business). It is linked to the purchases budget and the cash budget.

**Worked example**

The managers of Pavla Ltd provide the following information for the three months ending 30 June:

| | | $ |
|---|---|---|
| 1 April predicted amount owed to trade payables | | 14 000 |
| Budgeted purchases on credit terms for | April | 15 000 |
| | May | 16 000 |
| | June | 17 000 |
| Budgeted cash purchases | April | 2 000 |
| | May | 5 000 |
| | June | 3 000 |

All trade payables will be paid in the month following purchase. Pavla Ltd will receive a cash discount of five per cent on all credit purchases.

**Required**

Prepare a trade payables budget for the three months ending 30 June.

## Answer

**Trade payables budget for the three months ending 30 June**

| | April | May | June |
|---|---|---|---|
| | $ | $ | $ |
| Balances brought forward | 14000 | 15000 | 16000 |
| Credit purchases | 15000 | 16000 | 17000 |
| | 29000 | 31000 | 33000 |
| Cash paid to suppliers | (13300) | (14250) | (15200) |
| Discount received | (700) | (750) | (800) |
| Balance carried forward | 15000 | 16000 | 17000 |

**Worked example**

The managers of Berghaus Ltd provide the following budgeted information for the period ending 30 September:

| | | $ | |
|---|---|---|---|
| Budgeted credit purchases | May | 30000 | |
| | June | 24000 | |
| | July | 27000 | |
| | August | 32000 | |
| | September | 29000 | |
| 1 July predicted amount owed to suppliers | | 39000 | (payables from May $15000; payables from June $24000) |

Berghaus Ltd will settle 50 per cent of outstanding payables in the month following purchase of the goods; the remainder will be settled two months after purchase.

**Required**

Prepare a trade payables budget for the three months ending 30 September.

## Answer

**Trade payables budget for the three months ending 30 September**

| | July | | August | | September | |
|---|---|---|---|---|---|---|
| | $ | | $ | | $ | |
| Balance brought forward | 39000 | | 39000 | | 45500 | |
| Purchases on credit terms | 27000 | | 32000 | | 29000 | |
| | 66000 | | 71000 | | 74500 | |
| Cash paid to suppliers | (15000) | (May) | (12000) | (June) | (13500) | (July) |
| Cash paid to suppliers | (12000) | (June) | (13500) | (July) | (16000) | (Aug) |
| Balance carried forward | 39000 | | 45500 | | 45000 | |

➤ Now try Question 3.

## 44.7 Cash budgets

The managers of most businesses will prepare a cash budget. A cash budget shows estimates of future cash incomes and cash expenditures. It is usually prepared monthly and includes both capital and revenue transactions. It is drawn up to help management be aware of any potential shortages or surpluses of cash resources that could occur, thus allowing management to make any necessary financial arrangements.

The availability of cash is essential for the short-term survival of all businesses. Without it, resources required for the business to function cannot be acquired. Holding excessive cash will result in a less profitable business since cash held does not in itself yield profits.

Forecast **cash receipts** may be termed **positive cash flows**, while forecast **cash expenditure** may be termed **negative cash flows**. The difference between the forecast cash receipts and the forecast cash expenditure is the **net cash flow**.

The preparation of a cash budget:

- helps to ensure that there is always sufficient cash available to allow the normal activities of the business to take place
- will highlight times when the business will have cash surpluses, thus allowing management time to arrange short-term investment of those surpluses in order to gain maximum return
- will highlight times when the business might have cash deficits, thus allowing management to arrange short-term alternative sources of finance through the arrangement of overdraft facilities or the arrangement of extended periods of credit or the restructuring of existing longer-term debts.

A cash budget may be prepared weekly or monthly. The budget forecasts the cash (and cheques) coming into a business and the cash (and cheque) payments that the managers think will be made.

The net cash flow may be a positive amount if the forecast receipts exceed the forecast expenditure. It may be negative if it is forecast that expenditure is expected to be greater than receipts.

Tip 

It is possible to have a forecast negative cash balance at the end of a time period since receipts and payments will be made up of both cash and bank transactions.

### 44.7.1 Preparation of a cash budget

A cash budget is prepared in three parts:

- Part 1 shows the forecast receipts.
- Part 2 shows forecast expenditure.
- Part 3 shows a summary of the net cash flow for each period resulting from the forecast positive cash flow from Part 1 and the negative cash flow from Part 2. It will also show a forecast of cash balances to be carried forward at the end of each time period.

 Tip 

There are a number of different layouts for cash budgets. Choose the version that you feel most comfortable using and stick with it.

**Worked example**

Arvane opens a small store using $8000 savings. She estimates that her purchases and sales for her first three months of trading will be:

| | Purchases | Sales |
|---|---|---|
| | $ | $ |
| March | 8000 | 12000 |
| April | 7000 | 14000 |
| May | 11000 | 28000 |

Arvane will purchase fixtures and fittings for her store costing $11000. She will pay for these in April.

Her suppliers require payment for purchases in the month of purchase.

Her sales are 50 per cent cash sales.

Her credit customers are expected to pay in the month following sale.

Wages will amount to $1000 per month payable when due.

Rent for the store is $2000 for a three-month period. The first payment for rent is due on 1 March.

Other expenses are expected to be $1700 per month payable in the month following that in which they occur.

**Required**

a Prepare a cash budget for the three months ending 31 May.

b Comment on the results shown by the budget.

## Answer

a

**Cash budget for the three months ending 31 May**

| | March | April | May |
|---|---|---|---|
| | $ | $ | $ |
| Receipts | | | |
| Sales – cash | 6000 | 7000 | 14000 |
| credit | | 6000 | 7000 |
| | 6000 | 13000 | 21000 |
| Expenditure | | | |
| Purchases | 8000 | 7000 | 11000 |
| Wages | 1000 | 1000 | 1000 |
| Rent | 2000 | | |
| Other expenses | | 1700 | 1700 |
| Fixtures and fittings | | 11000 | |
| | 11000 | 20700 | 13700 |
| Net receipts/(payments) | (5000) | (7700) | 7300 |
| Balance brought forward | 8000 | 3000 | (4700) |
| Balance carried forward | 3000 | (4700) | 2600 |

b Arvane will have to arrange an overdraft with her bank to cover her expenditure during April and probably part of May. Hopefully she will in future have positive cash flows each month – understandably, the capital expenditure was the largest expense in her first three months of trading. Provided that the expenditure patterns are similar in future months it would appear that Arvane's cash flows should be positive.

**Note**

The heading should contain the word 'budget' or 'forecast' and the time period covered. Notice also that it is a forecast and so the heading tells us that the three months will end at 31 May.

### Self-test questions

1 Explain two reasons why a manager might prepare a cash budget.
2 Explain how there can be a negative cash balance shown in a cash budget at the end of a month.
3 A cash budget is another name for an income statement. True/False?
4 'There is no need to prepare a cash budget if my business is profitable,' a businessman was heard to say. Do you agree? Explain your reply to his statement.
5 Depreciation is only included in a cash budget in the final month. True/False?

➤ Now try Question 4.

## Worked example

The following budgeted figures relate to Cropp Ltd for the three months ending 30 September:

| | July | August | September |
|---|---|---|---|
| | $ | $ | $ |
| Cash sales | 10 000 | 10 000 | 12 000 |
| Cash received from credit customers | 26 000 | 28 000 | 27 000 |
| Payments made to suppliers | 9 000 | 11 000 | 12 000 |
| Cash purchases | 6 000 | 6 000 | 7 000 |
| Payment for rent | | 21 000 | |
| Payment for local taxes | | | 1 200 |
| Payment of wages | 8 000 | 8 000 | 8 000 |
| Payments for other expenses | 2 750 | 3 750 | 2 800 |

It is expected that cash in hand at 30 June will be $820.

**Required**

Prepare a cash budget for each of the three months ending 30 September.

## Answer

**Cash budget for each of the three months ending 30 September**

| | July | August | September |
|---|---|---|---|
| | $ | $ | $ |
| **Receipts** | | | |
| Cash sales | 10 000 | 10 000 | 12 000 |
| Cash received from customers | 26 000 | 28 000 | 27 000 |
| | 36 000 | 38 000 | 39 000 |
| **Payments** | | | |
| To suppliers | 9 000 | 11 000 | 12 000 |
| Cash purchases | 6 000 | 6 000 | 7 000 |
| Rent | | 21 000 | |
| Local taxes | | | 1 200 |
| Wages | 8 000 | 8 000 | 8 000 |
| Other expenses | 2 750 | 3 750 | 2 800 |
| | 25 750 | 49 750 | 31 000 |
| Balance brought forward | 820 | 11 070 | (680) |
| Receipts | 36 000 | 38 000 | 39 000 |
| | 36 820 | 49 070 | 38 320 |
| Payments | 25 750 | 49 750 | 31 000 |
| Balance carried forward | 11 070 | (680) | 7 320 |

The cash budget shows that overdraft facilities must be arranged to cover the cash deficit in August.

Cash budgets are the type of budget that you are most likely to be asked to prepare. It is well worth practising the layout shown.

There are alternative layouts. The one shown above is the version most frequently used.

**Note**

- Cash budgets include bank transactions. It is therefore possible to have negative balances in a cash budget.
- Only cash and bank items are included.

- Cash budgets deal only with transactions involving the movement of cash. They therefore will not include any non-cash expenses, such as a provision for depreciation or a provision for doubtful debts.
- Some business studies textbooks refer to cash budgets as 'cash flow forecasts'. Do not confuse cash flow forecasts with statements of cash flows (see Chapter 35).

## Worked example

Bradford Ltd sells one type of machine at a selling price of $6600 each. Fifty per cent is payable in the month of sale and 50 per cent the following month.

The machines are purchased from a supplier at a cost of $1500, paid in the month following purchase.

The following forecast information is available:

| | December | January | February | March | April |
|---|---|---|---|---|---|
| Budgeted sales (in units) | 4 | 6 | 3 | 5 | 7 |
| Budgeted purchases (units) | 6 | 3 | 5 | 7 | 8 |
| **Budgeted operating costs** | **$** | **$** | **$** | **$** | **$** |
| Rent | 1500 | 1500 | 1500 | 1500 | 1650 |
| Wages | 16000 | 19000 | 19000 | 19000 | 19000 |
| Other expenses | 4700 | 5200 | 5100 | 4800 | 5000 |
| Depreciation | 2500 | 2500 | 2500 | 2500 | 2500 |

All operating costs are paid in the month in which they occur.

The balance of cash in hand at 1 January is expected to be $1800.

**Required**

Prepare a cash budget for each of the three months ending 31 March.

## Answer

**Cash budget for the three months ending 31 March**

| | January | | February | | March | |
|---|---|---|---|---|---|---|
| | **$** | | **$** | | **$** | |
| **Receipts** | | | | | | |
| Cash received from trade receivables | 13200 | (Dec) | 19800 | (Jan) | 9900 | (Feb) |
| Cash received from trade receivables | 19800 | (Jan) | 9900 | (Feb) | 16500 | (Mar) |
| | 33000 | | 29700 | | 26400 | |
| **Payments** | | | | | | |
| Payments to trade payables | 9000 | (Dec) | 4500 | (Jan) | 7500 | (Feb) |
| Rent | 1500 | | 1500 | | 1500 | |
| Wages | 19000 | | 19000 | | 19000 | |
| Other expenses | 5200 | | 5100 | | 4800 | |
| | 34700 | | 30100 | | 32800 | |
| Balance brought forward | 1800 | | 100 | | (300) | |
| Receipts | 33000 | | 29700 | | 26400 | |
| | 34800 | | 29800 | | 26100 | |
| Payments | 34700 | | 30100 | | 32800 | |
| Balance carried forward | 100 | | (300) | | (6700) | |

**Note**

Depreciation has not been included – it is a *non*-cash expense.

➤ Now try Question 5.

## 44.8 The master budget

The master budget provides a summary of all the planned operations of the business for the period covered by the budgets. It is a sum of all the individual budgets prepared by the different parts of the business.

It is made up of:

- a budgeted manufacturing account (where appropriate)
- a budgeted income statement
- a budgeted statement of financial position.

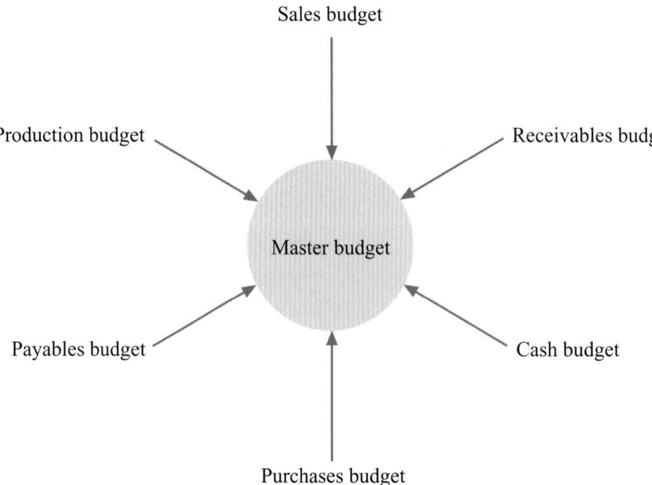


**Figure 44.1** Individual budgets used to prepare the master budget

**Tip**

It is possible that you could be asked to prepare a summarised income statement and/or a summarised statement of financial position from a cash budget.

Questions asking for summarised statements are designed to test your ability to:

- apply the concepts of accruals and realisation
- differentiate between capital and revenue expenditures and capital and revenue incomes
- distinguish between cash and non-cash expenses.

**Worked example**

The following budgeted information is given for Plum Ltd:

| | August | September | October | November |
|---|---|---|---|---|
| | $ | $ | $ | $ |
| Credit sales | 30000 | 40000 | 35000 | 45000 |
| Credit purchases | 15000 | 20000 | 15000 | 25000 |
| Wages paid | 7500 | 7500 | 7500 | 7500 |
| Other expenses | 8200 | 8400 | 8100 | 9000 |
| Purchase of machine | | 10000 | | |
| Depreciation of machine | | 100 | 100 | 100 |

Trade receivables will pay one month after goods are sold.

Trade payables will be paid one month after receipt of the goods.

All expenses are paid in the month in which they occur.

It is expected that cash in hand at 1 September will be $1200.

Inventory at 1 September is expected to be $2000.

Inventory at 30 November is expected to be $2500.

**Required**

Prepare:

a a cash budget for each of the three months ending 30 November

b a budgeted income statement for the three months ending 30 November.

## Answer

Always show the months separately when preparing a cash budget.

a

**Cash budget for the three months ending 30 November**

| | September | October | November |
|---|---|---|---|
| | $ | $ | $ |
| **Receipts** | | | |
| Cash received from credit customers | 30 000 | 40 000 | 35 000 |
| **Payments:** | | | |
| Cash paid to credit suppliers | 15 000 | 20 000 | 15 000 |
| Wages | 7 500 | 7 500 | 7 500 |
| Other expenses | 8 400 | 8 100 | 9 000 |
| Purchase of machine | 10 000 | | |
| | 40 900 | 35 600 | 31 500 |
| Balance brought forward | 1 200 | (9 700) | (5 300) |
| Receipts | 30 000 | 40 000 | 35 000 |
| | 31 200 | 30 300 | 29 700 |
| Payments | 40 900 | 35 600 | 31 500 |
| Balance carried forward | (9 700) | (5 300) | (1 800) |

Remember, depreciation does not involve cash leaving the business.

The heading should be precise and include the word 'budgeted', as well as the *time period covered.*

b

**Budgeted income statement for the three months ending 30 November**

| | $ | $ |
|---|---|---|
| Sales | | 120 000 |
| *Less* Cost of sales | | |
| Inventory 1 September | 2 000 | |
| Purchases | 60 000 | |
| | 62 000 | |
| Inventory 30 November | 2 500 | 59 500 |
| Gross profit | | 60 500 |
| *Less* Expenses | | |
| Wages | (22 500) | |
| Other expenses | (25 500) | |
| Depreciation of machinery | (300) | (48 300) |
| Profit for the three months | | 12 200 |

Do not show separate monthly figures in the budgeted income statement. This is probably the biggest single error made in answering questions on this topic.

The sales figure is the total of the budgeted figures for the three months under review – September $40 000, October $35 000 and November $45 000 – *not* the amounts shown in the cash budget. Do you remember the realisation concept in Chapter 7?

The purchases figure is the total of the budgeted figures for the three months under review – September $20 000, October $15 000 and November $25 000 – *not* the amounts used in the cash budget. Once again, the realisation concept is being applied.

Depreciation is included in the budgeted income statement because of the accruals concept – the machine is a resource that will be used to generate profits, so a charge has to be made.

## 44.9 Limiting factors

A **limiting factor** is defined by CIMA as 'anything which limits the activity of an entity'. It is also known as a **key factor**. (See also Chapter 29 Marginal costing.)

When budgets are being prepared it is essential that any limiting factors are identified and budgets amended to take into account any changes. Each individual budget is incorporated into a **master budget** (see above). Changes to one of the departmental or functional budgets will inevitably have a knock-on effect into other budgets. A change may be the result of a limiting factor. For example: a factory may be able to produce 40 000 units per month. It would be pointless for the sales budget to be prepared estimating sales volume at 50 000 units. Production of 40 000 units is a limiting factor.

This limiting factor would affect not only the sales budget but also the cash budget, the purchases budget, the receivables budget, the payables budget and, of course, the master budget.

Something that restricts a business from achieving its desired level of output is known as a **principal budget factor** (also known as a **key factor** or a **limiting factor**).

**Variances** arise when there is a difference between actual and budgeted figures.

**Favourable variances** increase profits.

**Adverse variances** reduce profits.

## 44.10 Flexed budgets

During the preparation of budgets it is important that any obstacle to achieving the desired outcomes is identified. There could be a shortage of materials or of a component used in the manufacturing process. Factory space might be limited. There could be a shortage of labour possessing a particular skill.

When the productive capacity of a business is restricted so that demand for the product cannot be met, the limiting factor must be identified. While individual budgets are being prepared it is essential that coordination takes place and changes are made to the budgets affected. For example, it would not be sensible to set a sales budget of 500 000 units if the factory is only capable of producing 450 000 units. Similarly, a production budget requiring 60 000 hours of labour input would not be met if only 50 000 hours was available locally.

Budgets are plans and may be used as control mechanisms when actual performance is compared to the budgeted performance. Variations from the budgeted data need to be investigated and action taken.

Adverse variances need corrective action to be taken.

The causes of favourable variances need to be identified and, where possible, applied to other areas of the business.

Actual results can be compared to a fixed budget based on a set level of sales or output. However, this type of comparison can give misleading results, which can lead to managers making inappropriate business decisions.

To overcome this problem, budgets should be 'flexed' to reflect changes in output and turnover.

**Example**

The production of 500 'tingels' is budgeted to require 200 kg of raw materials.

Actual usage is 180 kg of materials.

Budgeted use of materials was 0.4 kg per unit, whereas actual use was 0.36 kg per unit (180 kg ÷ 500).

Clearly, usage has been less than the budgeted amount – or has it?

In fact only 400 units of tingels were manufactured, so actual use has been 0.45 kg per unit.

---

According to CIMA, a flexible budget recognises '... different cost behaviour patterns ... as volume of output changes'.

In order to prepare accurate budgets capable of being used for budgetary control purposes, managers need to adjust budgeted levels of activity. If the actual level of activity is different to the budgeted level then managers will have to allow for differing levels of expenditure on the factors of production they use. Variable costs and revenues must be changed to reflect the actual level of activity achieved.

The budgets that are prepared should be based on the adjusted levels of activity. The flexed budget will reflect the different behaviour patterns of fixed and variable costs.

The process requires that variances are analysed and in the case of adverse variances any necessary remedial action is taken. Responsibility for variances rests with departmental heads.

The benefits and limitations of budgeting outlined in Chapter 31, page 328, also apply to budgetary control.

**Worked example**

The following data are available for Grizzel, a public limited company, for the year ending 30 September:

| | | Budget | Actual |
|---|---|---|---|
| | | $ | $ |
| Level of production (units) | | 8000 | 8500 |
| Variable costs – | direct materials | 15 200 | 16 000 |
| | direct labour | 19 200 | 21 000 |
| | variable overheads | 4 800 | 5 000 |
| Total variable costs | | 39 200 | 42 000 |
| Fixed costs | | 15 000 | 16 000 |
| Total cost | | 54 200 | 58 000 |

**Required**

Prepare a flexed budgeted operating statement for Grizell for the year ending 30 September.

## Answer

| | Flexed budget | Actual | Variances |
|---|---|---|---|
| Direct materials | 16 150 | 16 000 | 150 (favourable) |
| Direct labour | 20 400 | 21 000 | (600) (adverse) |
| Variable overheads | 5 100 | 5 000 | 100 (favourable) |
| | 41 650 | 42 000 | (350) (adverse) |
| Fixed costs | 15 000 | 16 000 | (1 000) (adverse) |
| | 56 650 | 58 000 | (1 350) (adverse) |

## 44.11 Budgetary control

As we saw in Chapter 31, budgetary control gives the responsibility of financial planning to managers. Budgetary control enables a company to evaluate the performance of its managers by continually comparing the actual results achieved by an individual department against the results set in the budget.

## Self-test questions

6 Identify one reason why a cash budget might be prepared.
7 Explain why depreciation is not included in a cash budget.
8 What is meant by the term 'master budget'?
9 Name one component of a master budget.
10 Explain the term 'variance'.
11 Why would a manager flex a budget?

➤ Now try Questions 6–8.

## Chapter summary

- Budgets are an important part of the management function.
- They are plans expressed in money.
- Budgets help with the planning and control of a business.
- Individual departmental budgets are summarised in the master budget.
- Care must be taken to ensure that data is entered in the correct month.
- Cash budgets are the most frequently examined budgets.
- Cash is vital for the short-term survival of all businesses.
- Cash budgets forecast future cash inflows and cash outflows.
- Preparation of cash budgets allows managers to make arrangements to invest forecast surpluses or to arrange overdraft facilities to cover any excess of expenditures over incomes.
- Only transactions that involve cash (or bank) transactions are included in a cash budget. Provisions for depreciation and doubtful debts do not appear, neither does any type of discount.
- Budgets must be flexed if there are changes in circumstances to those that prevailed when the budget was prepared.

# 45 Standard costing

## Content

### 2.3 Standard costing

- Understand the application of a system of standard costing to an organisation
- Calculate the following variances: direct material price and usage; direct labour rate and efficiency
- Reconcile standard cost to actual cost
- Reconcile standard profit to actual profit
- Explain the causes of the variances and their relationship to each other
- Discuss how standard costing can be used as an aid to improve the performance of a business
- Calculate the following variances: fixed overhead expenditure, capacity, efficiency and volume; and sales price and volume
- Discuss the advantages and disadvantages of a standard costing system

**By the end of this chapter you should be able to:**

- explain the uses of a system of standard costing
- calculate and interpret sales variances, materials variances, labour variances and fixed overhead variances
- understand the interrelationship of variances
- appreciate the usefulness of variance analysis to management.

## 45.1 Standard costing

**Standard costing** sets levels of costs and revenues that ought to be achievable when reasonable levels of performance are attained, together with efficient working practices to manufacture a product.

**Standard unit price** is the total of standard costs of all the factors of production that make up a finished unit of production.

A **budget** is a financial plan prepared in advance of a defined time period. It is based on the objectives of the business.

We all set standards in our everyday lives. Standards are goals – things that we hope to achieve.

- You may wish to save a certain sum of money in order that you can purchase a more up-to-date games console.
- You may wish to run 400 metres in a time of 1 minute 10 seconds or less.

All the examples may be realistic targets that we believe are achievable.

The same idea is widespread in manufacturing businesses. In order to achieve an efficient production process, a budget will be prepared. The details will set the targets that the business hopes to achieve – standards are set for future performance.

If you failed to accumulate sufficient funds to allow the purchase of the games console, you may need to investigate the reasons why. The failure could have been because:

- the target (standard) was unrealistic
- income was less than expected *or*
- other financial priorities took precedence.

If the desired time for completion of the 400 metres was not achieved, this could be due to:

- an unrealistic target
- poor training regime
- poor athletic diet, etc.

If a business does not achieve the standards set, the managers will also wish to find out why the standards were not achieved.

Estimated costs for labour, materials and overheads will be calculated and added together to give the standard cost for the product. The estimated or target costs are based on the costs that should be incurred under efficient production conditions.

The standard costs can be based on:

- past data used to forecast likely usage of materials and labour
- detailed study of the production processes involved in manufacturing.

Material standards are based on the quantity of materials that will be necessary to complete each unit of output.

Labour standards are based on production methods and the hours required by an average worker to complete each unit of output.

## 45.2 Types of cost standard

- **Basic cost standards** are unchanged over long periods of time. This enables managers to gauge efficiency of a process over time. Basic cost is rarely used because of the historical nature of the data.
- **Ideal standards** are based on achieving minimum costs that are possible using the most efficient production conditions. Once again, this type of standard is rarely used since these standards are almost impossible to achieve and can therefore act as a demotivating force.
- **Attainable standard hours** are costs that should be achievable using efficient operating conditions. Allowance is made for the 'usual' production problems such as lost time, machinery breakdowns and natural wastage.

A **standard hour** is the amount of work that ought to be achieved in an hour.

## 45.3 Materials variances

**Variance** is the difference between budgeted (standard) revenue and costs and actual revenue and costs. Variances arise when actual results do not correspond with predicted results.

**Sub-variance** is a constituent part of a total variance. Sub-variances added together give the total variance.

**Adverse variances** reduce predicted profits.

**Favourable variances** increase predicted profits.

**Total direct materials variance** identifies the difference between the amount that managers thought would be spent on direct materials (the standard set minus the budgeted amount) and the amount that was actually spent on the direct materials.

**Worked example**

Geoff Whyz has budgeted to use \$72 000 direct materials in October. When confirmation is available in November, Geoff discovers that the actual expenditure was \$75 000.

**Required**

Calculate the total direct materials variance for October.

### Answer

Total direct materials variance = \$3000 adverse (\$75 000 – \$72 000)

**Note**

The adverse total materials variance cost the business more than anticipated and will thus reduce profits (affect profits adversely).

---

**Worked example**

Ethel Bigome budgeted to use direct materials costing \$36 000 in January. In February Ethel was able to determine that actual direct materials cost \$34 800.

**Required**

Calculate the total direct materials variance.

## Answer

Total direct materials variance = $1200 favourable ($36 000 – $34 800)

**Note**

The favourable total materials variance cost the business less than anticipated and therefore would increase profits (thus having a favourable effect on profits).

---

It is fine that we can determine whether the price actually paid has cost us more or less than was anticipated but from a management point of view it would be much more useful if we could discover why the variance from budgeted figures had arisen.

The difference in the cost of direct materials used could be due to:

- more materials being used than was expected (adverse variance)
- fewer materials being used than was expected (favourable variance)
- an increase in the prices of materials since the budget was prepared (adverse variance)
- a decrease in the prices of materials since the budget was prepared (favourable variance)
- a combination of a change in the use of materials and a change in prices.

We can identify differences in budgeted and actual expenditure resulting from the above factors by calculating **sub-variances**.

## 45.3.1 Materials usage sub-variance

Materials usage sub-variance will calculate any changes in the total expenditure caused by changes in the quantity of materials used in the process.

- An adverse sub-variance will indicate that the production process used more materials than was anticipated. Once identified, remedial action can be taken.
- A favourable sub-variance will indicate that the production process used fewer materials than was anticipated. If the reasons can be identified, it should be possible to replicate any good efficient practices in other cost centres of the business.

**Worked example**

R.G. Bahgi provides the following information for raw materials:

| | Budgeted | Actual |
|---|---|---|
| Materials used | 2000 kg | 2100 kg |
| Materials cost per kg | $8 | $8 |

**Required**

Calculate the direct materials usage sub-variance.

## Answer

Materials usage sub-variance $800 adverse, caused by using more materials than were budgeted for

---

**Worked example**

T. Cup provides the following information for raw materials to be used in production during September:

| | Budgeted | Actual |
|---|---|---|
| Materials used | 830 $m^2$ | 810 $m^2$ |
| Material cost per $m^2$ | $4 | $4 |

**Required**

Calculate the raw materials usage sub-variances for September.

## Answer

$80 favourable sub-variance, caused by fewer materials being used than budgeted for

### 45.3.2 Materials price sub-variance

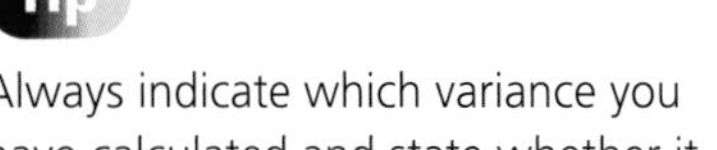

Always indicate which variance you have calculated and state whether it is a favourable variance or an adverse variance.

A direct materials price variance calculates any differences between budgeted and actual costs due to sub-variances that arise because of a change in the prices of the raw materials being used.

- A direct materials price sub-variance will arise when the price of the materials changes.
- An adverse price sub-variance will arise when the cost of acquiring the direct materials has risen.
- A favourable price sub-variance arises when the cost of acquiring the direct materials has fallen.

**Worked example**

Gwock provides the following information for raw materials to be used in her production process for December:

| | Budgeted data |
|---|---|
| Materials to be used | 1200 litres |
| Cost per litre | $9.60 |

In January, the following information relating to December became available:

| | Actual |
|---|---|
| Materials used | 1200 litres |
| Cost per litre | $9.80 |

**Required**

Calculate the materials price sub-variance for December.

## Answer

Materials price sub-variance $240 adverse, caused by an increase in the cost of acquiring each litre of the material used

### 45.3.3 Materials usage and price sub-variances

As you can see, the calculation to determine the variance is relatively straightforward if there is only one variable to consider. But what if there are differences in both the materials used and the price paid to acquire those materials from the amount used and price budgeted for?

The simple way to calculate and differentiate between the two types of sub-variances is to use the following grid:

$$Sq \times Sp$$
$$Aq \times Sp$$
$$Aq \times Ap$$

Where: S = the standard (or budgeted) figure
q = the quantity
p = the price
A = the actual figure

So: Sq = the standard quantity
Sp = the standard price
Aq = the actual quantity used
Ap = the actual price of the materials used

Sq × Sp = } Any difference (variance) between these two totals must be due to differences in the budgeted usage and the actual usage since the standard price remains the same on both lines.

Aq × Sp = } Any difference (variance) between these two totals must be due to differences in the budgeted price as the actual quantities remain the same.

Aq × Ap =

The two differences combined will amount to the total variance.

**Worked example**

The following information is given for the use of materials used to produce 'befures':

| | Budgeted | Actual |
|---|---|---|
| Direct materials | 720 metres | 730 metres |
| Direct material costs per metre | $3.00 | $3.50 |

**Required**

Calculate:

a the materials usage sub-variance
b the materials price sub-variance
c the total materials variance.

## Answer

Sq × Sp

720 × $3 = $2160 }

Aq × Sp } $30 Remember you also need to identify whether

730 × $3 = $2190 } these variances are adverse or favourable.

Aq × Ap } $365

730 × $3.50 = $2555 }

The first line tells us that budgeted total materials are expected to cost $2160.

The second line tells us that total materials actually cost £2190.

Materials in the second line cost $30 more than the budgeted costs on line 1. An increase in costs would have an adverse effect on profits, so $30 is an adverse usage sub-variance.

The second line tells us that materials actually used should cost $2190.

The third line tells us that materials actually used cost $2555.

Materials on the third line cost $365 more than the cost on the second line. An increase in costs would have an adverse effect on profits, so $365 is an adverse price sub-variance.

The materials usage sub-variance and the materials price sub-variance together will give the total materials variance. So:

Sq × Sp

720 × $3 = $2160

Aq × Sp — $30 Adverse materials usage sub-variance

730 × $3 = $2190

Aq × Ap — $365 Adverse materials price sub-variance

730 × $3.50 = $2555

$395 Total materials variance

We have successfully identified the three variances asked for in the question.

**Worked example**

The following information is given for the use of materials used in the manufacturing of 'trusmedas':

| | Budgeted | Actual |
|---|---|---|
| Direct materials | 2400 litres | 2250 litres |
| Direct materials cost per litre | $8 | $10 |

**Required**

Calculate:

a the materials usage sub-variance

b the materials price sub-variance

c the total direct materials variance.

## Answer

Sq × Sp

2400 × $8 = $19 200

Aq × Sp — $1200 Favourable materials usage sub-variance

2250 × $8 = $18 000

Aq × Ap — $4500 Adverse materials price sub-variance

2250 × $10 = $22 500

$3300 Total adverse materials variance

Materials cost $3300 more than budgeted for. This was because there was a price increase of $4500 and a saving of $1200 because of more efficient use of materials.

➤ Now try Questions 1 and 2.

# 45.4 Direct labour variances

Total direct labour variances identify the difference between the amount that managers thought that they would spend on direct labour costs (the standard set) and the amount that they actually spent.

**Worked example**

Tony has budgeted that direct labour costs for March would be $172 000. The actual amount spent was $178 000.

**Required**

Calculate the total direct labour variance for March.

## Answer

Total direct labour variance = $6000 adverse ($178 000 – $172 000)

**Worked example**

Magdalen budgeted to use $83 000 of direct labour in May. In early June, she discovered that she had actually spent $82 500.

**Required**

Calculate the total direct labour variance.

## Answer

The total direct labour variance = $500 favourable ($83 000 – $82 500)

In the first example above, labour cost more than was budgeted – this had an adverse effect on profits.

In the second example, $500 was saved on the budgeted amount – this would have a favourable effect on profit.

It would be useful for managers of a business to determine whether the total variance was caused by:

- workers being more efficient (favourable variance)
- workers being less efficient (adverse variance)
- workers being paid more (adverse variance)
- workers being paid less (favourable variance) *or*
- some combination of a change in efficiency and a change in wage rates.

We can use the same technique used to determine direct material sub-variances to calculate sub-variances in the budgeted and actual amounts spent on direct labour.

In order to calculate the sub-variances that make up the total direct labour variances we can refer to our grid:

Sq × Sp

Aq × Sp

Aq × Ap

However, we do need to make a couple of changes to our descriptions of the sub-variances.

- Labour 'usage' is referred to as 'labour efficiency'.
- Labour 'price' is referred to as 'wage rate' or 'labour rate'.

Labour is used more or less efficiently than budgeted for.

The price of labour, as you might know from a part-time job, is the 'wage rate' that you are paid.

Sq × Sp

Aq × Sp

Aq × Ap

S = the standard (or budgeted) figure

q = the number of labour hours

p = the rate at which direct labour is paid

A = the actual figure

So:

Sq is the standard number of hours thought to be necessary.

Sp is the standard wage rate.

Aq is the actual number of hours that were worked.

Ap is the actual rate paid to the employees.

Sq × Sp
Aq × Sp
Aq × Ap

Any difference between these two totals (Sq × Sp and Aq × Sp) must be due to the hours that managers thought would be worked by direct labour and the hours that were in fact worked.

Any difference between these two totals (Aq × Sp and Aq × Ap) must be due to any difference in the wage rate that had been budgeted and the wage rate actually paid.

As with materials, the two differences combined will amount to the total variance.

## Worked example

Katap Ltd provides the following information for the direct labour for November.

| | Budgeted | Actual |
|---|---|---|
| Direct labour | 37 000 hours | 39 000 hours |
| Direct labour wage rate per hour | $7.00 | $7.20 |

**Required**

Calculate:

a the direct labour efficiency sub-variance

b the direct labour wage rate sub-variance

c the total direct labour variance.

## Answer

Sq × Sp

37 000 × $7.00 = $259 000

Aq × Sp — $14 000

39 000 × $7.00 = $273 000

Aq × Ap — $6 200

39 000 × $7.20 = $280 800

Remember that you need to identify whether these sub-variances are adverse or favourable.

The first line tells us that the managers of Katap Ltd thought that $259 000 would be spent on direct labour wages.

The second line indicates the change due to budgeted hours not being achieved. There was an overspend of $14 000: this would affect profits adversely.

When the second line is compared to what actually happened, we can see that another overspend occurred. The profits would be adversely affected by $6200.

Both sub-variances are adverse.

- The direct labour efficiency sub-variance is $14 000 adverse.
- The direct labour rate sub-variance is $6200 adverse.
- The total labour variance is $20 200 adverse.

The three variances requested have been identified.

**Worked example**

Bash Ltd provides the following information for direct labour for April:

| | Budgeted | Actual |
|---|---|---|
| Direct labour | 6200 hours | 6250 hours |
| Direct labour rate per hour | $9.50 | $9.30 |

**Required**

Calculate:

a the direct labour efficiency sub-variance

b the direct labour wage rate sub-variance

c the total labour variance.

## Answer

| | | |
|---|---|---|
| Sq × Sp | | |
| 6200 × $9.50 = £58 900 | | |
| Aq × Sp | $475 | Adverse direct labour efficiency sub-variance |
| 6250 × $9.50 = $59 375 | | |
| Aq × Ap | $1250 | Favourable direct labour rate sub-variance |
| 6250 × $9.30 = $58 125 | $775 | Favourable total direct labour variance |

The workers took longer to complete their tasks – this cost Bash Ltd $475 more than the budgeted figure but workers were paid a lower hourly rate, so Bash Ltd saved $1250.

**Note**

The term 'standard' is used in place of 'budgeted' in the following questions, now that you have got used to the detailed calculations required.

➤ Now try Question 3.

You will often be faced with situations – in questions and in real life – in which you are given information for both direct materials and direct labour and are required to calculate all seven variances.

**Worked example**

The managers of Hasbec Ltd provide the following information for December:

Standard costs:

Direct materials: 430 kg costing $18 per kg

Direct labour: 170 hours at $7.50 per hour

Actual costs incurred in the manufacturing process:

Direct materials: 425 kg costing $18.10 per kg

Direct labour: 172 hours at $7.40 per hour

**Required**

Calculate:

a the direct materials usage sub-variance
b the direct materials price sub-variance
c the total direct materials variance
d the direct labour efficiency sub-variance
e the direct labour rate sub-variance
f the total direct labour variance
g the total direct expenses variance.

## Answer

**Direct materials:** Sq × Sp

430 × \$18 = \$7740.00

Aq × Sp

425 × \$18 = \$7650.00

Aq × Ap

425 × \$18.10 = \$7692.50

\$90 Favourable direct material usage sub-variance (a)

\$42.50 Adverse direct material price sub-variance (b)

\$47.50 Favourable direct materials variance (c)

**Direct labour:** Sq × Sp

170 × \$7.50 = \$1275.00

Aq × Sp

172 × \$7.50 = \$1290.00

Aq × Ap

172 × \$7.40 = \$1272.80

\$15 Adverse direct labour efficiency sub-variance (d)

\$17.20 Favourable direct labour rate sub-variance (e)

\$2.20 Favourable direct labour variance (f)

Total direct expenses variance \$49.70 favourable (\$47.50 + \$2.20) (g)

➤ Now try Question 4.

## 45.5 The flexed budget

One of the purposes of using a standard costing system is that problem areas in production are highlighted and so remedial action can be taken. The system will also identify areas of cost saving and therefore good practice which may be copied in other areas of the business.

The system identifies variances by making comparisons between standard (budgeted) costs and the costs that have actually been incurred.

One of the overriding principles involved in making any comparisons is that we should try, as far as is possible, to compare like with like.

This principle should be applied when comparing standard costs with actual costs. So, if actual activity differs from budgeted activity, the budget must be flexed to produce a budget which reflects actual levels of activity.

**Example**

The manager of Cottou plc has budgeted to produce 100 000 pairs of cotton trousers in August. She budgets for the use of 140 000 m² of cotton in the production process. The actual figures available in September show that only 120 000 m² of cotton was used and total production was 90 000 trousers.

Clearly, the production has used less cotton than had been anticipated but fewer trousers were manufactured, so one would expect that less material had been used (140 000 m² compared with 120 000 m²).

However, we are not comparing like with like.

- 140 000 m² should have made 100 000 pairs of trousers.
- 120 000 m² actually made 90 000 pairs of trousers.

In order to make a valid comparison to see if the materials have been used efficiently or not we need to adjust our budget – the adjustment is called **flexing**.

If we had known earlier, when the standard was set, that only 90 000 pairs of trousers would be made, the budgeted figures for materials to be used would have been:

- 126 000 m² (i.e. 90 000/100 000 or nine-tenths of 140 000 m²)

and the figures to be used would be:

- **Standard costs:**
  90 000 pairs of trousers requiring 126 000 m² of cotton

So a comparison can now be made quite easily:

- **Standard materials usage:**
  90 000 pairs of trousers requiring 126 000 m² of cotton
- **Actual materials usage:**
  90 000 pairs of trousers requiring 120 000 m² of cotton

We can now see quite clearly that less material has been used than anticipated – thus giving rise to a favourable materials usage sub-variance.

## Worked example

The managers of Getang Ltd provide the following information for the production of 'selvings' during March:

| Budgeted output | Actual output |
|---|---|
| 80 000 selvings | 70 000 selvings |
| **Budgeted use of direct materials** | **Actual use of direct materials** |
| 240 000 litres | 220 000 litres |

**Required**

Calculate the amount of direct materials saved or wasted during March.

### Answer

| Flexed budget | Budgeted use of direct materials |
|---|---|
| 70 000 selvings | 210 000 litres (7/8 × 240 000) |
| **Actual output** | **Actual use of direct materials** |
| 70 000 selvings | 220 000 litres |

So 10 000 litres of direct materials were used that had not been budgeted for. The reasons for this 'wastage' should be investigated and if possible a remedy sought.

It will also be necessary to flex the standards set for the use of direct labour.

**Worked example**

The following information is given for direct labour hours for July for the production of 'lingts':

| | Standard | Actual |
|---|---|---|
| Production | 250 000 units | 225 000 units |
| Direct labour hours | 70 000 hours | 65 000 hours |

**Required**

Calculate the direct labour hours to be used in a flexed budget for July.

## Answer

Production of 225 000 lingts should use 63 000 hours of direct labour (225 000/250 000 × 70 000 hours).

In fact 2000 further hours have been used.

An investigation should be undertaken to determine why this has happened and remedial action taken if possible.

**Tip**

Only flex the *standard* quantity of direct materials and/or the *standard* hours of direct labour to be used in your grid.

**Worked example**

The following information is given for the production of 'trapeds':

| Standard costs for 1000 trapeds | |
|---|---|
| Direct materials | 220 kg at $5 per kg |
| Direct labour | 60 hours at $9.50 per hour |
| **Actual costs for the production of 950 trapeds** | |
| Direct materials | 204 kg at $5.75 per kg |
| Direct labour | 58 hours at $9.30 per hour |

**Required**

Calculate:

a the direct materials usage sub-variance

b the direct materials price sub-variance

c the total direct materials variance

d the direct labour efficiency sub-variance

e the direct labour rate sub-variance

f the total direct materials variance.

## Answer

The budget must first be flexed. Only 95 per cent of the budgeted trapeds have been produced, so the standard usage of direct materials and direct labour should be calculated to construct an amended budget – a flexed budget.

(Remember, only the standard (budgeted) quantities will be changed.)

Standard costs for 950 trapeds (950/1000 = 0.95) should use:

- 95 per cent of budgeted materials, so 0.95 × 220 = 209 kg

  Standard costs for 950 trapeds (950/1000 = 0.95) should use:

- 95 per cent of budgeted labour hours, so 0.95 × 60 = 57 hours.

  Reworking the standard costs:

**Standard costs for 950 trapeds:**

Direct materials: 209 kg at $5.00 per kg

Direct labour: 57 hours at $9.50 per hour

These figures are used in the 'grid'.

| | | |
|---|---|---|
| **Direct materials:** | Sq × Sp | |
| | 209 × \$5 = \$1045 | \$25 Favourable direct materials usage sub-variance |
| | Aq × Sp | |
| | 204 × \$5 = \$1020 | \$153 Adverse direct materials price sub-variance |
| | Aq × Ap | |
| | 204 × \$5.75 = \$1173 | \$128 Adverse total direct materials variance |
| **Direct labour:** | Sq × Sp | |
| | 57 × \$9.50 = \$541.50 | \$9.50 Adverse direct labour efficiency sub-variance |
| | Aq × Sp | |
| | 58 × \$9.50 = \$551.00 | \$11.60 Favourable direct labour rate sub-variance |
| | Aq × Ap | |
| | 58 × \$9.30 = \$539.40 | \$2.10 Favourable total direct labour variance |

➤ Now try Question 5.

## 45.6 Fixed overhead variances

These variances seek to explain why there may be a difference between the actual amount of fixed overhead incurred and the amount that is charged to production through overhead absorption rates.

### 45.6.1 Total fixed overhead variance

The **total fixed overhead variance** calculates the difference between standard fixed overhead per unit absorbed by actual production and the actual fixed overhead incurred.

**Worked example**

Budgeted fixed overhead for September \$9080

- Budgeted output 908 units
- Actual production 900 unit
- Fixed overhead incurred \$10 000.

**Required**

Calculate the total fixed overhead variance for September.

### Answer

Standard fixed overhead per unit \$10

Total fixed overhead variance = standard fixed overhead absorbed by actual production less actual fixed overhead incurred (900 units at \$10.00) \$9000 – \$10 000 = \$(1000) adverse.

In this example there has been an under recovery of fixed overheads. There is therefore an adverse variance. This could be due to

- more expenditure on fixed overheads than was anticipated in the budget, or
- budgeted production not being achieved

The total fixed overhead variance does not give managers enough relevant information from which improvements to the production process can be made. This problem can be rectified by examining each individual item that makes up the total fixed overhead. In this way reasons for variances may be identified and, where possible, controlled.

The total fixed overhead can be separated into two parts to show these two possible explanations.

### 45.6.2 Fixed overhead expenditure (or spending) variance

This variance seeks to identify the amount by which the actual spending on fixed overhead differs from the budgeted amount.

**Worked example (based on the data used previously)**

**Required**

Calculate the fixed overhead expenditure variance.

#### Answer

Expenditure variance = Budgeted fixed overhead $9080 – Actual fixed overhead $10 000 = $(920) adverse

If the actual fixed overhead had been less than the budgeted figure the variance would have been favourable.

This may be caused by increases in the overheads incurred in the production of the product.

### 45.6.3 Fixed overhead volume variance

This variance identifies the amount by which actual production differs from budgeted production.

**Worked example (using same data used previously)**

**Required**

Calculate the fixed overhead volume variance

#### Answer

Volume variance = Budgeted fixed overhead $9080 – Standard cost absorbed by actual production $9000 = $(80) adverse.

If actual output had been greater than planned output the volume variance would have been favourable.

Variances may be due to changes in the volume of goods produced caused by shortages in the factors of production, machine breakdowns, industrial disputes, poor production scheduling, etc.

A favourable variance occurs when actual production exceeds budgeted production.

An adverse variance occurs when actual production is less than budgeted production.

**Note** that if the volume variance is combined with the expenditure variance the result is the total fixed overhead variance.

Volume variance $(80) + expenditure variance $(920) = total variance $(1 000)

### 45.6.4 Fixed overhead capacity variance

The capacity variance calculates the variance caused by the difference in the hours worked and the budgeted hours. An adverse capacity variance indicates that not enough overhead has been absorbed into production.

The capacity variance will be favourable when actual hours are greater than budgeted hours. For example the standard hours of input based on direct labour hours might be 4 hours per unit of production charged at $6.00 per hour. The budgeted output is 4000 units so the budget is based on the assumption that direct labour hours of input will be 16 000 hours. If in fact the actual hours of input were 15 000 hours the business has failed to use the planned capacity. If production had worked at the level of efficiency that had been planned a further 1000 hours would have been worked and $6000 more fixed overhead would have been absorbed.

### 45.6.5 Fixed overhead volume efficiency variance

The second reason why there may be a volume variance is that the labour force has failed to work at the level of efficiency anticipated by the budget.

The variance is the difference between the standard hours and the actual hours multiplied by the standard fixed overhead rate per direct labour hour.

**Worked example**

The following information regarding fixed overheads is available for Maketio for the month of February:

Budgeted fixed overhead (10 hours at $4.50 per direct labour hour) $45.00.

The budgeted production level was 1000 units.

Total budgeted fixed overhead was $45 000.

Actual fixed overhead cost $38 250.

900 units were produced in 8500 actual hours.

Maketio absorbs fixed overheads on the basis of direct labour hours.

**Required**

Calculate the

a expenditure variance

b capacity variance

c efficiency variance

d volume variance

e total fixed overhead variance.

#### Answer

a expenditure variance = actual expenditure – budgeted expenditure

= $38 250 – $45 000

= $6 750 favourable

The fixed overhead absorption rate was $6 750 greater than needed, so a favourable variance

b capacity variance = budgeted overhead – (actual hours worked x overhead absorption rate) $45 000 – $38 250 = $6 750 adverse Actual hours worked are less than the budgeted hours so not enough overhead has been absorbed into production.

c efficiency variance = total actual hours worked – total standard hours for actual production x standard fixed overhead rate per direct labour hour
8 500 hours – 9 000 hours = 500 hours × $4.50 per hour = $2 250 favourable
The work is worth 9000 standard hours but it only took 8500 hours to complete production.

d volume variance = budgeted overhead – actual hours worked × overhead absorption rate.

= $45 000 – $40 500 (9000 × $4.50)

= $4500 adverse

e Actual fixed overhead = $38 250 Total standard cost for actual production = $40 500

Total variance = $2250 favourable

## 45.7 Sales variances

Revenue is affected by both the price of the product being sold and the number of units that are sold. Sales variances analyse the effect that changes in the volume of sales and the selling price of the product has on overall profit.

The volume of sales is not flexed in order to calculate sales variances; they can be calculated by using the grid. However, do be careful when labelling the sales variances that you have calculated. After calculating the two sub-variances ask yourself whether the variance would make the business better off (A favourable variance) or worse off (an adverse variance).

**Worked example**

Budgeted sales of Redro were 11 000 units at $6.30 per unit. The actual sales were 10 800 at $6.40 per unit.

**Required**

Calculate:

a the sales volume variance sub-variance

b the sales price sub-variance

c the total sales variance.

### Answer

| | |
|---|---|
| Sq × Sp | |
| 11 000 × $6.20 = $68 200.00 | $1240.00 Adverse volume variance (an adverse impact on profit) |
| Aq × Sp | |
| 10 800 × $6.20 = $66 960.00 | $2160.00 Favourable price variance (a favourable impact on profit) |
| Aq × Ap | |
| 10 800 × $6.40 = $69 120.00 | $920.00 Favourable total sales variance (an overall favourable impact on profit) |

➤ Now try Question 6.

The type of question you will meet most often will relate to the calculation of total and sub-variances for direct materials and direct labour. So learn the grid!

## 45.8 Working with variance analysis

You must also be able to tell quickly whether a variance that you have calculated is favourable or adverse.

Calculating variances is only part of the process; with practice, the calculations can be mastered and you should be able to gain accurate results.

However, more important than merely calculating the variances is gaining information from your calculations.

Business managers introduce a system of standard costing because it can highlight variances between the predicted costs and the actual costs.

Variances lead to investigation into the causes of the differences.

Standard costing is the natural extension of budgetary control.

Budgetary control seeks to make sections and departments more efficient and hence improve the performance of the business as a whole.

Standard costing goes into much greater detail than budgeting. It examines in detail the costs of all the constituent parts of the production process for each product.

When variances are identified, action can be implemented to correct adverse variances.

Managers must know the cause of any deviation from standard in order to take remedial action.

You will probably be asked to comment upon or make observations about the variances you have calculated in response to a question.

Variance analysis highlights areas of concern and areas of good practice and you may be asked to explain possible reasons for the variances.

You may also be asked to identify some interrelationship between different sub-variances.

Many of the comments you may make could be speculative because you will have only a limited picture or scenario and thus may lack the detail necessary to arrive at a definitive conclusion. Your answer will require a lot of thought and the application of common sense.

The variances that we have calculated up to this point have been calculated in isolation from data prepared for setting standards and budgets. They have detailed individual costs, output and incomes.

A business that operates a standard costing system and a system of budgetary control should be able to use the systems to use the data to calculate its future profitability.

Changes in operations due to variances are going to affect profit earned; favourable variances in sales and costs explain how profits have improved from those budgeted; adverse variances explain the factors that have reduced budgeted profit.

Future performance can be compared with the standards set by management.

As part of a management control system, a standard costing income statement may be prepared reconciling budgeted profit with actual profit earned.

## 45.8.1 Reconciling standard cost to actual cost

The reasons why there may be a difference between the profit forecast in a budget and the actual profit earned are shown in detail by comparing the budgeted cost and sales variances with the actual costs and sales when these figures become available. These differences form the basis of remedial action where necessary.

The variances are summarised (after the budgets have been flexed) and the total is then used to adjust standard costs for materials, labour and overheads. The adjusted amount should total to the actual costs.

If the total of the variances calculated amounts to a total favourable variance this is deducted from standard costs since favourable variances reduced the amount of expenditure incurred. Conversely, a total adverse variance is added to the standard costs because the total represents more expenditure on the factors of production.

**Worked Example**

Hussain industries manufactures one product. Management uses a standard absorption costing system. Management prepared the following budget for February based on sales of 10 000 units

| **Budget for February** | **$** | **$** |
|---|---|---|
| Sales (10 000 units at $9.50 per unit) | | 95 000 |
| Direct materials (14 000 kgs at $3.00 per kilo) | 42 000 | |
| Direct labour (3750 hours at $7.20 per hour) | 27 000 | |
| Fixed overheads ($0.70 per unit) | 7 000 | |
| Cost of sales (10 000 units) | | 76 000 |
| Budgeted profit | | 19 000 |

**Hussain's actual sales for February were only 9500 units**

| **Actual results for February** | **$** | **$** |
|---|---|---|
| Sales (9500 units at $9.60) | | 91 200 |
| Direct materials (15 250 kgs at $2.90 per kilo) | 44 225 | |
| Direct labour (3500 hours at $8.00 per hour) | 28 000 | |
| Fixed overheads | 6 500 | |
| Cost of sales | | 78 725 |
| Actual profit | | 12 475 |

**Required**

Prepare a statement reconciling standard cost with actual cost.

## Answer

| | $ | $ | $ |
|---|---|---|---|
| Standard costs (10 000 units) | | | 76 000 |
| Only 9500 units produced so standard cost is actually | | | 72 200 |
| | **Favourable** | **Adverse** | |
| Direct material variances – usage variance | | 5 850 | |
| price variance | 1 525 | | |
| Direct labour variances – efficiency | 450 | | |
| rate | | 2 800 | |
| Fixed overhead variances – expenditure | 500 | | |
| volume | | 350 | |
| | 2 475 | 9 000 | 6 525 |
| Actual costs | | | 78 725 |

**Note**

- The direct expense variances have been calculated using 'the grid'.
- The fixed overhead expenditure variance is the difference between the budgeted figure and the actual figure. The volume variance arise because 500 fewer sales were made thus giving a shortfall in the absorption of overheads of 500 x $0.70 = $350.
- The total of the variances calculated is $6 525 adverse which means that further costs from standard have been incurred and this total needs to be added to the total standard costs.

## 45.8.2 Reconciling standard profit to actual profit

Budgeted profit is often different to actual profit; this is due to changes in the cost structure of the factors of production as well as differences in the volume of finished goods being produced and sold. The business may also have to change the selling price per unit to take into account changes in the price that customers are willing to pay.

Managers may prepare a standard costing income statement in order to reconcile the budgeted profit with the actual profit earned. They can then easily identify the reasons why actual profit might have deviated from the profit forecast in the budgeted income statement. The cost and sales variances replace the expenses and incomes found in a traditional income statement. Negative (adverse) variances allow management to identify areas of the business that need some form investigation to determine if remedial action is necessary; while the departments that produce positive (favourable) variances can be used as examples of good practice to be replicated elsewhere in tbe business.

An example of standard costing income statement is shown using the data for Hussain industries in section 45.8.1 above.

**Example**

**Hussain industries**

**Statement for February reconciling standard profit and actual profit**

| | $ Favourable variances | $ Adverse variances | $ |
|---|---|---|---|
| Budgeted profit for February | | | 18050 |
| Variances - Sales price variance | 950 | | |
| Direct materials - usage | | 5850 | |
| price | 1525 | | |
| Direct labour - efficiency | 450 | | |
| rate | | 2800 | |
| Fixed overheads - expenditure | 500 | | |
| volume | | 350 | |
| | 3425 | 9000 | 5575 |
| Actual profit | | | 12475 |

Workings for budgeted profit (after flexing based on actual sales of 9500 units)

| | $ | $ |
|---|---|---|
| Budgeted sales revenue (9500 × $9.5) | | 90250 |
| Direct materials (14000 × 0.95 = 13 300 × $3.00) | 39900 | |
| Direct labour (3750 × 0.95 = 3562.5 × $7.20) | 25650 | |
| Fixed overheads (9500 × $0.70) | 6650 | 72200 |
| Budgeted profit | | 18050 |

## 45.8.3 Causes of sub-variances

The actual results may differ from the standards because there have been errors in the standards set. These errors could be caused by:

- setting unrealistic targets
- managers deliberately setting low standards.

When answering an examination question show that you are aware of possible causes of deviations from standard figures, but do not labour the point; rather, make it as a general comment that will apply to all sub-variances.

**Table 45.1** Direct materials usage sub-variances

| Favourable sub-variance | Adverse sub-variance |
|---|---|
| Use of better-quality materials | Use of poorer materials |
| Use of highly skilled workers | Use of less-skilled workers |
| Use of 'state of the art' capital equipment | Use of poor capital equipment |
| | Theft of materials |
| | Deterioration of materials |

Note that the first three factors in both columns refer to wastage of materials.

**Table 45.2** Direct materials price sub-variance

| Favourable sub-variance | Adverse sub-variance |
|---|---|
| Deflation – either general or specific to the materials being purchased | Inflation – either general or specific to the materials being purchased |
| Supplier reducing price | Supplier increasing price |
| Use of a cheaper alternative material or poorer quality of the same material | Use of more expensive alternative material or better quality of the same materials |
| Increase in quantity purchased so better trade discount obtained | Decrease in quantity purchased so loss of trade discount |
| Increase in value of the dollar against the value of the euro or pound sterling, making imported materials less expensive | Decrease in value of the dollar against the value of the euro or pound sterling making imported materials more expensive |

**Table 45.3** Direct labour efficiency sub-variance

| Favourable sub-variance | Adverse sub-variance |
|---|---|
| Use of workers with higher skills | Use of workers with lower skills |
| Workers using better machinery | Workers using poor machinery |
| Good working conditions | Poor working conditions |
| High staff morale – highly motivated | Poor staff morale – poor motivation |
| Good levels of quality control | Poor levels of quality control |

**Table 45.4** Direct labour rate sub-variance

| Favourable sub-variance | Adverse sub-variance |
|---|---|
| Use of lower-grade workers earning lower rates of pay | Use of higher-grade workers earning higher rates of pay |
| Wage deflation | Wage inflation – general or specific to workers being employed |
| Reduction in overtime or premium rates being paid | Increase in overtime or premium rates being paid |

**Table 45.5** Sales volume sub-variance

| Favourable sub-variance | Adverse sub-variance |
|---|---|
| More aggressive marketing strategy | Less aggressive marketing strategy |
| Increased seasonal sales | Decrease in seasonal sales |
| Less competition in sector:<br>• fewer sales by competitors<br>• higher market share | More competition in sector:<br>• more sales going to competitors<br>• lower market share |
| Change in consumer tastes | Change in consumer tastes |
| | Defective product |

**Table 45.6** Sales price sub-variance

| Favourable sub-variance | Adverse sub-variance |
|---|---|
| Increase in price to compensate for increased costs | Reduction in selling price for bulk sales |
| Increase in price after use of 'penetration' (marginal cost) pricing | Reduction in price – to attract new customers; by using marginal cost pricing; to penetrate a new market; to quickly sell off goods, etc. |

### 45.8.4 Interconnections between sub-variances

There are interconnections between sub-variances and, generally, you would do well to identify these interrelationships where possible.

Here are a few interrelating sub-variances:

- Favourable materials usage sub-variance *and* Adverse labour rate sub-variance:

| | | |
|---|---|---|
| fewer materials being used | *because* | a higher skilled workforce is being used and has to be paid more |

- Adverse labour efficiency sub-variance *and* Adverse materials usage sub-variance:

| | | |
|---|---|---|
| workers taking longer to make goods because of faulty machinery | *which results in* | the machinery spoiling much of the materials being used |

➤ Now try Questions 7 and 8.

**Self-test questions**

1 Total variance = Standard cost – ___________
2 Copy out the 'grid' used to calculate sub-variances.
3 Usage is applied to direct materials. What is the word that replaces 'usage' in 'Direct labour ___________ sub-variance'?
4 We say 'materials price'. What word do we use for the price of labour?
5 Standard quantity direct materials information: 40 units; standard price $10.00. Actual quantity 50 units; actual price $10.00. Calculate the direct materials usage sub-variance.
6 X is a manufacturing business. Budgeted production is 1000 units. Budgeted materials used: 500 tonnes. Actual materials used: 550 tonnes. Which figure should be used in the grid for Sq?
7 Why is a budget sometimes flexed?
8 Explain a possible factor that would result in an adverse materials usage sub-variance.
9 Explain a possible factor that would result in a favourable labour rate sub-variance.
10 Explain how the use of poor machinery might affect a direct materials usage sub-variance and a labour efficiency sub-variance.

➤ Now try Questions 9–14.

**Chapter summary**

- Standard costs are predetermined and reflect possible levels of costs and revenues that ought to be achieved under conditions of acceptable levels of efficiency.
- Standard costs are used to prepare budgets and may be used in pricing policies.
- Variances identify differences between standards set and actual performance. They are composed of sub-variances.
- If actual performance is different from standard performance, the budget may have to be flexed.
- Analysis of sub-variances is necessary in order to eradicate problem areas in production or to copy good practice.
- A sub-variance in one area may cause a sub-variance in another connected area.

# 46 Capital investment appraisal

**Content**

**2.4 Investment appraisal**

- Understand the process of investment appraisal
- Ascertain future net cash inflows and outflows arising from the project, including the treatment of working capital
- Discuss the advantages and disadvantages of and apply the following capital investment appraisal techniques: net present value (NPV); accounting rate of return (ARR); payback; internal rate of return (IRR)
- Make investment decisions and recommendations using supporting data
- Evaluate, apply and discuss sensitivity analysis techniques in respect of the data prepared

**By the end of this chapter you should be able to:**

- understand the need for appraising capital investment options available to a business
- calculate net present values of future cash flows
- understand the payback, discounted payback, internal rate of return, accounting rate of return and net present value methods of capital investment appraisal
- analyse and evaluate capital investment proposals.

## 46.1 The need for appraisal of capital investment projects

We have seen that non-current assets are the wealth generators of a business. They are purchased with the intention that they will generate profits for the business for some years into the future.

The non-current assets used in a business usually comprise:

- land
- buildings
- machinery
- plant
- vehicles
- office equipment, etc.

They are used in the business for more than one financial time period.

The managers of a business are always looking for good value when they purchase non-current assets, just as you do when buying clothes, a mobile phone, etc.

Like you, the managers of a business do not have unlimited resources; as with you, available cash is a scarce resource; and, like you, the managers must plan their capital expenditure very carefully so that they get the best value for their money. They want to ensure that they earn maximum benefits from their purchase, just like you.

Since the money available to a business for a capital project is likely to be limited or in short supply, some form of rationing the available money is often required. Capital investment appraisal techniques are used by managers to assist them in their choice of appropriate investment opportunities.

Capital projects are appraised (evaluated) according to potential earning power.

Care must be taken when making a capital investment decision:

- Large sums of money are generally involved.
- The money may well be 'tied up' for a considerable length of time.
- The decisions cannot generally be easily reversed.
- The money committed is usually non-returnable.

Consider a family commitment to the purchase of their largest item of capital expenditure – property, i.e. a house or apartment:

- A large sum of money is involved.
- The money will probably be tied up for many years.
- It might be difficult to resell the property.
- Once purchased, the property cannot be returned to the previous owners.

A major investment in capital equipment needs careful appraisal.

It is equally important that managers of a business take care when making a capital investment appraisal. As much detailed information as possible should be obtained from all sources that may be affected by the decision, or that may affect the decision.

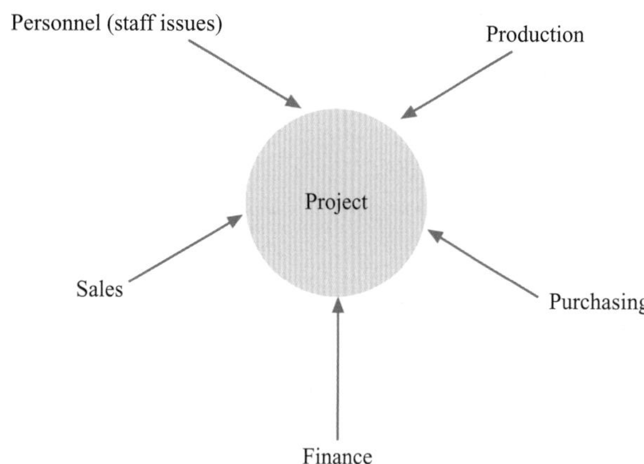


**Figure 46.1** Some sources of information that may affect or be affected by an investment decision

Capital projects are evaluated (appraised) in terms of their potential earning power. If the managers of a business need to replace an obsolete piece of machinery or purchase further pieces of machinery to complete a new project, they must decide which new machine to purchase. There would be no choice to be made if there was only one type of machine on the market that would do the job; they would not have to make a choice (other than to buy or not to buy!). In the real world there are usually alternative options from which to choose.

Machines might:

- have different prices
- have different qualities
- produce different quantities of goods
- produce different quality of goods
- have different life spans
- have different rates of obsolescence.

These differences apply to most capital purchases in both the business world and in the world outside of business, for example TV sets, DVD machines, computers.

There are five main methods of evaluating a capital project. They are:

- the **payback** method
- the **accounting rate of return** method (ARR)
- the **net present value** method (NPV)
- the **discounted payback** method
- the **internal rate of return** method (IRR).

All the methods require predictions about future flows of either cash or profits.

If the predictions are inaccurate, there could be serious problems for the business because of:

- the large sums of cash being involved
- the long-term commitment of cash and other resources
- the effect on profits.

**Opportunity cost** is the benefit from the alternative use of resources that is foregone when a new project is undertaken.

**Note:** From this point, reference will be made only to 'projects' but be aware that the text does also apply to the purchase of non-current assets.

So, managers will often use more than one method of appraising a project that could affect the business for many years.

**Sunk costs** are unrecoverable expenditures already incurred before a project is undertaken.

Capital expenditure appraisal only considers **incremental** revenue and **incremental** expenditure (the incremental expenditure may include opportunity costs). That is, any *additional* revenue generated by the project and any *additional* expenditure that may be incurred by the project.

Existing revenue and expenditure that has no influence on the new project is disregarded.

**Self-test questions**

1 Only large businesses need to evaluate capital projects. True/False?
2 Explain why the managers of a business would think it necessary to undertake a capital investment appraisal.
3 Identify two reasons why it is important to appraise capital investment decisions.
4 What is meant by the term 'opportunity cost'?
5 When undertaking a capital investment appraisal it is only necessary to consider the additional costs and additional revenues caused by the purchase of the new asset. True/False?

## 46.2 The payback method

The **payback period** is the length of time required for the total cash flows to equal the initial capital investment, i.e. how long will it take the project to pay for itself? The payback period is measured in years.

Risk is an important factor to be taken into account when considering a project lasting a few years. The sooner the capital expenditure is recouped, the better – this is the essence of the payback method.

The method is used widely in practice since most businesses are concerned with short time horizons.

Also, the longer the time horizon involved, the less reliable are the predicted inflows of cash. The earlier receipts are received, the sooner further investments can be made. A long payback period increases the possibility that the initial outlay will not be recouped at all.

Payback uses *cash flows* – so non-cash items, e.g. depreciation, accruals, prepayments, are ignored.

**Worked example**

Olive Branch is considering the purchase of a new machine. Two different machines will suit her purpose.

The cash flows are given:

| | Machine Argo | Machine Binko |
|---|---|---|
| | Cost $210 000 | Cost $180 000 |
| | Estimated cash flows | Estimated cash flows |
| | $ | $ |
| **Year 1** | 70 000 | 70 000 |
| **Year 2** | 80 000 | 70 000 |
| **Year 3** | 90 000 | 80 000 |
| **Year 4** | 90 000 | 80 000 |

**Required**

Calculate the payback period for each of the two machines.

## Answer

- **Machine Argo**
  The initial outlay will be paid back partway through Year 3.
  ($70 000 Year 1 + $80 000 Year 2 + $60 000 partway through Year 3)
  More precisely, 60 000/90 000ths through the third year
  Machine Argo payback is two and 60/90th years = 2.67 years.
- **Machine Binko**
  The initial outlay will also be paid back partway through Year 3.
  ($70 000 + $70 000 + $40 000 partway through Year 3)
  More precisely, 40 000/80 000ths through Year 3
  Machine Binko payback is two and 40/80th years = 2.5 years.

If Olive is only concerned with cash flows generated, then she should buy machine Binko.

**Note**

In the following questions and examples:

- the date of initial purchase is labelled Year 0.
- all cash outflows and inflows are deemed to accrue evenly throughout each year.

➤ Now try Question 1.

Some questions require that you calculate the projected cash flows to include in your calculations.

There are two types of question: when profits are given in the question, and when annual cash inflows and annual cash outflows are given separately.

## Type 1 When profits are given

(Remember, payback uses cash flows not profits.)

**Worked example**

The following information is available for two proposed projects:

| | Project 2178 | Project 2179 |
|---|---|---|
| | **$000** | **$000** |
| Initial costs | (14 000) | (12 000) |
| **Expected profits generated:** | | |
| **Year 1** | 3 500 | 3 500 |
| **Year 2** | 5 000 | 4 000 |
| **Year 3** | 8 000 | 5 500 |
| **Year 4** | 10 000 | 6 500 |

**Additional information**

The profit for each project has been calculated after providing for annual depreciation as follows:

| Project 2178 | Project 2179 |
|---|---|
| **$000** | **$000** |
| 1 500 | 1 200 |

**Required**

a Calculate the payback period for both projects.

b State which project should be undertaken.

## Answer

a

| | Project 2178 | Project 2179 |
|---|---|---|
| **Cash flows** | **$000** | **$000** |
| **Year 0** | (14000) | (12000) |
| **Year 1** | 5000 | 4700 |
| **Year 2** | 6500 | 5200 |
| **Year 3** | 9500 | 6700 |
| Payback | 2.26 years<br>(2 years 2500/9500) | 2.31 years<br>(2 years 2100/6700) |

b Project 2178 should be undertaken – it has the shorter payback period.

➤ Now try Question 2.

## Type 2 When annual cash inflows and annual cash outflows are given separately

In this type of question, simply deduct the annual cash outflows (expenses) from the annual cash inflows (receipts) to obtain the net cash flows.

**Example**

- **Year 1** Cash receipts $100000; cash expenditure $20000; net cash flow $80000
- **Year 2** Cash receipts $120000; cash expenditure $25000; net cash flow $95000
- **Year 3** Cash receipts $130000; cash expenditure $25000; net cash flow $105000

➤ Now try Question 3.

In the examples used and in the question, we have merely considered the financial aspects of deciding on a project. Clearly, the managers of a business would consider all the ways that a decision might impinge on the business. They would also consider, for example, how a decision might affect:

- the workforce – does the decision require more workers?
  – does the decision mean that some workers will lose their jobs?
- the environment – pollution
- the locality – is more space needed for expansion?
  – is the local infrastructure capable of supporting the 'new' project?

### 46.2.1 Advantages of using the payback method

- It is relatively simple to calculate.
- It is fairly easy for non-accountants to understand.
- The use of cash is more objective than using profits that are dependent on the accounting policies decided by managers.
- Since all future predictions carry an element of risk, it shows the project that involves the least risk because it recognises that cash received earlier in the project life cycle is preferable to cash received later.
- It shows the project that benefits a firm's liquidity.

The **time value of money**. Money received or paid in the future does not have the same value as money received or paid today. This concept recognises that $1 received today is worth more than $1 received in one year's time or in five years' time.

### 46.2.2 Disadvantages of using the payback method

- It ignores the time-value of money (but see below).
- It ignores the life expectancy of the project; it does not consider cash flows that take place after the payback period.
- Projects may have different patterns of cash inflows.

For example, consider:

| | Project 1 | Project 2 |
|---|---|---|
| | $ | $ |
| **Year 0** | (10 000) | (10 000) |
| **Year 1** | 10 000 | 1 |
| **Year 2** | 1 | 1 |
| **Year 3** | 1 | 50 000 |
| **Year 4** | 1 | 50 000 |

- Project 1 has a payback period of one year.
- Project 2 has a payback period of 2.2 years.

Payback in this case does not give a realistic appraisal.

If a machine has a scrap or trade-in value, this will be treated as an income in the year of disposal.

**Self-test questions**

6 Payback uses cash flows to appraise a possible capital investment decision. True/False?
7 A machine is purchased for $600. The net cash inflows are: Year 1 $250; Year 2 $250; Year 3 $250. In which year will the machine pay for itself?
8 Identify one advantage of using payback as a method of investment appraisal.
9 Outline two limitations of using payback as a method of appraisal.

## 46.3 The accounting rate of return method (ARR)

This method of appraisal has some similarities to the calculation of return on capital employed (ROCE). It shows the return on the investment expressed as a percentage of the average investment over the period.

Average investment seems rather complicated to calculate – have a look at the way it is calculated and then learn the formula.

**Worked example**

A machine is purchased for $100 000. It will be used for two years and will then be traded in for $20 000.

**Required**

Calculate the average investment on the machine over the two years.

### Answer

The machine will incur depreciation, using the straight-line method, of $40 000 per annum.

($100 000 – $20 000 = $80 000 ÷ 2 years = $40 000 per annum)

| | Start of year | End of year | Average investment over year |
|---|---|---|---|
| **Investment Year 1** | $100 000 | $60 000 | $80 000 ($160 000 ÷ 2) |
| **Investment Year 2** | $60 000 | $20 000 | $40 000 ($80 000 ÷ 2) |

So:

- in Year 1, average investment = $80 000
- in Year 2, average investment = $40 000

$120 000

$$\text{Average investment over two years} = \frac{\$120\,000}{2} = \$60\,000$$

**Worked example**

A machine is purchased for \$350 000. It will be used for five years, after which it will have a scrap value of \$50 000.

**Required**

Calculate the average investment in the machine over the five years.

## Answer

Average investment = \$200 000

Annual depreciation = \$300 000 ÷ 5 = \$60 000

| | | Start of year | End of year | Average investment over year |
|---|---|---|---|---|
| | | \$ | \$ | \$ |
| **Investment** | **Year 1** | 350 000 | 290 000 | 320 000 |
| | **Year 2** | 290 000 | 230 000 | 260 000 |
| | **Year 3** | 230 000 | 170 000 | 200 000 |
| | **Year 4** | 170 000 | 110 000 | 140 000 |
| | **Year 5** | 110 000 | 50 000 | 80 000 |
| | | | Total | 1000 000 |

Average investment over five years = \$1000 000 ÷ 5 years = \$200 000 per year

There is an arithmetic short cut which gives the correct answer without the long complicated calculation shown in the two worked examples given above:

**Formula**

$$\text{Average investment} = \frac{\text{Initial investment} + \text{Scrap value}}{2}$$

It does seem improbable that the scrap value is added, but it does work! Check the two worked examples above:

**Example**

### Example 1

Purchase price \$100 000 + Scrap value \$20 000 = \$120 000

$$\frac{\$120\,000}{2} = \text{Average investment } \$60\,000$$

### Example 2

Purchase price \$350 000 + Scrap value \$50 000 = \$400 000

$$\frac{\$400\,000}{2} = \text{Average investment } \$200\,000$$

This shorter method works! It always works!

The calculation of ARR uses *profits*, not cash flows.

**Formula**

$$\text{Accounting rate of return} = \frac{\text{Average profits}}{\text{Average investment}} \times 100$$

**Worked example**

Aoife is considering the purchase of a machine. There are two models that will suit her needs. All profits are assumed to accrue on the last day of the year.

| | Machine Ara | Machine Bibi |
|---|---|---|
| | Cost $160 000 | Cost $210 000 |
| | Estimated profits | Estimated profits |
| | $ | $ |
| **Year 1** | 50 000 | 70 000 |
| **Year 2** | 60 000 | 90 000 |
| **Year 3** | 70 000 | 110 500 |
| **Year 4** | 80 000 | 88 000 |
| **Year 5** | 60 000 | 84 000 |
| **Year 5 Scrap value** | 10 000 | 40 000 |

**Required**

a Calculate the accounting rate of return for both machines.

b Advise Aoife which machine she should purchase.

## Answer

| | Machine Ara | Machine Bibi |
|---|---|---|
| Average profit: | $\frac{\$320\,000}{5 \text{ years}} = \$64\,000$ | $\frac{\$442\,500}{5 \text{ years}} = \$88\,500$ |
| Average investment: | $\frac{\$160\,000 + \$10\,000}{2}$ | $\frac{\$210\,000 + \$40\,000}{2}$ |
| | $= \$85\,000$ | $= \$125\,000$ |

a Machine Ara: Accounting rate of return $= \frac{\$64\,000}{\$85\,000} \times 100 = 75.3\%$

Machine Bibi: Accounting rate of return $= \frac{\$88\,500}{\$125\,000} \times 100 = 70.8\%$

b Aoife should choose Machine Ara because this gives her a higher rate of return than Machine Bibi.

➤ Now try Question 4.

## 46.3.1 Additional working capital

Some projects will require an injection of additional working capital in the form of extra inventory and, as a result, more trade payables. The increase in working capital can be assumed to be a constant during the lifetime of the project. This means that there is no need to calculate the average increase in working capital over this time.

**Mutually exclusive** – the pursuit of one course of action will preclude the pursuit of any other action. For example, I can either go to a friend's house for a meal or I can go to a soccer match to watch my favourite team. I cannot do both. The two activities are mutually exclusive.

**Worked example**

Kosuke is considering an investment in a new project. The initial investment is $450 000. The project will require an increase in working capital of $50 000.

**Required**

Calculate the average investment in the project.

## Answer

Average investment $= \frac{\$450\,000}{2} + \$50\,000 = \$275\,000$

## 46.3.2 Advantages of using the accounting rate of return method

- ARR is fairly easy to calculate.
- Results can be compared to present profitability.
- It takes into account the aggregate earnings of the project(s).

### 46.3.3 Disadvantages of using the accounting rate of return method

- ARR does not take into account the time value of money.
- It does not recognise the timing of cash flows (see same disadvantage for payback).

**Self-test questions**

10 The accounting rate of return uses profits in the formula. True/False?
11 Average investment for the period = Half of the initial investment + Scrap value. True/False?
12 If a business has a return on capital employed of 23 per cent, what will be the minimum return necessary in order to undertake a new project?
13 Outline two advantages of using ARR as a method of capital appraisal.
14 Outline two disadvantages of using ARR as a method of capital investment appraisal.
15 Initial investment $100 000; additional working capital required $20 000. Calculate the average investment.

## 46.4 The net present value method (NPV)

Which of the following would give you the better value for money?

- spending $100 today
- spending $100 in ten years' time

I think that most people would say that $100 spent today would give them the better value.

Why?

The future is uncertain – there is an element of risk involved. Also, as time goes on, there is a tendency for money to become less valuable.

When your grandparents bought their apartment many years ago, they may have spent $2000. Would that buy the same apartment today? I don't think so!

If $1 were received and invested at five per cent per annum, it would be worth $1.05 in one year's time; if it were left to accumulate interest it would be worth just over $1.10 ($1.102) in two years' time and just under $1.16 ($1.158) in three years' time.

Looked at from another perspective:

- If 86.4 cents were invested today at five per cent for three years, this would yield $1.
- If 90.7 cents were invested today at five per cent for two years, this would yield $1.
- If 95.2 cents were invested at five per cent for one year, this would yield $1.

**Cost of capital** is based on the weighted average cost of capital available to a business.

A **discount factor** allows the value of future cash flows to be calculated in terms of their value if they were received today.

The **net present value method** of investment appraisal of a project is calculated by taking the present day (discounted) value of all future net cash flows based on the business's cost of capital and subtracting the initial cost of the investment.

Managers of a business invest in capital projects to provide security for the future through profits and cash flows.

As individuals, we invest to provide for the future, and we hope that the monetary rewards in the future will be worth waiting for.

In giving up the money today, we expect a reward. The reward is the interest that we will earn on our investment.

In the same way that we may invest in, say, a bank savings account to get a return on our investment, managers of a business will invest in projects that will pay a return on their investment.

Managers evaluate a project by comparing the capital investment with the return that the investment will bring in the future.

In order to make a meaningful comparison between the amount originally invested and the income generated in the future by that investment, there is a need to

**discount** the cash flows so that they are the equivalent of cash flows now. Thus we can compare like with like.

We can compare the initial investment at today's price with future cash inflows, discounted to give their values in today's world.

The discount factor used in net present value (NPV) calculations is generally based on a weighted average cost of capital available to the business.

## Example

Schiffe Ltd has the following capital structure:

| | $ |
|---|---|
| Ordinary shares (currently paying a dividend of 9% per annum) | 1000000 |
| 6% preference shares | 500000 |
| 7% debenture stock | 200000 |
| Bank loan (current interest rate payable 8%) | 300000 |

The weighted average cost of capital for Schiffe Ltd is:

| | Nominal value | Rate paid | Cost of capital per annum |
|---|---|---|---|
| | $ | | $ |
| Ordinary shares | 1000000 | 9% | 90000 |
| Preference shares | 500000 | 6% | 30000 |
| Debenture stock | 200000 | 7% | 14000 |
| Bank loan | 300000 | 8% | 24000 |
| | 2000000 | | 158000 |

$$\text{Average cost of capital} = \frac{\text{Cost of capital per annum}}{\text{Nominal value of capital}}$$

$$= \frac{158000}{2000000} = 7.9\%$$

This shows that the average cost of Schiffe Ltd raising further capital would be 7.9 per cent.

If you are given a number of discount factors to choose from, select the one identified as the cost of capital.

**Note**

The example is correct in principle. However, the interest on debenture stock and the bank loan are revenue expenditure (they reduce profits) – they would reduce the amount of tax payable by Schiffe Ltd. So, in reality, the two figures should be shown in the calculation net of taxation.

**More important note:** You will be given the discount factor (i.e. the cost of capital) in a question – 'thank goodness', I hear you say!

There is a misconception by students that a discount factor is used to take into account the effects of inflation on future cash flows – this is not so. The effects that inflation have on results are self-correcting.

The discount factor is based on the business's cost of capital (see above).

Generally, what we consider is what would happen if we were fortunate enough to be able to invest, say, $1000 in a bank account or a business project for, say, four years. We calculate how much our investment would be worth each year if the investment were earning, say, five per cent per annum.

At the end of:

| | |
|---|---|
| **Year 1** | $1050 |
| **Year 2** | $1102 |
| **Year 3** | $1158 |
| **Year 4** | $1216 |

Discounting uses the same principle but in reverse.

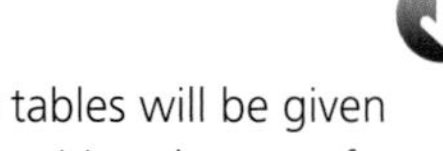

**Tip**

Net present value tables will be given in any question requiring the use of net present value.

If I require $1000 in four years' time and the interest rate, or rate of return, was five per cent, how much do I have to invest today? I would have to invest $823.

The present value gives the value of a future sum of money at today's values.

If you wish to have $100 in four years' time and the interest rates were seven per cent, you should invest $76.30 today.

Working this in reverse, we can say that $100 received in four years' time is equivalent to receiving $76.30 today.

($76.30 placed on deposit today and receiving interest of seven per cent per annum would produce a deposit of $100 in four years' time.)

How did I work these figures out? I used a set of present value tables!

### Worked example

Calculate the value of:

a $120

b $196

c $42

if the amount were invested for three years at three per cent per annum.

The following figures give the value of $1 at a compound interest rate of three per cent:

| | |
|---|---|
| **Year 1** | 1.030 |
| **Year 2** | 1.061 |
| **Year 3** | 1.093 |
| **Year 4** | 1.126 |

### Answer

a $1 invested today would yield $1.09 ($1.093) in three years' time, so $120 invested would yield $131.16 ($120 × 1.093).

b $214.23

c $45.91

### Worked example

Calculate the present value of:

a $926

b $62

c $1380

received in five years' time if the current cost of capital is nine per cent per annum.

The following figures give the present value of $1 at nine per cent:

| | |
|---|---|
| **Year 1** | 0.917 |
| **Year 2** | 0.842 |
| **Year 3** | 0.772 |
| **Year 4** | 0.708 |
| **Year 5** | 0.650 |

### Answer

a $1 received in five years' time would have a value of 65 cents if received today, so $926 received in five years' time has a value of $601.90 today.

b $40.30

c $897.00

The net present value method of capital investment appraisal compares the investment (at today's prices) with future net cash flows (discounted to give the values at today's prices).

Here is a table showing the present value of $1 at a number of different discount rates:

| | | 4% | 5% | 6% | 7% | 8% | 9% | 10% |
|---|---|---|---|---|---|---|---|---|
| **Period** | **1** | 0.961 | 0.952 | 0.943 | 0.935 | 0.926 | 0.917 | 0.909 |
| | **2** | 0.925 | 0.907 | 0.890 | 0.873 | 0.857 | 0.842 | 0.826 |
| | **3** | 0.889 | 0.864 | 0.840 | 0.816 | 0.794 | 0.772 | 0.751 |
| | **4** | 0.855 | 0.823 | 0.792 | 0.763 | 0.735 | 0.708 | 0.683 |
| | **5** | 0.822 | 0.784 | 0.747 | 0.713 | 0.681 | 0.650 | 0.621 |

## Worked example

James Squirrel is considering whether to purchase a new machine for his workshop. The machine will cost $12 000 and be used for five years, after which time it will be scrapped. The following cash flows relate to the machine:

| | Revenue receipts | Revenue expenditure |
|---|---|---|
| | $ | $ |
| **Year 1** | 8 000 | 4 000 |
| **Year 2** | 8 500 | 5 000 |
| **Year 3** | 7 000 | 4 000 |
| **Year 4** | 5 000 | 3 000 |
| **Year 5** | 3 000 | 1 000 |

The current cost of capital for James is ten per cent. All costs are paid and incomes received on the last day of each financial year.

The following extract is taken from the present value tables for $1:

| | 10% |
|---|---|
| **Year 1** | 0.909 |
| **Year 2** | 0.826 |
| **Year 3** | 0.751 |
| **Year 4** | 0.683 |
| **Year 5** | 0.621 |

**Required**

a Calculate the net present value of purchasing the new machine.

b Advise James whether he should invest in the new machine.

### Answer

| Year | Cash flows | Discount factor | Net present value |
|---|---|---|---|
| | $ | | $ |
| **0** (now) | (12 000) | 1.000 | (12 000) |
| **1** | 4 000 | 0.909 | 3 636 |
| **2** | 3 500 | 0.826 | 2 891 |
| **3** | 3 000 | 0.751 | 2 253 |
| **4** | 2 000 | 0.683 | 1 366 |
| **5** | 2 000 | 0.621 | 1 242 |
| | | Net present value | (612) |

James should not invest in the new machine as it will yield a negative net present value.

**Note**

The cash inflows are calculated from the revenue receipts less revenue expenditure. Any project that yields a positive net present value should be considered.

Projects that yield negative net present values should be rejected on financial grounds but may be considered on other grounds, for example to keep a good customer happy; to keep a good, skilled workforce within the business; perhaps to get further profitable orders in the near future.

## Worked example

The managers of Dvorak Ltd wish to purchase a new machine. They will use the machine for four years. There are three machines that are capable of producing the quality of goods that are desired. The current cost of capital for Dvorak Ltd is nine per cent. The following is an extract from the present value tables for $1.

| | 9% |
|---|---|
| **Year 1** | 0.917 |
| **Year 2** | 0.842 |
| **Year 3** | 0.772 |
| **Year 4** | 0.708 |

All cash flows arise at the end of the relevant year.

The following information is available for the three machines:

| Machine | 78/BA | 92/DC | 36/FE |
|---|---|---|---|
| | $ | $ | $ |
| Purchase price | 88 000 | 99 000 | 115 000 |
| **Forecast net cash flows:** | | | |
| **Year 1** | 44 000 | 47 000 | 50 000 |
| **Year 2** | 44 000 | 47 000 | 49 000 |
| **Year 3** | 40 000 | 47 000 | 48 000 |
| **Year 4** | 40 000 | 45 000 | 44 000 |

**Required**

a Calculate the NPV of each machine.

b Advise the managers of Dvorak Ltd which of the three machines they should purchase.

### Answer

a

| Machine | 78/BA | 92/DC | 36/FE |
|---|---|---|---|
| Present values | $ | $ | $ |
| **Year 0** | (88 000) | (99 000) | (115 000) |
| **Year 1** | 40 348 | 43 099 | 45 850 |
| **Year 2** | 37 048 | 39 574 | 41 258 |
| **Year 3** | 30 880 | 36 284 | 37 056 |
| **Year 4** | 28 320 | 31 860 | 31 152 |
| **Net present values** | 48 596 | 51 817 | 40 316 |

b The managers should purchase machine 92/DC because it yields the highest positive net present value.

**Note**

When a selection has to be made, the machine that yields the highest net present value should be chosen.

If all the machines yielded a negative net present value, then none of the machines should be purchased.

In this example, all machines will yield a positive NPV and, under different circumstances, they would all be worth purchasing.

## 46.4.1 Advantages of using the net present value method

- The time value of money is taken into account as adjustments are made to take account of the present value of future cash flows.
- It is relatively easily to understand.
- Greater importance is given to earlier cash flows.

## 46.4.2 Disadvantages of using the net present value method

Because the figures are projections, all the figures are of a speculative nature:

- Inflows are difficult to predict; outflows are equally difficult to predict.
- The current cost of capital may change over the life of the project.
- The life of the project is difficult to predict.

When the net cash flows to be discounted are the same amounts, time can be saved by totalling the discount factors for the appropriate years and multiplying the amount by this total.

**Worked example**

The following net cash inflows are given for a machine:

| | $ |
|---|---|
| **Year 1** | 40 000 |
| **Year 2** | 40 000 |
| **Year 3** | 40 000 |
| **Year 4** | 40 000 |

The present cost of capital is four per cent.

All cash flows arise at the end of the relevant year.

**Required**

Calculate the net present value of the cash flows.

### Answer

| | Cash flows | Discount factor | NPV |
|---|---|---|---|
| | $ | | $ |
| **Year 1** | 40 000 | 0.961 | 38 440 |
| **Year 2** | 40 000 | 0.925 | 37 000 |
| **Year 3** | 40 000 | 0.889 | 35 560 |
| **Year 4** | 40 000 | 0.855 | 34 200 |
| **Net present values** | | Net present value | 145 200 |

The same results would be given if 3.63 (0.961 + 0.925 + 0.889 + 0.855) is multiplied by the (constant) $40 000.

**Note**

This technique can only be used if the net cash flows are the same amount.

We said earlier that a major drawback in using the payback method was that it did not take into account the time value of money. We can take the current cost of capital into account by using discounting techniques (see below).

**Self-test questions**

16 NPV is an abbreviation of net positive value. True/False?
17 $1000 received in two years' time is worth more/less than $1000 received today? (Delete the incorrect response.)
18 Identify two disadvantages of using NPV as a method of capital investment appraisal.
19 The discount factor used in NPV calculations is based on the predicted average inflation rate over the period of investment. True/False?
20 NPV of machine A is $4760; NPV of machine B is $1920. Identify the machine that should be purchased.
21 NPV of machine X is $(2350); NPV of machine Y is $(1990). Identify the machine that should be purchased.

## 46.5 The discounted payback method

This method is widely used in business as a method of selecting a machine or project.

**Worked example**

Celeste Durrant is considering the purchase of a new machine at a cost of $120 000. The estimated net cash flows generated by the machine over the next five years are provided. It is assumed that all cash flows arise at the end of the relevant year.

| | $ |
|---|---|
| Year 1 | 30 000 |
| Year 2 | 45 000 |
| Year 3 | 50 000 |
| Year 4 | 55 000 |
| Year 5 | 45 000 |

The current cost of capital is six per cent.

Assume that cash flows accrue evenly throughout the year.

Extracts from the present value table for $1 at five per cent, six per cent and seven per cent are given:

| | 5% | 6% | 7% |
|---|---|---|---|
| Year 1 | 0.952 | 0.943 | 0.935 |
| Year 2 | 0.907 | 0.890 | 0.873 |
| Year 3 | 0.864 | 0.840 | 0.816 |
| Year 4 | 0.823 | 0.792 | 0.763 |
| Year 5 | 0.784 | 0.747 | 0.713 |

**Required**

Calculate the discounted payback period for the machine.

## Answer

The three tables are given because questions in examinations sometimes provide more than one. If this is the case, choose the table that corresponds to the current cost of capital. In this case, the six per cent table should be chosen.

| | Cash flow | Discount factor | Net present value |
|---|---|---|---|
| | $ | | $ |
| **Year 1** | 30 000 | 0.943 | 28 290 |
| **Year 2** | 45 000 | 0.890 | 40 050 |
| **Year 3** | 50 000 | 0.840 | 42 000 |
| **Year 4** | 55 000 | 0.792 | 43 560 |
| **Year 5** | 45 000 | 0.747 | 33 615 |

Payback will be partway through Year 4:

$120 000 – ($28 290 + $40 050 + $42 000) = $9670

$9670 ÷ $43 560 = 0.22 of Year 4

Therefore payback is 3.22 years.

➤ Now try Questions 5 and 6.

Two further points need to be considered:

- Many discounted cash flow questions are linked with social accounting issues, for example pollution issues, unemployment.
  You may have to discuss these issues once you have reached a decision about the project (or machine) that is recommended by the financial aspects of your decision.
- At the end of a project's life there may be some residual or scrap value to be considered. This should simply be treated as further income in the year in which it occurs.

### Worked example

The following cash inflows are generated by a machine:

| | $000 |
|---|---|
| **Year 1** | 240 |
| **Year 2** | 320 |
| **Year 3** | 650 |

At the end of Year 3 the machine will be sold. It is estimated that it will sell for $60 000.

**Required**

Prepare a schedule of cash inflows generated by the machine.

## Answer

| Schedule of cash inflows | |
|---|---|
| | $000 |
| **Year 1** | 240 |
| **Year 2** | 320 |
| **Year 3** | 710<br>($650 000 + $60 000) |

## 46.6 The internal rate of return method (IRR)

A business must be profitable in order to survive. A business must ensure that projects undertaken are profitable.

Net present value compares present day values of future estimated cash inflows with present day cash outflows. However, such a comparison does not give managers the rate of return expected on the investment.

The return on a project must cover the cost of capital, so if a business has a cost of capital of 12 per cent, any projects undertaken must yield a return that is greater than 12 per cent.

Managers need to be able to calculate the rate of return that any project being considered is likely to yield; this expected yield can then be compared with the cost of the capital needed to fund the project. The process involved is to calculate the present value of future cash flows which, when discounted, will equal zero.

The process used is to select two discounting rates: one that will give a positive net present value and a second that will give a negative net present value. The results are then used in the following formula:

**Formula**

$$\text{Internal rate of return} = P + \left[(N - P) \times \frac{p}{p + n}\right]$$

where $P$ = % rate giving positive NPV

$N$ = % rate giving negative NPV

$p$ = value of positive NPV

$n$ = value of negative NPV

**Note**

'$n$' is a negative value, so it should be added to the value of '$p$' in the denominator since mathematically the subtraction of a negative number will result in an increase in value.

**Worked example**

The managers of Kai Ltd are considering whether or not to invest in a new machine costing $9000. Their current cost of capital is 12 per cent. They have estimated that the future cash flows using a net present value of ten per cent will be $871.80 and at 15 per cent the value will be $(378.90).

**Required**

Advise the managers of Kai Ltd whether or not, on financial grounds, they should invest in the new machine.

### Answer

The machine should be purchased. It will yield an internal rate of return of 13.485 per cent, which is greater than the cost of capital.

**Workings**

$$\text{IRR} = P + \left[(N - P) \times \frac{p}{p + n}\right]$$

$$= 10 + \left[(15 - 10) \times \frac{871.80}{871.80 + 378.90}\right]$$

= 10 + (5 × 0.697)

= 10 + 3.485

= 13.485%

The managers of Kai Ltd should invest in the new machine since the IRR is greater than the company's current cost of capital.

---

**Worked example**

Hugo is considering the purchase of a machine which would require an initial outlay of $160 000. His current cost of capital is 12.5 per cent. The net present value of future cash flows for the machine are as follows:

NPV at 10% = $5408; NPV at 40% = $(52 242)

**Required**

Advise Hugo whether or not, on financial grounds, he should invest in the new machine.

### Answer

Hugo should invest in the new machine since it will yield 12.81 per cent, which is greater than his current cost of capital.

**Workings**

$$\text{Internal rate of return} = 10 + \left[(40 - 10) \times \frac{5408}{5408 + 52242}\right]$$

= 10 + (30 × 0.0938)

= 10 + 2.814

= 12.814%

**Note**

The internal rate of return can be calculated using two positive net present values. However, in such cases the '*n*' part of the denominator should be deducted from the value of '*p*'.

➤ Now try Question 7.

---

## 46.7 Sensitivity analysis

The time horizon involved in making sound capital investment decisions is generally long. Looking into the future makes the reliability of forecast data uncertain. **Sensitivity analysis** measures how responsive the outcome of such decisions is to the variability of revenues and costs.

**Example**

A project will require an initial outlay of $45 000. It is estimated that the project will generate net receipts of $15 000 over the next four years. The business's current cost of capital is ten per cent.

The present value of the project's net receipts is $47 535.

The internal rate of return is 12.73 per cent.

**Workings**

NPV at 10% = $15 000 × 3.169 (i.e. 0.909 + 0.826 + 0.751 + 0.683)
= $47535 – $45 000 = $2353

IRR requires a negative NPV, so let's try 16 per cent net present value:

NPV at 16% = $15 000 × 2.798 (0.862 + 0.743 + 0.641 + 0.552)
= $41970 – $45 000 = –$3030

$$IRR = 10 + \left[6 \times \frac{2535}{2535 + 3030}\right] = 12.733\%$$

If a project has a negative net present value, then the project should be rejected.

This project has a positive NPV and an internal rate of return that is greater than the cost of capital, so it should be acceptable.

However, the investment would not be worthwhile if:

- the initial outlay had been 5.6 per cent greater than \$45 000, that is \$47 535

$$\frac{\$2535 \times 100}{\$45\,000} = 5.6\%$$

- the NPV of the receipts had been \$2535 or 5.33 per cent less
- the current cost of capital faced by the business rises above 12.733 per cent, an increase of 27.33 per cent.

As you can imagine, in the 'real world' sensitivity analysis can be much more complicated than the examples used here and in Chapter 29.10. In a dynamic business environment, it is highly likely that several variables could change after the projected data was produced.

## Self-test questions

**22** Identify one method of capital investment appraisal that uses profits in the calculation.

**23** Which methods of capital investment appraisal are calculated using cash flows?

**24** Explain the term 'sunk cost'.

**25** How are sunk costs treated in a capital investment appraisal?

**26** Explain the term 'sensitivity analysis'.

➤ **Now try Question 8.**

## Chapter summary

- The availability of cash resources is generally limited.
- There are five main methods of capital investment appraisal:
  - payback
  - discounted payback
  - accounting rate of return
  - net present value
  - internal rate of return.
- The main disadvantage of payback is overcome by using discounted payback.
- All methods are used to appraise single investment opportunities and they are used to decide between competing strategies.
- Sensitivity analysis calculates the amounts by which factors affecting an investment decision can deviate from the projected data.

## Examination-style questions

1 The treasurer of the Boundary Cricket Club provides the following information for the year ended 30 September 2014:

| | at 30 September 2014 | at 30 September 2013 |
|---|---|---|
| **Assets and liabilities** | **$** | **$** |
| Land and buildings at valuation | 120 000 | 120 000 |
| Equipment at valuation | 27 000 | 26 000 |
| Life membership fund | ? | 12 800 |
| Café inventory | 2 146 | 1 790 |
| Amounts owed to café suppliers | 302 | 248 |
| Subscriptions in arrears | 140 | 350 |
| Subscriptions paid in advance | 490 | 630 |
| General expenses paid in advance | 387 | 842 |

The following receipts and payments account is available:

| | $ | | $ |
|---|---|---|---|
| Balance 1 October 2013 | 10 830 | Purchase of land | 25 000 |
| Subscriptions – annual | 22 470 | Purchases of equipment | 6 540 |
| life membership | 5 850 | Payments to café suppliers | 39 672 |
| Dinner dance receipts | 2 480 | Dinner dance expenses | 2 360 |
| Competition receipts | 3 726 | Competition expenses | 1 988 |
| Café takings | 83 444 | Café staff wages | 12 791 |
| Balance 30 September 2014 | 5 491 | Ground staff wages | 18 477 |
| | | General expenses | 27 463 |
| | 134 291 | | 134 291 |

It is club policy to transfer 10% of the balance standing in the life membership found at the financial year end to the income and expenditure account.

**Required**

Prepare:

a a café trading account for the year ended 30 September 2014 [3]

b an income and expenditure account for the year ended 30 September 2014 [9]

c a statement of financial position at 30 September 2014. [6]

d Evaluate methods of clearing the club's overdraft position. [7]

[Total: 25]

2 The following income statement for the year ended 31 August 2013 is given, together with statements of financial position at 31 August 2012 and 31 August 2013.

**Dratas plc**
**Income statement for the year ended 31 August 2013**

| | $000 |
|---|---|
| Profit from operations | 1123 |
| Interest paid | (29) |
| Profit before tax | 1094 |
| Tax | (447) |
| Profit for the year | 647 |

**Extract from statement of changes in equity**

| | $000 |
|---|---|
| **Retained earnings** | |
| Balance at 1 September 2012 | 544 |
| Profit for the year | 647 |
| | 1191 |
| Dividends paid | (298) |
| Balance at 31 August 2013 | 893 |

**Statement of financial position at 31 August**

| | 2013 | | 2012 | |
|---|---|---|---|---|
| | **$000** | **$000** | **$000** | **$000** |
| **ASSETS** | | | | |
| **Non-current assets** | | | | |
| Patents | | 174 | | 198 |
| Premises | 895 | | 1045 | |
| Depreciation | (186) | 709 | (199) | 846 |
| Machinery | 995 | | 770 | |
| Depreciation | (447) | 548 | (348) | 422 |
| | | 1431 | | 1466 |
| **Current assets** | | | | |
| Inventories | 932 | | 634 | |
| Trade receivables | 805 | | 656 | |
| Cash and cash equivalents | 462 | 2199 | 77 | 1367 |
| **Total assets** | | 3630 | | 2833 |

| | | | | |
|---|---|---|---|---|
| **EQUITY AND LIABILITIES** | | | | |
| **Equity** | | | | |
| Ordinary shares of $1 each | | 1170 | | 1020 |
| Retained earnings | | 893 | | 544 |
| | | 2063 | | 1564 |
| **Non-current liabilities** | | 300 | | 300 |
| **Current liabilities** | | | | |
| Trade payables | 820 | | 606 | |
| Tax | 447 | 1267 | 363 | 969 |
| **Total equity and liabilities** | | 3630 | | 2833 |

**Additional information**

There were no disposals of machinery during the year.

Part of the premises were sold during the year, for $175 000. The profit on the sale was $50 000. There were no additions to premises during the year.

Patents originally cost $240 000 and are being amortised over ten years.

**Required**

**a** Prepare a statement of cash flows for the year ended 31 August 2013. [18]

**b** Discuss the importance of preparing a statement of cash flows. [7]

[Total: 25]

**3** Tesda plc is a supermarket chain. They have been offered the choice of two five-year leases on supermarkets abroad. Lack of finance means that they can choose only one of them.

The directors have projected the following forecasts:

The lease on supermarket A will cost $5m.

The lease on supermarket B will cost $8m.

They expect cash receipts and payments to be as follows:

| Year | Without leasing either new supermarket $ | With supermarket A $ | With supermarket B $ |
|---|---|---|---|
| Total receipts | | | |
| 1 | 61m | 63.6m | 63.9m |
| 2 | 64m | 67.7m | 69.4m |
| 3 | 67m | 71.2m | 73.3m |
| 4 | 71m | 75.5m | 77.9m |
| 5 | 75m | 80.1m | 83.4m |
| Total payments | | | |
| 1 | 20m | 21.8m | 21.8m |
| 2 | 23m | 25.0m | 25.7m |
| 3 | 27m | 29.2m | 30.3m |
| 4 | 32m | 34.4m | 35.9m |
| 5 | 38m | 40.6m | 42.7m |

Assume all receipts and payments occur at the end of the respective year.

**Additional information:**

| Estimated additional costs | Supermarket A | Supermarket B |
|---|---|---|
| Additional working capital required at start of lease | $0.6m | $1m |
| Improvements end of year 2 | - | $1.8m |
| Improvements end of year 3 | $2.9m | - |
| Improvements end of year 4 | - | $1m |
| Depreciation | $0.5m per annum | $0.7m per annum |

**Required**

**a** Calculate the estimated annual net cash flows for

**i** Supermarket A [3]

**ii** Supermarket B [3]

**b** Calculate the accounting rate of return (ARR) for Supermarket A [6]

The following are extracts from present value tables for $1:

| Year | 8% | 14% |
|---|---|---|
| 1 | 0.926 | 0.877 |
| 2 | 0.857 | 0.769 |
| 3 | 0.794 | 0.675 |
| 4 | 0.735 | 0.592 |
| 5 | 0.681 | 0.519 |

The current cost of capital for Tesda plc is 8%.

**Required**

**c** Calculate the net present value for Supermarket B. [5]

The net present value for **each** supermarket using a cost of capital of 14% is estimated to be:

Supermarket A $1 057 900 negative

Supermarket B $2 127 600 negative.

**Required**

**d** Calculate the internal rate of return (IRR) for supermarket B. [4]

**e** Advise the managers of Tesda plc the supermarket that they should lease. [4]

[Total: 25]

*(Adapted from Cambridge International AS and A Level Accounting 9706/04, Paper 4 Q3 May/June 2007)*

4 Prescott, Rohini and Singh have been in partnership for many years with a profit sharing ratio of 2:2:1. Their statement of financial position at 30 June 2011 was as follows:

**Prescott, Rohini and Singh**
**Statement of financial position at 30 June 2011**

| | $ | $ | $ |
|---|---|---|---|
| **ASSETS** | | | |
| **Non-current assets** | | | |
| Property | | 100 000 | |
| Fixtures and fittings | | 34 500 | |
| Motor vehicles | | 16 750 | 151 250 |
| **Current assets** | | | |
| Inventories | | 23 500 | |
| Trade receivables | | 14 850 | |
| Bank | | 7 595 | 45 945 |
| **Total assets** | | | 197 195 |
| **CAPITAL AND LIABILITIES** | | | |
| **Capital** | | | |
| Capital Accounts – Prescott | 70 345 | | |
| – Rohini | 54 250 | | |
| – Singh | 38 150 | | 162 745 |
| **Non-current liabilities** | | | |
| Loan from Prescott at 12% | | | 25 000 |
| **Current liabilities** | | | |
| Trade payables | | | 9 450 |
| **Total capital and liabilities** | | | 197 195 |

The partners sold their business to Ashburton Ltd on 1 July 2011 for $215 000. Ashburton Ltd took over all of the assets and liabilities except the bank account.

The purchase consideration was satisfied by:

1 The issue of 100 000 ordinary shares of $1 at a premium of $0.50.

2 The issue of 8% debentures redeemable at par in 2020 to Prescott to ensure that he receives the same amount of annual interest that he received from the loan.

3 The balance was paid by cash.

On 1 July 2011 the partnership assets were revalued as follows:

| | $ |
|---|---|
| Property | 115 000 |
| Fixtures and fittings | 32 000 |
| Motor vehicles | 15 000 |
| Inventories | 22 000 |
| Trade receivables | 13 500 |

Ashburton Ltd's statement of financial position at 30 June 2011 was as follows:

**Ashburton Ltd**
**Statement of financial position at 30 June 2011**

| | | $ | $ |
|---|---|---|---|
| **ASSETS** | | | |
| **Non-current assets** | | | |
| Property | | 125 000 | |
| Fixtures and fittings | | 67 750 | |
| Motor vehicles | | 24 975 | 217 725 |
| **Current assets** | | | |
| Inventories | | 22 875 | |
| Trade receivables | | 14 363 | |
| Bank | | 28 462 | 65 700 |
| **Total assets** | | | 283 425 |
| **EQUITY AND LIABILITIES** | | | |
| **Equity** | | | |
| Capital accounts | Prescott | 200 000 | |
| | Rohini | 20 000 | |
| | Singh | 48 795 | 268 795 |
| **Current liabilities** | | | |
| Trade payables | | | 14 630 |
| **Total equity and liabilities** | | | 283 425 |

**Required**

a Prepare Ashburton Ltd's statement of financial position immediately after the acquisition of the partnership. [22]

b Explain one reason why the managers of Ashburton Ltd may have acquired the partnershiop of Prescott, Rohini and Singh. [3]

[Total: 25]

*(Adapted from Cambridge International AS and A Level Accounting 9706, Paper 43 Q1, October/November 2011)*

5 Len Zurker provides the following budgeted information:

| | 2016 | | | |
|---|---|---|---|---|
| | **February** | **March** | **April** | **May** |
| | $ | $ | $ | $ |
| Sales | 56 000 | 52 000 | 48 000 | 60 000 |
| Purchases | 32 000 | 30 000 | 28 000 | 40 000 |
| Wages | 6 200 | 6 200 | 6 500 | 6 500 |
| Rent | | 1 200 | | 1 500 |
| Other expenses | 11 400 | 10 200 | 12 500 | 19 700 |
| Depreciation | 1 200 | 1 200 | 1 200 | 1 200 |

It is expected that:

- the cash balance at 1 May will be $780
- 10% of all sales will be on credit
- 10% of all purchases will be for cash

- trade receivables will settle their debts in the month following sale
- trade payables will be paid two months after purchase
- wages, rent and other expenses will be paid for as incurred
- inventory at 1 April is expected to be $3460; at 31 May it is expected to be $4180.

**Required**

a Prepare a cash budget for the month of May. [7]

b Prepare a budgeted income statement for the two months ending 31 May 2016. [9]

c Discuss the advantages and disadvantages of budgeting. [9]

[Total: 25]

6 The managers of Tawanda plc have prepared a draft set of financial statements for the year ended 31 July 2015. According to the draft income statement, the profit for the year was $719 000.

The statement of financial position at 31 July 2014 shows retained profits $1 890 000.

The following information is now available:

1 Some items of damaged inventory have not been included in the income statement at 31 July 2015. These items cost $630; when perfect they have a selling price of $720. They could now be sold for $650 after repairs costing $110 have been undertaken.

2 Trade receivables have increased by $4800 during the financial year ended 31 July 2015. A provision for doubtful debts is made annually. No provision has been made in the current financial year.

3 A non-current asset is shown in the statement of financial position at a carrying amount of $15 000. Its value in use is expected to be $10 000 and its fair value is $8 000.

4 Land and buildings that cost $150 000 had been depreciated until the year ended 31 July 2014 at 2% on cost. In the past year property prices have fallen so no depreciation has been charged in the financial statements for the year ended 31 July 2015.

5 The following data refers to dividends paid and proposed:

| | |
|---|---|
| August 2014 | Directors propose a final dividend of $50 000 based on reported profits for the year ended 31 July 2014. |
| October 2014 | Shareholders approve the final dividend for the year ended 31 July 2014 |
| December 2014 | Final dividend of $50 000 for the year ended 31 July 2014 is paid to shareholders. |
| May 2015 | Interim dividend of $20 000 paid to shareholders based on profits for the half year ended 31 January 2015. |
| August 2015 | Directors propose a final dividend of $52 000 based on profits for the year ended 31 July 2015. |

**Required**

a Identify the International Accounting Standard (IAS) that should be applied to each piece of information (1–5) given. [5]

b Identify and explain **two** reasons for applying IAS's in preparing the financial statements of a limited company. [4]

c Prepare an extract from the statement of changes in equity taking into account the information (1–5) given. [9]

d Discuss your treatment of dividends as they appear in the extract from the statement of changes in equity. [7]

[Total: 25]

7 Orooj Choudhry is a manufacturer. The following information is available for the year ended 30 April 2015:

Revenue $525 342

Production cost of goods completed $258 600

| Inventories | 30 April 2015 | 1 May 2014 |
|---|---|---|
| | $ | $ |
| Raw materials | 3980 | 3720 |
| Work in progress | 7020 | 6140 |
| Finished goods | 9412 | 10530 |

Orooj transfers goods to her trading account at cost plus 30%.

**Required**

a Prepare the trading account for the year ended 30 April 2015. [5]

b Explain reasons why Orooj might transfer goods to her trading account at a price greater than the cost of production. [6]

c Prepare a provision for unrealised profit account for the year ended 30 April 2015. [3]

d Prepare a statement showing the total gross profit earned by Orooj's business for the year ended 30 April 2015. [4]

e Discuss why the managers of a manufacturing business might need to prepare a provision for unrealised profit account. [7]

[Total: 25]

8 Mpofu Manufacturing Limited produces one product. The budgeted costs and revenues for July are shown below:

- Units produced and sold 1000
- Standard selling price $125
- Standard direct materials 6 kilos at $8 per kilo
- Standard direct labour 5 hours at $10 per hour.
- All overheads are fixed.
- In July 1200 units were produced and sold. Selling price remained at $125 per unit.
- Actual costs were:

Direct materials 7100 kilos at a total cost of $57 510
Direct labour 6150 hours at a total cost of $60 270.

**Required**

a Prepare the original budget and the flexed budget for July to show budgeted contribution. [8]
b Calculate the actual contribution for July. [1]
c Explain the term 'contribution'. [2]
d Prepare a statement reconciling the contribution from the flexed budget with the actual contribution. [10]
e Suggest **two** reasons for the inter dependency of the material usage variance and the labour efficiency variance. [4]

[Total: 25]

9 Samira and Arun enter into a joint venture selling reconditioned air-con units. They agree to share profits and losses in the ratio 3:1 respectively. They provide the following information of the transactions undertaken:

| | $ |
|---|---|
| Samira supplies: air-con units | 2980 |
| materials | 1140 |
| Arun supplies materials | 860 |
| Samira paid warehouse costs | 520 |
| Wages paid: Samira | 6950 |
| Arun | 1800 |
| Freight and carriage paid: Samira | 1370 |
| Arun | 400 |

**Required**

a Prepare a joint venture with Arun account in the ledger of Samira. [7]
b Prepare a joint venture with Samira account in the ledger of Arun. [5]
c Prepare a memorandum joint venture account. [2]
d Explain what is meant by the term 'memorandum account'. [2]
e Calculate the amount of cash paid or received by each party to the joint venture. [4]
f Discuss the reasons that Samira and Arun might have considered before entering into the joint venture. [5]

[Total: 25]

10 The following information relates to Sandeal Ltd at 31 August 2015

| | |
|---|---|
| Gross margin | $33\frac{1}{3}$% |
| Profit margin | 10% |
| Rate of inventory turnover | 12 times |

**Additional information**

- Issued share capital was 800 000 ordinary shares of $0.50 each; 250 000 6% preference shares of $1 each.
- Retained earnings at 31 August 2015 was $416 000.
- Revenue for the year ended 31 August 2015 was $900 000.
- Inventory at 31 August 2015 cost $70 000.
- A final ordinary dividend of $0.04 per share for the year ended 31 August 2014 was paid in December 2014. The directors propose a final ordinary dividend of $0.05 per share for the year ended 31 August 2015. An interim ordinary dividend of $0.02 per share was paid in February 2015.
- The tax liability for the year ended 31 August 2015 is calculated at $40 000.
- A 9% bank loan of $50 000 is due for repayment in 2031.

**Required**

a Prepare a summarised income statement for the year ended 31 August 2015. [9]
b Prepare the retained earnings extract from the statement of changes in equity for the year ended 31 August 2015. [5]
c Explain the role of
 i shareholders [2]
 ii directors [2]
 iii auditors. [2]
d Discuss the role of the annual report as means of communication to shareholder. [5]

[Total: 25]

11 The summarised statement of financial position of Chaunte plc at 31 October 2015 was as follows:

| | $000 |
|---|---|
| **ASSETS** | |
| **Non-current assets** (carrying amount) | 2840 |
| **Current assets** | 638 |
| **Total assets** | 3478 |
| | |
| **EQUITY AND LIABILITIES** | |
| **Equity** | |
| Ordinary shares of $0.25 each | 800 |
| Share premium account | 200 |
| Retained earnings | 1328 |
| | 2328 |
| **Non-current liabilities** | |
| 6% preference shares of $1 each | 350 |
| 8% debentures (2025 – 2027) | 600 |
| | 950 |
| **Current liabilities** | |
| Trade payables | 93 |
| Other payables | 107 |
| | 200 |
| **Total equity and liabilities** | 3478 |

**Additional information**

- Chaunte's profit from operations for the year ended 31 October 2015 was $682 000.
- The tax liability for the year was $80 000.
- A dividend of $0.03 was paid on ordinary shares for the year.
- The ordinary shares had a market value of $1.20 each at 31 October 2015.

**Required**

**a** Calculate the profit or loss for the year ended 31 October 2015 attributable to equity holders . [3]

**b** Calculate the following ratios to two decimal places:

**i** gearing
**ii** earnings per share
**iii** price earnings ratio
**iv** dividend yield
**v** dividend cover. [10]

In July 2016 the directors of Chaunte plc plan to build an additional factory. This will require additional capital expenditure of $1 000 000. The new factory is expected to be profitable in 2020.

The directors are considering raising the additional funds needed to finance the building work by one of the following methods:

- an issue of 10% debentures (2040) at par
- a rights issue of ordinary shares of $0.25 at $1.05 per share
- an issue of 6% preference shares at $1 each.

**Required**

**c** Discuss each of the methods of raising the additional finance needed to fund the building work. Advise the directors the method they should choose. [12]

[Total: 25]

**12** The following information is available for Wakoso Ltd at 1 July 2014:

| | Non-current assets at cost | Accumulated depreciation |
|---|---|---|
| | $ | $ |
| Premises | 1 200 000 | 272 000 |
| Plant and machinery | 180 000 | 126 000 |
| Motor vehicles | 85 000 | 68 000 |
| Office equipment | 35 000 | 14 000 |

During the year ended 30 June 2015 the following transactions relating to non-current assets took place:

**1** Premises were revalued on 30 June 2015 at $3 000 000.

**2** Purchases of non-current assets:

| | |
|---|---|
| plant and machinery cost | $55 000 |
| motor vehicles cost | $112 000 |
| office equipment cost | $25 000 |

**3** During the year plant and machinery that cost $35 000 was sold. Accumulated depreciation relating to the machinery was $28 000. The profit on disposal was $1000.

**4** During the year vehicles that cost $47 000 were sold. Accumulated depreciation relating to the vehicles was $22 000. The loss on disposal was $5000.

**5** Depreciation is provided annually at the following rates using the straight line method:

| | |
|---|---|
| Premises | 2% |
| Plant and machinery | 10% |
| Motor vehicles | 20% |
| Office equipment | 10% |

**Required**

**a** Prepare a schedule of non-current assets at 30 June 2015. [10]

**b** Calculate the total amount of sale proceeds from sales of non-current assets during the year ended 30 June 2015. [6]

**c** Identify **three** causes of depreciation. [3]

**d** Discuss the statement 'The provision for depreciation of non-current assets provides cash to pay for their replacement.' [6]

[Total: 25]

# Index